Handbook

Of

Historical Free Will Baptist Burial Places

Compiled
by

Dr. Alton E. Loveless

To order additional copies of this book, contact:

FWB Publications
1006 Rayme Drive
Columbus, Ohio 43207
740--777-1944
www.forworthwhilebooks.org
www.fwbpublications.com

Published by
FWB Publications

Table of Contents

Acknowledgments

I am grateful to many who made this book possible. It has been an inexhaustible task and without their help it would not have been possible.

I wish to thank Winnie Yandell, Oklahoma, who furnished me hundreds of names and information from her research. She was a generous helper and worked tirelessley; Geraldine Waid, Archivist Georgia;   Karen Hollback, Ohio; Robert Picirilli, Tennessee; Gary Barefoot, North Carolina; Greg McCarty, Indiana; Deborah St. Lawrence, Tennessee; a descendant of David Marks; Jack Copet, Wisconsin; and various state promotional directors, who in their publications encouraged others to contribute information toward this project. And to many individuals whose names are lost to me and too numerous to itemize.

I do want to thank Eric Thomsen, editor of One Magazine, Free Will Baptist Historical Collection, National Assn. of Free Will Baptists and The Free Will Baptist Historical Collection, Mount Olive College for providing many photos for this book.

I sincerely thank everyone.

This will be a continuing project and if any of you have a father, brother, son or a friend that was a minister or missionary that you would like added in future editions, please forward to the address on the previous page.

Preface

This is the first revision of the book printed at the beginning of this year. That edition had less than 800 ministers. This new edition has 1820 covering 40 states and 3 foreign countries.

I am so happy for the co-operation of more during this last update. This edition, except of Georgia, there were more additions were from the Northern states, Randall movement, John Thomas Association and other bodies.

I have found the history with each minister fascanating. I hope you will also.

Below shows the states and their pioneer ministers burial cementeries.

Georgia	221
Maine	168
Ohio	150
Oklahoma	130
North Carolina	116
New Hampshire	90
New York	82
Tennessee	80
Arkansas	74
Missouri	67
Michigan	65
West Virginia	62
Illinois	56
Vermont	37
Rhode Island	36
Virginia	36
Iowa	35
California	28
Wisconsin	28
Alabama	26
South Carolina	26
Pennsylvania	22
Kentucky	21
Texas	19
Minnesota	18
Kansas	14
Nebraska	14
Indiana	11
Florida	10
Massachusetts	10
Mississippi	10
Connecticut	6
Canada	4
Washington	3
Colorado	2
Idaho	2
New Mexico	2
South Dakota	2
Africa	1
Arizona	1
District of Columbia	1
India	1
Louisiana	1
North Dakota	1

This book does not represent only the National Assn., but includes many of what we refer to as the Randall Movement (Northern). It includes those that are part of the Free Will Baptist movement, but never was a part of the national convention or who existed prior to it. Such as the Stone, John-Thomas, John Wheeler association, NC OFWB and more.

Many of the photos are poor quality, but it was all I could find. Likewise, I do not have photos or tombstones for many of them. The information about these ministers were all that was available to me or found in archives. I made every effort to include those for which they would be remembered. Some I had no information, but research had shown they were of our denomination. Others were with the National Association but left and I included their contribution to the movement.

There were some that somewhere, sometime, someone within these movements contributed to what we are today. It was not my purpose to promote any single group, but to let history present its own case. Likewise, the length of the column of the person does not denote the lesser or greater value of the person.

There are many words not spelled correctly, but were taken from the text of the history or book written about the person. E.g. Freewill, Free Baptist, Free Communion Baptists, Free Will Baptists, etc.. In different periods clergy were addressed as Elder, Rev., Dr. etc. I have made every effort to make it reliable, grammatically correct, but errors still reflect the time.

The sources used for accumulating these hundreds of men and women; were found in graveyard records, county histories, church records, genealogies, biographies, Google research, and valuable denominational resource materials such as: Cyclopedia of Free Baptists, pub. 1889 by Burgess and Ward. There is no way I could remember all of the resources used. But it is the product of hundreds of hours and the help of others to put this book together.

Please advise me at alton.loveless@prodigy.net to help me make the corrections for future editions.

We have a story to tell. Let us do it while we can.

Dr. Alton E. Loveless

As the old Episcopal Bishop Phillip Brooks said," *If God called you to preach never stoop to be a king*"

Dedicated

**To Those Pioneer Ministers Upon
Whose Labors We Now Work.**

"The steps of a good man are ordered by the LORD: and he delighteth in his way. Though he fall, he shall not be utterly cast down: for the LORD upholdeth him with his hand. I have been young, and now am old; yet have I not seen the righteous forsaken, nor his seed begging bread... For the LORD loveth judgment, and forsaketh not his saints; they are preserved for ever: but the seed of the wicked shall be cut off... But the salvation of the righteous is of the LORD: he is their strength in the time of trouble,"

(Psalm 37:23-25, 28, 39)

Rev. Selah Hibbard Barrett

Rutland, Meigs Co., Ohio
1822-1883

Minister, Educator, Writer, Author
Memoirs of Eminent Ministers in the Free Will Baptist Denomination
Auto-biography
Contributed to *The Morning Star* for 40 years

Africa

Missionary Glennda Leatherbury
Birth:
Kansas
Death:
October 15, 1994
Free Will Baptist Hospital
Doropo, Cote d'Ivoire, Africa
Buried:
Doropo, Cote d'Ivoire, Africa

Missionary Leatherbury had a heart failure in africa, departing this life at 43 years of age. She was converted to christ in 1973 and graduated from hillsdale fwb college and hutchinson community junior college. The kansas native was appointed to the mission field in 1985.

My Peace I Leave With you

Alabama

Brian Atwood
Birth:
June 7, 1956
Death:
March 9,, 2010
Huntsville,
Madison County, Alabama
Burial:
Maple Hill Cemetery, Huntsville,
Madison County, Alabama

For many years he was pastor of the Emmanuel FWB church in Wabash, Indiana. At the time of his passing he was pastor of the pathway church in huntsville, alabama at his untimely death.

Death is the fundamental human problem.

Elder Walter Pool Bond
Birth:
May 10, 1874
Death:
Jun. 26, 1943

Burial:
Nebo Church,
Limestone County, Alabama

He Was A FWB Preacher In The 30's In Jefferson Co., Alabama.

J A Brown
Birth:
Sep. 23, 1841
Death:
Jul. 20, 1916
Burial:
Old Corinth Cemetery
Lamar County, Alabama

Early Alabama Minister in the Vernon Association. He was married to Lydia C Barnes Brown (1841 - 1905) and secondly to Francis Brown (1882 - 1906).

Tommy Lynn Burch
Birth:
Aug. 1, 1924
Death:
Dec. 13, 1996
Burial:
Weavers Cemetery,
Brewton, Escambia County,
Alabama

He was an educator, minister and

builder. He was the social studies professor at Free Will Baptist Bible College. Nashville, Tn. For 20 years. He also built houses, churches and commercial buildings in several states.

WHATSOEVER EXCELLENCY YOU SEE IN ANY CREATURE IS AN IMAGE OF SOME EXCELLENCY IN God

Jackson Malone Cobb
Birth:
May 7, 1922
Alabama
Death:
Mar. 1, 1995
Fayette Co., Alabama
Burial:
Fayette Memorial Gardens
Fayette
Fayette County, Alabama

He pastored for 48 years, having been licensed in 1947, and ordained a Free Will Baptist minister in 1949. He attended FWB Bible College, Nashville, TN, from 1949-1951. His first full-time congregation was at the New Mission Church (now First FWB Church) in Fayette. His funeral was conducted at that same church 43 years later. He was a WW II Veteran, entering in 1942, fought in invasion of France and was wounded June 16, 1944. He met and married Clara Smith in 1946. He was an evangelist and had a missionary's heart, from which pastorates resulted from his own soul-winning efforts. He participated in a wide range of FWB activities, including being

elected to district home mission boards, in both Alabama and Georgia. In the 1950's, he served as a superintendent at the FWB Childrens Home in Al. He was pastor of union Chapel FWB Church in Crossville at the time of this death.

Charles B Craddock
Birth:
Feb. 17, 1922
Death:
May 24, 2000
Burial:
York Municipal Cemetery
York, Sumter County,
Alabama

Craddock, a native of Roper, N.C. was a pastor and minister in the Free Will Baptist Church for 26 years, serving at various churches. He served in Belk, Ala., Fulton, Miss., Ayden, N.C., Dothan, Marianna, Fla., Cottondale, Fla., and Wicksburg, Ala. He served as a Chief Petty Officer in the U.S. Coast Guard during World War II. A graduate of Free Will Baptist Bible College in Nashville, Tn., and attended Troy State University in Dothan, Alabama and Candler School of Theology in Atlanta, Georgia.

Tunis Michael Creech
Birth:
unknown
Alabama
Feb. 22, 2002
South Carolina
Burial:
Oak Hill Cemetery,
Jasper, Walker County,
Alabama

He attended the Free Will Baptist Bible College in Nashville, Tennessee. After ordination he served as an Associate Pastor of the Fellowship Free Will Baptist Church in Flat River, Missouri, then the following Free Will Baptist churches in Thomaston, Georgia; Smithville, Mississippi; and First Free Will Baptist Church of Florence, South Carolina beginning in 1994.

George Columbus Elliott
Birth:
Dec. 20, 1855
Alabama
Death:
Feb. 16, 1914
Burial:
Mount Pleasant Cemetery
Brilliant
Marion County, Alabama

Early minister in Vernon Assn. He was married to Lucinda A Elliott (1853 - 1927).

O. L. Fields
Birth:
Jan. 16, 1911
Death:
Mar. 31, 1989
Burial:
Millport City Cemetery, Millport.
Lamar County. Alabama

Joe Sephus Frederick
Birth:
1893
Death:
1973
Burial:
Union Hill Cemetery,
Hackleburg,
Marion County, Alabama

An ordained Free Will Baptist minister, well loved and esteemed.

Milton R. Gann
Birth:
unknown
Death:
Apr. 22, 1992
Hamilton,
Marion County, Alabama,
Burial:
Poplar Log Freewill
Baptist Church Cemetery,
Hamilton,
Marion County, Alabama

A Free Will Baptist minister for 37 years, serving four churches in Alabama and Florida. He served as a denominational leader in both states being the state association moderator in Florida and moderator of the Pastors and Deacons Meeting in Alabama. A navy veteran. He did studies at Free Will Baptist Bible College.

Ellis Gore
Birth:
Oct. 3, 1800
South Carolina
Death:
Oct. 5, 1883
Pickens County, Alabama
Burial:
Gore Cemetery
Pickens County, Alabama

Ellis Gore was pastor of Mount Moriah Free Will Baptist Church from spring 1846 until September 1883, a month before his death. See Tuscaloosa News, "Church's missionary spirit still alive after 150 years", June 5, 1996 his parents were: Thomas Tindall Gore (1776 - 1855) and Nancy Sanders Gore (1778 - 1831) and he had two spouses: Dorcas B Gore (1804 - 1866) Annie Mae Burdine Gore (1833 - 1896)

Whitaker W. Guyton
Birth:
1807
South Carolina
Death:
Feb. 4, 1860
McShan
Pickens County, Alabama
Burial:
Guyton Family
McShan
Pickens County, Alabama

Rev. Whitaker W. GUYTON, moved to AL by 1834, (date of his marriage) where he was associated with Rev. Ellis GORE, and J. Eddins, which records show when they petitioned for membership in the Baptist Union Association, Pickens Co. The Union Ass'n met in 1849, at the Mt. Moriah church which Gore had organized. By 1853 Minutes, (earliest after 1849) Mt. Moriah was no longer a part of the Association. It is reported to be the oldest Free Will Baptist church in Alabama. Rev. W. W. GUYTON, and the GORE family had kinship connections from genealogy of the families. Rev. Guyton married Luvina N (Bankhead) Nov. 29, 1834, Lamar Co. AL. Family Tree shows his parents as Abraham Guyton (1765-1816) and Martha Ellis, (1769-1838) Union Co. SC. U.S. Land records show he received 80 acres in 1839, Pickens Co, and the Alabama Homestead and Cash Entry Patents, show he received 40.015, issued May 1, 1849, from the Tuscaloosa Land Office.When the census was taken in 1860, Levina, age 48, was a widow, with

Sophrona A.J. Bird, age 21, and John J. Funderburk, age 28, in HH. In the 1850 census, there was also a Mariam Bird, male, b. AL, who d. in battle in the Civil War, son of James and Mary Guyton Bird, bur. in AR, with #70799738. (Mariam and Saphrona Bird, were possibly a nephew and niece, from the m/n name given as Marion's mother.)Not much is known about the ministry of Whitaker Guyton; there is old minutes of Macedonia Primitive Bapt. church, Lamar Co. AL, which states: "Macedonia Church convened on Saturday before the 3rd Sun in July 1832. Received by letter Bro. Whitaker Guyton." Then in conference Saturday before the 3rd Sun in November 1833, "Brother Whitaker Guyton applied for a letter and obtained." This ended his membership from that church.The number of churches increased in the confines of Pickens county with Rev. Gore, and we can probably surmise, that Rev. Whitaker was involved in some of those churches after he left the Lamar Co (formerly Marion Co) AL County. His name is linked with Rev. Ellis Gore..........This burial info was posted on Pickens Co. Message Forum by "redjugwadi, on Apr. 7, 2004, showing Whitaker and Luvina's graves here, and 2 or 3 small, unmarked ones. his spouse was Luvina N Bankhead Guyton (1812 - 1887)

Daniel George Washington Hollis
Birth:
Feb. 24, 1855
Marion County, Alabama
Death:
Feb. 4, 1930
Lamar County, Alabama
Burial:
Wofford Cemetery
Vernon
Lamar County, Alabama

Early Alabama minister. Daniel was the son of Jonathan Shelton Hollis and Barbara Milender Webb. He married Josephine

Millicent "Princess Millie" Pennington, 19 Nov 1874 in Sanford Co., AL. his parents were Jonathan Shelton Hollis (1815 - 1872) and Barbara Webb Hollis (1824 - 1904). And he was married to Josephine Millicent Pennington Hollis (1851 - 1910).

Eugene Howard
Birth:
unknown
Death:
May 9, 2011
Alabama
Burial:
Lawleys Chapel Cemetery,
Shelby County, Alabama

Mr. Howard was saved at the age of 21. He was ordained a deacon in 1953 and to be a minister in 1957 by the Cahaba River Free Will Baptist Association. He pastored many churches all over the area. He attended school at High Point which is now Davis Chapel church in Sterrett. He pastored Davis Chapel Church for 24 years, was assistant pastor for 3 years. Mr. Howard worked at the Stockhom Valve Fitting in Birmingham 38 years where he retired. Over the years he conducted 340 funerals, performed 213 weddings, and numerous revivals. He was a member of Ben M. Jacobs Masonic Lodge in Pell City. He served as Chaplain for many years.

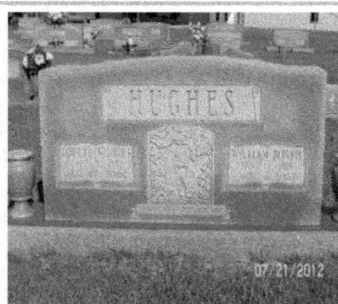

William Bonnie Hughes
Birth:
Nov. 15, 1919
Death:
Nov. 16, 2004

Burial:
Fulton Bridge Cemetery
Marion County, Alabama

William Bonnie Hughes died unexpectedly on November 16, 2004, one day after his 85th birthday. Mr. Hughes answered the call to preach shortly after returning from a tour of duty in World War II and spent the next 47 years pastoring churches in Florida, Tennessee, North Carolina and Alabama. A 1953 graduate of Free Will Baptist Bible College, he served on the Colleges' Board of Trustees for more than 10 years. Mr. Hughes was instrumental in establishing youth camp programs in Tennessee and Alabama. Although retired, Hughes remained an active member of Mt. Olive Free Will Baptist Church in Twin, Alabama.

Thomas Russell Hulsey
Birth:
Feb. 8, 1850
Death:
May 7, 1921
Burial:
Fairview Cemetery
Fairview
Cullman County, Alabama

Thomas married Mary Jane Mote on 16 Feb 1873 in Jefferson Co, AL. .Thomas was ordained as a Minister on 5 Jun 1884 and pastored a number of churches between 1901 and 1916 in Jackson Co AL. Churches he pastored were Pleasant Hill, Mt Tabor, Bethany, Friendship, Sulpher Springs and Center Point.

W R Latham
Birth:
Nov. 10, 1830
Death:
Mar. 23, 1909
Burial:
Shiloh Cemetery
Gordo
Pickens County, Alabama
Plot: 123A

Early Alabama minister.

Woodrow Matthews
Birth:
Mar. 4, 1919
Death:
Mar. 2, 2012
Burial:
Guin City Cemetery, Guin,
Marion County, Alabama

Woodrow Matthews, age 92, of Guin, Alabama passed away at the Northwest Regional Medical Center in Winfield, Alabama. Born in Mine LaMotte, Missouri. He was united in marriage to Blanche Huffman on October 28, 1939. Matthews answered the call to preach in 1939 and was ordained in 1940. He pastored churches in Missouri and Oklahoma. In 1973,

he moved to Guin, Alabama and pastored the Mt. Olive FWB Church until 1985. He then accepted the pastorate of Barnesville FWB Church in Hamilton, Alabama. In 1998 after 58 years of faithful service.

Bro. Matthews was actively involved in the Missouri FWB State Association, serving on the state youth camp board for many years, the state general board, and moderator of the Missouri State FWB Association.

As pastor of the Mt. Olive FWB Church, he was involved in the development of the Trinity Youth Camp, and served on the camp board for a number of years. He also served as moderator of the State Pastor and Workers Conference. Bro. Matthews was an active supporter of state and national programs, and especially missions. Numerous pastors, pastors' wives, home and foreign missionaries have come from his churches throughout his years of ministry. His philosophy of ministry was: "If you genuinely love your people, your people will love you."

Trellis L Mayhall
Birth:
Aug. 13, 1933
Death:
Jan. 29, 1998
Burial:
Winston
Memorial Cemetery,
Haleyville,
Winston County, Alabama

He was ordained to preach in 1964 as a Free Will Baptist minister. He served churches in Florida, Georgia, Indiana and Alabama. Three men answered the call to preach during his pastorate at the Free Water Free Will Baptist Church in Alabama. He was active in denominational work serving as moderator of Alabama's Jasper Association, Executive Board Member, General Board Member, and Ordaining Council Member. He graduated from the Alabama Bible Institute.

Just inside the Eastern Gate

Elihue Roy Mayo
Birth:
Sep. 13, 1923
Boyd County,
Kentucky
Death:
Sep. 17, 2011
Alabama
Burial:
New Home Cemetery,
Coffee County, Alabama

He was one of our WW II heroes, serving in the Army Aircorp. He received a purple heart, three bronze stars and many medals during his service and tour over Normandy during D-day. He was an ordained minister and had pastored churches in Gadsden, Wattsville, Pell City, Adamsville, Enterprise, Alabama and Houston, Texas. He served as a Home Missionary from 1973 to 1992.

W H McGee
Birth:
1843
Death:
unknown
Burial:
Hargrove Cemetery
Gordo
Pickens County, Alabama

A member of the Mt Moriah Association.

Luther D Nance
Birth:
Jul. 19, 1920
Death:
Dec. 9, 1993
Burial:
Cullman City Cemetery,
Cullman,
Cullman, County, Alabama

He was an ordained Free Will Baptist minister, pastor, and was in the early minutes of the Nat'l Ass'n of FWB, serving on the FWB League Board in 1945 to? He was living and pastoring in Detroit, MI at the time.

Herman A. O'Donnell
Birth:
May 20, 1896
Death:
Nov. 12, 1985
Burial:
Mount Zion Methodist Church Cemetery, Ragland, St. Clair County, Alabama

J R Robertson
Birth:
Apr. 22, 1839
Death:
Nov. 29, 1912
Burial:
Shiloh Methodist Episcopal Church Cemetery Hightogy Lamar County, Alabama

Minister in the Mt. Moriah Association.

Thomas Woods Springfield
Birth:
Mar. 11, 1854
Lamar County, Alabama
Death:
Aug. 25, 1922
Ethelsville, Pickens County, Alabama.
Burial:
Ethelsville Cemetery
Ethelsville
Pickens County, Alabama

He was an early minister that joined with Ellis Gore in the work in Alabama after which the churches multiplied in the countries throughout the region making it necessary to divide the Mt. Moriah Association. . He served 46 years. Springfield was the son of Thomas Springfield and Emily Woods. He married Amanda Catherine Guin on 10/10/1875 in Sanford County, Alabama.

William James Springfield
Birth:
Sep. 15, 1852

Death:
Jul. 6, 1883
Burial:
Vernon Cemetery
Vernon
Lamar County, Alabama

Early minister in Alabama. He was the son of Emily Calloway Woods and Thomas Walker Springfield, and was married toTessie M Haley (1858 - 1891).

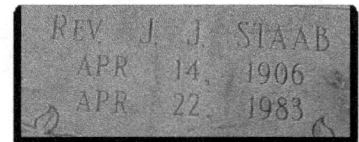

J. J. Staab
Birth:
Apr. 14, 1906
Alabama
Death:
Apr. 22, 1983
Alabama
Burial:
Forest Crest Cemetery, Birmingham, Jefferson Co., Alabama

He was an officer in the Alabama State Assn. serving as Assistant Moderator

Leon D. Vance
Birth:
1937
Death:
1994
Burial:
New Horizon Memorial Gardens, Dora, Jefferson County, Alabama

Arizona

Paul Timothy Thompson
Birth:
1951
Death:
2002
Burial:
City of Mesa Cemetery,
Mesa,
Maricopa County, Arizona

Before moving to Arizona, he served with his father at the Heritage Temple church in Columbus, Ohio. He was an able associate to his father and very capable speaker. He was on the pastoral staff of the Heritage Free Will Baptist Church in Gilbert, Arizona, before his untimely death. A great preacher, teacher and servant to the church.

The statistics on death have not changed. One out of one person dies.

Arkansas

J.W.Blanks
Birth:
Oct. 22, 1927
Flint, Genesee County, Michigan
Death:
Jan. 11, 2001,
Batesville,
Independence County,
Arkansas
Burial:
Egner Cemetery, Salado,
Independence County,
Arkansas

He was a Free Will Baptist Minister for 54 years, of which he was pastor of the Allen Chapel Free Will Baptist Church for 28 years, where he was a member at his death. He was elected multiple terms on the State Executive Board which became the State Youth Board and was a strong instrument in moving the state of Arkansas into a state youth camp program. He has a son, Ron Blanks who is also a Free Will Baptist Minister in Missouri. He served as a medic in the United States Army.

Joe Burney Braddy
Birth:
Dec. 8, 1940,
Green Forest,
Carroll County, Arkansas
Death:
Jan. 20, 1993,
Fredericktown,
Madison County, Missouri
Burial:
Pickens Cemetery,
Green Forest,
Carroll County, Arkansas

He was killed in an auto accident and was pastor at First FWB Church in Fredericktown, Missouri at his passing.

Henry P. Brown
Birth:
Oct. 16, 1926
Arkansas
Death:
Jun. 12, 2012
Springdale,
Washington County, Arkansas
Burial:
Mount Hope Cemetery,
Vesta,
Franklin County, Arkansas

Rev. Brown was a school teacher and a deacon before he became a preacher. Although a pastor himself, he did much to preserve history of ministers in making records and taping sermons and songs of other ministers. He was a denominational leader and a World War II Army veteran.

James F. Brown
Birth:
Aug. 17, 1854
Henderson County
Tennessee
Death:
Mar. 17, 1922

Cleveland County
Arkansas
Burial:
Friendship Cemetery
Friendship,
Cleveland County,Arkansas
James Franklin Brown was born near Lexington in Henderson Co., Tennessee. His parents were Abner S. Brown and Emma Amie Reed. James F. was the last of the children to be born in TN. His Father moved the family to Arkansas around 1858 and homesteaded land in what is today NE Cleveland County Arkansas. At one time, James F. was a "circuit preacher" and traveled to various churches in the area to serve as Pastor for those churches.There are still a number of FWB preachers in the area who are of his descent.

Inscribed on stone
"I have fought a good fight, I have finished my course,I have kept the faith"

George Washington Burris, Sr
Birth:
Jan. 18, 1856,
Atkins,
Pope County, Arkansas
Death:
Mar. 9, 1929,
Atkins,
Pope County, Arkansas
Burial:
Saint Joe Cemetery,
Atkins,
Pope County, Arkansas

From a October 4, 2007 newspaper article, noting the 120th anniversary of the

establishment of St. Joe Freewill Baptist Church on October 7, 2007: *"In the year of 1885, George W. Burris organized a Sunday school under a bunchy top Gum Tree at St. Joe on Pea Ridge 10 miles north of Atkins. They had logs for seats and took School Readers to Sunday school. The Freewill Baptist Church was organized there in 1886."* .
George W. Burris was the principal leader there during his entire life.

Clarence Elijah Campbell
Birth:
Aug. 9, 1920,
Lost Corner,
Pope County, Arkansas
Death:
Aug. 10, 2011,
Hanford, Kings County,
California
Burial:
Rock Springs Cemetery, Hector,
Pope County, Arkansas

He was raised and educated in Scotland and Greeley graduating from Dover High School in 1942. Clarence entered the U.S. Army and served in Europe until his discharge in 1945, earning the Good Conduct Medal, EAME Service Ribbon and Three Bronze Service Stars. Following his discharge, he obtained his AA degree in business. Clarence was ordained into the ministry in Russellville and served as pastor for Free Will Baptist Churches in Arkansas, Oklahoma and North Carolina for more than 30 years.

Glynn Campbell
Birth:
1925
Death:
Nov. 24, 2001,
Walnut Ridge,
Lawrence County,
Arkansas
Burial:
Lawrence Memorial Park,
Walnut Ridge,
Lawrence County,
Arkansas

Free Will Baptist minister who celebrated 50 years in the ministry. He pastored six churches in Arkansas and Missouri. He was an amateur ventriloquist. His son, Tim, became the Arkansas State Executive-Secretary.

Arthur Edward Coffman
Birth:
Jul. 20, 1932,
Jerusalem,
Conway County,
Arkansas
Death:
Dec. 11, 2009,
Russellville,
Pope County, Arkansas
Burial:
Cedar Creek Cemetery,
Jerusalem,
Conway County,
Arkansas

He was a member of the Dover Free Will Baptist Church. Bo was a Free Will Baptist Minister for 55 years (pastoring numerous churches over forty-nine years). He had numerous occupations over his lifetime: a farmer, a Dow

Chemical employee, a MacDonald-Douglas Aircraft employee, owner and operator of the Coffman Tile Company.

Joseph Dempsey Coffman
Birth:
Jan. 11, 1892,
Hector,
Pope County, Arkansas
Death:
May 24, 1975,
Russellville,
Pope County, Arkansas
Burial:
Walnut Grove Cemetery, Hector,
Pope County, Arkansas

Lawnie Coffman
Birth:
Feb. 22, 1922,
Arkansas
Death:
Jun. 3, 2008,
Arkansas
Burial:
White County Memorial
Gardens,Searcy,
White County, Arkansas

Coffman received numerous awards and honors for his action with the 35th infantry during the World War II, including two bronze stars, two silver stars, four battle stars, and two Purple Hearts for being wounded in action. When asked about his heroic service, Lawnie once replied, "I did not mean to be a hero, I just did what had to be done. In 2004, Coffman was invited by public officials in France to return for a hero's welcome. During the trip, three different French towns honored him for his role in their liberation. After being struck in the shoulder by a large caliber 37mm shell intended for a tank during a battle in the Rual Valley of Germany, Coffman promised God that if He would spare His life, He would spend the rest of it doing the Lord's work. Lawnie kept his promise, pastoring for more than 45 years, and serving the Free Will Baptist denomination on the local, state, and national level. He is especially remembered for his role in establishing Camp Beaverfork, the state youth camp in Arkansas. In his book, *My Leg of the Race,* Coffman said, *"This I believe to be the greatest achievement of my church work."* He was one of Arkansas' most decorated soldiers.

John M Crouch
Birth:
Jan. 5, 1890
Death:
Apr. 30, 1987
Burial:
Forks of the Creek Cemetery,
Hector,
Pope County, Arkansas

He was a Free Will Baptist Minister and pastored the Kenwood church from 1952. He was 93 in this photo.

Thomas Sewell "Tommy" Day
Birth:
Sep. 16, 1910
Henryetta
Okmulgee County, Oklahoma
Death:
May 7, 1997
Springdale
Washington County, Arkansas
Burial:
Friendship Cemetery
Springdale
Washington County, Arkansas

DAY spent 51 years in the ministry. He was the son of James Atlee Day (1888-1964) and Lula Lenorah (Nation) Day, (1889-1972). He was married to Mary Pearl (Shepherd) DAY for 61 years. She preceded him in death in 1993. Rev. Day was ordained as a Free Will Baptist preacher in January 1948. He was the founder of Phillips Chapel FWB Church in Springdale and pastored the church four years. He held membership there at the time of his death. Bro. Day pastored 12 FWB churches in Arkansas, Oklahoma and Missouri during his half-century long ministry. He also did extensive evangelistic work in those states as well as in Kansas. Rev. Day served on the state executive boards in Arkansas and Missouri. He was active in the ministry even after he retired in 1975. He taught Sunday School until he was 84 years old. Funeral services were conducted May 10 at Phillips Chapel FWB Church. Reverends Burton Perry, Cecil Garrison, Bobby Shepherd and Lonnie Burks officiated. ---From "Contact Magazine

Willard C. Day
Birth:
Aug. 25, 1913
Death:
Aug. 29, 1984
Burial:
Grace lawn Cemetery,
Van Buren,
Crawford County, Arkansas
He was the son of Francis Marion DAY (b. MO.) and Katherine (Catherine?) Mahalia (Hayes) DAY (b. AR.). He married Helen I. Chambers, May 1, 1934, in OK.
He was an ordained Free Will Baptist minister, who pastored in Oklahoma, Arkansas and Missouri. He was elected moderator and served the State Ass'n of Free Will Baptists in the 1950's. He was recognized as a teacher and taught from printed lessons on Biblical subjects he sent out to his radio listeners, and from which he taught in church schools. He was awarded a D.D. degree and was known among his brethren as Dr. Willard C. Day. He died of cancer problems in Ft. Smith, Arkansas.
He became the first Promotional Secretary in the state of Arkansas. He was also a member of the Foreign Missions Board in the early 50s.

Glenn G. Dipboye
Birth:
Jan. 9, 1903

Death:
Mar. 15, 1976
Burial:
Woody Memorial Cemetery,
Rudy, Crawford County, Arkansas

Oris Doggett
Birth:
Nov. 27, 1918
Death:
Nov. 7, 1999
Burial:
Pleasant Valley Cemetery,
Warren,
Bradley County, Arkansas
He was a very active leader in the Arkansas Free Will Baptist movement serving on many of their state boards.

Jefferson Davis "Judge" Doyle
Birth:
Sep. 21, 1861
Strawberry
Lawrence County, Arkansas
Death:
Feb. 13, 1945
Walnut Ridge
Lawrence County, Arkansas
Burial:
Lawrence Memorial Park
Walnut Ridge
Lawrence County, Arkansas
Plot: Section 10 -

Old Lane Block 4-9

He was a early Arkansas FWB preacher and leader.

Adrian E Duvall
Birth:
1881
Death:
Sep. 9, 1937
Russellville
Pope County, Arkansas
Burial:
Hudson Cemetery
Moreland
Pope County, Arkansas

Funeral services were held this morning for Adrian E. Duvall, 56, Moreland, who died at his home Wednesday. The services were conducted by Rev. Dempsey Coffman. FWB Baptist pastor at Hector. Note: posted in Arkansas Democrat Sept 10, 1937.

Cecil Oliver Garrison
Birth:
Oct. 2, 1909,   Pryor, Okla.
Death:
Nov. 6, 2003
Burial:
Bland Cemetery, Rogers,
Benton County, Arkansas

He began preaching in 1932. During his life, he helped organize 15 churches, preached more than 6,200 sermons, witnessed more than 2,000 professions of faith, baptized over 1,000 worshippers, conducted more than 1,200 weddings and about 2,600 funerals. His career included pastoring 12 churches, a radio ministry for 18 years with a broadcast every Sunday morning in his early years. Rev. Garrison was an evangelist with the Old Mount Zion Free Will Baptist Association for 19 years.

Kyle Elliot Goss
Birth:
Feb. 19, 1935
Pencil Bluff,
Montgomery County,
Arkansas
Death:
May 28, 2012
Arkansas
Burial:
Woody Memorial Cemetery,
Rudy, Crawford County,
Arkansas,

He was a retired ordained minister, having served at the 88 Freewill Baptist and Catcher Freewill Baptist Churches.

Herman A. Greenwood
Birth:
Dec. 2, 1917
Death:
Mar. 22, 1999
Burial:
Pleasant Valley Cemetery,
Warren,
Bradley County, Arkansas

Popular minister in the Saline Assn. in southern Arkansas.

William M. Guinn
Birth:
Aug. 8, 1885
Death:
Sep., 1977
Burial:
Oak Hill Memorial Cemetery,
Booneville,
Logan County, Arkansas
Plot: Section 3-3; Block 25;
Row Ac.

Guinn married Mary Elizabeth Fritz in 1906 in Branch, Franklin County, Arkansas. Rev. Guinn was a Free Will Baptist minister and records reveal he was in OKlahoma in 1946 at the State Conference in Tulsa.

Don P. Guthrie
Birth:
Sep. 21, 1953,
Gassville,
Baxter County, Arkansas
Death:
Jan. 27, 1998,
Hot Springs,
Garland County,Arkansas
Burial:
Memorial Gardens Cemetery,
Hot Springs,
Garland County,Arkansas

A Free Will Baptist, church planter, and denominational officer. He was listed in *"Outstanding Young Men of America."* Pastored in Oklahoma, Texas and Arkansas. Chairman of the Christian Education Board of the Oklahoma State Association. Board of Trustees for Hillsdale College, Member of the Texas Home Missions Board and the National Home Missions Board. Chairman of the State Youth Board in Arkansas. He was a member of the Optimist Club and the U. S. Army National Guard. He graduated from Hillsdale Free Will Baptist College, Moore, Okla. and had a Master's degree from Southern Nazarene University in Bethany, Oklahoma.

Mark Metcher Harris
Birth:
Aug. 8, 1861,
England
Death:
Oct. 12, 1935,
Coaldale,
Scott County, Arkansas
Burial:
Coaldale Cemetery, Coaldale,
Scott County, Arkansas

Harris was born in England and came to this country. He was found in the Chickasaw Nation, I.T. before statehood, and was affiliated with the Free Will Baptist. In 1901, the Center Ass'n approved him for license, and in 1902 he was ordained. He served as clerk of that conference for about two years, when he was elected to be moderator. He pastored churches in the association until about 1906 when he and some of his family moved to Scott Co. AR., where he lived until his death, remaining faithful.

John R. Hartley
Birth:
1863
Death:
1942
Burial:
Shady Grove Cemetery,
Glendale, Lincoln County,
Arkansas

He was Jim Puckett's great grandfather. He married Barbara Ellen Anderson, who was born in 1867 and died in 1931. He pastored in Arkansas all his life.. His daughter – Lillian Geneva Hartley –married James H. McClellan. She was a devout Christian woman who died following the birth of her eighth child. Her eldest was just a teenage boy, and Jim's mother Anna, was the oldest daughter. At age 11, Anna remembers her father gathering the children around her mother's bedside just before she died. She told them all that she loved them and wanted them to live for the Lord and meet her in Heaven. From that day forward, Anna cooked, cleaned, sewed and raised her siblings. The entire family lived for the Lord, and their family heritage of godliness continued. Anna's brother Elbert McClellan, was also a pastor.

Hartley pastored Macedonia Free Will Baptist Church from 1912-1914, and again from 1919 – 1925. Anna was born in 1919, during the time of his tenure. Rev. Hartley also had a son named Johnny who was a preacher. He never married . He did not pastor, but did preach. He adopted and raised a mentally retarded boy name Nonnie, and took care of him his entire life.

Carl Leo High
Birth:
Jul. 10, 1913
Death:
May 6, 1983,
Arkansas
Burial:
Pirtle Cemetery,
Peach Orchard,
Clay County, Arkansas

He served many years as a leader and pastor in the Social Band Association in Northeast Arkansas.

Terrell Holland
Birth:
Apr. 21, 1929
Duncan,
Greenlee County, Arizona
Death:
Jun. 8, 2012
Burial:
Glenwood Cemetery, Glenwood,
Pike County, Arkansas

Rev. Terrell pastored Free Will Baptist churches in Oklahoma and Arkansas for 48 years and served at the Glenwood Free Will Baptist Church for 13 years. He was always able to bring a smile through a story, joke or encouraging word as he was concerned and loved everyone.

James Monroe Holleman
Birth:
Aug. 25, 1895,
Rose Bud,
White County, Arkansas
Death:
May 31, 1973,
Rose Bud,
White County, Arkansas
Burial:
Mount Bethel Cemetery,
Rose Bud,
White County, Arkansas

He was a Free Will Baptist minister in the New Hope Assn.

Gaylord Huckaba
Birth:
unknown
Death:
Jan. 4, 2013
Rosie Independence County
Arkansas
Burial:
Maple Springs Cemetery,
Batesville,
Independence County, Arkansas

He was veteran and long-time Free Will Baptist pastor. His funeral message was preached by Rev. Shane King, pastor of the Blackland Chapel FWB church.

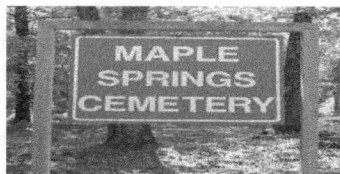

William Sherman Isbell

Birth:
May 4, 1891
Death:
Sep. 13, 1987,
Russellville,
Pope County, Arkansas
Burial:
Saint Joe Cemetery,
Atkins,
Pope County, Arkansas

He was a strong leader for Arkansas Free Will Baptist in the central part of the state. Most followed his leadership due to his wisdom and firm commitment to the FWB denomination.

William Rufus Jobe

Birth:
Aug. 11, 1865
Death:
Jul. 24, 1938
Burial:
Shiloh Cemetery
Atkins
Pope County, Arkansas

Son of James Robert and Lizzie (Choat) Jobe. Married first to Viola Jane Norris on 17 Jul 1887, and second to Alva Duvall on 20 Oct 1895, both in Pope Co., AR. His death notice in the Northwest

Arkansas Times, 25 Jul 1938: "Pea Ridge Minister Dies at Russellville: Russellville, Ark. July 25 - AP - Stricken while preaching at a revival, the Rev. W. R. Jobe, 73, Free Will Baptist minister of the Pea Ridge Community near here, died yesterday."

Keith Johnson

Birth:
Jun. 4, 1934,
Alton, Oregon County,
Missouri
Death:
Jan. 11, 2010,
Conway, Faulkner County,
Arkansas
Burial:
Crestlawn Memorial Park,
Conway, Faulkner County,
Arkansas

Bro. Johnson was the pastor of First Free Will Baptist Church in Conway until just months before his death and pastored churches in Missouri and Arkansas. He managed the Christian Supply Store in Conway for 23 years.

David A. Joslin

Birth:
Mar. 10, 1937,
Arkansas
Death:
Sep. 10, 2011,
Conway,
Faulkner County, Arkansas
Burial:
Mount Bethel Cemetery,
Rose Bud,
White County, Arkansas

Rev. Joslin is a son of the late Rev. Joel Arthur and Clara Flossie Jones Joslin. Rev. Joslin was licensed to preach at age 19 while working as a telegrapher for the Santa Fe Railroad on an Indian reservation near Albuquerque, New Mexico. He was ordained to preach in 1957. Joslin graduated from Free Will Baptist College in Nashville, Tenn. in 1960, then attended Arkansas College in Batesville. He was Executive Director of the Arkansas Free Will Baptist State Association for 30 years after pastoring 13 years in Arkansas and Tennessee. Rev. Joslin spent 43 years of his 49-year ministry in Arkansas, pastoring six churches and helping establish two others. He served on numerous Free Will Baptist Boards including the Christian Education Board, and the General Board, the Historical Commission, and 18 years on the Executive Committee of the National Association of Free Will Baptists. Rev. Joslin founded the Ministers' Benevolent Association for Arkansas Free Will Baptists, worked to create the guidelines for the Acts 1:8 Plan for missionary support and other denominational programs. He oversaw the publications of *"The Fifty-year Record,"* a brief historical book of the national association, and he collaborated with a group of writers in 1976 to publish *"History of Free Will Baptist State Association."* He also wrote adult Sunday School curriculum and prepared manuscripts for publication in *Contact,* the Free Will Baptist national magazine. He also edited *The Vision,* a monthly publication focusing on events and people among the 220 Arkansas Free Will Baptist churches for 30 years.

The saint of God is escorted to a land of joy and peace.

Joel Arthur Joslin
Birth:
Apr. 5, 1902,
Van Buren,
Crawford County,
Arkansas
Death:
Nov. 10, 1993,
Fort Smith,
Sebastian County, Arkansas
Burial:
Gracelawn Cemetery,
Van Buren,
Crawford County, Arkansas

He was a Freewill Baptist minister, a farmer and retired employee of Missouri Pacific Railroad. He was a member of Catcher Freewill Baptist Church and had been an ordained Freewill Baptist minister since 1921. He organized the Catcher Free Will Baptist Church near Van Buren in 1930 and re-organized it in 1943. He was the father Rev. David Joslin. He assisted in the Organization Of Several Other Free Will Baptist Churches in eastern Oklahoma and western Arkansas.

Charles Rice Kellam
Birth:
May 11, 1809
Vermont
Death:
Apr. 4, 1854
Burial:
Parks Cemetery
Charleston
Franklin County, Arkansas

He was founder of Charleston, Arkansas. Rev. Charles R. Kellam appeared in the southern part of Franklin Co. AR, via way of North Carolina, at least by 1846. In that year, he served as post-master for the area and opened the Post Office for Charleston on Aug. 10, 1846 (David Joslin, author of "The Arkansas State Association," , Randall House Pub, 1976).Rev. Kellam married his wife, Susan, in N.C. and they had two children, Charles and Edward P., both bn AR, in 1850 census (by 1860, they had added Mary B.) Rev. Kellam exerted a significant influence and the commuity was named Charles Towne--later, Charleston. Rev. Kellam organized a FreeWill Baptist church in 1846, the same year he opened the post office. He remained its pastor until 1850. His work may have been brief but it was here the Arkansas District Association was organized in 1869. The church he organized was later referred to by "Goodspeed's Hist of NW AR", as a Missionary Baptist Church, but the church changed hands a number of times, and probably was a M.B. Church by the time Goodspeed's was published in 1889. After Kellam's ministry ended there in 1850, the church remained w/o a pastor until 1857. It was later reorganized and numerous churches worshipped in the same 'meeting house,' and so confusion was not uncommon. Nevertheless, Rev. Charles Kellam did a good work and his name is found in old records and is noted here for it.He died at 45 years of age...unknown as to cause of death.

Darwin Eugene Kelton
Birth:
Mar. 13, 1937,
Roswell, Chaves County,
New Mexico
Death:
Dec. 12, 1999,
Atkins,
Pope County, Arkansas
Burial:
Oakland Cemetery,
Atkins,
Pope County, Arkansas

He was ordained to preach in 1974 in Fresno, California, where he chaired the Ministry Department at California Christian College. After teaching two years in Florida (1976-78), Rev. Kelton began pastoring the First Free Will Baptist Church in Berryville, Arkansas. He served the First Free Will Baptist Church in Athens, Hatfield and Pine Hill Free Will Baptist churches until declining health required him to cease full-time pastoral duties. He served as a Minister of Music at the Union Grove church at Athens until his death. He was a gifted musician, vocally, instrumentally, and began his first radio program at age 16. He later sang with gospel quartets, directed choral groups, teach guitar lessons and guide music programs on collegiate and local church levels. He had only one eye, but his ability far exceeded the handicap as he served the Lord in many areas of the United States.

Ernest McKinley Kennedy
Birth:
Jan. 11, 1905
Death:
Jun. 24, 1977
Burial:
Sutton Cemetery,
Pocahontas,
Randolph County, Arkansas

He was the first State Executive Secretary in Oklahoma, beginning in 1955. The office had been a part time office until the State Convention elected him. The office was in Oklahoma City.

Zane T. Kirkland
Birth:
unknown,
Arkansas
Death:
Feb. 2, 1992,
Little Rock,
Pulaski County, Arkansas
Burial:
Strangers Home Cemetery,
Alicia,
Lawrence County, Arkansas

Pastored Free Will Baptist churches in Arkansas. He was a state leader serving on the Arkansas State Mission Board for eight years and the state Executive Board for five. He was pastor of the Conway church at his death.

Robert Lee, Jr
Birth:
1814,
Tennessee
Death:
Apr. 22, 1887,
Madison County,
Arkansas
Burial:
Lee Family Cemetery,
Aurora,
Madison County,
Arkansas

An Arkansas pioneer Free Will Bapt. preacher in the late 1830's,

Herman A. Lewis
Birth:
Mar. 8, 1898,
Lebanon,
Laclede County, Missouri
Death:
Sep. 20, 1996,
Batesville,
Independence County,
Arkansas,
Burial:
Reeves Cemetery,
Melbourne,
Izard County, Arkansas

Pioneer Free Will Baptist preacher, pastor, and church planter. During his 73 years he pastored churches in Arkansas, California, & Washington. He had little education but memorized hundreds of Bible verses and quoted them extensively in his sermons. In his early ministry he pastored as many as seven churches at a time and was a widely-used revivalist he baptized hundreds of converts. He was a moderator of the Arkansas State Association during his ministry. A biography was written about him in 1974. To a grandson he wrote: "Observe with care of whom you speak, to whom you speak, and how and when and where you speak."

Curtis L. Lybarger
Birth:
Feb. 9, 1917
Death:
Jun. 29, 1993
Burial:
East Shady Grove Cemetery,
Greenbrier,
Faulkner County, Arkansas

Central Arkansas preacher.

Walter B. Maddox
Birth:
Jun. 6, 1887,
Arkansas
Death:
Sep. 12, 1982,
White County, Arkansas
Burial:
Honey Hill Cemetery,
Searcy,
White County, Arkansas

Most of his ministry was spent in the New Hope Association in central Arkansas.

Elbert McClellan
Birth:
Jun. 11, 1914,
Cleveland County,
Arkansas
Death:
Apr. 6, 2010,
Pine Bluff,
Jefferson County,
Arkansas
Burial:
Shady Grove Cemetery,
New Edinburg,
Cleveland County, Arkansas

McClellan pastored Macedonia Free Will Baptist Church from 1958-60, and 1964-1966. His daughter Geraldine is married to a preacher/Bible scholar, Rev. Dr. Cecil Sanders of New Edinburg, AR, and they have a son who is a pastor, Rev. Marvin Ray Sanders of Oklahoma City, OK.
He served many congregations in southern Arkansas and member of Macedonia Free Will Baptist Church. He was a farmer and carpenter.

James Samuel McClellan
Birth:
Nov. 13, 1834
Annibelle, Abbeville County,
South Carolina
Death:
Mar. 30, 1930
Ain, Grant County, Arkansas
Burial:
Camp Creek Cemetery,
Grant County, Arkansas

Born in South Carolina, Migrating with his parents first to Georgia then to Holmes County, Mississippi by 1846. Came to Arkansas from Mississippi after July 1860 - Holmes County, Mississippi Census to Hurricane Township in what was 'old' Bradley County Arkansas, which became Dorsey in 1873 and then Cleveland County in 1885. Served in the 2nd Ark Cavalry Co. D during the Civil War attaining the rank of Corporal. Was present at the Fall of Vicksburg in 1863 by his own statement and verified in the records at Vicksburg National Battlefield Park. After he was captured at the Fall of Vicksburg with his brother David and brother in Laws, Ben Tyler and Gus Muirhead with the Vaiden Mississippi Light Artillery, he was interred for a time at the Union POW Camp, Rock Island, Illinois eventually being 'paroled' returning to Arkansas debarking at what was known as 'Red River Landing'. His enlistment papers, pension application and war records held at the Old State Capital Archives; Little Rock, Arkansas. He did receive a war pension from the State of Arkansas for his service during the Civil War Pension Record from Arkansas State Archives. He was married in 1854 to Miss Huldah Scott Mathis of Attala County, Mississippi. Patriarch of the McClellan Clan of Arkansas and the progenitor of over 1300 descendants - one Grandson was Sen. John L. McClellan, also listed on this site, elected as one of Arkansas' United States Senators for thirty-five years.
He had a long list of Free Will Baptists in southern Arkansas and FWB preachers, namely; Elbert McClellan, James Puckett, Ray Sanders, Marvin Ray Sanders, Ron Puckett, etc.

William Franklin "Will" McGee
Birth:
Aug. 19, 1878
Death:
Jan. 2, 1959
Russellville
Pope County, Arkansas
Burial:
Saint Joe Cemetery
Atkins
Pope County, Arkansas

He was an early Free Will Baptist minister and leader in the state of Arkansas. His parents were George Washington McGee and Nancy Melvina Burris. He married Alice Clemons Oct 22 1899 in Pope County.

George W Million
Birth:
Sep. 25, 1877,
Randolph ,Arkansas
Death:
Jan. 8, 1969,
Pocahontas,
Randolph County, Arkansas
Burial:
Masonic Cemetery,
Pocahontas,
Randolph County, Arkansas

He was a well-known preacher and author of two books on the history of Free Will Baptists. He was remembered for the use of charts while he preached. He influenced many ministers in the

Social Band Association and tutored many of the early preachers that helped to form the National Association of Free Will Baptists in 1935.

Roy M. Moore
Birth:
Nov. 21, 1901
Death:
May 9, 1978
Burial:
Oak Grove Cemetery,
Yorktown,
Lincoln County, Arkansas

He was a popular preacher in Arkansas. It was common for him the pastored churches many miles away all the weekend should drive back to his job for Monday morning

James Monroe Patrick
Birth:
Mar. 12, 1854
Bradley County, Arkansas
Death:
Sep. 16, 1933
Herbine
Cleveland County, Arkansas
Burial:
Prosperity Cemetery
Pansy
Cleveland County, Arkansas
Rev. Patrick, was a pioneer Free Will Baptist Minister, spent a large portion of his life in this county and was the founder of the Free Will Macedonia church in Lee Township. He was a candidate for representative from this county several times, losing twice by narrow margins. He had many friends wherever he was known. Funeral services were conducted by Rev. J. R. Hartley, life-long friend.. His spouse was Celia Jane Johnson Patrick (1859 - 1918).

Raymond Armster Patrick
Birth:
Sep. 12, 1919,
Vilonia, Faulkner County,
Arkansas
Death:
Jun. 30, 2001,
Vilonia,
Faulkner County,
Arkansas
Burial:
Cypress Valley Cemetery,
Faulkner County, Arkansas

He was a minister and pastor in central Arkansas. During his retirement years, he was a member of the Center Point Free Will Baptist Church. He was a veteran of the Navy serving during WWII.

L D Payne
Birth:
Aug. 29, 1936
Death:
Oct. 27, 1997
Burial:
Oak Grove Cemetery,
Chicot County,
Arkansas

He was a popular Free Will Baptist minister serving in Arkansas pastorates. He served as Private First Class in the US Army in Korea.

Bruce Erwin Phillips
Birth:
Oct. 29,1902,
Washington,
Hempstead County, Arkansas
Death:
Mar. 13, 1995,
Springdale,
Washington County, Arkansas
Burial:
Burkshed Cemetery,
Washington County, Arkansas

During the time of his ministry, he was one of the strongest leaders in northwest Arkansas among some of the oldest churches in the state.

Death has no strength

Benjamin Perry "Ben" Pixley
Birth:
Feb. 17, 1890
Death:
Nov., 1981
Fort Smith,
Sebastian County, Arkansas
Burial:
Gracelawn Cemetery,
Van Buren,
Crawford County, Arkansas

The Rev. Benjamin Perry Pixley was a member of 88 Freewill Baptist Church. He was a minister for 65 years at several area Freewill Baptist churches. He was a former Mountainburg and Chester, Arkansas School board member and civic leader. He had twin sons, the Rev. Rupert Pixley and the Rev. Gilbert Pixley of Fort Smith, Arkansas who were greatly known as Free Will Baptist ministers throughout the United States.

Gilbert J. Pixley
Birth:
Jan. 25, 1920,
Rudy,
Crawford County, Arkansas
Death:
Sep. 17, 2006,
Van Buren, Crawford County,

Arkansas
Burial:
Gracelawn Cemetery,
Van Buren,
Crawford County, Arkansas

He was a minister, pastor, and evangelist for over 60 years in Arkansas, Oklahoma, California, Texas and other states. He pastored nine churches during his career. He sang, taught music schools, and wrote songs, including a popular one, *"My Child, You're Home at Last,"* which became his epitaph. He was a Navy veteran of WW II. He and his twin brother, Rupert, were an evangelistic team for years.

He baptized the author of this book.

Rupert E. Pixley
Birth:
Jan. 25, 1920,
Arkansas
Death:
Oct. 31, 2000,
Fort Smith,
Sebastian County, Arkansas
Burial:
Gracelawn Cemetery,
Van Buren,
Crawford County, Arkansas

He was a Freewill Baptist minister for 63 years, serving the First Freewill Baptist Church in Fort Smith for 44 years before his retirement. He led this church through seven major building programs including the 700 seat auditorium that was built in 1957. In 1984 the church built a 16 thousand square-foot multi purpose building and named it the R. E. Pixley Family Center. He was widely known as an evangelist and baptized more than 3000 converts during his ministry and the preformed over 2000 marriages. For years he had an ongoing radio ministry with a wide following. He and his twin brother, Gilbert, were known throughout the Free Will Baptists denomination as able evangelists. Many people and ministers owe their conversion to these brothers. In addition to his pastoral work, served 23 years on the Arkansas State CTS Board, a member of the State Executive Committee and served as the State Moderator. He moderated Zion Hope and Unity associations and served five years on the National Home Mission Board. At the time of his death, he was pastor of Bethlehem Free Will Baptist in Van Buren. He also was involved in the ownership of three local nursing homes.

> **The compiler of this book owes his conversion to him.**

Jesse E Pratt
Birth:
Jan. 13, 1898
Death:
Nov. 4, 1983
Burial:
Rose Bud Cemetery,
Rose Bud,
White County, Arkansas
Most of his ministry and pastorates were all within the New Hope Quarterly Meeting.

Reuben E Pruitt, Jr
Birth:
Sep. 8, 1929
Death:
Dec. 10, 2000
Burial:
White County Memorial Gardens,
Searcy, White County, Arkansas

He was a popular pastor and minister in the New Hope Association in central Arkansas.

Benjamin Randle "Ben" Scott
Birth:
Feb. 23, 1924,
Mountain Grove,
Wright County, Missouri
Death:
May 20, 2010,
Pocahontas,
Randolph County, Arkansas
Burial:
Sutton Cemetery,
Pocahontas,
Randolph County, Arkansas

He was a Free Will Baptist minister serving as full time pastor for more than 50 years. His early pastorates were in the states of Oklahoma Missouri, and in Arkansas. He pastored First Free Will Baptist Church in Pocahontas, First Free Will Baptist Church in Jonesboro, and for twenty-four years, the First Free Will Baptist Church in North Little Rock.
In semi-retirement Bro. Scott served as interim pastor for First Free Will Baptist Church in Myrtle, Missouri; United Free Will Baptist Church in Walnut Ridge and First Free Will Baptist Church in Jonesboro. He served on numerous boards within the denomination on all levels; District Assn's, State Convention and the National Association. Bro. Scott was a member of Sutton Free Will Baptist Church in Pocahontas.

J. C. Rauls
Birth:
Mar. 11, 1924,
New Edinburg,
Cleveland County,
Arkansas
Death:
Mar. 5, 2010,
Monticello,
Drew County, Arkansas
Burial:
Union Cemetery,
Rye, Cleveland County,
Arkansas

Bi-vocational pastor, retired from Burlington Industries and served as a Free Will Baptist minister in southeast Arkansas.

Melvin Lee Shelton
Birth:
Mar. 13, 1922
O'Kean Randolph County
Arkansas
Death:
May 26, 2012
Jonesboro
Craighead County Arkansas
Burial:
Randolph Memorial Gardens
Pocahontas
Randolph County Arkansas

Melvin was a pastor for 64 years and had been the pastor of Northside Freewill Baptist Church in Pocahontas for the last 35 years.

Robert S Shelton
Birth:
Aug. 3, 1888,
Mountain View,
Howell County, Missouri
Death:
Oct. 31, 1954,
Old Reyno,
Randolph County, Arkansas
Burial:
Sharum Cemetery,
Pocahontas,
Randolph County, Arkansas

He was a preacher along with running his merchandise store in Okean. He was very active in the Social Band Association and a leader in the state Association.

H. D. "Dick" Shipley
Birth:
Jul. 3, 1917,
Arkansas
Death:
Jan. 3, 1996,
Barling, Sebastian County,
Arkansas
Burial:
Gill Cemetery,
Van Buren,
Crawford County, Arkansas
He pastored a number of churches in Arkansas and Oklahoma and founded the First Free Will Baptist Church of Greenwood and the Cavanaugh First Free Will Baptist of Fort Smith. He also was employed by Harding Glass Co. for 31 years. He was a member of First Free Will Baptist Church for 46 years.

Berne Ora Stahl
Birth:
Dec. 8, 1913
Arkansas
Death:
Mar. 4, 1971
Dardanelle, Yell County,
Arkansas
Burial:
Bethel Cemetery,
Kingston,
Yell County, Arkansas

He had been an active minister for his last 14 years. Rev. Stahl was a native of Plainview, pastor of the Danville Free Will Baptist Church. He left many of his family active in the Lord's service. His legacy remains in them.

Charles R Staten
Birth:
unknown
Death:
Nov. 7, 1986
Burial:
Browns Chapel Cemetery,
Paragould,
Greene County, Arkansa,
Plot: 11, row 32

His ministry was mainly in the north eastern part of the state.

If God called you to preach-Preach!!

Ralph Lee Staten
Birth:
Jul. 11, 1911,
O'Kean,
Randolph County,
Arkansas
Death:
Oct. 6, 1997,
Knoxville,
Knox County, Tennessee
Burial:
Masonic Cemetery,
Pocahontas,
Randolph County,
Arkansas

He was a combination itinerant pastor and public school teacher in Northeast Arkansas in his early ministry. He later pastored in Arkansas, Alabama, Oklahoma, North Carolina and Virginia. In the early days of his ministry he was known for his debates with ministers of other denominations debating the doctrines of Free Will Baptists. He was also a writer beginning in his early ministry. He attended the 1935 organizational meeting in Nashville, Tenn. which formed the National Association of Free Will Baptists.

Roy Lathan Thompson
Birth:
Jan. 16, 1938
New Edinburg,
Cleveland County,Arkansas
Death:
Dec. 7, 2002
Heber Springs,
Cleburne County,Arkansas
Burial:
Hickory Springs
Cemetery,Hermitage,
Bradley County,Arkansas

Wayne Tucker, Jr
Birth:
Jul. 22, 1921
Death:
Jan. 31, 1996
Burial:
Pirtle Cemetery,
Peach Orchard,
Clay County, Arkansas

His ministry was mainly in the Social Band Association in north eastern Arkansas. He served with the US Army During WWII.

Christians have no fear of death.

Ruben Bunyan Venable
Birth:
Jul. 12, 1877
Arkansas
Death:
Jul. 19, 1954
Atkins
Pope County, Arkansas
Burial:
Saint Joe Cemetery
Atkins
Pope County, Arkansas

A Free Will Baptist minister and pastor from Pope Co. AR. Listed in a 1953 photo as a minister at the Ark. State Association of FWB. His spouse: Mary Ann Atkins Venable (1876 - 1959)

Reece G. Webb
Birth:
Jul. 10, 1900
Death:
Feb. 7, 1981
Burial:
Atkins City Cemetery
Atkins
Pope County, Arkansas

An ordained FreeWill Baptist minister in early Arkansas records. His name is listed in the roll of ministers in 1953 State Association Minutes. (see David Joslin's "History of Arkansas FWB." Spouse: Ada M. Littleton Webb (1900 - 1993)*

James E White
Birth:
Feb. 4, 1905
Arkansas
Death:
Jan. 10, 2000
Arkansas
Burial:
Willoughby Cemetery,
Warren,
Bradley County, Arkansas

Rev. White was the son of an ordained Free Will Baptist minister, as was his brother Stanton White. He had a long ministry in Arkansas completing over 70 years as a pastor, evangelist and church organizer.

He was 94 years of age at the time of his death which was just short of his 95th birthday. He was saved at age 12 and ordained to the ministry at age 25 in 1929. His ministry was basically a bi-vocational one serving during the great depression. He labored in both south Arkansas and north Louisiana, pastoring 14 churches and organizing three. He officiated at more than 700 funerals and finally lost the count of the number of his converts that he baptized. Rev. Ben Scott, who preached the funeral of, Rev. White, said of him, "He was a typical old-fashioned, Bible-toting, hard-hitting preacher. And was always where the action was. He was very forthright, but that the same time very tender and loving. His influence in the Saline Association was without equal. He was a moderator, served on the executive committee, examining board, and many other positions during his time as a pastor. He was well known for his doctrinal sermons and his compassion for the lost. Jack Williams, Former *Contact* editor was saved under brother Whites ministry, as well as many others. Brother Williams, said that the sermons of brother White still echo in his life after more than 50 years of service.

Stanton B. White
Birth:
Mar. 14, 1913
Death:
Oct. 31, 1997
Burial:
Willoughby Cemetery,
Warren, Bradley County,
Arkansas

He was a retired machine operator for Potlatch Corp., a Freewill Baptist minister and a member of Willoughby Freewill Baptist Church at Warren. He was the son of W.P. White and a brother of J.E. White, both FWB preachers. His daughter Sue White married Bobby Aycock and they served as missionaries in Brazil.

Founders and strong leaders in building Saline Assn in South Arkansas.

William Pleasant White
Birth:
Nov. 5, 1873
Death:
May 26, 1952
Arkansas
Burial:
Willoughby Cemetery,Warren,
Bradley County, Arkansas

He was an early ordained Free Will Baptist minister, who had two sons, James E. and Stanton, who were also FWB ministers and whose influence still exists in the Saline Assn. in Southern Arkansas.

Will S. White
Birth:
Aug. 29, 1890,
Death:
Mar. 27, 1973,
Randolph County,
Arkansas Burial:
Masonic Cemetery,
Pocahontas,
Randolph County,
Arkansas

He was a faithful servant coming to Christ later in life. Organizing churches and ministered the until a pastor came.

California

Bobby Lee Brown
Birth:
Jun. 1, 1945
Turlock,
Stanislaus County, California
Death:
Jun. 18, 1967
Modesto,
Stanislaus County, California
Burial:
Turlock Memorial Park. Turlock
Stanislaus County; California,
Plot: Lot 64 Block 27

Had not long been a minister when he was stricken with a deadly disease.

William E. B. Condit
Birth:
May 1, 1924
Locust Grove
Mayes County, Oklahoma
Death:
Jun. 24, 2013
Pryor
Mayes County, Oklahoma
Burial:
Cherokee Memorial Park
Lodi
San Joaquin County, California

Dr. William E. B. Condit was born to W. C. Pigeon (Ross) Condit. E. B. graduated from Locust Grove High School in 1943. He furthered his education at Northeastern State College where he graduated in 1953 with a degree in Industrial Arts. He finished his education by obtaining his Doctorate of Theology while living in Sacramento, CA. E. B. served his country proudly in the United States Navy from October 1, 1943 until January 11, 1946. On July 5, 1946, Mary Louise Littlefield and William E.B. Condit were united in marriage. This began a marriage of 67 years that coupled raising a family in the ministry, pastoring churches from North Carolina to California, ministering for over 64 years. On Aug. 1, 1949 Condit was ordained to preach as a Free Will Baptist Minister. In 1949 he organized the Little Rock Free Will Baptist Church east of Locust Grove where he was their first pastor. He then spent 1 year at Lowry Free Will Baptist Church before organizing Trinity Free Will Baptist Church in Muskogee. After 3 years there, E.B. was the pastor at Free Will Baptist Churches in Wewoka, OK, Bakersfield, CA, Ponca City, OK, Modesto, CA, Campbell, CA, Concord, CA, Ontario, CA, Farmville, NC, back to Campbell, CA, and Lompoc, CA. He also served as interim pastor for home missions at many churches in between. E.B. served on the California State Mission Board as well as the California Christian College Board for 17 years. Many pastors and Christian leaders were born from E.B.s ministry throughout the years. Before moving back to OK, they lived in Lodi, CA. Their ministry in California spanned over 38 years. He and his wife moved back to Mayes County, OK in 1998 where they lived west of Pryor. He remained an honorary member of Capital Free Will Baptist Church in Sacramento, CA. He always put God first. He also treasured the time he spent with his family provided a great fatherly image for his children grandchildren to follow. Every two months, his family would receive a hand written encouraging message from him. E.B. loved to watch football. He was a avid Oklahoma Sooner Football fan! He was also a fan of the San Francisco 49ers. E.B. was very patriotic was known to write governmental dignitaries to share what he believed to be right. For 5 years, E.B. played guitar sang in a family quartet that shared in song preaching by broadcasting at KOLS radio in Pryor. He was also a founding member of the original Cherokee Ramblers Band. E.B.'s life serves as an example to follow his ministry will flourish for many generations to come. Reverend Adrian Condit and Reverend Larry Condit officiated.

Osmondo Corrales
Birth:
Dec. 4, 1921
Pinar del Rio, Cuba
Death:
Mar. 7, 2013
Culver City
Los Angeles County, California
Burial:
Inglewood Park Cemetery
Inglewood
Los Angeles County, California

Osmundo Corrales was born in the small community of El Sábalo located in the Pinar del Rio province of Cuba.
His parents, Cerbellon Corrales Yut and Rosa Blanco Menéndez, were excellent examples and guided him well in his life especially in the areas of respect, honor and interpersonal relations. He was the next to the last among eight siblings: Antonio, Eusebia, Luz Maria, Josefina, Andrea, Cándido, Osmundo and Magdalena.
He embraced the Gospel of Jesus Christ during the decade of the 40's when he was 19 years old. In October 1941 he was baptized by immersion in a strong flowing river by Rev. Luis Díaz. In October 1944 he enrolled in the Free Will Baptist Seminary, "Cedros del Libano". During the summer of 1947 he was called as interim pastor of the church in the small town of Arcos de Canasí, in the Province of Matanzas. He later returned to the Seminary in the fall of 1948 to continue his Seminary studies. He received his graduation degree from the Seminary in 1950.One year later, May 16, 1951, he was ordained as a minister of the Gospel with the laying on of hands of the presbytery of the Seminary where he graduated and where they were celebrating the National Convention.In the fall of 1945, Osmundo met a young lady that had come to enroll as a student in the Seminary. For 62 years Celia was his faithful companion in the ministry which he had chosen in obedience to God's calling. From Osmundo and Celia's marriage were born two children, a daughter, Omayda and a son, Omar. Corrales was pastor of several churches: Free Will Baptist, Viñales, provincial de Pinar del Rio, Cuba, Free Will Baptist, La Lisa – Marianao, Cuba. Free Will Baptist Church, Bryan, Texas; Resurrection Free Will Baptist Church, Culver City, California. Brother Corrales was a living example of love for God. He has left a void in the pews of his church and in the hearts of all of his brothers and sisters in Christ, which will only be filled when we too are in the presence of our glorious Savior.

Luther R Crumb
Birth:
1891
Death:
1973
Burial:
North Kern Cemetery,
Delano,
Kern County, California

He began preaching in the many rural churches found in eastern OK. Where he was ordained is unknown, but was enumerated in old minutes of the Free Will Baptist Association of churches and was an active minister. Sometime after 1940, removed to central California, where he again, preached and carried on with church work, while working to provide for his family. During a time when he stopped to help a motorist, a fire ensued, burned his arm so badly, it was amputated from the elbow down. For sure, this was a great loss, but after some recovery, he went on working with one hand. He pastored and preached, attended meetings, until at last his health prevented it.

Death before Life

Orbin Hurst Doss
Birth:
Feb. 28, 1912,
Arkansas
Death:
Dec. 28, 1985,
Stanislaus County, California
Burial:
Turlock Memorial Park,
Turlock,
Stanislaus County, California,
Plot: Lot 233 Block 28

Native of Arkansas, he had lived in Turlock since 1979. He was a pastor in Arizona, Oklahoma, Arkansas, and in California at Hughson and Modesto. He served on various boards and committees during his successful ministry.

Oh, may I join the choir invisible
Of those immortal dead who live again.

Israel Bunyan Dunaway
Birth:
Apr. 7, 1884,
Hartselle,
Morgan County,
Alabama
Death:
Mar. 30, 1960,
Fresno County,
California
Burial:
Mountain View Cemetery,
Fresno,
Fresno County, California.

He was an ordained minister of the Free Will Baptist Church, and was elected moderator of the Eastern Association of Oklahoma in March of 1940. He was one of the founders. It is believed he came from the Texas West Fork Association to Oklahoma, probably from Eastland, where his family is shown in the census. His name was in records and old news items in the *Ada Weekly* of Pontotoc, Oklahoma. At what point he moved to California is not known. He was probably a bi-vocational minister as many were in his time.

Claudie Hames
Birth:
Nov. 22, 1925,
Kellyville,
Creek County, Oklahoma
Death:
Mar. 9, 2011,
Bakersfield,
Kern County, California
Burial:
Hillcrest Memorial Park,
Bakersfield,
Kern County, California

He attended schools in Sapulpa and started working at an early age at Liberty Glass Co. He joined the 503rd Regimental Combat Paratroop Division of the Army on February 10, 1944, to serve his country during World War II.
He served on Lyte, Corregidor and Negros, in the Philippine Islands. While on the Island of Corregidor, he was wounded by shrapnel with injuries to the spine. He was temporarily paralyzed and spent 59 days in the hospital before returning to battle. He was a recipient of the Purple Heart. He returned to Oklahoma and relocated to Taft to work in the oilfields after the war. He worked for Rocky Mountain Drilling Co.

On May 13, 1953, he accepted the Lord as his Savior. Mr. Hames accepted the call to preach the Gospel of Christ, and within a few months accepted the pastorate of the Lamont Free Will Baptist Church. He moved to Oxnard, California to pastor the Oxnard Free Will Baptist Church, a position he held for eight years before his move to Bakersfield in July 1964 to pastor the First Free Will Baptist Church. He pastored this church until his retirement in 2001. He also served on the National Home Mission Board of Free Will Baptists during this pastorate. His greatest joy in life was door-knocking, asking people to come and visit the church, and leading someone to the Lord.

Truman Niece Huddleston
Birth:
Jan. 19, 1910
Hartshorne, Pittsburg County,
Oklahoma
Death:
Sep. 8, 2004
Olympia, Thurston County,
Washington
Burial:
Chowchilla Cemetery
Chowchilla, Madera County,
California

Rev. Huddleston's parents were William Adam Huddleston and Nancy Belle (Allen) Huddleston. She died in 1918, when Truman was a child. His father remarried to Beulah Alice (unk) Huddleston, and both died in California. Truman N. Huddleston was ordained a Free Will Baptist minister when he was 35 years of age at the FWB Church at Non, OK. He was active in the church's ministry, and in the Center Ass'n meetings. He married Isadele and they removed to California in the

1940's. He lived at Chowchilla for years and held pastorates in the area.

John Jay Hull
Birth:
May 31, 1847
Death:
Aug. 8, 1933
Burial:
Chrome Cemetery
Chrome
Glenn County, California
An ordained FWB minister who labored in Wisconsin churches and with his father in South Dakota.

Edward "Butch" Johns
Birth:
May 7, 1924
Death:
Oct. 20, 2010
Burial:
Shafter Memorial Park
Shafter, Kern County, California
Edward "Butch" Johns, U.S. Veteran, who was faithful to the Free Will Baptist denomination serving as preacher and church planter for 60 years.

Paul Kennedy
Birth:
Apr. 4, 1921
Quinton, Oklahoma
Death:
Aug. 6, 2009
Tulsa, Tulsa County, Oklahoma
Burial:
Sunset View „
Amador County, California

Paul Kennedy was an active layman in California serving as a state leader and Pomotional Director. Paul was a generous man and shared his rare book denominational collection to the Historical Archives at Hillsdale College, Moore, OK,

Winston Benton Lawless
Birth:
Feb. 1, 1913
Death:
May 30, 1986
Burial:
Clovis Cemetery, Clovis,
Fresno County, California

Free Will Baptist ordained minister, pastor and leader. He was the California State Executive-Secretary of California FWB's and editor of *"Voice"*. He was manager of the state bookstore.

Archie J. Mayhew
Birth:
May 10, 1926,
Saint Cloud,
Stearns County, Minnesota
Death:
Oct. 26, 1997,
Modesto,
Stanislaus County, California
Burial:
Lakewood Memorial Park,
Hughson,
Stanislaus County, California

The Rev. Mayhew lived in Modesto for 32 years and for his past six years served the Free Will congregation. Previously, he spent more than 17 years as a missionary in Ivory Coast, West Africa. According to his wife, "The Lord called him to go to Ivory Coast and that's where he was happiest. Most of the work was village work. We would go and teach in the villages." Rev. Mayhew lived in Modesto from the time he was 12. He served in the Navy during World War II.

They served faithfully

Doice Lee McAlister
Birth:
Oct. 23, 1929
Pottawatomie County
Oklahoma
Death:
Apr. 27, 2010
Turlock,
Stanislaus County, California
Burial:
San Joaquin Valley National
Cemetery,
Santa Nella Village,
Merced County, California

He was the pastor of Tulock Free Will Baptist church for about 35 yrs. He preached for about 60 yrs. He was great brother and and good pastor and many people loved him. He had over 400 people at his funeral service in the church.
Inscription:
US ARMY Note: KOREA

George W McLain
Birth:
Jun. 6, 1894,
Oklahoma
Death:
Jan., 1965,
Fresno County, California
Burial:
Odd Fellows Cemetery, Fresno,
Fresno County, California

Rev. McLain was a pioneer minister in the state of Oklahoma and known for his successful evangelism and as a church planter. Rev. McLain was of Choctaw Indian descent, of which he was proud. He as a young man, worked closely with Rev. Elzie Yandell, an older minister, in eastern Oklahoma, who mentored him and held revival services with him. He was a motivator wherever he pastored. He often went to a church that was in a low state, and brought it to vitality and on successful financial footing. A son, Joy McLain, was elected delegate to the General Cooperative Ass'n. meeting in Denison, TX in 1934. When the State Ass'n met in Ada, OK; he was elected as Okla. State Evangelist in 1936, along with Dr. I.W. Yandell and Rev. Paul Purcell. In 1941, as state evangelist, he reported having eight revivals, 249 conversions, and organized three churches the past year. He was active in the state work, and often called upon to preach in their meetings. Rev. McLain pastored Ada First FWB in Oklahoma before moving to California, and then the Richmond First and Selma, churches.

Abundant life is waiting

Walter Stanley Mooneyham
Birth:
Jan. 14, 1926
Houston,
Chickasaw County, Mississippi
Death:
Jun. 3, 1991
Los Angeles,
Los Angeles County, California
Burial:
Desert Memorial Park,
Cathedral City,
Riverside County, California,
Plot: b-30,264

Dr. W. Mooneyham joined the U.S. Navy and served in the Pacific Theater (1943-45). He received his Bachelor of Science degree in journalism at Oklahoma Baptist University, Shawnee, Oklahoma (1950) while ministering as pastor at First Free Will Baptist Church, Sulphur, Oklahoma (1949-53). After working with the National Association of Free Will Baptists in Nashville, Tennessee (1954), he became Director of Information (1959) and Interim Executive Director of the National Assn. Of Evangelicals in Wheaton, Illinois (1964).

As a special assistant to Billy Graham, he coordinated the World Congress on Evangelism in Berlin (1966). One year later, he was appointed Vice-President of International Relations for the Billy Graham Evangelistic Association. From 1969 to 1982, he was the President of World Vision Intl., a service agency providing childcare, emergency relief assistance and missions research to Christian denominations in over 30 countries.

He was the recipient of three honorary doctorates: Houghton College, New York (1964), Taylor University, Indiana (1977) and Seattle Pacific University, Washington (1978). Dr. Mooneyham hosted and appeared in many television documentaries and prime-time specials such as *Come Walk the World*, a weekly documentary about Christian missions, and a weekly program, *Larry Jones Presents*, that he produced and which was aired on 200 stations. In 1980, he was the subject of a prime-time documentary about the refugee Vietnamese "boat people" who he helped rescue at sea.

He was the author of eight books and of innumerable magazine articles. His latest book was *Dancing on the Strait and Narrow* from Harper and Row, 1989.

He holds many honors such as the Polish Orthodox Church's Order of Mary Magdalene for extraordinary service to children and the Republic of Korea's highest award to foreigners, the Distinguished Service Award.

George N. Musgrove
Birth:
December 10, 1855
Kings County,
New Brunswick, Canada
Death:
1924
Burial:
Evergreen Cemetery
Los Angeles
Los Angeles County, California
Plot: Section I
He was converted when 19 years of age. He would was a student for the ministry ever made theological Seminary, received his

licensed to preach on December 1, 1879 and was ordained February 20, 1883 by Rev. Louis mild learned, EM. Eight. Quimby and others he held a few churches in New Hampshire before excepting the call to the Arlington church in Rhode Island.

Roy E. Pembrook
Birth:
Aug. 28, 1917
Death:
Dec. 10, 1993
Burial:
Westwood Hills Memorial Park
Placerville
El Dorado County, California
Plot: Parkcreek 74-A4-181
He was a retired minister at the time of His death at age 76. He was converted at age 12 and began to preach at age 15. He was ordained in Missouri on August 17, 1934 at the Mountain Grove FWB church. A native of Watson, Missouri he preached in various churches and held revivals in the state. After moving to California, he served on the Executive Committee and helped organize new churches. He organized or pastored the Martinez, Brentwoods, Antioch and Pleasant Hill churches.

John Lee Reel
Birth:
Jun. 7, 1905
Appleton
Pope County, Arkansas
Death:
Jul. 10, 1989
Visalia
Tulare County, California
Burial:
Visalia Public Cemetery
Visalia
Tulare County,California
Plot: Sect.A, Blk 16, Lot 15,
C/E Grave

His parents were james c. Reel, and Josephine (Prince) Reel.He married Elsie Violet "Vi" Eakin, Oct. 25, 1924, in Pope Co. AR. They had four children: .It was after 1940 census that John and Violet moved to Oklahoma, around the Tulsa area. He became an ordained Free Will Baptist minister, and later moved to California, where he pastored the Visalia FWB Church, and others. He was active in his district association of churches, serving on boards, and was a good pastor.

Tip Richardson
Birth:
Sep. 16, 1923
Norwood, Wright County,
Missouri
Death:
Mar. 3, 2013
Tulare County, California
Burial:

Visalia Public Cemetery
Visalia, Tulare County, California

Tip was born to Arthur and Dora Richardson. He Married the former Nina Kelley in Norwood, Missouri on December 6, 1942. Tip served in the navy during World War II as a dental assistant. In later years, he retired from Tulare County Family Support Division. He served as a minister of the Free Will Baptist Church in various valley locations. He was known for his love of singing and did so until he became ill. He left behind his wife of 70 years, Nina. (Published in Visalia Times-Delta and Tulare Adv-Register on March 6, 2013)

J L Roler
Birth:
Jan. 23, 1845
Racine, Ohio
Death:
Apr. 5, 1939
Burial:
Lindsay-Strathmore Cemetery
Lindsay
Tulare County, California

He was converted in January, 1866 and received his license to preach 10 years later. He was ordained in November, 1884. He was pastor of the Third Alexander and Lodi churches in South East Ohio. He was clerk of the Athens Quarterly Meeting. On March 11, 1869 he married to Alvira Smith.

Death is the entry to Life Evermore

Sheldon J. Smith
Birth:
Apr. 14, 1836
Elbridge
Onondaga County, New York
Death:
May, 1914
California
Burial:
Woodland Cemetery
Woodland,
Yolo County,California
Plot: Blk-17 Lt-31 Gr-15

Smith, son of Bliss and Priscilla (Rounds) SMITH, was married to Miss Emily Hakes Feb. 14, 1856. In 1882 she died, and he afterwards married Miss Susan Stevens.In September 1873. He was ordained by the Church of God. In 1885 he united with the Free Baptists, and pastored of the church at Corey HIll, Van Buren County, Mich. In 1882 he was elected department chaplain of the G.A.R. of the state of Michigan, having served in the late civil war in a New York Regiment."He moved from Michigan to Yolo Co. CA, where in 1910 census, he was living alone atage 74.

John Alexander Logan Waltman
Birth:
Dec. 13, 1886
Kirbyville,
Taney County, Missouri
Death:
Dec. 11, 1959
Turlock
Stanislaus County, California
Burial:
Turlock Memorial Park
Turlock,
Stanislaus County, California

He was married to Livia Elizabeth (Graham) sometime after he arrived in Oklahoma from Missouri, before 1910. They lived in Oklahoma for some years where their children were born. Shortly after 1940, they moved to central Calif., where Rev. Waltman began the Turlock Free Will Baptist Church March 22, 1942, with nineteen charter members. He was elected its first pastor. In the following months lots were purchased and in 1945, a new church auditorium was built at Landers and "C: streets. The church worshiped there for almost twenty years. Rev. Waltman was pastor from 1942-1946. He was active in the state work. He was a member of Turlock at the time of his death at 73 years lacking three days being 74 years. ---info from HISTORICAL CORNER, of the "Voice", official organ of the State Assn of Free Will Baptists.

James Clinton Wood
Birth:
Oct. 25, 1928
Oklahoma
Death:
Dec. 14, 200
Fresno, Fresno County, California
Burial:
Clovis Cemetery, Clovis, Fresno County, California

James Clinton Wood's parents were Walter F. and Hallie Wood. He was an ordained Free Will Baptist minister and pastor, pastoring at Salinas and Tulare, CA.

The saint of God is escorted to a land of joy and peace.

James M. Woodman
Birth:
Feb. 12, 1824,
Tamworth, Carroll County,
New Hampshire
Death:
Dec. 27, 1903,
San Leandro,
Alameda County, California
Burial:
Chico Cemetery, Chico,
Butte County, California

He united with the Free Will Baptist church in Sanbornton when fifteen years of age, and the following year was in preparatory studies of theology with Rev. J. Woodman at Lowell, Mass. He then studied at the Dracut Biblical School in Dracut, Mass, traveled as an evangelist two years and was ordained in 1844 at Limerick, Maine. He entered the Biblical School at Whitestown, N.Y., in 1845, and graduated two years later. He later attended the Botanico Medical College in Cincinnati, Ohio where he received a medical degree May 15, 1848. After preaching a short time at South Parsonfield and at North Berwick, Maine, he went West for his health and ministered to the Honey Creek, Wisconsin church during 1850-56, and the Mt. Pleasant church 1856-61, when in 1862 he went to California, where he has been principal of the Chico Academy. Sometime prior to 1866, Rev. Woodman erected a building for use as Mrs. Woodman's private school. On Nov. 12, 1874, the building was destroyed by fire, evidently the work of arsonists. The Academy was rebuilt and in 1884-5, the academy listed Rev. James M. Woodman, principal, his wife,

Selena, ass't principal; his son, Charles, teacher. In 1897 Rev. Woodman formally retired from active preaching and built a new home in San Leandro, CA. He is author of *"God in Nature and Revelation," "The Song of Cosmology;" "The Neptunian Theory of Creation"* and other articles for newspapers in Boston and Chicago.

Arvel Earl Woolery
Birth:
Feb. 14, 1912
Oklahoma
Death:
Jun. 20, 1982
Lindsay, Tulare County,
California
Burial: Hillcrest Cemetery,
Porterville, Tulare County,
California
Plot: Z-86-4

Woolery was a WW II Army veteran, enlisting 30 Oct. 1943 at Fresno, and mustered out, 09 Jan. 1946. After his service, he became a bi-vocational, ordained Free Will Baptist minister. He worked at different jobs that allowed him to have flexible time. He retired from the Kern Co. School District, in the 1970's. He became pastor of Selma Church, Porterville for several years, then at Earlimart for about a decade. Each place saw progress under his leadership. Rev. Woolery was a kind and generous man, soft spoken, and he usually thought before he spoke. His wisdom was useful to many of his peers and friends.

Joseph Elzie Yandell
Birth:
Feb. 5, 1880
Scott County, Arkansas
Death:
Jan. 23, 1970
Burial:
Clovis Cemetery
Clovis
Fresno County, California

He was ordained at Lodi (Latimer County Oklahoma) to preach for the Free Will Baptist Church in 1904. He farmed as most ministers did during this time, and went far and near to preach. He baptized probably more people in eastern minister of his day. He organized churches, held revivals, funerals and weddings, and was in demand as a speaker wherever he went. In 1929 he took his family to California. He was in the organization of the Oklahoma State Association of Free Will Baptists, at Holdenville, Oklahoma in 1908, where he was elected moderator, and his brother, Dr. I.W. Yandell, clerk. He had a serious demeanor, a good head, and was known for his honesty. He had an active life of faith and preaching for over 67 years. His memorial service was held in the Chapel of California Christian College, Fresno, with Dr. Wade T. Jernigan, officiating.

"He, that has learned to pray, as he ought, possesses the *secret* of a holy life."

Canada

William D Crowell
Birth:
Dec. 9, 1804
Barrington, Nova Scotia,
Canada
Death:
Mar. 7, 1869
Barrington, Nova Scotia,
Canada
Burial:
Old Meeting House Cemetery
Barrington, Nova Scotia,
Canada

Rev. William Donaldson Crowell's name is listed in records from Twenty-First Gen. Conference of Freewill Baptist, as having deceased in 1869, Nova Scotia. From the Crowell-Nickerson Family Tree, and their sourses from Barrington, Shelburne, Nova Scotia, he was the son of Heman Crowell, (1779-1858), and Abigail Young, (1786-1866) both listed as bur. in this cemetery also. Not much is known of his ministry, except that he was active in his area. He died of Stomach Cancer. Thomas Crowell, possibly a brother, is also listed as ordained in 182? and served in Barrington, N.S., area Free Baptist churches.

What a day!

What a place!

What a delight!

Chester Heard
Birth:
September 22, 1806
Newport, Canada
Death:
Sep. 3, 1887
Massawippi, Québec
Burial:
Massawippi Cemetery
Massawippi,
Quebec, Canada

He was a son of William Heard, who fought in the battle of Bunker Hill, and of Tirza, daughter of Col. William Williams, who fought in Bennington, Vermont. His father moved from Holton, Massachusetts to Newport, Canada, 30 miles into the wilderness, where in a log cabin, Chester was born. There was no church nor schoolhouse. Marcy Harvey, afterwards the mother of Dr. George H, Ball, taught school for short time in a log cabin on the farm of Mr. Heard. On his 16th birthday, after earnest prayers knelt alone in the woods by the side of a tree stump and began his first prayer. 'Oh Lord', were the only words that he could pray, but he'd read to the Bible for comfort and peace and erected a family altar. This was the beginning of revival that continued for years. Converted in September, 1822 he was licensed in September, 1841. He could not accept the doctrine of the

only church, a Calvinistic Baptist, in this vicinity. Finding himself in accord with the teaching of the Free Baptist treaties, he was ordained in September 1842. He was an earnest supporter of all of the Free Baptist missionary interest and a firm friend of his denomination. He took *The Morning Star* for over 50 years. He was present at the General Conference at Weare's, New Hampshire in 1880.

Death is not the end of the story for those who know the Lord

Jennie Johnson
Birth:
1868
Death:
1967
Burial:
Dresden Cemetery
Dresden, Ontario, Canada

After her conversion at a Baptist revival at sixteen, Jennie Johnson followed the call to preach. Raised in an African abolitionist community in Ontario, Canada, she immigrated to the United

States to attend the African Methodist Episcopal Seminary at Wilberforce University. On an October evening in 1909 she stood before a group of Free Will Baptist preachers in the small town of Goblesville, Michigan, and was received into the ordained ministry. She was the first ordained woman to serve in Canada and spent her life building churches and working for racial justice on both sides of the national border.

Asa McGray
Birth:
Sep. 18, 1780
Maine
Death:
Dec. 30, 1843
Nova Scotia, Canada
Burial:
Centreville Cemetery,
Centreville,Nova Scotia, Canada
Plot: McGray Burial Plot -
behind the church

From the Shelburne County Genealogical Society: The Free Will Baptist Church Records gives Asa's death date as 30 December, where as his gravestone gives 28 Dec.----. Information provided from a letter written by Arthur N. McGray (1862-1949) In 1871-72 my grandfather, Asa T. McGray, had decided to move all the McGray family who had been buried back of the old, first Meeting House, where the land was low and wet, to new graves on the higher land back of the present Church. He had recently

bought that property for a home for his daughter, Almira (McGray) Kenney.The morning of the day when the remains of the old Minister, Rev. Asa McGray, was to be removed, many of the family came to the new cemetery, for grandfather has announced that he would remove the wooden cover, over the glass face-plate to see what change had taken place in the 30 years of burial. Edgar Smith and I, on our way to school, were allowed to come close to the coffin, when grandfather took off the wooden coverage of the glass. Everyone gasped, for under that glass was a face that might have been alive only a day before. Silently, we all looked on, as tears flowed. The state of preservation was perfect. Then, as grandfather worked a small chisel under the glass, the outside air flowed in, and the film of features collapsed to dust forever.

Inscription:
In Memory of REV. ASA MCGRAY
WHO died Dec. 28, 1843
in the 64 year of his age.
A native of the United States and
first founder of the
Freewill Baptist Denomination in
Nova Scotia.

Written in Durham, ME History, that he was a successful evangelist and organizer of churches. Ordained Sept 26, 1814.

Their Works

Do Follow Them.

Colorado

Virgil Florence
Birth:
Dec. 25, 1906
Death:
Feb. 26, 1979
Burial:
Linn Grove Cemetery,
Greeley,
Weld County, Colorado,
Plot: Blk 17, lot 58, spc 2

Rev. Florence was licensed to preach in 1930, and in 1931,he was ordained to the gospel ministry by the Free Will Baptists.

He served as Evangelist for the Grand River Ass'n of Oklahoma, and then as moderator for the Grand River Association. He was the first Free Will Baptist minister to go to the Northwest Area of U.S. in 1951. He organized six new Free Will Baptist churches and pastored the following: (In chronological order: Oak Grove, OK; Watonga, OK; Shahan, OK; Coweta, OK; Duck Creek, at Mounds, OK; Bixby, at Bixby, OK; Broken Arrow, OK; In Idaho: he organized Buhl; In Oregon: Klamath Falls; California: Norwalk and Hughson; Shellenberger FWB at Bixby, OK; Guymon, Guymon, OK; and in retirement as pastor, he served as supply pastor, evangelist and mission worker. It was in Greeley, Colorado when he was working in mission work he went to his reward. He was also listed in *Who's Who Among Free Will Baptists.*

Roy L. Thomas
Birth:
Sep. 14, 1930
Greeley, Colorado
Death:
Mar. 23, 2003
Burial:
Linn Grove Cemetery, Greeley,
Weld County, Colorado,
Plot: Blk 24, lot 44, spc 1

Dr. Roy L. Thomas, former General Director of the Home Missions Dept. of the National Association of Free Will Baptists. He grew up on a farm near Buhl, Idaho. After high school, he attended the University of Idaho in 1948-49. He served in the U. S. Air Force the years of 1951-1955, with foreign service in Korea and Japan. He accepted Christ as his Savior in 1951 at the First FWB Church, Buhl, Idaho, but was immediately sent to Korea. After returning to the states, he was ordained as a FWB minister in 1954, and also was married to his wife, Pat, who is a native of Hobbs, New Mexico. He organized the First FWB Church of Artesia, New Mexico that same year. After serving the Artesia congregation for two years, he moved to Nashville, Tennessee to attend FWB Bible College. He graduated with honors from that institution in 1960 with a Bachelor of Arts Degree. While a student he pastored two different churches in Tennessee; Shady Grove Free Will Baptist Church and First FWB Church, Springfield, Tennessee.

Dr. Thomas was sent to Denver, Colorado as a home missionary by the National Home Missions Board in 1961 where he established the First Free Will Baptist Church of that city. He furthered his education by earning a Masters of Divinity Degree from Luther Rice Seminary in 1978, and was granted a Doctor of Divinity Degree from Bethany Seminary in 1989. In December 1970 he was appointed as Associate Director of the National Home Missions Department, Nashville, Tennessee, and became General Director in 1978. He served in that position until his retirement in December 1995, making a total of 25 years on the National Home Missions staff, and a total of 35 years' affiliation with the Department. While he served as General Director of the Home Missions Department, there were over 200 churches established throughout the North American continent and the U.S. owned islands of Puerto Rico and the Virgin Islands. Under his leadership, the Home Missions Department sponsored countless Evangelism and Church Growth Conferences, and the Old-ime Camp Meeting at the National Convention. He started the Church Extension Loan Fund, the Helping Hands Church Building Team, the Associate Missionary Program, the Aquila and Priscilla Program, the Tentmaker Program, and developed numerous Evangelism and Church Growth publications. He also authored the books, *Planting and Growing a Fundamental Church* and published *The Journal of Benjamin Randall*, and many other historical Free Will Baptist and church growth books and materials. Dr. Thomas has been an evangelist, conducting over 150 revival meetings and conferences in almost every state where Free Will Baptists have churches, and in some foreign countries.

Connecticut

Albert H Chase
Birth:
June 1, 1823
Killingly, Connecticut
Death:
1883
Burial:
Chase Cemetery #2
East Killingly,
Windham County, Connecticut

An early Freewill Baptist minister, editor, and leader. Served in several states. His ancestors were of Puritan stock and Oliver, his father, was a Revolutionary soldier. His thirst for knowledge lead him for a time to Smithville Seminary in Rhode Island. He married in 1844 and nine years later in the ministry. He then attended New Hampton Institution. In 1855 he became the pastor of the church at Cherry Valley, Ohio where he remained for two years and then entered upon a seven-year pastorate in New Lyme, Ohio. During the next three years he was employed in raising money for the Freeman's Mission. In January 1867 he became publishing agent and business manager of the *Christian Freeman,* a position he held for two years. He then labored in Cleveland, Ohio and in Harrisburg, Pennsylvania remaining with the latter church until he was elected corresponding Sec. of the Home

Mission Society. During his labors in this position he made Hillsdale, Michigan his home publishing for a time *The Evangelist.* Later he preached in various churches in the vicinity. On account of delicate health he visited Tennessee, yet gained but little. Called back to his home in New Lyme, Ohio to attend a wedding he was attacked with hemorrhage to his lungs where his earthly life ended. He was a man of positive convictions and found no time for neutral ground and disliked compromises. However, he had many warm friends and his influence was widely felt in the denomination. His children Roscoe and Mary graduated from Hillsdale College, Michigan and became successful educators.

William Dick

Birth:
Jan. 31, 1812
Bathgate
West Lothian, Scotland
Death:
Mar. 7, 1853
Danielson
Windham County, Connecticut
Burial:
Westfield Cemetery
Danielson
Windham County, Connecticut

Rev. William Dick was one of eleven children, four of whom became ministers of the gospel. At about nine years of age, he lost both his parents--his father drowned while bathing in the St. Lawrence River, while traveling to Quebec, Canada, and eight days later, their mother. The family travelled on with the company and settled at Lanark, Canada, their destination. William was licensed to preach in 1836, and his thirst for knowledge led him to prosecute studies while others slept. He entered Hamiliton Academy, now Madison Univ., 1836-37, with with his brother, Robert, but both dismissed for their adhering to an anti-slavery society. He entered Hamiliton

College, at Clinton in 1837, graduated in 1841. During this time he was a faithful member of the church of which Rev. Hiram Whitcher was pastor. He preached successively in Norway, Middleville, and Plainfield (NY). While a student of theology at Yale Seminary he preached much at Naugatuck, where he afterward married Maria L. Baldwin. He then spent several years in Canada where he organized churches. In the fall of 1851, he settled at Chepachet, R.I., but because of his views not well supported. He was unanimously chosen by the yearly Meeting to become the pioneer of an interest at Danielson, Conn. Here, in four short months, he drew together a large and permanent congregation, and completely won their affection and confidence. He died after a brief, distressing illness, March 7, 1853, aged 41 years. Martin J. Steere preached his funeral sermon; twenty ministers were in attendance. A stone marks his resting-place in Danielson, erected by his brethren of the Rhode Island Quarterly Meeting.

Louisa Arnold Fenner

Birth:
Jun. 22, 1832
Massachusetts
Death:
Jun. 17, 1909
Connecticut
Burial:
Grove Street Cemetery
Putnam
Windham County, Connecticut
Her parents were Nathaniel and Sarah Cook Buzzell. She was married twice; namely, Alvin Arnold and James Madison Fenner. She was converted in Providence, Rhode Island and was greatly blessed in Christian work.

After the death of her second husband she labored as an evangelist in several of the New England states with great success. She was ordained on March 5, 1878 at Foster. She passed at the Union Church in Foster, Rhode Island, the East Putnam, Connecticut church. Afterwards, an evangelist in Starksboro, Vermont. Her later ministry was spent in the state of Connecticut.

Josiah Graves

Birth:
September 27, 1775
Middletown, Connecticut
Death:
Jul. 24, 1825
Burial:
Old East Cemetery
Middletown
Middlesex County, Connecticut

He was the son of a Congregational clergyman, and was converted in the spring of 1794. In 1800, he united with the Baptist Church at Hartford. June 25, a Baptist Church was organized near his home which he joined and soon began to preach. He was ordained on October 31, 1811 and began an earnest ministry throughout the adjoining counties and met with some opposition but was blessed of God. Becoming convinced that close communion was unscriptural and un-Christian, he plainly told his church his position and began to preach free full salvation. In 1821, 12 persons put their trust in Christ and came out to form the first Free Will Baptist Church in Connecticut. At the close of the following year, Mr. Graves received a visit from David Marks, a nephew of Mrs. Graves. Marks stayed in the native place of his parents, comforting the people and introducing among them The Religious Former. Thus, Mr. Graves heard his own sentiments preach for the first time. After this, Rev. Eli Towne's saddlebags were stolen while passing through from Maryland to

Connecticut. A copy of the Buzzell's magazine, had been left in the woods as worthless by fell into the hands of Graves. On December 28, 1832, he wrote to The Informer, of his becoming known of the denomination. Two brethren from Rhode Island visited him in June, 1824 and the acquaintance was so mutually satisfying that in October the same year Mr. Graves attended the session of that body and with his church and united. The members of this church had greatly increased in opposition had ceased. He was a man of true convictions and with meekness he overcame opposition.He was a Elder for 50 years.

Clarissa H *Danforth* Richmond
Birth:
1792,
Weathersfield, Vermont
Feb. 15, 1864
Burial:
Westford Village Cemetery,
Westford, Windham County,
Connecticut

She entered John Colby's meetings in 1815 as a thoughtless, vain young lady, but she was awakened to a greater power, and began to follow in a new life.
She was well educated; had extraordinary talent and undoubted piety. Tall in person, dignified in appearance, easy in manners, and she had all the elements of a noble woman. As a speaker her language was ready and simple, her gestures appropriate, and her voice penetrated to the corners of the largest house. She held hundreds

with fixed attention for an hour, to listen to the claims of her heavenly Master. Revivals attended her labors wherever she went.
She preached in western Massachusetts, New Hampshire, and Rhode Island. Her many revivals resulted always in the organization of several churches. Many people of other denominations flocked to hear her preach and listened with deep emotion. She preached in 1820 in Vermont to large congregations with much success.

Zalmon Tobey
Birth:
Jul. 27, 1791,
Norfolk, Litchfield County,
Connecticut
Death:
Sep. 17, 1858,
Warren, Bristol County,
Rhode Island
Burial:
Canaan Valley Cemetery,
North Canaan
Litchfield County, Connecticut

A graduate of Brown University in 1817; an early minister of the Freewill Baptist church, uniting from the Calvinism to the Freewill Bapt. in 1826. He resided in Providence, Rhode Island between 1817-1831.

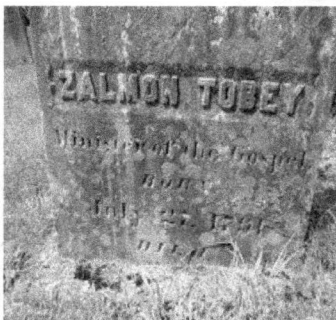

His name is linked in the early Minutes of the General Connection. He was elected moderator of Union Conference, 1824, in Cranston, RI, where a society was formed "for the purpose of furnishing interest in

preaching in destitute places in the state." He "rendered efficient service by publishing the *Freewill Baptist Magazine* for about four years. In January, 1828, at the Q.M. held in Pawtucket, Tobey gave a report as he had been a delegate this first General Conference in VT. He was a good scholar and a useful and estimable man.

Daniel Williams
Birth:
Oct. 6, 1790,
Rhode Island
Death:
Jul. 16, 1876,
Connecticut
Burial:
Bartlett Cemetery #1,
Killingly, Windham County,
Connecticut,
Plot: 1st sec R/E
He was baptized by Rev. John Colby in 1813. He organized the Foster church in 1824 and remained the pastor until his death. He was a descendant of Rev. Roger Williams.

District of Columbia

Richard M Lawrence
Birth:
Feb. 29, 1848
Dover, Kent, England
Death:
Dec. 25, 1934
Washington
District of Columbia
Burial:
Rock Creek Cemetery
Washington
District of Columbia
Plot: Section M, Lot 140, Site 5

Rev. Lawrence came to America with his parents at seven years of age, and lived on a farm in Wisconsin until twenty-one, when he entered Hillsdale College and graduated from the Classical Course in 1873. He was a loyal member of the Theological Society, and afterward, with his brother, founded the Lawrence Prize, which is still a stimulus to efforts of the noblest kind. He taught school in California the year following his graduation, and in October, 1874. sailed for India, where he labored for the next seven years as a Free Baptist missionary. In December, 1878, he was married to Miss Frankie Millard, who died in September, 1881.Mr. Lawrence then returned to the United States and took a course in the Grand Rapids Business College. After graduation he kept books for the Voight Milling Co., until opportunity opened to enter business for himself. He was a co-founder of the Valley Milling Co. in Grand

Rapids, Michigan.He was married a second time, May 1, 1884, at Grand Rapids, to Miss Mary J. Ford. After a successful business career of five years he retired to devote himself more exclusively to Christian work. He took charge of the "Free Baptist" for sixteen months, but left that position after getting it upon a self-supporting basis. After a period of comparative retirement he was, in the fall of 1896, called to the Presidency of Parker College, which post held for 4 years. His 2nd wife died in 1909 and in 1912, he married Charlotte Loukes who was from Fairwater, Wisconsin.

Now we know that if the earthly tent we live in is destroyed, we have a building from God, an eternal house in heaven, not built by human hand

Florida

Isaac Joshua Blackwelder
Birth:
Dec. 16, 1896
Death:
May 9, 1980
Burial:
New Zion Cemetery,
Lake Butler,
Union County, Florida

A very active pastor, minister and leader in the early part of the Free Will Baptist denomination. He was one of the committee members selected by the Co-operative General Association in Denison, Texas in 1934 to make farther plans for the merger with the General Conference to form the National Association of Free Will Baptists in 1935. He was a member of the Publication Board and the first Secretary-Treaurer of foreign missions in the newly formed association. He was active as a pastor, church planter, and provided leadership in the denomination during his 52 years as a minister. He served 24 churches in his pastoral services. He was the founder the Trinity

FWB church in Nashville, Tn. in 1942 and pastored in North Carolina, Georgia and Florida.

W. E. George
Birth:
Jun. 9, 1918
Death:
Apr. 20, 1998
Burial:
Bethany Baptist Church Cemetery, Holmes County, Florida

A veteran of the U.S. Army, serving as a staff sergeant in Europe during the Normandy Invasion. He was awarded the Good Conduct Medal for exemplary behavior and efficiency. He was ordained a Free Will Baptist Minister in 1955, serving several different churches in Northwest Florida and South Alabama. He retired from Salem Free Will Baptist Church on Sept. 19, 1995, after pastoring there for 24 years. He served as trustee and board member for the Free Will Baptist Children's Home in Eldridge, Alabama for 30 years. He received the "Pioneer Preacher" Award at Bethany Bible College in Dothan, Ala., on June 6, 1991. He conducted numerous revivals in Florida, Georgia and Alabama, and officiated over 1,000 funerals during his 43 years as a minister.

Ralph R Kennan
Birth:
Sep. 16, 1866
Minnesota
Death:
Nov. 18, 1948
Nassau County, Florida
Burial:
Oakwood Cemetery

Hilliard
Nassau County, Florida
Plot: Section 2, Grave 54

His parents moved to Michigan where they were active in church work, and their children could obtain an education. Rev. Ralph R. as well as his brother Rev. Albert L., obtained degrees from Hillsdale College, Hillsdale, Michigan, and Albert L. served in India as a missionary in the Free Baptist mission endeavor there. As seen from censuses, Rev. Ralph R. edited a church paper in Minneapolis, and then pastored until he moved to Florida, where he engaged in business where his brother, Albert, had already located. Ralph married Stella D. Cole, b. NY. Numerous city directories list him as being pastor of the Free Baptist church in Portland ME. His parents were Rev's. George Kennan (1832 - 1905) and Ada Montgomery Kennan (1839 - 1894).

Daniel Frederick Pelt
Birth:
Mar. 25, 1909
Death:
Jun. 22, 1975   Burial:
Comerford-Pelt Cemetery, Marianna, Jackson County, Florida

He attended Zion Bible School (1930-32) near Blakely, Georgia. He was ordained in 1930.
He attended Alabama State Teachers College in Troy where he graduated. He did graduate work at Emory University in Atlanta, Ga. He was a teacher and pastor, pastoring churches in Alabama, Georgia and Florida. He was one of the founders of the Florida State Association and served as the moderator for

eleven years. He attended some of the National Associational meetings, including the first one in 1935 in Nashville, Tennessee. He was writer for the Advanced Sunday School Quarterly for the Free Will Baptist Press.

Chester H. Pelt, Sr
Birth:
Apr. 3, 1912
Death:
Nov. 7, 1994
Burial:
Comerford-Pelt Cemetery, Marianna, Jackson County, Florida

He was licensed to preach at Marvin Chapel FWB church near Marianna, Florida in 1932 at age twenty. He attended Zion Bible School 1932-34 near Blakely, Georgia. In the fall of 1935 entered Bob Jones University in Cleveland, Tennessee. In 1938 he and his wife, Mildred Watson Pelt, moved to pastor churches in Pitt County, North Carolina. There he attended East Carolina Teachers College and then transferred to Atlantic Christian College, Wilson, N.C. and graduated in 1940. In 1941 he became pastor of the Edgemont Church in Durham, NC. He was commissioned on June 29, 1943 as a First Lieutenant in the Chaplains Corps to the Army Air Force and served as chaplain of the 39th Bomb Group, 314 Wing of the 20th Air Force on the Island of Guam until VJ Day in 1945. After returning from overseas in January 1946, he was stationed at Pope AFB at Fort Bragg, NC and was relieved from active duty in June 1948. He remained in active reserve in the Army until he was honorable discharged on April 3, 1972 with the rank of Colonel. He was the first Free Will Baptist

Chaplain. After the war he did graduate work at Florida State University and afterwards become the Director of Student Personnel at Chipola Junior College and a instructor in Psychology, while pastoring rural churches in Georgia and Alabama. Afterwards he resumed his education at Alabama State Teachers College, Troy, Alabama.

True to the will of the great Divine.

John M. Rich
Birth:
Apr. 6, 1919
Death:
Jul. 18, 2003
Burial:
Shiloh Baptist Church Cemetery
Chipley
Washington County, Florida

He was a minister serving in Georgia and Florida. He married Mary Velma Parker Rich (1915 - 1992).

Missionary
Mabel Alice Bailey Willey
Birth:
Jun. 13, 1905,
Huntsville,
Madison County, Alabama
Death:
Jan. 16, 1968,
Texas
Burial:
Woodlawn Cemetery,
Miami, Dade County, Florida

Mabel Alice Bailey Willey was a pastor's wife, missionary, mother, teacher and missions lecturer. Born in Huntsville, Alabama, she was a graduate of Toccoa Falls College in north Georgia and Nyack College in New York. In 1930. she and her new husband arrived in Miami to pastor the newly organized Alliance Gospel Tabernacle. A year later they had pastorates in North Carolina. In 1938 they went to Panama to work as missionaries among the Choco Indians. They returned to Miami a year later where Mrs. Willey survived a bout with black water malaria. In 1940, they packed the family and moved to Jaruco, Cuba where they assisted in a training program for Cuban pastors. In 1942 they moved to the province of Pinar del Rio and founded the Seminario Los Cedros del Libano, which trained pastors to serve in Iglesia Bautista Libre de Cuba (the Free Will Baptist Church of Cuba). Mabel Willey served as an instructor and the school administrator there for 16 years. Their days as missionaries to Cuba ended in 1960 and they returned to Miami due to Fidel Castro's regime. Undaunted, they opened the Free Will Baptist Refugee Center which responded to the needs of thousands of

Cubans fleeing from the oppression of Castro's communism. Mabel, after the death of her husband in 1968, embarked on an extensive ministry speaking to mission conferences, women's seminars and retreats in Japan and Europe. In her mid-60's she started a ministry to professional women in Panama, which included the wives of some of the high ranking government officials. In 1978, she was one of the first former U.S. missionaries allowed to return to Cuba for a visit. She returned six times before her death. In 1988, the government of Cuba allowed the re-opening of the Seminario. Her autobiography, *Through the Gate,* was published by Randall House Publications. She died in Bryan, Texas while living with daughter Barbara Willey Moehlman. In addition to her daughter she is survived by her son Tom Willey, Jr. the director of the Miami Office of World Relief. Her services were at the Iglesia Bautista Libre Ebenezer in Miami.

Thomas Willey, Sr
Birth:
Jan. 31, 1898,
New Jersey
Death:
Oct. 18, 1968,
Miami, Dade County, Florida
Burial:
Woodlawn Cemetery,
Miami-Dade County, Florida,

The Rev. Thomas H. Willey, veteran Free Will Baptist missionary to Latin America, died undergoing treatment for cancer.

Willey, was one of the denomination's early senior missionaries, serving in Latin America under Free Will Baptist auspices since 1936. The scene was a crude altar in a little Baptist church in the North. The year was 1898. The infant Willey was taken there by his loving, God-honoring, praying mother who gave her most cherished possession, the son of her own womb, to the Lord with a prayer that he would be used for the Lord's glory. The steps were all steps of faith. He was converted as a small lad and licensed to preach at age 14. He had an unforgettable encounter with a lost world at a missionary meeting in St. George Church, Philadelphia. He became Methodism's oldest enrollment at Asbury College for Christian training with no financial backing -a circuit riding ministry as a Methodist preacher in the rolling hills of Kentucky-a missionary assignment in the jungles of Peru - a home missions ministry then to Panama and, ultimately, Cuba. The Funeral service was held at Ebenezer Free Will Baptist Church (Spanish) in Miami. Foreign mission board Vice-Chairman Raymond Riggs of Detroit and General Director Reford Wilson of Nashville, long associates of the deceased, officiated assisted by other associates of the veteran missionary. They invited those wishing to express respects to do so by memorial contributions to the Thomas H. Willey Memorial Loan Fund, established by the family in cooperation with the foreign board to assist church construction in Panama. Surviving Mr. Willey are his wife, the former Mabel Alice Bailey; one son, Thomas, Jr., a Free Will Baptist missionary to Panama; and one daughter, Mrs. Barbara Willey Moehlman of Miami. Mr. Willey, known throughout the denomination as "Pop," was the first sent by his denomination to Latin America where he pioneered work in Panama in 1936 and in Cuba in 1942. He also made surveys leading to the

establishment of Free Will Baptist work in Brazil in 1958. Prior to appointment by Free Will Baptists, Mr. Willey served in Peru under auspices of the Christian and Missionary Alliance.

Charles Cecil Williamson
Birth
Bowling Green, Florida
February 20, 1940
Death
Lakeland, Florida
October 25, 2011

Cecil was a Minister and a member of the Freewill Baptist Organization and also a Army veteran. He was a well-known evangelist and pastored the Bartow church for many years.

Nathan Woodworth
Birth:
Mar. 29, 1824
Wayne, Ohio
Death:
Mar. 16, 1901
Welaka
Putnam County, Florida
Burial:
Oakwood Cemetery
Putnam County, Florida

He was a son of John Woodworth. He experienced the new birth in 1841. He was a student at Geauga Seminary and received license to preach in 1847 and ordained four years later. His pastorates were in Warren, Illinois; Rochester, Wheatland, and Wayne, Wisconsin; Crystal Lake and Nashua, Florida. He served as a delegate to the General Conference and was engaged in teaching during part of his ministry. He married Jerusha Bidwell in 1848.

Inscription:
"Blessed are the dead which die in the Lord"

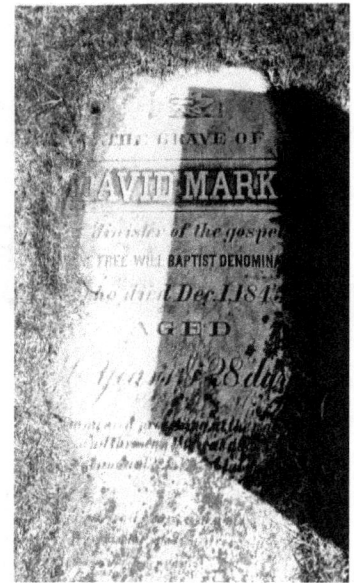

This marker is in the Oberlin Cemetery in Oberlin, Ohio.

Marks was one of the most able leaders in the Randall Movement of Free Will Baptists.

His funeral was preached by the lawyer turned preacher Rev. Charles Finney

Georgia

Amos Banks Adams
Birth:
Sep. 13, 1897
Death:
Nov. 12, 1953
Burial:
Satilla Freewill Baptist Church
Cemetery
Hazlehurst
Jeff Davis County,Georgia

His name appeared in the South Georgia Minutes in 1936 and during 1938-1953. He married Annie Warnock Adams (1904 - 1982).

William Amos Addison
Birth:
Apr. 14, 1907
Georgia
Death:

Nov. 17, 1977
Seminole County,Georgia
Burial:
Pilgrims Rest Church Cemetery
Colquitt
Miller County,Georgia

He served in the Martin and Little River Conferences according to the minutes of both Q.M's. Son of George M. Addison and Rosa Miller. His wife was Alma Monday (1907 - 1991).
Inscription:
In Heaven There is One Angel More.

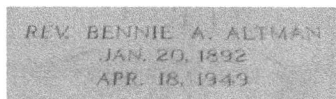

Bennie Allen Altman
Birth:
Jan. 20, 1892
Death:
Apr. 18, 1949
Burial:
Pineview Cemetery
Folkston
Charlton County,Georgia

According to South Georgia minutes he served there between 1940-48.He was a son ofMarion Altman (1866 - 1946) and Maggie Altman (1860 - 1926) he was married to Mattie Lou Mizell Altman (1896 - 1982).

John R Amburgey
Birth:
Apr. 30, 1940
West Virginia
Death:
Aug. 14, 2002

Patmos
Baker County,Georgia
Burial:
Patmos Free Will Baptist Church
Cemetery
Patmos
Baker CountyGeorgia

Amburgey,62-year-old pastor of Patmos Free Will Baptist Church in Newton. He was licensed to preach in 1979, ordained in 1980, and had served as pastor at Patmos since 1997. Rev. Amburgey, a native of W. VA, and U.S. Army Veteran, was an alumnus of Hillsdale FWB College, and Salem Bible College, Brevard Com. College (FL) and Bethany Theological Seminary in Dothan, AL. He had pastored churches in AL, MS, and FL, before coming to Patmos Church in GA. In addition to his pastoral ministry, Amburgey served on various boards and committees. He was elected Sec'y of Georgia State Board on Camping (1986-'88; 1998-2002). John Amburgey was known as a man with a sense of humor who supported and promoted every phase of denominational work.

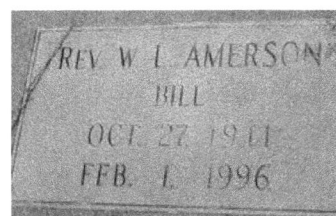

W L Amerson
Birth:
Oct. 27, 1911
Death:
Feb. 1, 1996
Burial:
Pine Level Freewill Baptist
Church Cemetery
Chester
Dodge County,Georgia

He was a Georgia minister serving in the Georgia Union.

H A Ammons
Birth:
1845
Death:
1915
Burial:
Memorial Freewill Baptist Church
Cemetery
Surrency
Appling County,Georgia

Early Georgia minister whose record is found in the 1907 South Georgia Minutes. He was a private in the CSA in Company A, 4th Regiment. he was married to Arvenie James Ammons (1848 - 1920.

Leonard Short Anthony
Birth:
May 28, 1881
Death:
Jan. 19, 1944
Burial:
New Life Freewill Baptist Church
Cemetery
Marion County,Georgia

Active minister whose name appears in the Chattahoochee, Little River, Midway, Union and Georgia Union Minutes.

Allen Bruce Ard
Birth:
Jul. 21, 1877
Death:
Mar. 5, 1966
Burial:
Salem Cemetery
Desser
Seminole County,Georgia

Early minister serving in the Martin Assn. according to their minutes from 1919 to 1964. His name also appears in the Midway Minutes in 1919.

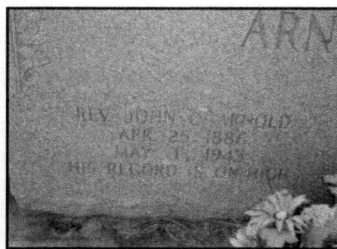

John Calvin Arnold
Birth:
Apr. 25, 1886
Death:
May 1, 1943
Burial:
Zion Hill Cemetery
Millwood
Ware County,Georgia

Minister in the Little River Conference.

Where death is, God was there beforehand to deliver.

Missionary Laura Belle Barnard
Birth:
Feb. 13, 1907
Death:
Mar. 10, 1992
Burial:
Ebenezer Cemetery,
Glennville,
Tattnall County,
Georgia,
Plot: E2

Free Will Baptist educator, missionary, humanitarian was born and reared in Glennville, Georgia. After graduation from high school, she attended South Georgia Teachers College in Statesboro, and then transferred to Columbia Bible College in South Carolina. She graduated from Columbia in 1932 and shortly thereafter she sensed a call to evangelical mission work. In 1935 she was commissioned for mission work in India by the General Conference of Free Will Baptists of the South. That year the General Conference merged with the Cooperative General Association of Free Will Baptists, a group in the Midwest and Southwest, to form the National Association of Free Will Baptists, becoming the first missionary of a newly formed denomination. Barnard began her mission in Kotagiri, South India, in the summer of 1935. She worked among the "untouchables," the lowest class in the Hindu caste system. In the early 1940s she moved back to the United States and served briefly as a teacher at the fledgling Free Will Baptist Bible College in Nashville,

Tennessee, but she soon returned to India, where she remained until 1957. Upon completion of her Master's Degree at Columbia Bible College in 1960, she became a Professor of Missions at the Free Will Baptist Bible College, from which she retired in 1972. Barnard wrote a number of books, including *His Name among All Nations* (1946), which is a theology of missions, and *Touching the Untouchables* (1985), her autobiography. Barnard retired to her hometown of Glennville, where she engaged in numerous ministries, including humanitarian aid to Mexican migrant workers.

John Nelson Barnes
Birth:
Sep. 18, 1895
Death:
Sep. 18, 1961
Burial:
Sowhatchee Cemetery, Blakely
Early County, Georgia

Gerald Baxley
Birth:
Sep. 17, 1943
Dothan
Houston County, Alabama
Death:
Oct. 25, 1995
Jesup
Wayne County, Georgia
Burial:
Omega Cemetery
Baxley
Appling County, Georgia

The 52-year-old minister pastored Surrency Free Will Baptist Church for seven years. Rev. Baxley was ordained to

preach in Feb. 1968. His first pastorate was at his home church, Corinth FWB in Midland City, Alabama. During his 27-year ministry, he pastored eight churches in three states--AL, KY, and GA. He was within 10 days of relocating to his ninth pastorate (New Lebanon FWB Church in Tishomingo, MS, when he died. In addition to pastoral work, Baxley was active in local associational outreach. He served as clerk of Alabama Cahaba River Ass'n, and Georgia's So. Georgia Ass'n. The Alabama Home Missions Board employed him for a time as interim pastor for the mission work in Enterprise.

John Lewis Batchelor
Birth:
Sep. 10, 1925
Death:
May 29, 2004
Burial:
Father's Home Church Cemetery
Camilla
Mitchell County, Georgia

Minister in the Martin and Midway Assn's. His wife was Margie Horn Batchelor (1931 - 2013).

Johnny Ralph Batchelor
Birth:
Aug. 1, 1893
Miller County, Georgia
Death:
Jul. 6, 1962
Mayhaw
Miller County, Georgia
Burial:
White Plains Freewill Baptist
Church Cemetery
Lucile
Early County, Georgia

Minister. Married to Pauline Inez Cooper Batchelor (1889 - 1963) and a son named Bruce Lawton Batchelor (1911 - 1985).

L R Beach
Birth:
1867
Death:
Jun. 12, 1950
Burial:
Live Oak Freewill Baptist Church
Cemetery
Milford
Baker County, Georgia
He was a minister in the Martin Assn.

Ed. C. Beers
Birth:
unknown
New York, USA
Death:
Sep. 18, 1872
Muscogee County, Georgia
Burial:
Rock Baptist Church Cemetery
Cataula
Harris County, Georgia

SPECULATIVE that this individual

is buried at Rehoboth (a.k.a. Rock) Baptist Cemetery - he was residing near Cataula at the time of his death and his son is buried at this cemetery. Said to have been of Dutch ancestry. Aged 74 years on the 1870 census, so evidently born about 1796. Married Sarah Unknown, who survived him. In 1854, he was preacher at the Providence Free Will Baptist Church on St. Mary's Road in Muscogee County, Georgia. They appear as Edmund BEARS (74, born in New York, retired tailor) and Sarah BEARS (61, born South Carolina), with William (38, grist miller), Victoria (33, farm hand), Emma (11, at home), James (9), Charles (7), Ida (5), and Clinton (3), as well as John McNEIL (30, farm hand), Mary WELLS (40, at home) and William WELLS (8) in the household. Sarah appears as a widow, aged 75 years, in the 1880 census household of her son, E. W. BEERS in Georgia Militia District #672 (Hamilton District) in Harris County, Georgia."E. C. BEERS KILLED.--We learn that when the workmen engaged in bridging Standing Boy Creek returned from dinner yesterday, they found the body of E. C. BEERS in the creek. His satchel was on the tressel at the end of the bridge. It is supposed from this fact that he was resting on the bridge and had fallen asleep and fell, and in the fall struck his head against one of the timbers. He was aged about 70 years. He left a wife and son (E. W. BEERS) who lives near Cataula, Harris county. This is in substance that we learned of the sad affair." [Columbus (GA) Sun newspaper, Thursday, 19 SEP 1872, p. 3.]"THE GEORIGA PRESS [news from around the state].

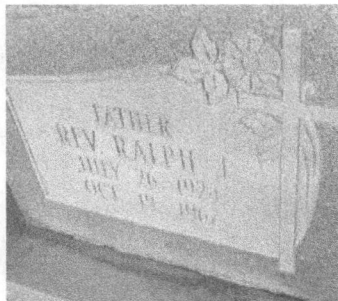

Ralph J. Bell
Birth:
Jul. 25, 1924
Death:
Oct. 19, 1967
Burial:
New Enterprise Freewill Baptist
Church Cemetery
Seminole County,Georgia

Member of Midway Conference.

David W Blanton
Birth:
Jun. 2, 1857
Death:
Nov. 12, 1916
Burial:
New Hope Free Will Baptist
Church Cemetery
Madray Springs
Wayne County,Georgia

Preacher in the Ogeechee and South Georgia Quarterly Meetings.

Isaac J. Blanton
Birth:
Feb. 14, 1861
Duplin County,North Carolina
Death:
Mar. 16, 1926
Surrency
Appling County,Georgia
Burial:
Memorial Freewill Baptist Church
Cemetery
Surrency
Appling County,Georgia

Isaac was born to Joshua Isham BLANTON (b. c1827) and Elizabeth "Bettie" BLAND (marr. 03 Jul 1852 Duplin Co, NC). He was a minister in the Oqeechee and South Georgia Assn's serving from 1903 to 1925 acccording from the minutes of said conferences.

David Louis Boatright
Birth:
Oct. 29, 1868
Death:
Nov. 14, 1950
Burial:
Lake Cemetery
Metter
Candler County,Georgia

Minister in the Ogeechee Assn. He married Lillian Cornelia Rogers Boatright (1870 - 1924) and they had son Reuben Lloyd Boatright (1894 - 1918).

Zachariah Taylor Bone
Birth:
Nov. 26, 1848
Butler
Taylor County,Georgia
Death:
Dec. 24, 1909
Butler
Taylor County,Georgia
Burial:

Mount Pisgah Cemetery
Butler
Taylor County, Georgia

He is recorded in the Chattahoochee minutes from 1891 until 1909. He was married to Sarah L. Decker Bone (1823 - 1912).

Seaborn Bowen
Birth:
May 29, 1882
Death:
Jul. 11, 1960
Burial:
Sunnyside Cemetery
Pearson
Atkinson County, Georgia

He was a minister and member of the South Georgia Conference.

Thomas J. Bowen
Birth:
Jan. 2, 1814
Death:
Nov. 24, 1875
Burial:
Greensboro City Cemetery
Greensboro
Greene County, Georgia
He was an early minister in the Chattahoochee Conference and appears in the minutes of 1842. Lurana H. Bowen (1832 - 1907) was his wife.

Barney B. Bradley
Birth:
Jul. 26, 1907
Death:
Jun. 24, 1949
Burial:
Oak Hill Cemetery
Griffin
Spalding County, Georgia
Plot: Section B; Block 2

Records show he was a member of the Chattahoochee assn.

David Rowan Braswell
Birth:
Jan. 8, 1877
Decatur County, Georgia
Death:
Jul. 1, 1947
Decatur County, Georgia
Burial:
Salem Cemetery
Desser
Seminole County, Georgia

He pastored in the Martin Association. He was married to Perry Lee Alday Braswell (1874 - 1968).

Benjamin F. Bratcher
Birth:
Apr., 1883
Georgia
Death:
Mar. 11, 1951
Georgia
Burial:
Carters Chapel Cemetery
Bacon County, Georgia

Minutes of the South Georgia record him as a minister from 1907 until 1931, He married twice.(1) Ella "Ellie" Carter, daughter of Jackson and Mary A. Carter. She is supposed to be buried at Fishing Creek in Pierce Co. GA and second to Lula Deen Powell (1915 - 1998).

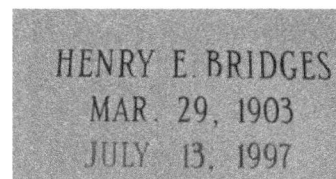

Henry Elmer Bridges
Birth:
Mar. 29, 1903
Death:
Jul. 13, 1997
Burial:
Mount Calvary Baptist Church Cemetery
Cary
Bleckley County, Georgia

COCHRAN--- Services for the Rev. Henry E. Bridges was held in Mount Calvary Baptist Church with burial in the church cemetery. Bridges, 94, died in a Cochran nursing home. The son of the late West and Cindy English Bridges, he was born in Laurens County but lived most of his life in Bleckley County. A Coast Guard veteran, he was retired from Paulk Lumber Company and as minister of Freewill Baptist Church. He was a member of Little Bethel Freewill Baptist Church. FROM: The Macon Telegraph 7-14-1997 Page 6B

Oscar C. Bridges
Birth:
Feb. 22, 1877
Death:
Apr. 20, 1948
Burial:
Parkhill Cemetery
Columbus
Muscogee County,Georgia
Plot: Garden 29

Listed in some of the Chattahoochee minutes of 1917-1947. He was married to Bessie Cromer Bridges (1890 - 1959).

James Edward Brodnax
Birth:
Dec. 11, 1822
Hancock Co. Georgia
Death:
Feb. 28, 1885
Muscogee Co. GA
Burial:
New Providence Baptist Church Cemetery
Muscogee County, Georgia

Rev. James Edward Broadnax, son of John Travis Brodnax and Hettie (Gordy) Brodnax, with his brothers settled near Columbus, GA, and was pastor of the Free Will Baptist Church where the Broadnax/Brodnax family have their burial plot. One of these brothers, John M. Broadnax, died from accidental wounds received during the War Between the States and is buried at Providence, with Irvin near him. (Rev.) James Edward Broadnax m. Martha Watkins [19 August 1847], and they had 7 children. John Travis Broadnax, a veteran of War of 1812. was living in Hancock, Co., Ga., in 1827, where he drew in that land lottery. The

goodness and faithfulness of Rev. Jas. E. Broadnax was appreciated by the whole neighborhood where he preached for 35 years."--from "History of Chattahoochee Co. GA, by N.K. Rogers, copyright, 1933...............
Inscription on slab:
"Pioneer Free Will Baptist Preacher; Gave the Land to Providence Free Will Baptist Church.

"I see Heaven open and Jesus on the right hand of God."

Gerald E. Brown
Birth:
Jan. 9, 1930
Death:
Aug. 14, 2006
Burial:
Cedar Creek Cemetery
Cordele
Crisp County,Georgia

He was a minister in the Georgia Union, Midway, Union, Little River and Chattahoochee conferences from 1895 through 1998. He was a veteran of the Korean War in the United States Army.

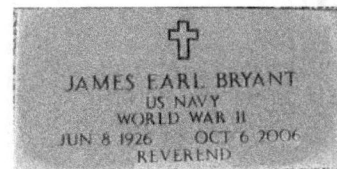

James Earl Bryant
Birth:
Jun. 8, 1926
Death:
Oct. 6, 2006
Burial:
Little Bethel Freewill Baptist Church
Cochran
Bleckley County,Georgia

He was a member of the Georgia Union Association and his ministry is recorded in its minutes from 1981 until 1999.

Robert L Burnett
Birth:
Feb. 26, 1883
Death:
Jun. 15, 1934
Burial:
Mount Nebo Primitive Baptist Church Cemetery
Charing
Taylor County,Georgia

An early Free Will Baptist preacher whose ministry is recorded in the Chattahoochee minutes from 1915 until 1933.

T. P. Carr
Birth:
Jan. 8, 1845
Death:
Oct. 26, 1909
Burial:
Mount Olive Freewill Baptist
Church Cemetery
Potterville
Taylor County, Georgia

Early minister in the Chattahoochee Association. His name appears in the Chattahoochee minutes in 1889 and in other editions until 1907.

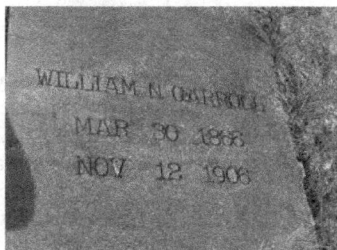

William N. Carroll
Birth:
Mar. 30, 1866
Death:
Nov. 12, 1906
Burial:
New Providence Baptist Church
Cemetery
Muscogee County, Georgia

Early minister that served in the Chattahoochee Association. His name appears in the minutes of 1908 and 1909.

J. C. Hubert Carter
Birth:
May 2, 1925
Death:
Oct. 7, 1988

Burial:
Blackshear City Cemetery
Blackshear
Pierce County, Georgia

He ministered in the Little River, Martin, and South Georgia Association's. His name appears in all three of the minutes of these conferences. he was married to Marjorie J. Carter (1925 - ___) .

T M Carter
Birth:
Apr. 25, 1900
Death:
Dec. 31, 1953
Burial:
Memorial Freewill Baptist Church
Cemetery
Surrency
Appling County, Georgia

He was a minister in the South Georgia conference. His World War I Draft Registration Cards, 1917-1918 Name: Theopheilus Marion Carter County: Appling State: Georgia Birth Date: 25 Apr 1900 Race: White FHL Roll Number: 1556940 Draft Board: His parents were Millard W Carter (1875 - 1940) and Dealphia Edenfield Carter (1879 - 1954).

Martin Franklin Cason
Birth:
Jun. 15, 1858
Ware County, Georgia
Death:
Mar. 31, 1939
Bemiss
Lowndes County, Georgia
Burial:
Royals Cemetery
Kirkland
Atkinson County, Georgia

Martin was a farmer and a minister serving in the South Georgia conference according to the minutes of 1905 and 1907. He is the son of Hillery William Cason and Pheby Walker Cason. he was married three times to Martha Frances Royal Cason (1868 - 1893),Alice Pafford Cason (1863 - 1910) and Emma Jane Smith Cason (1886 - 1955).

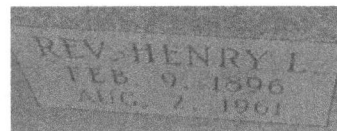

Henry L Catrett
Birth:
Feb. 9, 1896
Death:
Aug. 2, 1961
Burial:
Colquitt City Cemetery
Colquitt
Miller County, Georgia
He served in the Midway, Georgia

Union, and Martin Associations during the period of 1940 through the 1960s. his wife was Nettie S Catrett (1895 - 1959).

L J (James) Chambless
Birth:
Feb. 9, 1926
Alabama
Death:
May 30, 1998
Tift County,Georgia
Burial:
Tift Memorial Gardens and Mausoleum
Tifton
Tift County,Georgia

He was a minister in the Little River Association. His parents were Oscar H. Chambless (1898 - 1953) and Lonia Beasley Chambless (1908 - 1968). He was married to Betty Mason Chambless (1934 - 1994) and to this union was born Barbara Franks Chambless (1943 - 2011).

Edward S. Cheshire
Birth:
Apr. 20, 1842
Stewart County,Georgia
Death:
Mar. 31, 1926
Burial:

Friendship Cemetery
Hahira
Lowndes County,Georgia

He was an early minister in the Midway Association. He was married to Julia George Cheshire (1844 - 1918).

W C Coleman
Birth:
May 14, 1880
Death:
Jan. 21, 1959
Burial:
Bethel Free Will Baptist Church Cemetery
Appling County,Georgia

Early minister serving in the Georgia Union and South Georgia Associations during the periods from 1916 until 1957.

George W. Collins
Birth:
Apr. 10, 1880
Death:
Mar. 3, 1960
Burial:
Collins-McCullough Cemetery
Emanuel County,Georgia

He was a minister in the Ogeechee and South Georgia Assn's. His wife was Sarah McCullough Collins (1887 - 1964).

C C Coursey
Birth:
Aug. 2, 1872
Death:
Nov. 3, 1946
Burial:

Lyons City Cemetery
Lyons
Toombs County,Georgia

In the quarterly meeting minutes it revealed that he served as a minister in the South Georgia conference from 1913 until about 1946.

William Robert Crawley
Birth:
Jan. 9, 1912
Ben Hill County,Georgia
Death:
Mar. 28, 1990
Peach County,Georgia
Burial:
Sunset Memorial Gardens
Americus
Sumter County,Georgia

His parents were William Asberry Crawley (1882 - 1960) and Lillie Crawley (1888 - 1915) and he was married to Mary P. Lowell Crawley (1916 - 2007).

A man does not die of love

or even of old age;

he dies of being a man.

R. Paul Creech
Birth:
Oct. 11, 1962,
Durham,
Durham County,
North Carolina
Death:
Sep. 15, 2011,
Macon,
Bibb County, Georgia
Burial:
Glen Haven Memorial Garden,
Macon,
Bibb County,Georgia

Free Will Baptist Minister, missionary to Japan from 1987 to 1988, and to the Ivory Coast, West Africa, from 1989 to 1998. He served churches in New Brunswick, Canada and Georgia. He was a member of the Board of International Missions for the National Association of Free Will Baptists.

Madison Lamar Crook
Birth:
Dec. 20, 1867
Macon County,Georgia
Death:
Jan. 14, 1934
Burial:
Mount Olive Freewill Baptist
Church Cemetery
Potterville
Taylor County,Georgia

Minister in the Chattahoochee Association according to minutes of 1907-1912.

Gene Autry Cross
Birth:
Mar. 15, 1947

Death:
Dec. 5, 2004
Burial:
Dawn Memorial Park
Decatur
DeKalb County,Georgia

He served in the Oqeechee and Georgia Union conferences.

Joshua Edward Daniel
Birth:
Jun. 19, 1861
Death:
Aug. 6, 1928
Burial:
Forest Park City Cemetery
Forest Park
Clayton County,Georgia

Early minister in the Middle Georgia association. He was the son of Richard Daniel (1813 - 1891) and Sarah Norman Daniel (1831 - 1897). He was married to Mary J. Daniel (1861 - 1942).

Willie Dawson
Birth:
unknown
Death:
Sep. 12, 2012
Jamieson,Gadsden County,Florida
Burial:
Cool Springs Cemetery
Faceville, Decatur County, Georgia

He served churches in Florida and Georgia living to the age of 76 dying at his home in Jamieson, Florida. He served as a deacon at the First Free Will Baptist church in Quincy, Florida and after his call to the ministry served as a

bi-vocational preacher. By trade he was a construction worker. His last church was the First FWB in Bainbridge, Ga. He gave sacrificially to both home and international missions because missionary Sandra Payne was his sister.

G Thomas Dell
Birth:
Aug. 17, 1872
Death:
Mar. 10, 1956
Burial:
Wesley Chapel Methodist Church
Cemetery
Berlin
Colquitt County,Georgia

Minister in the Union Assn.

Damon C. Dodd
Birth:
Feb. 14, 1916,
Flat River,
St. Francois County, Missouri
Death:
Apr. 27, 2000,
Colquitt, Miller County,Georgia
Burial:
Donley, Bellview,
Miller County,Georgia

Free Will Baptist leader, pastor, and missionary. Bro. Dodd was converted at the age of 15 during an evangelistic crusade by the McAdams Evangelistic Team. The speaker on that blessed, fateful evening was a woman, Lizzie McAdams. He was ordained into the Gospel Ministry in 1936 at the St. Francois County Quarterly meeting in Missouri. Damon married Sylvia R. Wood in 1938, and God gave them two lovely girls and fifty-eight years of companionship and service together.

Sylvia's roots came from Joshua Wood who was one of three Wood families that came to St. Francois County Missouri from Ohio near 1866. They started most of the Free Will Baptist churches in the area. Damon attended Flat River Jr. College, but when the Free Will Baptist Bible College began in 1942. He and his wife, Sylvia, joined seven other students. Two years later they made up half of the first graduating class. Brother Dodd went on with his formal education until he received a Doctor of Ministries degree in the 1980s. Study was a joy and writing was a passion for him. He wrote as he spoke, with enthusiasm. He published, *All of Mine For Him*, 1954, *The Free Will Baptist Story*, 1956; *Go Home Tell Thy Friends*, 1957; *Trailways to Adventure, 1963; Study Guide for Revelation, 1967; Handbook for New Church Members*, 1970; *Marching Through Georgia*, 1977.

Damon and Sylvia were foreign missionaries to Cuba, 1945-48. He served as the fourth National Association Executive-Secretary, 1949-53. In 1953 he was the first full-time Promotional Secretary for the National Home Missions Dept. and opened its first national office. Damon was a Foreign Missions Board Member, 1944-46, and a Free Will Baptist Bible College Trustee Board Member, 1962-76.

In Georgia, Brother Dodd served as: the State Moderator; the state's Historical Commission; Chairman of the Committee that wrote the Standard and Doctrinal Examination for Licensing and Ordaining Free Will Baptist Ministers in Georgia, which was adopted by the state association, November 16, 1979. He served as an evangelist, church planter and pastor.

He served churches in Missouri, 1937-42, 1947-50; Tennessee, 1942-46; and in Georgia. His first Georgia pastorate was in Savannah, 1958-62, South Georgia Association. Later he served the congregations at Homerville, 1965-73, Little River Association; Bay, 1974-75, Union Association; New Home, Miller County, 1975-81 and 90, Martin Association; Bellview, 1983 and 1987, Midway Association.

Missionary
Sylvia *Wood* Dodd
Birth:
Jan. 25, 1917,
Missouri
Death:
May 5, 1996,
Colquitt, Miller County,Georgia
Burial:
Donley Cemetery,Colquitt,
Miller County,Georgia

She traveled with Texas woman preacher, Lizzie McAdams, playing the piano in her evangelistic ministry. Damon Dodd had been converted in her revival in Missouri. Lizzie was unhappy to lose her to Damon, but concluded that she'd be a blessing to Damon in his ministry. Sylvia's roots came from Joshua Wood who was one of three Wood families that came to St. Francois County Missouri from Ohio near 1866. They started most of the Free Will Baptist churches in the area.

E Allen Drake
Birth:
Aug. 1, 1864
Death:
Jan. 18, 1946
Burial:
Corinth Cemetery
Iron City
Seminole County,Georgia

According to the Martin conference minutes he served from 1902 until about 1943. he was married to Sallie W. Drake (1871 - 1962).

W A Drake
Birth:
1858
Death:
1930
Georgia
Burial:
Finch Cemetery
Philomath
Oglethorpe County,Georgia

He was an early minister serving in the Martin Association according records from1919 and 1921. his wife was Frankie M Drake (1864 - 1917) and their children was Hines Drake (1894 - 1908)* and Sibley Drake (1896 - ___).

William S Driggers
Birth:
Apr. 1, 1910
Death:
May 31, 1987
Burial:

Mount Gilead Freewill Baptist
Church Cemetery
Decatur County,Georgia
As a minister he served in the
South Georgia, Chattahoochee,
Midway and Martin Associations.
Inscription:
TEC 5 US ARMY WWII

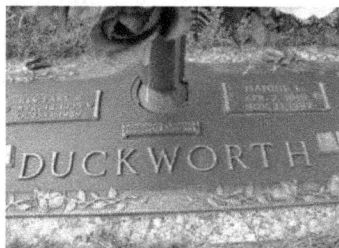

Earl B Duckworth
Birth:
Apr. 18, 1905
Death:
Oct. 11, 1989
Burial:
Glen Haven Memorial Garden
Macon
Bibb County,Georgia
Plot: Everlasting Life 163 D # 3

According to the South Georgia
and Georgia Union minutes he
served as a minister from about
1935 to 1988 in both of these
conferences.

Harold Keith Dunlap
Birth:
Nov. 3, 1926
Death:
Feb. 1, 1999
Burial:
Macon Memorial Park
Macon
Bibb County,Georgia

He was a member of the Georgia
Union Conference according to its
minutes from 1967 until 1979 his
record appears.

James M Dunn
Birth:
Mar. 5, 1856
Georgia
Death:
1929
Georgia
Burial:
Bay Springs Free Will Baptist
Church Cemetery
Plainfield
Dodge County, Georgia

The Georgia Union of minutes
show him serving as a clergyman
in their 1925 through 1927
records. He was married to
Isabella Jones Dunn (1875 - 1923)
to whose union was born Joseph T
Dunn (1914 - 1987).

J H Dupree
Birth:
Nov. 29, 1846
Death:
Jun. 12, 1922
Burial:
New Prospect Freewill Baptist
Coverdale
Turner County,Georgia

According to the Chattahoochee
minutes he ministered within the
Association from 1879 until 1913.
He also served in the Confederate
States of America Army.
Inscription:
Co C 55 GA INF
Confederate States Army

James Thomas Edwards
Birth:
Jan. 23, 1876
Baker County, Georgia
Death:
May 28, 1964
Baker County, Georgia
Burial:
Travelers Rest Freewill Baptist
Church Cemetery
Newton
Baker County, Georgia

He was a minister in the Martin
conference. He was married to
Rossie Bailey Edwards (1880 -
1964).

**In death we feel the
presence of the Holy
Spirit brush across our
souls with a deep
settled peace.**

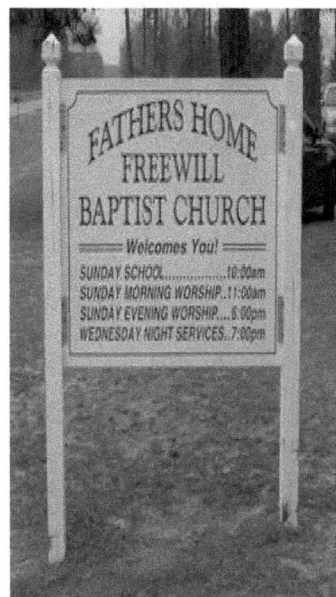

Adolphus Emanuel
Birth:
Oct. 29, 1868
Cumberland County, North
Carolina
Death:
Sep. 18, 1948
Emanuel County, Georgia
Burial:
Collins Cemetery
Oak Park
Emanuel County, Georgia

Named as one of the ministers in the promotion and organization of the GA Free Will Bapt. State Association in 1917.

John M Emanuel
Birth:
Sep. 24, 1875
Death:
Aug. 24, 1943
Burial:
Cool Spring Cemetery
Candler County,Georgia

He served as a minister in the Chattahoochee, Midway and South Georgia conferences from 1906 until about 1942.

George Troup Embry
Birth:
Dec. 4, 1832
Death:
Apr. 11, 1916
burial:
Morgan Methodist Church
Cemetery
Morgan
Calhoun County, Georgia

He was the son of Hezekiah Luckie Embry and Martha Slaton Lowe. He was an early minister in the Liberty and Martin Associations 1892 through 1894. He was married to Sarah Elizabeth Wolfe Embry (1834 - 1906) and they had one child Nancy E Embry (1854 - 1890).

Elder William H. Emerson
Birth:
Mar. 26, 1876
Georgia
Death:
Aug. 16, 1948
Macon County, Georgia
Burial:
Little Bethel Freewill Baptist
Cemetery
Ideal
Macon County, Georgia
Minutes show that he appeared as a minister from 1903 until 1948 in the Chattahoochee, Georgia Union and Midway Associations.

Charles B Ethridge
Birth:
May 1, 1886
Death:
Jul. 13, 1929
Burial:
Underwood Memorial Cemetery
Conyers
Rockdale County, Georgia

He served as a minister in the Chattahoochee and Georgia are Union Associations. He was married to Ludie Mae Ethridge (1891 - 1969).

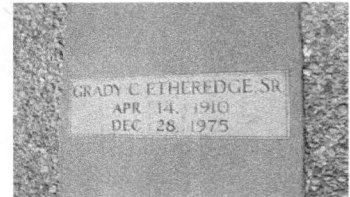

Grady C Etheredge, Sr
Birth:
Apr. 14, 1910
Death:
Dec. 28, 1975
Burial:
Live Oak Freewill Baptist Church
Cemetery
Milford
Baker County, Georgia

He was a minister in the Chattahoochee Association.

Alton Everson
Birth:
Sep. 4, 1922
Death:
Feb. 7, 1988
Burial:
Colquitt City Cemetery
Colquitt
Miller County, Georgia

His combined ministry was in the Little River, Georgia Union, South Georgia, Union, and an Martin associations.

Kenneth L. Faison
Birth:
May 23, 1935
Death:
Jul. 19, 1990
Burial:
Glennville City Cemetery
Glennville, Tattnall County,
Georgia
Plot: D5

Rev. Faison died at age 55 in Millen, Georgia after a long illness. He was a native of Moultrie, Georgia and pastor of the Deep Creek Free Will Baptist Church in Millen. He was a pastor and lifelong Free Will Baptist. The Reverends James Ussery, Larry Dale Williams, and Galen Dunbar officiated at his service.

Hoyt Duard Finley
Birth:
Sep. 21, 1920
Death:
Sep. 19, 1989
Hart County, Georgia
Burial:
Poplar Springs Baptist Church
Cemetery
Lavonia
Franklin County, Georgia

He was a minister in the Georgia Union and Chattahoochee Associations during a period of around 1954 through 1992. He was a S SGT US ARMY in WWII where he received a Purple Heart.

Joseph Otis Fort
Birth:
May 2, 1910,
Early County, Georgia
Death:
Mar. 7, 1976,
Early County, Georgia
Burial:
Jakin Freewill Baptist Church
Cemetery,
Jakin, Early County, Georgia

He was a minister in three of the Georgia associations, namely; Midway, South Georgia and Martin. His name appears in nearly all of the minutes beginning as early as 1933 until 1968.

Drew Floyd
Birth:
Sep. 5, 1882
Miller County, Georgia
Death:
Mar., 1971
Miller County, Georgia
Burial:
Rawls Cemetery
Colquitt
Miller County, Georgia

He was a minister in the Martin Association where records show he served from 1943 until about 1969. First wife: Eula Inez Pickren. Second wife: Linda Grimes Powell. Son of Thomas Newton Floyd and Eliza Rawls Floyd. Sibllings were: John ("Buddy"), William, Iona, Rebecca, and Joshua Franklin.

Herschel Greeley Fowler
Birth:
Nov. 8, 1888
Death:
Jul. 20, 1981
Burial:
Bethlehem Baptist Church
Cemetery
Condor
Laurens County, Georgia

He is listed as a minister in the Chattahoochee minutes.

Elder Harvey W Giddens
Birth:
Jul. 12, 1909
Death:
Apr. 14, 1981
Burial:
Bridge Creek Cemetery
Colquitt County, Georgia

During his ministry he served in the Chattahoochee, Little River and Georgia Union Associations.

Murray Elvin Giddens
Birth:
Nov. 15, 1930
Adel
Cook County, Georgia
Death:
Jan. 3, 2009
Moultrie
Colquitt County, Georgia
Burial:
Suncrest Memorial Gardens
Moultrie
Colquitt County, Georgia

The course of his ministry was spent in the Union, Little River, Martin Association's from about 1974 until 1990. A veteran, he was retired from the Marines and was a Free Will Baptist minister.In addition to his parents, He was preceded in death by his wife, Myrtice Foster Giddens.

Teedom M. Giddens
Birth:
Aug. 23, 1891
Coffee County, GA
Death:
Oct. 19, 1961
Burial:
Sunnyside Cemetery
Pearson
Atkinson County,Georgia

His ministry was confined to the Little River Association.Spouse: Beadie Mae Burch. Married: Abt. 1914 in Georgia and his parents were. Kindred Jasper Giddens (1861 - 1938) and Martha Lewis Giddens (1871 - 1954) and he married Beadie Mae Burch Giddens (1891 - 1972).

Chester A Gilbert
Birth:
Oct. 4, 1898
Death:
Feb. 12, 1977
Burial:
New Salem Cemetery
Miller County, Georgia

His ministry spanned from 1943 until 1969 in the Martin Association. Spouse: Ida Jane Nobles Gilbert (1902-36) Children: Mamie Gilbert Whatley (1921 - 2006), Hattie Sue Gilbert (1924 - 1926), Lawrence Lamar Gilbert (1926 - 1927), Garland Gilbert (1930 - 1951).

Benjamin Terrell Gill
Birth:
Jan. 2, 1890
Death:
Oct. 30, 1972
Burial:
Trinity Freewill Baptist Cemetery
Taylor County,Georgia

His ministry was held in the Chattahoochee Association and he is recorded in its minutes from about 1934 until 1971.

Walter D Gill
Birth:
Oct. 9, 1866
Death:
Apr. 18, 1934
Burial:
Trinity Freewill Baptist Cemetery
Taylor County,Georgia

His ministry appears in many of the minutes of the Chattahoochee Association ranging from 1903 until 1933.

Richard Harold Goolsby
Birth:
Jul., 1855
Jasper County, Georgia
Death:
Mar. 16, 1935
Monticello
Jasper County, Georgia
Burial:
Hebron Cemetery
Jasper County, Georgia

Records in 1897 show him as a minister in the Middle Georgia minutes.

William Hancil Gray
Birth:
Mar. 9, 1915
Death:
Apr. 16, 1995
Burial:
Chastain Memorial Park Cemetery
Blue Ridge
Fannin County,Georgia

He was a minister in the Georgia Union association.

For the name of Jesus and the protection of the church I am ready to embrace death.

Benjamin Franklin Green
Birth:
1873
Monroe County, Georgia
Death:
1938
Marion County, Georgia
Burial:
New Life Freewill Baptist Church
Cemetery
Marion County, Georgia

His parents were Thomas C Green (1824-) and Irena M (Helton) (1836-).He married Lucy Bone on Nov 17, 1892 in Taylor Co, GA. He was a minister in the union conference.

Doctor Evan Green
Birth:
Oct. 5, 1852
Death:
Jul. 6, 1936
Ideal
Macon County, Georgia
Burial:
Ideal City Cemetery
Ideal
Macon County, Georgia

Macon County Citizen-Montezuma Georgian July 9, 1936. Ideal, Ga. - July 8, Funeral services were held in the Free Will Baptist Church in Ideal Tuesday afternoon for Rev. D. E. Greene, 83, prominent minister and former postmaster of Ideal, whose death occurred at his home Monday following a lingering illness. Rev. Greene was the first citizen who moved to the town of Ideal and was postmaster here from the founding of the town until two years ago. For many years he walked and carried the mail from Oglethorpe to Ideal, a distance of 15 miles, until the A. B. C. Railroad was built, connecting these points. For 40 years he was a minister in the Free Will Baptist Church and served many charges. He was married to Miss Frances Dyson who died in 1922.

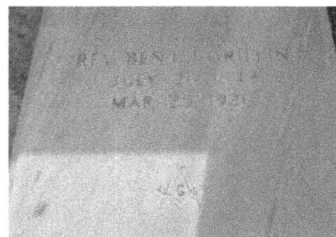

Benjamin J. Griffin
Birth:
Jul. 26, 1849
Death:
Mar. 25, 1926
Burial:
Leila Cemetery
Colquitt County, Georgia,

The Liberty minutes show him as early as 1895 as a minister in the Association.

THE LORD IS MY SHERPARD

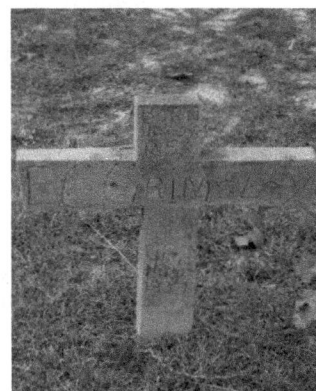

E C Grimsley
Birth:
Apr. 29, 1859
Death:
May 3, 1939
Burial:
New Life Freewill Baptist Church
Cemetery
Marion County, Georgia

The Chattahoochee minutes revealed that he appeared in their conference from 1898 until 1938.

William Thomas Grimsley
Birth:
Apr., 1879
Georgia
Death:
Oct. 20, 1942
Marion County, Georgia
Burial:
Parmer Cemetery
Oakland
Marion County, Georgia

He served as a minister in the Chattahoochee Association whose minutes revealed his presence from 1919 until 1942.

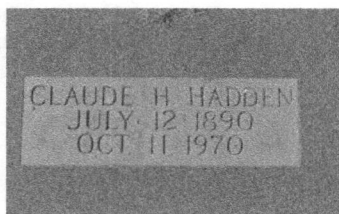

Claud H Hadden
Birth:
Jul. 12, 1890
Death:
Oct. 11, 1970
Burial:
Lake Cemetery
Metter
Candler County, Georgia

He served in the Ogeechee and South Georgia quarterly meetings from about 1940 untill 1960.

C W Harrell
Birth:
Oct. 13, 1943
Death:
Oct. 18, 1992
Burial:
Mizpah Primitive Baptist Church Cemetery
Cairo
Grady County, Georgia

He was a minister in both the Union and Martin Associations.

Kelly C Harrell
Birth:
Jan. 28, 1934
Death:
Apr. 16, 1997
Burial:
Mount Gilead Freewill Baptist Church Cemetery
Decatur County, Georgia

He served as a minister in the Martin Association.
Inscription:
AMN US AIR FORCE KOREA

James G Harris
Birth:
Sep. 7, 1883
Death:
Nov. 3, 1926
Burial:
Christ Methodist Church Cemetery
Baker County, Georgia

Minutes from the Martin and Midway Associations revealed him as a minister from 1916 until 1926 within their associations.

C J Harvey
Birth:
Jan. 6, 1889
Death:
Aug. 2, 1960
Burial:
Oakview Cemetery
Camilla
Mitchell County, Georgia

He was a minister in the Georgia Union, the Midway, and Union conferences during the period of 1929 until 1959.

R Slaten Hayes
Birth:
May 28, 1913
Death:
Nov. 9, 2002
Burial:
Forest Hill Freewill Baptist Church Cemetery
Adel
Cook County, Georgia

From 1952 until 1999 he served as a minister in the Little River and Union Associations.

Bessie *Widener* Hillis
Birth
April 23, 1890
Death
July 9, 1969
Burke County, Georgia
Burial
Corinth Cemetery
Burke County, Georgia

She was an early Free Will Baptist preacher in Georgia.

Joel I Hill
Birth:
Apr. 13, 1851
Early County, Georgia
Death:
May 10, 1914
Early County, Georgia
Burial:
Springfield Baptist Church Cemetery
Early County, Georgia

He was converted in 1872 and two years later and received license to preach. He was ordained in 1875 by J. B. McCullers and others. He ministered to the Howard's Grove church, Alabama; New Salem church, Georgia, and the Springfield church, Georgia.

Robert W Holmes
Birth:
Jun. 2, 1899
Death:
Oct. 12, 1976
Burial:
Pelham City Cemetery
Pelham
Mitchell County, Georgia
He was a minister in the Martin conference.

W. H. Holmes
Birth:
Jun. 10, 1870
Death:
Jun. 10, 1925
Burial:
Pine Level Church Cemetery
Alma
Bacon County, Georgia

Records in the Chattahoochee, the Georgia Union, and South Georgia minutes revealed his ministry among them from 1902 until 1924.

George Sherrod Holton
Birth:
Oct. 9, 1909
Death:
unknown
Burial:
Mount Zion Church Cemetery
Lyons
Toombs County, Georgia

He served in the South Georgia and Ogeechee Associations ranging from about 1952 until 1995.

Benjamin Franklin Horne
Birth:
Sep., 1866
Laurens County, Georgia
Death:
Oct. 6, 1944
Dodge County, Georgia
Burial:
Bay Springs Free Will Baptist
Church Cemetery
Plainfield
Dodge County, Georgia

The Georgia Union minutes record him from 1914 until 1943. He was married to Maryann Francis Jones Horne (1867 - 1934) and they had the following children: Joseph William Horne (1890 - 1967) John Benjamin Jefferson Horne (1896 - 1965) Charlton James Horne (1898 - 1985) Henry H Horne (1904 - 1958) Seaborn Horne (1905 - 1905) Athie Belle Horne Graham (1906 - 1947) Fannie C Horne Rodgers (1909 - 1999).

Carlton Robert Houston
Birth:
May 7, 1914
Death:
Aug. 10, 1983
Burial:
Roberts Cemetery
Miller County, Georgia
He served as a minister in the Martin and, Midway Associations.

**What a day that will
when my saviour I shall see!**

Dennis Oliver Irvin
Birth:
Oct. 25, 1926
Death:
Jun. 13, 1981
Burial:
Travelers Rest Freewill Baptist
Church Cemetery
Newton
Baker County, Georgia

His ministry was in the Midway and Union Associations.

Paul H Irvin
Birth:
Nov. 25, 1925
Baker County, Georgia
Death:
Dec. 2, 2008
Albany
Dougherty County, Georgia
Burial:
Travelers Rest Freewill Baptist
Church Cemetery
Newton
Baker County, Georgia

He had a broad ministry serving in the Georgia Union, Midway, Union, and Martin Associations.

He was a member of Travelers Rest Free Will Baptist Church. Rev. Irvin had pastored 12 churches in the past 47 years. He was preceded in death by four brothers, Herman Irvin, Price Irvin, Dennis Irvin and Lawrence Irvin,

Until Then

Von Deron Irvin
Birth:
Jul. 14, 1910
Death:
Dec. 9, 1985
Burial:
Travelers Rest Freewill Baptist
Church Cemetery
Newton
Baker County, Georgia

His ministry was in two associations: the Midway and Chattahoochee Quarterly Meetings.

John Pierce James
Birth:
Sep. 2, 1809
Rockingham county, North Carolina
Death:
Oct. 9, 1847
Burial:
Sardis Baptist Church Cemetery
McDonough
Henry County, Georgia
John professed conversion at the age of twenty-four, and was baptized by Rev. Cyrus White at Teman church, Henry county, Georgia. He was subsequently ordained to the gospel ministry at said church in 1835, by what presbytery the author is not informed. Though his ministry was thus commenced under those who were known as Whiteites, (and who were deemed as rather Arminian in sentiment,). He subsequently connected himself with the Central Association, in which body he was highly esteemed and eminently useful.

He was engaged in the ministry only about twelve years, yet he baptized about sixteen hundred persons. His labors were confined mostly to the counties of Jasper, Butts, Henry, Newton and Campbell. His burning zeal impelled him forward day and night, summer and winter. His first sermon was preached under a bush-arbor in Gwinnett county, and from that day until he ceased from his labors was his voice heard in the highways and hedges, inviting and urging the poor and needy to come to the gospel feast. It was by no means an uncommon thing with him to work hard on his farm all day, and, leaving his horse to rest, to walk from three to four miles and preach to his neighbors at night, after which he would return home, and resume his work in the morning. His last sermon was preached at Enon church, Jasper county, from Acts xx. 32: "And now, brethren, I commend you to God," etc.

In October, 1830, he was married to Miss Nancy Strickland, daughter of Colonel Solomon Strickland, of Henry county, who proved herself eminently qualified for the position she was called to occupy as a preacher's wife, and as the mother of six orphan children, which were left upon her hands by his death. His father, Martin James, was a soldier in the war of 1812, was taken prisoner, and died at Fort Johnson. His mother's maiden name was Martha Woodall. She died in 1869, in the ninetieth year of her age.

John H Jenkins
Birth:
Aug. 26, 1869
Georgia
Death:
Aug. 10, 1899,
Burial:
Sand Hill Cemetery
Fort Stewart
Tattnall County, Georgia
His name is recorded as a minister in the 1890s minutes of the Chattahoochee Association.

G W Jones
Birth:
Aug. 22, 1877
Death:
Jun. 23, 1938
Burial:
Satilla Freewill Baptist Church Cemetery
Hazlehurst
Jeff Davis County, Georgia

Minutes from the South Georgia conference revealed him serving in their area from their minutes dated 1916 until 1937.

Spurgeon Jones
Birth:
Dec. 22, 1914
Death:
May 29, 1970
Burial:

Mt. Ararat Free Will Baptist
Church
Chauncey
Dodge County, Georgia

He preached in the Georgia Union
conference.

Dr. Linton C. Johnson
Birth:
Feb. 3, 1914,
Alma, Bacon County,Georgia
Death:
Jun. 26, 2002,
Norfolk, Norfolk City, Virginia
Burial:
Pine Level Church Cemetery,
Alma, Bacon County,Georgia

He was a Free Will Baptist
minister, pastor, educator and
Bible college president. He
attended Middle Georgia College,
1932-33 and earned his degree
from Bob Jones college in 1939.
He pursued graduate studies at
Winona Lake School of Theology
in 1943, and Bob Jones Graduate
School in 1945.
Bob Jones University bestowed
the honorary Doctor of
Humanities degree on him in
1952.
He was the founding president of
Free Will Baptist Bible College in
Nashville, Tennessee in 1942,
where he served for 34 years until
his retirement in 1979. From
1979 until 1981 he was
Chancellor of the college. His
pastorates included Free Will
Baptist churches in Georgia,
Mississippi, Florida and
Tennessee.

He considered the Free Will
Baptist Bible College his great life
work and never allowed anything
to distract him from that focus. As
the president of the college,
Johnson became well known and
respected in academic circles.
He was listed in Who's Who in
American College and University
Administrations, served on
Executive Committee of the
American Association of Bible
Colleges, participated on the
program of the 1976 World
Congress of Fundamentalists in
Edinburg, Scotland and was a
member of the over view
committee for the New King
James Version of the Bible.
Dr. Johnson preached six times in
the national convention and was
elected as moderator of the
National Association of Free Will
Baptist twice. His influence
marked the denomination for
almost 70 years. In a 1999 tribute,
Dr. Robert Picirilli wrote of him,
"When the history of Free Will
Baptists in the last half of the 20th
century is written, the role of Dr.
L.C. Johnson will be perhaps the
most prominent of any,"
No one as touched more lives
within the Free Will Baptist
denomination.

Grace, Grace,
Wonderful Grace

Hughie J. Kelly
Birth:
Feb. 16, 1907
Death:
Jul. 20, 1957
Burial:
Evergreen Memory Gardens
Cemetery,
Columbus,
Muscogee County,
Georgia,
Plot: Christus Garden
His ministry was in the
Chattahoochee Association..

Hiram Leroy Knighton
Birth:
Jul. 20, 1906
Georgia
Death:
Jul. 31, 1984
Albany
Dougherty County, Georgia
Burial:
Parkhill Cemetery
Columbus
Muscogee County, Georgia
Plot: Section I-30

Hiram Leroy Knighton was first
married to Mary Elizabeth Hearn
and upon her death in 1939
married Sarah (Harrell) Knighton.
His ministry was in the
Chattahoochee and Midway
Associations.

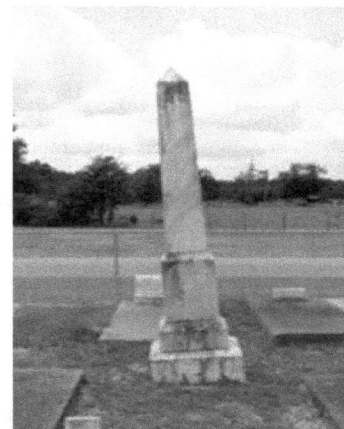

William Berrien Wesley Lane
Birth:
Jan. 24, 1854
Early County, Georgia
Death:

Mar. 5, 1893
Early County,Georgia
Burial:
Sowhatchee Cemetery
Blakely, Early County, Georgia

An early minister in the Chattahoochee and Martin Associations and is recorded in their minutes beginning in 1981 until 1892. He was the husband of Margaret J. (Anglin) Lane and son of Joseph William Lane, III and Chloe Elizabeth (Sheffield) Lane. He was converted in 1870, received license to preach in 1879, and was ordained the following year by Rev. C. C. Martin and J. E. Hill. His ministry was spent in the Chattahoochee Association, Georgia, where he baptized 125 converts organized two churches and aided in the gathering of three others.

Greenville L. Laney
Birth:
Mar. 5, 1941
Death:
Nov. 15, 1983
Burial:
Riverdale Cemetery
Columbus
Muscogee County, Georgia
Plot: 80 Sec. 10

His ministry was in the Chattahoochee Association.

Simeon Roy Lawhorn
Birth:
Feb. 23, 1879
Death:
Aug. 16, 1935
Burial:
New Providence Baptist Cemetery
Marion County, Georgia

He was a minister in the Chattahoochee Association whose minutes show him from 1921 until 1934.

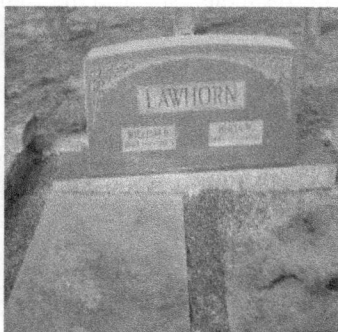

William Randolph Lawhorn
Birth:
Jun. 10, 1883
Death:
Feb. 8, 1971
Burial:
Sand Bethel Cemetery
Rupert
Taylor County, Georgia
He was the son of William H "W H" Lawhorn (1853 - 1897) and the husband of Effie Alberta "Berta" Watson Lawhorn (1884 - 1961). He was a member the Chattahoochee Association where the minutes revealed that he was active from 1918 until 1970.

Bruce V Lisle
Birth:
1901
Death:
1952
Burial:
Parkhill Cemetery
Columbus
Muscogee County, Georgia
Plot: Section F

He was a minister in the Chattahoochee Association.

Ralph Lightsey
Birth:
1918
Appling County,Georgia
Death:
Sep. 2, 2012
Statesboro, Bulloch County, Georgia
Burial:
Eastside Cemetery, Statesboro, Bulloch County,Georgia
Dr. Lightsey received his A.B. degree from Mercer University in 1945, a B.D. degree in Theology from Emory University in 1951, a Master's in Theology from Columbia University in 1955 and a doctorate degree in Education from the University of Georgia in 1965. He was ordained to the gospel ministry in 1940. He served churches in Georgia, Alabama, North Carolina and Mississippi. After serving as an active pastor for more than 52 years, he served as a supply speaker at more than 50 churches in Bulloch and surrounding counties. In addition, he was an educator. He served 16 years as professor of Educational Research at Georgia Southern University and as an assistant to the vice-president. Upon his retirement, the Board of Regents conferred on him the title of Professor Emeritus of Educational

Research. In keeping with his concern for his fellow human being, he received the Dean Day Smith Service to Mankind Award. He was also the original owner of Lightsey Construction Company, Inc.

Tom Joseph Lightsey
Birth:
Jun. 24, 1929
Appling County
Georgia
Death:
Jan. 25, 2010
Palm Garden Rehabilitation
Center
Jacksonville
Duval Co. Florida
Burial:
Piney Grove Free Will Baptist
Church Cemetery
Appling County, Georgia

He was a member of the Piney Grove Free Will Baptist Church and was an ordained Free Will Baptist minister. He served several churches as pastor in Southeast Georgia including Alabaha Free Will Baptist in Pierce County. After teaching for several years in the public school system, he completed his career at West Georgia University in Carrollton, from which he retired. Rev. Dr. Charles Thigpen and the Rev. Steve Hughes officiated. According to the South Georgia minutes he is recorded from 1956 through 1998 as a minister.

James D. Little
Birth:
Mar. 3, 1875
Death:
Aug. 16, 1958
Burial:
Sunnyside Cemetery Pearson
Atkinson County Georgia

Minutes of the Chattahoochee, Georgia Union and Little River associations from 1910 through 1957 record him as a minister.

Joel H. Little
Birth:
Dec. 23, 1869
Death:
Mar. 29, 1937
Burial:
New Prospect Freewill Baptist
Coverdale
Turner County, Georgia

He was an early Free Will Baptist minister in the state of Georgia. He was a minister in the Georgia Union Association. He was married to Ola McCarty Little (1876 - 1953).

S. N. Little
Birth:
Apr. 3, 1848
Death:
Mar. 3, 1932
Burial:
New Prospect Freewill Baptist
Coverdale
Turner County, Georgia

He was an early Free Will Baptist preacher in Georgia.

Come

Quickly

Theron Wyndell Long
Birth:
Nov. 24, 1935
Death:
Aug. 1, 2011
Coffee Regional Medical Center,
Burial:
Surrency Cemetery
Surrency
Appling County, Georgia

Rev. Long, a former Free Will Baptist minister and a native of Appling County, was a Southern Baptist Minister for many years. He was an Alumnus of the Freewill Baptist College of Nashville, Tennessee. He was the son of the late Doric Quitman Long and the late Ola Evelyn Carter Long. He was also preceded in death by a brother, Wyndell Long. Funeral Services were held at the College Avenue Baptist Church, with Rev. Don Harper, Rev. Luther Burns, and Rev. J. E. Blanton officiating.

James B Lovering
Birth:
Feb. 7, 1912
Death:
Dec. 4, 1976
Burial:
Colquitt City Cemetery
Colquitt
Miller County, Georgia

He was a minister in the Midway, Martin, Little River, and George Union associations recorded as early as 1940 until 1963 in their minutes. Spouse: Flora Newsom Lovering (1915 - 1997).

L O Lovett
Birth:
Mar. 9, 1882
Death:
May 10, 1965
Burial:
Pine Grove Baptist Church
Cemetery
Nashville
Berrien County, Georgia

He was a minister in the Union Association.

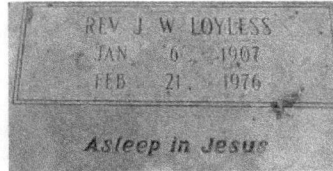

J W Loyless
Birth:
Jan. 6, 1907
Death:
Feb. 21, 1976
Burial:
Oak City Cemetery
Bainbridge
Decatur County, Georgia

He was a minister in the Midway Association.

Henry Lewis Lumpkin
Birth:
Mar. 9, 1878
Talbot County, Georgia
Death:
Dec. 26, 1946
Taylor County
Georgia
Burial:
Pine Level Cemetery
Mauk
Taylor County, Georgia

He married Emma Virginia Whitley in Talbot County on July 28, 1897. His parents were William J. and Sarah Lumpkin and he was the grandson of J.L and Jane (Hancock) Lumpkin. He was called to preach at the age of 18. He served in the Free Will Baptists denomination. He was a member of Woodmen of the World. He was the father of seven children. His two sons, William Robert and John Beverly were well known preachers. Henry and his two sons, William Robert and John Beverly all at some time were Pastors at New Life Church. During his ministry he preached in the Chattahoochee, Georgia Union and South Georgia conferences from about 1903 till 1942.

Johnnie Beverly Lumpkin
Birth:
Oct. 29, 1906
Georgia
Death:
Jan. 30, 2002
Georgia,
Burial:
Pine Level Cemetery
Mauk
Taylor County, Georgia

Husband of Blanche Hart Lumpkin. He was the son of Henry L. Lumpkin and Emma Watson Lumpkin. During his ministry he preached in the Chattahoochee, Georgia Union, Little River, Union, and Martin associations.

William Robert Lumpkin, Sr
Birth:
Aug. 19, 1904
Taylor County, Georgia
Death:
Jun. 13, 1991
Blountsville
Blount County, Alabama
Burial:
Pine Level Cemetery
Mauk
Taylor County, Georgia

W.R., attended Mauk and Berry High School. He worked with Goodrich in Silvertown, Thomaston, Georgia. He was raised on a farm. He was a Mason in the late 1920's and early 1930's. He was a member of

Woodmen of the World. He was saved in his bedroom in 1938. He was called to preach the Gospel and pastored several churches including; New Life in Talbot County, Spring Hill in Marion County, Trinity in Charing, Eastman in Dodge County, Cloud Springs in Ft. Oglethorpe, Temple in Rossville and Ft. Perry in Taylor County. He was married to Leila Foster on January 2, 1927 by and at the residence of Rev. J.L. Whitley in Mauk, Georgia.

John T Lunsford
Birth:
May 4, 1884
Death:
Oct. 27, 1940
Burial:
Mothers Home Cemetery
Miller County, Georgia

He was an early minister in the Martin Association.

Levi B. Manning
Birth:
Dec., 1879
Death:
1956
Burial:
Manningtown Presbyterian
Cemetery
Manningtown
Wayne County, Georgia

Early minister in the South Georgia Association.

Charles Courtney Martin
Birth:
Mar. 9, 1827
Jasper County, Georgia
Death:
Nov. 25, 1910
Randolph County, Georgia
Burial:
Martin Family Cemetery
Randolph County, Georgia

He was one of six brothers, four of whom were preachers of the gospel. He united with the Free Will Baptist when 14 years of age; received license to preach at 21 and was ordained when 22. At this time many of the churches of his vicinity united with the larger Baptist body, but brother Martin remained faithful to the smaller denomination. He went to work seriously and incessantly to propagate a free salvation and his labors were blessed of God to the saving of many. He assisted in the organizing of numerous churches and two associations, one named the Martin Assn., and baptized 1531 converts. For more than 30 years he was a pastor of two churches in the Chattahoochee Association.

Robert M Massey
Birth:
Jun. 6, 1872
Death:
Nov. 26, 1966
Burial:
Oak Ridge Cemetery
Tifton
Tift County, Georgia
Plot: Annex III

He pastored in the Chattahoochee, Little River, and Union associations from about 1925 until 1946.

Newton Elmore Massey
Birth:
Aug. 25, 1850
Muscogee County, Georgia
Death:
Nov. 3, 1914
Worth County, Georgia
Burial:
Hillcrest Cemetery
Sylvester
Worth County, Georgia
He was a minister in the Chattahoochee Association where records show that he was a pastor in 1892 through 1903. He was married to Julia Hill Massey (1850 - 1926) and they had two Children: Newton Elmore Massey (1878 - 1947) and Emma Massey Heath (1882 - 1952).

If the Spirit of him that raised up Jesus from the dead dwell in you, he that raised up Christ from the dead shall also quicken your mortal bodies by his Spirit that dwelleth in you.

Romans 8:11

Jordan B. McCullers
Birth
May 30, 1831
Dooley County, Georgia
Death:
Nov. 22, 1887
Burial:
Hodges Cemetery
Jakin
Early County, Georgia

He was converted in 1852, licensed in 1868, and ordained in April, 1874 by Bishop Pierce of the Methodists denomination. Since uniting with the Free Baptists his ministry has been in the Chattahoochee and Martin Associations baptizing over 100 converts and organized four churches, one of them in Thomas County, Georgia while laboring as a missionary.
Inscription:
Confederate Memorialco. D32 Ga. Inf. C.S.A.

Solomon Oscar McCorvey
Birth:
Mar. 31, 1879
Death:
Oct. 30, 1955
Burial:
Oak Ridge Cemetery
Tifton
Tift County, Georgia
Plot: Annex III

The Liberty minutes show that he was recorded in the 1926 edition as a minister.

Frank Steely McDanal
Birth:
Aug. 9, 1914
Death:
Jun. 21, 1966
Burial:
Parkhill Cemetery
Columbus
Muscogee County, Georgia

He was a minister in the Chattahoochee Association.

John D McDaniel
Birth:
May 28, 1879
Death:
Jun. 24, 1947
Burial:
Satilla Freewill Baptist Church Cemetery
Hazlehurst
Jeff Davis County, Georgia

He was in the Ogeechee Association.

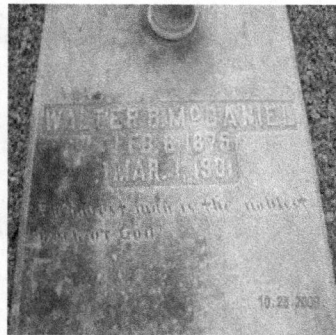

Walter Ballenger McDaniel
Birth:
Feb. 6, 1875
Death:
Mar. 1, 1931
Burial:
Oak Grove Cemetery
Americus
Sumter County, Georgia

Walter married Willie Adkins on 10 AUG 1902. He served as a minister in the Chattahoochee and UnionAssociations.
Inscription:
An Honest man is the noblest work of God

Warren Arthur McDonald
Birth:
Dec. 25, 1848
Death:
Jul. 28, 1933
Burial:
Shepard Cemetery ,
Miller County,Georgia

Rev. McDonald started several churches in the area, was quite prominent in his community and was a surveyor in Miller county as well. An old newspaper article concerning him stated there had been some stealing going on in the community; pigs, chickens, and homes entered and pilfered. No one knew who was doing it and could not seem to catch the thieves. One Sunday after church, Warren was going home in the mule and wagon. Suddenly, two unknown men jumped from the ditch bank and tried to hold him up. They apparently believed he would have the Sunday offering money with him. He told them to allow him to get it out of his inside coat pocket. He reached into the pocket, came out with a pistol instead, and shot and killed both men. He then left them lying there while he went to town and got the sheriff. He had no charges filed against him, and the stealing in the area stopped.

Richard B. McFadden, Jr
Birth:
Mar. 17, 1951
Death:
Jul. 12, 2008
Burial:
Macon Memorial Park
Macon
Bibb County, Georgia

He ministered in the Georgia Union Association

Peter McLain
Birth:
Nov. 19, 1843
Death:
Oct. 27, 1939
Burial:
New Hope Free Will Baptist
Church Cemetery
Madray Springs
Wayne County, Georgia

He was a minister in the Ogeechee and South Georgia Associations between 1903 and 1941 being recorded in the minutes of both associations on a regular basis.

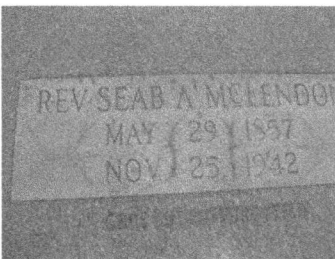

Seab A McLendon
Birth:
May 29, 1857
Death:
Nov. 25, 1942
Burial:
New Salem Cemetery
Miller County, Georgia

The Martin Association minutes from 1892 to 1921 record him as a minister.

Clarence McMillan
Birth:
Jul. 14, 1920
Death:
Dec. 19, 1994
Burial:
Sardis Cemetery
Folkston
Charlton County, Georgia

He was a minister in the South Georgia and Little River associations and whose record is found in the 1955 through 1988 minutes.He was married to the Leona Mock McMillan (1924 - 2011).

Thomas B. Mellette
Birth:
Apr. 25, 1892
Death:
Oct. 31, 1962
Burial:
Sowhatchee Cemetery,
Blakely
Early County,Georgia

He was one of the first educators in the early days of the denomination, who created Zion Bible School near Blakely. Mellette, who held degrees from several schools, including Columbia Bible College in Columbia, South Carolina, Zion served as the training ground for numerous ministers in Georgia, Florida, and Alabama. Many Zion graduates went on to become leaders in the national association. In 1942, after the national association established the Free Will Baptist Bible College in Nashville, Tennessee, Zion closed its doors and donated all its assets to the new school. He

had been on the joint Education Committee that had been working together for the purpose of establishing a Free Will Baptist school. Mellette was from the Eastern General Conference.

Henry Mills
Birth:
Dec. 28, 1908
Death:
Dec. 20, 1988
Burial:
Oakland Cemetery
Waycross
Ware County, Georgia
Plot: Section K Lot 9C

Minister in the South Georgia Association.

Cecil C Mock
Birth:
Oct. 25, 1917
Death:
Feb. 27, 1983
Burial:
Corinth Cemetery
Iron City
Seminole County, Georgia
He was a minister in the Martin Association. He was the son of John Henry Mock (1893 - 1966) and Alma Womble Mock (1898 - 1961).

H. S. "Monty" Montgomery
Birth:
1919
Death:
1973
Burial:
Carroll Memory Gardens
Carrollton
Carroll County, Georgia
Plot: Sec 3, Row 11

He was a member of the Chattahoochee Association.

Donald W. Moore
Birth:
May 24, 1919
Dodge County
Georgia
Death:
Oct. 12, 2002
Bibb County
Georgia
Burial:
Bay Springs Free Will Baptist
Church Cemetery
Plainfield
Dodge County, Georgia

He was a minister in the Georgia Union Association. His parents were Jim Moore and Mary Hogan. He was married on July 14, 1941 in Dodge County to Ruby Lee Horne Moore (1913 - 2006)Service Info.: S1 US NAVY WORLD WAR II.

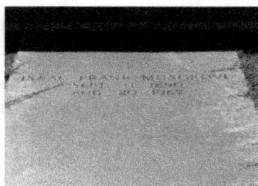

Isaac Frank Musgrove
Birth:
Sep. 11, 1890
Death:
Aug. 20, 1967
Burial:
Liberty Hill Baptist Church
Cemetery
Hartsfield
Colquitt County, Georgia

Was a member of the Martin Association.

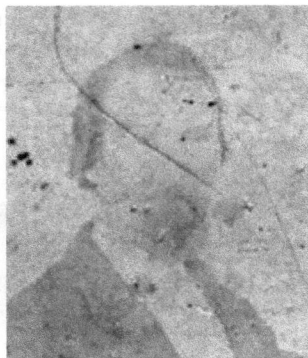

Franklin "Seab" Myers
Birth:
Oct. 28, 1846
Gordon
Wilkinson County, Georgia
Death:
Feb. 8, 1911
Douglas
Coffee County, Georgia
Burial:
Carver Baptist Church Cemetery
Douglas
Coffee County, Georgia

He was the son of David and Mary Myers in Gordon, Wilkinson county Ga. On 09, July 1861 He along with Brother William, enlisted in Co. "B" 14th Ga Infantry Regiment CSA. They were joined later by their two brothers, John, and Daniel. William, John, and Daniel were all released before war end from illness, or wounds sustained in battle. But Seab served till surrender at Appomattox Courthouse, Virginia on April 09, 1865. He had been captured a month earlier, on March 25, near Petersburg Va, and was released on May 15th, at Point Lookout Maryland. He returned to Ga, and Married Susanna (Susan) Hersey on March 21, 1872 in Coffee county. His grave is marked with a confederate stone. Susan died at her daughter Ida's home in Perry, Taylor county Florida, and is buried in that county at New Hope cemetery. Her gravestone reads, Susan wife of S.F Myers Dec 22 1849-April-6-1918   Having finished life's duty, she now sweetly rest. He was a member of the South Georgia conference.

William T. Park
Birth:
Oct. 30, 1830
Death:
Sep. 6, 1919
Burial:
Boynton Cemetery
Catoosa County, Georgia
Plot: Row 6

He was an early minister in the Chattahoochee Association and is recorded in the 1848 minutes of that conference.
Inscription:
2nd Co. "D", Ist Ga Inf., C.S.A.

William H. Parkman
Birth:
Jan. 8, 1831
Death:
May 7, 1907
Burial:
Fort Benning Cemetery #02
Fort Benning
Chattahoochee County, Georgia

In the 1848 minutes of the Chattahoochee Association listed as a minister. Confederate Civil War Veteran. 1850 Census McNortons, Muscogee Co GA. Film M432_79 pg 403A in household with his parents, John and Susan V. A Parkman and a lot of siblings. U.S. Civil War Soldier Records and Profiles Name: William Parkman Residence: Muscogee County, Georgia Enlistment Date: 5 Dec 1862 Rank at enlistment: Private State Served: Georgia Survived the War: Service Record: Enlisted in Pemberton's Company G, Georgia 54th Infantry Regiment on 16 May 1862. Mustered out on 25 May 1862 at Savannah, GA. Sources: Roster of Confederate Soldiers of Georgia 1861-1865.

C. L. Torbett Funeral Home, Columbus, GA Funeral Services Billed for May 7, 1907 $28.00.

Neal H Parrish
Birth:
Jul. 13, 1880
Death:
Sep. 6, 1962
Burial:
Friendship Cemetery
Hahira
Lowndes County, Georgia

Records revealed in four different associations that he pastored or was a minister there in. Namely; South Georgia, Georgia Union, Little River and Union Associations.

Oliver Hazard John Perry
Birth:
Jan. 7, 1865
Death:
Mar. 14, 1942
Burial:
Cedar Springs Cemetery
Cedar Springs
Early County, Georgia

He was an early minister in the Martin and Midway Association at the turn-of-the-century from 1902 until 1926.

August Jonathan Peters
Birth:
Dec. 5, 1847
Death:
Aug. 31, 1917
Burial:
Jesup City Cemetery
Jesup
Wayne County, Georgia

The minutes of the Martin Association record him in the 1893 edition. Then he is found in 1902 in the Midway Association.

James L Pittman
Birth:
Mar. 27, 1892
Death:
Jan. 22, 1977
Burial:
Smyrna Baptist Church Cemetery
Deepstep
Washington County, Georgia

A record of him is found in 1961 Chattahoochee minutes.

Roscoe Pitts
Birth:
Feb. 23, 1923
Georgia
Death:
Nov. 2, 1994
Columbus
Muscogee County, Georgia

Burial:
Riverdale Cemetery
Columbus
Muscogee County, Georgia

Roscoe was married to Avie Lou Howard. He was a preacher in the Chattahoochee and Georgia Union Association's ranging from about 1955 until 1987. He is recorded numerous times in these record books.

James Monroe Posey
Birth:
Mar. 5, 1852
Taylor County, Georgia
Death:
Aug. 1, 1918
Burial:
New Prospect Free Will Baptist
Church Cemetery
Reynolds
Taylor County, Georgia

His name is recorded in the Chattahoochee mintues from 1885 until 1917 in most all editions.

James L Poston
Birth:
Jul. 7, 1881
Death:
Jul. 20, 1952
Burial:
Pine Level Freewill Baptist
Church Cemetery
Chester
Dodge County, Georgia

His ministry was confined to the Georgia Union Association.
Spouse: Eunice T Poston (1889 - 1982)

James W. Potter
Birth:
Aug. 15, 1931
Death:
Jan. 24, 1991
Burial:
Middle Georgia Memory Gardens
Jones County, Georgia

He ministered in three Georgia associations. Namely; South Georgia, Chattahoochee and Georgia Union Associations.

William S Powell
Birth:
Jul. 24, 1875, USA
Death:
Mar. 13, 1932
Georgia
Burial:
Satilla Freewill Baptist Church
Cemetery
Hazlehurst
Jeff Davis, Georgia

He was an early minister in the South Georgia conference whose name is recorded in the 1929 and 1931 minutes.

William L Presley
Birth:
Apr. 8, 1820
Death:
Aug. 31, 1887
Burial:
Mount Zion Baptist Church
Cemetery
Towns County, Georgia

He is a minister whose name appears in the Chattahoochee minutes of 1842, 1847 and 1848.

William Lester Purvis
Georgia Birth:
Feb. 20, 1899
Death:
Aug. 8, 1979
Burial:
Purvis Cemetery
Coffee County, Georgia

He preached in a number of conferences in Georgia, namely; South Georgia, Georgia Union, Chattahoochee, Union and Little River Conferences.

Calvin C Quinn
Birth:
Jan. 3, 1870
Death:
Dec. 13, 1942
Burial:
Satilla Freewill Baptist Church
Cemetery
Hazlehurst
Jeff Davis County, Georgia

He preached in the South Georgia conference and his name appears in the 1907 minutes. He was married to Rebecca A Bland Quinn (1893 - 1927) and they had two children: Alvin H and Esther Lee.

They preached about this time and the hereafter

Henry Smith Reese
Birth:
Nov. 21, 1827
Jasper County, Georgia
Death:
Nov. 11, 1922
Turin
Coweta County, Georgia
Burial:
Tranquil Cemetery
Coweta County, Georgia

He is in the 1848 minutes of the Chattahooche Assn. He was a twin brother of John Palmer Reese. He was the son of Reverend James Reese and Rebecca (Smith) Reese. He was an ordained Baptist minister despite his lack of a formal education as well as a prominent writer and singer of Sacred Harp music. His ministry covered almost seventy years at churches throughout Georgia. In 1857, he married Amanda Brawner and this union produced one daughter. In 1865, he married a widow, Martha Jane (Leavell) Brooks, and there were seven children born of this union. He was also a teacher of Sacred Harp music according to the Baptist Biography (1920).

C D Rentz
Birth:
May 7, 1916
Death:
Jun. 22, 2001
Burial:
Memorial Freewill Baptist Church
Cemetery
Surrency
Appling County, Georgia

He is recorded many times in the South Georgia and Georgia Union conferences.

Charlie T Rentz
Birth:
1894
Death:
1952
Burial:
Westview Cemetery
Moultrie
Colquitt County, Georgia
Plot: Lane 10 East; Section 6,
Block C, Lot 45 (6 C 45 10th East)

He was a minister in the Union Conference.
Inscription:
RENTZ Rev. Charlie T.
Rentz 1894 ----- 1952
At Rest

Wilbur L Rentz
Birth:
Nov. 16, 1923
Death:
Aug. 29, 2007
Burial:
Memorial Freewill Baptist Church
Cemetery
Surrency
Appling County, Georgia

He was a preacher in the Midway and Martin conferences

G W Rhodes
Birth:
Mar. 6, 1870
Death:
Mar. 9, 1941
Burial:
Bethlehem Schley Baptist Church
Cemetery
Moultrie
Colquitt County, Georgia

He was a preacher in the Union Association.

Charles W Rickerson
Birth:
1868
Death:
1930
Burial:
Oak Ridge Cemetery
Tifton
Tift County, Georgia
Plot: old sect. blk 21, lot 4;
C W Rickerson plot

He was a preacher in the Chattahoochee Association.

Death brings eternal Life

Bill Robinson

Birth:
Apr. 11, 1927,
Liberty, Tennessee
Death:
May 13, 2005
Bainbridge, Georgia
Burial:
Mount Gilead
Freewill Baptist Church Cemetery,
Brinston,
Decatur County,Georgia

He was a United States Navy veteran of World War II and a 1962 graduate of Free Will Baptist Bible college in Nashville Tennessee. He was very active in denominational affairs and served for 12 years on the Board of Trustees of Free Will Baptist Bible College. He pastored churches in Tennessee, Michigan, Mississippi, North Carolina and Georgia. He retired as a Minister after 45 years of service and his retirement was only because of his health. He had diabetes for 35 years, had an open heart surgery, and only months before his death he lost a leg. He also had a brother of whom he was proud, Paul Robinson, who was a Free Will Baptist missionary to Uruguay.

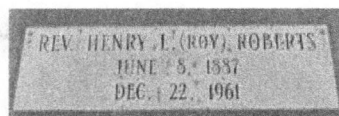

Henry Leroy "Roy" Roberts

Birth:
Jun. 8, 1887
Miller County, Georgia
Death:
Dec. 22, 1961
Miller County, Georgia
Burial:
Primitive Union Cemetery
Colquitt
Miller County, Georgia

He was a minister in the Martin and Midway conferences between the years of 1921 until 1959 according to the minutes of both associations.

Harris Edgar Rogers

Birth:
Aug. 13, 1888
Death:
Feb. 3, 1969
Burial:
Roberta City Cemetery
Roberta
Crawford County, Georgia
Plot: 351B

He is recorded as a minister in the Union minutes in 1952.

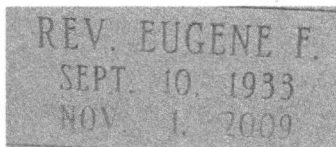

Eugene F. Ross

Birth:
Sep. 10, 1933
Dodge County, Georgia
Death:
Nov. 1, 2009
Cochran
Bleckley County, Georgia
Burial:
Bethany Baptist Church Cemetery
Bleckley County, Georgia

His ministry is recorded in the Georgia Union, Union and Chattahoochee minutes.

Vester Sadler

Birth:
Aug. 31, 1934
Death:
Jan. 13, 2007
Burial:
New Hope Cemetery
Cairo
Grady County, Georgia

Minister in Martin Association.

Pete Allen Sangster

Birth:
Jun. 12, 1872
Dooly Co, GA
Death:
Dec. 20, 1944
Burial:
Blackshear City Cemetery
Blackshear
Pierce County, Georgia

He was a minister in the Georgia Union conference.

Coming Home,

Coming Home

Never More To Roam.

Leon L. Sapp, Jr.

Birth:
Jan. 2, 1928
Death:
Oct. 13, 1974
Burial:
Lone Hill Cemetery
Coffee County, Georgia

He was a preacher in the following four conferences; Chattahoochee, Georgia Union, South Georgia and Union conferences. He was married to Heloyse Turner Sapp.

REVERAND JOSEPH WASHINGTON SAULS
OCT. 18, 1847
MAR. 7, 1919

Joseph Washington Sauls
Birth:
Oct. 18, 1847
Death:
Mar. 7, 1919
Burial:
Bethlehem Freewill Baptist
Church Cemetery
Shellman
Randolph County, Georgia

Brother Sauls was born and reared in Randolph County, and there he spent his entire life and raised a large and useful family. He became converted, joined the church, was baptized and soon afterwards began to preach and was ordained as a minister of the Gospel, and served a number of churches in the Bethel Association. In his own home church and community he was most useful. The lives of such men as this are jewels and they become the very foundation of the church and community life wherever they live. He and some of his family migrated from NC to Georgia..

Kenneth V. Shutes
Birth:
Jul. 9, 1905
Death:
Dec. 18, 1962
Burial:
Floral Memory Gardens, Albany,
Dougherty County,Georgia

Shutes for many years directed the Superannuation Board, which administered an insurance program for full-time ministers in the denomination.

Death is not the end.

Dr. Eugene Louis St. Claire
Birth:
Jun. 9, 1865,
Georgia
Death:
Feb. 6, 1916,
Florida
Burial:
Ebenezer Cemetery, Glennville,
Tattnall County,Georgia

Prominent evangelist of the Free Will Baptist denomination. At the time of his death, not yet 50 years old, he was living in Live Oak, FL, trying to regain his health following several paralytic strokes. Dr. St. Claire had been pastoring the church in Glennville, GA, and his body was returned for burial in the Ebenezer F.W.B. cemetery. Reverend O. B. Rustin officiated at his funeral. An account of his death appeared in the *Free Will Baptist* published. in Ayden, North Carolina. on Feb. 16, 1916, with a tribute to his life and ministry. Editor Phillips stated, "Dr. St. Claire, had conducted many revival campaigns there and had won many friends by his kind and genial disposition. Especially was he remembered for the great zeal and energy he had put in building and strengthening the Free Will Baptist Seminary in Ayden, N.C.
He was orphaned at age four years, and it is unknown if he had any siblings. Both parents were of English descent. He spent his early life on an old-fashioned plantation. He pursued his higher education at the University of Alabama, with Master of Arts, and in one paper, the editor states he studied and graduated from "several theological colleges."
The Doctor of Divinity designation appears wherever his name appears in print. Upon completing his secular education, he embarked upon a successful business career, but soon felt the call to the ministry. In his relatively short period of twenty-three years of ministry, his accomplishments were nothing short of phenomenal. In several of our Southern states he has done a great work. Association after association has been organized and put in working order. Thousands of souls have been led to the Lord in his meetings. In his first year of ministry, he helped to organize three associations. In his autobiography, he stated he organized 73 churches and won and baptized 4,879 persons.
FWB church records at Glennville, show that Dr. St. Claire was its founder in the year 1899. He pastored this church off and on up until his death.
Dr. St. Claire was also known as an orator, writer, and public debater. Debating was one of his skills, done in a witty manner, and at least five of these occasions are on record. He is acclaimed as one of the foremost preachers of the land, of scholarly ability, a man of culture and zeal, and service to his denomination.
For Dr. St. Claire's entire life as a Christian and as a minister of the Gospel, he was almost totally blind. This would mean that his Bible and theological education was acquired in spite of his lack of physical vision. How he acquired such vast and thorough knowledge of letters is hard to imagine for that time. However it came to him, he got it. This is a tribute to his indomitable spirit, for such a man cannot be defeated. His wife died shortly before he did. [It is unknown where she is buried]

Tombstone of Dr. St. Claire

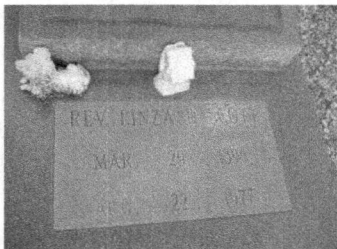

Linza D Scott
Birth:
Mar. 29, 1896, USA
Death:
Aug. 22, 1977, USA
Burial:
Brinson Cemetery
Brinson
Decatur County, Georgia

He was a minister in the Martin conference according to its minutes from about 1943 until 1975.

Farest W Sellers
Birth:
May 26, 1912
Death:
Jun. 16, 1984
Burial:
Branchville United Methodist Church Cemetery
Camilla
Mitchell County, Georgia

He pastored in the Martin, Union and Ogeechee conferences according to the minutes of all three conferences beginning in 1946 until 1983.

Willie A. Sellers
Birth:
Jan. 23, 1881
Death:
Jul. 14, 1975
Burial:
Branchville United Methodist Church Cemetery
Camilla
Mitchell County, Georgia

He pastored in the Liberty, Union and Martin conferences according to the records of all three beginning in 1926 and continuing until 1969.

Thomas J. Strickland
Birth:
Aug. 1, 1861
Tattnall County, Georgia
Death:
Mar. 18, 1920
Wayne County, Georgia
Burial:
Hopewell Methodist Church Cemetery
Tattnall County, Georgia

He is found in the Ogeechee minutes in 1903 and later in the South Georgia 1905-1911. He was married to Caroline Surrency.

James R. Stroup
Birth:
Nov. 16, 1914
Death:
Jun. 29, 1987
Burial:
Middle Georgia Memory Gardens
Jones County, Georgia

He was a minister in the Chattahoochee and Georgia Union Associations.

Grover Cleveland Sullivan
Birth:
Oct. 31, 1893
Dooly County, Georgia
Death:
Jan. 27, 1986
Perry
Houston County, Georgia
Burial:
Snow Methodist Church Cemetery
Unadilla
Dooly County, Georgia

Was a minister in Georgia Union Association.

John Taylor
Birth:
Feb. 14, 1818
Emanuel County, Georgia
Death:
Jan. 12, 1896
Worth County, Georgia
Burial:
Old Shiloh Cemetery
Tift County, Georgia

He was a clergyman in the Chattahoochee Association according to its minutes in 1891-92.

J. L. Tedder
Birth:
Jul. 18, 1886
Death:
Dec. 6, 1960
Burial:
Sowhatchee Cemetery
Blakely
Early County, Georgia

From 1923 until 1960 he was a minister in the Midway and Martin Associations.

James Alfred Thompson
Birth:
Sep., 1849
Appling Co, Georgia
Death:
1910
Burial:
Bethel Free Will Baptist Church Cemetery
Appling County, Georgia

He preached in the Ogeechee and South Georgia associations in the early part of the 1900s.

Allen L Thornton
Birth:
Dec. 5, 1872
Death:
May 18, 1953
Burial:
Satilla Freewill Baptist Church Cemetery
Hazlehurst
Jeff Davis County, Georgia

He was a preacher in the South Georgia Association and is recorded in most of the minutes from 1919 until 1953.

A J Tomlinson
Birth:
Aug. 6, 1870
Death:
Mar. 18, 1951
Burial:
Pine Level Cemetery
Cairo
Grady County, Georgia

He was a minister in the Liberty and Martin associations from 1921 until 1950.

Moutrie H Touchton
Birth:
Aug. 22, 1876
Death:
Feb. 3, 1961
Burial:
Boney Bluff Cemetery
Echols County, Georgia

He was a preacher in the Little River Association.

Thomas J. Touchton
Birth:
Sep. 28, 1905
Death:
Jul. 15, 1907
Burial:
Macedonia Baptist Church Cemetery
Mayday
Echols County, Georgia

He was a minister in the Union Association.

Willie Gus Turner
Birth:
Jun. 29, 1922
Sale City
Mitchell County, Georgia
Death:
Aug. 9, 2012
Cairo
Grady County, Georgia
Burial:
Carter-Banks Cemetery
Grady County, Georgia

Rev. Turner was born to the late David Glenn Turner and Blanchie M. Johnson Turner. On March 23, 1946, he married Nancy Elizabeth Banks Turner. Rev. Turner was a minister for 66 years (32 years at First Freewill of Cairo, Georgia). He served his country in the U. S. Army, as an honorable veteran, fighting on the front line in the European Theatre of WWII. His ministry was spent in the Martin and Union associations.

James Edwary Usury
Birth:
May 6, 1935
Graham
Appling County, Georgia
Death:
Mar. 16, 2013
Jeff Davis County, Georgia
Burial:
Satilla Freewill Baptist Church Cemetery
Hazlehurst
Jeff Davis County, Georgia

He graduated from Jeff Davis high

school. He desired for education and took correspondence courses after graduation, including some courses from Welch College (then Free Will Baptist Bible College). After graduation from High School he worked at a news agency. He married Janice Quinn who was a real asset and blessing in his Christian Ministry.James was called to the ministry at the age of 21 and was ordained the next year. He was ordained in the South Georgia Association and those serving on the Ordaining Committee were: Dr. Tom Hamilton, Dr. Ralph Lightsey and Rev. C. D. Rentz.His first pastorate was at the Oak Hill Church and then at the Corinth Church both in the South Georgia Association. In 1967 he was called to the Midway Church, Moultrie, in the Union Association and was there until 1976. The Lord led him to the First Church in Columbus, Twin Cities Association until 1982. Then they went back to the South Georgia Association, First Church in Jesup until 1990. He then served the New Home Church in the Martin Association until 1999 when he officially retired from active ministry because of health problems and went back home to Hazlehurst.During his ministry there were at least five young men called to ministry: Rev. Steve Hughes, Dr. Billy Lewis, Rev. Irvin Murphy, Rev. Ken Murphy and Rev. Curtis Alligood.James was totally involved in Free Will Baptist ministry. In the districts where he pastured he served in various capacities including committees and moderator. At the State level, he was on the Resolution Committee; served as music director for the State Meeting; served on Board of Christian Education; Budgeting Committee; was Chairman of the Board of Mission and in 1985 was elected Clerk of the State. Officiating the services were Rev. Paul Smith, Rev. Herbert Waid and Rev. Steve Hughes.

Julian Vickers
Birth:
Dec. 20, 1923
Death:
Mar. 27, 2002
Burial:
Hebron Cemetery
Coffee County, Georgia

He preached in the Union and Little River associations.

Edgar Jackson Wade
Birth:
Jan. 1, 1881
Georgia
Death:
Jan. 11, 1952
Cordele
Crisp County, Georgia
Burial:
Sunnyside Cemetery
Cordele
Crisp County, Georgia

He preached in the Georgia Union conference.

Frank W Wade
Birth:
Feb. 22, 1884
Death:
Nov. 12, 1954
Burial:
Colquitt City Cemetery
Colquitt
Miller County, Georgia

He was a preacher in the Martin Association.

Samuel Watkins, Jr
Birth:
1779
Richland County, South Carolina
Death:
Apr. 15, 1855
Columbus
Muscogee County, Georgia
Burial:
New Providence Baptist Church Cemetery
Muscogee County, Georgia

Rev. Samuel Watkins, Jr. was the son of Samuel Watkins, Sr,and Elizabeth (unknown). He married Charity (unknown) about 1808 in Richland Co., SC and they were the parents of six children: William, Zachariah, Samuel, Ervin, Epsey and George Washington Watkins. He migrated from Richland Co., SC to Muscogee Co., GA about 1833. He was an early pastor of the New Providence Freewill Baptist Church. The dates for Samuel and Charity were accidently reversed on the tombstone.

Benjamin Blanton Watson
Birth:
Aug. 24, 1829
Marion County, Georgia
Death:
Feb. 13, 1915
Taylor County, Georgia
Burial:
Trinity Freewill Baptist Cemetery
Taylor County, Georgia

The 1842 Chattahoochee Assn minutes record him as a minister. He was the son of Richard William Ansley Watson (1803 - 1871) and Sealia R Waller Watson (1802 - 1870). He married Sarah Frances Rebecca Lawhorn Watson (1834 - 1921).

John R. Weeks
Birth:
Apr. 24, 1891
Death:
Dec. 30, 1947
Burial:
Weeks Chapel Cemetery
Norman Park
Colquit County, Georgia

He was a minister in the Little River conference.

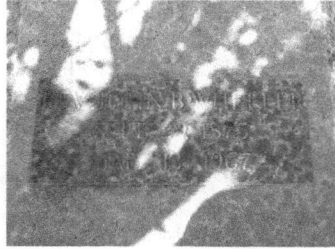

John B Wheeler
Birth:
Sep. 29, 1875
Death:
Mar. 13, 1967
Burial:
Oak Ridge Cemetery
Tifton
Tift County, Georgia

He preached in both the Little River and South Georgia conferences.

Connie C White
Birth:
Oct. 27, 1878
Death:
May 22, 1975
Burial:
White Plains Freewill Baptist Church Cemetery
Lucile
Early County, Georgia

Son of Andrew Jackson White (buried at Blakely City Cemetery) and Linton Ann Malinda Mills White. Married Ola Barbrie on 17 Aug 1899 in Early County, Georgia.
The minutes of the Midway Association beginning in 1916 record him in most all minutes until 1971. Inscription:In thee o Lord have I put my trust

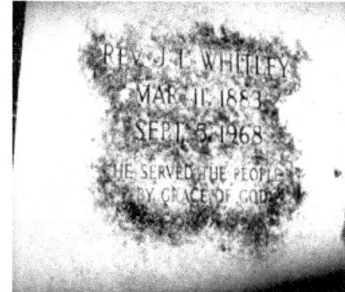

James L. "Jim" Whitley
Birth:
Mar. 11, 1883
Death:
Sep. 5, 1968
Burial:
Pine Level Cemetery
Mauk
Taylor County, Georgia

He was a minister in the Chattahoochee Association.He was the son of James M. and Polly Whitley, who married Fannie Lucinda Lee Hayes Whitley (1882 - 1956).

L B Whitley
Birth:
1855
Death:
1929
Burial:
Brushy Creek Cemetery
Adel
Cook County, Georgia

He is recorded in the Liberty minutes in 1895.

Death is not annihilation.

Green Thomas Wiley
Birth:
Apr. 10, 1845
Death:
Sep. 14, 1917
Burial:
Sowhatchee Cemetery
Blakely
Early County, Georgia

His ministry began in 1879 in the Chattahoochee Association where he served until 1885. Afterwards, he joined the Martin Association in 1892 and remained there until 1902. He joined the Midway Association in 1902 and served there until 1909. He was the husband of Margaret (Walter) Wiley and son of Jacob Wiley, Jr and Mary D. (Lane) Wiley.

William T Wiley
Birth:
Sep. 6, 1868
Georgia
Death:
Jun. 26, 1952
Burial:
Sowhatchee Cemetery
Blakely
Early County, Georgia

He joined the Martin Association in 1887 and in 1902 he united with the Midway Association and remained there until 1948 as a clergyman. He married Ella G. Alston Wiley (1873 - 1975).

Samuel Longstreet Wilkinson
Birth:
May 13, 1933
Death:
Apr. 11, 1988
Burial:
Ebenezer Cemetery
Glennville
Tattnall County, Georgia
Plot: Section B2

His name appears in the South Georgia minutes on a regular basis from 1954 until 1985. He was a Minister, Missionary in Brazil 19 years, and a professor at Hillsdale FWB College. Husband of Volree June Goode. Inscription: Children: Kevin, Kimberly, Kenan

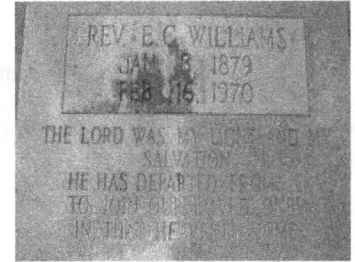

E. C. Williams
Birth:
Jan. 8, 1879
Death:
Feb. 16, 1970
Burial:
New Enterprise Freewill Baptist
Church Cemetery
Seminole County, Georgia

He served in the Midway and Martin Association's from 1919 until 1969. He was married to Abbie Rebecca Williams (1887 - 1947) and to them had the following children; Infant Son William (1905 1905), Anderson Williams (1906 - 1971), Nita Williams Tyler (1907 - 1998), J. T. Williams (1913-1934) Modainer R. Williams (1914 - 1930).

Kinnebrew Willis, Sr
Birth:
1812
Morgan County, Georgia
Death:
Dec. 12, 1880
Lee County,, Alabama
Burial:
Emmaus Baptist Church Cemetery
Muscogee County, Georgia

His name appears in the Chattahoochee minutes of 1879. It is SPECULATIVE that this individual is buried at Emmaus Baptist Cemetery - at least two of his children, one who died during the Civil War in 1864 and another who died in 1934, are buried here. Said to be son of Robert L. Isabel (Frazier) Willis, Sr. Married ca. 1837, probably in Muscogee County, Georgia, to Nancy Motley. Father of fifteen children.

Harvey J. Wilson
Birth:
Dec. 28, 1902
Death:
Aug. 24, 1932
Burial:
New Hope Free Will Baptist
Church Cemetery
Madray Springs
Wayne County, Georgia

He was a member of the Union conference.

Riley H Windham
Birth:
Feb. 12, 1908
Death:
Jun. 22, 1987
Burial:
Mount Olive Freewill Baptist
Church Cemetery
Potterville
Taylor County, Georgia

The Chattahoochee minutes record him from 1930 until 1948.

Needham Graham Yarbrough
Birth:
Nov. 28, 1842
Williamsburg County, South
Carolina
Death:
Mar. 10, 1928
Wayne County, Georgia
Burial:
George Cemetery
Wayne County, Georgia

Rev. Yarbrough's parents were: Needham Madison and Rebecca

Wright Yarbrough. He enlisted in Clarendon County, South Carolina with Co. H 26th Regiment, South Carolina Volunteers along with his brothers John Edward, William, his brother in law John McCaskill and his uncle John Yarbrough during the war between the states. Before the war he was working as a farm hand on the Jones farm in Clarendon, South Carolina where he met and fell in love with Eliza McCaskill. Family members said he came to the field one day and ask her to marry him and off they went to Charleston, SC and was married that very day Dec. 24, 1860. During the war his father Needham Madison Yarbrough went to South Carolina and brought his sons family to his home in Liberty Co., Georgia. After the war Needham G. moved his family from Georgia to Starke Florida. In a letter he wrote back to his father, he wrote it took 3 months by ox and cart to get there and they had to fight off Indians during the journey. Years later he and the family moved back to Georgia and settled in Wayne County, Georgia. The Ogeechee minutes showed him as a clergyman in their Association in 1903 and later the South Georgia minutes in 1905 through 1907 showed him as a minister.

Thomas Patrick Young
Birth:
Jan. 15, 1843
Columbus
Muscogee County, Georgia
Burial:
Riverdale Cemetery
Columbus
Muscogee County, Georgia
Plot: Section 7, North 1/2 of Lot 93

Son of Marmaduke N.and Elizabeth (McSWAIN) YOUNG. The local newspaper said:."MR. T. P. YOUNG DIED YESTERDAY: Was 66 Years of Age and a Confederate Veteran--Funeral Tomorrow

Morning. The deceased was a member of the Free Will Baptist church and was held in high esteem by all who knew him. The news of his death will bring sorrow to many homes in the community in which he lived. He was a gallant soldier in the service of the south during the civil war and the following page from an old family record bears out the fact of his loyalty to his state: Enlisted in Company B, Captain R. F. PARDY, (of Muscogee county) Thirty-first Georgia regiment, volunteers, October 4th, 1861. Was captured at Appomatax, Va., May 12th, 1864, carried to Fort Delaware. Paroled March 10th, 1865. During the war he served under Generals A. R. LAWTON, John B. GORDON, Clement A. EVANS, Jeb. A. EARLY, and a member of JACKSON's corps, Army of Northern Virginia. Was wounded on the 13th of December, 1862, and afterwards joined the ranks.' Besides his devoted wife, he is survived by five children, as follows: Messrs. F. B. YOUNG, of Chattanooga; F. R. YOUNG, Jr., of the United States navy; W. L. YOUNG, C. L. YOUNG, of Columbus, and G. N. YOUNG, of Milledgeville. He is also survived by two brothers, Messrs. F. R. YOUNG, of Columbus, and O. C. YOUNG, of Girard. The funeral will take place tomorrow morning at ten o'clock from the late residence, and 'Taps' will be sounded over the grave by Messrs. Marion Schley DAVIS and Gurlin F. DAVIS, of the Columbus Guards." [Columbus (GA) Enquirer-Sun newspaper, Saturday, 19 DEC 1908, p. 3.]" Sunday morning at 10 o'clock, the services being conducted by the Rev. Mr. KIDD. The funeral was largely attended by relatives and friends of the deceased. Camp Benning was also represented at the funeral, as Mr. YOUNG was a member of the camp and served the south well during the civil war. Interment was in Riverdale cemetery and the following members of Camp Benning acted as pallbearers: Probably the most impressive feature of the ceremony at the grave was the sounding of 'taps' immediately after the services by Mr. Marion Schley DAVIS, leader of the Columbus Guards drum and bugle corps." [Columbus (GA) Enquirer-Sun newspaper, Tuesday, 22 DEC 1908, p. 8..Entry in Sexton's Card File for Riverdale Cemetery:

Death is a trade-in.

One day we will trade in our broken down bodies for a new body. Look what Paul says about that new body.

It is from God. It is not made with hands. It is eternal. It is heavenly, not earthly.

Idaho

Romanzo Alexander Coats
Birth:
Jul. 3, 1842
Fabius
Onondaga County, New York
Death:
Mar. 17, 1927
Ontario
Malheur County, Oregon
Burial:
Canyon Hill Cemetery
Caldwell, Canyon County, Idaho

UNION WISCONSIN VOLUNTEERS 23rd Regiment, Wisconsin Infantry Romanzo Alexander CoatsRegiment Name 23 Wisconsin Infantry. Side Union Company K Soldier's Rank_In Fifer Soldier's Rank_Out Fifer also...He was an ordained minister in Spencer, Iowa .He was a teacher and a school superintendent in Idaho. He was a farmer in Minnesota."Rev. R.A. Coats, son of Rev. D. N. Coats was born in Chenango Co., NY, July 3, 1842. He studied at Spring Green Academy, Wis., and served three years in the 23d Wis. Vol Infantry at Vicksburg, New Orleans, etc. He was converted Jan. 1, 1863, and ordained June 23, 1872. As missionary for the Little Sioux Valley Quarterly Meeting in the winter of 1871-72, he was engaged in revivals at Lost Island, Iowa, and Elm Creek and Freedom, Minnesota. In April

1883, he entered upon a seven years' pastorate with the Spencer, Iowa church, during which he served the Minnesota Southern Yearly Meeting in soliciting funds at the time of the famous "grasshopper scourge."In 1880 he became pastor of the Mitchell, Burr Oak and Lincoln churches, enjoying a gracious revival with the latter, and three years later returned to Spencer. In 1887, he removed to Idaho. Rev. Coats was a member of the General Conferences of 1874 and 1880; has served as superintendent of schools in Clay Co. IA, two terms; has been a member of the Iowa Home Mission Board six years and an assistant editor of the *Free Baptist* from commencement. His varied labors have been very helpful to the cause in that region, and he is widely known and respected. His parents were David N Coats (1815 - 1889) and Elizabeth Eleanor White Coats (1822 - 1910)and his spouse was Lephe H Wells Coats (1844 - 1924).

Rue Thomas
Birth:
Apr. 15, 1907
Arkansas
Death:
Jul. 17, 1992
Twin Falls
Twin Falls County, Idaho
Burial:
Sunset Memorial Park Cemetery
Twin Falls
Twin Falls County, Idaho
Thomas, was converted when Oklahoma preacher Jake Gage conducted a revival in Idaho. He soon answered the call to preach, left his farming career in 11953 and invested the next 39 years as a Free Will Baptist minister. Although he did not organize any of the Idaho Free Will Baptist churches, Rue Thomas had a part in each of them. He was a charter member of the Buhl Church, formed the nucleus of the Jerome Church and preached in the Boise church.Born in Kingston, AR, he pastored the only Free Will Baptist church that ever existed in the state of Nevada. He also pastored churches in Midland and San Angelo, TX., and at Artesia, N.Mex. While pastoring small, struggling churches, Bro. Thomas earned a living working for the C.R. Anthony Co. where he received numerous awards as top manager and salesman.He retired from the C.R. Anthony Co., at age 66, then spent more than 15 years on occasional special assignments with the Home Mission Dept. going into churches where a missionary had become discouraged and left. Every time Bro. Thomas left a church, the congregation was debt-free with money in the bank and a larger

membership than when he came. His last pastorate was in Rupert, Idaho.

**Burial Place of
Benjamin Randall
Spafford County, Dover, N.H.**

Illinois

A L Asberry
Birth:
Oct. 17, 1827
Death:
Aug. 23, 1876
Burial:
Glenn Cemetery, Glenn
Jackson County, Illinois

Early Free Will Baptist Church in western Illinois.

D. W. Ashby
Birth:
January 7, 1851
Hopkins County, Kentucky
Death:
unknown
Burial:
DeSoto Cemetery
De Soto, Jackson County, Illinois
APlot: Second Addition Row 7

He experienced religion in January, 1869 and received license to preach in 1871. He was ordained on April 4, 1875 with his connection first being with the General Baptist. About 1885 he united with Freewill Baptist. And began to minister churches in the Makanda Quarterly Meeting in Illinois

J. H. Bagwill
Birth:
1874
Death:
1936
Burial:
Looney Springs Cemetery,
Campbell Hill,
Jackson County, Illinois

Early Free Will Baptist minister in Southwest Illinois.

Matthew Baker, Jr
Birth:
Oct. 21, 1791,
Stamford,
Bennington County, Vermont
Death:
Jan. 19, 1852,
Coles County, Illinois
Burial:
Hurricane Cemetery,
Hutton Township,
Coles County, Illinois

Matthew was a prominent minister, marrying many of the local couples in Coles County.

Stephen Bathrick
Birth:
May 27, 1810
New York
Death:
Sep. 26, 1880
Frankfort, Will County, Illinois
Burial:
Pleasant Hill Cemetery
Frankfort, Will County, Illinois

A native of Cayugo Co. N.Y. He died at Frankfort, Ill, aged 70 years. In 1830 he commenced preaching and in 1832 married Miss Cynthia M. Bartholomew. He was ordained Sept. 28, 1833, a Free Will Baptist minister, and became pastor of the N. Parma church, N.Y. He was successful in his efforts in other places. After nine years, he settled at Conneaut, Ohio, where many were added to the church. His labors in the Ashtabula Q.M. were greatly profited by his earnest efforts. After spending some time in his native State, he spent time in Saco and Biddeford, ME, and with the exception of a short period at Lexington, MI, most of his last twenty years were spent in Central New York. At the urgent request of the church at Frankort, Ill, where he had recently pastored, he settled there some two years before his death. His beliefs were positive; his preaching practical and earnest. He loved truth and condemned error. It is thought by many that he preached over 7,000 sermons, and they were remembered by thousands who felt a loss at his death.

Loren Bixby
Birth:
1810
Death:
1900
Burial:
Bloods Point Cemetery
Boone County, Illinois
Plot: 108

Parents: Ebenezer and Hannah Tracy (Flint) Bixby, both bur. VT. His bro., Newell W, also a FWB minister, is bur. in Iowa.

Richard A. Bradley
Birth:
1802
Death:
1859
Burial:
Looney Springs Cemetery,
Campbell Hill,
Jackson County, Illinois

Richard A. Bradley was born in Sumner Cty, Tennessee. Richard was in his mid-teens when the family moved to Randolph County, Illinois. At age 22 Richard was a member of the survey party that finalized the disputed county line between Jackson and Randolph County. The Bradley's found the majority of their land was now in Jackson County, Illinois. The Black Hawk war broke in the early 1830s and Richard served as a Corporal in the 3rd Regiment, Illinois volunteers commanded by Gabriel Jones. From 1838 to 1840 Richard served as a County Commissioner, and in 1842 he was elected a Representative to the Illinois State Legislature. He served in this capacity until 1846 and then again from 1848 to 1852. During his first term in the State Legislature he Chaired the Elections Committee and presented the bill that moved the Jackson County seat to Murphysboro. In 1848 he Chaired the Committee on Public Buildings and Grounds and presented the bill which reduced the fees of many county officials and also presented the bill that chartered the Chester and Wabash Railroad. Richard joined the Looney Springs Free Will Baptist Church in 1850 and was ordained a minister in 1852. For many years he served as Pastor at Looney Springs, as well as at the Campbell Hill Free Will Baptist Church. Richard died on April 16, 1859.

Death is not reincarnation.

William Bradley
Birth:
Feb. 13, 1814
Death:
Aug. 10, 1887
Burial:
Holliday Farm Cemetery,
Murphysboro,
Jackson County, Illinois

William Bradley was born in Sumner County, Tennessee. Through his early years he studied on his own and acquired a liberal education. In April 1839 William was one of the 32 men who pooled their funds to purchase 80 acres of land to be used in establishing Shiloh School and Meeting House to serve both Jackson and Randolph Counties. In December he, along with his brothers James, Benjamin, and Richard and six other men, was elected Trustee for the incorporation of Shiloh College which was approved on January 8th, 1840 by the Illinois House and Senate. He remained a trustee for several years and was a member of the committee which drafted the resolutions which governed the board of the college. He was appointed postmaster of the town of Bradley from its formation in 1846 until 1853. He served as Associate county Judge from 1849 to 1853 and County Judge from 1853 to 1857. In 1858 he unsuccessfully ran for the State Legislature. In October 1852 he was ordained a Freewill Baptist Minister by Reverend Henry S. Gordon. He served as Pastor at Looney Springs Baptist Church near Campbell Hill and at Sato Baptist Church. In 1860, he and Reverend Gordon organized the Ava Free Baptist Church, where

William served as pastor until 1864. In 1869 William and Serena moved to the growing city of Murphysboro where they lived the rest of their lives. From 1869 to 1873 William once more served as County Judge and through his remaining years stayed active in the church.

Samuel S. Branch
Birth:
Dec. 27, 1801
Vermont
Death:
Jan. 29, 1862
Geff, Wayne County, Illinois
Burial:
Pleasant Grove Christian Church
Cemetery
Geff, Wayne County, Illinois

He had 11 children by three wives, the first two wives dying in childbirth in Meigs Co, Ohio. He moved his family and congregation to Wayne County, Illinois in 1852 and started the Oak Valley Free Will Baptist Church. The HISTORY OF WAYNE CO:Free-Will Baptists, pg 121-122-- The first church organized in this county about two miles west of Jeffersonville, Sept 2 1854, by Rev. S. S. Branch, and consisted of six members: S.S. Branch, Elizabeth Branch, Densy TUBBS, Samuel BRANCH, Jacob S. HAWK AND Mary HAWK. S.S. Branch was chosen pastor; J.S.Hawk clerk, and Samuel

Branch, deacon a cousin to S.S. Branch, his wife is Phoebe and they had no children. He is buried in the Geff cemetery]. The Saturday before the third Sabbath of each month, was appointed for covenant meetings. Regular services were held on the Sabbath. Rev. S.S. Branch was born in Vermont in 1794 [bible records say 27 Dec 1801], removed to Ohio in 1802; professed religion April 1831; baptized by Rev. Eli STEADMAN, his brother-in-law, was ordained 1841, removed to Illinois 1853; and died leaving a wife and eight children. His widow Elizabeth Branch lived in Big Stone Co. Minneasota with her son Joseph. The membership of the church was 92.

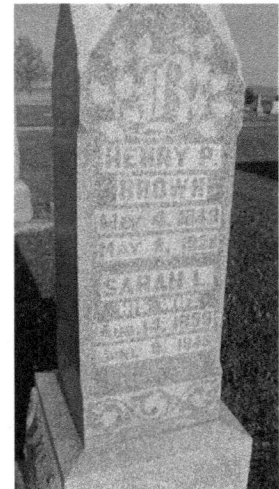

Henry Brown
Birth:
Mar. 4, 1843
Virginia
Death:
Mar., 1928
Illinois
Burial:
Harvel Cemetery
Harvel, Montgomery County,
Illinois

He was converted in 1859 and married in 1878. And receivined his license to preach in 1886 and at one time ministered the church in East St. Louis, Illinois.

Obed W Bryant
Birth:
Mar. 9, 1815
Death:
Aug. 2, 1882
Burial:
Wyoming Cemetery
Paw Paw, Lee County, Illinois
Bryant, a native of New Vineyard, Me., was converted when about nineteen years of age and went to reside in Illinois two years later. He joined the Baptist church and later the Free Baptist, near Lamoille. Later, he moved to Four Mile Grove, where he was instrumental in raising a church. He was ordained at that place in August 1859, and remained a member until his death, when 67 years of age. He labored zealously and successfully. He was faithful in his care of the widely separated churches, punctual at the general meetings, persistent in revival efforts, true in positions of public trust and active in moral enterpnses.

William Riley Burton
Birth:
Sep. 21, 1881,
Ewing, Franklin County, Illinois
Death:
Nov., 1963,
Ewing, Franklin County, Illinois
Burial:
Shiloh Cemetery
Ewing, Franklin County, Illinois

A retired minister and native of Franklin Co. and was a member of Rescue Free Will Baptist Church at Whittington, with Rev. Marsh Harpool officiating

No More Death
The beginning of life

Lyman Chase
Birth:
Oct. 2, 1839,
Rutland, Ohio
Death:
1918
Burial:
Tamaroa Cemetery,
Tamaroa, Perry County, Illinois

He began his new life in 1857, and received license in 1859, and ordination in 1868, having graduated from Hillsdale College (Michigan) in 1866. He became principal of Atwood Institute in Ohio, the year of his graduation, and was there five years. He has also served as editor of the Huntington, West Virginia., *Independent*, and as superintendent of the city schools.

His pastorates were at Conneaut, Sheffield and Madison, Ohio; Fairview, Ill, and Mt. Pleasant, Kan. He was superintendent of the work in the northern Kansas and southern Nebraska Yearly Meeting, and in connection with his ministerial duties prepared a book entitled, *Contending for the Faith*.

Claude B Childers
Birth:
Jun. 17, 1882
Death:
Mar. 29, 1962
Burial:

Wakefield Cemetery,
Wakefield,
Richland County, Illinois

Early preacher in Illinois.

Charles Dwight Dame
Birth:
Jan. 15, 1922,
Waltonville,
Jefferson County, Illinois
Death:
Oct. 9, 2009
Burial:
Maple Hill Cemetery,
Sesser, Franklin County, Illinois

Dwight was ordained a Free Will Baptist minister in 1952 and served as a minister for over 50 years at several different churches. He was the chaplain for the Sesser VFW and American Legion, giving the Memorial Day address every year. He attended grade school at White Oak and high school in Sesser. He entered the United States Army on Sept. 8, 1942, serving until Jan. 1, 1946, with two years, 11 months and 24 days overseas, serving in battles at Ardennes, Rhindland and Central Europe. He received six overseas service bars, one service stripe, American Campaign, European and African and Middle East Theater Ribbons, three Bronze Battle Stars, Asiatic Pacific Theater Ribbon, Good Conduct Medal and a World War II Victory Medal, while becoming a sergeant. Dwight raised cattle and farmed his entire life and loved to hunt quail. He worked at Valier Coal Company before World War II and at Freeman United Coal for 30 years after the war. He worked as a United Mine Workers Association member, a supervisor and plant superintendent. He was also a college mining instructor at

Rend Lake College for five years before retiring. He served on the Sesser School Board for eight years and as president for four years. He was also the mayor of Sesser for four years and got the city hall built during his term in office. Military rites were conducted by the Sesser VFW and American Legion.

James Charles Gilliland
Birth:
1874
Death:
1958
Burial:
Grandview Cemetery, Freeport, Stephenson County, Illinois

Free Will Baptist minister in Illinois.

George Alexander Gordon
Birth:
Apr. 14, 1842,
Alton, Madison County, Illinois
Death:
Aug. 25, 1922,
Ava ,Jackson County, Illinois
Burial:
Calvary Cemetery,
Campbell Hill,
Jackson County, Illinois

Active early leader and church builder in Illinois. Respected and looked to for guidance by other ministers in his area in southern Illinois.

Floyd Harley
Birth:
unknown
Death:
unknown
Sesser,
Franklin County, Illinois
Burial:
Maple Hill Cemetery,
Sesser,
Franklin County, Illinois

**Missionary
Evelyn *Lawrence* Hersey**
Birth:
Mar. 2, 1930,
Vroman,
Otero County,Colorado
Death:
Oct. 4, 1993,
Nashville,
Davidson County, Tennessee
Burial:
Zion Cemetery,
Ozark, Johnson County, Illinois

She served many terms as a missionary to Japan under the International Mission Board of Free Will Baptists. She was married to Fred Hersey.

James Walter Hicks
Birth:
Sep. 18, 1930
Jefferson County, Illinois
Death:
Sep. 9, 1987
Burial:
Knob Prairie Cemetery
Waltonville, Jefferson County, Illinois

Hicks, a son of Travis and Sadie (Dees) Hicks. On Dec 4, 1954, in Mt. Vernon, he married Anna Marie Fairchild. Services were at the Waltonville Free Will Baptist Church with the Rev Geraldine Lewis officiating. Hicks was a U. S. Navy veteran of the Korean War and a member of VFW 9153 and Disabled American Veterans of Mt. Vernon. He was a Free Will Baptist minister in the Waltonville area for several years and was a member of the Free Will Baptist Church in Nason.

John J. Hiltibidal
Birth:
Jan. 24, 1908
Death:
Apr. 21, 1973
Burial:
Old Covenanter Cemetery
Marion County, Illinois,
Plot: Back of church

He was a retired Carmen and welder for the Illinois central railroad and a retired minister in the Free Will Baptist denomination. For 50 years he served as a minister for several Free Will Baptist Churches throughout southern Illinois. He was a member of the Pleasant View Free Will Baptist Church where he established his original membership in 1934.

Opal P. Hiltibidal
Birth:
Apr. 28, 1914
Illinois
Death:
Sep. 6, 2008
Walnut Hill,
Marion County, Illinois
Burial:
Old Covenanter Cemetery,
Marion County, Illinois

Opal passed at the age of 94 years. Opal was a resident of Walnut Hill, Illinois at the time of her passing. She was a student of the first class of FWB Bible College of Nashville, Tenn. She was also a minister in the state of Illinois.

George B. Hopkins
Birth:
April 11, 1855
Oakfield, New York
Death:
Nov. 13, 1941
Illinois
Burial:
Oakwood Cemetery
Geneseo, Henry County, Illinois

He graduated from Pike Seminary in 1879, from Hillsdale College in 1884, and completed the theological course in Bates College in 1887. He made a public confession of Christ in 1876 and received his license to preach for the Genesee, New York Quarterly Meeting in January 1886. He served churches in Maine and New York before coming to Illinois.

Andrew J. Hoskinson
Birth:
August 4, 1816
Athens County Ohio
Death:
1892
Illinois
Burial:
Peaceful Valley Cemetery
Odin, Marion County, Illinois

He experienced religion in 1837, and in 1843 was ordained by Rev. S. S. Branch and others in South East Ohio. He labored as an evangelist among the destitute churches and has organized several churches and baptized about 80 converts.

George H. Hubbard
Birth:
Feb. 16, 1823
Burlington, New York
Death:
1911
Burial:
Oakwood Cemetery
Waukegan, Lake County, Illinois

He was converted in 1836, receiving baptism at the hand of Elder Wm. Hunt, and united with the Free Communion Baptist church. He studied at Clinton Seminary, received license from the Otsego QM, about 1852, and was ordained June 28, 1857, at Libertyville, Ill. Since October, 1855, with the exception of one year, his ministry has been with the churches of the Wisconsin YM, the longest pastorate being with the Honey Creek and Caldwell churches. He has been clerk of the Honey Creek QM seventeen years, and has held other positions of trust for long terms. The sermons preached number 3,700, and have resulted in much good. The assistance of his faithful, consecrated wife, Mary Wilbur Hubbard, since their marriage, Jan. 6, 1848, has aided him materially amid the toils and trials incident to a minister's life, and will ever be remembered with appreciation.

Orville E. Huggins
Birth:
Jan. 31, 1832
New York
Death:
Sep. 14, 1855
Illinois
Burial:
Mount Hawley Cemetery
Peoria, Peoria County, Illinois

Huggins, removed in 1847 from Penfield, N.Y., to Illinois, where he united with the Osceola church in 1852, and was soon licensed to preach by the Walnut Creek Quarterly Meeting. He was a young man of much promise, and his death, Sept. 14, 1855, at the age of 23, was much lamented."The Glendale School, though not known in the beginning by that name, was opened in the fall of 1849 in a little log cabin. Orville Huggins was the first teacher, and pupils of all ages attended. A huge fireplace that was kept filled with great logs heated the cabin.On April 3rd, 1850, Enoch Huggins and wife deeded a piece of ground eight rod square in the N. W. corner N.W. Quarter of Section 36, Radnor Township, to School District No. 5. A short time thereafter, a schoolhouse was built which has always been known as Glendale.
Inscription:
ORVILLE. HUGGINS
DIED Sep. 14, 1855
23Ys,7Ms,14Ds.

Arthur W Kern
Birth:
May 4, 1919
Death:
Aug., 1992
Illinois
Burial:
Oak Hill Cemetery, Ewing, Franklin County, Illinois

He pastored the Plasters' Grove Free Will Baptist Church, Thompsonville, Illinois and the Aiken Grove church, Benton, Illinois. He was the founding pastor of the Belle Rive Free Will Baptist Church in Belle Rive, Illinois.

Columbus Jackson "Jack" Ketteman
Birth:
Apr. 3, 1899
Death:
Jan. 10, 1994
Burial:
Liberty-Ridlin Cemetery,
Macedonia,
Franklin County, Illinois

He was a very active Free Will Baptist pastor and minister in southern Illinois. He preached his first sermon in 1938 and pastored at least 14 churches in southern Illinois. He was 94 at his passing. He was the father of Jack Ketteman and Mrs. Bobby Jackson.

H. Wallace Malone
Birth:
Jan. 16, 1917,
Mulkeytown,
Franklin County, Illinois
Death:
Nov. 29, 2006,
Decatur, Macon County, Illinois
Burial:
Greenwood Cemetery,
Coello, Franklin County, Illinois

Throughout his 66 years of ministry, the Rev. Malone was pastor of several Free Will Baptist Churches throughout the state of Illinois and was the founding pastor of Bethel Free Will Baptist Church in South Roxana. He pastored Decatur Free Will Baptist Church in Decatur until his retirement. He was a member of IBEW, a former member of Illinois Mission Board, and a member of the Alumni Association of Free Will Baptist Bible College in Nashville, Tenn. The Rev. Malone was co-founder of Illinois Free Will Baptist Youth Camp, now known as Camp Hope. He was on the Executive Committee of the National Association of Free Will Baptists.

E Leon McBride
Birth:
Dec. 29, 1917
Death:
Apr. 21, 2006
Burial:
Zion Grove Cemetery, Kell,
Marion County, Illinois

He spent most of his life in the Centralia area. He served in the Army Air Force during World War II in the South Pacific. Upon returning home from war, he farmed the family farm near Walnut Hill. Leon was a minister and pastor of several Free Will Baptist Churches, including Johnsonville, Bear Point in Sesser, Blue Point and Oak Valley in Cisne, First Free Will Baptist Church in Johnston City and Zephyr Hills in Asheville, N.C. Celebration services of his life will be conducted by Rev. Tom Malone

and Rev. David Shores. Graveside military rites will be conducted by the VFW and American Legion of Mount Vernon.

George McMillan
Birth:
May 23, 1832
Belfast, Ireland
Death:
1902
Burial:
Woodlawn Cemetery
Creston
Ogle County, Illinois

His studies were pursued at Grand River Institute, Austinsbourgh, Ohio and in 1855 he graduated from Oberlin college, Oberlin, Ohio. He was a professor of the Greek language and literature at Hillsdale College, Michigan, from 1860 until 1876 and later held a similar position in the University of Nebraska. He married Josephine young in 1858 and they had two children. One son received a Master Of Arts from the University of Nebraska and later was an instructor in Botany at the University of Minnesota.

John W. McMillan
Birth:
Jun. 16, 1844
Death:
Jan. 12, 1912
Burial
Calvary Cemetery, Campbell Hill,
Jackson County, Illinois

He was an early Free Will Baptist minister and served with Co A 80th Illinois Infancy during the Civil War.

Thomas O. McMinn
Birth:
Dec. 20, 1869
Death:
Feb. 13, 1936
Burial:
Tamaroa Cemetery,
Tamaroa, Perry County, Illinois

He was baptized at age 17 (by his future father-in-law) and later ordained 10 Nov 1875 by Rev. W. H. Blankenship, J. C. Gilliland, J. S. Gullege at Cottage Home, T.O. founded the Cottage Home Baptist Church. It was built in 1883. Those who followed the leadership of McMinn organized themselves into the Cottage Home Baptist Church a Free Will Baptist Church. He was a member of the 1883 General Conference at Minneapolis and in 1895 at Winnebago MN.

In the early days he was a real circuit rider, serving several churches at the same time going from church to church and farm to farm on horseback. He helped start or grow several churches. Some churches he was involved with: Campbell Hill Free Will Baptist Church, 1886 helped reorganize Ava Free Will Baptist Church, 1897-1900 Scheller Church,1901 Murphysboro Church. He had 3 main churches where he served for many years: Tamaroa IL, Little Cedar IA, and one in Nebraska. In his later years, Thomas worked for the American Baptist association of churches after returning to IL in 1918. His earlier association with the Free Will Baptists were thought an aid to convert people to the new association. He retired in the 20s as he became quite forgetful.

George W Minton
Birth:
Jul. 16, 1860
Union County, Illinois
Death:
Jan. 21, 1904
Burial:
Friendship Cemetery
Union County
He was ordained in 1884 and was connected with the Rock Springs Church of the Looney Springs Quarterly Meeting.

William J. Mishler
Birth:
1916,
Colville, Stevens County, Washington
Death:
Oct. 20, 1995,
Johnston City, Williamson County, Illinois
Burial:
Lakeview Cemetery, Johnston City, Williamson County, Illinois

He was a Free Will Baptist minister for 61 years pastoring 11 churches in five states: Missouri, Tennessee, Michigan, Arkansas and Illinois. He was the State Moderator in both Arkansas and Illinois. He was a member of the national Sunday School Board and later served as the first Promotional Secretary beginning in 1954. He set up the first Sunday School Department in the National Offices in Nashville, Tennessee. He served 17 years on the Board of Trustees at Free Will Baptist Bible College being Chairman 14 years. He served 18 years on the General Board of the National Associaton. He was a graduate of Free Will Baptist Bible College.

Samuel Reddick Modlin
Birth:
May 28, 1828
Davidson County, Tennessee
Death:
Mar. 10, 1904
Blue Mound
Macon County, Illinois
Burial:
Hall Cemetery
Blue Mound
Macon County, Illinois

His record was taken from death certificate; there is no grave stone.

Jacob Overocker
Birth:
Jul. 5, 1795
Minden
Montgomery Count, New York
Death:
Feb. 28, 1877
Franks
DeKalb County, Illinois
Burial:
Cronktown Cemetery
Kirkland
DeKalb County, Illinois
Ordained in 1826, a Freewill Baptist minister, and preached extensively in this vicinity, as his health would permit until "called to his reward." Married 1/8/1815 in NY State to Anna Delavergne, and was the father of nine children.

Kevin Payne
Birth:
Aug. 19, 1956
Mount Vernon,
Jefferson County, Illinois
Death:
Aug. 18, 2012
Franklin,
Williamson County, Tennessee
Burial:
Kirk Cemetery,
Ina, Jefferson County, Illinois

He was bi-vocational and had been pastor of the Cornerstone Free Will Baptist Church in Murfreesboro, Tn. Shortly before his death. Dr. W. Stanley Outlaw and the Rev. Brad Ryan officiated

Orrin D Patch
Birth:
Jan. 23, 1861
Eaton, New Hampshire
Death:
Oct. 16, 1915
Burial:
Roseville Cemetery
Roseville
Warren County, Illinois

When he was 18 years of age he moved to Illinois and was educated in his hometown at Prairie city Academy, Illinois, where he also taught for two years and studied theology under a private instructor. His life was consecrated to God in 1861; licensed to preach was granted in 1865, and ordination received in July, 1867. Prof. Ransom Dunn preached the sermon of his ordination. He ministered the church and Kewanee, Illinois until 1874 when under the direction of the home mission board he took

charge of the work at Cleveland, Ohio were under his direction the church reorganized and a house of worship was erected in a new location and an interest became greater. In 1881 he moved to Greenville, Rhode Island and had a successful pastorate. Then at the Main Street Church in Lewiston Maine as well. But the Cleveland church demanded is labor and he returned to Cleveland in 1884. He was for many years a member of the home mission board and is now a member of the conference Board in one of the corporators for the Free Will Baptist Printing Establishment.

Peter Wells Perry
Birth:
January 24, 1830
Stockbridge, Massachusetts
Death:
1916
Burial:
Bronswood Cemetery
Oak Brook
DuPage County, Illinois

He was educated at Ohio University, Athens, Ohio. He licensed on November 3, 1855 and was ordained at Canaan, Ohio on September 14, 1856. In June, 1861, he was married to Julia Hall. His pastorates in Ohio with the Free Will Baptist were at Chester, Mainville, Rutland, Blanchester and Pleasant Plain. He also pastored in Jackson, Michigan, Lowville, New York and Great Falls, New Hampshire. For about seven years he was connected with the Congregationalists. He was the principle of Cheshire Academy for five years at

Cheshire, Ohio, and a member of the Free Baptist Foreign Mission Board for six years. He baptized more than 500 converts

Jacob B Prickett
Birth:
October 30, 1834
Springfield, Ohio
Death:
May 11, 1886
Belvidere, Illinois
Burial:
Davis Cemetery
Winnebago County, Illinois

In 1836 his parents moved to Indiana where he united with the Washington church in 1846. He received his licensed to preach in 1856 and after serving the Fifth-Fifth Illinois infantry and honorably discharged, he was ordained in 1863 at the Noble County Quarterly Meeting. His ministry was confined primarily in that quarterly meeting in Indiana and the Fox River Quarterly Meeting in Illinois.

Andrew Jackson Rendleman
Birth:
Mar. 3, 1867
Williamson County, Illinois
Death:
Oct. 2, 1940
East Saint Louis
St. Clair County, Illinois,
Burial:
Mount Hope Cemetery
Belleville
St. Clair County, Illinois

Early Free Will Baptist, preacher, principal, supervisor and County Superintendent of Schools in Jackson, Perry, Williamson and Madison Counties, and newspaper editor. He was a member Illinois State Teacher's Assn. and Historical Secretary of the Illinois Baptist State Convention-1938-39. He researched and wrote several historical papers.

George Edward Ritter, Jr
Birth:
Jul. 21, 1923,
Johnston City,
Williamson County,
Illinois
Death:
Nov. 18, 2009,
Marion,
Williamson County, Illinois
Burial:
Sunset Lawn Cemetery,
Harrisburg, Saline County, Illinois

He served in the U.S. Air Force from 1943 to 1949. Rev. Ritter pastored churches in Illinois, Arkansas and Alabama until he retired in 1993. He was former owner of Ritter's Custom Cabinets and a member of the Scottsboro Baptist.

Wiley L. Smart
Birth:
1833
Wilson County, Tennessee
Death:
Aug. 6, 1891
Saline County, Illinois
Burial:
Ward Cemetery
Saline County, Illinois

He married Mary A. Allison in 1854, KY, and they had eight children. He was converted in 1859, began to preach the next year and was ordained in 1865. His pastorates have been Oak Grove and Bell City, KY; and Harmony, Mt. Pleasant, Pleasant Ridge, Mt. Moriah, Mt. Zion and Freedom, Illinois. He was active in the work of the ministry until about 1884, when he was unable to bear the burdens longer.He has baptized 530 converts.

Caleb Marsh Sewall
Birth:
Nov. 6, 1811
Maine
Death:
Nov. 21, 1875
Hamilton, Illinois
Burial:
Greenwood Cemetery
Hamilton
Hancock County, Illinois

He was converted when 19 years of age and ordained in Chesterfield, Maine on April 13, 1842. The same year he was sent by the Home Mission Board to Illinois, where he labored with great devotion 33 years within the bounds of the Hancock and Quincey Quarterly Meetings he was a man of strong faith and fix purpose and was instrumental under God interning many souls to Christ.

Inscription:
The Lord is my rock and my fortress and my deliverer.

Emma Serena *Snider* Uhles
Birth:
Sep. 25, 1863
Campbell Hill
Jackson County Illinois
Death:
Jun., 1914
Illinois
Burial:
Cottom Cemetery,
Denmark, Perry County, Illinois

She was an early Free Will Baptist preacher in Southern Illinois.

Jonathan Noel Thigpen
Birth:
Dec. 17, 1951
Death:
May 20, 2001
Burial:
Wheaton Cemetery, Wheaton, DuPage County, Illinois

Dr. Thigpen was president emeritus of the Evangelical Training Association. He had ministered in various church and Para-church organizations for 34 years. He was a member of College Church in Wheaton.

Born in Nashville, Mr. Thigpen graduated from Free Will Baptist Bible College and earned degrees from Tennessee Temple Theological Seminary in Chattanooga, Tenn. and Trinity Evangelical Divinity School in Deerfield, Illinois. Before joining the association, Mr. Thigpen was an editorial manager for Randall House Publications and a professor at Free Will Baptist Bible College. His last job before the association was as an advertising manager for Christianity Today.

Dr. Thigpen was an innovator who helped modernize the delivery of Christian educational materials as president of Evangelical Training Association in Wheaton.

He died in his home of amyotrophic lateral sclerosis after a six year battle with Lou Gehrig's disease.

George Douglas Ward
Birth:
Mar. 5, 1831,
Tennessee
Death:
Nov. 4, 1915,
Bradley Twp, Jackson Co. Il.
Burial:
Evergreen Cemetery, Ava,
Jackson County, Illinois,
Plot: Lot #52, Bl #4

Early Free Will Baptist minister in southwestern Illinois.

India

Missionary Marie Hanna
Birth:
Plattesville, Wisconsin
Death:
April 23, 1998
Buried:
India

Missionary Hanna suffered a heart failure in mid-April in North India, departing this life at 70 years of age. When her body arrived at the mission station, Christians started ringing the church bell. Hindu and Muslim shops in the market closed out respect for her. Her body was placed on the veranda and thousands of people filed past. Due to the conditions in India, and the lack embalming, she was to be buried that evening, but a large crowd caused them to wait until Friday morning, when she was buried in the church compound in Sonapurhat near the bell tower.
She attended Harris Teachers College in St. Louis, Mo. and was the first woman to graduate from Free Will Baptist Bible College. Memorial services were conducted at the First Free Will Baptist Church in Florence, South Carolina, and Free Will Baptist Bible College in Nashville, Tennessee.

Indiana

Caleb W. Collett
Birth:
May 1852
warning County, Ohio
Death:
1926
Burial:
Maplewood Cemetery
Anderson, Madison County,
Indiana

He was educated at Ridgeville college in Indiana. He turned to God in 1870 and receive license to preach in 1886 and thereafter became the clerk of the Salem Quarterly Meeting in Indiana.

John E. Cox
Birth:
October 14, 1850
Posey County, Indiana
Death:
Dec. 5, 1932
Evansville
Vanderburgh County, Indiana
Burial:
Stewartsville Cemetery
Stewartsville
Posey County, Indiana

His conversion took place in 1872 and he was ordained in

September 1878 by the Liberty Association, Indiana. In 1879 he founded, edited and published *The Golden Rule* at Evansville, Indiana and later *The Open Door* Enfield, Illinois; and in 1884 The *Free Will Baptist Herald* was established by him to aid his work in the Kanawha Valley and in the South generally. He held pastorates in Indiana and Illinois and in the spring of 1883 settled in the Kanawha Valley, West Virginia where he was the acknowledged leader in founding the West Virginia Yearly Meeting and from which place he has made several journeys South exerting a wide influence. He organized 10 churches and assisted in organizing many others and baptized about 400 converts since 1885. He was aVeteran of service in the Indian Wars. And a minister of over 40 years in Owensville, Oakland City and Evansville. He left a legacy through his children namely Daughters: Eva Grace Cox. Sons: Dr. James E Cox, Dr. Harvey C Cox and Arthur S Cox.

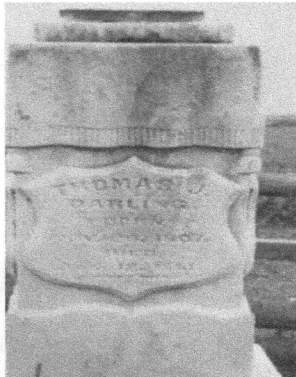

Thomas Jefferson Darling II
Birth:
Nov. 20, 1807
Essex County, New York
Death:
Jan. 12, 1881
Dearborn County, Indiana
Burial:
Darling Family Cemetery
Bonnell
Dearborn County, Indiana

Son of Thomas J. Darling Sr. (1784 - 1865) and Ruth Ann Beech Darling (1785 - 1866). DARLING, Rev. Thomas J., a native of New York, died at aged 73 years. He moved with his parents to Wright's Corners, Ind., married Julia A .Martin in 1829, received license from the Miami Quarterly Meeting Oct. 18, 1839, and was ordained at the Second Creek church,Aug. 20, 1841. He preached to churches in the vicinity of his home, was earnest in exhortation, fervent in prayer, zealous in preaching and hence useful in his calling.

Ichabod S. Jones
Birth:
February 23, 1833
Niles, New York
Death:
Indiana
Burial:
Woodland Cemetery
Wolcottville
Lagrange County, Indiana

When quite young, with his parents, he moved to Indiana. In 1861 he enlisted in the Union Army, and was appointed sergeant, and in two years he was promoted to the office of a major. He began preaching in 1871 and was ordained in 1872. For some time he preached at churches in the Lagrange Quarterly Meeting.

M H Jones
Birth:
unknown
Death:
Dec. 21, 1876
Burial:
Oak Park Cemetery
Ligonier, Noble County, Indiana
Plot: 2-3

Israel Luther
Birth:
Mar. 29, 1810
Canaan, Vermont
Death:
Oct. 1, 1888
New Haven, Indiana
Burial:
Eel River Cemetery
Dunn
MillAllen County, Indiana

He was converted in 1835 and ordained in 1851 by the Noble Quarterly Meeting in Indiana. He traveled in the early part of his ministry through Ohio, Indiana and Michigan holding revival meetings and organizing churches. He baptized over 300 people.

Ives Marks
Birth:
Jan., 1812
Connecticut
Death:
Sep. 9, 1884
Scipio, Jennings County,
Indiana
Burial:
Cave Springs Cemetery,
Jennings County,Indiana

Parents: David Marks (1778 - 1852) Rosanna Merriman Marks (_- 1821) Spouse: Emily Leaming Marks (1810 - 1902). Children: Jared Marks (1842 - 1883), William Marks (1851 - 1900), Ives J. Marks (1856 - 1933).

Preacher in Freewill Baptists, brother of Rev. David Marks, noted FWB in NH, then Ohio. Rev. Ives helped build several churches in Kansas and Nebraska with son Rev. William Marks.

Thomas J Mawhorter
Birth:
Dec. 10, 1852
Noble County, Indiana
Death:
1921
Indiana
Burial:
Cosperville Cemetery
Wawaka
Noble County, Indiana
Plot: 3-5

Mawhorter, was the son of William and Prudence (Pierson) Mawhorter, of Scottish descent, an early family in Noble Co. Indiana. He attended local schools, graduated from Fort Wayne College, 1872. He was converted in June 1873, and baptized by Rev. Dodge. He felt his need to do more, but also felt he was unqualified. He married Arminda "Mindie" Rendel in May 17, 1874, in Noble Co. Ind. To this union was born ten children. He served as deacon, SS Supt., and other offices in his church, but in 1885, he entered Hillsdale College, MI, to pursue more education, having worked on the Railroad to obtain funds. Soon after, however family sickness called him home. He began to preach in local churches and his church asked that he be ordained. He was ordained to the Freewill Baptist ministry, May 15, 1887. Several ministers, including Rev. Rendel, Prof. Ransom Dunn, and others were on his ordaining council. He immediately began pastoring the Wawaka Church,

(now Cosperville Freewill Bapt). Other pastorates included Pleasant Ridge, Haw Patch, S. Milford, and he served Jones Chapel and Rome City churches, as well .He attended the Gen. Conference when held at the Minneapolis; and in 1897 he was delegate to the Gen. Conf. at Lowell, Mass; then delegate to Ocean Park Gen. Conference, 1898, and a delegate to Harpers Ferry Conference in 1901. He was recognized as a strong and forceful speaker, and in Noble County was an advocant in the cause of temperance.

We will have a new body - not the same as before.

Wilton R McKee
Birth:
1830
Shelby County, Indiana
Death:
1899
Burial:
Liberty Cemetery
Martinsville
Morgan County, Indiana

He was converted in December, 1849, and ordained in 1858. From 1856 to 1870 he was a member of the Separate Baptist. He then united with the Free Baptist Church, and during his ministry witnessed many revivals and organize several churches. In 1852 he married Kathryn Hawkins, and after her death, he married Elizabeth Bock, August 15, 1860. He was the father of 13 children. All the churches he pastored were in the state of Indiana.

Michael Mills
Birth:
May 28, 1787,
Death:
May 17, 1864
Burial:
Liber Cemetery
Portland, Jay County, Indiana

Mills was born in Pennsylvania and the year 1817 began a life unto God. He soon began to preach with the Calvinistic Baptists; but having Arminian views finally became a Free Baptist. In 1838 he moved to Jay County, Ind., and continued his work, being ordained at about this time, and aided in building upthe Salem Q. M. His native talent made him a close reasoner with a firm purpose.

Jared H Miner
Birth:
Feb. 27, 1795
Death:
May 26, 1863
Otsego, Indiana
Burial:
Clark Cemetery
Steuben County, Indiana

He was ordained in 1829 and labored successfully for many years in Sheldon, New York and in adjacent towns and later in northern Indiana and southern Michigan where many were converted and churches were gathered under his labors. He baptized about 400 converts of whom several entered the ministry.

Death is the setting free from the warfare of the soul.

Eli Noyes
Birth:
Apr. 24, 1814,
Jefferson,
Lincoln County, Maine
Death:
Sep. 10, 1854,
Lafayette, Tippecanoe County,
Indiana
Burial:
Greenbush Cemetery,
Lafayette, Tippecanoe County,
Indiana,
Plot: Section 3, lot 208

His parents were deeply pious and taught their children religion, missions, and stories of missionaries. He pursued an education, and taught a few months and studied till he commenced preaching in 1834. In Jan. 1836, he offered himself to the Foreign Mission Board of Freewill Baptists as a candidate for missionary service to Orissa, India. He and his wife were accepted and on 22nd of Sept. 1835, they sailed to Calcutta, India, along with Rev. Jeremiah Phillips, who sailed in the same vessel, and took charge of the bazaar schools connected with the General Baptist mission in Balasore. In a few months, their bright hopes were succeeded by suffering and disappointments. They lost a 16-month old daughter, as well as Rev. Jeremiah Phillip's wife. They became prostrated by disease and his became of a chronic type. Mr. Noyes made rapid progress in the language, and became a ready and able preacher, and for a time encouraging results attended his ministry. But, he was not able to shed the disease, and in 1841, they returned to their native home. For a time, he pastored small churches in Maine, and Lynn, Mass., then went to Roger Williams church in Providence, R.I. Here the congregation grew until they had to add a balcony of seats. His health failed and he retired from the pastorate forever. He did recover enough to make a trip to England with Rev. Jonathan Woodman, to visit the General Baptists of England.

His knowledge of languages exceeded all but few, and he was an able theologian, lecturer and a writer. He was taken with consumption and in his debilitated state, he went to Lafayette, Indiana where his brother-in-law, Mr. M.L. Pierce, had generously provided a home for him and his family. He died the 10th of Sept. 1854, age 40 years. *"A Hebrew Reader," "Strength of Hindooism", "Lectures on the Truth of the Bible;"* and two or three sermons, were published before his death. He instructed what would be inscribed on his tombstone: ELI NOYES First Freewill Baptist Missionary To India, and it was carried out.

William C. Parson
Birth:
May 6, 1933
Morehead, Kentucky
Death:
Feb. 7, 2011
Anderson,
Madison County,Indiana
Burial:

Carthage Cemetery,
Carthage, Rush County,Indiana

The Rev. Parson was an ordained Free Will Baptist minister for more than 40 years. He pastored several churches, retiring in 2007 from East 16th St. Separate Baptist Church in Muncie. His secular occupation was as a machinist and grinder, retiring from Delaware Tool and Machinery after 19 years of service. Prior to that, he had worked at Nicholson File. He was a member of the 38th Street Free Will Baptist Church in Anderson.

John Prickett
Birth:
1811
Death:
Oct. 24, 1856
Indiana
Burial:
Metz Cemetery
Noble County, Indiana
Plot: 11

A native of Ohio, he was converted under the labors of Rev. Elias Hutchins in 1831 and was ordained in Indiana in 1842. He preached in the Noble Quarterly Meeting for his untiring labors were blessed to the conversion of many.

John W Rendel
Birth:
March 24, 1849
Wayne County, Ohio
Death:
1917
Burial:
Lake View Cemetery
Kendallville
Noble County, Indiana
Plot: Section D
Row 3 Circle 11

He was converted in 1865 and attended Auburn and Kendallville high schools for two years. Received ordination on June 2, 1878. His pastorates were all in the state of Indiana. In these churches he had many good revivals resulting in a large number of conversions.

Fredrick Stovenour
Birth:
Oct. 18, 1834
Morrow County, Ohio
Death:
Mar. 6, 1923
Burial:
Green Park Cemetery
Portland
Jay County, Indiana

He began his religious life in 1863 and in the following year was ordained by the Richland and Licking Quarterly Meeting, Ohio. He was a pastor also in the Saline Quarterly Meeting in Indiana.

David A. Tucker
Birth:
May 20, 1845
Jennings County, Indiana
Death:
Jul. 10, 1927
Burial:
Union Flat Rock Cemetery
Ripley County, Indiana

He was a student one year at Moores Hill college and one year at Hillsdale. His conversion was in 1859 and he was licensed in 1870. He was ordained in 1872 to the gospel ministry. He pastored a number of churches in Indiana. He was also a veteran of the Civil War serving in Co. K 18th Ind. Inf. He enlisted in 1861 as a private in reenlisted on January 1, 1864. He mustered out in all this 1865 at Savannah Georgia as a Sgt. He married first, Susanna Dorsh Tucker (1845 - 1888) and after her passing Sarah A. Snow Tucker (1861 - 1949)

William Tucker
Birth:
Oct. 7, 1820
Beaver County, Pennsylvania
Death:
Dec. 21, 1905
Ripley County, Indiana
Burial:
Union Flat Rock Cemetery
Ripley County, Indiana
Plot: Row 7 Lot 24

He married Mary Oldham (1816 - 1894) with whom they had nine children. Three of whom

served in the Civil War. And David was also a Free Will Baptist preacher. When he was one year old his father died leaving four children to the mother's care. There were no free schools where he lived at the time and hence his education was very limited. His family moved to Indiana and there and his early years were spent in clearing the wildland by day and studying the Bible by fire-light at night. He was converted in 1843 and in 1873 he was ordained to the ministry. He preached in several churches in the Ripley and other quarterly meetings and his labors were blessed with the conversion to larger number of converts.

Henry W. Vaughn
Birth:
May 31, 1820,
East Greenwich, Kent County,
Rhode Island
Death:
Aug. 13, 1900
Burial:
Greenwood Cemetery, Lagrange,
Lagrange County,Indiana,
Plot: Big Old

His conversion took place in 1842 and his ordination to the ministry in 1856, the council being composed of Freewill Baptist Elders Seth Parker, E. Root and

Thomas Dimm. He had the care of several churches in Ohio, Indiana and Michigan. He was twice a member of the General Conference, and he organized two churches and had several revivals.

Joseph Winch
Birth:
unknown
Death:
February 10, 1854
Galena, Indiana
Burial:
Foster Cemetery
Hesston
La Porte County, Indiana
Plot: 1-4-8

The last two years as his life were the only years devoted to the ministry. His death was one of the most triumphant every witness. His early life was spent in Massachusetts, Vermont and Ohio.

Iowa

Oscar E. Baker
Birth:
Jan. 9, 1826,
Marion County, Ohio
Death:
Jul. 31, 1893,
Minneapolis,
Hennepin County,
Minnesota
Burial:
Elmwood Cemetery,
Waterloo,
Black Hawk County, Iowa,
Plot: C E Lot 17 E

Oscar was in the 141st Regiment, Ohio Infantry, during the Civil War. Born at Marion, Ohio, the son of Rev. George Washington Baker. Oscar's grandfather, was one of the founders of the town of Marion, OH. He, as his father, were Free Will Baptist ministers. Oscar was licensed to preach when he was 17 yrs old. And by his nineteenth birthday, he was ordained by the Free Will Baptist church, because of his work and dedication. From time to time he endeavored to go to college, but the demands of the churches interfered with his plans. Meanwhile he applied himself to study and with the aid of private teachers acquired at length an elective collegiate and theological course. Rev. Baker preached in Ohio, moved to Iowa and became pastor of Wilton Junction church, and took charge of the Seminary

at that place. The Seminary grew into a college of which he became president. His health failing, he resigned. Then he took charge of the church at Waterloo, IA. In 1881 he was called to the church in Marion, OH, his native city. In 1884, he accepted a call to the Roger Williams church, Providence, R.I. where he remained until 1888, when he was called to Lincoln, Nebraska. He served his denomination for many years through the several benevolent societies and as a member of the Board of Corporators of the Printing Establishment. He was a frequent contributor to the denominational papers.

Tappan Batchelder
Birth:
Jan. 25, 1817,
Bridgewater, Grafton County
New Hampshire
Death:
Oct. 29, 1885,Linn County,
Iowa
Burial:
Jordan's Grove Cemetery,
Central City,
Linn County, Iowa

Rev Batcheler was a Methodist minister but ordained a Free Will Baptist minister in 1841 in R.I. In 1855 he moved from Taunton, Mass. to Olive Twp, Clinton Co,

Iowa. In 1865 he moved to Clay Twp, Jones Co, Iowa. In 1876, he moved to Linn Co, Iowa and farmed near Central City, and served as pastor at Free Will Baptist churches in Central City and Waubeek.

Newell Willard Bixby
Birth:
Jan. 18, 1809
Death:
Jan. 31, 1903
Burial:
Edgewood Cemetery
Edgewood, Delaware County,
Iowa

Son of Ebenezer Bixby and Hannah Flint. Husband of Ruby Knapp, married 09 Nov 1842 Vermont. Was an ordained Freewill Baptist minister, prominent and successful among the pioneer ministers of Iowa.

Ruby Knapp Bixby
Birth:
1818
Death:
Jan. 5, 1877
Burial:
Edgewood Cemetery
Edgewood, Delaware County,
Iowa

Both she and her husband, Rev. N. W. Bixby, where prominent Free Will Baptist ministers in the early days of Iowa.

David E. Champlin
Birth:
1825
Ohio
Death:
Feb. 20, 1871,
Waterloo
Black Hawk County, Iowa
Burial:
Fairview Cemetery, Waterloo
Black Hawk County, Iowa,
Plot: Block 19, Lot 100

He was converted when sixteen years of age, and baptized by Rev. I. Eaton. He was licensed to preach by the Freewill Baptists, while connected with the Fox River Q.M. (Ill), about 1856. He remained a few years with the Ohio Grove church which was much increased during his connection with it. About 1860, he moved to the Waterloo Q.M., IA, and was connected with the Oxley Grove, Pleasant Valley, Spring Creek and Waterloo churches. He was in the organization and the first pastor of the Waterloo Freewill Baptist church, which

was organized with twelve members. The church grew but in 1896, all 49 members joined the regular Baptist church, just before the Freewill Baptist denomination was merged with the American Baptist. Rev. David Champlin, was a zealous, faithful laborer, an advocate of all moral reform, and active in the work, until a brief illness carried him away from the earth.

David N Coats
Birth:
Dec. 7, 1815
Litchfield
Tioga County, New York
Death:
Jan. 20, 1889
Spencer
Clay County, Iowa
Burial:
Riverside Cemetery
Spencer, Clay County, Iowa

He was converted under the labors of Elder David Marks. While yet a young man he moved to Wisconsin, where he was ordained in 1859. At about this time he became a pioneer in northwestern Iowa, and made his home at Spencer, where he died. He was an untiring worker and his labors were blessed to the

good of many. The results of his labors in Iowa will be manifest for years to come. He was married to Miss B. E. White. They have two children, Rev. R.A. Coats, and Mrs. Frank Wells.

Isaac W Drew
Birth:
May 11, 1823,
Quebec, Canada
Death:
1893,
Black Hawk County, Iowa
Burial:
Fairview Cemetery,
Waterloo,
Black Hawk County, Iowa

He was converted about 1850 and soon began to preach, receiving ordination by the Freewill Baptists in 1858 while connected with the Coaticook church of the Stanstead QM. His later ministry has been chiefly with churches of the Waterloo, Ia., and the Fond du Lac, Wis., QM's.

Edward Dudley
Birth:
Dec. 11, 1811.
Brentwood,NH
Death:
Feb. 19, 1890
Burial:
Agency Cemetery
Agency, Wapello County, Iowa
Plot: Section 36

Son of Daniel Dudley and Jane Campbell; m. 10 Jun 1841 Eliza A. Dudley; Free Will Baptist minister, ordained 1844. Did a good work and passed to his reward.

Yea, saith the Spirit, that they may rest from their labours; and their works do follow them.

L. D.. Felt
Birth:
1821
Death:
Nov. 29, 1889
Burial:
Greenwood Cemetery
Masonville,
Delaware County, Iowa

He experienced the new birth in 1837 and was ordained in 1863. He held pastorates in the state of Wisconsin and Iowa. In these fields he enjoyed a good degree of prosperity and that churches was strengthened. He was a delegate to the General Conference of 1866.

Marcus B Felt
Birth:
October 3, 1832
Brutus, New York
Death:
unknown
Burial:
Osage Cemetery
Osage, Mitchell County, Iowa

He was a brother of L. D. Felt. He was converted in January, 1855 he was ordained in February, 1866 and spent the first nine years of his ministry was churches and Root River Quarterly Meeting in Minnesota. During his ministry he served the churches in Nebraska, three churches in Illinois and in Burnett, Wisconsin. He was very efficient in the pastorate and organized four churches. Marcus served in Company H 6th Minnesota Infantry then served as a 2nd Lt in Company E 121 United States Colored Infantry and then transferred to Company I 13 United States Colored Heavy Artillery.

Henry Elijah Gifford
Birth:
Dec. 18, 1809
Pawlet, Rutland County, Vermont
Death:
Jun. 26, 1881
Burial:
Elkader Cemetery
Elkader, Clayton County, Iowa

Gifford, died at his residence near Elkader, Iowa. aged 72 years. He was baptized by Rev. S. Howe at Otselic, N. Y., and later received license at Portage. He moved to Iowa in 1842, and was ordained May 27, 1849, at the fifth session of the Delaware and Clayton Q. M.

His was the first ordination in Iowa among the Free Baptists, and in this vicinity his ministry was spent. The Boardman Grove (later Farmersburg), West Union, Cox Creek and Volga Bottom churches enjoyed his labors. He was a man of good natural abilities, a close student of the Bible and hence sound in doctrine. His wife, who had toiled with him more than fifty years, survived at his death. He was chaplain of the Old Settlers' Association, whose president pronounced a fitting eulogy at the grave.

Abel Gleason
Birth:
Jun. 4, 1795
Rome
Oneida County, New York
Death:
Jan. 3, 1874
Burial:
Oakview Cemetery
Clinton County, Iowa

He went in his youth to Genesee County, New York where was baptized at the age of 13 and ordained when he was about 28. Then on to Michigan in 1838, and two years later he was found in Illinois continuing on to Iowa in 1853. He was a gentle and affectionate gifted man of prayer and faithful in the Lord's vineyard

David Demaree Halstead
Birth:
Feb. 24, 1811
New Paltz, Ulster County,
New York
Death:
Dec. 3, 1887
Fort Dodge,
Webster County, Iowa
Burial:
Oakland Cemetery,
Fort Dodge,
Webster County, Iowa,
Plot: lot 95

He was converted in 1831 and in 1853 united with the Free Will Baptist and soon was ordained. He pastored churches in Greene and Mecca, Ohio and also preached in other places. In 1859 he moved to Marion County, Ohio, where he labored with success. In 1872 he moved to West Fort Dodge, Iowa where he died.

Erastus C Harvey
Birth:
Mar. 8, 1789
East Haddam
Middlesex County,
Connecticut
Death:
Aug. 27, 1872
Castalia, Winneshiek County, Iowa
Burial:
Pleasant View Cemetery
Castalia,
Winneshiek County, Iowa

Erastus Harvey, sixth child of William and Jane (Beebe) Harvey. In the year 1807, he enlisted in the regular army and was in the War of 1812. He played the tenor drum in the battle of Plattsburg, in September, 1814. At the close of the war he returned to Lyndon, Vermont, and in the year 1816 he married Betsey Bettis, who was born September 27, 1798.
Erastus Harvey was a member of the Free Will Baptist church at Cabot, Vermont, in 1821. The Wheelock Q. M., licensed him to preach in 1822. In 1825 he was ordained. From the time of his marriage until he entered the

ministry he had farmed at Lyndon, Vermont. His obituary speaks of his preaching first in Vermont; then he went to Littleton, New Hampshire, for one year, returning to Vermont. Thence to Barnston, in Stanstead county, Canada, Province of Quebec. A call came to Rev. Erastus Harvey to preach to a congregation at Woodstock, Champaign county, Ohio which was gladly accepted and he moved his family to that place sometime about the year 1838. He purchased a farm in the woods and soon a log house was built and some land cleared.

He preached to Baptist congregations in Champaign and Union counties, and for a while at Pitchin, in Clark county. After six or seven years he sold this farm and purchased one in Perry township, Logan county, Ohio, near North Greenfield. He continued to preach and acted as Q. M. clerk "making full proof of his ministry." After a residence of about five years, he sold this farm and purchased another near Walnut Grove. After a long illness from dropsy the wife and mother died on the Walnut Grove farm July 31, 1855. In a month or two the father sold the farm and with his sons, William and Albee, he moved to Castalia, Winneshiek county, Iowa. In 1857 he married Mrs. Hannah Sargent, who was a native of Vermont. He preached to a number of congregations in northern Iowa and did so occasionally till a few days before his death. "As a preacher Brother Harvey was earnest, animated

and spiritual. He had received and had retained the Holy Anointing which gave him strength and boldness in the presence of the people. His sermons were eminently Scriptural, evangelical, and comforting to the saints. He succeeded well as a pastor. He died of bilious diarrhea and was first buried in Mt. Grove cemetery; but was later removed to Pleasant View cemetery, Castalia, Iowa

Orrin Hix
Birth:
September 11, 1807
Montpelier, Vermont
Death:
Mar. 5, 1880
Benton, Iowa
Burial:
Brooks Cemetery
Hedrick, Keokuk County,
Iowa

He went to Ohio in his youth and married Sally Gregory in 1831 and commenced ministerial work in 1840 receiving his ordination five years later. He continued to labor in Ohio until 1854 and then took up the work in Van Buren Quarterly Meeting, Iowa.

Charles Holroyd
Birth:
1823
England
Death:
Oct. 22, 1875
Iowa
Burial:
Campton Cemetery
Lamont, Buchanan County, Iowa

Charles Holroyd was born in England. He came to the United States in 1850 with his wife, Mary (Patch) and their family. Holroyd was a stone mason and carpenter by trade. On Nov. 20, 1858, he received his license to preach in the United States at the Union Free Will Baptist Church of Wingville, Grant County, Wisconsin. When he moved to Delaware County, Iowa, he helped build the Campton schoolhouse and the Campton church where Free Will services were held. He preached there and everyone loved him. The little children used to sit around his feet while he was preaching.

Enoch Jenkins
Birth:
1808
Death:
1892
Burial:
Fairview Cemetery
Waterloo
Black Hawk County, Iowa
Plot: blk. 16 - lot 41

Rev. Enoch Jenkins, was born in western New York. He was son of Rev. Herman and Nancy (Brown) Jenkins, and grandson of Rev. N. Jenkins. He was licensed by the Chautauqua Q.M. [Freewill Baptist] and ordained about 1855, his first pastorate being with the Heart Prairie, Wis., then recently organized. His ministry continued in Wisconsin and Iowa, being characterized by great loyalty to the denomination.

My Friends.

I Go To Glory.

John Lucius Lesher
Birth:
Sep. 20, 1830
Batavia
Genesee County, New York
Death:
Oct. 28, 1890
La Porte City
Black Hawk County, Iowa
Burial:
Pleasant Hill Cemetery
Ireton, Sioux County, Iowa
Plot: Block 3, Lot 3

He was converted in his early life and received ordination on November 22, 1863 periods to churches were organized by him and more than 100 converts were baptized.He married Nancy Jane Allred of Perrysville, Indiana on 24 Apr 1852.

Amaziah Loomis
Birth:
Aug. 8, 1800
New York
Death:
April 30,1873
Riceville, Mitchell County, Iowa
Burial:
Riverside Cemetery
Riceville, Mitchell Count, Iowa

Loomis, died at age 72 years. He was licensed by the Catlin church, August 21, 1830, and ordained by

the Chemung Q. M. (N. Y.), Sept. 7, 1834, continuing his labors with this and adjoining Q. M's until 1855, when he removed to Iowa. He was a pioneer preacher, and devoted himself to the work with great perseverance.

James Cram Marston
Birth:
Aug. 14, 1804
Parsonfield, Maine
Death:
Jun. 25, 1865
Iowa
Burial:
Postville Cemetery
Clayton County, Iowa

Son of James Marston and Elizabeth Cram.He first married Cordelia Sutton who died before 1850. then he married Nancy Maria Fisher. He emigrated to western New York at an early age. In 1854 he went to Iowa and the following year united with the Postville church, where he became deacon. He received license from the Elgin Quarterly Meeting in 1859 and ordination in 1861, serving the Postville and Bloomfield churches as pastor until his death in 1865. All the benevolent enterprises of the day received his hearty co-operation.

Thomas Proctor Moulton
Birth:
Apr. 19, 1808
Hatley
Quebec, Canada
Death:
Feb. 25, 1893
Newell
Buena Vista County, Iowa
Burial:
Newell Cemetery
Newell
Buena Vista County, Iowa

In January, 1840, he was married to Louisa Moore who he shared fifty years of happy life together. In early life they entered upon the work of the Christian ministry, being connected with the Freewill Baptist denomination. His father was a Rev. Avery Moulton, who was the ancestor for many Free Will Baptist preachers. For more than forty years, Thomas Proctor continued in the active ministry in the following places: Walden and Lyndon, Vt. Conneaut, Ohio, Pelham, N. H., Coaticook, .P. Q., and West Derby, Vt. At Coaticook P. Q., he organized the first church and labored there for fifteen years. His active ministry was closed at West Derby, Vt., in 1873, at which time he came to Newell to be near his daughter, Mrs. S. A. Parker.

John Russel Mowry
Birth:
Oct. 30, 1853
Lyons
Clinton County, Iowa
Death:
Feb. 14, 1908
Des Moines
Polk County, Iowa
Burial:
Woodland Cemetery
Des Moines
Polk County, Iowa

He was the son of Rev. Juni Mowry. He was converted in 1871 and studied at Wilton Collegiate Institute and at Hillsdale College. He was ordained of by President Durgin at Hillsdale in April 8, 1883. He ministered to churches Michigan and Ontario, Canada, and was later employed as the state evangelist for Michigan. He was successful in pastoral and revival work can baptized over 100 converts.

Junia Smith Mowry
Birth:
Jul. 18, 1805
Smithfield,
Providence County,
Rhode Island
Death:
Apr. 27, 1890
Calamus,
Clinton County, Iowa
Burial:
Mowder Cemetery,
Clinton County, Iowa

In 1829 he was licensed by the Free Baptist Church to preach, and that year commenced his ministerial labors. In 1832 he was licensed by the Elders of the Free Baptist Conference, and in August of that year was ordained at North Taunton, and was pastor there and in Rehoboth until the spring of 1835. He then went to Tiverton and served as pastor of a congregation in that place until the fall of 1840, when he went to Apponaug and continued his ministerial labors for a year and a half. From Apponaug, Mr. Mowry went to Johnson, R.I., where he preached for some eleven months, being at the same time an agent for the Smithville Seminary, located in North Seituate. He then received a call from a congregation at Georgiaville, in Smithfield Township, and there resided until the spring of 1847. He next went to Hebronville, Mass., where he preached for two years and taught school one winter and again returned to Georgiaville and preached to different congregations in that region until 1851. He was also on the School Board of the town of Smithfield.

Rev. Mr. Mowry was first united in marriage Dec. 2, 1835, to Rev. Salome Lincoln. She was born in Raynham, Mass., Sept. 13, 1807. She was a good, kind-hearted, Christian woman, and, as well as her husband, was engaged in ministerial labor. She died July 21, 1841.

The second marriage was solemnized Dec. 2, 1841, when Miss Nancy Manchester became his wife. She died Feb. 24, 1868. She was a woman of superior abilities, both as a wife and mother, and had few equals. A son, John R. attended Wilton Institute, Iowa, and Hillsdale College, Mich., and is a preacher of the doctrines of the Free Baptist Church.

The third marriage was solemnized July 15, 1869, when Mildred M. A. Holmes, widow of Rev. Luther Holmes, became his wife. She died March 11, 1879, and June 8 of that year he was married to Susan Mott. She was born in Ohio, and they lived together as man and wife until the 15th of March, 1885, the date of her demise. Oct. 11, 1885, our subject was married to Nancy Dubois, who came to Iowa with her husband in 1841. She was a native of Pickaway County, Ohio.

Live so death will have its reward.

Benjamin F Morrill
Birth:
1848
Blanchard
Ontario, Canada
Death:
1913
Burial:
Lawn Hill Cemetery
Stanhope
Hamilton County, Iowa

His conversion to Christ was in 1874, and his marriage to Miss Mary O'Dell was in 1875. He received licensed to preach the following year and was ordained in November, 1886, taking pastoral charge of the Fostoria and Buffalo Valley churches in Kansas. His ministry later took him to Iowa.

Joshua Gaskill Newbold
Birth:
Sep. 30, 1802
Fayette County, Pennsylvania
Death:
Aug. 31, 1887
Burial:
Hillsboro Cemetery
Hillsboro
Henry County, Iowa
Plot: Row 18

Ordained to the Freewill Bapt. ministry Sep. 10, 1826; He ministered in western Penn, organizing churches, until 1854, when he moved to Iowa, and organized the Hillsboro church there and pastored as long as his health would permit. He baptized over 800 converts and ministered sixty years.He was first married to Rebecca Davis who passed away in 1855. After which he married Mrs.'s Susannah Dudley Hoyt, sister of Rev. Edward Dudley who died in 1881.

Nathaniel A Odell
Birth:
1816
Wayne County, New York
Death:
Aug. 19, 1882
Elliott, Montgomery County, Iowa
Burial:
West Point Cemetery
Bremer County, Iowa

Rev. Nathaniel Alvah ODELL, was the son of Augustine Odell, and Lydia Odell. When a young man, he emigrated to Newton, Calhoun Co. Michigan, in 1835. He joined the Freewill Baptist Church in 1844, and soon began to preach, being connected to Barry Co. Quarterly Meeting. After opposing the wave of spiritualism then sweeping over the vicinity, he moved to Delhi, IA, where he was ordained, May 25, 1856.He labored with good success, especially in Revivals, nearly 20 years, when he went to Montgomery Co. where the closing years of life were spent.He married Mahala May Bruce and they raised a large family.

Asahel Palmer
Birth:
1835
New York
Death:
Dec. 6, 1879
Horton
Bremer County, Iowa
Burial:
Horton Cemetery
Horton, Bremer County, Iowa

Palmer, a Free Will Baptist minister, was a worthy man, well loved and respected, and lamented by his untimely death. His death was caused by a fall from a staging while assisting in repairing the house of worship.
This is noted in the "Butler and Bremer Counties, IA History" as also being the eighth pastor of Horton Church.. He and his wife were converted under the labors of the Rev. Mrs. Ruby Bixby in 1866 and united with the Madison church. He was ordained in 1873 having served with a license for

two years. He pastored many churches in the Delaware, Clayton, and Cedar Valley Quarterly Meetings.

William Small
Birth
1812
Death:
Jun. 17, 1883
Burial:
Upper Bay Cemetery
Delhi, Delaware County, Iowa

Small, Rev. William, was born in Scarboro', Me., in 1812. He and his brother James were ordained to the ministry in the Exeter Q. M., Jan. 13, 1842. He continued to labor in the Exeter and Montville Q. M's until 1855, when he went to Wisconsin and preached at Monticello and other places in the La Fayette Q. M. In 1868 he moved to Manchester, Ia., and continued to preach in various churches of the Delaware and Clayton O. M. until his last sickness. His death occurred at the residence of his son, near Earlville, Ia., in his 71st year, His earnestness and love for the work seemed to increase as he approached the close of life. He had baptized over two hundred converts.

Justus H Steward
Birth:
Aug. 4, 1819
Erie County, Pennsylvania
Death:
Jan. 8, 1877
Tama County, Iowa
Burial:
Rock Creek Cemetery
Tama County, Iowa

He was the fifth son of Lemuel Steward and Elizabeth Roush. Justus studied for the ministry and was licensed with the larger Baptist body before uniting with the Free Baptists soon after his marriage to Amanda Main on August 29, 1846. They made their home in Ashtabula County, Ohio, where they settled on a homestead. He was ordained on September 28, 1863 and soon after moved to the state of Iowa where he pastored a number of churches as well as organizing the Fairview church where he remained its pastor until his death. He also taught school many years. The family consisted of three sons, and two daughters. Rev. Justus H. Steward was stricken with typhoid fever in the fall of 1876 at his home in Tama County, Iowa, suffering many weeks, then the infection settled in one leg, necessitating an operation, and the leg amputated.

Even death is not to be feared by one who has lived wisely.

David Smutz
Birth:
Mar. 30, 1814
Washington County, Maryland
Death:
May 6, 1858
Van Buren
Jackson County, Iowa
Burial:
Hillsboro Cemetery
Hillsboro
Henry County, Iowa
He was licensed by the Cook's

town quarterly makes the meeting, Pennsylvania and in two years he was ordained in September, 1845 where he labored with some churches in the Somerset quarterly meeting, Pennsylvania. Their after he moved to Iowa and assisted in forming the Van Buren quarter meeting in that state. Minister of the Free-Will Baptist Church. He and his wife both died in a typhoid epidemic.
Inscription:
Rev. D. SmutzDied May 6 1858AE. 44 Yrs 1 Mo 6 Ds Not lost blessed thought But gone before Where we shall meet to part no more.

Spencer Summerlin
Birth:
May 27, 1828
Norwalk, Ohio
Death:
Feb. 1, 1907
Burial:
Horton Cemetery
Horton
Bremer County, Iowa

He married Sarah P Cook (1830 - 1921) in April 1858. He was ordained in 1861 and pastored a number of churches in Ohio as well as many churches in Iowa. He was active in the work of the denomination serving offices in the quarterly and yearly meetings. He was a member also of the Home and Foreign Mission Boards. His been a general missionary for the yearly meeting and was a member of the General Conference of 1883. He conducted many revivals which produced the organization of at least five churches.

John Sweatt
Birth:
1806
Gilmanton, New Hampshire
Death:
December 18, 1884
Toledo, Iowa
Burial:
Woodlawn Cemetery
Toledo
Tama County, Iowa

He was ordained on September 30, 1841 at Orange, New Hampshire. In January 1843 he moved to Fort Jackson, New York where he organized a church and remained until 1856 when he returned to New Hampshire. Here he held official positions in the town and served in the legislature. In 1865 he settled on a farm in Iowa but continued be faithful to the end.

Robert T Valentine
Birth:
1812
North Carolina
Death:
unknown
Burial:
Pleasant Hill Cemetery
Fayette
Fayette County, Iowa
Plot: Row 9 Lot 22

Because of his race he enjoyed no advantages in his birth state. He was ordained in Fairfield, Iowa in May, 1877 and ministered to the all but the church. He was a good man and faithful to his Lord. Unmarked grave near wife .

Joseph Whittemore
Birth:
Sep. 10, 1813
Salisbury
Merrimack County, New Hampshire
Death:
May 9, 1891
Iowa
Burial:
Harlington Cemetery
Waverly
Bremer County, Iowa

His parents were Eleazer and Lydia (Richards) Whittemore, of a well-known New Hampshire family. He was a brother of Rev. David Richards Whittemore, bur. in R.I. He studied medicine in Concord, N.H., and in 1834, and theology in Dr. Mott's school at Nashua. He was licensed by the Congregationalists in 1836, and ordained in Freewill Baptists

about 1841, at Tiverton, R.I., by a council of the Rhode Island Quarterly Meeting. His pastorates were Tiverton, Pawtuxet, Pawtucket, and South Providence, R.I., Grafton and Taunton, Mass., and Randolph and Charleston, VT. He baptized about three hundred converts, and served as delegate to the General Conference. About 1865, he went to Iowa. NOTE:Zorn Family Tree shows he married Sarah M. Williams, Dec. 1876

William Wright
Birth:
1803
Otsego County, New York
Death:
Aug. 11, 1877
Delaware County, Iowa
Burial:
Spring Branch Cemetery
Delaware County, Iowa

Wright was converted at the age of seventeen years. He was connected with the Erie Quarterly Meeting, and after his ordination in 1842, with the Chautauqua and French Creek Q.M's. Later he resided in Iowa, being in feeble health, and died at age 74 years. He was a Free Baptist minister. He married Lovica (Unk) abt 1824 in NY; [Louisa: 1808-1884]

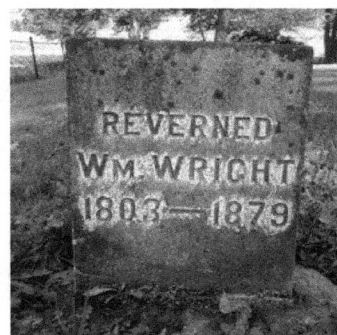

Today is not a day of defeat
But a day of victory.
Today is not a day of demotion,

Amos C. Zabriskie

Birth:
Nov. 17, 1836
La Porte County, Indiana
Death:
Aug. 6, 1915
Stanley,
Buchanan County, Iowa
Burial:
Stanley Cemetery, Stanley
Buchanan County, Iowa

Amos C. served in the Iowa 32nd Inf., Co. K, Union Army until the close of the War. Throughout his life, he retained a great interest in the Grand Army. For years he was in great demand as a speaker at encampments throughout the state and the few remaining comrades in the vicinity were his chosen pall bearers. He was converted in 1867, and labored as a licentiate among the United Brethren, engaging in itinerate work. In 1886, having united with the Free Will Baptists, he was ordained and became pastor of the Buffalo Grove and Madison churches in Iowa. For more than thirty-five years he preached the gospel in the pulpits of various denominations in country places and in villages and towns. For although thoroughly orthodox he was broad in his sympathies and understanding of religious principles. For a number of years he conducted revival meetings during the winter. The saving power of Christ was his great theme---On account of his clear thinking and his deep moral conviction, he was a extemporaneous speaker. The power that he processed was an inheritance and a special "inducement from on high" rather than the result of education. He performed weddings and funerals in the hundreds. It was said, "he was a friend maker and a faithful and helpful friend to many of all classes. For forty years he was a poplar auctioneer. And for 35 years he was an agent for the Hawkeye Insurance Co. He was highly esteemed by both his company and patrons.

Kansas

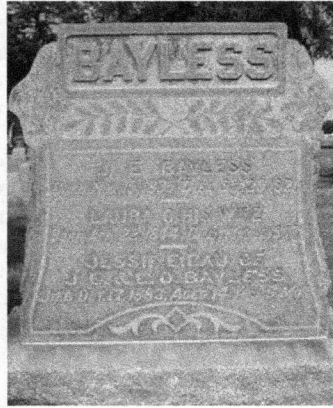

Joseph E. Bayless

Birth:
Nov. 13, 1835
Huron County, Ohio
Death:
Sep. 20, 1921
Kansas
Burial:
Elmwood Cemetery
Chanute
Neosho County, Kansas

Joseph was the son of Jacob and Sally Bayless. He was born in Ohio, but by age 15 he was living in Fulton County, Illinois. He came to Christ in 1848 in the Fiatt, Illinois church. He married Laura O. Tharp, and in 1860 the couple was living on her parents' farm. He was a licensed in 1861; and stated for three years at the Prairie city Academy, and was ordained in 1869. Except for three years in Wisconsin, which was of between 1872-75, he ministered with the church there in Illinois. His ordination came in 1882 when he moved to Kansas and organized the Village Creek church and labored to build up the cause in the vicinity. By 1880 Joseph had become a minister and was the father of three. In 1895 he and Laura were living in Wilson County, Kansas. By 1905 they had moved to Chanute, Neosho County, Kansas.

Milo William Dodge

Birth:
Mar. 14, 1851
Erie, Erie County, Pennsylvania
Death:
1919
Great Bend, Barton Count, Kansas
Burial:
Great Bend Cemetery
Great Bend, Barton County, Kansas

Milo married (1) Annie E. Morey 01 March 1871. She died 04 April 1890. He married (2) Harriet Aurelia 'Hattie' Buffum 01 October 1890 in Manila, Erie County, New York. Dodge, was the son of Rev. Calvin and Sharlotte Dodge. He was educated at Pike Seminary, New York, and in 1871, married (3) Annie E. Mowry. .His conversion took place in 1864, and his ordination in 1880. With the exception of two years at Bliss, where he assisted in organizing the church, and one year at Odessa, his ministry has been with the churches of the Owego Quarterly Meeting (PA). In 1886 extensive revivals resulted from his labors with the Warren and Windham Churches. After Annie died., he married (4) Hattie Buffon in 1890.

But godliness is profitable unto all things, having promise of the life that now is, and of that which is to come.

John Blosser Fast
Birth:
Oct. 12, 1814
Pennsylvania,
Death:
May 1, 1897
Burial
Columbus City Cemetery,
Columbus, County, Kansas,
Plot: Section 10

He went to Orange, Ohio where he joined the Freewill Baptists in 1835, and received license to preach the next year, and was ordained in Adams Co. Ill, April 3, 1840. He took a prominent place among the early workers in Illinois, and did much good in the work of the church. He was instrumental in gathering some fifteen churches and assisted in establishing other church Quarterly and Yearly meetings. The Prairie City Academy was established largely through his instrumentality. Many years he served as clerk of Quarterly and Yearly meetings, and in 1859, he represented Illinois Y.M. in the General Conference of Freewill Baptists in Lowell, Mass. His later years were spent in Kansas and the pastor of Ness City Church.

Arlie Z. Hoover
Birth:
Feb. 24, 1903
Death:
Oct. 19, 1978
Burial:
Grinnell Cemetery,
Grinnell,
Gove County, Kansas

He was active both of Missouri and Kansas and serve both states in its early ministries. He was an early contributor to the *Free Will Baptist GEM.*

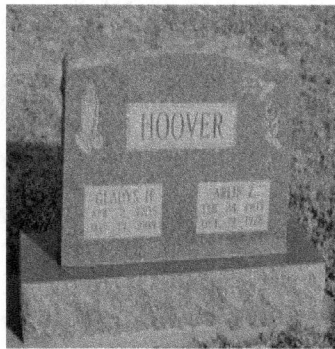

Farewell, Death is the deliverance from a body wracked with pain.

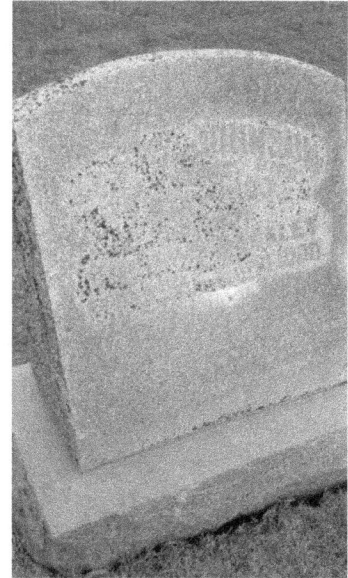

David Johnson
Birth:
June 16, 1822
Bethany, New York
Death:
1903
Burial:
West Cedar Cemetery
Phillips County, Kansas

His conversion took place in 1839; he received license to preach in 1846, and years later was ordained in Wisconsin. After preaching for some time in the state of Wisconsin, he moved to the state of Kansas where in 1886 he organized the Plum Creek church in Phillips County, Kansas. He baptized more than 180 converts during his ministry and accomplished much good.

Samuel Keyes
Birth:
May 5, 1819
West Boylston,
Massachusetts
Death:
Feb. 13, 1901
Burial:
Fairview Cemetery
Fulton,
Bourbon County,Kansas

In 1843 he married D. E. Johnston. He spent his early years in DeKalb, New York and was converted in 1843 receiving license to preach in 1858. He was ordained by the Cherokee Quarterly Meeting in Kansas on September 27, 1870. He organized the West Liberty church. He baptized 60 the year following his ordination and continued his labors in that vicinity.

George S Latimer
Birth:
Nov. 7, 1864
Iowa
Death:
Feb. 19, 1958
Vinland, Douglas County, Kansas
Burial:
Blocker Cemetery,
Haddam,
Washington County, Kansas

He was an ordained Free Will Baptist minister, who pastored the FWB Church at Hadden, KS, and in 1900, in Elm, Putnam Co. Missouri, as well as others. Rev. G.S. Latimer, and Rev. John H. Wolfe, planned the organization of a Western Conference of FWB after the 1911 merger of FWB with the Northern Baptists. They met with the Missouri State Association with their proposal, and perfected the organization, with representatives from Kansas, Nebraska, Missouri, Oklahoma and Texas, in Old Philadelphia Church, Plattsburg, MO. on Dec. 16, 1916. This became the Cooperative General Association. Rev. Latimer was faithful minister to his denomination and carried out the work he was called to do.

Willis Jackson "Jack" Ledbetter
Birth:
Apr. 5, 1913
Drakes Creek
Madison County, Arkansas
Death:
Feb. 24, 1995
Wichita
Sedgwick County, Kansas
Burial:
Wichita Park Cemetery and
Mausoleum
Wichita
Sedgwick County, Kansas

He was a retired minister, founding pastor and pastor emeritus of the Westside Freewill Baptist Church. He was licensed as a FWB minister in 1951 and ordained in 1952. He pastored four churches, three in Arkansas and one in Kansas. Of his 44 years in the ministry, 24 was invested at the Westside FWB church, that he founded. He was a leader in Kansas and served 16 years on the state Executive Board and chaired the Examining Board also for 16 years. He was father of the 'Singing Ledbetter Family' who recorded more than 30 albums and tapes. His close preacher friends nicknamed him 'Tig' short for Tiger, because of his boldness for Christ. At the time of his death the Ledbetter family number 62 members, eight of whom are ministers.

Henry S. Limbocker
Birth:
Sep. 10, 1807
Death:
Jan. 28, 1893
Burial:
Sunset Cemetery, Manhattan,
Riley County, Kansas
Entered the Gospel Ministry January 28 1839 as Freewill Baptist ordained minister from NY to Mich, then Kansas. Honored and esteemed by many. A true pioneer.

Horace Washington Morse
Birth:
Jan. 24, 1822
Williamsfield
Ashtabula County, Ohio
Death:
May 23, 1894
Fostoria
Pottawatomie County, Kansas
Burial:
King Cemetery
Pottawatomie County, Kansas

He was a son of Rev. Horace Morse, who is buried in Ohio. He began his religious life as a young boy and was baptized by Rev. Ransom Dunn on January 17, 1839, as was also Melvinia Prindle whom he married on March 30, 1842. He was ordained in 1861 having served as a licensed minister for two years and ministered to churches in the Ohio and Pennsylvania Yearly Meeting until this removal to Illinois in 1864. Later he moved from Illinois to Kansas in the year 1870 and organized the Fostoria and other churches and was the founder of the Blue Valley Quarterly Meeting.

Francis P. Newell
Birth:
Feb. 9, 1813
Boston
Suffolk County, Massachusetts
Death:
Dec. 23, 1899
Cedar
Smith County, Kansas
Burial:
Cedar Cemetery
Cedar
Smith County, Kansas
Plot: Section 4, Row 1-9

Rev. Francis P. Newell, was born

in Mass. and educated at Whitestown Seminary, NY, and New Hampton College, New Hampton, NH. He married Miss Hannah B. Ramsey, in New Hampton, on 30 May 1847. He was ordained a Freewill Baptist minister, and after school he moved west to Iowa, where he was the the fourth pastor of a church in Butler Co. Some years later, he moved to Smith Co. Kansas, where he was minister and lived with his family. It was written in Butler and Bremer Co. Iowa Histories, that he was an able man and preacher.

No word of God must be incredible to us, as long as no work of God is impossible to him.

William H Northrup
Birth:
September 4, 1826
Otsego County, New York
Death:
Oct. 20, 1878
Burial:
Womer Cemetery
Womer
Smith County, Kansas

In 1856 he received his licensed to preach and settled in Kansas in 1872 where he was ordained by the Blue Valley Quarterly Meeting on November 20, 1876.

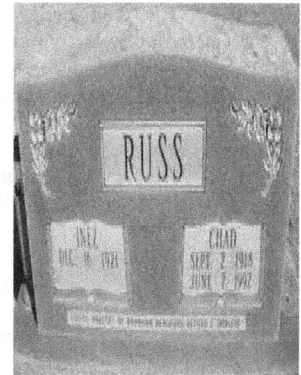

Chad Russ
Birth:
Sep. 2, 1918
Death:
Jun. 7, 1992
Burial:
Sumner Memorial Gardens,
Wellington,
Sumner County, Kansas,
Plot: C L25

Charles Smith
Birth:
Jul. 26, 1824
La Roy, New York
Death:
Jun. 25, 1904
Burial:
Powhattan Cemetery
Powhattan
Brown County, Kansas

He was converted very early united with the Protestant Methodist Church. In March 1852 he was married to Maria E. Fish in Mason, Michigan. In 1856 he moved to Kansas uniting with the Free Baptist denomination, and was licensed and began preaching. He was ordained in 1874 and traveled and preached in the states of Kansas and Nebraska doing pioneer work.

George W Thompson
Birth:
1846
Wisconsin
Death:
1918
Burial:
Mound Valley Cemetery
Mound Valley
Labette County, Kansas

After serving in the Civil War he was brought to God in 1872 and united with the United Brethren in Kansas receiving from them license to preach. Three years later he united with the Free Baptist receiving ordination soon after. In 1882 he moved to Clearwater, Nebraska where he assisted in organizing several churches and continued to minister to them baptizing 50 converts.

Jules Legender Williams
Birth:
Mar. 2, 1841
Merthyr
Tydfil, Wales
Death:
Jul. 14, 1878
Jefferson County, Kansas
Burial:
Pleasant View Cemetery
Oskaloosa
Jefferson County, Kansas

When he was quite young his parents emigrated to Canada. His father died when he was about seven years of age. He early prepared himself for a teacher, and in 1859 went to Hillsdale College, Michigan, expecting to remain there until he graduated, but in '61 he enlisted in the 4th Michigan Infantry regiment and was sent immediately to the front. He was in both battles at Bull Run, and other engagements. He remained with the regiment only a year being discharged for disability, having contracted a lung disease. He remained at home until he partially recovered, and then enlisted in the 137th Pennsylvania Volunteers. The 137th enlisted for nine months and were discharged at the expiration of that time. The ensuing fall he enlisted for one year on board the U. S. Receiving ship "Grampus." He was promoted to Master's Mate. When he left the Navy he received a commission at Lieutenant in the U.S. colored Infantry, but was not assigned to duty. He then returned to college and remained during the winter tern of 1864-5, and in May 1865, was ordered to report for duty in the 42nd Regular Colored Infantry stationed at Chattanooga, Tenn. In November 1865 he obtained leave of absence, came north and was married to Lovina A. BATES of Spring, Crawford Co., Penn., who returned with him to his Regiment, then stationed in Huntsville, Ala. In Feb. '66, he was discharged from the Army. He came to Kansas and settled in Sarcoxie township, Jefferson County, May 4, 1866. He taught school in the Tibbots district, Pleasant Valley and Stringtown. He commenced to preach during the first years of his residence in Sarcoxie. He was a member of the Free Will Baptist Church, having professed religion before he entered the army and lived true to his profession through all the temptations of army life. When the Mud Creek Baptist Church was organized he walked to Brown county, Kansas, sleeping on the prairie, with his shoes for a pillow, to get an ordained Minister to administer the church ordinances. He was himself soon after ordained by Rev. Keniston, of Walarusa. He was elected Probate Judge of Jefferson county in 1872, and re-elected in 1874. From October 9, 1873, to April 11, 1878, he was connected with a paper as Editor, which he assisted in establishing. He was buried July 15 and followed to the grave by a very large procession of friends and mourners. The funeral services were conducted by Rev. L.D. Price, in a most appropriate manner.

Now we know that if the earthly tent we live in is destroyed, we have a building from God, an eternal house in heaven, not built by human hand

Kentucky

Roger Lee Blair
Birth:
Sep. 21, 1959
Death:
Oct. 9, 1993
Burial:
Highland Memorial Park
Cemetery
Staffordsville
Johnson County, Kentucky

He was a FWB minister and a member of the John-Thomas Association.

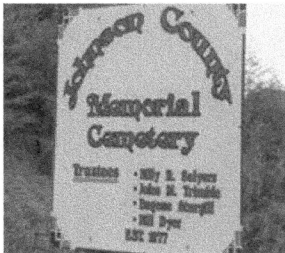

Steve Branham
Birth:
Aug. 15, 1901
Johnson County, Kentucky
Death:
Apr. 7, 1978
Prestonsburg,
Floyd County, Kentucky
Burial:
Johnson County Memorial
Cemetery,
Staffordsville
,Johnson County, Kentucky

Rev. Steve Branham, 76, died at Highland Regional Medical Center. Rev. Branham was born the son of Turner and Martha Engle Branham. He was a resident of Sitka, a retired coal miner, and an ordained minister since 1969. Rev. Branham was pastor of the Collista Freewill Baptist Church for four years. Funeral services were held in the Sitka Freewill Baptist Church with Reverends Richard Williams, Herb Arms, and

Mark Daniel officiating. Paintsville Herald Wednesday April 12, 1978

Scott Castle
Birth:
Jul. 7, 1902
Johnson County, Kentucky
Death:
Nov. 29, 1997 Salyersville,
Magoffin County,
Kentucky
Burial:
Staffordsville Church Cemetery,
Staffordsville,
Johnson County, Kentucky

C Z Cavin
Birth:
1875
Death:
1956
Burial:
Rose Hill Park and Mausoleum,
Ashland,
Boyd County,
Kentucky,
Plot: D

Lawrence E Colliver
Birth:
1899
Death:
1999
Burial:
Crown Hill Cemetery,
Sharpsburg,
Bath County, Kentucky

Harvey Burns Conley
Birth:
Sep. 3, 1861
Paintsville
Johnson County, Kentucky
Death:
Feb. 1, 1941
Paintsville
Johnson County, Kentucky
Burial:
Conley Cemetery
Johnson County, Kentucky

Family genealogy states "he had always lived in Paintsville, managed several hotels in the city and had been interested in several business enterprises. He

was a poplar man with a large following, elected Judge at one time. He was a leading minister of the Free Will Baptist church and did much to advance its cause. He has probably married more couples than any man living in the county. He officiated at many, many, funerals. Rev. Conley, was a son of the Judge Hiram E. and Clerinda Rice Conley. He was the County Judge for 5 years, served 1 term as County Assessor, 1 term as Master Commissioner, 2 terms as a member of the Board of Education of Paintsville City Schools, and was a Baptist minister for the Freewill Baptist Church for 58 years. site. Rev. Burns Conley helped lead the Kentucky FWB into organization of that State's Association in 1939, at Tom's Creek church, where he explained the purpose of the organization.

John Elliott Conley
Birth:
Nov. 30, 1856
Johnson County, Kentucky
Death:
Jan. 6, 1945
Auxier
Floyd County, Kentucky
Burial:
C C Meade Cemetery
Hagerhill
Johnson County, Kentucky

An early FWB minister of note who came out of Toms Creek church who with others, offered leadership and counsel to the denomination for a number of years. His name is mentioned in History of FWB in KY. Conley married Susan James January 17, 1877, Johnson Cty, Kentucky.

Scott Daniels
Birth:
Feb. 13, 1884
Thealka
Johnson County, Kentucky
Death:
May 23, 1975
Johnson County, Kentucky
Burial:
Greenlawn Cemetery
Louisa
Lawrence County, Kentucky

Rev. Scott Daniel was in the Tri-State Association organized on Oct. 4, 1919, and included the Scioto Yearly Meeting, Ohio; the Big Sandy Yearly Meeting in KY, in the early movement in Johnson Co. KY. and the West Virginia Yearly Meeting. Rev. Scott Daniel was listed as one of several leaders for that year. He worked as a coal miner.

Death is not the greatest loss in life.

John B Dills
Birth:
1890
Death:
Jan. 5, 1972
Paintsville,
Johnson County, Kentucky
Burial:
Sycamore Cemetery, Nippa, Johnson County, Kentucky
He was a retired miner and was affiliated with the Freewill Baptist

church by Revs. Millard VanHoose and Claude Preston at the Mouth of Rush Freewill Baptist Church.

Ted Greene
Birth:
Jan. 21, 1916
Floyd County, Kentucky
Death:
Sep. 1, 1996
Morehead
Rowan County, Kentucky
Burial:
Lee Cemetery, Morehead, Rowan County, Kentucky

He was a Free Will Baptist pastor for nearly 50 years pastoring four churches, organized 10 churches and was a full-time evangelist. He pioneered radio and television ministries in the Morehead area. He organized the Kentucky Bluegrass Association and moderated it often and the Kentucky State Association for six years. For seven years he represented Kentucky on the General Board of the National Association of Free Will Baptists. Seventy-five men answered the call to preach under his ministry. He attended Booth Business College, Free Will Baptist Bible College and Emmanuel Bible Seminary.

James A. Hayes
Birth:
Dec. 29, 1931
Georges Creek Kentucky
Death:
Apr. 25, 2012
Louisa, Key
Burial:
Pine Hill Cemetery, Louisa,
Lawrence County, Kentucky,
James A. Hayes was a Freewill Baptist minister having been ordained in 1955. He had served the Louisa Free Will Baptist Church for 25 years stepping down in 1997. Before that he had pastored the Columbus First Free Will Baptist Church in Columbus, Ohio. He is well-known for his

leadership and participation. Funeral service was at the Louisa Freewill Baptist Church and the burial with military honors.

"The mouth, the instrument, the articulation was theirs; but the words were God's."

Jesse Eugene Meade
Birth:
Jun. 27, 1941
Magoffin County, Kentucky
Death:
Jan. 18, 2000
Paintsville, Johnson County, Kentucky
Burial:
Meade Cemetery, Flatgap, Johnson County, Kentucky

He was the son of Rev. Wayne Meade, Sr. Jesse. A graduate of Free Will Baptist Bible College, and Army veteran. He pastored in Tennessee and Kentucky.

The South-Central Q. M. of Tennessee's Cumberland Assn, where Meade had pastored for 15 years, established a Memorial scholarship in his honor at the Free Will Baptist Bible College. He was a man of powerful and deep held convictions carried through with his magnetic personality and a sense of humor, which were legendary. Besides his father, he had 3 brothers who were Free Will Baptist ministers. His funeral was held at the Southside Free Will Baptist church in Paintsville, Ky.

Tommy Moore
Birth:
Sep. 19, 1928
Adams, Lawrence County
Kentucky
Death:
Sep. 23, 1967
Columbus,
Franklin Co., Ohio
Burial:
Yatesville Cemetery,
Louisa, Lawrence County,
Kentucky

He was born to Hubert and Delphia Adams Moore. The obituary of Rev. Moore notes that he was 39 years of age at his passing in his home in Columbus following a long illness. He had been a Free Will Baptist minister for 21 years. The service was conducted at the Welch Avenue Church in Columbus where he was its third pastor..

Earlist Mullins
Birth:
Apr. 29, 1921
Pike Co., Kentucky
Death:
Jun. 9, 1994
Burial:
Salem Cemetery
Irvine
Estill County, Kentucky

A FWB minister, retired sheet metal worker and a World War II veteran. He attended Hylton Freewill Baptist church, Ashcamp, Ky.

Charlie Pennington
Birth:
1888
Death:
1970
Burial:
Dixon Cemetery, Westwood,
Boyd County, Kentucky

Jay Francis Preston
Birth:
Feb. 15, 1893
Death:
May 27, 1994
Lawrence County, Kentucky
Burial;
Preston Family Cemetery
Georges Creek
Lawrence County, Kentucky

He was ordained as a Free Will Baptist minister in 1926. The picture of Rev. Preston was taken at his 100th birthday gathering being celebrated by his children. At his party he preached a sermon for about 10 minutes. He married first Marie Burgess who died in a home fire in 1966. His second wife was Gladis R. Preston who died in 1992. He was a veteran of World War I. His funeral was held at the Bell's Chapel Free Will Baptist Church, where he at one time had been pastor. The ancestry of the Preston family in Kentucky and Virginia is quite large and one of his ancestors was Moses Preston who was born in 1700. There are eight Preston Cemetery's in Lawrence County where he also is buried. He was the father of 13 children of which 10 lived to adulthood. One of his daughters, Helen, taught Sunday school for more than 73 years before retiring at age 90. These were in Free Will Baptist churches.

> **As a doorman opens the door to a place, so death opens the door for the soul to take its flight.**

Oliver W Privett
Birth:
Mar. 12, 1918
Death:
Sep. 29, 1983
Burial:
Mill Creek Cemetery
Sawyer
McCreary County, Kentucky

Well-known Free Will Baptist preacher in West Virginia and Kentucky. Helped organize a Chapman Memorial Free Will Baptist Church in Chapmansville, West Virginia. He was the first moderator of the West Virginia State Association when it reorganized in 1949. His parents were James Harmon Privett (1895 - 1957) and Hannah Perry Privett (1898 - 1956) His spouse was Ella Rose Privett (1923 - 1997). He was a PFC in the US Army during WW II.

Carl Lee Senters
Birth:
Aug. 14, 1901
Death:
Apr. 27, 1969
Burial:
Davidson Memorial Gardens,
Ivel, Floyd County, Kentucky

Joe Slone
Birth:
1941
Death:
Aug. 24, 2009
Prestonsburg
Floyd County, Kentucky
Burial:
Annie E. Young Cemetery
Pikeville, Pike County, Kentucky

Joe was born to the late John M. and Stella Thacker Slone. Joe worked as a coal miner for many years and was a member of the Chapter 166 Disabled American Veterans Society of John's Creek KY .Joe was a minister for the lord for 30 plus years and loved to preach the Gospel to all. He was a member of The Owsley Freewill Baptist Church.

Eliphas Preston VanHoose
Birth:
Feb. 29, 1836
Floyd County, Kentucky
Death:
Oct. 5, 1911
Johnson County, Kentucky
Burial:
VanHoose-Fairchild Cemetery,
Tutor Key,
Johnson County, Kentucky

A Free Will Baptist minister in the early days in the Paintsville, Johnson Co. KY area. He was a farmer. He served in the Civil War, the 10th KY Calvary, Co B.

Frew Stewart VanHoose
Birth:
Sep. 4, 1883 Johnson
County,
Kentucky
Death:
Apr. 6, 1967
Johnson County,
Kentucky
Burial:
Wells Buckingham Cemetery,
Paintsville,
Johnson County,
Kentucky

F. S. VanHoose, 83, president and manager of VanHoose Lumber Company for the past 50 years, died in Paintsville after a long illness. Mr. VanHoose was born Sep. 1, 1883 in Johnson County, a son of the late Harry and Elizabeth Dixon VanHoose.

He was an active Republican, a member of the Paintsville Rotary Club, a member and minister of the Third Street Freewill Baptist Church. His company had outlets in Louisa, Prestonsburg, and Paintsville.

Millard VanHoose
Birth:
Jun. 24, 1883
Johnson County, Kentucky
Death:
Sep. 16, 1973
Johnson County, Kentucky
Burial:
Highland Memorial
Park,Staffordsville
,Johnson County, Kentucky

An ordained Free Will Baptist minister, pastor and leader, who served mostly in Johnson Co. in early times.

O Lord, into Thy hands I commit my spirit; for Thou hast redeemed my soul.

Richard Scott VanHoose
Birth:
Oct. 30, 1977
Ashland,
Boyd County, Kentucky
Death:
Apr. 9, 2004
Johnson County,
Kentucky
Burial:
Johnson County
Memorial Cemetery,
Staffordsville,
Johnson County, Kentucky

Owned VanHoose Funeral Home and in the later stages of his life became a Free Will Baptist Pastor and preacher.

Louisana

Robert Martin
Birth:
Dec. 29, 1814
Union County, South Carolina
Death:
Dec. 25, 1899
Bossier Parish, Louisiana
Burial:
New Bethel Baptist Church
Bossier Parish, Louisiana

His parents moved to Georgia when he was a child, where he was raised.In 1839 he was married to Miss Indiana Dillard, and was ordained to the ministry in 1840. In 1852 he moved to Louisiana, and settled six miles from Rocky Mount, where he lived until 1886, when he moved to Fisher county, Texas, residing there six years, when he returned to his old home in Louisiana, where he remained to his death. The deceased raised nine children, seven. Full of years and honors Rev. Robert Martin was on Christmas morning gathered to his father. He was a man of positive force of character, and ever exerted that force for the cause of his God, and his country and his people. He was one who [sent] luster to the citizenship of his country and inspired those who came in contact with him to greater effort in the struggle to reach higher ideals.-> From the Bossier Banner, Thursday, December 28, 1899, page 3a. He was one of four brothers that preached the gospel, one of which was the founder of the Martin Association in the state of Georgia as well as one other association. Since there were family roots into South Carolina one of which had been buried in the Cemetery of the Horse Branch Free Will Baptist Church that I am assuming that the other three brothers that went on west also carried the Free Will Baptist doctrines.

Whatever you do, work heartily, as for the Lord and not for men, knowing that from the Lord you will receive the inheritance as your reward. You are serving the Lord Christ.

Colossians 3:23-24

Maine

George J Abbot
Born
Dec. 3, 1830
Death:
Nov. 3, 1883
Burial:
Pond Cemetery 1, Unity,
Waldo County, Maine,
Plot: row 6

He was baptized by the Rev. Dexter Waterman, under whose labors he was converted about 1852. He joined the church in South Jackson, Maine and in June of 1856 he was licensed by the Unity quarterly meeting. Soon after this, he went to the theological school at new Hampton, New Hampshire where he was highly esteemed by his teachers and fellow students. He was ordained in June of 1858 during a session of that same quarterly meeting. His pastorates were in South Montville, Wayne, and Dover, Maine and also in Bristol, Hampton, New Hampshire. He was pastor of the Apponaug church in this state of Rhode Island. The Rev. E Knowlton, a well-known Free Will Baptists at the time, knew him in his first church and said of him that he was one of the best spirited man he had ever known and for a young man his sermons were both spiritual and instructive.

John Quincy Adams
Birth:
Jan. 19, 1848
Death:
Apr. 16, 1897
Burial:
Riverside Cemetery, Lewiston,
Androscoggin County, Maine

He graduated from Bates College 1876 and from the Divinity school in 1881. He was baptized by the Rev. Elisha Purington, his pastor. In April, before his graduation, he accepted the call to the South Parsonsfield, Maine church. He also pastored a church in Dover, Maine, but due to failing health he resided in Lewiston and supplied the Kennebunk and Kennebunk Port churches for one year. In 1883 he was a delegate to the General Conference from the Maine Western quarterly meeting. In 1885 and 1886 he was the corresponding secretary of the Maine Association and delivered addresses at its annual meetings.

William Abbott
Birth:
1793
Livermore
Androscoggin County, Maine
Death:
Jul. 16, 1877
New Portland
Somerset County, Maine
Burial:
East New Portland Cemetery
New Portland, Somerset County,
Maine

He became a Christian when about 26, was baptized by Rev. Samuel Hutchins and united with the church in New Portland. He was a faithful minister for over fifty years and instrumental in bringing many to Christ. He was a strong advocate of education and reforms. He won the affection of his brethren by whom he was venerated.

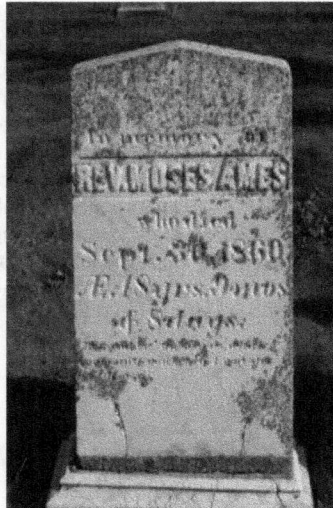

Moses Ames
Birth:
Dec. 8, 1812
Dover-Foxcroft,
Piscataquis, Maine
Death:
Sep. 30, 1860
South Dover, Me.
Burial:
South Dover Cemetery
Dover-Foxcroft
Piscataquis County, Maine
Plot: North Section, Row 2

Moses Ames was a FWB clergyman, At the age of 4, the family moved to Bradford, where after twelve years his parents were reclaimed, and he had the conviction strongly forced upon his heart that he was a sinner. In the spring of 1834, through a protracted meeting, he and others were converted, and in July following he began preaching. He had been baptized by Rev. Nathaniel Harvey, uniting with the church in Bradford. The destitute churches in the Sebec Q. Y. were objects of his labor. He was licensed by the Quarterly Meeting September, 1838, and labored in Garland and Danville. Sept. 22, 1839, he was ordained. In May 1838, he began his ministry at Corinth. In 1840 he saw from his preaching a great revival at Garland, and in a short time baptized over twenty. His work in Bradford was blessed. In 1841 he saw revivals both in the Wellington and in the Springfield Q. M's. In October he was present at the eleventh General Conference at Topsham. He moved his family to Corinth in December, where for some months he had preached half the time. In January 1842, in a revival at Hunting's Mills, in Corinth, twenty-three were added to the church. A revival attended him in Garland where he preached part of the time. During the summer he baptized there forty-six. and in 1845 moved there. He attended the thirteenth General Conference in Sutton, Vt., in October 1847, as a delegate from the Penobscot Y. M. The next year he moved to Veazie for a pastorate of two years. Here a church was organized. In November 1850, he began his labors with the Dover and Foxcroft church, where his strength failed him. During the last year of his ministry seventy were added to the church. He was a man highly gifted in natural talent; he possessed good business ability. His devotion to the ministry cost him his health. He was a gifted speaker and drew multitudes after him.

"His power is infinitely strong,

so is his wisdom infinitely clear,

and his will infinitely pure."

Otis Andrews
Birth:
Mar. 14, 1817
Livermore Falls
Androscoggin County, Maine
Death:
May 5, 1897
Industry
Franklin County, Maine
Burial:
Weeks Mills Cemetery
New Sharon
Franklin County, Maine

He studied in the common schools and was converted on January 1, 1836. He was licensed in 1838 and then ordained by the Bowdoin Quarterly Meeting In 1843. He pastored a number of churches and enjoyed many revival meetings. He saw 100's converted, married over 100 couples and attended over 200 funerals.
Inscription:
REV. OTIS ANDREWS
MAR. 14, 1817-MAY 5, 1897

Hezekiah Atwood
Birth:
unknown
Death:
Dec. 26, 1870
Burial:
Gibbs Mill Cemetery
Livermore
Androscoggin County, Maine

He studied at the Farmington Academy and served his denomination for many years in the state of Maine. He organized the church at Barkers Island, Booth Bay, Maine. He had a son A. C. Atwood that was a pastor in Cape Sable Island, Nova Scotia.

Inscription:
HEZEKIAH ATWOOD
Died
Dec. 26, 1870
AGE. 72

Aaron Ayer
Birth:
Apr. 3, 1802
Buxton, York County, Maine
Death:
Oct. 8, 1866
Naples
Cumberland County, Maine
Burial:
Naples Village Cemetery
Naples, Cumberland County, Maine

Ayer was a Freewill Baptist Minister. He filled pulpits in Maine and New Hampshire, and was widely known and beloved. (His stone says 1866).

Inscription:
AARON AYER
Died Oct. 8, 1866
Age. 64 yrs. 5 mos.
Blessed are the dead that die in the Lord.

John M Bailey
Birth:
1764
Death:
Oct. 5, 1857
Burial:
Grover Cemetery
Woolwich, Sagadahoc County, Maine

He was born in Woolwich in 1764, and was converted by the preaching of Benjaman Randall and baptized by Rev. E. Lock about 1787. In 1798, when the denomination had less than a score of ministers, he was ordained by Timothy Cnnningham and Dea. Daniel Dunton, neither of whom were then ordained ministers. He entered upon a long ministry. In 1823, the best of feeling was restored by the aid of a council between him and his church, and with the help of Rev. Allen Files a revival sprung up in which over 100 were converted. He retained his mental faculties to the end of his long and useful life, and died in peace, fully resigned to his Master's will. Revolutionary War veteran. An ordained Freewill Baptist minister, died at age 93 years

John Buzzell
Birth:
Sep. 16, 1767
Barrington, Strafford Cty
New Hampshire,
Death:
Mar. 29, 1863
Parsonsfield, York County, Maine
Burial:
North Parsonsfield
North Parsonsfield,
York County Maine

Rev. John Buzzell, a Free Will Baptist clergyman, married Anna Buzzell, b. 1770, d. 1839. They had 11 children. His attainments were above average, early becoming a teacher of common schools. He along with Dr. Moses Sweat, and Rev. Rufus McIntire, founded the Old Parsonsfield Seminary, the first school in the denomination.

He, with Elder Benjamin Randall founder of FWB in NH, came to Maine before 1800, and he is known to have pastored churches in Maine for more than 50 years. He was a noted and powerful preacher, dignified in his demeanor, yet in spirit humble. He did as much as any in extending the work and influence of the FWB church. It was said that he also had a talent for painting, 'as good as the old masters' and even painted a portrait of a young couple a week after their marriage as a gift to them. He had a far-reaching view of education, and had a commanding influence in exerting and molding political and religious opinions of the people. He was first editor of his denomination's "Morning Star"

paper, which position he held seven years; He was instrumental in establishing the Orissa Mission (India.) He wrote a biography of his mentor, *"Life of Rev. Benjamin Randall."* He died at his home in North Parsonsfield at the advanced age of ninety-five years, and 6 months.

Oliver Butler
Birth:
Feb. 25, 1809
Berwick, York County Maine
Death:
Dec. 6, 1897
Chelsea,
Suffolk County,
Massachusetts
Burial:
Woodlawn Cemetery,
Biddeford,
York County, Maine

A graduate of Bowdoin College and for years publisher of the *"Biddeford Journal,"* a member of the Maine Legislature, two yrs president of the Senate, and at present (1889) attorney at law in Boston, Mass. Rev. Oliver Butler studied with a tutor and at Parsonfield Seminary in theology in 1843. He was licensed in June 1840 and ordained Jan. 28, 1842 a Free Will Baptist clergyman at Great Falls, N.H., by a council from the Rockingham Q.M., with Rev. Silas Curtis as Chairman. His first

pastorate was at Effingham Falls where he organized a church and built a meeting house, adding during fourteen years, about 100 to the membership. He pastored Middleton, Wolsbourough, East Andover and at Parker's Head, ME, and for twelve years at Meredith Centre, N.H., where a hundred were baptized. He also pastored at Buxton, and Lyman, Me. He went into the publishing business in 1872, but continued preaching until 1880. When enfeebled by disease he moved to Chelsea, Mass, where he has served three yrs in a Baptist city mission. At nearly 80 years, he retired active service. He was three years a member of the Home Mission Board, and a member of Gen. Conference at Sutton, VT, in 1847, and Lowell, MA in 1852.

John J. Banks
Birth:
Dec. 20, 1826
Levant, Penobscot County,
Maine
Death:
Mar. 13, 1917
Burial:
Corinthian Cemetery,
Penobscot County, Maine,
Plot: Div. 9 Lot 8

He became a Christian at the age of 26. He was two years a member of a Baptist church. He received license on Sept. 29, 1855, and on Jan. 3, 1857, was ordained by the Free Will Baptist Springfield Quarterly Meeting. He had a revival in Lincoln, Me, in 1856, and raised up a church of thirty-six members of which he was chosen pastor. In 1858, he had a revival in Chester. He had a revival in Kenduskeag in 1866. A church was organized there two years later of which he has been pastor. He supplied the Congregationalist church of Kenduskeag part time eight years.

Favel Bartlett
Birth:
Apr. 12, 1792
Plymouth, Mass.
Death:
Mar. 22, 1873
Auburn, Me
Burial:
Norway Pine Grove Cemetery
Paris, Oxford County, Maine

In early manhood he was an active minister in Franklin County, Me., but disease of the throat and lungs forced him to turn aside and engage in business. He became a merchant, but preached occasionally as long as health permitted. Fifteen years before his death he moved to Auburn, where he soon retired from business, in still feebler health. He lived a quiet, cheerful, Christian life till his departure, and was much respected and beloved.

John Batchelder
Birth:
Feb. 15, 1813
Rhode Island
Death:
Jun. 21, 1865
Burial:
Evergreen Cemetery,
Garland,
Penobscot County, Maine

John Batchelder moved to New Hampshire at the death of his father in 1823, and went out as a tanner's apprentice. At the age of

21 he was baptized, joining the Free Baptist Church. Having moved to Garland, Maine, he united with the church there in April 1842. He was licensed by the Exeter Q.M.in March 1854 and for a while was connected with the Biblical School at New Hampton. He was ordained in Parkman, Maine in January 1858, in which field he organized a church and became it's pastor. During the last four years of his life his work was crippled through ill health. His last season was spent with the church at South Dover. He was a good preacher and was much beloved.
Inscription:
Died at age 53 yrs. and 4 mos.

The resurrection of the body is the final step in our salvation.

Edwin Blake
Birth:
1843
Death:
1915
Burial:
Riverside Cemetery, Farmington, Franklin County, Maine

Freewill Baptist minister. He served Co. A 8th Me. Vol. Sept. 1861 to Nov. 1865 during the Civil War. His wife was Elsie W. Cross, who lived between 1842-1926.

Stephen S Bowden
Birth:
Oct. 18, 1806
Penobscot, Maine
Death:
Nov. 3, 1878
West Waterville, Maine
Burial:
Old Cemetery
Oakland
Kennebec County,Maine

He was converted in 1829, when 22 years of age, under the labor of Rev. Cyrus Stilson and baptized by him on November 22 and joined the church. He was chosen clerk of the church and served it for 12 years. He was licensed on January 15, 1842. His ordination occurred at the Pittsfield church in June 1844. While not specifically an evangelist, he did have a circuit of some 12 towns in the Waterville Quarterly Meeting and was graciously favored by his ministry. For 30 years before his death he rarely spent a Sunday at home, though few loved home more ardently or more fully honored the relationship of husband and father. His preaching was sound, clear, and persuasive. He attended many funerals and solemnized many marriages. At the time of his death he was clerk of the Quarterly Meeting and had served in this office 17 1/2 years out of the last 20 attending every session. He was chosen delegate to the last General Conference before his death but yielded his place to his alternate.

The Divine power appears fearful in its holiness

Levi Brackett
Birth:
1813
Westbrook, Maine
Death:
1890
Burial:
Growstown Cemetery
Brunswick
Cumberland County, Maine

He was converted at age 26, and graduated from the Theological School at Whitestown, New York about 10 years afterwards in 1849. He received license to preach in 1844 and was ordained by the Bowdoin quarterly Meeting in 1849. After pastoring in New Hampshire for many years he moved to West Lebanon, Maine and supplied in Northfield and elsewhere. He also pastored in North Parsonsfield. Revivals and baptisms he enjoyed in nearly in all his pastorates. On December 20 field, 1852 he married Mrs. Nancy J Cram, of Brownfield, Maine. He had four children and the oldest was a professor at the Colorado State University. The older daughter was a teacher in the Classical Institute at Hallowell, Maine, and the second daughter is Librarian of the Spear Library at Oberlin College. These three were graduates of Bates College, Lewiston Maine.

Nancy Jane Cram Brackett
Birth:
1827
Death:
1897
Burial:

Growstown Cemetery
Brunswick
Cumberland County, Maine

She had been a Free Will Baptist preacher prior to the marriage to Rev. Levi Brackett.

Though policy teacheth us not to trust our enemies, yet piety teacheth us to love them.

Ebenezer Brown
Birth:
1771
Death:
Mar. 27, 1838
Wilton, ME,
Burial:
East Wilton Cemetery
Wilton
Franklin County, Maine

Rev. Ebenezer BROWN, d. at age 67 yrs. He was ordained a minister of the Freewill Baptist church May 19, 1805. He was married to Hannah, who d. May 29, 1852, age 76. Their daughter, Hannah (Brown) Fletcher, m. Asa Fletcher. She d. Jan. 27, 1877. Brown, after a pastorate of the First church at for many years died after a hurtful and distressing illness. He was excellent as a counselor, and zealous in his work for the Savior.

Jonathan Brown
Birth:
1772
Death:
Sep. 10, 1850
Burial:
Curtis Cemetery, Bowdoinham,
Sagadahoc County, Maine

Jonathan Brown was born in Phippsburgh, ME. At the age of twelve he was converted and baptized. About the year 1803 he began to preach. He was ordained to the Free Baptist ministry in 1808. He was afflicted through much sickness in his family, but as far as possible, he prosecuted his holy calling.

Georges E S Bryant
Birth:
October 28, 1818
Dover-Foxcroft,
Piscataquis, Maine
Death:
1871
Burial:
South Dover Cemetery
Dover-Foxcroft
Piscataquis County, Maine
Plot: North Section, Row 8

George married Nancy S Dexter on 21 Nov 1844 in Dover-Foxcroft, Piscataquis, Maine.He became a Christian at the age of 15 and joined the church. He was ordained about 1860 and license several years before. He was 12 years clerk of the Penobscot Yearly Meeting and preached at Milo and other places. He had an excellent mind and was a good scholar and for a time a student in the biblical school. His sermons were carefully prepared, were instructive, suggestive and plain. He was an acceptable preacher until his health failed. He was a radical supporter of reforms, but was a kind and accommodating person. He was very efficient in the business affairs of the church. In him the churches and institutions of the denomination had a true friend and helper.

God will not let death win

Almira Wescott Bullock
Birth:
1797, USA
Death:
Apr. 25, 1859
Maine,
Burial:
Forest Hill Cemetery
Bridgton
Cumberland County, Maine
Plot: Chap. 19

Minister and wife of Andrew Cobb
Former wife of Rev. J. Bullock.

Jeremiah Bullock
Birth:
1797
Death:
Dec. 16, 1849
Maine
Burial:
Forest Hill Cemetery
Bridgton
Cumberland County, Maine
Plot: Chap. 19

An ordained Free Will Baptist minister.

Wescott Bullock
Birth:
Jul. 7, 1818
Limington
York County, Maine
Death:
1900
Burial:
Greenwood Cemetery
Biddeford
York County, Maine

He received his education in the common schools and at Parsonsfield Academy, and was a teacher in early life. He embraced religion in 1842 and soon after began to preach. The twofold and wonderfully woven mantle of his parents had fallen on him; that part received from his father, coarse, hard twisted and substantial, proved a panoply of security amid the storms that sometimes gathered about the minister's pathway; that inherited from his saintly mother and dyed by her gentle spirit, was of soft and silken texture designed to keep the heart warm and tender. This sacred mantel was "reversible" and sometimes changed in the pulpit, alternating between the rough and silken sides. He was ordained at Saco, in August 1856, preaching the sermon to a vast assembly of people in the town hall. He says "I have preached in various towns of Maine and New Hampshire, sometimes in a fine pulpit, sometimes in school house and sometimes standing on stone walls; wherever I had a thus saith

the Lord." He has always preached what he believed and lived as he preached. In personal appearance both commanding and attractive; his voice pleasant and melodious, and his language plain and pure. He has been a very useful man, who was widely known and much beloved; now passing the snowy years of venerable age, cheered by the sunshine of the Christian's undying hope. He has been incapacitated for active service from paralysis, and says he "lives by praying"; resides in Biddeford, Maine. indicates Ord. 1856. Son of Jeremiah Almira (Wescott) Bullock..

Cyrus Campbell
Birth:
Sep. 29, 1817
Bowdoin
Sagadahoc County, Maine
Death:
Jun. 13, 1893
New Sharon
Franklin County, Maine
Burial:
Weeks Mills Cemetery
New Sharon
Franklin County, Maine

He was converted 25 years of age. He was a student of Whitestown, New York. On October 7, 1846 at the age of 29, he received license to preach and was ordained the following year in September. He pastored a number of churches in the area. On December 8, 1846 he married Adaline Lenpest.

Joseph Chadbourne
Birth:
Jun. 28, 1807
Greene
Androscoggin County, Maine
Death:
Nov. 20, 1877
Bradford
Penobscot County, Maine
Burial:
Corner Cemetery
Bradford, Penobscot County,
Maine

Joseph Chadbourne, at the age of nineteen, while a student in the Seminary at Kent's Hill, became a Christian. Ten years afterwards he became a member of the church in Bradford. He was for a time the efficient deacon of the church. In 1858 he took a letter and joined the Christian denomination, by which he was ordained March, 1859. He was highly esteemed among them.Four years before his death, he again became a member of the church in Bradford. He was much interested in education and a successful teacher. He was frequently elected to officesof trust and responsibility.
Inscription:
JOSEPH CHADBOURNE died
November 20, 1877
age 70 years   4 months
22 days

Edward R. Chadwick
Birth:
Jun., 1861
China
Kennebec County, Maine
Death:
1926
Burial:
Chadwick Hill Cemetery
China
Kennebec County, Maine

He was converted in 1878 and later graduated at the Maine Central Institute in 1880 and then from Bates College in 1884. He was of the class of 1888 of the Cobb Divinity School. In July, 1888 he settled in Milton, New Hampshire and on August 23 he was ordained by the New Durham Quarterly Meeting.
His parents were: Abner D. Chadwick (1831-1911) and Drusilla Newcomb Chadwick (1836 - 1920)

Oren Burbank Cheney
Birth:
Dec. 12, 1816
Ashland, Grafton County,
New Hampshire
Death:
Dec. 22, 1903
Lewiston,
Androscoggin County, Maine
Burial:
Riverside Cemetery, Lewiston,
Androscoggin County, Maine

Dr. Cheney attended Parsonfield Seminary and New Hampton Institution, and graduated from Dartmouth College in 1839. He was converted in the spring of 1836 and, walking from Dartmouth to his native place, he was baptized by Rev. Simeon Dana, and united with the Ashland church. After graduation he became principal of the Farmington ME Academy in the autumn of 1839. He became principal of the Strafford Academy in 1841. Then he taught the Greenland, N.H., Academy near Portsmouth and was licensed by the Portsmouth church. He was ordained in the Effingham Hill, N.H. church, in the autumn of 1844, by Rev. John Buzzell, Rev. Benj. S. Manson, and others. He held anti-slavery sentiments, and this pastorate was laid down because of opposition to his views. In 1851-52, he was sent to the Legislature by the Whigs and Free-soilers, and voted for the original Maine Temperance Law. In 1852, he went to Augusta for five years as pastor of the church. On Sept. 22, 1854, he received a letter from Rev. J. A. Lowell, principal of Parsonfield Seminary, announcing that the Seminary building had been burned the day before. From that day Dr. Cheney consecrated himself to build for the Free Baptists an efficient literary institution in a more central place. President Cheney held many important positions of confidence and trust in this denomination. Twice was moderator of General Conference, and occupied important position on the Conference Board. He represented his denomination as delegate to the General Baptists of England. He has been recording secretary of both the Foreign and Home Mission Societies, and president of the Education and Anti-Slavery Societies. He was foremost in vision to merge the Free Baptists with the larger open-communion Baptist, and worked to that end not only with Baptists but with Christian and other denominations until his demise. He is best known for being the founder and first president of Bates College in Lewiston, Maine. The college was chartered in 1862 and was founded as the Maine State Seminary in 1855.

Blessed *are* the dead which die in the Lord

Hubbard Chandler
Birth:
Jan., 1798
Death:
Nov. 5, 1866
West Poland,
Androscoggin County,
Maine,
Burial:
Highland Cemetery,
West Poland,
Androscoggin County,
Maine

Rev. Chandler was converted and baptized before age 20 by his mother's brother, Rev. Jeremy Bean. He then began to preach and connected himself with the Second Wilton church, preaching in all the towns around and doing evangelistic work, holding revivals with great success. He was ordained at Phillips, ME, June 9, 1822, by Rev's Samuel Hutchins and John Foster. His travels as an evangelist in Maine extended to 120 towns and plantations. All the while, he supported himself, not receiving $50 a year for his labors. Though he was not favored with an extensive education, yet, he was gifted by nature. He was very conversant with Scripture. As a speaker, he was dramatic and was mighty in persuasive powers to move sinners. His earnestness and consecration enabled him to accomplish a great work. He raised up quite a number of churches in the new settlements he visited.

George Colby Dyer Chase
Birth:
Mar. 15, 1844
Death:
May 27, 1919
Burial:
Pond Cemetery 1,Unity,
Waldo County, Maine,
Plot: row 22

Professor of Rhetoric and English Literature in Bates College, Lewiston, Me., was born in Unity, Me. He prepared for college at the Maine State Seminary (afterwards Bates College), and immediately, entered Bates College, where he graduated in 1868.The next two years he was teacher of Greek, Latin and Mental Philosophy, at New Hampton Institution, N.H. He then spent a year in Bates Theological School, and was at the same time a tutor of Greek in the college. He was at this time elected a professor in the college, and after taking a post-graduate course of one year at Harvard College, entered upon the work of the professorship. He was a member of the Lewiston School Board and twice chosen . president in 1883 and 1887. In 1894 George Colby Chase, Class of 1868, succeeded President Cheney. Known as "the great builder," He oversaw the construction of eleven new buildings, including Coram Library, the Chapel, Chase Hall, Carnegie Science Hall, and Rand Hall. Chase tripled the number of students and faculty, and the endowment. He discontinued the Cobb Divinity School and Nichols Latin School departments of the College. In 1907 at the request of Chase and the Board, the legislature amended the college's charter removing the requirement for the President and majority of the trustees to be Free Will Baptists; this change to a non-sectarian status allowed the school to qualify for Carnegie Foundation funding for professor pensions He was for several years a contributor to the "Morning Star."

Aaron Clark
Birth:
unknown
Death:
Dec. 11, 1880
Hennon, Maine
Burial:
Light Cemetery
Knox County, Maine,

He was converted at the age of thirteen. When seventeen years of age, he was licensed by the Methodists as an exhorter. He afterwards united with the Free Baptists, by whom he was ordained about 1840. He preached in several places within the limits of the Montville Q. M. His name appears in the Register in connection with the Washington church from 1848 to 1869; then as pastor of the Second Montville church till 1872; then as pastor of the Washington church till 1875; then as pastor of the South Montville church one year. He remained a member of the latter church till his death.

John Clark
Birth:
unknown
Newcastle. Me.
Death:
Aug. 8, 1871
Prospect
Waldo County, Maine
Burial:
Clark Cemetery
Prospect, Waldo County, Maine
He married and moved to Monroe in early manhood, and in 1824, during a great revival in that section, he was converted and united with the church. He was licensed in1832, and ordained as an evangelist in 1838. He worked hard to support his family, and preached Sabbaths. He was in the ministry about forty years, and traveled in that time about forty thousand miles, at least one half of the distance on foot. He baptized 125, attended 100 funerals; and. Married sixty couples. He preached till within a few days of his death. Though born of poor parents and with limited education, his willing mind enabled him to do a good work Reverend John Clark for whom the Cemetery was named. He was a Veteran of the Battle of Hampden, War of 1812 and began the Clark Settlement, in Prospect, Maine. His broken gravestone is down and buried and no flag marks him as a veteran. He died at age 78 years 8 months, 19 days.

Jonathan Clay
Birth:
December 13, 1775
Buxton Maine
Death:
Feb. 20, 1849
Maine
Burial:
Highland Cemetery
Buxton
York County, Maine

He was converted in 18 and five and was one of the early members of the Buxton church. He began to preach soon after his baptism and was ordained in 1815. His labors were mostly confined to Buxton and in 1831 he took his destination from his church and united with a few others who constituted a church near his home.

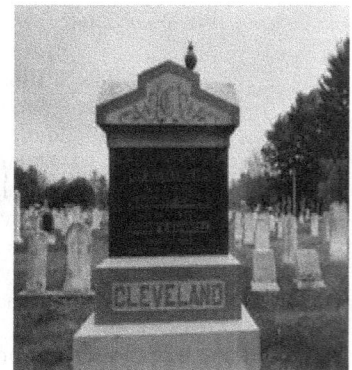

Edward Lindley Cleveland
Birth:
Nov. 6, 1813
Camden
Knox County, Maine

Death:
Mar. 9, 1897
Rockport
Knox County, Maine
Burial:
West Rockport Cemetery
West Rockport
Knox County, Maine

He became a Christian at the age of 24 and was ordained in 1845 by Rev. John Hampton and others. He has preached an evangelist and labored in many revivals. He was a member of the Rockville Church, Camden, and preached as opportunity was offered him.

William G Cobb
Birth:
1779
Otisfield
Oxford County, Maine
Death:
Jun. 2, 1850
Otisfield
Oxford County, Maine
Burial:
Cobb Hill Cemetery
Otisfield
Oxford County, Maine

He was converted to the age of 22 and was baptized by Rev. Zachariah Leach and after preaching considerably for 16 years was ordained in March, 1824. Ill health confined his labors near his home. Note: Age 70 yrs

There is victory for the children of God.

Greenleaf H Coburn
Birth:
Mar. 7, 1839
Turner
Androscoggin County, Maine
Death:
Jul. 11, 1865
Maine
Burial:
Gray Village Cemetery
Gray
Cumberland County, Maine

Died aged 26 years. He early showed a fondness for books. At fourteen he went to Boston, where he was employed till he was seventeen. He was converted in 1857, at Gray, ME, under the labors of Rev. W. T. Smith. He was baptized at once uniting with the church (Freewill Baptist) at Gray. In the spring of 1858, he returned to Boston for another year. Early in 1859, he went to Lewiston and entered Bates College, enjoying the love and esteem of his instructors, graduated from his preparatory course in July 1862. He then entered the Theological School at New Hampton (NH) and after three years graduated being ordained there July 17, 1865. A fortnight later he came to Lewiston and arranged with President Cheney to enter the Junior Class of the College. But in two weeks he was dead from a fever. A gentleman offered to start him in business in Boston, and give him half the profits. "No," young Coburn replied. "I must get an education and enter upon a higher calling." President Oren B. Cheney, Bates College, preached his funeral sermon.

George Warren Colby
Birth:
Dec. 8, 1836
Vassalboro
Kennebec County, Maine
Death:
Jan. 22, 1913
Augusta
Kennebec County, Maine
Burial:
Mount Hope Cemetery
Augusta
Kennebec County, Maine

He was converted to the age of 23. He received license to preach from the Montville Quarter Meeting in March 1874 and was ordained on June 20, 1875 by Rev. Aaron Clark and others. In his many revivals he had between three and 400 conversion, baptized 73. Records show that he married 23 couples and attended 75 funerals. He married Ayrobine DAMON on 16 JAN 1879 in Vassalboro, Kennebec Cty, Maine.
Inscription:
COLBY /CONANT
George Warren
Colby 1836-1913

Joshua B. O. Colby

Birth:
Jan. 13, 1808
Maine
Death:
Mar. 27, 1891
Denmark
Oxford County, Maine
Burial:
Colby Cemetery
Denmark
Oxford County, Maine

He studied for a time at Fryeberg Academy. He became a Christian at the age the 26 and was baptized by Elder Jonathan Tracy and joined the church at Denmark. He was first ordained as a Deacon but soon after on October 6, 1852 was ordained by Rev. James Rand and others. The church in Denmark was under his care for 40 years.

Inscription:
Rev. J. B. O. Colby
Born Jan. 13, 1808
Died Mar. 27, 1891

Jacob D. Couillard

Birth:
Nov. 24, 1815
Frankfort, Maine
Death:
Jul. 18, 1888
Maine
Burial:
Smith Cemetery
Palermo
Waldo County, Maine

He was converted in 1832, and an in Exeter, Maine was licensed in 1834. Two years later he was ordained. He had an itinerant ministry in which he baptized a good number of people and assisted in organizing several churches. After driving for some time in Massachusetts he moved to North Palermo, Maine and did a good work among the destitute churches. He also served during the Civil War.

John Cook

Birth:
May 7, 1809
Alton, Belknap, New Hampshire
Death:
Jan. 4, 1891
Burnham, Waldo, Maine
Burial:
Burnham Village Cemetery
Burnham, Waldo County, Maine

His obituary appeared in the *Morning Star* published on 2 Apr 1891.

Mary Jane (Adams) Cook married Rev. John Cook on 8 Nov 1846. His parents were Jacob and -- (Hubbard) Cook. His education he received from the common school Before he was sixteen his father moved on a new lot in Exeter, Me., where, in the midst of "black logs and flies," he was educated to work with his hands so effectively, that he could support himself and family' by working half the time and have the rest for preaching in destitute places without hire. He found a region of four towns without a preacher. In a town where there had been no religious meetings for ten years, he proclaimed the" glad tidings."He was converted at the age of twenty, received license to preach in 1833, and was ordained June 26, 1837, by Rev's Nathan Robinson, Roger Copp, and John B. Copp. He had revivals, baptized 141 converts in twelve different towns, assisted in organizing seven or eight churches, and married ninety-eight couples. He was chosen pastor of the Burnham church at its organization, July 2, 1857. During the war their church edifice was built. Though his pastorate ceased some time ago, he supplied the church from time to time,. He attended every monthly conference since 1860, and can tell how many times each member had been present for the last eighteen years. He was married Dec. 29, 1833, to Miss Sally P. Kenisten on Nov. 8, 1846, he was married again.

Lavina Carr Coombs

Birth:
Nov. 23, 1849
West Bowdoin
Sagadahoc County, Maine
Death:
1927
Burial:
Woodlawn Cemetery
West Bowdoin, Sagadahoc County, Maine

Coombs, Miss Lavina C., daughter of David and Sarah Coombs, She commenced the Christian life in 1862; attended Litchfield Academy 1864-66, the Normal School at Farmington 187273, and the Lewiston High School in1880. She taught ten years in the schools of Maine, and in November, 1882, was sent by the Woman's Missionary Society as a missionary to India. She located at Midnapore, and took chargeof the Zenana work and the Ragged Schools at that place. Was a Free Will Baptist missionary in India for forty years, teaching in a school and helping the team there. 1882- 1922.

Freeman Cooper
Birth:
February 6, 1835
Wakefield, Maine
Death:
Apr. 11, 1900
Maine
Burial:
Oak Hill Cemetery
Windsor
Kennebec County, Maine

He was converted to the age of 35 and send began to preach the gospel. He received his license on February 15, 1873 and was ordained by the Montville quarterly meeting on September 20, 1874. He pastored many of the churches in that area of Maine and held revivals throughout the region.He was a Member of Co.F 21st Me. Reg during the Civil War.

Charles T. D. Crockett
Birth:
Mar. 15, 1833
Woodstock
Oxford County,Maine
Death:
Jun. 25, 1899
Maine
Burial:
Hunts Corner Cemetery
Albany
Oxford County, Maine

He Was A Student At Gould's Academy In Bethel, Maine. After His Conversion On February 8, 1875 He Attended Bates Theological School, Lewiston, Maine. With his wife he was baptized at Mechanic Falls on May 16 1875 by Rev. B Menard. He was licensed to preach on January 27th, 1876 and ordained at Canton on June 8, 1877 by Rev. J. M. Pease, and others. He preached at West Paris where the church was revived and the next four years at Canton. After preaching at many churches in the area he settled at Jackson, New Hampshire where a house of worship was thoroughly repaired and well furnished and the church strengthened by the addition of excellent members. In 1888 he became the pastor of the church at Steep Falls, Maine and served branched churches..

True W. Dore
Birth:
Nov. 6, 1806
Death:
Mar. 26, 1879
Garland, Maine
Burial:
Hathaway Cemetery
Garland
Penobscot County, Maine

Converted in early man hood, he soon began to hold meetings. Gifted in prayer and song he labored as an evangelist with success. He first united with the Methodists, but it Ripley, Maine, he joined the Free Baptists and was ordained by them in June 1842. He preached at Ripley, Garland, and in the vicinity for other.

Inscription:
I have kept the faith.

Because he rose, we too shall rise.

Joseph Dyer
Birth:
1774
Boston
Suffolk County,
Massachusetts
Death:
Jan. 31, 1859
Phillips
Franklin County, Maine
Burial:
Riverside Cemetery
Phillips
Franklin County, Maine

Rev. Joseph DYER, was the son of a sea-captain, and was one of the memorable party who threw the British tea into Boston harbor. His mother's was Elizabeth Nichols, of Malden, MA. At the age of eight years, Joseph's father died, and Joseph was bound out to learn the Morocco shoe trade. He married Miss Sally Merritt, of Malden,where he resided till he removed to Hallowell, ME, in October 1806. He had already experienced religion and joined the Calvinistic Baptist church in Massachusetts. He was ordained in 1810, and when the Free Baptist church which had been established by Benjamin Randall in 1795, was reorganized, Nov. 12, 1819, Rev. Dyer was one of the eleven included in the reorganization. With this church he was worthily connected until Sept. 17, 1831, when with others he organized a new church in

Madrid, where his labors had been blessed. Over this flock he watched with ceaseless interest for more than a score of years, when failing health induced him to resign the charge to a younger brother.Though engaged in pioneer work in this section, making his way with his precious message on horseback through the wilderness, guided by spotted trees and preaching the gospel chiefly in log cabins, yet he was progressive and was practically interested in the moral and educational enterprises. He was devout and eminently spiritual in prayer. He lived to see his great-great-grandchild. He was universally esteemed for his kindliness of heart and the purity of his life.

Ebenezer G Eaton
Birth:
Jul., 1808
Death:
Aug. 13, 1883
Lewiston, Me.
Burial:
Oak Hill Cemetery
Auburn, Androscoggin County,
Maine

Eaton died at age 76 years. He was thoroughly converted in1831. He studied at Parsonfield Seminary and held meetings in Freedom, N. H., where sixty were converted. He was ordained at Freedom July 14, 1833, by Rev's Hosea Quinby and John Buzzell. He was for a time a missionary in the Otisfield Q. M., being the first preacher in the Q. M. who received a salary. He preached in Otisfield, Harrison, Bridgton, Brunswick, Auburn, Buckfield, Canton, Livermore, Greene, Poland, South Lewiston, Bethel and Sabattus. He also preached three years in Nova Scotia, and in a great revival there one hundred and seventy-five were added to the churches. During his ministry, he baptized 1000 persons. He was a schoolmate of President Cheney,

who wrote of Eaton, "He was a good man and full of the Holy Ghost and of faith, and much people was added unto the Lord."

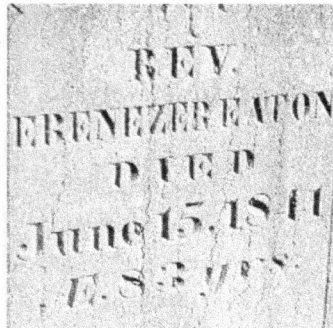

Ebenezer Eaton
Birth:
unknown
Death:
Jun. 15, 1841
Androscoggin County, Maine
Burial:
Sedgwick Rural Cemetery
Sedgwick
Hancock County, Maine

Rev. Ebenezer Eaton Died June 15, 1841 (Age 83 years.). Ebenezer Eaton was the son of Theophilus Eaton and Abigail Fellows. He was married about 1777 to Abigail Herrick, the daughter of Joshua Herrick and Huldah Brown. Abigail is buried in Southwest Harbor, Maine,

where Reverend Ebenezer Eaton was the town's first established minister. He was converted in 1831 after which he stated to attend Parsonfield Seminary and held meetings in Freedom, New Hampshire, where 60 were converted. He was ordained at Freedom on July 14, 1833, by Rev. Hosea Quinby and John Buzzell. He was for a time a missionary in the Otisfield Quarterly Meeting being the first preacher in the quarter meeting who received a salary. He preached in the churches at the following towns of Otisfield, Harrison, Bridgton, Auburn, and numerous other places in the area. He also preached three years in Nova Scotia and in the and in a great revival where 175 were added to the churches during his ministry he baptized 1000 people. He was a schoolmate of Pres. Cheney, who wrote of him, "he was a good man and full of the Holy Ghost and of faith, and much people were added unto the Lord."

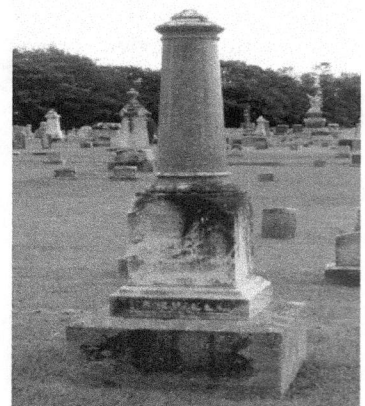

Josiah Farwell
Birth:
unknown
Death:
Mar. 10, 1872
Burial:
Pittsfield Village Cemetery,
Pittsfield,
Somerset County, Maine

Ordained a Free Will Baptist minister in 1817 in Maine, but after a time he left the church.

Charles W. Foster
Birth:
Feb. 3, 1836
Harrison, Maine
Death:
Sep. 16, 1902
Burial:
Evergreen Cemetery
Phillips
Franklin County, Maine

He attended the Bridgeton Academy and Westbrook Seminary. He was converted on May 30, 1870 in the Methodist Church at South Harrison. After three years he yielded to a call to the ministry and preached his first sermon in the Grand Hill schoolhouse in York. He was licensed in 1874 and ordained by the York and Cumberland Christian conference on October 19, 1875. On June 21, 1878 he united with the Free Baptist Church in Bridgeton. He was also treasurer of the town of Bridgeton for three years. In the Civil War he served in Battery A 1st. Reg. Me. Vol. Lt. Art._____Regt.

Joseph Foss
Birth:
1765
Lee, Strafford County, New Hampshire,
Death:
Dec. 28, 1852
Brighton,
Somerset County, Maine
Burial:
Mount Rest Cemetery, Athens, Somerset County, Maine
An ordained Free Will Baptist minister. He went west to Brighton, ME, in 1812, and began holding meetings. He became pastor there and stayed pastor for forty years, doing much ministerial work in towns that

had no regular minister. He preached more than fifty years and died in his 88th year of age.

William E. Foy
Birth:
1818
Death:
Nov. 9, 1893
Burial:
Birch Tree Cemetery
East Sullivan
Hancock County, Maine
Plot: Very back of the cemetery on the right

William was born a free black boy. His parents were Joseph and Betsy Foy. His home was near Augusta, Maine. Even though slavery was not tolerated in the north, free people of color were not considered equal to whites. There isn't a lot of information about Foy's parents, but seems that Foy was allowed to read books and attend school. William Foy had a friend whose name was Silas Curtis. Silas was an ordained Freewill Baptist. It was through the ministry of Silas that Foy became converted at the age of 17. Foy continued to study and followed his mentor's footsteps in becoming a minister. Foy was an unusual black man. Foy was tall and light skinned. He was gifted as an eloquent speaker. Witnessing for God, however, wasn't always easy for Foy. He worked hard among both the blacks and whites and led many people to know Jesus. Early in 1842, Foy had experienced two visions about Christ's second

coming and the reward of the righteous. Because of the visions, he joined the Millerite movement. However, he was reluctant to relate the visions publicly because he was aware of the prejudice displayed toward blacks. Foy was attending ministerial school in Boston at the time. A fellow pastor of the Episcopal Methodist Church encouraged Foy, and he began relating the visions to large audiences throughout New England.

The third and last vision Foy experienced was in 1844. That vision showed three levels. #1...God guiding his people from truth to truth; #2...testing the truths God's people had discovered; and #3...ultimate victory when the saved reach the Holy City because they believed and followed God's messages. Foy was experiencing financial pressures and there were things about the vision that he could not understand. Therefore, he stopped recounting them. Foy moved back to Maine and continued to minister to the FW Baptist and Methodist congregations. William Foy is considered as a prophet for the time prior to the Great Disappointment.

Inscription:
Rev. William E. Foy.
Died in Plantation at Age 74 years.
Also buried here is his daughter,
Laura, age 7 years

"What shall be the end of all
covetous persons?
—Eternal damnation."

Thomas Flanders
Birth:
Unknown
Alton, New Hampshire
Death:
1839
Burial:
Knowlton Mills Cemetery
Piscataquis County, Maine

He was ordained in 1825 and labored to in New Hampshire

and Maine.

Jarius Fuller
Birth:
May 27, 1805
Maine
Death:
Jan. 23, 1877
Maine,
Burial:
Harding Cemetery
Brunswick, Cumberland County,
Maine

Jarius married Sophia (Cargill) Fuller. He was an ordained minister/pastor in the Freewill Baptist church in Maine, and pastored in Greene, ME, where in 1826, revival was seen in that church, resulting "in twenty being added to the church." He also pastored at So. Monmouth, and other places, and was known to be a faithful man.

William F Gallison
Birth:
Windham, Me,
Jan. 14, 1799
Death:
Mar. 9, 1858
Burial:
Dover Cemetery,
Dover-Foxcroft,
Piscataquis County, Maine,
Plot: North Section, Row 3

At age eighteen, he professed Christ, and was baptized by Rev. C. Phinney in Feb. 1817. He moved to eastern Maine at age twenty-five, and settled in Charlotte. He united with the Christian church in that place and maintained an outward life beyond reproach. He served his townsmen as officer in the militia and as magistrate. In 1832, he was a member of the State Legislature. In 1834, moving to Dover, Me, he joined the Free Will Baptist church, and the next year began his gospel ministry. He had in early life received a good academic education. He was licensed by the Sebec Quarterly Meeting, in January, 1840, and was ordained in Dover, July 8, 1841. His labors in the ministry were confined mostly to the Sebec Q.M. Fourteen ministers attended his funeral.

For me to live is Christ, To die is gain.

Mark Gatchell
Birth:
May 17, 1812
Litchfield
Kennebec County Maine
Death:
Jul. 28, 1887
Burial:
Litchfield Plains Cemetery,
Litchfield Plains,
Kennebec County, Maine

He became a Christian under the labors of the Rev. Dexter Waterman and was baptized at the age of 16. He began to preach at the age of 20 and was licensed two years afterwards. He was ordained by a council at the Bowdoin Quarterly Meeting at 24 years of age. He pastored many churches in Maine and records show that he was asked 25 times to harmonize difficulties in churches. He was a member of the legislature the year that a grant was made to the Maine State Seminary.

William Getchell
Birth:
Dec. 6, 1793
Vassalborough, Me.,
Death:
Oct. 30, 1867
Pittsfield, Me.
Burial:
Carr Cemetery
Pittsfield, Somerset County, Maine

He married, Aug. 22, 1814, Miss Mary Leavitt, of Clinton. In the summer of 1818 he was converted and united with the Christian church at East Pittsfield. In August, 1823, having moved to another part of Pittsfield, he was instrumental in organizing a Freewill Baptist church and was chosen one of its deacons. In September 1826 he was ordained by a council from the Exeter Q. M. as pastor of the church with which he was connected. This relation he held till death. He also acted as pastor of the Second Pittsfield church and of the Burnham church for over twenty years. He solemnized over one hundred and fifty marriages and attended hundreds of funerals.

Harry O Gidney
Birth:
July 9, 1829
Cambridge
New Brunswick
Canada
Death:
Nov. 11, 1895
Maine
Burial:
South Amity Cemetery
South Amity
Aroostook County, Maine

He became a Christian at the age of 20. In 1860 he moved on Houlton, Maine, where he lived 16 years and then moved on to Amity where he resided for some time. He received license in 1868 and was ordained in the same year. His pastorates were at the Glenwood church, a Littleton, second Hodgdon, and other churches in that area of Maine. He had revivals in each of the churches where he pastored and baptized over 100 converts. He organized a Littleton and Haynesville churches.

Capt Philip Gilkey, Sr
Birth:
Jan. 25, 1788
Islesboro
Waldo County, Maine
Death:
Jan. 5, 1872
Searsport
Waldo County, Maine
Burial:
Gordon Cemetery
Searsport, Waldo County, Maine

He lived in Islesborough till forty years of age, and the rest of his life in Searsport. He was converted in youth, but did not decide to preach till he was more than fifty years of age. He was then a Baptist. His first efforts were in the town of Eden, Mt. Desert, where some were converted. He was then ordained by the Free Baptists, and preached mostly in Eden. Philip was married to Jane Pendleton (1789 - 1821) They had 7 children. After Jane died, Philip married Deborah Cushing (1787 - 1865). They had 6 children. Deborah was the widow of Philip's brother Jacob. After Deborah died, Philip married Judith Pendleton (1794- 1892), they had no children.

**There is no
sting
when you die in the Lord.**

Lincoln Given
Birth:
Nov. 7, 1827
Wells, Maine
Death:
Oct. 8, 1894
Maine
Burial:
Pond Road Cemetery
Androscoggin CountyMaine

He was a brother of the Arthur Given. He was converted at the age of 15 and was baptized by Rev. E. J. Eaton and United with the church in Wales in the spring of 1843. He received his early education at Litchfield Institute, and his theological in the Biblical School at New Hampton. In June 1854 he received license to preach from the Bowdoin Quarterly Meeting and in June 19,1859 he was ordained at a session of the Springfield Quarter Meeting At Weston by Rev. L. M. Hagget and others. Most of his pastorates was in Maine and New Hampshire. However he did spend 18 months in Minnesota and six months in Illinois where many were converted for his efforts. He was a member of the General Conference three different times. He taught 15 terms of school and served as a supervisor 15 years. In 1851 he married Miss Lucy A. Colby who died in 1869 and afterwards he married in December 1873 Miss Carrie Weymount.

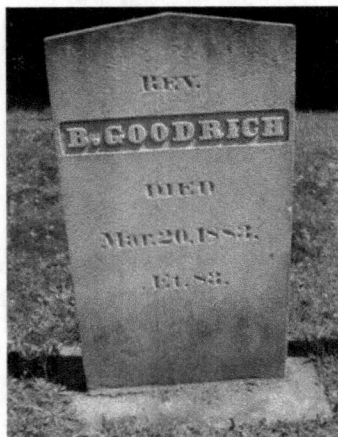

Barnard Goodrich
Birth:
1800
Nottingham, N. H.
Death:
Mar. 20, 1883
Burial:
Ripp Cemetery
West Gardiner
Kennebec County, Maine

He became a Christian in early life. About 1831 he moved to Maine. He preached and baptized in Monmouth, West Gardiner, Greene, Litchfield, South Gardiner and Richmond. He supported himself at the trade of blacksmith and preached as opportunity offered.

Joseph Goodwin
Birth:
Jul. 10, 1788
Death:
Mar. 21, 1850
Wells, Maine
Burial:
Goodwin Cemetery
Oxford County, Maine

He was converted in 1801, and on August 28 joined the Baptist church. The next year his name appears as one of the committee who transcribed the articles of faith and records of this newly organized church. Later difficulties some years distracted the church and the radical preaching of the election by the pastor caused some to question the doctrine. He and 13 others were expelled on June 4, 1807. They associated themselves for worship with himself as the leader. In 1808 a revival followed and a Free Baptist church was organized over which he was ordained as pastor in 1812 and for 13 years this relationship existed. He supported his family by labor in the ship-yards but his excellent gift of exhortation frequently gave him wholely to the Lord's work.

Oh! How precious is the dust of a believer!"

John Grant
Birth:
unknown
Death:
Oct. 25, 1882
Bucksport
Hancock County, Maine
Burial:
Oak Hill Cemetery
Bucksport
Hancock County, Maine

He was a native of the Province of New Brunswick, but moved to Maine in 1839. He was converted to the age of 16 and publicly professed Christ eight years later and in 1842 was baptized uniting with the Hodgdon church. He was licensed by this church in 1859 and ordained a few years later. His preaching was characterized by interesting expositions of Scripture.

Andrew Gray
Birth:
Sep. 2, 1823
Brooksville, Maine
Death:
Mar. 24, 1901
Burial:
Otter Creek Cemetery
Hancock County, Maine

He was converted at the age of 28, and was licensed to preach on December 12, 1854 and ordained on June 17, 1872. He had for pastors and baptize 83 converts at four churches.

Stephen Gross
Birth:
unknown
Death:
Nov. 27, 1887
East Bucksport
Hancock County, Maine
Burial:
Granite Cemetery
Orland
Hancock County, Maine

He died at age 85 and his wife only two days later. Throughout his earnest early ministry many of the churches in the Ellsworth Quarterly meeting were strengthened, if not planning. He was loyal to his denomination and an early subscriber and devoted reader of *The Morning Star*. He was earnest in securing the salvation and especialty of the young, and in urging them to seek good learning as an advantage for their life work.

Throughout his faithfulness many found their saviour.

S. M. Haggett
Birth:
Nov. 8, 1818
Edgecomb
Lincoln County, Maine
Death:
Aug. 23, 1878
Springfield
Penobscot County, Maine
Burial:
Mills Cemetery
Springfield, Penobscot County, Maine

At the age of seventeen he became a Christian and united with the church in his native town. Soon he felt called to the ministry, and received encouragement from the church.In 1840, he went to Parsonfield Seminary, and was a student there three years. The Edgecomb Q.M. gave him license in 1842. He traveled and preached in New Hampshire and Vermont with good success. From 1845 to 1849, he preached in Penobscot. In 1849 he settled at Monroe. The next year, in June, he was ordained by the Prospect Quarterly Meeting. After several years at Monroe he went to North Bangor, where many were converted under his labors. At this place in 1852, he married Miss Delia H. Rollin.The next year he preached in the Springfield Q.M. At Chester he held meetings and where he organized a church. He was a delegate to General Conference in 1856. The same year he became pastor of the Springfield church. He served as clerk of the Q.M. sixteen years and attended all its sessions and all the Yearly Meetings. He was the town clerk nine years. In 1871, he resigned the pastorate of the Springfield and Carroll church, and in 1873 he served as missionary in the Springfield Q.M. The next two years he preached in Gardiner, ME, and then returned to Springfield. He baptized over four hundred, and attended over eight hundred funerals.

Ephraim Harding
Birth:
December 23, 1809
New Sharon, Maine
Death:
1892
Burial:
Corinthian Cemetery
Corinth
Penobscot County, Maine
Plot: Div. 3 Lot 25

His father was Jedediah Harding M.D.who was buried at sea when Ephraim was only 13 months old. At the age of seven he was sent away on among strangers. He was converted on October 25, 1825, at the age of 13 and was baptized by Rev. Samuel Hutchins, united with the church in his native town. In 1838, he began to preach and on October 13 received his license. January 29, 1843, he was ordained at New Portland by the Anson Quarterly Meeting. He was pastor of 14 churches and had revivals in 15. He baptized over 150 people. He organized eight churches during his ministry. Five times he was a delegate to the General Conference and wants to the Free Christian Baptist Conference of New Brunswick.

We are made for a new life and a new body and a new existence with the Lord.

Lot L Harmon
Birth:
1826
Madison, New Hampshire
Death:
1905
Burial:
Mount Auburn Cemetery
Auburn
Androscoggin County, Maine

He became a Christian when 10 years old and studied at Parsonsfield Seminary and Bangor Theological Seminary. He was licensed in 1856, and was ordained March 5, 1857 by Rev's. M.J. Steere, P. S. Burbank and J. R. Cook. He pastored churches through out the area and after graduating from the Seminary he continued to pastor the North Bangor church and made a specialty of Sunday school work, mostly in Maine. Being a gifted musician and singer, sometimes for weeks he talked and sang with the children three or 3 1/2 hours a day. He was a member of the Maine legislature in 1866 and assisted in getting the charter of the Maine Central Institute. He was a general agent of the Sunday School Union from 1868 to 1883 and recording Sec. of Free Baptist Sunday School Union from 1877 to 1882. Before he entered the ministry he was a justice of the peace and had charge of schools in Madison, New Hampshire.

Samuel Hathorn
Birth:
Sep. 14, 1794
Bowdoinham
Sagadahoc County, Maine
Death:
Dec. 13, 1858
West Gardiner
Kennebec County, Maine
Burial:
Ridge Road Cemetery
Bowdoinham
Sagadahoc County, Maine

Rev. Samuel Hathorn was converted in 1817 in revival conducted by Asa Foster. He was active and consecrated, and 1819, in connection with Andrew Rollins and one other,

he purchased a tract of land and began clearing it. In Jan. 1821, Rollins began to preach, and Hathorn soon sold the land and began his labors with the Rock River church in the vicinity in Sept. 1825. The First Church in town grew from this church. He was licensed by the Bowdoinham Quarterly Meeting, in Oct 1825, and Jan. 12, 1826 was ordained. After an itinerant ministry of five or six years in his QM, he extended labors over the state. Late in 1836 he went to Indiana and after a brief visit to Maine in the summer of 1837, he returned and settled at Milan, Ripley Co. Indiana with his wife, and lived there three years. Finding the climate ill suited to their health, they returned to the home of their early years. Before 1844, he had made four tours through the Western States. In 1852, his wife died of consumption. In July 1853 he married Cordelia Clough, who survived him. They spent the following winter in the Western States and on their return to Maine they purchased a farm at West Gardiner. He preached his last sermon May 30, 1858 at Bowdoinham Ridge from Hosea 6:3. He spoke of his uninterrupted peace and joy, and of the brightness of his hope beyond. During his ministry he baptized 1350 persons. Many churches were gathered and organized.

George W Haskell
Birth:
Dec.9, 1814.
Poland,ME.
Death:
Dec. 31, 1874
Hodgdon, Aroostook County, Me.
Burial:
Hodgdon Cemetery
Hodgdon, Aroostook County,
Maine

He became a Christian in early life, and resisted for some time a call from God to the ministry. He was ordained in 1840, and after three years of very successful evangelistic work, moved to Aroostook County. In 1844 he married Miss Hannah M. Smith, of Hodgdon, and resided in the town of Hodgdon the remainder of his life. His labors in Aroostook County were very extensive, and resulted in the conversion of about one thousand, the most of whom he baptized. His last work for the Master was the erection of the house of worship at Hodgdon. He identified himself with the anti-slavery movement, and represented his district in the Legislature in 1855, 1866, and 1867. As the result of his benevolence and large heartedness, he had great popularity.

Inscription:
In Memory of
Rev George W Haskell
Died Dec. 31, 1874 AE 60 yrs
He being dead yet speaketh

Asa Hathaway
Birth:
Sep. 26, 1842
Atkinson, Maine
Death:
Apr. 20, 1914
Burial:
Hathaway Cemetery

Garland
Penobscot County, Maine

He was educated in the public schools of his time and converted in 1875 and ordained in September, 1884. He was the father of Rev. Leonard Hathaway who also served in Maine. He married Vivania R. Batchelder Hathaway (1846 - 1933) on January 5, 1869.

Leonard Hathaway
Birth:
1802
Middleborough, Mass.,
Death:
Nov. 7, 1876
Burial:
Hathaway Cemetery
Garland, Penobscot County, Maine

A preacher in the F.W.Baptist Denomination fifty-one years. Ordained in 1826. His labors have been in Maine. Died at age 74 yrs.29 ds.

*Inscription:
Front *I have finished the work which thou gavest me to do.*
Back:*The gospel which he preached for more than fifty years sustained him to the last.*
Right:*Faithfully he done the work of the ministry Firmly he kept the faith Surely he wears the crown. Sacred is his memory.*

Joseph Higgins
Birth:
1776
Death:
1837
Burial:
Thorndike Center Cemetery
Thorndike, Waldo County, Maine

Rev. Joseph Higgins of Thorndike, Maine, aged 91 years, and his wife, Betsey Higgins, aged 89 years, both died on the 5th of February, 1867, and within ten hours of each other, by no especial sickness except the gradual breaking down of old age. Father Higgins was born in Eastham, Mass., in 1776. Mother Higgins, whose maiden name was Files, was born in Gorham, Maine, in 1778. He came to Thorndike, then called Lincoln Plantation, and felled the first tree on the farm where he ever afterwards lived, in 1797, being one of the very first settlers in town. They were married in 1804, were blessed with eight children, all of whom lived to have families of their own. One of the two sons, Joseph Higgins, Esq., has always lived on the farm with his father and had three children. Still there had never been a death on that dear old homestead until father and mother Higgins passed over the Jordan together. He retained his mental faculties and physical strength in an unusual manner - enjoying life, and contributing to the enjoyment of others till the last days of his life. She was a devoted and cheerful Christian and a most affectionate wife and mother, and although her memory failed, and she was quite childish for the last few years, yet her happy disposition and social, buoyant spirit continued with her to the end. Father Higgins had a good education for his time and taught the first three schools ever taught in Thorndike.

He experienced religion in 1803 and joined the Freewill Baptist Church organized there in that year. He commenced preaching in 1806 and was ordained in 1811. He was an honor to his profession to the day of his death. He worked on his farm through the week and preached on the Sabbathentirely without salary, as was the custom in those days. His preaching was candid, Practical, and very scriptural, the Bible being his chief book of study. The Freewill Baptist Church in Thorndike owes much of its strength and prosperity to father Higgins. For years he preached and lived when many ministers would have been discouraged. And for many years last past, having voluntarily resigned the pastorate, his life, advice, sympathy and means have been a great help to those who have ministered to that church and people.He was a most conscientious and exemplary man in his daily life, showing love to God, man and his country. He was prompt and accurate in his business affairs and quite successful in temporal as well as spiritual things.They gave their eight children a good home and school education, so that they are among the most respectable and influential members of society. Seven of them are living, and they were all present at the funeral, and the aged parents lived to see all their children worthy members of Christian churches. Their life work so perfectly done, there is a pleasing sublimity in the fact that these venerable parents were taken together from earth to heaven. And it adds to the moral grandeur of the scene when we remember that it can literally and truthfully be said of them in the language of scripture, "And they were both righteous before God, walking in all the commandments and ordinances of the Lord blameless." (Written by E. Knowlton in the *"Morning Star"*

Albert G. Hill
Birth:
Apr. 27, 1838
Newfield
York County, Maine
Death:
Jan. 26, 1907
Garland
Penobscot County, Maine
Burial:
Mount Pleasant Cemetery
Dexter
Penobscot County, Maine

He attended the Parsonfield Seminary and New Hampton Institution. In 1858 he was converted and was licensed in 1867 and ordained by the Cumberland Quarterly Meeting in 1869.

Andrew Hobson
Birth:
Sep. 10, 1795
Buxton,
York County, Maine
Death:
May 1, 1877
Cambridge,
Middlesex County,
Massachusetts
Burial:
Steep Falls Cemetery,
Steep Falls,
Cumberland County, Maine

He was converted at age 21, under the labors of Rev. Clement Phinney, was baptized by Rev. Jonathan Clay, and united with the Free Baptist church in Buxton. He began to preach in 1821, and was ordained two years after. He pastored several churches, including So. Gorham, Buxton, fifteen yrs and built a new

meeting house there, Fort Hill, Steep Falls, ten yrs. He returned to Steep Falls in 1862, and in ten years baptized over fifty. In 1871, he entered upon his last pastorate which was at Hollis. He was one of a committee of twelve in favor of establishing a General Conference, and was a member of the first and of several other General Conferences. He was one of the original trustees of the "Morning Star" (newspaper). Every genuine interest received his sympathy. He had one son, Pelatiah M. who became a Free Will Baptist minister.

God pours life into death and death into life without a drop being spilled.

Pelatiah M. Hobson
Birth:
Jul. 20, 1818
West Buxton,
York County, Maine
Death:
Jan. 8, 1888
Steep Falls,
Cumberland County, Maine
Burial:
Steep Falls Cemetery,
Steep Falls,
Cumberland County, Maine

He was educated at Parsonfield Seminary (later Bates) and Gorham Academy, and was a member of the first class in the Biblical School at Parsonsfield. He received license from the Gorham Quarterly Meeting in 1842, and was ordained by the Bowdoin QM, at Bath, ME, in July, 1843.He was pastor of the North Street church, Bath, and remained two years, baptizing about twenty. He engaged in business with his father at Steep Falls. He helped build up the church there, which was organized in 1847. Beginning in the spring of 1856, he was pastor of this church three years, and added sixty to its membership, forty by baptism.

Alphonso L Houghton
Birth:
May 3, 1847
Weld, Me
Death:
Oct. 2, 1881
Weld, Me
Burial:
Oak Grove Cemetery
Bath, Sagadahoc County, Maine

He was the eldest child of Azel E. and Betsey (Hawes) Houghton. "When about sixteen years of age he became a Christian, was baptized by Rev. Orin Pitts
and united with the church. He graduated from Bates College in 1870, as valedictorian of his class, and at once entered the Theological School. During
this course he was a tutor in the college. In May, 1872, he received a unanimous call to the church in Lawrence, Mass. He accepted the call and began his labors there in July ; was ordained and installed Sept. 4. Jan. I, 1873, he married Miss Hattie B. Mallet, of Bath, Me., in whose death, three years later, he was grievously afflicted. He

held the pastorate eight years, when broken health compelled him to resign. As a minister, the scholar and pastor were most finely blended. He was an organizer. Besides the addition of nearly three hundred members to the church during his pastorate, he trained the church into such order and efficiency that, when he was cut off, the church went on steadily with its work. For several years he served on the school committee in Lawrence. He was a member of the executive board of the Foreign Mission Society, and a trustee of Bates College. He left his excellent library and $1,000 to this institution, $500 to the permanent fund of the Bible School in India, and a microscope and cabinet of minerals to Maine Central Institute. After seeking recovery in Europe and in Colorado, he returned to his native place shortly before his death.

Francis Howard
Birth:
Nov. 2, 1810
Ward, Maine
Death:
Feb. 11, 1892
Washington
Knox County, spaceMaine
Burial:
Howard Cemetery
Knox County, Maine

His conversion happened

when he was 13 years of age. In 1843 he was licensed and the same year ordained. He labored in many revivals and was a pastor eight years. He has baptized 74 and attended 412 funerals.

Eld Samuel Hutchins
Birth:
Nov. 29, 1790
New Portland, Me.
Death:
Apr. 9, 1876
West Waterville, Me.
Burial:
East New Portland Cemetery
New Portland, Somerset County, Maine

He was converted when twelve years of age, and began to preach at the age of nineteen. In 1810, at the age of twenty, he was ordained and became the first settled minister in New Portland. Previous to his marriage, he taught school and preached in Madison. He witnessed several revivals there. In Mt. Vernon many were converted under his labors. He also preached in Boston, Mass., Portland, Bangor, and Augusta. He was pastor at Norridgewock several years. He then moved to Belgrade, and was pastor of the church there and at the same time at Smithfield, till his death. He baptized more than 1,000 persons, and his labors "were widely known and appreciated throughout the Kennebec Y. M. For several years he was military chaplain. He was a representative in the Legislature two or three years, and while there preached in Portland. He was a member of the Second andThird General Conferences. Inscription: Age 85y 4m 10d.

Leonard Hutchins
Birth:
April 20, 1828
New Portland, Maine
Death:
1915

Burial:
East New Portland Cemetery
New Portland
Somerset County, Maine

His mother died when he was 12 years old and three years later he was converted. He studied in the schools near him, and dwelt with his father until the father's death in May, 1868. He had been licensed in June, 1853 and was ordained September 21, 1856. He entered Bangor Theological Seminary in 1869. He pastored a number of churches in the area and had revival interest in each of his churches, baptizing 50 in Garland, and about 150 and other pastorates. From 1883 through 1887 he was employed in missionary work by the Maine State Mission Society in Anson Quarterly Meeting having under his care the churches in Stark, Freeman and Salem, Lexington and Dead River. He was the clerk and treasurer of the Anson Quarterly Meeting and also was a trustee of the Maine Central Institute.

Asa Foster Hutchinson
Birth:
Aug. 1, 1824
Buckfield, Maine
Death:
Dec. 2, 1893
South Portland, Maine
Burial:
Mountain View Cemetery
Auburn
Androscoggin County, Maine

His parents were Rev. Samuel and Mercy (Randall) Hutchison, and a cousin to Rev. C. T. Keen. He was converted at 15 and studied in North Bridgeton Academy, Maine and in Strafford Academy and in the Biblical School at Whitestown, New York. He was licensed in September, 1845 and ordained in September, 1850. He pastored many churches in that area and baptized 185 converts. He was on school committees in various towns and in 1865 he represented the towns of West Garndiner, Farmingdale, and Pittston in the legislature.

Benjamin Jaques
Birth:
1790
Death:
Jul. 16, 1878
Lisbon, Me
Burial:
Riverview Cemetery
Topsham, Sagadahoc County

Jaques died at aged 87 years and 8 months. He was converted in April, 1825, and baptized the next year. He was in the ministry more than forty years.

John B Jordan
Birth:
September 30, 1850
Auburn, Maine
Death:
1925
Burial:
Oak Hill Cemetery
Auburn
Androscoggin County, Maine

He was converted as a boy, and at the age of 16 was baptized. He united with the Court Street church, Auburn. His early education was with a business life and view. In March, 1868, when 17 years of age he accepted the position of messenger and

bookkeeper in the First National Bank of Auburn, and was promoted in 1871 to the position of Teller, and in February, 1874, was elected cashier, which office he held until 1882, when he resigned and accepted a call to the pastorate of the Pine Street church, Lewiston, Maine. For a number of years he was active in evangelistic work in connection with the YMCA. He received license to preach June 11, 1878 and was ordained on may 25, 1882. During his pastorate with the Pine Street church 122 were added to its membership, 100 by baptism. In August 1883, he accepted a call to the first church, in Minneapolis, Minnesota. He remained with this church until October,, 1885 but not before 53 had been added to the church. There after he became pastor of the Augusta church in July, 1886. During the first year, 30 were added to the church. In December, 1886 he was elected chaplain of the Maine Insane Hospital. He was a member of the General Conference in 1886. He was the corresponding Sec. of the Maine Home Missionary Society and clerk of the Maine Central Yearly Meeting. He was a member of the city Council of Auburn for two.

William P. Kinney
Birth:
Mar. 7, 1833
Queensberry
New Brunswick, Canada
Death:
1916
Maine
Burial:
Old Baptist Cemetery
Yarmouth
Cumberland County, Maine

He became a Christian at the age of 16 and was educated in the Houlton Academy and Bangor Theological Seminary.

His license to preach was granted on March 15, 1873, and on March 17, 1881 he was ordained. He held eight pastorates and several revivals and baptized 20 convert. He helped organize four churches. He was clerk of the quarterly meeting for a number of years and was a trustee of the Maine Central Institute and a member of the legislature of 1876.

Ebenezer Knowlton
Birth:
Dec. 6, 1815
Pittsfield, N. H.
Death:
Sep. 10, 1874
Montville, Me.
Burial:
Pine Grove Cemetery
South Montville, Waldo County,
Maine

His father moved to Montville in 1828. He obtained a thorough academic education and became a teacher in early life. He was converted in 1832, and united with the church in Montville. The day that he decided to preach the gospel was the day he was elected speaker in the Legislature of his state. He preached his first sermon at Hallowell, Aug. 9, 1846, from the words" We love him because he first loved us." He was ordained Dec. 17, 1848. His labors covered a wide territory in eastern and central Maine. He preached in Rockland two years at different times. The rest of his ministry was in connection with the Montville churches. He went far and near to solemnize marriages, attend funerals and deliver temperance and Sunday-school addresses. At the close of 1852, he wrote in his journal: "number' of funerals attended during the year, sixty; sermons preached, 171; religious meetings attended, 332; temperance and Sunday school lectures, twenty-three." In 1853 the Legislature elected him State Treasurer, but he declined the honor. He consented, however, in 1854, to be elected to Congress, upon the advice of his brethren, but declined a re-electiion in order to devote himself to the work of the ministry and also to work for the Maine State Seminary. When he accepted the nomination to Congress he informed the convention that nominated him, that if elected, he should go to Congress as a Christian minister devoted to the interests of humanity; that he would accept the nomination only as from freemen desiring to be represented by a freeman; that he should allow no allegiance to any clique or party in any way to interfere with a strict adherence to freedom, country, and God. While in Congress he wrote weekly letters to the *Morning Star,* subscribing himself "Daniel" This correspondence attracted considerable attention. He took an interest in the colored people and preached the gospel to them. He preached one half of the Sabbaths during the time he was in Congress. In 1869, there was a general desire among the Republicans of Maine that he should be their candidate for Governor. But although great pressure was brought to bear upon him and he was himself disposed to consent for the sake of the principles of temperance, he finally refused to allow his name to be used. Mr. Knowlton had all the mental and moral qualities that go to make up the real statesman, such as ability, strength, foresight, decision, honesty, integrity, love of humanity, and fear of God; and the only reason he did not rise to higher positions in the affairs of state was because he declined to do so, believing that, as a minister of Christ, he was holding the highest office on earth. When urged to become a candidate for Governor, he wrote to a leading religious politician saying, among other things: "You urge me to be Governor so as to enforce prohibition. I know rum-selling is a crime and grog-shops are a nuisance. A radical law with front teeth and grinders should be kept on the statute book and be lived up to. But a correct moral sentiment among the people is the only means to secure this end. This moral sentiment grows only out of the gospel. The Christian ministry is the leading agency in spreading the gospel. So do let me alone, that what there is left of me may be devoted to the appropriate work of my profession. It is easier to find good and suitable material to make governors of, than it is to find good and suitable material to make ministers. It is but little I can do anywhere, but I would rather see one young man in my congregation soundly converted to Christ than to have any office in the gift of man." He was often appointed to preach at denominational gatherings, but accepted with extreme diffidence. He was desired as pastor in Lewiston, Auburn, Augusta, Portland, Boston, New York and other places, but accepted none of these positions. He was very firm in his denominational loyalty. He was one of the projectors of the Maine State Seminary, which grew into Bates College. Other positions of responsibility were as follows: Trustee of Colby University, trustee of Bates College, president of the Foreign Mission Society, corporator of the Printing Establishment, and moderator of three General Conferences. He died suddenly while taking a bath in a pond near his home, where he was accustomed to fish and swim. His death was conspicuously noticed by resolutions in town meeting, and by the denomination in which he was a pillar of strength.

Zina Knowlton
Birth:
Sep. 20, 1813
Swanville
Waldo County, Maine
Death:
Sep. 7, 1885
Monroe
Waldo County, Maine
Burial:
Mount Solitude Cemetery
Monroe
Waldo County, Maine

Married Nov 2 1833 in Swanville and was a Free Will Baptist minister.

George Lamb
Birth:
1788
Lincolnville,
Waldo County, Maine
Death:
Dec. 14, 1836
Brunswick,
Cumberland County, Maine
Burial:
Growstown Cemetery,
Brunswick,
Cumberland County, Maine
He became interested in religion when but a boy, and was converted and joined the Free Will Baptist Church. His circumstances afforded him little advantage of an education, but he had an inquisitive and well-balanced mind, he worked with a clergyman in his preaching endeavors, and his success was such that he was licensed and ordained in 1813.He gathered a church in Bangor Me, but he declined settlement. His brethren wanted him to go to Topsham where the church was waning.

There was a remarkable revival commenced and he baptized about 40. (It was here that the later eminent scholar, Prof. John J. Butler, was influenced by good from Rev. George Lamb, with whom he stayed while a student there.

John Lamb
Birth:
Jun. 7, 1776
Nova Scotia, Canada
Death:
Jun. 4, 1828
Waldo County, Maine
Burial:
Center Lincolnville Burying Ground
Waldo County, Maine

In 1805 he was ordained and for 20 years he had a useful ministry. He preached the gospel without any salary and at the same time supported with hard labor a large family. For some time his public ministry was hindered by asthma.

Zachariah Leach
Birth:
Jun. 7, 1765
Raymond
Cumberland County, Maine
Death:
Nov. 3, 1841
Raymond
Cumberland County, Maine

Burial:
Raymond Village Cemetery
Raymond
Cumberland County, Maine

He was ordained a Free Will Baptist minister on Nov. 6, 1794 by Rev. Benjamin Randall, and others. In 1799 he became clerk of the Edgecomb Q. M. In 1808 he had an extensive reformation at Standish, in which Joseph White was converted and soon became an efficient minister. He preached three times at the Y. M. at Edgecomb in September 1811. He was followed by John Buzzell and John Colby. March 18,1812, he wrote to the *Religous Magazine* of an agreeable journey he had among the churches of the Sandy River country. He made the ordaining prayer while Joseph White preached the sermon at the ordination of Clement Phinney at Standish Neck in 1816. In 1834 he added forty-six to his church by baptism and the next year twenty-nine.

Samuel Lewis
Birth:
1825
Buxton, Maine
Death:
Oct. 12, 1850
Burial:
Hackett-Notch Cemetery
New Vineyard
Franklin County, Maine

At the age of 24 he married Phepe Irish. He was converted at the age of 28 and was baptized by John Buzzell. He moved to Chatham, New Hampshire and began to preach and some years later he moved to Harrison, Maine where he had great revivals. He was ordained in Sebec Quarterly Meeting in 1832 and was instrumental in promoting revivals in this new section and organizing and substaining several of the churches that composed Springfield Quarterly Meeting.

Almon Libby
Birth:
Oct. 10, 1816
Minot, Maine
Death:
Nov. 1, 1895
Burial:
Stroudwater Burying Ground
Portland
Cumberland County, Maine

He became a Christian at the age of 16 and was a student in the Parsonfield Seminary. In 1837 he was ordained by the Cumberland Quarterly Meeting. All of his pastorates were in the state of Maine. He labored in many revivals and baptized a large number of converts. In 1886 he was an agent for the Androscroggin County Bible Society. He has been a member of the General Conference. He had two sons that graduated from Bates College; one is a civil engineer, and the other is a district attorney in Colorado. His youngest daughter was on the

staff of the Lewiston Journal.

David Libby
Birth:
Jun. 2, 1822 Portland,
Cumberland County,
Maine
Death:
1901
Burial:
Lisbon Cemetery, Lisbon,
Androscoggin County, Maine

He was a younger brother of Rev. Almon Libby. He became a Christian when fourteen years of age; was licensed in June 1845, and ordained by the Bowdoin Quarterly Meeting, two years later. He had pastorates in South Lewiston, Harrison, Harpswell, Freeport, Poland and Lisbon. He baptized a large number of converts.

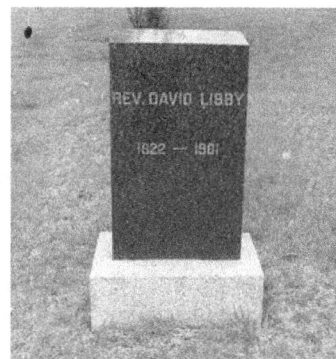

James Libby
Birth:
Oct., 1796
Auburn,
Androscoggin County, Maine
Death:
Mar. 6, 1884
West Poland,
Androscoggin County, Maine
Burial:
Highland Cemetery,
West Poland,
Androscoggin County, Maine

Rev. James Libby, became a Christian at the age of twenty, was baptized by Elder Leach and joined the church in that vicinity. In 1828, after serious conviction, he consecrated himself to the ministry, and was ordained at Danville by Rev's Z. Jordan, J. White and J. Clay. In 1832, he moved to West Poland, and for thirty-three years was pastor of that church. Early in his pastorate a meeting house was erected. There were several extensive revivals with large additions to the church. The Second Poland church grew out of this church. In the course of his ministry of more than sixty years, he baptized about one thousand converts, married several hundred couples and attended the funerals of 1500 persons. His valuable labors were frequently sought by various pastors in protracted meeting

Jason Mariner
Birth:
November 14, 1824
Lincolnville, Maine
Death:
Nov. 18, 1891
Burial:
Union Cemetery
Lincolnville Center
Waldo County, Maine

He was converted through the Ministry of Rev. John Stevens who baptized him at the age of 18 when he fully gave his heart to God. He preached his first sermon on 14, 1843 in the same church where he was converted. He was a student at Whitestown, New York after which he was licensed at Montville Quarterly Meeting and ordained at Lincolnville with Rev. Ebenezer Knowlton preaching. He held numerous pastorates in New York, Maine, Massachusetts, and Rhode Island. He was a trustee of the Maine State Seminary and Bates College for 25 years.

Moses McFarland
Birth:
unknown
Death:
Nov. 1, 1865
Burial:
Mount Repose Cemetery
Montville
Waldo County, Maine

He was ordained in 1806 and nine in May. In 1818, 40 were converted under his labors and the Second Montville church was organized. Early in 1827, he was charged with preaching Universalism. Rev. Ebenezer Knowlton of Pittsfield, New Hampshire had moved to the area in time to save the church from defection. At the June Quarterly Meeting a charge was brought against McFarland. In September a committee of seven was appointed, with Rev. Benjamin Thorn as chairman. McFarland finally separated from the quarter meeting in December, 1827.

Elbridge L McKindsley
Birth:
1839
Whitefield, Maine
Death:
1911
Burial:
Whitefield Cemetery
Whitefield
Lincoln County,, Maine

He was converted to the age of 13 and studied at Pittston Academy he was licensed in September 1883 and was ordained in September 1886. He preached as an evangelist most of his ministry.

John Miller
Birth:
May 13, 1806
Durham
Androscoggin County, Maine
Death:
Dec. 5, 1869
Durham
Androscoggin County, Maine
Burial:
Union Cemetery
Auburn, Androscoggin County,
Maine

He was converted in 1829 and began to preach with the Methodists in 1837. He afterwards joined the Free Baptists and continued a good and acceptable minister with them until his death. He felt especially called to preach to the poor, and his labors were fruitful. He was a man of much prayer, strong faith, fervent love, and deep piety. He was married to Hannah, dau. of Samuel and Catherine (Clark) Robinson on 2 Dec 1830.

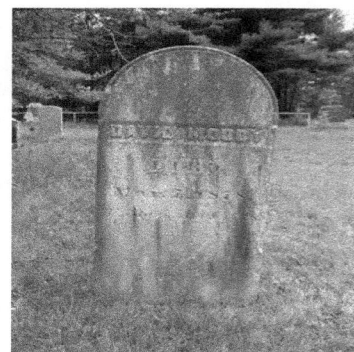

David Moody
Birth:
December 3, 1804
GilmanTon, New Hampshire

Death:
Mar. 7, 1878
Burial:
Mount Solitude Cemetery
Monroe
Waldo County, Maine

He was converted at age 18, and received his license the following of May, 1824 and was ordained two years later by Rev's. Enoch Place, S. B. Dyer, and Moses Bean, Ebenezer Knowlton and Arthur Caverno. He was in the ministry more than 63 years. The first 10 years was spent in evangelism, with his ministry beginning at Bethlehem, where he had an extensive revival. He helped numerous churches throughout New Hampshire and during this time baptized 171 converts, married 197 couples and attended 572 funerals. On March 19, 1827, he married Miss Sally Bean.

Samuel Plummer Morrill
Birth:
February 11, 1816
Chesterville, Maine
Death:
1892
Burial:
Chesterville Hill Cemetery
Chesterville
Franklin County, Maine

He was a student at the Farmington Academy, and was converted at the age of 18, licensed in 1839 at the age of 23, and ordained in 1841 by the Rev. Dexter Waterman. He held many pastorates in the state of Maine after his ordination, but in 1885 he settled in Vienna, Maine where

a good revival was enjoyed. In his 11 pastorates he baptized in all 75. In 1886 he lay aside an active ministry due to poor health. He was a member three times at the Gen. conference; and assisted in organizing several churches. He was elected to the 41st Congress of the United States and served during 1869-70. On November 28, 1838, he married Mary J. Chase.

Levi Moulton
Birth:
1812
Death:
May 10, 1846
Burial:
Academy Cemetery
Lee
Penobscot County, Maine

He drowned while crossing a lake in a boat with others coming out of the woods from a lumber drive, when a squall hit the boat. The body was found and buried in June on the lake shore. His funeral was attended by Rev. Moses Ames of Garland. He experienced religion about 1834 and was baptized by the Rev. Samuel Lewis, after which he joined the church at Lee. This Sebec Quarterly Meeting granted him a license in January, 1838 and ordained him the following July. He was blessed by revivals in his tours through the Springfield Quarterly Meeting. He had a deep love for the Bible, and was a friend of the Bible school at Whitestown and especially advocated the cause of the slave.

Joseph Nickerson
Birth:
Apr. 10, 1833
Litchfield. Maine
Death:
Feb. 27, 1909
Burial:
Litchfield Plains Cemetery
Litchfield Plains
Kennebec County, Maine

Converted at 17. In December, 1878 he received his licensed to preach and on October 11, 1883 was ordained by Rev. Mark Getchell and others. His pastorates were in the vicinity of his conversion.

Joseph N. Noble
Birth:
Apr. 29, 1847
New Brunswick, Canada
Death:
Feb. 2, 1912

Burial:
Evergreen Cemetery
Houlton
Aroostook County, Maine
Plot: Section 6, Block 13, Grave

He was converted on September 27, 1866 in Canning, Nova Scotia under Rev. Charles Knowles. He yielded the call to preach in May 1882. He was licensed to preach at Upper Woodstock, New Brunswick. In October he began working with the Bridgewater, Maine church, where upon his labors he was ordained by the Houlton Quarterly Meeting on December 18, 1886.

Lemuel Norton
Birth:
Jun. 21, 1785
Edgartown
Dukes County, Massachusetts
Death:
Sep. 18, 1866
Burial:
Hillrest Cemetery
West Tremont, Hancock County, Maine

Son of Noah and Jerusha (Dunham) Norton. (Noah served in Revolutionary War and died in Mass.) He married Mary "Polly" Norton. Rev. Lemuel Norton, was ordained in 1817, in the Calvinist Baptist, but after ten years preaching, changed his views and united with the Freewill Baptist in 1828, and organized a church at Mt. Desert. In 1840, he became pastor of the Belmont Church, and served in the ministry faithfully until his death from cancer of the stomach, at the home of his daughter, Mary. He requested to be "buried on Mt. Desert Island," where he had organized the first Freewill Baptist church in Hancock County, ME.

Albert Pease
Birth:
Oct. 21, 1811
Norridgewock, Maine
Death:
Jul. 16, 1898
Burial:
Pease Cemetery
Avon
Franklin County, Maine

He came to Christ in 1830 and in 1832 was licensed. In 1843 he was ordained by the Farmington Quarterly Meeting. At first he was an itinerant preacher preaching mostly in Maine. However, thereafter he preached in Massachusetts and Rhode Island, but due to his health he lived with his father in Maine and therefore held many pastorates at the time while his health was poorly. He finally engaged in farming and became a successful writer for agricultural papers. He also wrote the *History Of Phillips*, the city where he lived. He married on February 24, 1830 Ms. Ann Huntoon. His eldest son was a captain of the 17th Regiment New York volunteer's.
Inscription:
"Preacher - Poet - Farmer"

Ezekiel Gilman Page
Birth:
Dec. 25, 1814
New Sharon
Franklin County, Maine
Death:
Jun. 17, 1909
Kennebec County, Maine
Burial:

Litchfield Plains Cemetery
Litchfield Plains
Kennebec County, Maine

His parents were Reuben and Elizabeth (Jackson) Page...He married in March, 1837, Miss Mary G. Bursley, deceased, and has one son living. He married Mrs. Mary Bates, of Oakland, Sept. 12, 1885. He was ordained Dec. 10, 1839" according to "Ordinations" on page 164 of Volume II, Number 1, June 1840, the *Freewill Baptist Quarterly Magazine.* He has been pastor in Edgecomb, Booth Bay (sic), Woolwich, Westport, Brunswick, Georgetown, Richmond Village, West Gardiner, Winnegance, Bowdoinham, Richmond Corner, Litchfield Plains and West Bowdoin. During his ministry he had charge of two churches at the same time and never without a pastorate or appointment in his 47 years of ministry. Baptized between 400-500, and married 211 couples.

Inscription:
Rev.E. G. Page
Died June 17, 1909
age. 94 yrs.

John Page
Birth:
Feb. 11, 1787
Wentworth
Grafton County, New Hampshire
Death:
Aug. 17, 1834
Garland
Penobscot County, Maine
Burial:
Hathaway Cemetery
Garland
Penobscot County, Maine

He was converted in 1805 and began to preach in 1808. On March 20 of that year he was married by the Rev. Hezekiah Buzzell to Susan Clark and moved to Alton where he served the church at East Bridge. He was ordained they are in 1811 and was pastor of the church 12 years engaging at the same time successfully as an evangelist in the country around assisting in the organization of several churches. In 1820 he moved Maine and begin preaching in that area and organized a church at Garland where he was the pastor for 10 years.

Inscription:
That gospel he preached for twenty two years triumphantly supported him in the hour of death.

William Paine
Birth:
Nov. 19, 1760
Woolwich
Sagadahoc County, Maine
Death:
Oct. 14, 1846
North Anson
Somerset County, Maine
Burial:
Gray Cemetery
Embden
Somerset County, Maine

He was converted under the preaching of Reverent Edward Locke after which he joined the Free Baptist Church. Two years later his wife was converted and united with the church. He was ordained as a minister in the Anson church in October, 1808, with which he remained till death. He was a husband for 60 years and the father of 15 children. He fought in the Revolutionary War as a private in Capt. Wiley's company, Col. Michael Jackson's regiment in 1777. He enlisted at age of 17 and served about three years. Lived in North Anson, Maine. A son of John Payne. A headstone marks his grave. Ref: Daughters of the American Revolution Magazine, Vol 36 January-June, 1910

The dead in Christ will rise first.

Benjamin P Parker
Birth:
May 16, 1835
Kittery, Maine
Death:
Aug. 3, 1924
Burial:
Hillside Cemetery
North Berwick
York County, Maine

His father was ordained as a Christian minister about 1867. When he was about two years of age, his parents moved to Newburysport, Massachusetts, where his early life was spent in study in the public schools. He was converted on April 18, 1852 and on his 17th birthday was baptized by Rev. Daniel Pike, joining the Christian church there. In the spring of 1859 he united with the First Baptist Church at Greenwood, Maine and on June 2, was licensed at the Otisfield Quarterly Meeting. His first pastorate was at New Gloucester, Maine; in 1862 he moved to Kittery, his birthplace, and was employed at the Navy Yard for six years. Thereafter, he held a number of pastorates in Maine, New Hampshire and Vermont. He was the first vice president of the Maine Home Mission Society, clerk of the Strafford, Vermont Quarterly Meeting and attended one of the General Conferences.

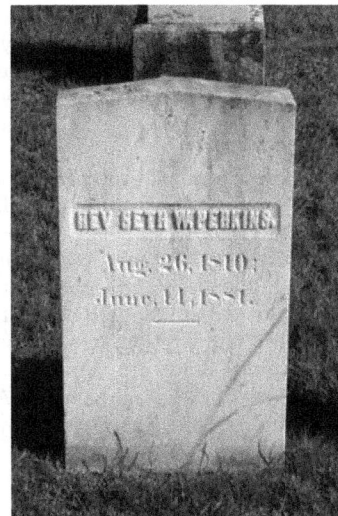

Seth W Perkins
Birth:
Aug. 26, 1810
Death:
Jun. 14, 1881
Hollis, Me.
Burial:
Riverside Cemetery
Dixfield, Oxford County, Maine

About the year 1866 he settled in South 'Wheelock, Vt., and remained three years; then he was pastor of the

Eaton and Newport church, Province of Quebec, three years. After this he was pastor one year in each of the following places in Maine: Canton, Wiltoll, Weld, New Sharon, South Montville and New Gloucester.

Clement Phinney
Birth:
Aug. 16, 1780
Death:
Mar. 2, 1855
Burial:
Western Cemetery,
Portland
Cumberland County,
Maine

He became a minister in the early 1800's. He served at the Free Will Baptist Church, Standish, Maine from 1816-1825. Had a talent for singing, and frequently used it in meetings and at school. He had an unusual wit, won many friends and could hold the undivided attention of large audiences. A book on his life was written by D.M. Graham.

Joseph Phinney
Birth:
unknown
Death:
December 3, 1869
Harrison, Maine
Burial:
Saint John Cemetery
Pembroke
Washington County, Maine

He died in his 81st year and for many years he preached the gospel with a particular power and success until he was trouble with ill health.

John Pike
Birth:
Aug. 25, 1793
Cornish,York County, Maine
Death:
Nov. 29, 1877
East Fryeburg
Oxford County, Maine
Burial:
Pike Cemetery
Fryeburg, Oxford County, Maine

He was the son of John and Nancy (Thurston) Pike He married Hannah (Hubbard) Pike March 23, 1819, East Fryeburg, Oxford County, Maine. He was in the ministry about fifty years, and preached in Fryeburgh, Brownfield, Harrison, Chatham, Conway, Sweden, Hiram and Sebago. He usually preached to more than one church at a time. His ministry was successful in the conversion of souls. In his former years he did much justice and probate business. He was an earnest advocate of reforms, including abstinence from tobacco.

Inscription:
Age: 84 yrs, 3 mos

John Pinkham
Birth:
Jan. 25, 1808
Death:
Jan. 18, 1882
Burial:
Cook Pinkham Cemetery, Casco, Cumberland County, Maine

He was converted at the age of sixteell and joined the church.

When about eighteen years of age, he began to hold meetings in his own and adjoining towns with good results. At the request of his church the Q. M. licensed him. In 1830, at the age of twenty-two, he was ordained in Freedom, N. H. His pastorates were, Sandwich seven years, Gilford eight years, and Alton five years. He lived at Dover two years, and preached as an evangelist at Great Falls and Portsmouth. In the latter place a church was organized. His health became impaired so that he ceased to preach. He then moved to Casco, Me., and cared for his aged parents while they lived. As soon as health permitted he entered into the work again and preached to churches in the Otisfield and Cumberland Q. M's. As formerly, his labors were very fruitful. The Second Poland church, of which he was a member when he died, held him in high esteem, as did also the community in which he lived.

Inscription:
REV JOHN PINKHAM
BORN
JAN 25 1808
DIED JAN 8 1892
Rest, sweet rest

George Plummer
Birth:
Apr. 7, 1826
Durham
Androscoggin County, Maine
Death:
Jun. 17, 1897
Lisbon Falls
Androscoggin County, Maine
Burial:
Hillside Cemetery
Lisbon Falls
Androscoggin County, Maine

He was the son of Henry and Wealthy (Estes) Plummer. He was licensed to preach in the Free Baptist Church, March 1856, and ordained 22 Dec. 1861.He was pastor in Durham five years, at Lisbon Falls five years, at Freeport one year and W. Bowdoin one year. He baptized 60, married 190 couples, and attended 636 funerals.He was a Member of Maine Legislature in 1859.

Albert Pratt
Birth:
unknown
Death:
Oct. 19, 1886
Sebec, Maine
Burial:
Foss Cemetery
Piscataquis County, Maine

He was converted it to age of 31 and was baptized for the Reverend E. Harding on his 32nd birthday and united with the Sebec church. Three years after, in 1856, he was licensed by the Sebec Quarterly Meeting and at the next annual session was ordained. He preached several years, mostly within the limits of this quarterly meeting with good success.

Henry Preble
Birth:
January 9, 1815

Norridgewock, Maine
Death:
May 5, 1892
Burial:
Maplewood Cemetery
Fairfield
Somerset County, Maine

He was licensed to preach in 1841 and was ordained the next year. For some years he was an evangelist in the Farmington Quarterly Meeting. For nearly 20 years he spent his time pastoring within this body. Thereafter, he labored in the Anson Quarterly Meeting and the Bowdoin Quarterly Meeting as well. He organized a number of churches within the confines of these associations. During his ministry of 46 years he has traveled over 80,000 miles with his own team, not having received as much as four cents a mile for his services. But he served over 40 churches and hundreds were converted and baptized. He was firm in moral reforms and genuine in his loyalty to his denomination.

Nehemiah Preble
Birth:
Sep. 15, 1819
Death:
Jan. 6, 1891
Waterville, Maine
Burial:
Litchfield Plains Cemetery,
Litchfield Plains,
Kennebec County,
Maine

In 1849, he was ordained to the gospel ministry in the Free Will Baptist church. He labored with remarkable results wherein many hundreds were converted and baptized. He was much loved and very successful as a pastor, having held that position in the Free Baptist churches in Gardiner, Manchester, West Gardiner, Richmond Corner, Bowdoinham and Litchfield Plains. Of the last mentioned church, he was pastor for eighteen years. In Litchfield, where a large portion of his work was accomplished, he is held in loving remembrance by hosts of

friends who recall his faithful labors. Elder Preble was a residence in the town of Richmond for nearly half a century.

Jesus is the Life

Elijah H Prescott
Birth:
Feb. 14, 1831
Death:
Sep. 14, 1872
Burial:
Whitaker Cemetery
Albion
Kennebec County, Maine,

Rev. Elijah H. Prescott was a Free Will Baptist minister, noted in the History of the town. He pastored Candia Village, NH FWB church.

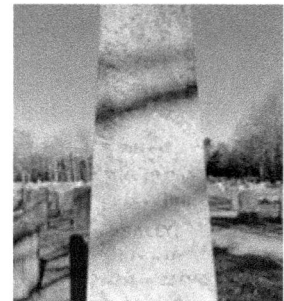

Albert W Purinton
Birth:
Jun. 2, 1811
Bowdoin, Sagadahoc County,
Maine
Death:
May 10, 1878
Maine
Burial:
West Bowdoin Cemetery
West Bowdoin,
Sagadahoc County, Maine

He was the oldest son of Rev. Nathaniel Purinton. He became a Christian when about twenty-two years, influenced by a sermon of

Rev. Joseph White. He was baptized by his father and joined the Second Lisbon church, where he was elected a deacon. After a great struggle, he consented to preach, and was licensed by the Quarterly Meeting in 1841. He preached first to his own church and in other places in his own and adjoining towns. His labors were fruitful, and Jan. 8, 1843, he was ordained. His pastorates were E. Bowdoin, Freeport, two years; Sabattusville, Freeport a second time six years, Bowdoin in all nine years, and Woolwich five years. In 1865 he returned to his native place, where his wife and two daughters died. He then became pastor at Bath four years and afterwards settled at Lisbon, where at the close of an address on Decoration Day in the cemetery, May 30, 1874, he was stricken with paralysis, and after four years of patient waiting he passed to be with his Saviour. In all his pastorates he had marked religious interest, and at Freeport and Bath, houses of worship were build. His second wife, who had faithfully cared for him, was called away seven months before his death

---

Charles W Purinton
Birth:
Apr. 27, 1849
Bowdoin, Sagadahoc County, Maine
Death:
Oct. 21, 1910
West Bowdoin, Sagadahoc County, Maine
Burial:
West Bowdoin Cemetery
West Bowdoin, Sagadahoc County, Maine

He became a Christian at the age of 15 and graduated from state normal school in 1870 and was a student at Lewiston, Maine for three years. In March 1875 he was licensed by that Bowdoin quarterly meeting and on December 27, 1877 he was ordained. He was a member of the General Conference in 1880 and on October 4, 1882 he married

Hattie Newman. He pastored churches in the area. His father was Joseph C. PURINTON, and his mother was Octavia,

Humphrey Purinton
Birth:
Aug. 16, 1758
Bath, Sagadahoc County, Maine
Death:
Jan. 25, 1832
Bowdoin, Sagadahoc County, Maine
Burial:
Old Bowdoin Cemetery
Sagadahoc County, Maine

He was converted at 17 uniting with the Congregationalists at Harpswell. He was a Revolutionary War Patriot from Prov. of Maine serving during 1 Jul 1775-31 Dec. 1777. After his service in the war of the Revolution, in about 1779, he settled in Bowdoin, then a wilderness. He was active in supporting divine worship, and preached some. It became evident that an Arminian element existed in the Baptist church. In the separation which occurred, Bro. Purinton and others united under the name of "Christian Band." Through his ministry large accessions occurred. When the Freewill Baptist movement reached Bowdoin, Purington and his followers joined them. He was ordained in December, 1807. His labors were especially blessed as a revivalist. Finally, with mind bright and soul tranquil, he fell asleep in his 75th year. He was married to Thankful Snow, and they had a large family. Many of his descendants were ministers, deacons and workers in the Free Baptist Church, especially, the West Bowdoin Free Baptist,

Bowdoin, ME.

Nathaniel Purinton
Birth:
Aug. 20, 1787
Maine
Death:
Jun. 12, 1862
Bowdoin, Sagadahoc County, Maine
Burial:
West Bowdoin Cemetery
West Bowdoin, Sagadahoc County, Maine

First pastor of West Bowdoin Free Baptist church. Ordained June 4, 1818. Rev. Nathaniel Purinton was the son of Rev. Humphrey Purinton and Thankful Snow. He was converted in December 1808, when he entered at once upon a faithful Christian life. He commenced a membership for life with the Second Lisbon church at its organization in May, 1818, and the next month he was ordained as its pastor. This relation he sustained till death with but slight interruptions. He was married to Pricilla Wilson, 20 Sept. 1810, Lincoln, ME. He was frequently absent to serve destitute churches, and sometimes had two or three under his pastoral care. He possessed a discerning mind, clearness of utterance, a warm, true heart, and was progressive in regard to the benevolent enterprises of his day. He was constant in his attendance of the Quarterly Meetings, and was frequently engaged on ordination councils and at church organizations. At times he took up the mason's trowel (He was a mason by trade) to enable him to preach the gospel to the poor. He died respected and beloved. One son (Rev. A. W. Purinton), one brother and two nephews entered the Free Baptist ministry.

The Anchor Holds

Constant Quinnam
Birth:
Feb. 9,1807
Wiscasset, Me.
Death:
Apr. 24, 1865
Bowdoinham, Me.
Burial:
Ridge Road Cemetery
Bowdoinham, Sagadahoc County,
Maine

At the age of eighteen, while listening to Rev. E. Hutchins, he decided to accept Christ and was baptized by Hutchins. The woe rested upon him by day and by night, at home and abroad, till he began to preach. He was licensed by the Edgecomb Q. M., Jan. 16, 1830, and was ordained in Whitefield, N. H., Nov. 17, 1831. After an itinerant ministry of several years, during which he saw many converted, teaching school frequently at the same time, he settled as pastor. He was one year each in Georgetown, Booth Bay, Harpswell, Waterville, Hallowell, Richmond and Bowdoin. In 1851 he was pastor of the interest at Litchfield, till in 1855 he entered upon a pastorate at Bowdoinham Ridge which terminated with his death some ten years later. He had good natural abilities, rendered efficient by a good academical training. For several years he served on school committees, and represented both Litchfield and Bowdoinham in the State Legislature. Spouses: Betsey Quinnam (1807 - 1835), & Sarah Swett Quinnam (1809 - 1893).

John Holmes Rand
Birth:
Aug. 3, 1838
Parsonfield, Maine
Death:
Nov. 7, 1907
Burial:
Riverside Cemetery
Lewiston
Androscoggin County, Maine

He was a nephew of Rev. James Rand and was fitted for college at Limerick Academy, Parsonfield Seminary and Maine State Seminary. He was a member the first class of Bates College, graduating in 1867. He at once became a teacher of mathematics and of mental and moral philosophy in the New Hampton Institution and continued in that position until 1876 when he was elected to the professorship of mathematics at Bates College. In 1868, he made a public profession of religion and united with the Free Baptist Church at East Parsonfield, Maine. He was married on November 24, 1881 Miss Emma J. Clark of Lewiston a graduate of Bates College in the class of 1881.

Appleton W Reed
Birth:
Jul. 16, 1821
Albion, Maine
Death:
1911
Burial:

Whitaker Cemetery
Albion
Kennebec County, Maine

He was a student at read to feel Seminary. Converted in August, 1835 he was sliced Sunday in 1840, and ordained that Skowhegan, February 8, 1843. He was for 20 years pastor of the Christian denomination and has been 20 years pastor with the Free Baptists. His pastorates were in New Hampshire and Maine.

John N Rines
Birth:
Apr. 3, 1807
Maine
Death:
Dec. 16, 1874
South Thomaston
Knox County, Maine
Burial:
Pine Grove Cemetery,
Appleton, Knox County, Maine

Rines was married to Mercy Dunham (Pease), daughter of James PEASE and Abigail Dunham. He became a Christian when about twenty-six years, and after a long struggle with duty, he entered the ministry. His fields of labor were Lincolnshire, Dixmont, Plymouth, Carmel, Mt. Desert, Thorndike, Brooks, Montville, Monroe, Waldo, ME. He had great success in most of these places. About 1859 his health failed after which he preached only occasionally. He was an earnest and effective speaker, and a devoted Christian.

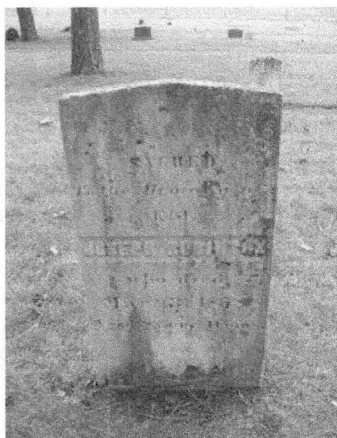

Joseph Robinson
Birth:
1774
Death:
Mar. 3, 1858
Burial:
Litchfield Plains Cemetery
Litchfield Plains
Kennebec County, Maine

He was ordained in Maine in 1818. After of which he assisted in many of the churches and revival seem to follow him in most places he went in Maine.

What is your life? You are a mist that appears for a little while and then vanishes"
(James 4:14b).

Andrew Rollins
Birth:
Sep. 5, 1799,
Topsham, Maine
Death:
Aug. 15, 1859
Burial:
Growstown Cemetery
Brunswick
Cumberland County, Maine

Feeling a call to the ministry in January 1821, he went into the Sandy River country and began holding meetings, and the next year he was ordained by the Gorham Quarterly Meeting at Danville, and had a useful itinerant ministry of eighteen or twenty years.On May 17 1829, he married Miss Huldah Freeman. He accepted a call to Brunswick, and a revival at once beginning over one hundred were baptized. Some four years later, in a protracted meeting of twenty-one days, assisted by Rev. Clement Phinney, he saw another revival in which a hundred were baptized, mostly among the young. In 1841 he became pastor of the church at Topsham, and after two or three years returned to his itinerant ministry. He journeyed preaching through southern New England.

John Alvin Rogers
Birth:
Apr. 29, 1830
Ossipee
Carroll County, New Hampshire
Death:
Feb. 6, 1866

West Newfield
York County, Maine
Burial:
Rogers Family Graveyard
York County, Maine

He was baptized at Lowell, Massachusetts by Rev. A. K. Moulton. At the age of 22 with his family he moved to West Newfield where he married Miss Julia Nealey in 1854. In June 1863, he was licensed up by the Parsonfield Quarterly Meeting. He was ordained at is home on June 21, 1864.

Varnum S Rose
Birth:
Nov. 23, 1810
Islesboro, Maine
Death:
Dec. 14, 1865
Burial:
Islesboro Cemetery #2
Islesboro, Waldo County, Maine

Converted at the age of seventeen, he united with the Baptist church. Ten years later, feeling called to the ministry, on the ground of doctrine he united with the Free Baptists and in 1831 was ordained. He moved later to Monroe on the mainland, seeking for greater usefulness.His last sickness was long and severe. He had good talent as an evangelist.

Psalm 90:5-6, **"You sweep men away in the sleep of death; they are like the new grass of the morning-though in the morning it springs up new, by evening it is dry and withered."**

Nathaniel Kennard Sargent
Birth:
Mar. 23, 1797
Wells
York County, Maine
Death:
Jan. 13, 1876
Kennebunk
York County, Maine
Burial:
Hope Cemetery
Kennebunk, York County, Maine

He was born in the southern part of Wells, and was married Sept. 17, 1818, to Miss Susan Brooks, of Sanford, with whom he lived fifty-four years. He moved to Wells Beach in 1826, became a Christian in 1827, and united with the church in that place. He was ordained at Acton June 8, 1837, by Samuel Burbank and others. In the same year he moved to Kennebunk, and was one year pastor of the church. After this, he preached as he had opportunity in destitute places. He was clerk of the York County Q. M. four years. He was a pioneer in the temperance and anti-slavery causes.

His zeal, conscientiousness and sterling integrity gave him influence in these enterprises. He was appointed collector of customs by President Lincoln in 1861, and held the office till 1875.His wife Susan is recorded as being blind. He was the son of William SARGENT{born - 2 June 1752 at York, Maine who died - 13 November 1824 at Wells, York, Maine Occupation - Farmer; Owner of schooner 'Elmira'

Served in the Revolutionary War}. and wife Susannah ALLEN {born - 26 March 1757at York, York, Maine}.

Inscription:
NATHL. K. SARGENT
died January 13, 1876
aged 78 years 10 months.

Edward Savage
Birth:
Nov. 21, 1766
Woolwich
Sagadahoc County, Maine
Death:
Aug. 27, 1856
Solon
Somerset County, Maine
Burial:
Murphy Cemetery
Embden
Somerset County, Maine

Reverend' Edward Savage moved to Embden, where he was converted in March 1789, and was baptized the same month, being the first person baptized in Seven Mile Brook. A church was organized at Anson in August and united with the Farmington Quarterly Meeting. In 1801, he was ordained, and was devoted to the spiritual welfare of his people and deeply interested in all the benevolent causes of the day.In June 1838, he removed his standing to the Embden and Concord church. He died in his 90th year at the residence ofhis son, at Solon, Maine. Edward and Sarah married on 8 June 1790 at Woolwich, Sagadahoc, Maine left thirten children, seventy-five grandchildren and twenty-five great-grandchildren.

Sargent Shaw
Birth:
Dec. 16, 1791
Standish, Me.
Death:
Mar. 4, 1866
Burial:
White Rock Cemetery
White Rock, Cumberland County, Maine

His father left Congregational church for the Free Baptist church, and he early became acquainted with Randall, Tingley, Buzzell and Stinchfield, as they made his father's house their home. In the revival of 1808-09 in Standish, in which Z. Jordan, A. Files, C. Phinney and J. White found the Saviour, he was converted. After deferring his call to the ministry for years, he was ordained in September, 1828, through the encouragement of Joseph White. He still labored with his hands, preaching as opportunity offered. He was a safe counselor and a true friend to the slave.

Just waiting for the resurrection

Humphrey Small
Birth:
July 26, 1828
Bowdoin, Maine
Death:
1910
Burial:
Rose Cemetery
Brooks
Waldo County, Maine

He was converted when he was 12 years of age and for four years was a member of a Methodist church. He was licensed by the Prospect Quarterly Meeting on June 25, 1858 and then ordained

March 10, 1860. He pastored many churches in the area for many years.

James Small
Birth:
1821
Death:
Feb. 26, 1885
Montville, Maine
Burial:
Halldale Cemetery
West Montville
Waldo County, Maine

He accepted Christ as an early age and was baptized by Rev. J. B. Copp and united with the Exeter church. He began to preach at the age of 19 and was ordained in the Exeter Quarterly Meeting. He preached in countless churches during his 45 years of ministry and baptized a large number of converts

Fred Albertis Snow
Birth:
Nov. 23, 1861
North Berwick
York County, Maine
Death:
Oct. 9, 1931
Islesboro
Waldo County, Maine
Burial:
Burr Cemetery
Freeport, Cumberland County,
Maine

Rev. Snow was the first member of his church, the Freewill Baptist Church of North Berwick, to go to divinity school and to be ordained as a Baptist preacher. He went to Colby College, Waterville Maine and later to Newton Seminary, Andover Massachusetts. He was known as a Hebrew and Greek scholar.

What shall be the end of all covetous persons?
—Eternal damnation.

Moses Stevens
Birth:
1794
Death:
May 28, 1866
Burial:
West Mills Cemetery
Industry, Franklin County, Maine

He was converted in early life, joining the Christian Connection. He united with the Free Baptists from doctrinal preferences, and was licensed *by* the Sebec Q. M. He was ordained in 1832 at Bradford, Me. He joined the Springfield Q. M. at its organization, and for many years was a itinerant ministry. He contributed of his hard earning to the cause of missions and education. He was faithful to truth and a humble Christian.

Freelon Starbird
Birth:
September 14, 1841
Woodstock, Maine
Death:
Jan. 29, 1910
Burial:
Riverside Cemetery
Farmington
Franklin County, Maine

In February, 1877, he was licensed to preach and on June 3, 1880 he was ordained at Milton, Maine by the Otisfield Quarter Meeting. He organized the Carthage church on May 5, 1880

and became it's pastor. He later pastored a number of churches in the area. He was married to Myra C. George and after her passing married on January 30, 1864 to Miss Mary Oldham.

Live For Eternity

William S Stevenson
Birth:
Feb. 3, 1818
Montville, Maine
Death:
May 2, 1891
Burial:
Halldale Cemetery
West Montville
Waldo County, Maine

His father, the Col. William Stevenson, was born in Liverpool, England. He was converted at age 13 and joined the church in North Montville. He yielded his call to the ministry in 1868 at the age of 50 and was ordained in June, 1871 at a session of the quarterly meeting at his church. Rev. Ebenezer Knowlton preached the sermon. He has preached mostly as an itinerant and has seen many revivals.

God ESTEEMS AND CALLS

Joseph Stinson
Birth:
October, 1798
Bowdoin, Me.
Death:
Feb. 27, 1864
Burial:
Tilton Corner Cemetery
Pittsfield, Somerset County, Maine

Stinson, Rev. Joseph, son of Rev. William Stinson of the Christian Connection. He married in 1823 Miss· Mary Whittemore, after which for several years he resided in Litchfield, where he was converted and baptized by Rev. S. Hathorn, uniting with the Free Baptist church there in 1838. In March, 1842, he was ordained by Rev's N. Purington, C. Quinnam and M. Getchell. In 1844 he moved to Pittsfield of the Exeter Q. M., and joined the church there, a relation which continued during life. He served this church with acceptance to their edification. He was deeply interested in the Sunday-school of which he was superintendent.

William C Stinson
Birth:
February 14, 1803
Richmond, Maine

Death:
Jul. 20, 1886
Pittsfield, Maine
Burial:
Pittsfield Village Cemetery
Pittsfield
Somerset County, Maine

He was converted in a revival under Rev. Dexter Waterman. He was ordained in 1857 and in 1861 became pastor away from that area until 1870 when he returned back to Pittsfield where he remained until his death. He was an important factor in the establishment of the Maine Central Institute at Pittsfield. He helped to raise the first $10,000.

If God has Called, Never stoop to be a King.

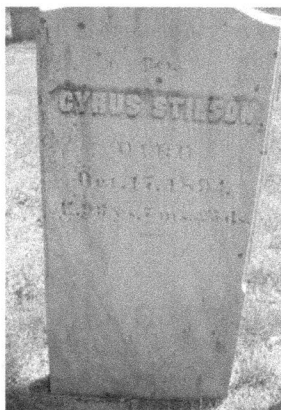

Cyrus Stilson
Birth:
1801
Sydney, Maine
Death:
Oct. 17, 1894
Burial:
New Sharon Village Cemetery
New Sharon
Franklin County, Maine

He was ordained in 1828 and the next year with Leonard Hathaway, entered New Brunswick, Canada, by way of Houlton and for a month preached to large and attentive audiences up and down the St.

John's River. At Hodgdon, where a revival was in progress before they arrived, a church was organized and Stilson remained till August. In the meantime making a tour 100 miles further into the Providence where he not only preached but baptized. Age 93 yrs. 7 mo. 25 days at his death.

Alvah Strout
Birth:
Apr. 28, 1810
Limington
York County, Maine
Death:
Aug. 24, 1881
Burial:
Mills Cemetery
Bradford
Penobscot County, Maine

His ministry extended over 45 years and he did much for the cause of Christ in the Sebec quarterly meeting.

James Strout, Jr
Birth:
Apr. 24, 1800
Limington
York County, Maine
Death:
Sep. 25, 1878
Exeter Center
Penobscot County, Maine
Burial:
Chamberlain Cemetery
Penobscot County, Maine

Rev. James Strout died in Exeter, ME. At the age of seventeen he was converted but lapsed. While in Harrison he lost his wife and a child, and in his affliction he turned to God. After removing to Bradford, ME, he united with the church in March 1834, and soon began to preach. About 1835 he was licensed, and was ordained in March 1839. He traveled extensively, often on foot, and preached mostly without compensation. He was a workman that needed not to be ashamed. He was a good citizen and elected to offices of trust. He was clerk and treasurer of the Penobscot Yearly Meeting. Though the church where he lived was broken up, he continued a zealous supporter of the denomination. His health and hearing failed a few years before his death.

Virgil D Sweetland
Birth:
Sep., 1837
Palmyra, Maine
Death:
unknown
Burial:
Warren Hill Cemetery
Palmyra
Somerset County, Maine

His grandfather was a Revolutionary War soldier and a native of Providence Rhode Island. Virgil studied at the Academy and was a member of the First Main Heavy Artillery in the Civil War serving two years. He took part in the desperate charge of May 18, 1864 at Spottsylvania and was wounded. His conversion, which was sudden and radical, occurred in the autumn of 1862. He began to preach in 1876 and was licensed on June 9, 1877 and ordained at Palmyra by Rev's. James Boyd, John Cook, M. H. Tarbox and others on June 18, 1879. He pastored many churches in the area and at one time even pastored four churches at once. He is attended about 200 funerals and married 61 couples. He has been supervisor of schools, the town clerk, and represented his town in the legislature.

David Swett
Birth:
Jun. 22, 1792
Gorham, Me.
Death:
Jul. 13, 1869
Burial:
Libby Hill Cemetery
Albion, Kennebec County, Maine
Plot: row 1

He was ordained in 1822. In the Montville Q. M. in 1824 at Dixmont and Newburg, he baptized 106 during three months. His ministry was confined to Maine, New Hampshire and Vermont.

Because He lives all fear is gone

Jesse Swett
Birth:
1807
Gorham, Maine
Death:
Mar. 15, 1840
Burial:
Ridge Road Cemetery
Bowdoinham
Sagadahoc County, Maine

He was converted in 1827 and baptized by the Rev. Clement Phinney and united with the church at Windham. In 1828, while in Dover, New Hampshire, with his brother, trying to advance the cause of Christ, he became to consider the duty of the ministry. He already had three brothers in the ministry at that time. He continued to exhort at home until 1830 when he spent some time in Bowdoinham and Litchfield. His work with blessed and in January, 1831 he was licensed by the Gorham quarter Meeting and in June 1832 was ordained by the Bowdoin Quarter Meeting. In September of the following year he formed the Second Richmond church with 15 members and resided there until the spring of 1837 during which time the church and had grown to 50 members. He died at the home of his father-in-all Capt. Sanford in Bowdoinham where his sermon was preached by the Rev. Stephen Purington.

Bradbury Sylvester
Birth:
Nov. 19, 1815
Leeds, Maine
Death:
Aug. 31, 1889
Burial:
Evergreen Cemetery
Wayne
Kennebec County, Maine

He was licensed in 1868 and on September 29, 1877 was ordained by the Bowdoin Quarter Meeting.

Friend D. Tasker
Birth:
Jul. 31, 1850
Jackson, Maine
Death:
Oct. 24, 1904
Burial:
Mount Pleasant Cemetery
Dexter
Penobscot County, Maine

He became a Christian at 28 and on January, 1879 he was licensed, and in December, 1880 was ordained. He held several pastorates in Maine.

Sophia Thomas
Birth:
December 14, 1814
Limerick, Maine
Death:
Jan. 22, 1888
Burial:
Woodlawn Cemetery
Biddeford
York County, Maine

On April 30, 1836 she married Samuel Thomas. She was converted in her childhood and early felt the call to preach. She made a resolute struggle for an education and was greatly interested in God's word. In 1845 she gathered all the Free Will Baptist she could find in Biddeford to her home, where January 15, 1848 a Free Will Baptists church was organized. Her husband became its first Deacon. After many years of devoted ministry she died at her daughter's home.

Thomas W Thompson
Birth:
181
Litchfield
Kennebec County, Maine
Death:
Apr. 26, 1894
Sumner
Oxford County, Maine
Burial:
Fields Hill Cemetery
Oxford County, Maine

His parents were Joel and Rachel (Wilson) Thompson. He became a Christian at the age of eighteen, and was Ordained Freewill Baptist by Rev. C. W. Goule. He had been pastor of the Carthage, Weld, and Livermore churches, and from 1880, of the Summer church. He has organized one church and had three revivals. He was married in 1837 to Miss Hannah Hammond.

Edward Toothaker
Birth:
May 20, 1813
Bowdoinham
Sagadahoc County, Maine
Death:
Feb. 12, 1879
Rangeley
Franklin County, Maine
Burial:
Evergreen Cemetery
Phillips, Franklin County, Maine

His parents moved to Rangeley when he was eight years of age. He became a Christian and a member of the church there in early life. He began to preach when about twenty-one, and was ordained at the June session of the Farmington Q. M. in 1849. His ministry was mostly within the limits of the Farmington and Ansoil Q. M's. His last pastorate was with the Phillips church. He was highly esteemed by those among whom he had faithfully preached the gospel forty-five years and lived an exemplary Christian life.

The LORD *is* my shepherd;
I shall not want.
He maketh me to lie down
in green pastures:
He leadeth me beside the
still waters.
He restoreth my soul:
He leadeth me in the paths
of righteousness for his
name's sake.

Christopher Tracy
Birth:
Oct. 2, 1758
Falmouth,
Cumberland County,
Maine
Death:
Nov. 12, 1839
Burial:
Littlefield Cemetery,
Lisbon Falls,
Androscoggin County, Maine

Eld. Tracy was baptized by Eld. Benjamin Randall in 1781, and was one of the original members of the Free Baptist Church of Durham, organized 1790, of which he remained a member until his death. He was ordained a minister of the gospel, Aug. 31, 1808, by Elders Ephraim Stinchfield, Adam Eliot, and Benjamin Thorn. Rev. Tracy was an evangelist; a well-read and educated man for his time, of excellent judgment; earnest and forceful as a public speaker. He had four sons who were licensed to preach: Jonathan, Asa, Christopher, Jr., and Daniel.

Etta G Goodwin Tracy
Birth:
Oct. 8, 1865
Kennebec County, Maine
Death:
Oct. 17, 1917
Skowhegan,
Somerset County, Maine
Burial:
Mount Auburn Cemetery,
Auburn,
Androscoggin County, Maine

Etta was the daughter of Charles N. and Emma C. (Ellis) Goodwin, both of Maine. She attended Bates College and became a teacher before she was ordained a minister in 1910. She served churches at So. Berwick, ME; Pittsfield and Meredith Center, N.H. churches. She was a resident of New Hampton, NH.

Olin Hobbs Tracy
Birth:
Jul. 4, 1857
Minot,
Androscoggin County, Maine
Death:
Aug. 7, 1944
Stoneham,
Middlesex County,
Massachusetts
Burial:
Mount Auburn Cemetery,
Auburn,
Androscoggin County, Maine

Olin H. Tracy was the son of Ferdinand Tracy and Sylvia J. (Hobbs) Tracy. (He was grandson of Rev. Jonathan and Abigail (Small) TRACY). He was a resident of Lewiston Maine in 1857, where he attended Nichols Latin School, a preparatory school. He then went to Bates College, Lewiston, where he was graduated in 1882. On 3 Nov. 1884, he married Miss Susan Elizabeth Barbarick, at Ossippee, Carroll Co. NH. He was ordained

to the Free Will Baptist ministry on 24 June 1885, by Prof. J. Fullerton, D.D. In 1885, he was graduated from Cobb Divinity School. He moved to Oakland, Alameda Co. CA. after his graduation, and there his wife, Susan died in childbirth in 1891. He moved to Minneapolis, MN, where he was found in 1891. In 1896, he was married to Rev. Etta Gertrude Goodwin, in Kennebec, ME. (She was not ordained until 1910, some years after her marriage). In 1901, at age 44 years, he was awarded the D.D. degree from Hillsdale College, MI. In 1910, he was a resident in Pittsfield, Merrimack, NH, age 63...probably a pastor. Cem., Auburn, Androscoggin Co. Maine.

Jonathan Tracy
Birth:
Dec. 28, 1782
Durham,
Androscoggin County, Maine
Death:
Jan. 24, 1864
Wales Corner,
Androscoggin County, Maine
Burial:
Mount Auburn Cemetery
Auburn,
Androscoggin County, Maine

Jonathan; Christopher, Jr; Asa, and Daniel. Jonathan and his father, Christopher, Sr., were ordained

Free Will Baptist ministers in that part of Maine and did great work. (Hist. of Durham, ME, by Everete Stackpole, Lewiston, 1899.)Rev. Jonathan was named for is grandfather, Jonathan Tracy of Gouldsboro. It was said he was a good type of his ancestors and showed his Norman origin in his extremely light hair and blue eyes. He had a sturdy and powerful frame, though only of medium height. Rev. Jonathan moved to Minot, now Auburn, when a young man. Ordained 24 Feb. 1828. Was called "Scripture Tracy" for his remarkable familiarity with the Bible. He baptized between 700-800 converts, and one time 45 through a hole cut in the ice. He was an earnest advocate of temperance and anti-slavery. He d. at Wales, aged 81 yrs. The text at his funeral was I Cor. XV 58, "Steadfast and unmovable always abounding in the work of the Lord." Two of his grandsons, Rev. A.P. Tracy of VT and Rev. Olin H. Tracy of Boston, entered the ministry of the Free Bapt. Church.

Pelatiah Tingley
Birth:
Jan. 3, 1735
Middlesex County,
Massachusetts
Death:
Sep. 3, 1821
Waterboro,
York County, Maine
Burial:
Woodward/Tingley,
Waterboro,
York County, Maine
At age sixteen, he had serious reflections regarding religion and

was encouraged to obtain a collegiate education. so he went through the preparatory studies, and in 1757, at the age of twenty-two, entered Yale College, in New Haven, Conn. He graduated in 1761. His class at the time of graduating, consisted of thirty young men, of whom ten afterward became ministers, and one of them, several years later, was chosen governor of the state of Georgia. He heard Rev. Benjamin Randall, founder of the Free Will Baptist in NH, preach and felt he had the same sentiments for a general atonement and other biblical doctrines. He joined that church and was ordained a Free Will Baptist Minister in 1764, which he followed until his death. He was the first FWB minister of Waterboro, ME. On Dec. 26, 1787, the town of Waterboro, voted to send the first representative to the Convention in Boston, to ratify the Constitution. The person they chose was Rev. Pelatiah Tingley. (some info from *Memoirs of Eminent Preachers in the Freewill Baptist Denomination--1874* by Selah Hibbard Barrett of Rutland, Ohio.)

Death is a debt

we all must pay.

Sophia Thomas
Birth:
December 14, 1814
Limerick, Maine
Death:
Jan. 22, 1888
Burial:
Woodlawn Cemetery
Biddeford
York County, Maine

On April 30, 1836 she married Samuel Thomas. She was converted in her childhood and early felt the call to preach. She made a resolute struggle for an

education and was greatly interested in God's word. In 1845 she gathered all the Free Will Baptist she could find in Biddeford to her home, where January 15, 1848 a Free Will Baptists church was organized. Her husband became its first Deacon. After many years of devoted ministry she died at her daughter's home.

One never understands Life --until he knows God.

Abel Turner
Birth:
14 Mar 1811
Death:
1878
Burial:
South Dover Cemetery
Dover-Foxcroft,Piscataquis
County,Maine
Plot: South Section, Row 9

He moved to Foxtrot, ME, among the early pioneers. Eld.Turner heard of Baptist meetings in the area when a young man, went to hear, and began his life as a Free Will Baptist, rejecting his Calvinistic upbringing. There is a book, *The Life and Travels of Abel Turner, Minister of the Gospel*--Written by himself, Written for his Wife, dated 1839----------"His father, Abel Turner, it said, was born in Pembroke, Mass, a descendent of John Turner, one who came over with the Pilgrims. He moved to Foxtrot, ME, among the early pioneers, where the last two of his eight children, Adam B., ca 1817, and Betty B, late 1818, were born. Eld. Abel Turner heard of Baptist meetings in the area when a young man, went to hear, and began his life as a FreeWill Baptist, rejecting his Calvinistic upbringing. He was ordained at age 21 yrs, in about 1832. His ministry was in Maine, Vermont, and Western New York. He lived out his life as a FWB preacher in Chester, Penobscot Co. ME.

Matthias Ulmer
Birth:
1809
Death:
Jun. 24, 1878
Appleton, Me.
Burial:
Pine Grove Cemetery
South Montville, Waldo County,
Maine

Ulmer died at age 69 years and 9 months. His father died when he

was young, and being the oldest, the care of his mother and a large family devolved upon him. He fulfilled his trust well. He early became a Christian and was a pioneer worker in every good cause. He organized the first temperance society in that part of the state, in March, 1828. His bold stand against slavery gave him a prominent position in political matters. He lost a son in the war. His labors were mostly with the people of the Montville Q. M., and for fifty years he spared neither time nor money for their advancement. His fine business talent made him efficient in the management of churches.

Sidney Wakely
Birth:
Oct 7, 1850.
Trowbridge Wiltshire, England
Death:
1937
Burial:
New Village Cemetery
Clinton
Kennebec County, Maine

He came to the United States in 1869, when about eighteen years old. He was converted when sixteen and joined the Wesleyan Methodist church in Trowbridge. He joined the Free Baptist church at Lisbon Fallls, ME, and was baptized by immersion. His early education was in the English Church school. He was licensed by his church Feb. 1, 1879, and by the Bowdoin Quarterly Meeting June 1881, and was ordained at West Poland, Maine, by the Cumberland Quarterly Meeting, Oct. 4, 1882. He was pastor at West Bowdoin over a year, West Poland one year, Casco two years, at the same time a year at East Otisfield, and Bow Lake, N.H., three years. He settled at Kittery Point, Maine, March 1, 1855.He was married Aug. 22, 1870, to Miss Emma White of his native place, and had eight children.

John B. Wallace
Birth:
Jan. 31, 1787
Mystic, Massachusetts
Death:
Aug. 19, 1851
Freeman
Franklin County, Maine
Burial:
North Freeman Cemetery
Farmington
Franklin County, Maine

After his birth he was carried by his parents the next year to New Brunswick, Canada. In 1809 he experienced religion with the Baptists. Two years later he married a pious lady, and in 1814 he moved to Marmashe. In 1818, having moved to Belgrade, Maine, he became interested in the reformation there prevailing, and joined the Free Baptist Church. In 1830, he moved to Freeman, near the kingfield line, and by his labors a small church was revived and strengthen till it became large and flourishing. August, 1838 he was licensed by the Anson Quarterly Meeting and on May 11, 1845 he was ordained. He helped organized a church in the center of the town of Freeman where he afterwards lived till his death.

Dexter Waterman
Birth:
Jun. 13, 1807
Litchfield, Me.
Death:
Feb. 8, 1890
Burial:
Growstown Cemetery,
Brunswick,
Cumberland County, Maine

In Jan. 1828, he was licensed to preach for the Free Will Baptist.

He was ordained in July 1828, by Rev's Robbins, Joseph Robinson, and Silas Curtis, and for six years led an itinerant ministry, witnessing many revivals in the Bowdoin and Edgecomb Q.M's. In the twenty-five churches he served, as many as 375 were converted and baptized. Four churches were organized by his help. He became interested in the temperance and anti-slavery movements, preaching, lecturing and voting; has been two years president of the Foreign Mission Society, a member of the board of corporators of the Printing Establishment since 1844, nine times a delegate to General Conference. He was one of the four brethren that originated the call for the convention that organized the Education Society, Jan. 18, 1840, and joined in the efforts to endow that society. His two winters, of seven months each, at Harper's Ferry, were especially blessed. He is now trustee of Bates College and of Storer College. During more than fifty years of active labors at over eighty years of age he was still active, conducting the preaching service every Sunday, and attending the other meetings of the church.

Nathaniel F Weymouth
Birth:
Oct. 3, 1818
Gray, Maine
Death:
Oct. 1, 1887
Burial:
Rogers Cemetery
Troy
Waldo County, Maine

He was licensed in September, 1852 at the age of 34. After this, he was a student five terms at New Hampton, New Hampshire mostly during his 38th year. He was ordained June 18, 1857 by the Exeter Quarterly Meeting. His pastorates were basically in the Exeter area. The Exeter church was organized during his pastorate there. He also assisted

in the organization of several churches and had revivals at Exeter, Pittsfield and Burnham. He gave liberally in the building of churches and for the Maine Central Institute of which he was a trustee. He was also clerk of the Exeter Quarterly Meeting for 12 years. He married Judith P. (Simons) in 1843.

Samuel Wheeler
Birth:
May 20, 1801
Chesterville, Maine
Death:
Apr. 6
Burial:
Chesterville Center Cemetery

Chesterville
Franklin County, Maine

His grandfather came to the United States from England about 1770 and served in the Revolutionary War with courage and gallantry under Commodore John Paul Jones. Mr. Wheeler became a Christian at the age of 17 and was licensed in June, 1841. He was Ordained at Vienna, Maine the following year in June by a Council of the Farmington Quarterly Meeting. He pastored numerous churches in the area. However, he was the most successful as a pastor that Chesterville church which he pastored for 40 years. In 1864 he represented his town in the legislature. He married to November 11, 1823 to Miss Nancy W. Keniston.

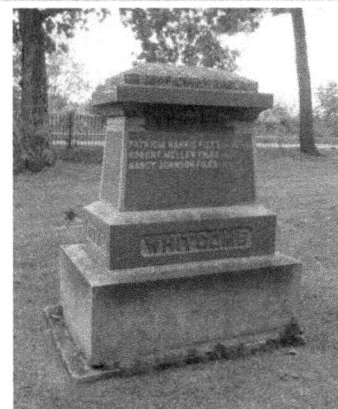

Simeon Coffin Whitcomb
Birth:
Jan. 16, 1845
Thorndike
Waldo County, Maine
Death:
Feb. 24, 1918
Bangor
Penobscot County, Maine
Burial:
Mount Hope Cemetery
Bangor
Penobscot County, Maine

He was a student at Hampden, Maine where he studied at the Academy and later at Maine State Seminary. In 1862, he enlisted in the Army as a private and rose to a second sergeant before the close of the war. At age 22, he was converted and soon felt called to preach. He was licensed in September 1874. He graduated from Bangor Theological Seminary and was ordained at Dover, Maine on July 1, 1875. He held a number of successful pastorates and became a trustee of the Maine Central Institute, Pittsfield, and was clerk of the Maine Central Yearly Meeting. On August 1, 1877 he was married to Miss Celestia Cates.

Joseph White
Birth:
May 24, 1789
Standish, Maine
Death:
May 17, 1837
Burial:
Harding Cemetery
Standish
Cumberland County, Maine

At the age of 20 he witnessed a baptismal of 150 in his town by the Rev.'s Z. Leach and Silas Hutchison. As Leach was coming up out of the water, he noticed a young man of serious face gazing earnestly and said, "come now and let us reason together saith the Lord." These words God blessed to the conversion of Joseph White. In 1814, he became deeply impressed with Colby's petition for help in Rhode Island, and in company with Rev. George Lamb on May 1, 1815 he set out for this field, which for the next 10 years was to be so richly blessed by his ministry. He joined John Colby and for three months they preached together there and in surrounding towns. He returned to Maine and was ordained on November 4 at a session of the yearly meeting held in Fort Hill in Gorham. During the next 22 years of his ministry he was engaged in the Master's work. By June, he left the state to visit the yearly meeting in New Hampshire and make a tour in Maine, at his home administering his first baptism. A little previous to Colby's death in 1817, Colby urgently solicited White to re-visit Rhode Island. A revival attended his efforts at Parsonsfield, Maine. For the next six years he spent most of his time in Rhode Island. On May 16, 1820 he organized the First Smithfield church at Greenville which prospered greatly under his care. At the Rhode Island meeting in October, 1821 the church numbered 144 members. He presented the organization of the quarterly meeting and at that time assisted in the ordination of the first Free Baptist minister ordained in the state. He was greatly used in his state and neighboring states. He was a member of the sixth and seventh General Conferences. With John Buzzell, Henry Hobbs, Enoch Place and Hosea Quinby. He was chosen by the General Conference on the committee of revision for the denominational treatise published in 1834. Two days before his death he said, "I find support in the Christian religion, my soul rest in the bosom of God." And also, "life is none too good to wear out in the service of God." He first married Elizabeth White (1796 - 1863) day next year after their marriage leave you a baby child. Thereafter he married her sister, Catherine White (1798 - 1822).

Thomas White, II
Birth:
1806
York County
New Brunswick, Canada
Death:
Dec. 19, 1859
Hodgdon, Maine
Burial:
Hodgdon Cemetery
Hodgdon
Aroostook ,

He was converted in 1822 uniting with the Christian church in his location. In 1829 he married and moved a Hodgdon where he joined the Free Baptist church under the evangelistic labors of Elder's Leonard Hathaway and Stillson. In 1840, he was called to God and entered the Christian ministry. He was ordained in 1853. Note: Marker placed beside stone by GAR.

Stephen Williamson
Birth:
Feb. 16, 1795
Maine
Death:
Jul. 2, 1873
Stark
Somerset County, Maine

Burial:
Tupper-Williamson Cemetery
Starks, Somerset County, Maine

Williamson, died in Stark, Me., his native town. When twenty-one years of age he became a Christian and united with the First church in Stark. He was licensed to preach Aug. 10, 1822 and again by the Farmington Q. M. Feb. 5, 1824. Dec. 4, 1826, he was ordained. He labored successfully in many revivals, particularly at New Portland, Anson, Mercer and Stark. In business he was wise and successful and the benevolent causes found in him sympathy and support. He was a friend of freedom and temperance. His name is frequently found on the records of Q. M's, Y. M's and General Conferences.

Inscription:
Rev. Stephen Williamson
Died July 2, 1873 Age 78

Ezra Winslow
Birth:
Apr. 13, 1808
New Vineyard, Franklin County, Maine
Death:
Jul. 27, 1884
New Portland, Somerset County, Maine
Burial:
West New Portland Cemetery
New Portland,
Somerset County, Maine

He was the son of Rev. Howard, an M.E. minister, and Polly Winslow. He was an acceptable teacher for many years. His conversion in early life was thorough. He joined the M.E. class and was soon licensed by "camp-meeting" John Allen. Having become convinced that baptism should be by immersion only, he took a letter and joined the Free Baptists.He was united in marriage with Miss Mary Thomas, of Farmington, March 24, 1831.He was ordained by a council appointed by the Anson Quarterly Meeting in June 1850. His labors were in many towns in Somerset and Franklin counties, and were abundant and fruitful.He remembered each of the benevolent causes of the denomination in his will. He died at age 76 years, 3 months.

Lewis H Witham
Birth:
July 6, 1817
Milton, N. H.
Death:
Jan. 26, 1880
Biddeford, Me.
Burial:
Woodlawn Cemetery
Biddeford, York County, Maine

His father was Obadiah Witham, of Wakefield, N. H., and his mother, Abigail Hanson, of Milton. He was a teacher in a large number of schools. In 1834 he became a Christian, and three years later began to preach. He was licensed the next year, and was ordained Sept. 13, 1839, by the Waterboro Q. M. Rev. H. Hobbs preached the sermon. In 1840 he was married to Miss Martha A. Richardson, of Limington. He spent some time in missionary work in his Q. M., and supported himself by teaching. During his ministry he baptized 182 persons: fifty in Saco, forty-one in Biddeford, twenty-six in South Buxton, and the others in Kennebunk, Kennebunk Port, Hollis, Lyman, and Lebanon, Me., Portsmouth, and Contoocookville, N. H., and two in Bristol, Pa., while connected with the army. He enlisted in the Thirty-second Maine Volunteers in February, 1864, and finally acted as chaplain. Through ill health he was mustered out of service in July, 1865. He was pastor at Shapleigh two years, and South Buxton six years. He preached six months at Kittery, and was supplying at Kennebunk Port when he was prostrated by the disease which resulted in his death. He was clerk of the Maine Western Y. M. twelve years.

John Whitney
Birth:
unknown
Death:
Mar. 9, 1851
Burial:
Elmwood Cemetery
Dexter
Penobscot County, Maine

In June 1785, to attend the Q. M., and there related his Christian experience and call to the ministry. The question of his ordination was referred to the next Q. M., when it was decided in the affirmative, and he was ordained at Westport, Sept. 7; Randall himself preached the sermon, Tingley made the consecrating prayer, and Hibbard gave the hand of fellowship. He was the first to be ordained to the ministry in the denomination, and for thirty years he was successful especially in awakening sinners in his evangelistic work. He frequently met with opposition in his preaching tours. He visited the frontier settlements with Tingley the year of his ordination, and souls were saved and a few churches organized. He went to reside at Edgecomb, where a church of twenty members was organized by the aid of Hibbard. In 1787 a remarkable revival was enjoyed by him at Royalsborough. In 1788 he baptized several at Lewiston and visited the "Eastern country." He moved his family to Leeds, where they resided for several years. He organized churches at Canaan, Bristol, aild at the present Camden. In 1791 from the revival in Kittery, a church ,vas embodied. In September, 1793, with Randall, Tingley, Hibbard, and Deacon Otis he went from the Y. M. to answer the call for help from the churches in the Sandy River valley. In 1813 he moved to Newfield, and through faithful labors the place of death soon bloomed as a garden. One hundred and fifty were converted during the year. Samuel Burbank, the teacher, with many pupils was among the number.

A minister's reward is out of this world!

William Woodsum
Birth:
Feb. 1, 1792
Saco
York County, Maine
Death:

Jul. 24, 1872
Dickvale
Oxford County, Maine
Burial:Dickvale Cemetery
Dickvale
Oxford County, Maine

He was converted at the age of sixteen and soon felt called to preach, but being an orphan and having little education he put it off until he should be settled in life.In January, 1814, he married Miss Rosannah Woodman, of Leeds, Me. They had eleven children.He soon began with trembling to preach the gospel. He was ordained in Sumner, Sept. 20, 1823 (and there for about 17 years). Many were led to Christ through his efforts. In 1831 he settled in Peru, and resided there till his death. History shows that he founded the Free Baptist Church there, and he was its pastor for nearly 40 years. He also preached in various places in Maine and New Hampshire, attending about four hundred funerals.He repeatedly served his town in public offices, and in 1833, he represented his district in the Legislature.

Samuel Wormwood
Birth:
Jun. 24, 1793
Saco, York County, Maine
Death:
Mar. 25, 1865
North Berwick
York County, Maine
Burial:
Mount Pleasant Cemetery
North Berwick, York County, Maine

He was converted and baptized by Rev.John Buzzell when about eighteen years old, and at the age of twenty-one was ordained. Meeting with opposition in his early Christian life, he yet stood firm and -remained true. His labors were confined mostly to the Wellington Q M. on the St. John River. In Brighton seventy were converted under his labors in about three weeks. At that time another baptized the candidates, as Brother Wormwood was afflicted with lameness from which he never afterwards was free. His life was characterized by the spirit of true piety, sound doctrine, and indomitable perseverance. He moved his family to North Berwick two years before his death, where his health gradually declined.

Massachusetts

John C Ball
Birth:
unknown
Death:
Feb. 7, 1872
Leverett, Franklin County,
Massachusetts
Burial:
Gardner Cemetery
Leverett, Franklin County,
Massachusetts

Ball, Rev. John C., died at age 33 years. He became a Christian when quite young and united with the church in Ashfield, Mass. He began to preach in 1862 and was ordained at the September session of the Rensselaer Q. M., in 1867. His ministry was mostly in that Quarterly Meeting. He preached as he had opportunity in Leverett, Shutesbury and Ashfield, Mass. till 1868 when he became pastor of the, church in Stratton, Vt., and preached also for the West Jamaica church. His death was most painful. While watching with a sick daughter, he fell asleep and overturned the lamp. The oil saturated his clothes so that he was fatally burned before he could be relieved. He was a devoted and consistent Christian, and willing to do what he could.

Isaiah M. Bedell
Birth:
Jul. 11, 1820
Springvale,
York County, Maine
Death:
Feb. 9, 1893
Massachusetts
Burial:
Pine Grove Cemetery,
Lynn, Essex County,
Massachusetts,
Plot: Catalpa Path-Section-C,
Lot-33,Grave-8

He studied at Parsonsfield Seminary, and in the Biblical School at Whitestown, N. Y. Converted in 1834, he was licensed in 1850 and the next year ordained by Rev's G.P. Ramsey, W. H. Littlefield, C. B. Mills, and L. H. Witham. His pastorates were Woolwich, Farmington and Topsham, ME, and Meredith, Belmont and Strafford Centre, N.H. He has seen revivals in seven of the churches with which he has labored.

> While we in the dust
> and the shadows
> wait
> The will of the One
> who understands.

Andrew Hobson
Birth:
Sep. 10, 1795
Buxton
York County
Maine
Death:
May 1, 1877
Cambridge
Middlesex County
Massachusetts
Burial:
Steep Falls
Cumberland County, Maine

Andrew was converted at age 21, under the labors of Rev. Clement Phinney, was baptized by Rev. Jonathan Clay, and united with the FB church in Buxton. He began to preach in 1821, and was ordained two yrs after. He pastored several churches, including So. Gorham, Buxton, fifteen yrs and built a new meeting house there, Fort Hill, Steep Falls, ten yrs. He returned to Steep Falls in 1862, and in ten years baptized over fifty. In 1871, he entered upon his last pastorate which was at Hollis. He was one of a committee of twelve in favor of establishing a General Conference, and was a member of the first and of several other General Conferences. He was one of the original trustees of the "Morning Star" (newspaper). Every genuine interest received his sympathy. He had one son, Pelatiah M. HOBSON, who became a Freewill Bapt. minister.

Larkin A. Lang
Birth:
February 17, 1822
Brighton, Maine
Death:
Jun. 23, 1894
Massachusetts
Burial:
Pine Grove Cemetery
Lynn
Essex County, Massachusetts
Plot: Bignonia Path
Lot-3,Grave-8

He studied at Conway, New Hampshire and in 1841-42. He was converted in March, 1837, and was licensed at Conway in 1845 and ordained the same year by the Conway Quarterly Meeting. During his pastorate of 16 years at Conway, he enjoyed frequent revivals, baptizing about 120. He also was engaged in the practice of medicine. In September 1845, he married Harriet W Leavitt.

Lewis Malvern
Birth:
Jun. 9, 1846
England
Death:
May, 1939
Burial:
Pine Grove Cemetery
Lynn
Essex County, Massachusetts

Plot: Plot-C,Lot-118 ,Grave-1

He studied in the school at Cheltenham with Rev. H. H. Hayman, D.D., as head master, and at New Hampton, N.H. He was converted in 1867, and the same year licensed. He was ordained June 3, 1874, by the Sandwich Quarterly Meeting and supplied at Barrington, Ashland, and Dover. His pastorates have been Bristol, Manchester, and Laconia, where he is now located [1889]. He has had important positions of trust on the state Home Mission board, as Q.M. chairman, and on committees of the Yearly Meeting [Y.M.]. He has been on the Laconia school board, and is Grand Master of Odd Fellows in N.H.

John H Roberts
Birth:
April 17, 1860
Providence, Rhode Island
Death:
Mar. 23, 1925
Burial:
Meeting House Hill Cemetery
West Springfield
Hampden County, Massachusetts

He was converted in 1873 and 10 years later, while employed at a hardware store which was in Lowell, Massachusetts, where he was a member of the Paige Street

Church, he felt called of God to the ministry. He lay aside his secular occupation and spent some six months as an assistant secretary of the YMCA. The year later he was called to be acting secretary, but in the spring of 1886 he entered Cobb Divinity School. And later was a pastor

Warren Chase Stafford
Birth:
1823
Death:
May, 1857,
Burial:
Pine Grove Cemetery
Lynn
Essex County, Massachusetts
Plot: Dahlia Path, Lot-478,Grave-8
He is known for the work he did as a minister in the Free Baptist Church, in ME, NY, VT, NH and MA.

Edmund March Tappan
Birth:
Sep. 3, 1824
Sandwich
Carroll County, New Hampshire
Death:
Dec. 12, 1860
Lawrence
Essex County, Massachusetts
Burial:
Bellevue Cemetery
Lawrence
Essex County, Massachusetts

Edmund was the son of Jonathan and Dorothy (Beede) TAPPAN, was the eldest of ten children.In the Autumn of 1841, went to high school in Douglas, MA, and taught his first school the following winter in Uxbridge with success and satisfaction. In 1846, he entered Smithfield Seminary as a

pupil, then under the charge of Rev. Hosea Quinby, also from Sandwich, and a Freewill Baptist educator, he remained until August 1847, when he entered Dartmouth College. The year before, he was converted and was baptized by Rev. H. Quinby at which time he announced his Christian purpose, and united with the Freewill Baptist Church, at North Scituate, R.I. At Dartmouth, he and his wife, Lucretia Logee, whom he had married Aug. 15, 1849, by practicing rigid economy while they both taught, he graduated 29 July 1852, from Dartmouth, free of debt. He accepted the Principalship of Geauga Seminary in Ohio. He was ordained Aug. 18, 1852, only a few days before starting his work in Ohio.He then went to pastor Waterford Church in May 1853...then to Lawrence, MA in 1857, his last sphere of labor. He enjoyed a pleasant revival and added a goodly number to the church.Here his health began to fail, and in May 1860, retired for a season. In Sept. 1860, he preached once more, his last, with great feebleness, that he did not attempt again. He passed away at 36 years of age, leaving a wife and daughter of six years.Rev. Dr. George T. Day, D.D., Providence, R.I., delivered the sermon; Rev. Ransom Dunn, D.D., of Boston, followed with a brief and touching address to the bereaved family, friends, and church. The services closed with singing of Hymn 322 in the "Choralist" that Rev. Tappan, himself, had composed. He had for some years, beem an efficient co-laborer in sustaining the literary department of the "Quarterly," and had contributed material for the "Morning Star," a leading denominational paper, and had actively co-operated in all the great general enterprises.He was esteemed by his peers, twenty ministers attending his funeral, along with many in the town who had great respect for his dedication and work....taken from *Memoirs of Eminent Preachers in the Freewill Baptist*

Denomination, (1874) by Selah Hibbard Barrett of Ohio. Some info from state records; more info in Tappan Family Genealogy, Sandwich, NH.

Good-by; but oh, it is not forever

We say good-by as we turn away;

We shall be rejoined, no more to sever.

Charles Tedford
Birth:
September 24, 1850
Topsham
Minot
Androscoggin County, Maine
Death:

Jan. 12, 1911
Boston
Suffolk County, Massachusetts
Burial:
Rock Hill Cemetery
Foxboro
Norfolk County, Massachusetts

He prepared for college at Nichols Latin school and was a student at Bates College. He was licensed in June 1872 and was ordained February 22, 1887 by a Council called by the church at Limerick, Maine. He pastored a number of churches in Maine and also served as superintendent of schools in Limerick for three years. He married December 10, 1885 minutes Eva M. Mears.

Charles P Walker
Birth:
May 14, 1832
Scituate, Rhode Island
Death:
Jan. 31, 1877
Johnston, Rhode Island
Burial:
Jonathan Wheeler Cemetery
Rehoboth
Bristol County, Massachusetts

In 1850 he married, and about 18 months after he was converted and united with the church at Johnston. He was ordained in installed pastor of this church on November 28, 1861. He received only donations for his services and worked in a cotton field, of which he became superintendent. He preached neighboring districts in his zeal for winning souls characterize him both as a layman and as a pastor. He was faithful in diligent in business in his Christian life was uniform and exemplary.

I don't know about tomorrow but I know who holds my hand.

Michigan

James Ashley
Birth:
Nov. 18, 1850
Toronto, Ontario, Canada
Death:
Mar. 23, 1882
Cass County, Michigan
Burial:
Adamsville Cemetery, Adamsville,
Cass County, Michigan,
Plot: Row 7

In 1826 the family removed to Huron County. Ohio, where his father followed farming. In 1841 he was ordained and commenced preaching as a Free Will Baptist minister in the Huron Quarterly Meeting; but most of his pastoral and evangelist work for fourteen years was in new fields where churches were gathered and the Seneca Q.M. was organized. In 1855, he removed to Mason township, Cass county, MI, where he preached at Summerville for twelve years and organized the church at Berrien Center, and preached there nine years. He also did much missionary work and was never idle, working as a carpenter to supply his needs. Through his instrumentality the churches at Adamsville and Mason were built. He labored mostly in the St. Joseph Valley Yearly Meeting where he spent the remainder of his useful life. He was a Representative in the legislature of 1869-70 as a Republican.

George T. Baxter
Birth:
Jul. 11, 1837
Long Island City
Queens County, New York
Death:
Jul. 16, 1912
Oceana County, Michigan
Burial:
Otto Township Cemetery

Rothbury
Oceana County, Michigan

He was converted in 1878 and labored with success as a licensed preacher among the United Brethren in the White River mission. Afterwards he United with the Free Baptists being connected with the East Otto church of the Holton and White River Quarterly Meeting in the state of Michigan.

Archibald Bennet
Birth:
Jan. 22, 1807
Otsego, N.Y.
Death:
Oct. 22, 1889
Waverly, Michigan
Burial:
Covey Hill Cemetery
Van Buren County, Michigan
Archibald Bennet married Harriet C. (Whitcher) Bennet when 25 years of age and began to preach at age 29 receiving his ordination two years later. He labored as a revivalist for seven years in Columbus and vicinity and for four years in North Clarkson. In about 1849 he moved to Michigan where he ministered and organized Free Will Baptist churches. He was engaged in about 20 revivals and saw over 1000 conversions and baptized several hundred.At his death he was 61 yrs, 9 mos.

David Daniel Brown
Birth:
1822
Ontario, Canada
Death:
Aug. 3, 1869
Macomb County, Michigan
Burial:
Centennial Cemetery
New Haven, Macomb County,
Michigan

Rev. Brown was an ordained Freewill Baptist minister, baptized by Rev. S. Griffith, and ordained in 1845, after which he moved to Lexington, MI and preached in the Oxford Quarterly Meeting, with considerable success, and in June, 1867, settled as pastor of the Bruce Church, where he remained until his death in Bruce Twp of Macomb County, Michigan, when forty-seven years of age. He is recorded as having served in Michigan's 22nd Reg. Inf., Co. K, from 1864-1865, mustering out at Murfreesboro, TN, from the 29th Inf. Reg. having previously transferred from 22nd to 29th. It's possible he contracted his "consumption", i.e. TB, while exposed in the War. Inscription:Died Aug 3, 1869 Aged 47 yrs. 4 mos. 29 days Here he will sleep till that great day when Heaven and earth shall pass away when saints with joy their graves forsake.

William C. Burns
Birth:
1854
Death:
1955
Burial:
Macon Cemetery
Macon
Lenawee County, Michigan

He was converted in 1868 and was ordained to the ministry in 1880 and was a minister to the churches at Paw Paw, Michigan and Fairport, New York. He baptized 35 converts during his ministry and has been active in the Young Peoples Society Of Christian

Endeavor and served as an instructor in history at Oak Park Seminary in Paw Paw, Michigan. On September 9, 1885 he married Alice Collins. His education was received at Hillsdale College and the Theological School. He also did postgraduate work at Auburn Theological Seminary in New York.

John Jay Butler
Birth:
Apr. 9, 1814
Berwick,
York County, Maine
Death:
Jun. 16, 1891
Hillsdale,
Hillsdale County, Michigan
Burial:
Oak Grove Cemetery,
Hillsdale,
Hillsdale County, Michigan,
Plot: Sect. 15 - Row 5

Prof. John J. Butler, when quite young became interested in politics and religion. He united with the Free Will Baptist church of Great Falls, NH. When the Free Will Baptists established a Seminary at Parsonsfield, ME, he became a student and prepared for college. While there he lived with the family of Rev. George Lamb, an eminent minister of the village, for whom he formed a deep attachment and under whose direction he began holding meetings and delivering addresses. John was ordained a minister in 1846. He was Professor Emeritus of Systematic Theology in the early Free Will

Baptist movement in New England. He graduated at Bowdoin College in 1837. Following his graduation, he began teaching as an assistant teacher in the Seminary in Parsonsfield. In Dec. 1839, he entered Andover Theological Sem. Mass. The highlights of his teaching career included holding the professorship of systematic theology in the Whitestown Seminary at Whitestown, New York for 10 years, as well as holding the professorship of systematic theology in the Seminary at New Hampton, New Hampshire for 16 years, and in Bates College at Lewiston, Maine for 3 years. In 1860, Bowdoin College gave him the degree of Doctor of Divinity. In 1873, Butler took the chair of Hebrew Language and Literature at Hillsdale College, in Michigan. A large number of his pupils became worthy ministers and missionaries abroad. No less than fifteen hundred pupils were under his instruction, and a third prepared for the Gospel ministry. He retired from teaching in Hillsdale in 1883. He was the author of: Natural and Revealed Theology (Dover, New Hampshire, 1861) Commentary on the Gospels (1870) Commentary on the Acts, Romans, and First and Second Corinthians. (1871) Lectures on systematic theology: embracing the existence and attributes of God, the authority and doctrine of the scriptures, the institutions and ordinances of the gospel (with Ransom Dunn, 1892) In 1834, Dr. Butler became the assistant editor of The *Morning Star*, a Free Will Baptist publication.

Missionary Julia Emma
Phillips **Burkholder**
Birth:
Jun. 5, 1845,
India
Death:
1931
Dickinson County, Michigan
Burial:
Oak Grove Cemetery,
Hillsdale,
Hillsdale County, Michigan

Julia Emma was the daughter of Jeremiah Phillips, D.D., and Hannah (Cummings) Phillips, missionaries for the Free Will Baptist church. She was one of six of their children to serve in India. She was born in Jelasore, India, Orissa Province. She was married to Thomas Wesley Burkholder, M.D., Nov. 8, 1879, by her brother, James Liddell Phillips, M.D., in India. She and her husband as a physician served many years in India, where he died and is buried, as well as her brother, Dr. James L. Phillips, and her mother, Hannah Cummings Phillips. Julia E. studied at Hillsdale College, Michigan, and served as missionary in India from

1865-1917. Her father, Jeremiah, is bur. in Oak Grove, as well as sisters, Ida Orissa, Mary Anne Platt(s) and bro.-in-law, Dr. Richard Gilbert Platt(s), M.D., and other kindred.

Inscription:
Missionary to India
1865-1917

Dudley E Clark
Birth:
Jul. 18, 1855
Ashtabula County, Ohio
Death:
Nov. 24, 1884 Arlington,
Rhode Island
Burial:
Northlawn Cemetery,
North Adams,
Hillsdale County, Michigan

He was graduated at Hillsdale College, Mich., in 1879, and from the Theological Department of this college in 1881. He was ordained in 1880, and preached while in school, at Woodstock, Mich., where he witnessed a revival and a score of conversions. After his graduation he preached and taught school at Davison Station, Mich., where his labors were highly esteemed. In 1883, he was called to Arlington, R.I., where he endeared himself to many in the short time before his early death.

Elijah Cook
Birth:
Jul. 17, 1793
Rensselaer County, New York
Death:
Jan. 31, 1872
Eckfor, Calhoun County, Michigan
Burial:

Cook's Prairie Cemetery
Clarendon, Calhoun County,
Michigan

Cook, Rev. Elijah, of Cook's Prairie, Mich., died aged 78 years. He was converted when fourteen, and soon moved from Oneida County; N. Y., to Clarkson, where his home welcomed the fathers of those times. In 1835 he moved to Michigan, locating at Cook's Prairie, where he saw the need of ministerial labor and took up the work. He was ordained in 1845, and his zealous labors were crowned with success. About 1858 he united with the Girard church. He and his companion of fifty-seven years, were highly esteemed.

Dr Ransom Dunn
Birth:
Jul. 7, 1818
Bakersfield,
Franklin County, Vermont
Death:
Nov. 9, 1900
Scranton,
Lackawanna Cty,
Pennsylvania,
Burial:

Oak Grove Cemetery,
Hillsdale, Hillsdale County,
Michigan,
Plot: Sect 5, Lot 150

He grew up in Vermont one of ten children of John and Abigail Dunn. All four of their sons became ministers, including Ransom. His eyesight was poor but he never ceased to study. He became an orator, writer and sought-after pastor in the northeastern Free Will Baptist movement. He came west to preach and teach in the newer states, finally lending his time and influence to the growth of Hillsdale College in its formative years, and forward.

He became the "Grand Ole Man" of Hillsdale College, serving the College in various capacities (professor, fund-raiser, and president) from 1852 to 1900. From 1853 to 1855, he obtained over $10,000 of the original college funding by travelling 6,000 miles by carriage through frontier Illinois, Wisconsin, Iowa and Minnesota.

Dr. Dunn was a long-time anti-slavery activist. In 1891, a book of lectures by Prof. Dunn, and co-educator Prof. Butler entitled, *"Butler and Dunn's Systematic Theology"*, was published, which instantly became a favorite of scholars interested in biblical doctrines, and is still a sought-after volume. Within the cornerstone of Central Hall is the prayer of Ransom Dunn: "May earth be better and heaven richer because of the life and labor of Hillsdale College." He had extensive work in Ohio at Geauga Seminary and Rio Grande College where he was the first president.

Francis Wayland Dunn
Birth:
Jan. 29, 1843 Ohio
Death:
Dec. 13, 1874
Hillsdale
Hillsdale County Michigan
Burial:
Oak Grove Cemetery Hillsdale
Hillsdale County Michigan

The second son of Rev. Dr. Ransom Dunn. He graduated from Hillsdale College in 1862, and went into the 64th Reg. of Illinois Volunteers for the War, along with his brother, Newell Ransom. They served in Mississippi, going thru several battles, and when his brother died of typhoid fever, he was with him and took responsibility to ship the body back to Hillsdale. After the war he became editor of *The Christian Freeman*, a denominational publication. His health continued to decline from the exposures of war. 'He accepted the chair of belles letters at Hillsdale, but it was only a matter of months until his brief professorship would end.' He suffered from tuberculosis and died in 1874, an outstanding young man, loved by his family and college friends.

James Harvey Darling
Birth:
Dec. 2, 1828
Spafford,
Onondaga County,
New York
Death:
Jul. 31, 1916
Paw Paw,
Van Buren County,
Michigan
Burial:
Covey Hill Cemetery,
Van Buren County, Michigan

He studied at Cortland Academy, Homer, N.Y., and at the Biblical School at Whitestown, a Free Will Baptist institution. His father was also a FWB minister, having died in Eleroy, Ill. James' life was consecrated to God in 1848 and the same year license to preach was granted. He was ordained a Free Will Baptist minister by Rev. R. Ide and others, Sept. 20, 1853. After ministering to the Spafford and Summerhill churches, N.Y., he moved to Michigan, where the remainder of his ministry, except three years at Prairie Centre and Homer, Ill., was been spent. He has ministered to the Summerville, Paw Paw, Waverly, Oshtemo, Gliddengurg, Arlington, Gobleville, Porter and Ortonville churches. He organized three churches and baptized over one hundred converts.

Wellington DePuy
Birth:
Aug. 20, 1849
Mount Morris
Livingston County, New York
Death:
Mar. 22, 1919
Grand Ledge
Eaton County, Michigan
Burial:
Oakwood Cemetery
Eaton Rapids
Eaton County, Michigan

He graduated from Hillsdale College, Michigan in 1878. He had been converted in 1872 and license by the Hillsdale Quarter Meeting in 1876. In 1880 he

graduated from Bates Theological School, Lewiston, Maine and in April 1881 he settled in Ortonville, Michigan. On December 11, 1881 he was ordained to the Free Will Baptists ministry. In 1882 he became the pastor of the Grand Ledge, Michigan church and thereafter became a Congregationalist in 1885.

Gilbert G. Durfee
Birth:
unknown
New York
Death:
Dec. 23, 1868
Burial:
Forest Home Cemetery
Greenville, Montcalm County,
Michigan
Plot: sec 7

He affiliated with the Free Baptists in Michigan in 1865, but due to failing health, soon had to retire from active ministry. Ordained Freewill Baptist minister, bn NY, abt 1819, moved to Michigan, where he died relatively young.

Nathaniel Ewer
Birth:
1800
Death:
Aug. 9, 1836
Burial:
Perry McFarlen Cemetery
Grand Blanc
Genesee County, Michigan

An ordained Freewill Baptist pioneer minister from Vermont. Died young.

Nor pain, nor deathcan enter there.

Micaiah Fairfield
Birth:
Apr. 3, 1786
Vermont
Death:
Feb. 19, 1858
Burial:
Oak Grove Cemetery
Hillsdale
Hillsdale County Michigan

Micaiah Fairfield graduated Middlebury College, Vt, with highest honors, and studied theology at Andover, Mass. His roommates there were Judson, Newell and Rice, and no one of the number was more devoted to missionary work than he. One of their children was Rev. Edmund Burke Fairfield, D.D., LL.D, who became president (1848) of Hillsdale College, Hillsdale, MI. Rev. Micaiah Fairfield, was for

fifty years engaged in the work of the ministry, and whether missionary or pastor, his aim was for the promotion of the gospel.

William Penson Fifield
Birth:
Jul. 7, 1813
Salisbury,
Merrimack County,
New Hampshire
Death:
Feb. 12, 1880
Jackson County, Michigan
Burial:
Fifield Cemetery,
Blackman Township,
Jackson Cty, Michigan

William P. Fifield came to Michigan with his parents, Enoch and Abigail (Stevens) Fifield, in 1830, locating on a farm near Jackson. He united with the Baptists in 1834, but shortly afterward became connected with the Freewill Baptists. He firmly

maintained the principles he so dearly loved to the end. He was deeply interested in all the denominational work.

Newton Preston Gates
Birth:
Feb. 18, 1894
Clay County, Arkansas
Death:
Nov. 1, 1977
Detroit,
Wayne County, Michigan
Burial:
Roseland Park Cemetery,
Berkley, Oakland County,
Michigan

He was the founder of the First Free Will Baptist Church in Hazel Park, which was the very first Free Will Baptist Church in the state of Michigan after the 1935 merger of the present FWB Natl' Association. He was the founder of the Liberty Association of Free Will Baptist churches in the state and was founder of the Free Will Baptist Temple in Detroit. He was widely known as a song writer and singer. He was awarded the Professor of Music degree from the Arkansas State Normal Music College. His daughter, Winona, married Raymond Riggs which continued a large legacy of FWB ministers and leaders.

Thomas Grinnell
Birth:
1794
Exeter
Washington County, Rhode
Island
Death:
Feb. 4, 1882
Bethel
Branch County, Michigan
Burial:
Snow Prairie Cemetery
Bethel
Branch County, Michigan

A native of Exeter, R. I., died at age 89 years. Shortly after his marriage he made his home in Genesee County, N.Y., where he was ordained in 1826. Two years later he moved to Chautauqua County, where his ministry was marked by persevering efforts for the cause he loved. Later he labored in Wisconsin and Illinois, making his home in Michigan.
Note: *Chautauqua Co. NY history.*The Free-Will Baptist Church, in the town of Cherry Creek, was formed About the year 1826, by Rev Thomas Grinnell; and is said to have been the earliest religious organization in the town.

Elisha Wesley Harding
Birth:
Jan. 15, 1852
Warsaw
Jefferson County,
Pennsylvania
Death:
Jan. 3, 1951net
Corunna
Shiawassee County, Michigan
Burial:
Yerian Cemetery
Vernon
Shiawassee County, Michigan

He died at the age of 44. He was converted when he was 16 years of age, licensed by the Leicester church in 1838 and ordained 10 years later in 1848. He preached at Warsaw, New York for six years and in the Elk County Quarterly Meeting in Pennsylvania. In 1855, they moved to Michigan where he was pastor at Venice and Vernon until his death.

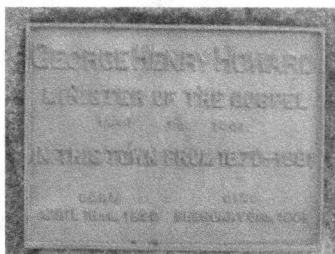

George Henry Howard
Birth:
Apr. 18, 1829
Union
Bloome County, New York
Death:
Feb. 3, 1907
Michigan
Burial:
Ortonville Cemetery

Brandon Gardens
Oakland County, Michigan

He consecrated his life to God in November, 1857 and received ordination on June 16, 1867 in the Wolf River Quarterly Meeting, Wisconsin. He began his work with the Rosendale, Wisconsin church and then removed to Ortonville, Michigan and later to Lisbon, Michigan. He baptized at 200 converts.

Edward J. Howes
Birth:
Oct. 17, 1838
Ontario County, New York
Death:
Mar. 16, 1906
Michigan
Burial:
Knauss Cemetery
Kinderhook
Branch County, Michigan
Plot: Lot 92

The family moved to Hillsdale County, Michigan in 1848, and nine years later Howe was converted and united with the North Reading church. He was ordained by the Hillsdale Quarterly Meeting at Cambridge in 1864. His pastorate was with the Salem and Green Oak churches of the Oakland Quarterly Meeting In 1865. He was married in 1870 and the next year became pastor of the Fairfield, Michigan church. After 12 years as a faithful leader there he was again compelled to abandon the work because of poor health.

Thomas Huckins
Birth:
1795
Lee, New Hampshire
Death:
1853
Lexington, Michigan
Burial:
Huckins Cemetery
Croswell
Sanilac County, Michigan

Left an orphan in early life, after serving in the war of 1812, he married and moved to Canada where he joined the first Free Will Baptist church organized in that locality. In 1819 he moved to Dunwick, and later to London. In these places churches were organized and the latter he served as a Deacon until 1827, when he was ordained to the ministry, which occurred soon after. He labored in that vicinity for 10 years gathering three churches and then moved to Lexington, Michigan where his remaining years were spent. Here he soon organized a church to which about 60 members were added during his pastorate.

Alonzo O. Jenne
Birth:
1822
Hartland, Vermont
Death:
1892
Michigan
Burial:
Needmore Cemetery
Needmore
Eaton County, Michigan

He was converted in 1837; received license to preach in 1847, studying at Whitestown Seminary, New York and was ordained in April, 1853. Much of his ministry was done in the Grand River Quarterly Meeting.

Anson Green Kalar
Birth:
Nov. 8, 1833
Stamford, Ontario, Canada
Death:
Jan. 31, 1902
Richfield Center, Genesee County, Michigan
Burial:
Cottage Cemetery
Richfield Center, Genesee County, Michigan

Parents were William Kalar and Winifred Hawley. A minister of the Freewill Baptist, licensed in April 1877, and pastor in Genesee Quarterly Meeting, Michigan.

Good-by; but oh, it is not forever
We say good-by as we turn away;
We shall be rejoined, no more to sever

Ada Montgomery Kennan
Birth:
Jun. 4, 1839
Madison
Lake County, Ohio
Death:
Apr. 14, 1894
Hillsdale
Hillsdale County, Michigan
Burial:
Oak Grove Cemetery
Hillsdale
Hillsdale County, Michigan

Freewill Baptist minister and pastor. Wife of Rev. George Kennan (1832 - 1905). She was also the mother of Ralph Kennan who was also an effective Free Will Baptist minister.

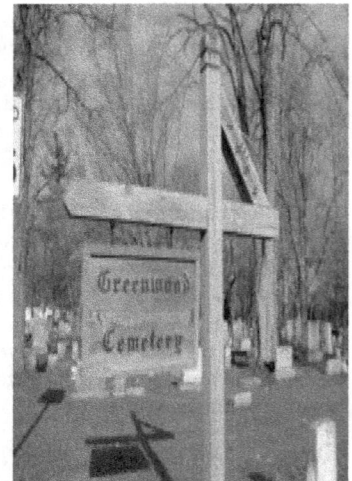

Moses Rice Kenny
Birth:
Sep. 6, 1816
Townshend
Windham County, Vermont
Death:
Mar. 25, 1905
Hillsdale
Hillsdale County, Michigan
Burial:
Oak Grove Cemetery
Hillsdale
Hillsdale County, Michigan

An ordained Free Will Baptist minister and pastor, born in VT but lived in mid-west for many years. Married Elizabeth "Betsey" Ross, -16 Nov. 1843-Ashtabula County, Ohio. Married Caroline Gage-15 April 1863-Ashtabula County, Ohio.

Samuel Ketcham
Birth:
Feb. 2, 1807
Chautauqua, New York
Death:
May 6, 1889
Mason, Cass County, Michigan
Burial:
Five Points Cemetery
Edwardsburg
Cass County, Michigan

He was converted in early manhood and went to Michigan about the time of his marriage to Abigail Pullman, which was consummated on March 13, 1831. She was his companion for more than half a century. On July 15, 1848 he was ordained at Gillead and his ministry was spent in the St. Joseph Valley Quarterly Meeting.

Elijah Kingsbury
Birth:
unknown
Death:
Aug. 16, 1862
Oakland County, Michigan
Burial:
Kingsbury Cemetery,
Oxford, Oakland County, Michigan
Plot: Lot 8 Grave 1

Minister and also the father of Rev. Leonard Kingsbury.

Leonard Kingsbury
Birth:
1794
Death:
Oct. 19, 1879
Oakland County, Michigan,
Burial:
Kingsbury Cemetery, Oxford,
Oakland County, Michigan,
Plot: Lot 8 Grave 2

He was converted under the labor of Rev. E. Hannibal. He began to preach and was licensed by the Free Will Baptist Church in Clarkston, New York. He continued to labor in that vicinity until 1834. After which, he moved to the state of Michigan where he was ordained and was accepted into the Oakland quarterly meeting with the Bruce church. His labors were well known since the established several churches in the Oxford quarterly meeting. He loved the denomination and carefully gave of his time and money and aiding it's evangelistic work and benevolent enterprises.

Arnold D. Knight
Birth:
Apr. 8, 1803
Oneida County, New York
Death:
Mar. 18, 1889
Burial:
East Hill Cemetery
Osseo
Hillsdale County, Michigan
Plot: Sec. A, Lot 161

On January 2, 1823 he married Harriet M. Knight. At the age of 18 he was converted and before 1840 he was ordained at the Pittsfield church. He held long pastorates with the Pittsfield, Spencer, and Rochester churches along with some other churches for a brief time. In all these pastorates there were revivals. He baptized over 200 converts and assisted in gathering's six churches.

John Beal Lash
Birth:
Jan. 25, 1841
Athens County, Ohio
Death:
Jul. 17, 1901
Hillsdale,
Hillsdale County, Michigan
Burial:
Oak Grove Cemetery,
Hillsdale,
Hillsdale County, Michigan

An ordained Freewill Baptist minister from Ohio, who moved to Michigan and was a great warrior for Christ.

J. B. Leavenworth
Birth:
Jun. 5, 1820
Sandgate, Vermont
Death:
Sep. 20, 1905
Michigan
Burial:
Novi Cemetery
Novi
Oakland County, Michigan

He was born of Puritan ancestry in Vermont but later settled in Novi, Michigan about 1844 and received ordination 18 years later and his ministry was in this vicinity.

Our birth is nothing but our death begun.

David H Lord
Birth:
Aug. 9, 1814
Rumney
Grafton County, New Hampshire
Death:
Jun. 14, 1889
Hillsdale
Hillsdale County, Michigan
Burial:
Oak Grove Cemetery
Hillsdale
Hillsdale County, Michigan

Rev. D.H. Lord was the son of Thomas H. and Louisa (Avery) Lord. He consecrated his life to God in Aug. 1832, and soon began to preach, studying at Parsonfield Seminary, ME, in 1835-36, and on Sept 28, 1836, was ordained to the gospel ministry in the Free Will Baptist Church. He ministered successively to churches in Portsmouth, NH, Springvale, E. Lebanon, and others in Maine, and Newport and Pascoag in RI, in Medina, OH, and in Howard City, MI. He baptized over five hundred converts. His voice having failed, he studied medicine at Brunswick, ME, and Vermont Medical College, graduating in 1849. In Sept. 1838, he married Elmira Clark of Dover, NH, who died seven years later. In 1848, he married Annette M. Merrill, of Parsonfield, ME.After a brief illness at Hillsdale, MI, he died and was buried there.By his wide and benevolent life, he exerted a wide influence for God.

Joseph William Mauck
Birth:
Aug. 17, 1852
Cheshire
Gallia County, Ohio
Death:
Jul. 7, 1937
Hillsdale
Hillsdale County, Michigan
Burial:
Oak Grove Cemetery
Hillsdale
Hillsdale County, Michigan

Dr. Mauck was a graduate of Hillsdale College, Class of

1875, after which he became Professor of Classical Languages at the college. He later served as Chancellor of the University of South Dakota. Dr. Mauck was President of Hillsdale College for 20 years, retiring in 1922 to his beloved home, Sunnycrest, with the title President-Emeritus. Inscription:President of Hillsdale College 1902-1922

John H Maynard
Birth:
November 29, 1830
Junius, New York
Death:
1905
Burial:
Greenwood Cemetery
Sparta
Kent County, Michigan

After his marriage to Mary Williams in 1853, years later they moved to the state of Michigan. He was ordained in the Hillsdale Quarterly Meeting in January, 1866 with Rev. John Thomas, who had baptized him, preaching the sermon. Most of his pastorates were in the state of Michigan where he served as the Michigan Yearly Meeting clerk for many years and for three times a delegate to the General Conference.

Charles Blunt Mills
Birth:
May 5, 1823
York County, Maine
Death:
Mar. 11, 1896
Mayville
Tuscola County, Michigan
Burial:
Fremont Township Cemetery
Mayville
Tuscola County, Michigan

He received a good common and high school education, and at an early age he became a minister in the Free Baptist denomination. He was a close student and gave frequent lectures in addition to his regular pastoral work. He removed to Ohio, and from there, in 1856, to Tuscola County, where he bought a farm. He was a State senator in 1869-70 and a representative in 1877 and was judge of probate for Tuscola County eight years. He was a trustee of Hillsdale College for many years and several years acted as its secretary and treasurer, and was one of the incorporators of the Free Baptist printing house at Dover, N. H. he was a member of the executive Board of the Home Mission Society, and a corporator of the Morning Star and served in the General Conference.

I am come that you may have life abundantly

Samuel A. J. Moody
Birth:
Feb. 25, 1825
Chautauqua County, New York
Death:
1891
Michigan
Burial:
Fairfield Cemetery
Adrian
Lenawee County, Michigan

He was born in Chautauqua Co. New York, Feb. 26 1825. His parents were Samuel and Martha (Thompson) Moody.He married Roxey E. Emmery in 1859, and had six children.He was converted in 1839, and received ordination May 26, 1861.He ministered to the Liberty and First and Second Augusta churches in Michigan and engaged in revival work at Rose, but for several years was hindered in the work because of disease.He also received certification to teach school in 1855, in the Lenwanee Co. schools.

Inscription:
"In God's Care"

Marcus Mugg
Birth:
Aug. 12, 1809
Yates County, N. Y.
Death:
Jun. 23, 1865
Mason, Mich.
Burial:
Five Points Cemetery
Edwardsburg, Cass County, Michigan
Plot: Section 1, Row 8, Stone 2

Marcus was the son of Rev. John Mugg, and died at aged 56 years. His conversion took place in York, Ohio, where he soon began to preach and was ordained June 6, 1840. He spent most of his ministerial life with the churches of the Huron and Seneca Q. M's, Ohio, where his general influence and exemplary life were appreciated. Some twelve years before his death he moved to Michigan, where bereavement and sickness awaited him. His wife passed to a better world and his eldest son was slain in the war. But the sustaining grace of God was present.

Erastus W Norton

Birth:
Sep. 9, 1818
Richmond, Ontario County, New York
Death:
Aug. 9, 1887
Sparta, Kent County, Michigan
Burial:
Greenwood Cemetery
SpartaKent County, Michigan
Plot: O-2-1

Rev. Norton's parents were John and Norma (Short) NORTON.He married 1) Minerva Gardener, Feb. 14, 1839, and 2) Laura A. Compton, July 17, 1851.He was converted when twelve years of age, and ordained in the Freewill Baptist church in Michigan when twenty-three years (ca 1841). He went to Kent County in 1850, where his principal work in the ministry was done. The Sparta and Lisbon churches enjoyed his services many years, and both built houses of worship during his pastorate. He was strongly denominational, a good preacher, and an energetic business man. His wife and ten children were left to mourn his passing.

William R Norton

Birth:
February 12, 1822
Richmond, New York
Death:
1902
Burial:
Rose Cemetery
Bath
Clinton County, Michigan

He was converted in 1843 and the same year received licensed to preach. He moved to Michigan in November of that year and commenced to labor in the Oakland Quarterly Meeting where he was ordained in 1848. In 1854 he moved to Clinton County and also the Lansing Quarterly Meeting where he organized the Bath church which he served for 22 years. He later became a missionary in the vicinity of Boyne City in the northern peninsular of Michigan. He had two sons both of whom graduated from Hillsdale College with Walter E., being a soldier in the Civil War and William A., a successful lawyer.

The Story Does Not End here...

Linus S Parmelee

Birth:
August 20, 1815
Spafford, New York
Death:
1895
Burial:
Maplewood Cemetery
OldReading
Hillsdale County, Michigan
Plot: Old Part Sec E Lot 30

On May 3, 1835 he married Julia A. Jones and their son, Horatio, became a trustee of Hillsdale College, Michigan. Linus was converted the year following his marriage. In 1847 he received licensed to preach and that next year was ordained. He ministered the Salford, Ontario, Canada church for seven years, and two years the Innerskip church which he organized. He then moved to Reading, Michigan and assisted in organizing that church and was its pastor for 21 years. He also assisted in organizing the Woodbridge and West Reading churches and served them also as pastor. Four of these churches build houses of worship during his pastorates and he had baptized more than 210 converts. He also spent some time in Chicago and raised several thousand dollars for the interest of Free Will Baptist. He also raised $18,000 for the Hillsdale College from which he also served as a trustee for 15 years.

Jeremiah Phillips
Birth:
Jan. 5, 1812
Plainfield Center,
Otsego County, New York
Death:
Dec. 9, 1879
Hillsdale,
Hillsdale County, Michigan
Burial:
Oak Grove Cemetery,
Hillsdale,
Hillsdale County, Michigan

He studied at Hamilton Literary and Theological Seminary, N.Y; ordained at Plainfield, NY, Sep. 2, 1835. Was among the very first missionaries for Free Will Baptists, going to India in 1835, aged twenty-three, with his colleague, Rev. Eli Noyes, and founded the Free Baptist Mission in Orissa, India. He began work among the Santals, an aboriginal tribe, reduced their language to writing, and also prepared a dictionary and grammar, and translated the gospels and other portions of the Bible. He married Mary Spaulding Beede in 1835, who died soon after arriving in India. In 1839, he married Mary Anne Grinditch, Serapore, India, who also died. Thirdly in 1841, mar. Hannah W. (Cummings) who had gone to India at twenty-two years of age, died there in her ninetieth year, having had but two furloughs during the intervening sixty-seven years.

Dr. Jeremiah Phillips was the father of fourteen children, eleven of whom lived to mature age, six of whom and three granddaughters became workers in the same field, while five remaining in America were nearly, or quite all active workers for missions.

On his retirement from the field in 1879, with health completely shattered by privations and strenuous labors during one of India's terrible famines, the Lieutenant-Governor of Bengal addressed to him a letter in which he said he could not allow him to retire without expressing his high appreciation of the valuable service he had rendered to India.

His eldest son, a medical doctor, James L. Philips, spent twenty-five years in the same field and was the Field Secretary of the India Sunday-School Union, in whose service he remained until in 1895. Also, a daughter, Dr. Nellie M. Phillips, and Dr. Thomas Wesley Burkholder, a son-in-law, were medical missionaries. Eleven of Dr. Phillips' family are buried in India, including his last wife, Hannah Cummings Phillips, while Dr. Phillips himself, and those of two missionary daughters and one daughter-in -law, rest in Oak Grove Cemetery.

One daughter, Mrs. Julia P. Burkholder (widow of Dr. T.W. Burkholder), served 50 years as a missionary in India. A fine brick church now stands in Khargpur, India, a memorial to Dr. Phillips, erected in 1906-07 by Mr. and Mrs. I.L. Stone, (Harriet Phillips Stone) of Battle Creek, the latter a daughter of Dr. Phillips, and for twenty-six years a member of the mission. This family did great service for God in helping the poor and down-trodden, and gained for themselves, a great reward.

Nellie Maria Phillips
Birth:
Jun. 15, 1852,
India
Death:
Mar. 7, 1906
Rochester,
Olmsted County, Minnesota
Burial:
Oak Grove Cemetery,
Hillsdale,
Hillsdale County, Michigan
She graduated from Hillsdale College, MI in June 1875. She engaged in teaching and the study of medicine until 1881, graduating at that time from Adelbert Medical College, Cleveland, Ohio. She served with her parents and a rather large, extended family as a medical missionary to India, from 1881 to 1903. Dr. Phillips died in Rochester, MN.

Richard Gilbert Platts
Birth:
Nov. 4, 1838
Old Saybrook,
Middlesex County,
Connecticut,
Death:
Jan. 3, 1873,
India
Burial:
Oak Grove Cemetery,
Hillsdale,
Hillsdale County, Michigan,
Plot: Plot: Row 3

Gilbert Platts, M.D. was a student of Hillsdale College, MI, and was graduated at Buffalo Medical College, N.Y., Feb. 1866, as a physician. He married Mary Anne Phillips, the daughter of Jeremiah Phillips, D.D., and Mary Anne Grimditch Phillips, Free Will Baptist missionaries to India, on Dec. 15, 1866, at Bethany, NY. Death occurred in India in January 1873, and presumed re-interment in 1874, in Oak Grove Cem. as Feb. 1, 1874, is shown as date of burial He died a young man at 34 years of age. His wife is also interred in Oak Grove. The children are buried at the Riverview Memorial Cemetery in Ft. Pierce, Florida.

O thou who choosest for thy share
The world, and what the world calls fair,
Take all that it can give or lend,
But know that death is at the end

Ida Orissa Phillips
Birth:
Jan. 24, 1856
Death:
Jul. 5, 1889
Winnebago,
Faribault County,
Minnesota
Burial:
Oak Grove Cemetery,
Hillsdale,
Hillsdale County, Michigan

Daughter of Jeremiah L. Phillips, DD, and Hanna (Cummings) Phillips, Free Will Baptist missionaries to Orissa Province India. She graduated from Hillsdale College, MI. in 1877 and was a missionary to India from 1877-1889, at the time of her death, at age 32 yrs and 5 months. She came from an extended family of medical missionaries and ministers. Her mother lies buried in India with other family members there. Ida came to U.S. at age 16, probably to attend college, in Dec. 30, 1870 with a clergyman's family, Rev. Obadiah B. Batchelder, M.D., who worked with the Phillips family in India. Most info is from a book, pub. 1912, *"Jeremiah Phillips, DD, Family Missionaries to India"* by Harriet Phillips Stone.)

Mary Anne *Phillips* Platts
Birth:
Feb. 20, 1842,'
India
Death:
Apr. 25, 1911 Winnebago,
Faribault County, Minnesota
Burial:
Oak Grove Cemetery, Hillsdale,
Hillsdale County, Michigan,
Plot: Row 3

Mary Anne was the daughter of Free Will Baptist missionaries to India, Dr. Jeremiah Phillips, and Mary Anne (Grimditch) Phillips She married R. Gilbert Platts, MD, Dec. 15, 1866, in Brittany NY. She studied at Whitestown Seminary, NY and Prairie City Academy, Illinois, and New Hampton Seminary, N.H. They served at missionaries with her extended family in Orissa Province, India, where her husband died at the early age of 34 yrs.

Mary R *Sayles* Phillips
Birth:
unknown
Death:
Feb. 6, 1911
Battle Creek,
Calhoun County, Michigan
Burial:
Oak Grove Cemetery, Hillsdale,
Hillsdale County Michigan

Married James L. Phillips, M.D., at Pasoag, R.I., Aug. 10, 1864, a Free Will Baptist missionary to India. She died at 73 years, after serving with her husband in India. He died there in 1895.

Chauncey Reynolds
Birth:
August 28, 1805
Argyle, New York
Death:
1890
Burial:
Oak Grove Cemetery
Hillsdale
Hillsdale County, Michigan

In the winter of 1819 the family moved to Bethany, New York. During that first year he became interested in religion, but delayed baptism until 1827. He went to Michigan in 1828 and was married to Sarah Harper, October 30, 1828. He was ordained at the Grand River Quarterly Meeting in October, 1845 and soon organized the church and Shiawasasee County. He also organized a church and Du Plain, Clinton County, and another in North Plains, and assisted in the work in other places. He was a trustee of Michigan Central College at Spring Arbor and served also as a trustee at Hillsdale College for 20 years and he served as a delegate to the Gen. conference in 1853.

William T. Risner
Birth:
1847
Prussia
Death:
1919
Burial:
Novi Cemetery
Novi
Oakland County, Michigan
He married Sarah Hammond in 1868. In 1874 he was led to Christ's and licensed to preach was granted four years later. He received his ordination on February 14, 1883. His pastorates were in Michigan.

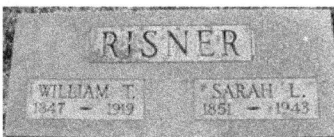

J. C. Robinson
Birth:
April 14, 1836
Harrison County, Ohio
Death:
1922
Burial:
Oak Grove Cemetery
Coldwater
Branch County

His parents migrated from Virginia to Ohio where he turned of God in August, 1851. Seven years later he was licensed to preach having received his education Albany University, Ohio. On August 24, 1862 he was ordained by Rev. H. J. Carr and others. His labors have been in Ohio, Minnesota, Illinois, Wisconsin and Michigan. He has organized five churches and baptized 125 people.

E B Rolf
Birth:

Vermont
Death:
Nov. 16, 1872
Bristol, Indiana
Burial:
East Union Cemetery
Union
Cass County, Michigan

After his conversion he joined the Sodus, New York church. The Holland Purchase Conference granted him a license to preach in 1843 and his ordination took place on July 12, 1844. 21 years of his ministry was spent with the Galen and Savanna churches of Wayne Quarterly Meeting, New York. About 1865 he assisted in organizing the church at Porter, Michigan and remained its pastor until he died.

Charles A Shattuck
Birth:
Feb. 19, 1815
Leyden, Mass.,
Death:
Apr. 9, 1887
Burial:
Mount Hope Cemetery
Litchfield,
Hillsdale County,
Michigan
Plot: Section 9 Row 1 Lot 3

His manhood was spent in Hillsdale County,Mich., where he engaged in the work of the ministry for some twenty years before his death. He was faithful in duty, and none could leave a better reputation for sincere piety.

John Silvernail
Birth:
November 17, 1828
Greene County, New York
Death:
1917
Burial:
Brigham Cemetery
Monroe County, Michigan

He was brought to Christ in 1852 and was ordained in April 1867. His ministry was mainly in Michigan.

Paul M. Sparks
Birth:
1959
Ivory Coast, West Africa
Death:
1992
Indianapolis, Indiana
Burial:
Edwardsburg Cemetery,
Edwardsburg,
Cass County, Michigan
He was the minister of the Antlers Free Will Baptist Church in Oklahoma at the time of his passing. He had formerly served churches in Winona Lake and Elkhart, Indiana and before was a missionary to Spain.

Federal Alcander Stanford
Birth:

March 15, 1815
Oneida County, New York
Death:
1901
Burial:
Mount Hope Cemetery
Middleville
Barry County, Michigan

He was married to Miss Sophia Hicks in 1838. His conversion took place in 1832 and he was ordained in February, 1854. His ministry was spent in Pennsylvania, Ohio and Michigan with the longest continuous pastorate being in watch in Michigan.

Norman Starr
Birth:
unknown
Death:
Sep. 16, 1865
Burial:
Hart Cemetery
New Baltimore
Macomb County, Michigan

He was an ordained minister connected with the Southfield church of the Oakland Quarterly Meeting, Michigan as early as 1856. He remained with this church until about 1859 when he became pastor of the Chesterfield and Lenox church of that Oxford Quarterly Meeting where he remained until his death. Note: age 42 yrs.

Tilton E. Smith
Birth:
1840
Ontario, Canada Michigan.
Death:
Feb. 4, 1890
Lapeer
Lapeer County, Michigan
Burial:
Mount Hope Cemetery
Lapeer
Lapeer County, Michigan

He was converted in 1860 and in 1880 received license to preach with his connection being with

the Oxford Quarterly Meeting. He was a Civil War VeteranTilton E. Smith serving as Corporal 33 New York Infantry Company-E. Enlisted: May 9, 1861 Discharged: June 2, 1863 Enlisted In: Yorktown, New York

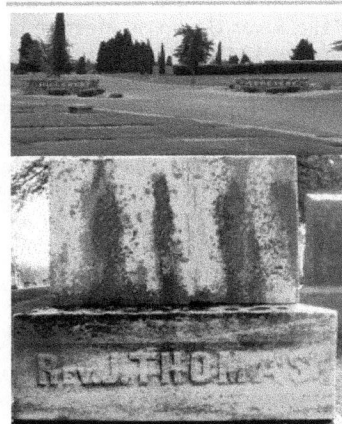

John Thomas
Birth:
unknown
Death:
Oct. 10, 1874
Burial:
Fairfield Cemetery
Adrian, Lenawee County,
Michigan

Thomas, a native of New York, while yet young consecrated himself to God and his work. Soon after receiving license in Royalton, N. Y., he commenced laboring in Michigan, receiving ordination at the Michigan Central Q. M. Feb. 23, 1839. There were then few Free Baptist churches in the state, but giving himself, soul and body, time and talents, to his work, neither the poverty of the churches nor the. roughness of the roads weakened his courage or diminished his fervor. Many log cabins were cheered by his genial presence, many rough schoolhouses were made houses of God and gates of heaven to converted souls. After laboring several years as an evangelist, he settled as pastor and spent nearly twenty-five years with the Wheatland and Fairfield churches of the Bean Creek (later Hillsdale) Q. M. His sermons were short and earnest, sprinkled at times with a little natural eccentricity and wit, and full of love. His sermons were practical and forcible, his life godly and earnest, and the whole enveloped in a cheerful, affectionate spirit, which seemed to be the most forcible element of his nature. After spending a little time in labor at Blackberry, Ill., he returned to the scenes of his former labors, and died Oct. 10, 1874, aged 58 years. He was an early and constant friend of Hillsdale College, and for some time a trustee. He was the Pastor of Fairfield Baptist Church from 1864-1870.

Nelson Thomas
Birth:
1820
Death:
Aug. 7, 1848
Constantine, Michigan
Burial:
Five Points Cemetery
Edwardsburg
Cass County, Michigan
Plot: Section 1, Row 8, Stone 10
He was 27 years old at his death which came only three years after his ordination. However during that three years he organized three churches and was a preacher of much promise.

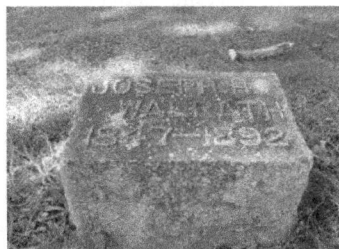

Joseph Harvey Walrath
Birth:
Jan. 14, 1847
Canajoharie
Montgomery County, New York
Death:
Aug. 31, 1892
Michigan
Burial:
Oak Grove Cemetery
Hillsdale
Hillsdale County, Michigan
Plot: Section 14

In 1847 he married Miss L. M. Mount. Entering Hillsdale College in 1871, he passed through both the academical and theological departments graduating in 1878. He was ordained by the Hillsdale Quarterly Meeting in September, 1876 and had the pastoral care of many churches within this state of Michigan, Iowa, South Dakota and Wisconsin. For four years he was secretary treasurer of the Wisconsin Home Mission Board. Other positions which he occupied were: agent of the Free Baptist Western Association, State Agent and Evangelist of the Iowa Yearly Meeting, and was the Corresponding Editor of *The Free Baptist* from its beginning to February 15, 1888. In pastoral and evangelistic work and in his life of official work for the denomination he was successful.

John T. Ward
Birth:
Jan. 20, 1847
Norway,
Herkimer County, New York
Death:
Dec. 9, 1918
Yokohama, Kanagawa, Japan
Burial:
Oak Grove Cemetery, Hillsdale
Hillsdale County, Michigan

He graduated from Whitestown Seminary in 1867, from Hillsdale in 1870, and from Andover Theological Seminary in 1873. While a student in Hillsdale he was a member of the Amphictyon society and the Hillsdale chapter of Delta Tau Delta fraternity,

being one of the seven charter members of the latter when it was founded in 1867. He received ordination to the ministry in the Freewill Baptist church on Dec. 14, 1873. As pastor, Dr. Ward served several of the leading Free Baptist Churches in Ashland, NH; Georgiaville, R.I; Park Street, Providence, RI, and Jackson, MI, and was prominent in the activities of the denomination. He was elected as delegate to the national conference and was on educational boards, and served six years on the Home Mission Board. He was also a member of the General Conference Board and trustee of Hillsdale College from 1889-1898. He became editor and manager of *"The Free Baptist"* at Minneapolis, the first religious paper in the northwest, founded by Rev. A. A. Smith, a former pastor of the College Church in Hillsdale. He managed and edited the paper with distinct efficiency for a number of years, and was instrumental in merging it into *"The Morning Star"* in Boston. During his service as pastor and editor he and two fellow clergymen edited *"The Free Baptist Encyclopedia,"* a large volume of significant ecclesiastic and historic value, which passed to the sole control of Dr. Ward shortly after he and the one surviving collaborator received it from the press and bindery. He had positive convictions on the doctrines and practices of the Church, but was of a practical vision, and was one of the most consistent advocates of co-operation of the denominations in their foreign missions, federation and union at home and abroad, openly supporting the organic union of the Baptists and Free Baptists which was wrought out while he was in Hillsdale. He entered the faculty of Hillsdale College in 1898 where he served until 1913, with one intervening year of leave of absence which he and his wife spent with Mrs. Phelps in Japan. His subjects were theology and homiletics. During a part of the residence of the family in

Hillsdale, the daughter Mary, the only child and a graduate of the University of Minnesota, was an instructor in Hillsdale College, and was active in the religious and club life of the college and city. On her marriage to Mr. Phelps they went to Japan, where he is one of the most prominent of the international secretaries of the Young Men's Christian Assn. Probably remembered now more as the co-author of *"Free Baptist Cyclopedia"* with Gideon Burgess, pub. 1889.

Abraham H Whitaker
Birth:
June 9, 1845
Kirklin, Indiana
Death:
1917
Burial:
Bankers Cemetery
Hillsdale County, Michigan
Plot: Sec 1 Row 2 Lot 16

On January 1, 1868 he married Sarah Ellen Balcom. Brother Whitaker was converted11 years of age, was a student at Centerburg Academy, Ohio and four years at Hillsdale College in Michigan and received his ordination in January, 1871. He pastored many churches in Michigan, and, also churches in Ohio and Wisconsin. He nearly all of these revivals were enjoyed under his labor. He organized three churches and baptized about 200 converts. He was active in temperance and every good work, and was highly esteemed among his brethren both as a preacher and a pastor.

Elder Samuel Whitcomb
Birth:
June I, 1788
Lisbon, N. H
Death:
April 7, 1867
Clarendon, Mich
Burial:
Cook's Prairie Cemetery
Clarendon, Calhoun County, Michigan

Aug. 5, 1813, he married Miss Nancy Jacobs. In 1816 he was thoroughly converted. Soon after he moved to Lyons, N. Y., and joined the Presbyterian church. Disagreeing with them in doctrine, in December, 1819, he united with the Free Baptist church in his place. He moved to Hartland in April, 1822, and soon to Shelby, where he organized a church in 1824, and was its pastor till he moved to Michigan in 1838. Here the next year he organized the Cook's Prairie church in Clarendon, where he retained his membership till death. Oct.10, 1844, his wife died, and he afterwards married Miss Lydia Cowles, of Burlington, Mich. He was in sympathy with all denominational enterprises, a safe counselor, a practical preacher. He was once a member of General Conference.

William E. Whitney
Birth:
1812
Penfield, Monroe County, New York
Death:
Sep. 17, 1893 Leslie
Ingham County, Michigan
Burial:
Woodlawn Cemetery Leslie
Ingham County Michigan

He began his Christian life in 1832, moved to Canada in 1834, commenced to preach in 1844, and was ordained a Free Will Baptist minister in 1846. He moved to Michigan in 1849, and worked with various churches there. He served as a soldier in the Civil War in the Mich. 12th Infantry, Co G, in the early part of the war, and re-enlisted in 1864. He lost a limb, but on his return resumed the work of the ministry and was a faithful servant of God.

Samuel Wire
Birth:
1786
Goshen, Conn
Death:
Jun. 6, 1870
Commerce, Mich.
Burial:
Wixom Cemetery,
Wixom, Oakland County
M ichigan

His father served in the British army and was present at the defeat of Braddock; he also served in the army of the Revolution. Brother Wire moved to western New York in early manhood, and was baptized with his wife by Elder Z. Dean in May, 1819.

Immediately he began to preach and was ordained the same year. In July of that year he and Elder Dean sought out David Marks and introduced him to his life of usefulness, and from that time Brother Wire was active in carrying forward the work. His labors were abundant and successful in western New York and northern Pennsylvania until 1833. when he removed to northeastern Ohio, and labored in the Ohio and Pennsylvania Y. M. Subsequently he returned to New York, where in 1843 his companion of thirty-eight year was parted from him. He afterwards married 'Widow Colby of Sodus. N. Y., and removed to Michigan, where his remaining years were spent. Brother Wire was a man of unusual natural ability and of extraordinary energy. which made his life an exceedingly active one. For many years he is prominently mentioned in the field of his labors, and he did much to strengthen the denomination. His love of preaching was intense, and in the days of his strength, his soul burning with holy zeal, there was sometimes a power in his sermons which was well-nigh irresistible.

Faith is not believing that God can,

It is knowing that God WILL!

Minnesota

John D. Batson
Birth:
Feb. 16, 1835 Otsego
County, New York
Death:
Jan., 1919 Farmington,
Dakota County
Minnesota
Burial:
Corinthian Cemetery
Farmington,
Dakota County
Minnesota

Batson,was born of English parents. He united with the Free Will Baptist Church at Fairwater, Wis., where he was ordained Sept 29, 1861. He settled in Dakota Co. Minn., and began to preach in that new country as congregations could be gathered. He served in the Civil War, in the 4th Minn. Vols., Co. I. until the close of the war. He continued this work and in 1869 organized the Castle Rock church, and later the East Castle Rock church, both of which have been continually favored with his efficient ministry. His education was obtained at Ripon and Carleton Colleges. His sister, Mrs. W.I. Price, was a missionary in Burma. He served for years as clerk of Minnesota YM and a member of the State Mission Board.

A P Corey
Birth:
October 6, 1795
Amherst, Massachusetts
Death:
October 14, 1882
Minnesota
Burial:
Money Creek Cemetery
Money Creek
Houston County, Minnesota

He was ordained by a Council of the Winona and Houston Quarterly Meetings in Minnesota on December 11, 1857. His ministry was largely spent within the bounds of this quarterly meeting having moved there at a very early day. He worked earnestly to establish sabbath schools and churches and he was very highly esteemed for his devoted Christian life.

Frank Llewellyn Durgin
Birth:
1851
Maine
Death:
Sep. 23, 1935
Winnebago,
Faribault County,Minnesota
Burial:
Rosehill Cemetery,
Winnebago,
Faribault County,Minnesota

He married Lucy M. Phillips, dau. of Dr. Jeremiah and Hannah C. Phillips, in Hillsdale, MI, Aug.6, 1877, by Prof. Ransom Dunn, D.D., of Hillsdale College, of which he graduated. He also was graduated from Adelbert Medical College, Cleveland, OH, Mar. 15, 1882.
Many of Lucy's family (eleven siblings) served as Freewill Baptist doctor, missionaries to Orissa Province, Belasore,India.
Inscription:Frank L. Durgin, M.D.

Lucy Marilla *Phillips* Durgin
Birth:
Sep. 6, 1854
New Hampshire
Death:
Mar. 6, 1938
Winnebago,
Faribault County, Minnesota
Burial:
Rosehill Cemetery,
Winnebago,
Faribault County, Minnesota

Lucy M. Durgin was the daughter of Dr. Jeremiah Phillips, Sr., and Hannah (Cummings) Phillips. She, as well as most of her siblings, were medical missionaries with the Freewill Baptist church, her father going to the Orissa area in India when he was 23 yrs of age. Her mother died in India and is bur. there, as well as several other of her family. Lucy married Dr. Frank L. Durgin in Hillsdale, Michigan, Aug. 6, 1877, by Prof. Ransom Dunn, D.D., Hillsdale College, from which she was graduated. Frank Durgin became a medical doctor. Lucy was Lady Principle of Parker College, Minnesota, from 1889-1897.

Wentworth Hayden
Birth:
Oct. 28, 1813 Skowhegan,
Somerset County, Maine
Death:
Feb. 8, 1886
Minneapolis, Hennepin County,
Minnesota
Burial:
Champlin Cemetery, Champlin,
Hennepin County, Minnesota

He was ordained at Mayfield, ME in 1838, ten years after his conversion. In Maine he labored for some time as a home missionary. His ministry was attended with many revivals and several churches were organized. In 1856. Because of impaired health he went to Minnesota, where he organized a church at Champlin and was pastor of the Minneapolis church. He served in the Maine Legislature in 1854, and later in the Minnesota Territorial and State Legislatures, and was the only member of the Minnesota Constitutional Convention that voted against excluding the black man from the ballot.

Josiah Lorenzo Heath
Birth:
1822
New York
Death:
Apr. 12, 1864
High Forest, Olmsted County,
Minnesota
Burial:
High Forest Cemetery
High Forest, Olmsted County,
Minnesota
Plot: Section 1SW 16

He married Candace Louise Fisher She was b: Feb 05, 1820 in Jefferson County, New York and died Oct 28, 1907 in Bangor (LaCrosse) Wisconsin.A native of NY, he moved to Wisconsin about 1844, where in 1859, he was ordained by the Saulk Co. Q.M, among the churches of which he labored, when because of failing health he moved to High Forest, MN, where he died. He was a man of excellent spirit.

Charles Augustus Hilton
Birth:
Jul. 22, 1845
ParsonsfielD
York County, Maine
Death:
Oct. 24, 1912
Minneapolis
Hennepin County, Minnesota
Burial:
Lakewood Cemetery
Minneapolis
Hennepin County, Minnesota
He was converted in 1856. He served two years in the Civil War and returned with an impaired health, in 1868 he was licensed and soon after was ordained. He helped many pastorates including Maine, Illinois, New York, and Massachusetts before coming to Minnesota.

Ruth J *Canney* Keith
Birth:
Feb. 7, 1827
Farmington, Strafford County,
New Hampshire
Death:
Nov. 11, 1898 Minneapolis,
Hennepin County,
Minnesota
Burial:
Lakewood Cemetery, Minneapolis,
Hennepin County, Minnesota

She united with the Free Will Baptist church and was connected with the "Mission Column" of the

'Free Baptist.' In 1883-86. She was a member of the Foreign Mission Board, and for several years has been a member of the board of managers of the Woman's Missionary Society, holding other responsible positions in it. In her service to the cause of missions, especially in connection with the 'Free Baptist, she has been widely known among the FWB people and universally appreciated.

Albert Josiah Marshall
Birth:
Nov. 3, 1847
Death:
Jul. 30, 1924
Burial:
Wadena Cemetery
Wadena
Wadena County, Minnesota

MARSHALL's parents were Josiah H. MARSHALL, and Elizabeth O (Wood) MARSHALL.In January, 1864 he entered the army (WI) and was with Sherman's army on its famous march to the sea and thence north, to the end of the war.He was converted in 1869 while at Rochester Seminary, Wisconsin. After this he studied at Evansville Seminary and at Hillsdale College, Mich., where he completed the theological course and the larger part of the college course. He received license to preach in 1870 and ordination April 26, 1872, in the Freewill Baptist denomination. While at Hillsdale he was pastor successively of the churches at Butler, St. Joseph River, gathered by his labors, and Cook's Prairie, where a considerable revival resulted. While in the Junior class at Hillsdale, the needs of the foreign work were so great that he devoted himself to it, and set sail for India in September, 1873. He was accompanied by his wife, Emily L., a daughter of Rev. Jeremiah Phillips, and a graduate of Hillsdale in the class of 1870, whom he married July 15, 1871. On reaching India they were located at Balasore, where they labored with success until their return in 1882. After a period of recuperation, Brother Marshall was called to the pastorate of the Evansville, Wis., church, and a year and a half later he became principal of Rochester Seminary, which prospered under his direction. He then served a year as editor of the Free Baptist, and entered upon his duties as president of Winnebago College.

Franklin B. Moulton
Birth:
Feb. 15, 1835
Adams, New York
Death:
Jun. 20, 1902
Minnesota
Burial:
Pleasant Prairie Cemetery
Rochester
Olmsted County, Minnesota

Soon after his conversion in 1849, he united with the Methodist Church and entered large university, Wisconsin. His first learning of the Free Will Baptist was in 1855 and he united with this denomination for they held his own doctrinal views. In the March session, 1858, of the Zumbro Quarterly Meeting, Minnesota, he was licensed and excepted the call as the quarterly meeting missionary of the Hennepin Quarterly Meeting which was then on the extreme frontier. In 1861, he assumed the pastorate of the Rolling Prairie church, Wisconsin. The Americans Sunday school Union in 1866 called him to engage in their work which he did for several months. He resigned this work traveling in the interests of the Western Freeman's Mission. In the spring of 1867, he took the pastorate of the Stockbridge church, Wisconsin. His next pastorate was with the Vineland church where a church of 110 members was organized and a church building erected. For many years he labored in Wisconsin, but in 1884 he returned to Minnesota and ministered with some churches there and organizing the Winona church. In 1887, he removed to Diamond Bluff and engage in mission work under the direction of the state home mission board.

A holy war is better than the peace of the devil's palace

Nathan J. Robinson
Birth:
unknown
New Brunswick, Canada
Death:
Sep. 20, 1871
Burial:
Minneapolis Pioneers and
Soldiers Memorial Cemetery
Minneapolis, Hennepin County,
Minnesota
Plot: LOT 34 BLOCK P

C. L. Russell
Birth:
April 21, 1824
Brighton, Maine
Death:
Oct. 25, 1891
Burial:
Lakewood Cemetery
Minneapolis
Hennepin County, Minnesota
Plot: Section 6, Lot 188, Grave 2

He was converted when 12 years of age and on August 16, 1848 married Tryphen Hutchins, who died on January 8, 1885. He was ordained on March 8, 1863 and was pastor at Wellington, Maine for five years, as Sangerville, Maine, three years; at Champlin, Minnesota for 12 years. Revivals were enjoyed in all these places and some have been baptized every year church being materially strengthened he was the quarterly meeting clerk many years and president of the state mission board.
Spouse: Tryphena D. Russell (1829 - 1885)

Levi N Sharp
Birth:
Mar. 18, 1831
New Brunswick, Canada
Death:
Oct. 19, 1894
Minneapolis, Hennepin County, Minnesota
Burial:
Lakewood Cemetery
Minneapolis, Hennepin County, Minnesota

He was born in New Brunswick, March 18, 1832. He was married to Miss E.A. Fenwick {Ellen Adelaide Finwick, Can]. He pursued his preparatory studies at Sackville, N.B., and graduated at the Pennsylvania Medical College. After a short practice in his native place, he graduated at the Royal College of Surgeons of Physicians in Edinburgh, Scotland.Dr. Sharp was converted when a child and has been active in religious work. In 1882, he moved to Minneapolis, Minn., and uniting with the First church there, he has taught in the Sunday-school and serves it as clerk. Since the organization of the Western Free Baptist Publishing Society, he has held, with credit, the responsible position of treasurer. He has moved in political life in New Brunswick and has held many important positions of trust in the community. He is now a lecturer in the Minnesota State Medical College and also in the Winnebago City College.Mrs. Sharp has served jointly with Mrs. H. C. Keith in editing the department of the Woman's Missionary Society.

Andrew A Smith
Birth:
Nov. 5, 1840
North Randolph
Orange County, Vermont
Death:
Jan. 5, 1887
Minneapolis
Hennepin County, Minnesota
Burial:
Lakewood Cemetery
Minneapolis
Hennepin County, Minnesota
Plot: Sec. 7, Lot 115, Grave 5.5

He was married to Laura A. Chubb in 1864, whom he survived less than two years, leaving a son and daughter at his death.Converted to Christ in 1857, he entered New Hampton Institution with the preparation afforded by the North Randolph schools, and fitted for the ministry. His first pastorate was at Topsham, ME, where he was ordained in 1865. His earnestness, fervor, passion for saving souls, and a felicitous way of meeting men won their hearts and their acceptance of the saviour. Leaving Topsham he held a successful pastorate of three years at Portlan, ME, when he was called to the responsible duties as pastor of the college church at Hillsdale, Michigan, in 1873. Here his lively sympathy for the young found full play, his genial temperament gaining for him a ready welcome to the rooms and meetings of the students. During this pastorate he led a large number into the baptismal waters.Accepting a call to the First Free Baptist church of Minneapolis in 1878, his old-time zeal broke forth into a flame that rapidly consumed his expanding life. He deeply felt the need of organization and concentration in that vast field where churches were many miles from each other. He was a leader in uniting the brethren in the ministry by correspondence, and cooperation, among the churches, until a general organization of the churches was agreed upon, and the "Association of the Free Baptist Churches of the Northwest," was the direct result. He saw the need for a Western paper to help unify the churches, and his conviction and tenacity resulted in "The Free Baptist" paper at Minneapolis. Soon after resigning the pastorate of the First Church in Minneapolis, he continued his labors with a mission Sunday-school which he organized in a store building in 1881. He hoped this would be the nucleus for a second church, which was realized in January 1884, when he organized the Stevens Avenue church, of which he became the pastor in connection with editorial and other work, and continued in these relations until his death, when he left a self-supporting church, moved with much of the missionary zeal of their leader and pastor.

Freeborn W Straight
Birth:
1806
Washington County, New York
Death:
Dec. 23, 1878
Monroe County, New York
Burial:
Beach Ridge Cemetery
Brockport,
Monroe County, New York
Plot: B.R. II 165

Soon after his birth, with his father, William Straight, moved to Walworth, Wayne Co. NY. When about twenty-one years of age he ws converted under the labors of Elder Lyon and united with the Walworth Free Baptist church. In about a year he was licensed to preach and soon after, with Elder David Marks, he went to Ontario, Canada, where they traveled and labored with great success. Marks, returning, but Straight remained in Canada and supplied the Woodstock and London churches, forty miles apart, and preached at intervening points. More than a hundred were converted during the winter, and he was sent to New York for ordination in March 1828. He remained in Canada several years and churches were formed which grew to become the Ontario Yearly Meeting. Returning to New York, he was inactive for a time. In 1841, he took up the work and a year later he assisted Brother Bathrick at Conneaut, Ohio, and Bro. Dunn at Mecca, with many being converted at each place. He was pastor at Conneaut two years and assisted in a great revival in Pennfield, N.Y., and later settled as pastor of the church at Fairport for eight years. In the winter of 1851-52 he assisted Bro. Bathrick again at Saco, Maine and more than four hundred were converted in the congregation with the revival being one of unusual power and extending also to other congregations and towns. He seemed almost inspired in his labors there. A part of the following winter was spent in revival work in Saco. After a year at Brockport, he settled at Manchester, New Hampshire., where he remained for three years, and eighty were converted the first winter. After one year at Boston, Massachusetts, and two at Saco ME. he went to Conneaut Ohio in 1861, and two years later to Jackson, Michigan. He remained there nine years, reorganizing the church and carrying it through many difficulties. He then made his home in Lansing, intending to rest, but could not.

Live for eternity

He gathered fragments of several churches together at Grand Ledge, encouraged them to build their beautiful brick church, and by his visits aided the churches at Reading, Cambridge, Paw Paw, Bath, Macon, Delta and Leslie. Then in 1877, visiting the scene of his early labors in Ontario, he took charge of two churches in Zorra, and worked with the zeal and ardor of his youth until his sudden death. Straight was a man of large and commanding form, and of robust health, rather diffident unless aroused by some exigency, pre-eminently social and companionable. His intellect was of a high order, quick, discriminating and logical. He was several times a member of the General Conference. He died at the post of duty near where he preached his first sermon fifty-one years before, and was buried at Brockport, N.Y., near the scenes of his early ministry. He was married to Sarah (unk) Straight,(said to be born in Canada?)and their Family Tree says they married in Lowell, MA. His wife, died on Mar. 4, 1855, at age 43. He was then married to Miriam F. Jenkins, on 27 May 1856, Lowell, MA.

Austin Wheeler
Birth:
unknown
Death:
Feb. 7, 1873
Burial:
Rice Lake Cemetery
Delavan, Faribault County,
Minnesota

Wheeler, a native of Gilead, Me., died in Prescott, Minn., aged 72 years. He was licensed at the age of twenty-six, and ordained the following year. He moved to Otisfield in 1837, and subsequently labored in Hebron, Gardiner, Minot and Canton. Going in May, 1862, to reside in Minnesota, he soon organized a church, and aided in building up the Minnesota Southern Y. M. His baptisms numbered 231. He was a safe counselor and a good preacher, enforcing both with an exemplary life.

Tombstone for
A.K. Moulton
Cleveland, Ohio
Strong leader, preacher,
writer.

On that bright and cloudless morning when the dead in Christ shall rise,

And the glory of his resurrection share;

When his chosen ones shall gather to their home beyond the skies,

And the roll is called up yonder, I'll be there.

Mississippi

Matthew Ranson Allen
Birth:
Oct. 5, 1888
North Carolina
Death:
Jul. 21, 1953
Mississippi,
Burial:
Sherman Cemetery
Sherman
Pontotoc County, Mississippi

Minister, teacher; who pastored churches in Monroe Co. MS. His name is listed in book by Rev. G. C. Lee, Sr., in 1949. College educated he taught school after college. As a minister of the gospel it was said that he served the Lord in pastoring several churches in N. E. MS including Pearce's Chapel in Monroe County near Smithville, MS. Allen married Lillian L. Brasfield, 19 Dec 1914. Born to that union included sons: Doyle, Thomas, an Eustace Dorsey Allen.

William Fondren
Birth:
Dec., 1855
Alabama
Death:
Mississippi
Burial:
Gauley Cemetery, Pittsboro,
Calhoun County, Mississippi

He came to Mississippi sometime between 1870 and 1880, where records show him as performing a number of marriages. He was a Free Will Baptist minister, but it is unknown where and when he was ordained.

Luther D. Gibson
Birth:
Aug. 20, 1920
Mississippi
Death:
May 2, 1992
Booneville,
Prentiss County, Mississippi
Burial:
Tuscumbia Baptist,
Old Hwy 145, Booneville,
Prentiss County, Mississippi

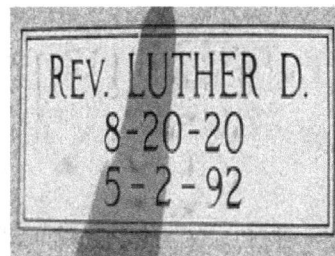

A well-known Free Will Baptist pastor and denominational leader. He pastored for 49 years in Mississippi except for 5 years in Missouri. As a leader, he was the moderator of two district associations and for 25 years served on the Board of Trustees of the Free Will Baptist Bible College in Nashville Tennessee. *The Lumen*, the college yearbook, was dedicated to him in 1976. A Navy veteran serving in World War II. He was a pastor's pastor and a role model for many. He held a Bachelor of Arts degree from Free Will Baptist Bible College and did graduate study at Columbia Bible College in Columbia, South Carolina.

He who has gone, so we but cherish his memory, abides with us, more potent, nay, more present than the living man.
~Antoine de Saint-Exupery~

M. L. Hollis, Sr.
Birth:
Sep. 1, 1898
Death:
Feb. 18, 1974
Amory, Mississippi
Burial:
Masonic Cemetery
Amory, Monroe County, Mississippi

The 17 year old saw mill worker had only completed eight years of school, but God had called him to preach and for several years he fought that calling. Mr. Hollis was licensed to preach in June, 1918. He began holding services and revivals, but somehow he just couldn't shake the conviction that God wanted him to finish school. He tried several ways to get the money to further his education, but each time the door was closed. Finally, Damascus Free Will Baptist Church near Meridian, Mississippi asked Brother Hollis to come to their church for a revival. Meridian seemed to be very far from his home in Vernon, Alabama, yet, he realized this was a call from the Lord. He soon found himself standing on the train depot in Meridian waiting to be met by two

men from the church. However, these two men mistook him for a young boy and they left without the evangelist! Brother Hollis finally managed to get to the church - just in time for the service. As he walked to the pulpit, an elderly man with a beard stroking his belt, said in tones loud enough for that frightened 17 year old to hear, "lf that is our chance for a preacher, we are out!" But God hadn't struck out. At the close of the revival the church offered to call the teenage preacher as pastor of the church and pay his expenses while he finished school. So, Mr. Hollis started back to school in the ninth grade. He finished high school graduating second in his class. The Damascus Church then sent Brother Hollis to Beason Jr. College in Meridian for two years. Several years later, in 1927, Brother Hollis received a scholarship from the John D.Rockefeller Foundation to attend Vanderbilt School of Religion in Nashville, Tennessee. He attended six weeks a year for four years. He later went to Moody Bible lnstitute in Chicago, lllinois. After God had called and prepared His vessel, He began to open doors of service. In 1927 he went to a full time church in Bryan, Texas. He then returned to Red church Bay, Alabama in 1929, where he served as it's pastor for 21 years. Following his five year ministry at the Damascus church, Mr. Hollis accepted the pastorate of five country churches in Alabama for four years. However, during these churches he was already serving, he also had the times the newly organized churches had the responsibility of simultaneously having services on Saturday night or Sunday ministering in five to eleven other mornings at nine o'clock, or Sunday churches, preaching five to six sermons in the afternoon to enable Brother Hollis to pastor or preach every weekend. This schedule was maintained as a typical story repeated 24 times during these years of his ministry Brother

Hollis organized many Free Will Baptist churches. As far as is known there were no Free Will Baptist known who organized more churches as he did. He began as a Free Will Baptist minister in extensive evangelistic endeavors and organizing churches. Because of his ability and dedication, he was elected chairman of the National Home Missions Board in 1938. Not only is Mr. Hollis known for his pastoral and organizational work. but he has been one of the most widely used evangelists in 20th century in Free Will Baptist history. Whether the revival was held in brush-arbors, tents, churches, or auditoriums, God blessed the revival work of M. L. Hollis. One of the best remembered revivals in this evangelist's ministry was held at Pearce Chapel Free Will Baptist Church in Smithville, Mississippi. At the close of the week 78 converts were baptized. Because of the large number of baptismal candidates several hundred people gathered at the river to watch. Many doubted that the short evangelist could accomplish the strenuous task by himself. However, he not only baptized all 78, but he did ¡t ¡n exactly 32 minutes! Manv called Mr. Hollis aga¡n and again as evangelist. The Damascus Church where he first pastored has had him in revival 33 times. Brother Hollis' ministry spanned over 55 years with his longest pastoral tenure being 35 years at the Pearce Chapel Church. During these years he had become well-known for his prophetic messages. One of the highlights of his ministry was his visit to he Holy Land. Even though in his 70s he thrilled to see the area where many Biblical prophecies, of which he has so long preached, will be fulfilled. It is impossible to fully realize what this veteran preacher has meant to the Lord's work. A numerical summary of his work is given in his own words: "l have organized 24 churches, held revivals in 23 states, baptized more than 6,000 converts, received into Free Will

Baptist churches over 10,000 members, married numerous couples and average over 100 funeral a year. His spousd were Effie Mae Hollis (1898 - 1969) who married in 1922 and Helen Streety who he married have the death of Effie..

Inscription:
A Devoted Husband, A Loving Father.And A Faithful Soldier Of The Cross Of Jesus Christ

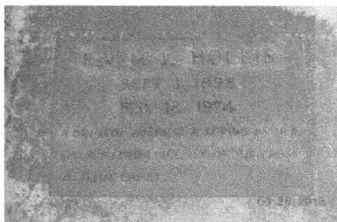

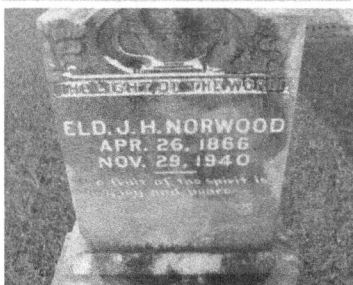

James H. Norwood
Birth:
Apr. 26,1866
Death:
Nov. 29,1940
Mississippi
Burial:
Antioch Cem.,
Toccopola
Pontotoc Co. MS

Daniel Wyatt Jones, Jr
Birth:
Mar. 23, 1930
Death:
Apr. 20, 2011
Burial:
Little Brown Cemetery,
New Site,
Prentiss County, Mississippi

He was a member of New Lebanon Freewill Baptist Church, a retired Freewill Baptist preacher and a sheet metal mechanic. He was the son of Rev. D.W. Jones Sr.

John A. Killingsworth
Birth:
Dec. 5, 1852
Mississippi
Death:
Jan. 4, 1925
Calhoun County, Mississippi
Burial: Pittsboro
Cemetery, Pittsboro,
Calhoun County, Mississippi

A Free Will Baptist pioneer minister/pastor in Mississippi.

George Cullen Lee
Birth:
May 3, 1887
Calhoun County, Mississippi
Death:
Jul. 12, 1971
Calhoun County, Mississippi
Burial:
New Gauley Cemetery,
Calhoun City,
Calhoun County, Mississippi

A Mississippi FWB minister for over 62 year and a man of faith. From the Calhoun newspaper, "Rev Lee was one of Calhoun County's best citizens and in addition, is a forceful, eloquent and successful preacher. If we were called on to name most valuable citizen of Calhoun City, Rev. Lee would be among those who would come to our mind. He lives his religion every day of his life; he meddles with no person's affairs, but is ever ready to help and advise when there is trouble or sorrow. He is not the spectacular, egotistical type of preacher--he goes about his work quietly, confidently, full of high purpose. George Lee is a product of Calhoun and we are proud of him." He was called to preach in his home church of Gauley Free Will Baptist Church west of Calhoun City, MS and pastored there from 1909 until the late 60's or approximately 60 years. He married Estelle Whitworth in 1909 and they had 8 children. Clara Mae, who died in infancy, Marie, Lillian, Lora, Nellie Helen, Wanda and G.C., Jr. followed.

He pastored country churches in Mississippi during his ministry and a partial listing of them were: New Gauley, New Life, Priceville, Antioch, Bethlehem, Lee's Chapel, Stetson's Chapel, Beech Springs, McGregor's Chapel Springdale. Those are some of the ones I recall going to with him but this is an incomplete list. (GC Lee,Jr.)
He married hundreds of couples and conducted at least 500 funerals.

Iris Lyndon Stanley
Birth:
Mar. 19, 1906
Saltillo, Lee County, Mississippi
Death:
Sep. 27, 1993
Saltillo, Lee County, Mississippi
Burial:
Spring Hill Cemetery,
Saltillo,
Lee County, Mississippi

He was the first Superintendent of the Free Will Baptist Home for Children in Greenville, Tennessee. He served in this position for 25 years. He started the Harris Memorial Free Will Baptist Church in Greenville so the children would have a Free Will Baptist church to attend. He was a World War II veteran of the U.S. Army and a former school teacher with the Lee County school system. He was a well known music director assisting the late Rev. H. L. Hollis in starting many Free Will Baptist churches in Mississippi and Alabama. He was frequently used as the song leader of the National Association at its annual sessions.

To be cursed by God, one need not do the *wrong* thing, just *nothing*.

George W. Wages
Birth:
May 5, 1886
Death:
Jun. 27, 1972
Burial:
Blue Mountain Cemetery
Blue Mountain
Tippah County, Mississippi

Rev. Geo. Washington Wages, was a FWB minister, mentioned in a book pub. in 1949, by Rev. G.C. Lee, Sr., who had association with him. In the 1940 census he states his occupation. as 'minister.' He was esteemed by those who knew him. George W. Wages married Viola Sewell on September 15, 1907. They had 6 children.

To call his soul to the life immortal Where souls a-weary shall rest with God.

Missouri

O. T. Allred
Birth:
Sep. 12, 1895
Death:
Apr. 29, 1976
Burial:
Bethel Cemetery, Masters,
Cedar County, Missouri

Well-known Free Will Baptist preacher and pastor in the Southwest region of the state of Missouri. He was one of the early writers for the Free Will Baptist Gem and was a contemporary with B.F. Brown the first editor. He, with John Rollins, Ken Turner and Winford Davis, were all the early pastors in the Indian Creek Association.

Earl Edward Altis
Birth:
Mar. 14, 1933
Death:
Apr. 12, 1986
Springfield
Greene County, Missouri
Burial:
Providence Cemetery, Cabool,
Texas County, Missouri

He received his bachelor's degree from Southwest Missouri State University in 1961, his Master's degree from the University of Denver in 1964 and an advanced studies certificate in 1974. He was a teacher and librarian in Missouri and Oklahoma colleges and schools. He also served as a Free Will Baptist pastor in Missouri and Colorado. He helped organize the Church Training Services organization in Missouri and served as the editor of the Free Will Baptist Gem. He married Judy Shrewsbury in Nashville, Tennessee in 1979.

Lewis P. Barker
Birth:
1913
Death:
Nov. 24, 2002
Oklahoma City, Okla.
Burial:
Licking Cemetery, Licking,
Texas County, Missouri

He was a member of the First Free Will Baptist Church in Moore, Okla. He pastored FWB churches in Arkansas and Missouri. Surviving are one daughter, Willie Jean Deeds, retired missionary to Brazil, of Moore, Okla.; two sons, Charles Berton Barker of Licking and Dr. Robert Lewis Barker of Oak Park, Calif.

Harry Howard Beatty
Birth:
Aug. 16, 1911
Oregon County, Missouri
Death:
Feb. 27, 1994
Owasso,
Tulsa County, Oklahoma
Burial:
Thayer Cemetery, Thayer,
Oregon County, Missouri

Beatty was converted at the age 19 and began his ministry in the Thayer area. He was a well known Freewill Baptist minister for many years in Missouri and Oklahoma as a pastor and church planter. He was the first Missouri Promotional Secretary of Free Will Baptist and served in that capacity from 1961 until 1975. During his tenure led the state of Missouri in becoming one of the strongest co-operative giving states in the denomination.

Lue Bequette
Birth:
Apr. 16, 1922
Death:
Jan. 4, 2008
Burial:
Mine La Motte Cemetery,
Mine La Motte,
Madison County, Missouri

He was an early Free Will Baptist minister and pastored in the St. Francois Association in Southeast Missouri.

Manuel Eugene Bingham
Birth:
May 7, 1924
Death:
Apr. 22, 2007
Burial:
New Home Cemetery, Falcon,
Laclede County, Missouri

He worked as a cattle farmer and in the timber. Manuel followed the Free Will Baptist faith throughout the years.

Miles Evans Brasher
Birth:
Sep. 6, 1855
Death:
Feb. 23, 1948
Burial:
Crossroads Cemetery,
Lebanon,
Laclede County, Missouri

Benjamin F. Brown
Birth:
Jan. 6, 1870
Death:
Aug. 29, 1964
Barry County, Missouri
Burial:
Purdy Cemetery, Purdy,
Barry County, Missouri

Rev. B. F. Brown was the second president of Tecumseh College in Tecumseh, Oklahoma until after 1927 when the school burned. At that time there was a committee considering a publication that would be located in Missouri, but a publication for everyone in the denomination. This committee offered B. F. Brown the opportunity to be the first editor, even though he still resided in Tecumseh. The first issues of the *Free Will Baptist GEM* were published in Tecumseh, beginning January 1929. In May of 1930 the paper was moved to Purdy, Missouri. Rev. Brown moved to Purdy and continued as editor until 1939 when he retired. At that time, the publication was moved to Monett, Missouri. However, in 1946 he was called upon to rescue the magazine and became the acting editor from December of 1946 until August of 1947. B. F. Brown during the time between 1929 until 1935 had become a leader in the Cooperative Association which existed throughout the Midwest. It later was to merge with the General Conference, a conference mainly in the Southeast, in 1935 at Nashville, Tennessee. Rev. Brown would sign for the Cooperative Association to accept the agreement with the General Conf. This agreement in 1935 formed the National Association of Free Will Baptists. Rev. Brown was a member of the executive board and served as its secretary. Later, he became a member of the Home Missions Board of the National Convention. Records revealed that he attended the national convention until about 1946.

Claude R Bryan
Birth:
May 13, 1884
Death:
Nov. 26, 1981
Burial:
Thayer Cemetery, Thayer, Oregon County, Missouri

He was an early Free Will Baptist preacher in the south-central part of the state of Missouri.

Cecil Herbert Campbell
Birth:
Sep. 28, 1910 Stella, Newton County, Missouri
Death:
Jul. 18, 1999
North Little Rock,

Pulaski County, Arkansas
Burial:
Jones Chapel Cemetery, Stella, Newton County, Missouri

He served churches in Missouri and North Carolina. He conducted revivals in Texas, Oklahoma, Missouri, North and South Carolina. He was an active denominational leader on state and national levels, with a good ministry where ever he served.

Mike S. Cleaver
Birth:
Nov. 21, 1897
Death:
Dec. 6, 1971
Burial:
Oakside Cemetery, Summersville, Shannon County, Missouri

Fred E Comber
Birth:
1857
Canada
Death:
1917
Galveston
Galveston County. Texas
Burial:

Weiss Cemeter
Doe Run
St. Francois County, Missouri
Born in Canada; immigrated to Bonne Terre, Mo. to work as an engineer at about 18 years of age. Married Elizabeth Weiss of Doe Run about 1885. About 1895 he began preaching and helped to organize Free Baptist Churches. He had served the Free Baptist Churches at Doe Run, MO, Murphysboro and Ava, IL and various other localities in this area as well as southern Illinois.He was preceded in death by his wife Elizabeth early in 1915, after which he located in the Galveston, TX area for health reasons and where he had accepted a pastorate. Funeral Services were conducted by his friend and co-worker of many years, Reverend George Gordon of Ava, IL. Note: per Gib Weiss - a neighbor's team of Percheron horses were used to skid the tombstone up to the cemetery. Tombstone was donated by some of his parishoners (from another state) and shipped to the Weiss farm in Doe Run.

Henry Clay Crase
Birth:
1865
Death:
1966
Burial:
Garfield Cemetery, Garfield, Oregon County, Missouri

He had a long ministry in the Free Will Baptist denomination and was very active as a district and state leader.

William Elvin Crews
Birth:
Sep. 22, 1893 Alton,
Oregon County,
Missouri
Death:
Aug. 24, 1946 Oregon
County, Missouri
Burial:
Shiloh Cemetery, Alton,
Oregon County, Missouri
He was a Veteran of the U.S Army (Pvt; Btry D, 342 Inf) serving in World War I. Minister of the Freewill Baptist Church.

Winford C. Davis
Birth:
Dec. 8, 1904
Death:
May 5, 1997
Burial:
Bethel Cemetery, Monett,
Barry County, Missouri

Davis lived to be 93 years old and had been a Free Will Baptist preacher for more than 70 years in which time he was a very active leader in the denomination.
He was converted at age 12 at a brush arbor revival. He preached his first sermon in the Macedonia Free Will Baptist Church in 1926 and was a member of that church at the time of his death. He pastored churches for 60 years including 40 years at the Macedonia church in various tenures. He served for 19 years as Secretary-Treasurer of the Missouri State Association. He was a member of the National Board Of Education that led the denomination to establish the Free Will Baptist Bible College. He was Secretary-Treasurer of the Foreign Missions Board and made three trips to Cuba: in 1942; in

1944; and in 1946. He helped to establish Missouri's magazine, *THE GEM*, and served 3 1/2 years as its editor and manager from a printing office in Monett. He kept a comprehensive record of his ministry which recorded he had preached 9,100 sermons, won 2,170 souls to the Lord, and received 1,385 members into the church. He traveled 330,772 miles, not counting three trips to Cuba and three trips to Israel. He conducted 159 revivals, officiated at 173 weddings, and conducted 621 funerals. He organized 13 churches, baptized 40, and ordained 30 deacons. He attended the organizational meeting of the National Association in 1935 and was a member of the Treaties Committee. He was truly a pioneer within the Free Will Baptist denomination.

Christian Benjamin Dees
Birth:
Jun. 28, 1902
Fredericktown,
Madison County, Missouri
Death:
May 19, 1973
St. Louis City, Missouri
Burial:
Woodlawn Cemetery,
Leadington,
St. Francois County,
Missouri

An active pastor and leader in Missouri. He was editor of the Free Will Baptist Gem, serving in that position for a number of years. He was a member of the St. Francios Association in South East Missouri.

Alice M Dickey
Birth:
1907
Death:
2001
Burial:
White Chapel Memorial Gardens,
Springfield,
Greene County, Missouri

She was a longtime minister and known for founding the First Free Will Baptist Church of Kansas City, Missouri.

Claude A. Dotson
Birth:
Aug. 23, 1891
Death:
Apr. 29, 1954
Burial:
Huddleston Cemetery,
Alton,
Oregon County, Missouri

An early Free Will Baptist pastor in south central Missouri.

William Driver, Sr
Birth:
1859
Jefferson City, Missouri
Death:
1934
Burial:
Iberia Cemeter
Iberia
Miller County, Missouri

Was born in in 1859, the son of a slave woman named Amanda/Mandy Dixon. At an early age he was adopted by a black family named Driver and carried that name the rest of his life.William Driver, Sr. moved to Laclede Co., MO in the early 1880's and located near the small town of Eldridge. He became a preacher in the Free Will Baptist Church and traveled around central Missouri as an evangelist. About 1916 he moved his wife and children to Miller County and located southwest of Iberia near the Pleasant Hill community and the old Rankin Wright Cemetery. Driver was a well-known minister in the area as he traveled around preaching the Holy Word and playing loudly on his large drum. When he died in 1934, his funeral was held at the Iberia Nazarene Church, conducted by Rev. Otto Shearrer. He was buried at the Iberia Cemetery (per his obituary) but no stone marks his grave today.

Eunice S. *Jenkerson* Edwards
Birth:
Jan. 5, 1912
Death:
Jul. 30, 1997
St. Francois County, Missouri
Burial:
Parkview Cemetery, Farmington,
St. Francois County, Missouri

She served as pastor at the Leadington Freewill Baptist Church in Missouri and then she served the National Free Will Baptist Women's Auxiliary for seven years as Director. A great leader and servant of God.

Warren Franklin
Birth:
Mar. 12, 1879
Osseo, Wisconsin
Death:
May 25, 1957
Burial:
Lone Rock Cemetery,
Plad,
Dallas County, Missouri

He was an early Free Will Baptist minister.

Tom C Ferguson
Birth:
1870
Death:
1957
Burial:
Alta Vista Cemetery
Alta Vista, Daviess County,
Missouri

Ross H. Green
Birth:
May 7, 1929
Death:
Apr. 28, 1989
Burial:
Parrack Grove Cemetery,
Macks Creek,
Camden County, Missouri

He was a veteran and Cpl in the US Air Force. He was a minister & pastor in the Free Will Baptist denomination.

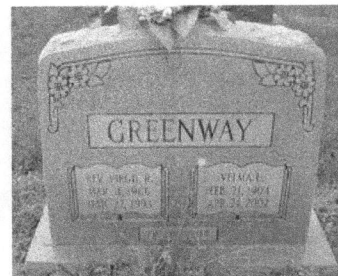

Virgil R. Greenway
Birth:
Mar. 4, 1906
Missouri
Death:
Mar. 27, 1993
Joplin,
Jasper County, Missouri
Burial:
Leann Cemetery,
Leann, Barry County, Missouri,
Plot: Row 30, Plot 419

Early Free Will Baptist preacher in the state of Missouri serving mostly in the region around Monett and southeast Missouri.

Benjamin F Henderson
Birth:
1874
Death:
1950
Burial:
Bethel Cemetery, Monett,
Barry County, Missouri

Early Free Will Baptist preacher in southwestern Missouri.

William C Hill
Birth:
Jul. 22, 1920
Death:
Jul. 8, 1986
Burial:
Polk Memorial Cemetery
Ellington
Reynolds County, Missouri:

He served as pastor of the Flat Woods Free Will Baptist Church in St. Francois QM.

Elmer Hodges
Birth:
May 7, 1883
Alton,
Oregon County, Missouri
Death:
Sep. 19, 1960
Alton,
Oregon County, Missouri
Burial:
Smyrna Cemetery, Alton,
Oregon County, Missouri

He was a pastor and minister in southcentral Missouri serving in the early days of the denomination in that region.

King David Hudgens
Birth:
Sep. 16, 1847
Phipps County, Missouri
Death:
Jul. 16, 1920
Burial:
Dunkard Cemetery
Saint Robert
Pulaski County, Missouri

He entered the ministry among the Presbyterians in 1875 and a few years later became a Free Will Baptist with the Big Creek Quarterly Meeting, Prosperity Assn, Missouri ministering to the Liberal church.

E. Marie Hyatt
Birth:
1920
Death:
April 1, 2002
Burial:
Warrensburg Memorial Gardens Cemetery,
Warrensburg,
Johnson County, Missouri,
Plot: Section 2
Lot 147 Space 1

Rev. E. Marie Hyatt, and Myron E. Hyatt were married at the Free Will Baptist Church, Monett. She served 40 years in church ministry, with the first 12 years with the Free Will Baptist Church. She was a member of Professional Women, Chaplain of AARP and the Western Missouri Medical Center

Lloyd T. Jeffrey's
Birth:
Apr. 23, 1917
Death:
Mar. 4, 1972
Burial:
Monett IOOF Cemetery,
Monett,
Lawrence County, Missouri

He was a retired Army officer and pastored in the Indian River Association of Free Will Baptist in Southwest Missouri. His wife was the Rev. Opal Jeffrey's and they both pastored Merl's Chapel Free Will Baptist Church near Cassville.

Opal Ethel McClerren Jeffrey's
Birth:
Jul. 8, 1921
Death:
Oct. 2, 2000
Burial:
Monett IOOF Cemetery,
Monett,
Lawrence County, Missouri

She was a well-known Free Will Baptist minister and pastor in southwest Missouri serving for many years the Merl's Chapel Free Will Baptist Church near Cassville. She was married to the Rev. Lloyd Jeffrey's a retired Army officer.

Arthur A. Kicenski
Birth:
Dec. 21, 1896
Death:
Dec. 29, 1970
Burial:
Clintonville Cemetery,
El Dorado Springs,
Cedar County, Missouri

He was active Free Will Baptist minister serving in the Missouri & Kansas region.

Absalom Sussdorf Lick
Birth:
Jul. 31, 1853
Illinois
Death:
Jul. 17, 1942
Springfield,
Greene County, Missouri
Burial:
Dixon Cemetery, Dixon,
Pulaski County, Missouri

He served in central Missouri.

Charles Earl Mann
Birth:
Jul. 8, 1875
Glenwood,
Schuyler County, Missouri
Death:
Mar. 20, 1943
Jackson County, Missouri
Burial:
Jimtown Cemetery,
Queen City
Schuyler County, Missouri

He was an early minister and pastor in central Missouri.

Thomas J. Mann
Birth:
1880
Death:
1943
Burial:
Pendleton Cemetery
Doe Run
St. Francois County, Missouri

He was pastor of the church in Flat River in 1918.

Samuel H Marcum
Birth:
Aug. 14, 1891

Death:
Mar. 19, 1975
Burial:
Evergreen Cemetery,
Cameron,
Clinton County, Missouri

An early Minister and active leader in the state of Missouri.

John D McKown
Birth:
Apr. 29, 1892
Daviess County, Missouri
Death:
Mar., 1982
Jamesport,
Daviess County, Missouri
Burial:
Clear Creek Cemetery,
Lock Springs,
Daviess County, Missouri

His ministry was basically confined to Daviess County Missouri. Note: his life and ministry extended 90 years.

Wm. F. Millard
Birth:
Aug. 18, 1874
Death:
Aug. 15, 1958
Burial:
Lebanon City Cemetery,

Lebanon
Laclede County, Missouri,
Plot: 18-5 Blk 14
An early Free Will Baptist minister in Laclede County Missouri.

George Miller
Birth:
Sep. 3, 1834
Death:
Jan. 11, 1900
Burial:
Elmwood Cemetery,
Kansas City,
Jackson County, Missouri
One of the early Free Will Baptist ministers in western Missouri.

James F. Miller
Birth:
Sep. 3, 1894
Bollinger County,
Missouri
Death:
May 14, 1965
Farmington,
St. Francois County, Missouri
Burial:
Union Light Cemetery, Loyd,
Bollinger County, Missouri

During his ministry he pastored in four different states: Missouri, Texas, North Carolina and Tennessee. He was elected the Missouri State Moderator for Free

Will Baptists in 1933 where he served eleven years.

He was elected as Moderator of the National Association of Free Will Baptists in 1938, a position he held for seven consecutive years. He served as a member of the Board of Trustees to the Free Will Baptist Bible College for sixteen years. The college yearbook was dedicated to him in 1963. He received a life time honorary membership in the college Alumni Association in April, 1965. He became a representative of the college in his later years and traveled in 16 states in the interest of the school. Funeral service were held at the Farmington Free Will Baptist Church by the Rev. Charles Thigpen, Dean of the college in Nashville, Tennessee. He was assisted by the Rev Everett Hellard, pastor of the church.

"Jesus Christ is in the noblest, and most perfect sense, the realized ideal of humanity."

John H Noble
Birth:
Jun. 24, 1832
McMinn County, Tennessee
Death:
Jul. 13, 1903
Burial:
Ashland Cemetery
Saint Joseph
Buchanan County, Missouri

In 1861 he married Betty Tuck. His conversion took place in 1866 and ordination in 1872. He united with the Free Baptists in 1876 and has conducted several revivals and organized four churches. Besides pastorates in Tennessee he also pastored in Missouri where he died.

James Coy Powell
Birth:
Dec. 25, 1923
Dunklin County, Missouri
Death:
Jan. 4, 1994
Flint
Genesee County, Michigan
Burial:
Mount Gilead Cemetery
Clarkton
Dunklin County, Missouri

His parents were Colombus Powell, and Luella Powell. He was one of several children. He married Sally Jane McFarland 8 Feb. 1943, in St. Louis, MO. A Free Will Baptist minister. He was pastor of the Friendship FWB in Flint, Michigan for many years.

John Postlewaite
Birth:
Apr. 5, 1926
Graff, Missouri.
Death:
Oct. 21, 2012
Sentera Leigh Hospital
Norfolk, Virginia
Burial:
Hillcrest Cemetery
Mountain Grove, Wright County, Missouri

He was the 8th son of the late John Jefferson and Lucy Jane (Crewse) Postlewaite. He was 86 years, 6 months, and 16 days of age at his death.John was saved at the age of 12 at the No. 1 Free Will Baptist Church near Huggins, Missouri, when his teacher dismissed school for the students to attend an 11:00 revival service. He answered the call to preach at the age of 19. After attending Free Will Baptist Bible College (now Welch College) in Nashville, Tennessee, he was ordained as a minister of the gospel in 1947. He married Leah Mae Scott on September 21, 1948 at the home of Rev. Homer B. Smith near Mountain Grove. To this union were born 4 children. John's first pastorate was at Faith and Hope Free Will Baptist Church near Willow Springs, Missouri. There John and Leah lived in a small log cabin, which was the church parsonage. Throughout the next 53 years, he pastored churches in Oklahoma, Arkansas, Illinois, and Missouri. He planted 7 churches in Washington and Oregon under the auspices of Free Will Baptist Home Missions. He was a well-known evangelist, soul winner, supporter of missions, and mentor to many young people. After moving back to Mountain Grove in his retirement years, he served as Senior Citizens' Pastor at First Free Will Baptist for almost 8 years. He had a lovely tenor voice and often sang in church and at home. He was also a lover of the Scripture and committed many passages to memory. Even in his last days, he spent several hours a day reading the Bible and could still quote many passages. He and his wife, Leah, shared 64 years.His four children were: Joe and Pauline Postlewaite of Florence, South Carolina; Sue and Earl Larson of Brentwood, Tennessee; Sam and Diana Postlewaite of Virginia Beach, Virginia; and Ruth and Donnie McDonald of Tokyo, Japan. Only eternity will reveal how many spiritual children were saved because of his faithful witness.

William T. 'Bill' Reeves
Birth:
Jan. 1, 1902
Death:
Sep. 15, 1994
Burial:
Big River Cemetery, Irondale,
Washington County, Missouri

He ministered in central Missouri and was a regular contributor to the Free Will Baptist Gem. An influential officer and leader in the state Sunday school convention. In later years he was superintendent of the youth camp at Niangua which continues today as a beautiful and well attended camp for Missouri youth.

Elder Samuel Nelson Reid
Birth:
1868
Death:
1946
Burial:
Crossroads Cemetery,
Lebanon,
Laclede County, Missouri

He was an early pastor and minister in the central region of the state of Missouri.

John Byron Rollins
Birth:
Jul. 16, 1912
Stone County, Missouri
Death:
Jul. 6, 2003
Jefferson City,
Cole County, Missouri
Burial:
Hawthorn Memorial Gardens,
Jefferson City,
Cole County, Missouri

He was a 1932 graduate of Purdy High School in Purdy, Missouri. He was a Free Will Baptist

minister who as early Minister and pastor began work with the Free Will Baptist GEM as a printer and writer.

When the founder B. F. Brown retired at age 70, he was succeeded by Rev. Rollins. In this position he traveled much of the State of Missouri. He was a prolific writer, theologian, and well respected by his peers. He moved to Jefferson City where he united with the Southern Baptist, serving the Russellville Baptist Church, New Hope Baptist Church, Elston Baptist Church, Enon Baptist Church, Cole Springs Baptist Church, and the Little Flock Baptist Church in Vienna. He began to work with the *Word and Way* newspaper for the Missouri Baptist and by the time of his death at age 90 had performed 1648 weddings in the Jefferson City area.

John F. Schebaum
Birth:
Aug. 7, 1918
Death:
Jul. 7, 2000
Burial:
Big Creek Cemetery
Yukon
Texas County, Missouri

He was converted in 1955 and was ordained as a Deacon before answering his called to preach in 1963. During his 37 years of ministry he pastored six Free Will Baptist churches in Missouri and one in Tennessee. He also served as a supply pastor for several churches and maintained an active tape ministry and Bible study at two nursing homes. At the time of his passing he was a member of the First Free Will Baptist Church in Waynesville, Missouri. He was married to Lorene Emeline Dixon Schebaum (1918 - 2011).

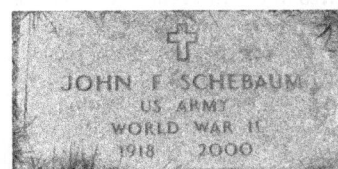

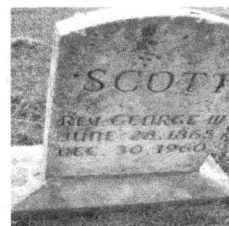

George Washington Scott
Birth:
Jun. 28, 1865
Ozark County, Missouri
Death:
Dec. 30, 1960 Wright
County, Missouri
Burial:
Mountain Valley Cemetery,
Mountain Grove,
Wright County, Missouri

He pastored several churches in the area.

James W Sellards
Birth:
Jun. 28, 1835
Floyd County, Kentucky
Death:
Aug. 8, 1897
Missouri
Burial:
Barber-Whitener Cemetery
Zion
Madison County, Missouri

He was brought to God in 1861, and ordained by the larger Baptist body in 1864 laboring with them in Minnesota. He experienced much difficulty because of his open communion views; and, on moving to Missouri and learning of the Free Baptists at Fredericktown in 1885 where he united with the church.

Elza Elisha Simpson
Birth:
Dec. 13, 1898
Wilderness,
Oregon County,
Missouri
Death:
Sep. 25, 1994
St. Louis County,
Missouri
Burial:
Smyrna Cemetery, Alton,
Oregon County,
Missouri

Richard 'Milo' Standley
Birth:
Jun. 14, 1859
Pennsylvania
Death:
Dec. 31, 1935
Couch, Oregon County,
Missouri
Burial:
New Salem Cemetery,
Couch, Oregon County,
Missouri

Son of William Richard Standley and Mary (Mathias) Standley. He first married Virgiline Crowell (1869-1932) on 07-Sep-1884 at Oregon Co., MO. Afterwards he married Caroline Mary Harder (1860-1892) about 1894. He was a farmer and preacher. Standley, of Cave Springs Association, gave his life for the cause of Christ. He traveled many miles in a buggy, pulled by a white mule named Maude. He preached in the Missouri and Arkansas Lapland: Many Springs, Walnut Grove, Bonds, New Salem, Hideout School House, Corning and Paragould, Arkansas, to name a few. Many were saved and baptized under his preaching. He and his wife, Caroline Harder, foster daughter to Judge John F. Harder of Many Springs, lived at Couch, Missouri.

William Preston Stogsdill
Birth:
Jan. 31, 1870
Oregon County, Missouri
Death:
Jul. 18, 1944
Oregon County, Missouri
Burial:
Cave Springs Cemetery,
Alton, Oregon County, Missouri

Free Will Baptist minister in south central Missouri.

A Star that shines in darkness

John C Swaffar
Birth:
Jun. 19, 1904
Death:
May 31, 1996
Burial:
New Site Cemetery, Monett,
Barry County, Missouri

Minister in South west Missouri.

John H Tally
Birth:
Dec. 25, 1878
Ash Flat,
Sharp County, Arkansas
Death:
Aug. 22, 1948 Thayer,
Oregon County,
Missouri
Burial:
Walker Cemetery,
Thayer,
Oregon County, Missouri

Ministry was mainly in southern Missouri.

Grover V Terry
Birth:
Apr. 7, 1913
Death:
Sep. 8, 1999
Burial:
Marshfield Cemetery
Marshfield
Webster County, Missouri

One of the leading Missouri pastors and very active in denominational affairs prior to his retirement.

Roena C Thomas
Birth:
1898
Death:
1959
Burial:
Worsley Cemetery,
Bronaugh,
Vernon County, Missouri

She was a Free Will Baptist Minister for 26 years in the state of Missouri.
Inscription:
Minister -
26 years

Lawrence Delmon Thompson
Birth:
May 16, 1925
Salem, Dent County, Missouri
Death:
Sep. 17, 1980
Saint Louis, St. Louis County, Missouri
Burial:
Salem Grove Cemetery, Salem
Dent County, Missouri

Lawrence Thompson was a WWII Navy Vet, and was a pastor for 28 years. He was killed in a light plane crash along with 2 other pastors from the St. Louis area. He is remembered for his strong leadership in the state of Missouri.

Kenneth Turner
Birth:
Nov. 27, 1907
Death:
Feb. 8, 1998
Burial:
Jones Chapel Cemetery,
Stella,
Newton County, Missouri

Minister, pastor, and able denominational leader. He pastored churches in Missouri, Arkansas, Oklahoma and Kansas. He was on a Joplin TV station doing magic acts in the middle 50's. He went to Cuba three times filming the mission work there and traveled for 15 years in the United States raising funds for foreign missions. He served five years as president of the Free Will Baptist League and served in numerous roles in denominational offices during his 66 years of ministry.

Robert J Warner
Birth:
Mar. 16, 1941
Death:
Feb. 15, 1997
Fredericktown,
Madison County, Missouri
Burial:
Mine La Motte Cemetery,
Mine La Motte,
Madison County, Missouri

A minister, and denominational officer. He retired after 20 years in the military and returned to Missouri where he farmed and pastored. He was the Clerk of the Missouri State Association at the time of his death.

Ira Waterman
Birth:
Nov. 6, 1873
Missouri
Death:
Nov. 23, 1926
Laclede County, Missouri
Burial
Hufft Cemetery
Eldridge, Laclede County, Missouri

Free Will Baptist minister and public school teacher.

His Grace is Sufficient

Mary Elizabeth *Retherford* Wellbaum
Birth:
1887
Death:
1972
Burial:
Greentop Cemetery, Greentop, Schuyler County, Missouri

She was a well-known and respected Free Will Baptist minister in central Missouri.

Willie K. Weston
Birth:
Sep. 30, 1904
Death:
Apr. 9, 1988
Burial:
Monett IOOF Cemetery, Monett, Lawrence County, Missouri

He was a well-known pastor and minister in Indian Association in southwestern Missouri and was a regular contributor to the Free Will Baptist GEM.

The saint of God is escorted to a land where there is no more dying.

Paul Williams
Birth:
Feb. 9, 1918
Carterville,
Jasper County, Missouri
Death:
Jan. 12, 1963
Duquesne,
Jasper County, Missouri
Burial:
Carterville Cemetery,
Carterville,
Jasper County, Missouri,
Plot: Section 4A, Lot 48

He founded the Joplin Free Will Baptist Church where he served for eight years before an unexpected heart attack. Prior to this he pastored the Carterville Free Will Baptist Church. He was an active member of the Joplin Ministerial Alliance and the Niangua Youth Camp Board. He was also an officer on the State Executive Board and the Indian Creek Association Executive Board.

Jeremiah Wood
Birth:
Apr. 24, 1824
Virginia
Death:
Jan. 9, 1913
Doe Run,
St. Francois County, Missouri
Burial:
Doe Run Memorial Cemetery,
Doe Run,
St. Francois County, Missouri

Rev. Jeremiah, brother of Rev. John Wood, was born in Randolph County, Va. He was converted in 1847, was licensed to preach by the United Brethren in 1868, and ordained by the Freewill Baptists the next year. He assisted in organizing four churches, baptizing over one hundred converts. His labors have been in the St. Francois County, Mo., Q. M. which is the oldest in the state of Missouri. The results of his earlier work is still existent in that area.

Joshua Wood, Jr
Birth:
Apr. 12, 1857
Meigs County, Ohio
Death:
Jan. 11, 1928
St. Francois County, Missouri
Burial:
Cedar Falls Cemetery, Desloge,
St. Francois County, Missouri

He received license to preach Dec. 25, 1885. He has been for several years a student at Carleton Institute, Farmington, Mo., and was clerk of the St. Francois County Q. M. He is a part of the early Wood families that migrated to this part of Missouri from Ohio who were founders of the oldest existing quarterly meeting in Missouri.

WOOD

MARY C.
MAR. 26, 1876
MAR. 3, 1947

JOSHUA J.
APR. 12, 1857
JAN. 11, 1928

John Wood
Birth:
Nov. 23, 1829
Virginia
Death:
Jan. 26, 1903
Doe Run,
St. Francois County,
Missouri
Burial:
Doe Run Memorial Cemetery,
Doe Run,
St. Francois County,
Missouri

John Wood was born Randolph County, Va. He was married in 1850 to Fidelia Nichols. Of their seven children one was commissioner of schools in California. His early education was limited. With commendable devotion he learned to read after his conversion, which took place in 1853. In 1871 he received license to preach, and three years later he was ordained. He has since engaged in revival and pastoral work. His labors have been largely instrumental in building up the St. Francois County Q. M., Missouri, all the churches of which, except two, he has either organized or assisted in organizing. He was a minister of the Free Will Baptist Church, having taken out his license in 1875. He was a member of the "Missouri Board", whose function is to secure a union between the Free Will Baptists and the General Baptists of Southeast Missouri.

Merl Wright
Birth:
Jun. 3, 1903
Cassville, Barry Co. Missouri
Death:
May 6, 1977
Wichita, Kansas
Burial:
Oak Hill Cemetery, Cassville,
Barry County, Missouri

She was born June 3, 1903, near Cassville. After her ordination, she and Winford Davis established Merl's Chapel Church on Nov. 14, 1929, north of Cassville.

Ferrell C Zinn
Birth:
Aug. 28, 1902
Death:
Mar. 24, 1984
Burial:
Brown Cemetery, Cedarcreek,
Taney County, Missouri

He was a Free Will Baptist minister and school teacher in southern Missouri. He was an active contributor to the *Free Will Baptist GEM* and served on various committees and boards of the state Association.

Nebraska

Kinsman R Davis
Birth:
Dec. 8, 1816
Quebec, Canada
Death:
Apr. 26, 1898
Burial:
Maple Cemetery
Salem, Richardson County,
Nebraska

Parents: Silas L. Davis, b. VT, d. WI; and Phoebe (Bennett) DAVIS. Spouse: Sarah Ann Brooks, bn ME."Rev. Kinsman R. Davis, a brother of Rev. Jarius E. Davis assisted in gathering the LaFayette Quarterly Meeting at its organization, about 1850. His ministry was chiefly spent in Wisconsin, a part of the time in the Rock and Dane QM, until about 1869, when he moved to Nebraska, was connected with the Salem church.

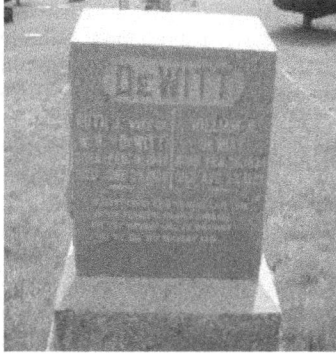

William Robert DeWitt
Birth:
Feb. 26, 1834
Pike County, Indiana
Death:
Aug. 23, 1903
MillsKeya
Paha County, Nebraska
Burial:
Olive Branch Cemetery
MillsKeya
Paha County, Nebraska

William Robert wed Ruth Jane Bartlett on Oct 27, 1869 in Knox co. Ill. he was brought to God in 1871, license in 1880 and ordained on February 19, 1886. He has since been actively engaged in revival work in Nebraska.

William Henry Edger, Jr
Birth:
Feb. 5, 1874
Wisconsin
Death:
Dec. 6, 1955
Central City
Merrick County, Nebraska
Burial:
Central City Cemetery
Central City, Merrick County, Nebraska

He was the son of Rev. William H. Edger,Sr, and Elizabeth and himself a Free Will Baptist minister.

Peter Alexander Lansing
Birth:
May 9, 1808 Saratoga,
Saratoga County
New York
Death:
Sep. 7, 190
Saunders County, Nebraska
Burial:
Pleasant View Cemetery,
Leshara, Saunders County, Nebraska

Rev. Lansing was converted in 1833, and ordained in 1844, taking charge of the Providence church and residing at Laurenceburgh, Indiana. In an anti-slavery article in the "Morning Star" he offended some of his parishioners, but also the same article became known to people of Mainville, Ohio, where he ministered to them until 1850. After spending three years in Jasper Co. Indiana, and organizing a church there, he settled in Wisconsin, where he remained thirteen years and organized seven churches. Then, after a revival in Iowa, he moved to Nebraska and organized two churches. During his ministry he has engaged much in revival work, and baptized 1,014 converts. He represented the Ohio Y.M. in the General Conference of 1844. He has served in several local offices and has always stood firm for temperance and every moral interest in the community. He was 92 yrs of age when he died.

William Marks
Birth:
Mar. 10, 1851
Death:
Oct. 26, 1900
Burial:
Shelton Cemetery,
Hall County, Nebraska
Plot: Lot 523

Free Will Baptist denomination in which Rev. Wm. Marks was ordained and labored until death. He was a nephew of David Marks the influenical minister of this denomination. His father was Rev. Ives Marks.

John Morrow
Birth:
Mar. 1, 1833
Pike County, Illinois
Death:
Feb. 4, 1912
Nebraska
Burial:
Mount Hope Cemetery
Scotia
Greeley County, Nebraska

He was ordained in 1887 and labored with the Bethel and Paddock Nebraska churches.He was also a veteran of the civil war serving and Sergt. Co. I 148 Ill. Inf.

Joseph H. Reeves
Birth:
Jan. 28, 1841
Burlington Island, Illinois
Death:
Dec. 7, 1927
Burial:
Greenwood Cemetery
Lexington
Dawson County, Nebraska

He was a son of Rev. M. D. Reeves, and like his father followed in the ministry. He was educated at M.E. Seminary and at Wasioja, Minnesota. His religious life began in 1860 and in September, 1879 he was ordained by the Root River Quarterly Meeting, Minnesota. He pastored numerous churches in Minnesota and in connection with his pastoral work he was a member they state home mission board, a trustee of the Western

Association, an active supporter of the Free Baptists and a leading worker in founding the Winnebago City College.
Inscription:
39 IL Infantry Co. G

Edward Root
Birth:
Feb. 4, 1822
Litchfield County, Connecticut
Death:
Oct. 22, 1901
Weeping Water, Cass County, Nebraska
Burial:
Oakwood Cemetery
Weeping Water, Cass County, Nebraska

ROOT was the son of Anson and Sally (Brooks) ROOT, and was born in Litchfield Co. in 1822. Twenty years later, he was married to Lucy S. Palmer (15 Mqy 1842, Ohio). Brother Root received license from the Williamsfield church [Freewill Baptist] of the Ashtabula Quarterly Meeting (Q.M.) Ohio, in 1839, and two years later, was ordained by the Huron Q.M. He ministered ten years to the Greenfield and New Haven church, in Ohio; fifteen years to the church in Porter, Mich., and ten years to the church of Centreville, Nebraska, and to other churches for brief periods. He has engaged in many revivals and assisted in organizing ten or more churches. He was a member of the Executive Board of Nebraska and pastor of the Long Branch and Grand View churches..

But none of these things move me, neither count I my life dear unto myself, so that I might finish my course with joy, and the ministry, which I have received of the Lord Jesus, to testify the gospel of the grace of God.

George W. Sisson
Birth:
May 13, 1837
Bradford, Pennsylvania
Death:
Jul. 8, 1925
Burial:
Wyuka Cemetery
Lincoln
Lancaster County, Nebraska
Plot: Sec-17 Lot-47 Gr-5

In 1868 he married Miss Annie C. Griffith. He obtained his education at Kingsville, Ohio; Millersville, Pennsylvania and at Hillsdale College, Michigan. He was ordained in 1867 and Latrope, Pennsylvania by Rev. J. S. Burgess preaching the sermon. He held pastorates in Pennsylvania and Ohio and conducted revivals in several other places. In 1862 he entered the Army and served with Co. F of the 169th PA Infantry, was stationed at Fort Keyes,

Yorktown, Virginia nearly 6 months. He established Sunday schools for the freemen in the old Baptist Church of Yorktown. He was discharged from the army in 1863 engaging himself in the American Home And Foreign Mission Society of New York and was sent to Beaufort, South Carolina where he labored two seasons. In 1865 under the appointment of the Philadelphia Freeman's Aid Society he took up the work in Nelson County, Virginia before moving to Nebraska.

Samuel F Smith
Birth:
Aug. 2, 1825
Martinsburg
Lewis County, New York
Death:
Sep. 18, 1898
Brown County, Nebraska
Burial:
Grandview Cemetery
Long Pine, Brown County, Nebraska,

He was educated at Geauga Seminary, OH, and at Whitestown Seminary, NY. He was converted in 1839 under the labors of Rev. Ransom Dunn.He was ordained July 4, 1844, by direction of the Ohio and Pennsylvania Yearly Meeting.He moved to Wisconsin in 1848, and assisted in revivals and in organizing churches at Fayette and Wayne, and preached at the Willow Springs church. He organized churches in Caledonia, and at Elgin, and McHenry, Ill. In 1853-55 where he worked assisted by Eld. Dunn, and a church at Racine, WI, was organized. He was seven years at Fairwater, Wis. while assisting in a revival at Winnegago; four years at Berlin, WI, and one yr at Fairbury, IL, and five years commencing 1871, at Postville, IA. After this, moving to Nebraska he organized churches at Rose, Fairburg, Marshall and Dry Branch, Neb. and at DeWitt, KS. He covered a period of forty years, baptized move than four hundred converts, and assisted in organizing two Quarterly and two Yearly Meetings. He also manifested his benevolence and love for the cause of education by munificent gifts to Hillsdale College, Mich., of which he is an honored trustee.

Wilmetta Marks Wheeler
Birth:
Dec. 26, 1879
Death:
Dec. 18, 1973
Burial:
Shelton Cemetery,
Hall County, Nebraska

She was a niece of David Marks and a minister in Nebraska.

Alvin Dighton Williams
Birth:
Oct. 13, 1823 Smithfield,
Fayette County,
Pennsylvania
Death:
Dec. 31, 1894
Kenesaw,
Adams County, Nebraska
Burial:
Kenesaw Cemetery, Kenesaw,
Adams County, Nebraska,
Plot: Blk 2, Row 6

He was converted at age thirteen and commenced preaching two and a half years later, gaining some notoriety as the "boy preacher." He was ordained a Free Will Baptist minister at Carolina Mills, R.I. in May 1848, and graduated at Hamilton College, NY in 1849.

He was pastor of churches at Carolina Mills, and Pawtucket, R.I., Lawrence, MA, Minneapolis, and Fair Point, Minn., and Cheshire, and Middleport, Ohio, and has baptized nearly five hundred converts. He has assisted in organizing churches at East Killingly, Conn.; Elk River, Otsego, Ramsay, Iowa; Lebanon, Minn.; Flemington and Fairview W.VA; Kenesaw, Marshall, Pleasant Plain, Long Branch and Lincoln, Neb.; also, the Hennepin Q.M. Minn., the W.VA Ass'n and the Hastings, Autora and Nemaha River Q.M's in Nebraska. He has been superintendent of schools for Lawrence, Mass., and in W.VA, president of the Northwestern and West Virginia Colleges, principal of Nebraska State Normal School, and member of the Nebraska State Board of Agriculture. The degree of Doctor

of Divinity was conferred in 1871 by Quincy, now Chaddock College, Ill. He did the *Freewill Baptist Quarterly* and is the author of "The *Rhode Island Freewill Baptist Pulpit,*" "The Support of the Ministry," *"Memorials of the Free Communion Baptists,"* and of *"Four Years of Co-operation in Nebraska and Kansas."* He was several times a member of the General Conference. From Kenesaw Cem. Neb cemetery records, it is stated that the first settlers to Kenesaw were Dr. A.D. Williams and his widowed sister, Mrs. Norton, with her four children. Other local history, tells that they lived in the wagon box for three weeks after arriving, a stove outside, and the horizon for the walls; that he had the first house, and the first well dug in Kenesaw. He bought up large tracts of land and left a sizeable estate when he died. He had a quest for learning that took him into many areas and avenues for service and progress.

John H. Wolfe
Birth:
Jan. 7, 1863
Jones County, Iowa
Death:
Dec. 30, 1954
Pawnee County, Nebraska
Burial:
Pawnee City Cemetery,
Pawnee City,
Pawnee County, Nebraska

He was an ordained Free Will Baptist minister, a graduate of Hillsdale College, MI, in 1897, was a church planter and educator. He married Delia Scriven, 14 Oct. 1884 in Marshall, Iowa. Rev. Wolfe established churches in Nebraska and in their pastoral care, and in 1917, was called upon to be president of Tecumseh College in Tecumseh, OK. After the college burned in 1927, and was not rebuilt, they returned to Nebraska. He wrote articles for church magazines regarding FW Baptist work in the state of Nebraska, which is very helpful to church historians. He was one of the voices who tried to stem the decision to merge with Northern Baptists in 1911.

Delia *Scriven* Wolfe
Birth:
Oct. 14, 1863
Fort Wayne
Allen County, Indiana
Death:
Jan. 7, 1949
Plattsmouth
Cass County, Nebraska
Burial:
Pawnee City Cemetery,
Pawnee City,
Pawnee County, Nebraska
Married John Wolfe on October 14, 1884, in Marshalltown, Marshall County, Iowa. They went to college together, took the same courses, and both graduated from Hillsdale College in Michigan in 1897. She was an ordained minister who taught and ministered beside her husband.

New Hampshire

Austin Wakefield Avery
Birth:
Nov. 18, 1838
Campton
Grafton County, New Hampshire
Death:
Oct. 5, 1865
Haverhill
Essex County, Massachusetts
Burial:
Blair Cemetery
Campton
Grafton County, New Hampshire

At 16 he took a public stand for Christ in revival. He entered the New Hampton Institution to prepare for the ministry in 1856. Two years later he was licensed to preach. Shortly after he went to Paducah, Kentucky in early 1859 to visit his brother and to make a tour through nine of the southern states and saw slavery as it was. He returned to Dover, New Hampshire to supply for three months. And 51 requested interest in Christian prayers. For a while he served as an agent of the New York City church raising funds for building. When a revival broke out where he had settled. He resigned that job and settled in Parishville, where he was ordained at the age of 21 on March 24, 1860. In January 1861 he went to Boston to study with Rev. Ransom Dunn and on March 13 he became pastor of the Boston church. Through his four years of pastorate, a great interest continued till 1865 had been added to the church 156 of them by baptism. With the ministry of only six years he baptized 175, when an illness overtook him and he died in his 27th year. He was buried in his native state with the funeral being preached by Dr. Isaac the Stewart.Note: Additional information from Native Ministry of New Hampshire

J. Franklin Babb
Birth:
May 20, 1873
New Hampshire
Death:
May 31, 1938
Laconia
Belknap County, New Hampshire
Burial:
New Hampton Village Cemetery
New Hampton
Belknap County, New Hampshire
Plot: 165

His parents were John W. Babb and Josephine H. (Damon) BABB. Was married to Candace Porter Ladd, 11 Oct. 1897, at Ladd's Hill, Belmont, NH. She was the dau of Arthur S. Ladd and Ellen M. (Porter) LADD. Rev. Babb was fondly called "the sporting parson" by editors and those who knew his affinity for the outdoors and his hunting and fishing expeditions. He was often called upon by groups to speak as he always drew a crowd for his entertaining way of presenting his subject. He was the last pastor of the New Hampton Freewill Baptist church, before it became the New Hampton Community church after 1911. It was originally built as a Freewill Baptist church in the 1800's and is now on the National Registry of Historic places.He pastored for some years in Mass. before the last one at New Hampton.

The saint is escorted to a land of perfect day.

Wm. S Babcock
Birth:
Nov. 15, 1764
Death:
Aug. 29, 1821
Burial:
Babcock-Cate Cemetery,
Barrington,
Strafford County,
New Hampshire

Son of a wealthy merchant, who sent him to Yale College to prevent his being drafted as a soldier. After school, he settled in Springfield, VT, where he began a study of the Scripture to refute its teachings. But it mightily convinced him of its truth, and he was converted in 1800, and at once began to preach. Becoming acquainted with the Freewill Baptists, he found himself in agreement with them, was baptized and ordained by Rev. Jeremiah Ballard of NH. He gathered a church together, of 25 members, sent a letter to the Quarterly Meeting requesting instruction and fellowship, whereupon another church under Rev. Stephen Place, joined with Rev. Babcock's church and were in fellowship. These were pioneer days for the church in Vermont. Rev. Wm. Babcock and Nathaniel Marshall, convinced Rev. John Colby, the young FWB Vermont evangelist, to be ordained, before his trip to Ohio. Rev. Babcock's father's estate continued to yield him an annual remittance and he preached the word with acceptance. His life was cut short by consumption, but he died in the triumphs of faith,

Henry M. Bacheler
Birth:
Jun. 16, 1849,
India
Death:
unknown
Burial:
New Hampton Village Cemetery,
New Hampton, Belknap County,
New Hampshire,
Plot: #219

Henry M. Bacheler, M.D., was the son of Rev. Dr. Otis Robinson Bacheler and wife Sarah P. (Merrill) Bacheler. He was born in Balasore, India where his parents were medical and ministerial missionaries. He entered work in India at the close of 1886.

Otis Robinson Batchelder
Birth:
Jan. 17, 1817 Andover,
Merrimack County,
New Hampshire
Death:
Jan. 1, 1901
New Hampton, Belknap County,
New Hampshire
Burial:
New Hampton Village Cemetery,
New Hampton, Belknap County,
New Hampshire,
Plot: Lot 219

In preparation to become a missionary he studied at Holliston & Wilbraham, MA and Kent's Hill, ME academies, 1835-1839. He studied medicine at Dartmouth & Cambridge Medical colleges. He was licensed to preach by the Boston Quarterly Meeting, Lowell, MA, April 1839 and was ordained an evangelist in Lowell, May 7,

1840.He received his M D from Dartmouth College, 1850; and DD, Hillsdale College, 1881. He sailed for India, May 16,1840 where he was a missionary at Balasore, Orissa, India, October 1840-52; Midnapore, Bengal, 1865-83. Otis returned to the United States, September 1883 and was without charge in New Hampton, 1883-6. Again he sailed from Boston for India, January 23, 1886. He published "A Medical Guide in Oriya and Bengalee." The funeral services for Otis were held in the Free Baptist Church at New Hampton, with the Reverend Atwood B Meservey, DD, PhD, the venerable ex-principal of the New Hampton Literary institution, was to have preached the sermon, but was prevented by sickness, consequently his address was read by Reverend Professor Shirley J Case, of the institution. Others taking part in the services were the Reverend J Burnham Davis, late of Ocean Park, Maine, the Reverend Arthur Given, DD, of Providence, Reverend Robert Ford, of Campton, and Reverend George L White of New Hampton.

Benaiah Bean
Birth:
Jun. 30, 1793
Salisbury,
Merrimack County,
New Hampshire
Death:
Dec. 17, 1856 Colebrook,
Coos County,
New Hampshire
Burial:
North Road Cemetery,
Wilmot,
Merrimack County,
New Hampshire

He was converted under the preaching of John Colby and baptized in Feb. 1812, by Rev. Joshua Quimby. He moved to Whitefield in 1821 and became a member of the Freewill Baptist church in that place at its organization. In 1823, he was licensed to preach by the Sandwich Quarterly Meeting. He was ordained August 24, 1828, at

Whitefield, where he was pastor for about ten years, witnessing several revivals. At one time he baptized forty-one, at another forty. During the revival which began July 1, 1832, ninety were hopefully converted. While in Whitefield, he labored in Concord, VT, Jefferson and Bethlehem, NH. In 1838 he moved to Bethlehem and was pastor of the church there for eight years. In 1850 he organized the Clarksville and Pittsburg church of fifteen members and became their pastor. Four years later the church numbered sixty. In 1855, the history of Colebrook give the account that Rev. Benaiah Bean organized a Freewill Baptist Church at Colebrook. A church about this time was also organized at Stewartstown, of which he was pastor till his death.

Death is not the greatest loss in life. The greatest loss is what dies inside us while we live.

Lewis P Bickford
Birth:
Oct. 4, 1844
Center Harbor,
Belknap County, New Hampshire
Death:
Aug. 3, 1917
New Hampton,
Belknap County, New Hampshire
Burial:
New Hampton Village Cemetery,
New Hampton,
Belknap County, New Hampshire

He experienced the new birth in 1857 and received license in 1868. He graduated from the New Hampton Institution In 1869 [later Cobb Divinity School, then Bates College]. He received ordination June 31, 1871.

Israel Blake
Birth:
1765
Death:
May 1, 1839
Grafton County, New Hampshire
Burial:
Blake Cemetery
Stinson Lake
Grafton County, New Hampshire

He was ordained in the Sandwich Quarterly Meeting in 1800. Here he continued to reside for 40 years. The year 1811 was one of marked revival for his church and quarterly meeting. In 1824 David marks visited him, and in the month of protracted meetings that followed, the church was revived and enlarged. In 1833, 27 members were added by baptism. On May 1, 1839, brother Blake closed a long service for the master. The Rev. Thomas Perkins preached his funeral sermon from First Thessalonians 4:14.

Joseph Boodey, Jr
Birth:
unknown
Death:
May 12, 1876
New Hampshire
Burial:
Old Boodey Place,
New Durham,
Strafford County,
New Hampshire

Approx. year of birth: 1782. He was the nephew of another Rev.

Joseph Boodey born 1752, who was shown as companion of Rev. Benjamin Randall, whose house was where Eld. Randall and his group of Free Will Baptists organized their church by that name in New Durham. Free Baptists Cyclopedia, pub. 1889, records that this Eld. Joseph Boodey was the first to preach free salvation in northern Vermont. He had good success but for six months he saw not a minister who gave him a word or cheer. He was ordained Oct. 18, 1798, at a session of the Q M in New Durham Schoolhouse, with Elder Benjamin Randall, delivering the sermon and Eld. Daniel Lord giving the prayer. He helped organized Quarterly Meetings from the churches that were organized.

The fear of death follows from the fear of life.

~Mark Twain~

Nahum Brooks
Birth:
Jun. 11, 1811
East Wakefield,
New Hampshire
Death:
Mar. 17, 1883
Manchester,
New Hampshire
Burial:
Valley Cemetery,
Manchester,
Hillsborough County,
New Hampshire,
Plot: 973-3

He was baptized in Aug. 1834 by Rev Samuel Burbank, and joined the church in Wakefield. He acquired a thorough academic education at North Parsonfield under the instruction of the Rev. Hosea Quinby, D.D. He afterward went to Dover, New Hampshire, and was employed in the "Morning Star" office. He began preaching in 1837. Through his efforts a church was organized at Laconia, NH, March 17, 1838, which began with 9 members. He was ordained the following May in 1838 in a session of the Q.M. During this pastorate of six years, he baptized 166 persons. A fine house of worship was built and dedicated Jan 6th, 1841. His next pastorate was at Great Falls, where he baptized 192 converts. In all his pastorates he baptized 653 persons before he contracted a severe cold in a meeting in Candia, which caused partial paralysis of the vocal cords, and in consequence, he was obliged to cease preaching. After his ordination, he attended every

session of the NH Yearly Meeting, except four. He was deeply interested in the benevolent enterprises of the denomination and contributed generously to their support. For twenty years, he was an active member of the Foreign Mission Board and two years treasurer of the society. He was also one of the founders of the Maine State Seminary at Lewiston, ME (now Bates)

Amos Brown
Birth:
Sep. 4, 1800
Bristol, Grafton County,
New Hampshire
Death:
Dec. 7, 1867
Eaton Center, Carroll County,
New Hampshire
Burial:
Homeland Cemetery,
Bristol, Grafton County,
New Hampshire,
Plot: Sec. 11E, Lot 3, Grave 7

Amos Brown was licensed to preach by the Sandwich Quarterly

Meeting, of the Free Baptist denomination 16 Dec 1829, and was ordained at Alexandria, Grafton, New Hampshire, 30 Sep 1832, by council of elders of the Sandwich Quarterly Meeting, composed of Rev. John Hill, of Alexandria, Rev. Simeon Dana, MD, Rev. Thomas Perkins, of New Hampton, and Rev. Devi Smith. He labored one-half the time at Alexandria from 1837 till 1853, and had pastoral oversight of the church for thirty-seven years. During his labors there, 160 were added to the church. He also labored successfully in Nashua, Orange, Center Harbor, New Hampton, Hill, and Bridgewater.

He represented Bristol in the legislature of 1847 and 1848. In May 1867, he accepted a call to the pastorate of the Free Baptist Church at Eaton, where a revival of religion was very general.

William Burr
Birth:
Jun. 22, 1806
Hingham Center,
Plymouth County,
Massachusetts
Death:
Nov. 5, 1866
Dover, Strafford County,
New Hampshire
Burial::
Pine Hill Cemetery,
Dover,Strafford County,
New Hampshire

While in his early teens, he apprenticed with a Boston

printer, learning the trade he would put to good use for the Free Will Baptist Printing Establishment. Their books included his name among those they hold in high esteem.

A biography, *Life of William Burr*, was written in 1871 by Rev. J. M. Brewster.

An inscription on the 12-ft marble monument erected over his grave reads: WILLIAM BURR, age 60. This Monument, erected by the Freewill Baptist Denomination stands as a tribute to his memory. He had charge of the Printing Office at the opening in 1826, and was Editor of the *Morning Star* and Agent of the Printing Establishment during a period of more than thirty years. By his integrity in business, his urbanity in social intercourse,

His broad and philanthropic sympathies, especially by his devout earnestness and as a Christian, he won and retained the high esteem of all who knew him.

He was a member of the City Government in Dover, the Legislature of New Hampshire; and for twenty-five consecutive years was elected Treasurer of the Benevolent Societies. He was a strong abolitionist and at a anti-slavery meeting sat beside President Abraham Lincoln.

Elder Hezekiah D Buzzell
Birth:
Dec. 16, 1777
Alton,
Belknap County, New Hampshire
Death:
Sep. 6, 1858
Alton, Belknap County,
New Hampshire
Burial:
Hurd Cemetery, Alton,
Belknap County, New Hampshire

Buzzell was ordained in Gilmanton, New Hampshire on Jan 25, 1803, then preached in Alton, Gilmanton and Weare for fifty years. He was a minister at the Free Will Baptist Church in Weare (established October 20, 1806) from March 8, 1812 to 1829. He served as a State Rep in the New Hampshire House of Representatives from 1814 to 1816 and again 1819-1820, and as a State Senator in the New Hampshire 3rd District 1822-1823.

Aaron Buzzell
Birth:
Dec. 31, 1764
Gilmanton,
Belknap County, New Hampshire
Death:
Oct. 21, 1854
Barrington, Strafford County,
New Hampshire
Burial:
Pine Grove Cemetery,
Barrington, Strafford County,
New Hampshire

Rev. Aaron and his brother Rev. John Buzzell and Rev. Benjamin

Randall were the people who started the Free Will Baptist Church of Middleton in 1790. The branches of both brothers and family members were all Free Will Baptists.

In God is my salvation and my glory: the rock of my strength, and my refuge is in God. **(Psalm 62:7)**

Alvah Buzzell
Birth:
Apr. 12, 1807
Parsonsfield,
York County, Maine
Death:
Apr. 2, 1888
Southborough,
Worcester County,
Massachusetts
Burial:
Lake View Cemetery,
East Andover,
Merrimack County,
New Hampshire

Reverend Alvah Buzzell, son of Reverend John Buzzell, was born in Parsonfield, Maine on April 11, 1807. He was converted at the age of eighteen and ordained as pastor of the church at Barnstead, New Hampshire in June 1834 by Reverend Enoch Place. He has had the care of twelve churches and helped organized six churches. He has baptized many hundreds. At the breaking out of the Civil War, when he was fifty-four, he followed his sons Frank and John to the front, caring for the sick and wounded, and preaching the gospel and helping the Negro to school privileges.

David Calley
Birth:
Nov. 8, 1815
Holderness, Grafton County
New Hampshire
Death:
Dec. 23, 1906
Bristol, Grafton County
New Hampshire,
Burial:
Green Grove Cemetery
Ashland, Grafton County
New Hampshire

David Calley's career as a clergyman was a remarkable one. At the age of 23 years he professed religion, and the next year, 1837, he received a license to preach. In May 1942, at a session of the Sandwich Quarterly Meeting he was ordained, and a month later became the pastor of the Free Baptist Church at North Tunbridge, Vermont, where he remained until 1847. In September 1852 he began his second pastorate at Bristol, which continued for seven years. He then returned to Tunbridge, Vermont. where he remained three years, and again assumed the pastoral charge of the church at Bristol and continued for another seven years. He thus served the Bristol church as pastor for sixteen years. To no other man does the Free Baptist Church of Bristol owe so much as to the Reverend David Calley. He was a man of great natural ability, an excellent preacher, devoted, godly and his pure life and labors endeared him to all classes in the community. He was of fine personal presence, standing six feet two inches. Mr Calley four times had a seat in the Legislature. He represented

Holderness in 1853, Bristol in 1872, and 1873 and Sandwich in 1885.

Arthur Caverno
Birth:
Apr. 6, 1801
Strafford, Strafford County,
New Hampshire
Death:
Jul. 15, 1876
Dover, Strafford County,
New Hampshire
Burial:
Pine Hill Cemetery,
Dover, Strafford County,
New Hampshire

Caverno died at aged 75 years.
He was the son of Jeremiah and Mary Brewster Caverno, and great-grandson of Arthur Caverno (or Cavano), of Scotch Irish nationality, who came to this country soon after 1735.
He was born in Strafford (then Barrington), N. H., He was in a twofold sense one of the fathers of the denomination. He had been more than fifty-four years in its ministry, and, at a formative period of its history, he exerted a controlling influence.
When seventeen years of age he became a Christian, after a severe struggle with unbelief occasioned by deep conviction of sin. He was baptized by Rev. Enoch Place, Oct. 11, 1818. He attended Gilmanton Academy six months, and afterwards studied in th academy at Newfield's village in New Market. He obtained what was, in those days, an excellent academic education and taught school successfully in various places. He yielded more cheerfully than many to the call to preach, and began at the age of nineteen. Aug. 23, 1822, at the age of twenty-one

he was licensed by the New Durham Q. M. He was ordained June 17, 1823, in an oak grove on his father's homestead by a council consisting of Rev's Samuel B. Dyer, Moses Bean, David Harriman, Enoch Place and William Buzzell. David Harriman preached the sermon.
He was married December 23d to Mrs. Olive H. Foss of Strafford.
The next year he taught school in Epsom.
Through his ministry there a church was gathered of which he was pastor till the autumn of 1827. The revival, the first year, was extensive. He also preached and baptized in Nottingham and Raymond. Rev. D. P. Cilley and two other ministers were converted ouring this time.
His second pastorate was at Contoocook. His first sermon there was published in the *Morning Star.* Text, "The Powers Of Heaven Shall Be Shaken."
The first year, 1830, a revival of remarkable power and extent was witnessed. People were converted at their homes, in their shops, on their farms, going to and returning from meetings. The church more than doubled its membership and the good influence of the work lasted many years. He continued there five years. For three years, ending in 1836, he was pastor at Great Falls; the next two years financial agent of Strafford Academy; pastor of Roger Williams church, Providence, R. I. one year, eliding in the fall of 1839; assistant pastor in Lowell, Mass., six months; pastor in Charleston, Mass., two and a half years; pastor in Bangor, Me., three years, ending in the fall of 1845; stated supply in Portsmouth, N. H., at the Old South, until the spring of 1847; pastor in Candia two years; pastor in Dover three years, when the house of worship was changed to its present locality on Charles Street; stated supply in Concord several months in 1852, and several months in South Berwick, Me.; then pastor two years in Biddeford, Me.
His wife, who had helped him

thirty-one years, died in Dover, N. H., Jan. 30, J854.

The next year he married Mrs. Isabel J. Sule, of Bath, Me.

He preached for the First church, Dover, a year, then in New Market a year. For two years, ending in 1860, he was pastor in Gardiner, Me. He then preached in Strafford Centre, Laconia, and Alton Corner, a few months in each place. For two years, ending in 1866, he was pastor at South Parsonfield, Me.

He next lived in Great Falls, N. H., and preached for the Baptist church at Little River Falls in Lebanon, Me., and in Berwick at Cranberry Meadow. Then he was pastor in North Berwick two years, and lastly in Candia again two years. In some places there were revivals, in others he trained the forces.

He was a preacher fifty-six years, an ordained minister fifty-three years. He preached 6,000 sermons, baptized 480 persons, married 320 couples, and attended 500 funerals. As a preacher, he was systematic in his presentation of truth, apt and forcible in his illustrations. He was a diligent student of the Bible and a careful observer' of men and things about him. His usual method was to preach from a well-prepared skeleton, and many of his sermons were afterwards 'written out in full. He possessed a voice of more than ordinary sweetness and power.

He was affable and courteous in manner, social in disposition, and a general favorite in all the families where he was known.

He helped forward every denominational enterprise.

He began to write for the *Morning Star* the first year of its existence, and contributed more or less every year during his life. His last article appeared in the number issued during the week of his death. He early published a series on the "Support of the Ministry," which helped to introduce the practice of stipulated salaries. He was himself the first minister in the denomination who received a stipulated. salary.

He had great influence in removing the practice of feet washing which prevailed in some measure.

He was a member of the first General Conference, and assisted in organizing the Home and Foreign Mission Societies. He was greatly interested in all the educational movements. Other good causes received his earnest support. He lectured often in many places on temperance, and helped in the organization of some of the earliest Total Abstinence Societies in New Hampshire. He labored much for the abolition of capital punishment.

His last years were spent in Dover. The Sunday before his death he preached in Alton. His funeral services were conducted by Rev. Joseph Fullonton one of his early converts.

Peter Clark
Birth:
October 8, 1781
Upper Gilmanton, New Hampshire
Death:
November 25, 1865
Upper Gilmanton, New Hampshire
Burial:
Highland Cemetery
Belmont
Belknap County, New Hampshire
Plot: D

He was born in Dialogue and had the example and instruction of a faithful mother who early told him the value of prayer. He was converted in June 1798 and was baptized by Elder R. Martin. In the next September he began his ministry in his native place. Elder Martin pointed them out to a bystander as a boy was hard to handle it in argument. In January 8, 1810 he was ordained by the Rev.'s Winthrop Young, R. Martin, and Hezekiah D. Buzzell. He became the pastor of the newly organized Third Gilmanton church. Great revivals followed and there were added on April 20, 24; August 22, eight; June 25, 1814, 22; October, 18, 31. In 1826 this independent church joined the New Durham Quarterly Meeting. In the 1829 session of the quarterly meeting a revival commenced which continued for months, spreading elsewhere, and in November there were 18 added to the church in others through the winter. A healthy growth existed in the church for years. And in its early days beginning in about 1830 the church began to have great interest in the cause of temperance. He represented his town in the legislature and was given to Christian hospitality.

Inscription:
Died in his 63rd yrs of Ministry.

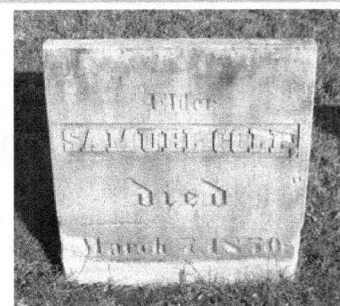

Samuel Cole
Birth:
Unknown
Salem, New Hampshire
Death:
Mar. 7, 1850
Lisbon, New Hampshire
Burial:
Sunny Side Cemetery
Grafton County, New Hampshire

In 1798 he moved to Landaff

where at the age of 21 was converted. After deep conviction, he began to hold meetings and was ordained in 1827. His labors as a minister were confined mostly to Lisbon and Landaff. He supported a large family by diligence and yet found time to engage much in the labor for his master.

Solomon Cole
Birth:
July 8, 1821
Whitefield, New Hampshire
Death:
1902
New Hampshire
Burial:
Glenwood Cemetery
Lebanon
Grafton County, New Hampshire
Plot: sec a; Lot O

In a session of the New Hampshire Yearly Meeting about 1836, he was converted under the preaching of David marks and four years later was baptized by the Rev. Beniah Bean of Whitefield. At that time he felt called to the ministry, but put off the work for 20 years because of his lack of preparation. However, during this time he began holding meetings in needy places. He received license to preach about 1870 and was ordained in 1876 by Rev. C. N. Nelson and others. His early ministry enjoyed revivals and saw hundreds come to the Lord. He was a member of the firm of S. Cole and Sons Iron Founders and Machinists, Lebanon, New Hampshire, so he was able to preach the gospel to the needy without compensation. In 1846 he married miss Caroline F. Peasley. He also served four terms in the New Hampshire legislature. *Calculated relationship

Charles Corson
Birth:
1788
Lebanon, Maine
Death:
1860
New Hampshire
Burial:
Rochester Cemetery
Rochester
Strafford County,
New Hampshire

He was converted about 1820 and was baptized by Rev. David Blaisdell joining the Free Baptist Church in Lebanon. He began preaching soon after. After preaching several years he was ordained about 1840 and was associated with Rev. Blaisdell and Copp. He was not a revival preacher, but was instructive. His words were mighty through the excellent character of the man behind them.

Arthur Elmes Cox
Birth:
May 25, 1858
Princes Risborough,
Buckinghamshire, England
Death:
May 21, 1942
New Hampshire
Burial:
New Hampton Village Cemetery
New Hampton
Belknap County New Hampshire,
Plot: #182

Rev. Cox immigrated to the U.S. in 1872. He married Elizabeth Anna Hayes, daughter of Prof. Benjamin F. Hayes, of Lewiston, ME. Cox studied at Richmond College, Virginia, and theology at Cobb Divinity School. He was converted in 1869, and was ordained to the ministry June 24, 1883, by Rev's J.J. Hall, C.E. Cate, J. Fullerton, B.F. Hayes, and J.S. Burgess. He was a Freewill Baptist minister and held pastorates at Garner, W. Pike, Pennsylvania; Little Falls and Windham Center, Maine.

Jesse Cross
Birth:
June 9, 1790
Newbury, New Hampshire
Death:
November 1, 1865
New Hampshire
Burial:
Church Place Cemetery
Wilmot
Merrimack County, New Hampshire

In his early years he committed to memory, through the example in inspiration of the pious mother a large portion of the Bible. He acquired the rudiments of education in the common schools and when he was about 20 he was converted under the preaching of Rev. Timothy Morse and 10 years later was licensed by Weare Quarterly Meeting meeting. In 1840 he was ordained by the same body as pastor of the Springfield church, of which he had been many years a member. For 40 years he labored among the churches in Sullivan and Merrimack County and witnessed a precious outpourings of the spirit of God. His sermons were highly biblical, ernest and pathetic; his prayers were tender and suppository, yet wonderfully full of faith and power. He preached much in secret. He was a member of the Second Wilmot Church at the time of his death.

Silas Curtis
Birth:
Feb. 27, 1804
Minot,
Androscoggin County, Maine
Death:
Jan. 27, 1893
Concord,
Merrimack County,
New Hampshire
Burial:
Blossom Hill Cemetery,
Concord, Merrimack County,
New Hampshire

In the schools of Lewiston and Greene he laid the foundation of his education. He prepared for College in the Maine Wesleyan Seminary at Kent's Hill, but had health problems and could not continue. He was converted at age 17 was baptized by Rev. B. Thorn, and joined the Free Will Baptist church at Lewiston in May 1821. After his 21st year, he taught school several winters in Lewiston and Lisbon. In the spring of 1827, at age 23, he began to preach the gospel. He was ordained Oct. 4, 1827, when Bowdoin Q.M was in session at Topsham, Maine.

Ordaining members were Rev's Geo. Lamb, Aliezer Bridges, and Allen Files. He travelled and preached all around the area for the next three or four years. He pastored in Lynn, Mass, but the ocean air did not agree with his health, and thus, he became pastor of the Lowell church for five years. In Lowell. From 1852-1856, he pastored in Pittsfield, NH, and from there to Concord, NH, where he pastored.

During his ministry he baptized 800 converts, assisted in organizing several churches and preached at the dedication of twelve church edifices. he was active and influential in every denominational enterprise.

He was foremost in the era of publication and educational institutions and organization of benevolent societies. In 1832, he was selected as one of the printing committee of the Printing Establishment and continued on that board for over 40 years, and was interim agent after William Burr's death. He was appointed agent, and raised $17,000 for the New Hampton Institution, and gathered funds for Chapel Hall. He was corresponding Secretary of the Home Mission Society from 1839-1869, when he resigned. Also, he served on the Foreign Mission Society. In 1865, he spent several weeks in South Carolina and Virginia, superintendent of the work among the freedmen, and afterwards visited the schools and mission stations in Shenandoah Valley, and Storer College at Harper's Ferry. He was clerk of the General Conference in 1835 until 1868. He attended 20 of the 26 General Conferences. He made his home in Concord, New Hampshire for more than 30 years. In Concord, he was an esteemed member and Vice-President, of the "New Hampshire Bible Society" until his death. They recorded in their 1893 minutes at his death, "Rev. Silas Curtis, D.D., was removed by death"

Robert Dickey
Birth:
Jun. 11, 1764
Boston
Suffolk County, Massachusetts
Death:
Jan. 2, 1849
Burial:
Bunker Hill Cemetery
Wilmot
Merrimack County, New
Hampshire

He was a member of Benjamin Randall's church and at New Durham, New Hampshire and went from Epsom, N.H. to Work as a laborer with a relative in Stafford, Vermont. The young man was touched by the spiritual needs of the place and began his preaching and witnessed over 30 converted. On September 10, 1791 a letter was addressed to the New Durham church desiring church orders. Benjamin Randall and John Buzzell and several times visited these brothers. It was the first Free Will Baptist church in Vermont to be organized in the spring of 1793. In june 1794 Robert Dickey was a delegate of this church with a letter to the New Hampshire Yearly Meeting for membership. He subsequently became a useful minister being ordained in 1814, but later his usefulness was lost when he joined the Shakers.

Andrew J. Eastman
Birth:
Jul. 23, 1846
East Parsonsfield,
York County, Maine
Death:
1918
Burial:
Blair Cemetery,
Campton Lower Village,
Grafton County,
New Hampshire,
Plot: A 85

He graduated from Bates College in 1974 and the Bates Theological School in 1977. He was ordained in the Steep falls, Maine Quarterly Meeting on November 1, 1877 by the Cumberland Quarterly

Meeting. He held a number of pastorates in the state of Massachusetts and recorded many baptisms.

Being faithful has its reward beyond the grave.

Daniel Elkins
Birth:
1760
Lee
Strafford County, New Hampshire
Death:
Jun. 4, 1845
Jackson
Carroll County, New Hampshire
Burial:
Jackson Village Cemetery
Jackson
Carroll County, New Hampshire

He moved to Gilmanton and in 1797. In 1799 he held meetings on Meredith Hill. In 1804 he had a revival in Jackson, and by request of the converts he was ordained at the quarterly meeting held at Sandwich, by Rev. Benjamin Randall and John Buzzell. He immediately returned to Jackson, where he baptized several, formed a church and soon made his home. Here he had a useful ministry for 40 years.

David Garland
Birth:
Dec. 18, 1791
Death:
Feb. 6, 1863
Burial:
Garland Family Cemetery,
Center Barnstead,
Belknap County, New Hampshire

His ministry was confined to the New Hampshire area.

Moulton Hackett
Birth:
1772
New Hampshire
Death:
Oct. 10, 1830
New Hampton, Belknap County,
New Hampshire
Burial:
Chandler Cemetery,
New Hampton,
Belknap County, New Hampshire,
Plot: Grave 9

New Hampshire FWB Minister.

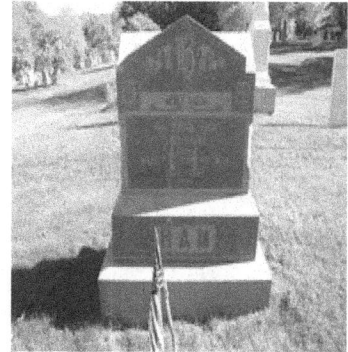

Ezra Ham
Birth:
Mar. 7, 1797
Farmington, Strafford County,
New Hampshire
Death:
Feb. 16, 1880
Gilmanton,
Belknap County, New Hampshire
Burial: Smith Meeting
House Cemetery,
Gilmanton,
Belknap County, New Hampshire

He became a Christian in early life, but did not enter the ministry till forty-three years of age. He was ordained a Freewill Baptist minister at Gilmanton Iron Works, New Hampshire, in 1840. He was instrumental in the organization of the church there and it was largely through his efforts that the meeting house was built. He was pastor of the church several years. In 1867-68, he represented his town in the Legislature; the latter term he served as chaplain of the House.

Moses Hanson
Birth:
Aug., 1792
Ossipee
Carroll County, New Hampshire
Death:
Nov. 21, 1868
Wolfeboro
Carroll County, New Hampshire
Burial:
Ossipee Town Cemetery
Ossipee, Carroll County,
New Hampshire

His father died when he was seven, and he was put out in a good home till he, reached his majority. In the war of 1812,as a musician, he served his country several months at Portsmouth. He married Oct. 1, 1815, Miss Joanna Hansom. At the death of his second child, in 1821, he was seriously convicted, but he did not yield his heart till the winter of 1829,and in 1830 was baptized by Rev. John Pinkham, joining the Second Ossipee church. The next year he was chosen deacon, and served the church well till he was dismissed with others to form the Fourth Ossipee church. He was licensed in 1838, and ordained in 1840. In June,1842, his wife died; in 1843 he married Miss Hannah Seavey, who survived him.He preached in Effingham, N. H., andin Porter, Me., and finally came to Wolfborough,where he finished his course. He was earnest in reform and eminently a man of prayer.
Inscription:
"With heavenly weapons I have foughtThe battles of the Lord. Finish'd my course,and kept the faith,And wait the sure reward."

Pelatiah Hanscom
Birth:
1796
Kittery, Maine
Death:
Apr. 20, 1857
Epping, New York
Burial:
South Hampton Cemetery
South Hampton
Rockingham County,
New Hampshire

Early in his life he went to Barnstead, where he was converted and baptized by the Rev. n. Wilson. Receiving a license to preach, he moved to Lyman, Maine where he enjoyed a good revival. In 1837, he moved to Exeter, New Hampshire and connected himself with the Stratham church and did a good work in that locality. On July 5, 1839, he was ordained by a Council consisting of the Reverends John Kimball. S. P. Fernald, E. True, and J. Fullonton. He soon had the satisfaction of baptizing his wife and his only daughter. After moving to Epping, he organized a church there in 1840.

Joseph Morrill Harper
Birth:
Jun. 21, 1787
Limerick
York County, Maine
Death:
Jan. 15, 1865
Canterbury
Merrimack County, New Hampshire
Burial:
Canterbury Village Cemetery
Canterbury

Merrimack County,
New Hampshire

He attended Fryeburg Academy, studied medicine, and in 1810 began a practice in Sanbornton, New Hampshire, later moving to Canterbury, where he was a physician for 30 years. Converted in October 1810 he was baptized uniting with the church in Canterbury. He was ordained on April 11, 1838 and preached for more than 27 years. He was the moderator of the Ninth General Conference at Greenville, Rhode Island in October 2018; of the 10th at Conneaut, Ohio in October 1837; of the 11th, at Topsham, Maine, in October 1841. Harper was a veteran of the War of 1812, serving as Assistant Surgeon of the Fourth Infantry Regiment. He served in the New Hampshire House of Representatives from 1826 to 1827, and was Canterbury Justice of the Peace from 1826 until his death. Harper served in the New Hampshire Senate from 1829 to 1831. He was President of the Senate and became Governor ex officio upon the resignation of Matthew Harvey, serving from February to June 1831. In 1830 Harper was elected to the U.S. House of Representatives as a Jacksonian and served two terms, 1831 to 1835. He then returned to his Canterbury medical practice, and also became involved in banking, serving as President of Mechanics' Bank of Concord from 1847 to 1856.

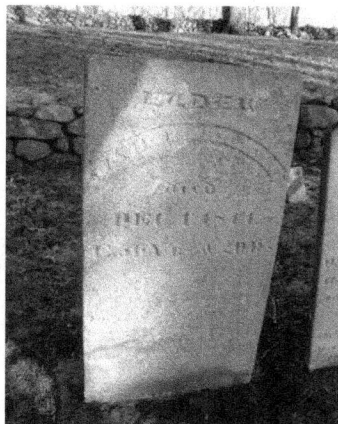

David E Harriman
Birth:
November 11, 1788
Plaistow, New Hampshire
Death:
Dec. 1, 1844
Hillsborough County, New
Hampshire
Burial:
Hadley Cemetery
Weare
Hillsborough County,
New Hampshire

He was converted in 18 and seven and baptize by Rev. Timothy Morse in May. He soon began to teach and to preach. Then in 1808 he taught at Bangor, Maine and saw a good revival. Early in 1809 he returned to his hometown and married. He then moved to Candia where he was ordained on November 30, 1817.

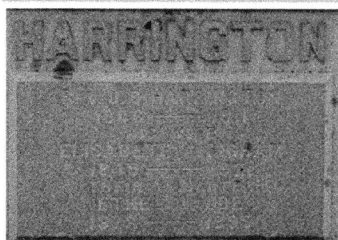

John Sherman Harrington
Birth:
Dec. 17, 1846
Woodstock
Ontario, Canada
Death:
Dec. 30, 1911
Burial:

Pine Grove Cemetery
Farmington
Strafford County,
New Hampshire

He received an academic education, was converted at the age of 12, licensed March 5, 1870, and ordained by Rev's J. Ingram and George Donmocker on May 12, 1872. He graduated from Hillsdale Theological Seminary in 1880, and in July, 1881 took charge of a mission in Elmira, New York. Besides this church he pastored churches in New Hampshire, Michigan and had revivals in all of his pastorates. He was the father of Virgil Dewitt Harrington who ran the Oceanwave Hotel in Rye, NH.

A life well used brings happy death.

Samuel Hill
Birth:
1784
Death:
Dec. 27, 1852
Loudon, New Hampshire
Burial:
Hill Cemetery
Loudon
Merrimack County,
New Hampshire

He was converted at the age of 18 and baptized at Canterbury, July 12, 1803 by Rev. Winthrop Young and remained a worthy member of the church there for 50 years.

He was chosen a deacon in 1819 but was an ordained to the Free Will Baptist ministry in 1821 by the New Durham Quarterly Meeting. He held offices of trust in his town; was a member of the legislature during Jackson's administration. Many were baptized by him. He died respected and honored.

Marilla *Turner* Marks Hills
Birth:
Mar. 20, 1807
Vermont
Death:
Nov. 28, 1901
Dover,
Strafford County,
New Hampshire
Burial:
Pine Hill Cemetery, Dover,
Strafford County,
New Hampshire

She married Rev. David Marks, 20 Sep 1829, a Free Will Bapt. minister. They were involved in evangelizing, book publishing, and many works of the church. She was elected treasurer of the Woman's Mission Society in 1848, and after the office of the treasurer was dissolved she became the corresponding secretary and remained such till the society dissolved. She edited and had published a Memoirs of David Marks, in 1846, taken from his diary and journals. She and her husband adopted and raised a niece, Julia Marks. Rev. David Marks died at age 44 in Oberlin, Ohio, where he is buried in

Westwood Cemetery, Oberlin. Marilla and her husband were both active in the abolition causes at the Oberlin College. Marilla then married another esteemed FWB minister, Rev. Elias Hutchins, 26 Dec. 1846, a widower, in New Hampshire, where he pastored the Washington Street church in Dover. This union was not to endure for long as Rev. Hutchins' health failed in a few years and he died Sept. 11, 1859. Marilla then married Mr. Hills, who preceded her in death. She continued to live in Dover to the age of 93, a respected and beloved Free Will Baptist church woman.

Death is the surest calculation that can be made

Hiram Holmes
Birth:

October 3, 1806
Rochester, New Hampshire
Death:
May 1, 1863
Merrimack County, New Hampshire
Burial:
Presbury Cemetery
Bradford
Merrimack County,
New Hampshire

He consecrated himself to the Savior on November 8, 1827 and the next August was baptized at Crown Point by Rev. Enoch Place. Thereafter, he began to have meetings and appointments and on January, 1830 the New Durham Quarterly Meeting licensed him. He was ordained in Strafford, February 8, 1831 with Rev. B. S. Manson preaching the sermon. October 19, 1837 he married Miss Susanna Brown of Weare and in 1838 settled in Raymond. In 1839 he went to Bradford. During the next 20 years he made tours among the destitute churches of the Weare Quarterly Meeting. He was a member of the sixth, seventh, and eighth sessions of the General Conference.

**Today is not a day of distress
But a day of delight.**

Henry B Huntoon
Birth:
Oct. 9, 1840
Salisbury
Merrimack County, New Hampshire
Death:
Jun. 18, 1909
Bristol
Grafton County, New Hampshire
Burial:
Lakeview Cemetery
Hampstead

Rockingham County, New Hampshire

He studied in the common schools and was converted in 1854. Licensed in 1883 and ordained in 1886 by the Wolfborough Quarterly Meeting. Besides his pastorates in that area he also served as a justice of the peace. Information from NH Vital Records at State Archives, Concord.

Elias Hutchins
Birth:
Jun. 5, 1801
New Portland,
Somerset County, Maine
Death:
Sep. 11, 1859
Dover,
Strafford County,
New Hampshire
Burial:
Pine Hill Cemetery,
Dover,
Strafford County,
New Hampshire,
Plot: Sect. 4, Lot 91

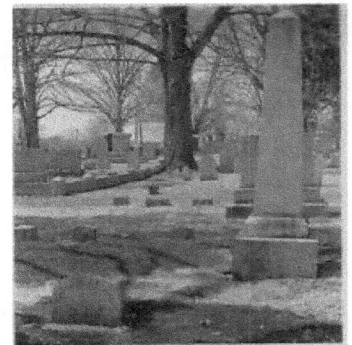

He was baptized by his uncle, Rev. Samuel Hutchins, in 1818, and joined the church. He felt called to preach and on 8 Jan 1823, he was licensed at the age of eighteen. He purchased a horse and saddle and entered upon an itinerant ministry for two years in the Farmington and Edgecomb districts.

He was ordained a minister at Wilton Feb. 1, 1824.

He set out as an evangelist in Ohio and Indiana for two years, principally in Marion, Clark, and Warren Counties, Ohio, and in Dearborn and Switzerland Counties, Indiana. The winter of 1829 he spent among Free Will Baptists in North Carolina, where many slaves flocked to hear him preach.

He returned to New England in 1831 in New Hampshire and Maine. In Oct. 1833, he became pastor in N. Providence, Rhode Island, until 1838, when he went to Lowell, Mass.

He entered a pastorate of five years at New Market, N. H. He was elected Corresponding Sec'y of Foreign Mission Society, an office he held until his death.

In May 1845, he accepted a call to Washington St. church in Dover, New Hampshire, and for a time was editor of the "Myrtle" and the "Gospel Rill" books used in Sunday School for children.

Dec. 26, 1846, he married Mrs. Marilla Marks, the widow of Rev. David Marks. He was 58 years at the time of his death. He died as he lived, a sweet, loving example of Christian trust. The heathen and the slave found a firm friend in him.

He represented Ohio in the Second Gen. Conference, and was a member of the committee on an itinerant ministry. He served the General Conference in 1835, and 1850, on the committee on correspondence.

In 1842 he was president of the Home Mission Society, and in 1848-52 of the Education Society; in 1840-41 of the Sunday-School Union. He was a trustee 11 years, and corporator twenty-four years for the Printing Establishment.

We all have the same body, the same human flesh, and therefore we will all die.

Lorenzo Dow Jeffers
Birth:
Mar., 1821
East Haverhill
Grafton County, New Hampshire
Death:
Sep. 6, 1893
Grafton County, New Hampshire
Burial:
Number 6 Cemetery
East Haverhill
Grafton County,
New Hampshire

He was converted to the age of 21; began to preach in 1846; and was ordained in 1854. He pastored a number of churches in the area where he was converted and ordained. He labored as an itinerant preacher and had revivals in his work. He was clerk of the Wentworth quarterly Meeting for a number of years.

Oh, may I join the choir invisible Of those immortal dead who live again.

Reuben Varney Jenness
Birth:
May 5, 1836
Strafford County, New Hampshire
Death:
Jun. 25, 1861
Dover
Strafford County,
New Hampshire
Burial:
Pine Hill Cemetery
Dover
Strafford County,
New Hampshire

Rev. Reuben V. Jenness, was the son of Nathaniel (1796-1882) and Lydia (Varney) JENNESS.He was converted at age fifteen, and baptized by his teacher, Rev. O.B. Cheney, joining the church in West Lebanon. He afterwards transferred his membership to Washington St. church, Dover, where his parents resided, and remained a devoted member for ten years. Feeling called to preach, he prepared for college principally at South Berwick, Maine, under the tuition of Dr. Grey. He entered Darmouth a year in advance, and graduated with high honors in 1859.He was married to Miss Emily C. Smith, of E. Randolph, VT, July 29, 1862, and was ordained Sept. 10, 1862, as pastor of the Pine Street Church in Manchester, not long before his failing health caused him "to go home to die." (i.e. Dover).He was a member of the FWB Foreign Mission Board, and especially excelled as a writer. He and had a bright future ahead of him, when he died at age 27 years.

Abner Jones
Birth:
Apr. 28, 1772
Worcester County,
Massachusetts
Death:
May 29, 1841
Burial:
Winter Street Burial Ground
Exeter
Rockingham County,
New Hampshire

He was a medical doctor, minister, and early church reformer. He was married 1804 to Damaris Prior, b. 6 Dec 1768 in Canaan, Conn., dau. of Clothier and Anna (Bramble) Prior.

Francis Kenerson
Birth:
Dec. 25, 1828
Albany, New Hampshire
Death:
Jan. 13, 1858
New Hampshire
Burial:
Chickville CemeteryCenter
Ossipee
Carroll County,
New Hampshire

He was 14 months old when his father died. At the age of nine, his mother moved with him to Great Falls. At 13 he returned to near the place of his birth to live with Joseph Bennett of Tamworth. At this time under, Rev. James Emery, experienced religion at age 14. Three years later he went to Hingham, Massachusetts to learn the trade of Carpenter. In the summer of 1851 he preached in Tamworth and vicinity till early in 1852 when he accepted a call to the Second Eaton church. Later he pastored a number of churches in the area. However, in November, 1857, his health failed and he preached his last sermon on November 29, at Tamworth in the very church where he preached his first sermon. Add age 29 years and 19 days.

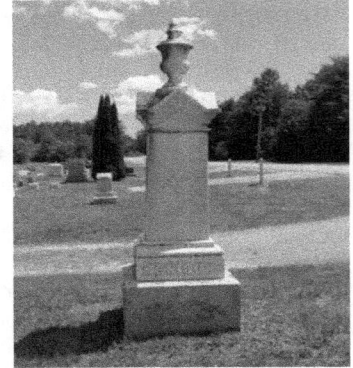

Spencer Kenison
Birth:
1806
Death:
Mar. 10, 1884
Bartlett
Carroll County,
New Hampshire
Burial:
Garland Ridge Cemetery
Bartlett
Carroll County,
New Hampshire

Rev. Spencer Kenison, died in Bartlett, his native town, at age 75 years. He early married Miss Judith Hazelton, daughter of Rev. Samuel Hazelton, of Jackson, afterwards of Bethel, ME. He cleared a farm and made himself a comfortable home. At the age of twenty-seven, he was baptized by Elder John Pinkham, and with his wife united with the church in Bartlett. From this time he was the leader of the church, and for many years successfully ministered to them as a licensed preacher. A lady visitor having offered $200 toward the erection of a meeting house, he and his neighbors took their oxen, and went to the woods, cut the timber, and soon had a neat chapel built.In 1864 he was ordained, and continued the acceptable pastor of the church fourteen years. The last six years he was unable to work. He suffered severely before death came to his relief.

"I see Heaven open and Jesus on the right hand of God"

Thomas Keniston
Birth:
Dec. 9, 1819
Woodbury, Burma
Death:
Dec. 25, 1901
New Hampton
Belknap County,
New Hampshire
Burial:
New Hampton Village
Cemetery
New Hampton
Belknap County,
New Hampshire

He studied one year at New Hampton and was converted in his 21st year. He was licensed in February, 1842 and ordained the next year by the Lisbon Quarterly Meeting at Bethlehem. He labored for a number of years in Maine and New Hampshire where he baptized more than 1400 people.

Samuel Knowles
Birth:
1777
New Hampshire, USA
Death:
Nov. 15, 1850
Ossipee
Carroll County, New
Hampshire
Burial:
Fall Cemetery
Ossipee
Carroll County,
New Hampshire

About 1830 he joined the Free Baptists and was ordained to their ministry. In 1832 he became a pastor at Sandwich, New Hampshire. After a year and a half he moved to Eaton. In 1843 he went to Ossipee and continued to preach until a few months before his death of palsy.

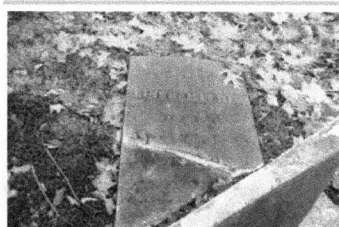

Lincoln Lewis
Birth:
1799
Waterville, Maine
Death:
Apr. 21, 1858
Upper Gilmanton,
New Hampshire
Burial:
Sleeper Burial Ground
Gilmanton Ironworks
Belknap County,
New Hampshire

He was ordained in 1822. His ministry was confined to Maine and New Hampshire.

Nathan Chase Lothrop
Birth:
Jun. 19, 1839
Norton
Bristol County,
Massachusetts
Death:
Feb. 15, 1920
Bristol
Grafton County,
New Hampshire
Burial:
Homeland Cemetery
Bristol
Grafton County,
New Hampshire
Plot: Sec. 20E
Lot 7, Grave 7

Son of Solomon Lothrop and Fanny Chase. He was converted at the age of 17, after baptizing united with the church at Colton. He graduated from New Hampton institution in 1861 and from the theological school in 1864. He was ordained in the South Berwick, Maine, where pastored 18 months. Most of his pastorate was in the confines of the state of Maine. He married on November 16, 1865 to Sarah J Lovejoy of Laconia, New Hampshire.

Francis H Lyford
Birth:
September 19, 1820
Pittsfield, New Hampshire
Death:
1891
Burial:
Union Cemetery
Laconia
Belknap County,
New Hampshire
Plot: Section 392-E
Grave 6

He was converted at the age of eight and studied at Pittsfield Academy, Clinton Grove Seminary, and the Friends Institution at Weare, New Hampshire. In 1859 he was licensed and in 1860 was ordained by the Strafford Quarterly Meeting, Vermont. His pastorates were in East Randolph and Thetford, Vermont; West Lebanon, Maine, Hampton, Laconia, and Meredith Ctr., New Hampshire; Haverhill, Massachusetts; Littleton, New Hampshire, to name a few. He was the author of the history of his hometown. In 1845 he married Miss Eunice Pickering and 1852 Miss Catherine S. Cox.

Josiah Magoon
Birth:
Jun. 25, 1758
East Kingston
Rockingham County,
New Hampshire
Death:
Feb. 5, 1841
New Hampton
Belknap County,
New Hampshire
Burial:
Magoon Cemetery
New Hampton
Belknap County,
New Hampshire
Plot: 4

He served his country faithfully in its struggle for independence and was present at Newcastle, Winter Hill and Ticonderoga. He accepted the Lord Jesus in the spring of 1780 and was baptized, joining a Baptist church. After he resided at New Hampton, in 1800, a remarkable revival was conducted by Rev. Winthrop Young. He was ordained in 1804 and remained faithful for nearly 40 years. Under the lead of brother Magoon, the church had almost yearly additions. For 10 years from 1833, 120 united with the church by baptism. He made occasional visits to Maine and Vermont, but most of his preaching was done in and around New Hampshire. He died at the age of 82
Note: Some information from the Inventory of New Hampton's Rural Burial Grounds, provided by the Town Clerk

John McClary
Birth:
1784
Epsom,
Merrimack County,
New Hampshire
Death:
Dec. 22, 1821
Epsom,
Merrimack County,
New Hampshire
Burial:
McClary Cemetery,
Epsom,
Merrimack County,
New Hampshire

He was killed almost instantly by the fall of a piece of timber from the frame of a shed under which he was standing. From his earliest youth he possessed a remarkable degree the affection of his friends, and the confidence of his fellow citizens. He was repeatedly elected a Representative from his native town in the Legislature of this State, and two years he was chosen a Senator, by the fourth district.

James McCutcheon
Birth:
unknown
Death:
Sep. 2, 1855
Burial:
Old North Pembroke Cemetery
North Pembroke
Merrimack County,
New Hampshire

He was ordained in 1828 and his labors were in New Hampshire.

Asa Merrill
Birth:
Mar. 10, 1783
Stratham, N.H.
Death:
Nov. 13, 1860
Burial:
Congregational Cemetery
Stratham
Rockingham County,
New Hampshire

His conversion occurred 9, 1800 at the age of seventeen the Congregationalists and feeling call to the ministry he began study the pastor of his church. Through differing from his church he was baptized uniting with the Christian church. After preaching much in the southern part of the town he was ordained there May 9 1827. Rev Mark Fernald of Kittery, Me. preaching the sermon. He served this church till 1834 when he and the church united with the Free Baptists. During the eight following years he enjoyed frequent revivals and a number were baptized. In 1842 the church lost its visibility and he joined the Raymond church and preached there for several years. He afterwards removed his standing to the New Market church. To his first wife were born twelve children. Sarah P. is the wife of Rev. O. R. Bacheler missionary to India, another daughter married Rev JT Eaton a Methodist minister, a son Daniel P. Merrill graduated from Dartmouth College in 1836 and for many years taught in Mobile Ala, As a preacher Brother Merrill was practical spirltual and rich in experience. Four years before his death he was prostrated with paralysis.

Nathan Merrill
Birth:
unknown
Death:
Aug. 28, 1836
Burial:
Highland Cemetery
Rumney
Grafton County, New
Hampshire

He was ordained in the church at Gray, Me. by Randall and Tingley Oct 2 1787. Stinchfield says,' Merrill ran well for a while. He has been useful to the church by occupying his proper gift which was of exhortation.' He was pastor of Gray and New Gloucester church. When Stinchfield attempted to preach in 1793 he found little to help him. Merrill encouraged the church in military display declaring that they might innocently engage in parades, which annoyed his ministerial brethren. The matter was brought before the YM for four years where it occasioned serious discord. Alienation finally ensued and Nathan Merrill ceased to co-operate with the people of his early choice.

Inscription:
"A soldier of the revolution"

Atwood B Meservey
Birth:
Sep. 30, 1831
Appleton,
Knox County, Maine
Death:
Feb. 21, 1901
Belknap County,
New Hampshire
Burial:
New Hampton Village Cemetery,
New Hampton, Belknap County,
New Hampshire,
Plot: 307

Mr. Merservey chose medicine as his profession and attended lectures at Bowdoin College. He decided to become a clergyman and came to New Hampton in 1855 to prepare for college. He graduated from the literary department there in 1857 and past three years in the study of theology, also attending for six months the Andover Theological Seminary; plus, lectures on physical geography and geology at Brown University. In 1861 he was ordained pastor of the Freewill Baptist Church at Meredith Village. In 1867 he became principal of the Seminary at Northwood, returning to New Hampton after a year, to become principal of that town's Seminary. The school honored him by establishing the "Meservey Medal" in his name, which is still awarded to a person for outstanding contribution to the academic and social life of the school. Mr. Meservey received the degree of A.M. from Brown University and a Ph.D. from Bates College. Republican in politics he represented New Hampton in the State Legislature in 1867.

Nathan H Milton
Birth:
1811
Death:
1839
Dover, New Hampshire
Burial:
Trickey
Brookfield
Carroll County, New Hampshire

He was ordained for five years prior to his death and was able to preach the gospel until failed in health took his life.

As a doorman opens the door to a place, so death opens the door for the soul to take its flight.

Timothy Morse
Birth:
1765
Newbury, Massachusetts
Death:
Oct. 30, 1832
Burial:
South Newbury Cemetery
South Newbury
Merrimack County,
New Hampshire

In 1815 he was chosen to represent his town, and for several years said in the state legislature, and preaching as occasions offered. At one time three other ministers of Free Will Baptists denomination had seats in the legislature and boarded at the same house. When the days the work was ended they held religious meetings and evenings to as many as would come. Later, he abandoned his legislative career and gave himself wholly to the work as an itinerant preacher. His first tour was to Windsor, Vermont, where he was blessed in the gathering of the church of 60 members in 1822. In October, he returned to Rhode Island and added 42 to the Pawtucket church. Remaining there with the Rehoboth Free Communion Baptist Church, which was organized in 1777, and through his influence he so the church added to the Rhode Island Quarterly Meeting in August, 1823. In the summer of 1824, he saw large numbers converted in Randolph, Vermont. In July, 1825 he had good additions to the church in Danville. He remained in the area of Lyndon, Sutton and then removed to Strafford, Vermont where he had more than

300 people converted. His itinerant preaching took him into many states and regions. In October, 1830, he was an active and influential member of the fourth General Conference which was held at Greenville, Rhode Island. He had also been a member of the first General Conference. There was power in his presence which nothing could resist. He felt the power of Christ, and during his ministry baptize over 500 people.

Inscription:
Elder Timothy Morse
died Oct 30, 1832, aged 67 years.
The gospel was his joy and song,
E'en to his last breath, The truth
he had proclaimed so long, Was
his support in death.

William Alson Nealy
Birth:
Nov. 3,
Bolton
Chittenden County, Vermont
Death:
Jan. 28, 1890
Bristol
Grafton County, New Hampshire
Burial:
Homeland Cemetery
Bristol
Grafton County, New Hampshire
Plot: Sec. 15W, Lot 10, Grave 7

Rev. Wm. A. Nealy, studied at Green Mountain Seminary, and ordained Dec. 22, 1872. Pastored in Vermont, NY, and R.I. In 1887, took pastorate of Bristol, NH. Son of John Nealy and Sarah Cooper. William was a pastor of the Free Baptist Church in Bristol, Grafton, New Hampshire 1888-1890.

As the rain from heaven refreshes the parched ground, so death provides the saint to partake of the refreshing of the soul in the presence of Jesus.

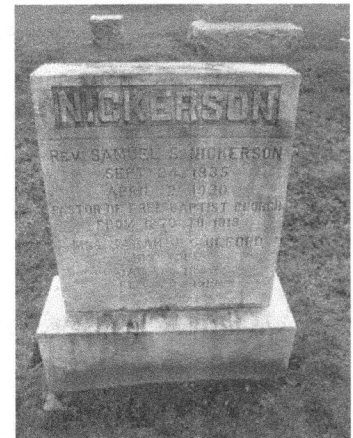

Samuel S Nickerson
Birth:
Sep. 24, 1835
Albany, New York
Death:
Apr. 2, 1930
Burial:
Sunny Side Cemetery
Grafton County, New Hampshire

He graduated from New Hampton Literary Institution in 1859 and from the theological department in 1863. He was licensed to preach on May 26, 1863 and ordained in Providence, Rhode Island on October 13, 1864 under the direction of the executive board of home missions. He was for four years a missionary to the Freeman in North Carolina and Virginia, from October 1863 to October 1867. He arrived at Roanoke Island, South Carolina and later was the society's first missionary to bear the word of life to this suppressed race. He pastored a number of churches in Vermont and also later in New Hampshire. He served faithfully the Free Baptist denomination from 1873 to 1918.

John Norris
Birth:
June, 1804
Death:
Aug. 15, 1870
Burial:
Glenwood Cemetery
Littleton
Grafton County, New Hampshire

He was married in October 1825 to Polly Sleeper. He was converted in March, 1828 and baptized in May by the Rev. Nathaniel Bowles joining the church in his town. Began to preach in 1839 and was soon ordained. He served for many years in New Hampshire and Vermont. After the death of Polly he married Mrs Ruth Nurse in December, 1861. He was thrown from a wagon receiving fatal injuries from which he died.

Micajah Otis
Birth:
May 21, 1747
Barrington,Strafford County,
New Hampshire
Death:
May 20, 1821
Barrington, Strafford County,
New Hampshire
Burial:
Center
Strafford Cemetery,
Strafford, Strafford County,
New Hampshire

Otis was very instrumental in the development of the early northeastern Free Will Baptist Church, along with Elders John Buzzell, and other church fathers. He was dedicated to his church and its doctrine of Free Grace, Free Will, and Free Salvation to all. He preached until he died at nearly 74 years of age. In 1776, Micajah signed the Pledge to Support the American Revolution at Barrington, N. H. He was ordained a Free Will Baptist clergyman, and was a very respected and effective minister.

God himself took a day to rest in, and a good man's grave is his Sabbath.

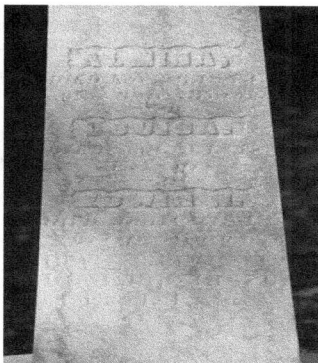

A. C. Peaslee
Birth:
May 29, 1832
Death:
Jul. 1, 1876
West Topsham
Orange County, Vermont
Burial:
Old South Sutton Cemetery
Sutton
Merrimack County,
New Hampshire

Rev. Arthue C. Peaslee, the son of Rev. Isaac and Hannah Peaslee, was born in Sutton, N.H. He was converted at the age of thirty-three, and soon after, he attended school at New Hampton, NH with the ministry in view. He was ordained at Newfield, ME, May 5, 1868, where there had been a revival under his labors. In the fall of 1874, he attended the Vermont Yearly Meeting at West Topsham. He with others, remained and held a series of meetings which resulted in his being chosen pastor. The work prospered under his labors. He held seven pastorates, in nearly all of which there was revival interest.

Isaac Peaslee
Birth:
Jun. 9, 1795
Death:
May 11, 1884
Sutton
Merrimack County,
New Hampshire
Burial:
Old South Sutton Cemetery
Sutton
Merrimack County,
New Hampshire

He was an active Christian for more than seventy years. He was deacon for several years in the Sutton Church, and on Feb. 15, 1832, he was ordained a Freewill Baptist minister and entered upon his ministerial labors, which were mostly in the Weare Quarterly Meeting (District). He baptized nearly one hundred in his own town.

Inscription:
Rev. ISAAC PEASLEE
DIED
May 11, 1884AE 89 yrs.

David Marks Place
Birth:
Feb. 4, 1831
Strafford County,
New Hampshire
Death:
May 13, 1900
Strafford County,
New Hampshire

Son of Rev. Enoch Hayes Place. Served in Co. C, 324 Reg. Mass. Volunteers (Civil War).

Blessed are the dead which die in the Lord

Enoch Hayes Place
Birth:
Jul. 13, 1786
New Hampshire
Death:
Mar. 23, 1865
Strafford, Strafford County,
New Hampshire
Burial:
Center Strafford Cemetery,
Strafford, Strafford County,
New Hampshire, Plot: 83

Elder Place was a very active and respected minister in the northeastern Free Will Baptist movement, and rode horseback, or in a carriage, to attend far away meetings, where he was in demand as a speaker. He kept detailed records in journals which were transcribed by William E. Wentworth, entitled "Journals of Enoch Hayes Place, 1810-1865." These volumes were published by New Hampshire Society of Genealogists in Concord, New Hampshire in 1998. Church records and books note that he always had sound words and wise counsel. His work as a pastor or preacher was of an inestimable value to his church.

Joshua Quimby
Birth:
Nov. 5, 1766
Rockingham County,
New Hampshire
Death:
Mar. 31, 1844
Grafton County,
New Hampshire
Burial:
Sunny Side Cemetery,
Grafton County,
New Hampshire

He began to preach in 1792. He was ordained at Lisbon in 1800. He was at first a Baptist, and in 1811 he became a Free Baptist and was for more than thirty years pastor of that church on Sugar Hill and his pure Christian character and exemplary life carried an influence that can hardly be estimated. During his long ministry he doubtless officiated at more funerals and united more people in marriage than any other clergyman in town or who ever lived in town." (History of Lisbon, ME., by Guy S. Rix.) Others helping in this church were Rev. Josiah Quimby, Moses Aldrich, Timothy Tyler and Jonathan Bowles. They erected the first church building in 1829 which served until 1884 when a new one was erected. Records state it would seat 300-400 and valued at $3,500. From this small beginning, the Lisbon Quarterly meeting has arisen, numbering now about 1200 members. Rev. Quimby was a man of good judgment, and a Christian of sincerity and honesty. He was one of the most faithful and capable men of his day in church labors and difficulties. He travelled to sit on committees and councils. Many old church records mention his ministerial labors, such as "Rev. Joshua Quimby here (Whitestown Free Will Baptist) in 1816-17, forming a Religious Society and several persons were baptized." (Rev. Benaiah Bean, an associate, was the first resident minister of Whitestown. He traveled all over the North Country, preaching his faith, and organizing churches.

Moses A. Quimby
Birth:
Oct. 5, 1821
Lyndon,
Caledonia County, Vermont
Death:
Dec. 7, 1895
Pittsfield,
Merrimack County,
New Hampshire
Burial:
Floral Park Cemetery,
Pittsfield,
Merrimack County,
New Hampshire

He was a grandson of the Rev. Daniel Quimby. He received his early education at the Lyndon Academy and at Geauga Seminary, Ohio and took the three years course for the ministry at Whitestown, New York. In January, 1842 he received license to preach and on December 3, 1845 he was ordained by reference Daniel Quimby, Jonathan Woodman and others.

He had the care of 10 different churches and his pastorates have averaged nearly 4 years. He closed the fourth pastorate with the Epsom church where he had been pastor for 10 years. He baptized 160 converts. He was a member of two General Conferences and several years on the Home Mission Board. He built the new FWB Meetinghouse in Epson, N. H., 1854, which in 2007, has been moved into town and is being preserved for historical purposes.

Goram Parsons Ramsey
Birth:
Jan. 16, 1813
New Hampton,
Belknap County,
New Hampshire
Death:
Aug. 23, 1876
Dover,
Strafford County,
New Hampshire
Burial:
Pine Hill Cemetery,
Dover,
Strafford County,
New Hampshire,
Plot: Sect 4, Lot 91

At age seventeen he was converted and baptized by Rev. E. Fisk. Soon after, he attended school at Parsonsfield Seminary, a foundation he built upon to the end of his active ministry. He was ordained at Falmouth, Maine in Nov. 1839, and in June, 1840, settled in Epsom, New Hampshire. He spent one year at Hillsdale, Michigan, in charge of the Boarding Hall, and Mrs. Ramsey was lady principal. His pastorates always were fruitful, and under his ministry, churches obtained solidity, spirituality and efficiency. He was active in his denomination's Anti-Slavery Committee, of which he served as Recording Secretary from 1843-44.He died in New Berwick about a year and a half after his last pastorate. Rev. O.T. Moulton conducted his funeral service. Rev's Hosea Quinby, his teacher, and Silas Curtis, who married him, assisted.

Vienna G. *Morrell* Ramsey
Birth:
Jan. 8, 1817
North Berwick
York ,County, Maine
Death:
Jan. 16, 1905
Dover, Strafford County
New Hampshire
Burial:
Pine Hill Cemetery
Dover, Strafford County
New Hampshire,
Plot: Sect. 4, Lot 91

At fourteen she taught school, and then went to Parsonsfield Seminary. She also studied at New Market Academy and Philadelphia Collegiate Institute. She married Rev. Goram P. Ramsey, a Free Will Baptist minister, in Aug. 1840. She was converted at age nineteen and soon became a contributor to the "Morning Star" and the Boston "Saturday Evening Post," and took a prize from the latter Aug. 5, 1840. She was a faithful helper to him in his several pastorates. When he served Hillsdale College in Michigan., she became the first lady principal there. She was deeply interested in foreign missions, and was very active in promoting the interests of the FWB Woman's Missionary Society. In 1851, she was elected as its president, serving several years. Before this, she was its corresponding secretary for three years. The Society often called upon her to deliver public addresses. Though she sacrificed her literary aspirations to home and parish work, her pen was not idle.

James Rand
Birth:
Sep. 15, 1815
York County, Maine
Death:
Dec. 24, 1888
Dover
Strafford County, New Hampshire
Burial:
Pine Hill Cemetery
Dover
Strafford County, New Hampshire
Plot: Section S-6 Lot 137 Grave 1

His father was John H. Rand, who was for more than 50 years a deacon of John Buzzell's church. He was converted at age 14 and baptized on January 18, 1830 by Rev. Elias Libby. He attended Parsonfield Seminary so he could teach. He was licensed from the Parsonlield quarterly meeting on September 11, 1833 and on September 25, 1840 was ordained

by Rev. John Buzzell, B. S. Manson and others. He married on December 26, 1839 Miss Dorothy Fernald and they had four children. He pastored many churches in Maine and then in New Hampshire. Because he received meager offerings for his preaching he had to teach school and to engage in farming along with his work as a minister. He was for several years Pres. of the Home Mission Society and at one time member of its executive board. He also was a member of the Foreign Mission Board and was for 12 years its president. There were more than 16 ministers of the Free Will denomination present at his funeral.

Benjamin Odger Randall
Birth:
Feb. 7, 1749
Newcastle,
Rockingham County,
New Hampshire
Death:
Oct. 22, 1808
Burial::
Randall Cemetery,
Strafford County,
New Hampshire

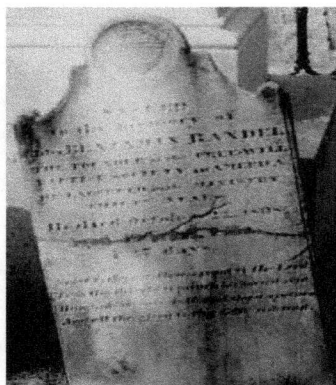

He was the son of a sea captain. From age nine he followed his father at sea until age 18, when he tired of it, and at his request, his father put him as an apprentice to learn the art of sail making, which he followed until age 21. He served in the Revolutionary War as assistant commissary officer in the New Hampshire militia. He re-enlisted Sept. 10, 1776, and became a Sgt. in the company of Capt. John Calf., Col. Pierce Long's Regiment, New Hampshire Militia. A fellow officer, Joshiah Magoon, said that "He was accustomed to visit the sick and administer to them the consolations of religion; indeed doing largely the duties of a chaplain.

Thus many a desponding heart was cheered and made strong by his efforts."Upon hearing the Rev. George Whitefield, one of England's great preachers who came to America to preach, following his religious convictions, broke with his traditional religion of predestination and in 1780, founded the First Free Will Baptist Church of New Durham, New Hampshire, from which spread that church's beginnings in the northeast United States. His preaching was effective and he went near and far to preach, establish churches, and propagate the gospel. It was largely because of the exposures of the severe northeastern winters, that his health failed and after 30 years of selfless service, died from lung disease, age 59 years, 7 mos. 27 days. The churches in that area erected a monument and slabs over his grave. His will was made 4 June 1808; a codicil was added 1 Oct; the will is on record at the county office.(taken from the book, "The Life of Elder Benjamin Randall, pub. 1827, Limerick. MA. by Eld. John Buzzell, a comtempary, who read Randall's notes and also had personal knowledge.) He was a great man who stood by his convictions and 'the Book.' His work, like the proverbial grain of mustard seed, grew to spread in all directions. He is remembered in books written about him and in many other ways after all these years. The large monument was erected a few years after his death by a grateful church to this great leader. Inscription: West side of tall monument reads "Benjamin Randall died October 22, 1808, 59 years, 8 months and 15 days. Founder of the Free Will Baptists.

Benjamin Walton Randall
Birth:
May 4, 1776
New Durham
Strafford County, New Hampshire
Death:
Sep. 24, 1843
New Durham
Strafford County, New Hampshire
Burial:
Randall Cemetery
New Durham
Strafford County, New Hampshire

He followed his father on the homestead. Parents: Benjamin Odger Randall (1749 - 1808) Joanna Oram Randall (1748 - 1826) Spouse: Sarah Titcomb Parsons Randall (1774 - 1860) Children: Josiah Parsons Randall (1801 - 1808)* Sarah Sewell Randall (1803 - 1805)

Sarah Titcomb Parsons Randall
Birth:
1774
Maine
Death:
Nov. 8, 1860
New Durham
Strafford County, New Hampshire
Burial:
Randall Cemetery
New Durham
Strafford County, New Hampshire

For several years prior to her marriage Sarah, historically known as Sally Parson, traveled on horseback doing missionary work and was a early evangelist with Benjamin Randall. Sarah's father threw her out of the house for being a despised Baptist, but finally relented and invited her home just before her marriage to Benjamin W. Randall, the son of the founder of the Free Will Baptist of the north. Her spouse was Benjamin Walton Randall. and their children were Josiah Parsons Randall (1801-08) Sarah Sewell Randall (1803 - 1805).

Caleb H. Richardson
Birth:
February 17, 1787
Death:

Apr. 25, 1868
Canaan, New York
Burial:
Wells Cemetery
Canaan
Grafton County, New Hampshire

He preached 35 years in Wilmot, Danbury, Grafton and vicinity. He took The Morning Star for over 40 years.

George Washington Russell
Birth:
Jun. 11, 1802
Woodstock
Grafton County, New Hampshire
Death:
Aug. 10, 1886
North Woodstock
Grafton County, New Hampshire
Burial:
Parker Cemetery
Grafton County, New Hampshire

He became a Christian when about 18 years of age and soon began to preach. He was ordained at Thornton Gore. He helped to form the Woodstock church, of which he continued a member until his death. The church edifice was built by him and in 1851.He was the son of Joseph and Mary (Robbins) Russell. He married 1st, Margery W. Pinkham. She died and he married Sally Mills.

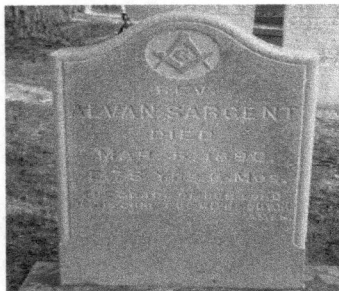

Alvan Sargent
Birth:
1814
union, Maine
Death:
1890
Burial:
Church Place Cemetery
Wilmot
Merrimack County
New Hampshire

He read theology and homiletics in Lowell, Maine. In 1844 and in 1845 he received license to preach. He was ordained in 1847 by the Weare Quarterly Meeting, in New Hampshire. He mainly pastored churches in New Hampshire. He baptized 203 converts, married 287 couples and attended 414 funerals. He was a Quarterly Meeting Clerk, a member of the General Conference and of the Home Mission Board. He served one term in the legislature. He was married in 1836 to Nancy Hayward who died and in 1880, then he married Miss Sarah Greely.

Seth Sawyer
Birth:
1808
Alton, New Hampshire
Death:
1892

Burial:
Riverside Cemetery
Alton
Belknap County, New Hampshire

He was converted in 1831 and ordained in 1857. His labors were mostly confined to supplying churches where they had no settled pastor. He labored at Guilford village, new Durham, Middletown, Wakefield, East Alton, and Alton. He baptized among his converts a granddaughter of Rev. Benjamin Randall.

John Langdon Sinclair
Birth:
Jul. 10, 1809
Meredith,
Belknap County,
New Hampshire
Death:
Aug. 16, 1888
Burial:
Blossom Hill Cemetery,
Concord,
Merrimack County,
New Hampshire

He studied in the common school and at New Hampton he listened to the preaching of many of the fathers and before his twenty first year he was baptized by Rev B.S. Manson. In 1832 he was licensed. In 1833 he supplied the church in Lowell, Mass. and in May 1834 probably went to Dover, New Hampshire. On June 30 1835 he was ordained by Fisk Dana Hill and Pinkham and settled at Lynn, Mass. For nearly thirty years he was a member of the board of corporators of the Printing Establishment retained there for his business ability. He was twice president of the Home Mission Society.

He was President, Recording Secretary and Corresponding Secretary of the Sunday School Union. He was President of the Anti-Slavery Society. He was a strong and bold advocate of the right by prudence and economy he gathered in order that he might bestow upon the benevolent work of the denomination. From the time says Dr Brackett more than forty years ago when he as a pastor was laboring to build a church in Manchester and living on a meager salary gave the first hundred dollars of savings to our struggling Biblical School on to the day of his death he was a regular and liberal giver to all our benevolent causes. Many a poor student at New Hampton or elsewhere has received a regular donation from term to term to enable him to go on with his studies. Among the larger gifts already executed are $10,000 to Storer College. $1,000 to the Sinclair Orphanage in India. $1,000 to Hillsdale College. $1,000 to the Concord church and $500 to the Lake Village parsonage. No man in our denomination minister or layman with so small an income has given so much money to benevolent work.

Levi Streeter
Birth:
unknown
Lisbon, New Hampshire
Death:
Jul. 22, 1886
North Lisbon, New Hampshire
Burial:
Glenwood Cemetery
Littleton
Grafton County, New Hampshire

He was a member of the Littleton church. He was born within the bounds of the Lisbon Quarterly

Meeting. He was a Christian over 40 years and 35 of those who use as an ordained minister.

Hiram Stevens
Birth:
December 12, 1806
New Chester, New Hampshire
Death:
Jun. 6, 1880
Meredith village,
New Hampshire
Burial:
Meredith Village Cemetery
Meredith
Belknap County,
New Hampshire

He began to hold meetings when he was about 15 and soon went to New York and for most of the time until 1827 preached with success in the various adjoining towns in the area. In April, 1825 he was licensed by the Ballston Christian church. He returned to New Hampshire in 1827 and in the following spring began to preach in Lowell as a Free Baptists. In June he was received as a licensed preacher by the New Hampshire Yearly Meeting at Strafford and in August of the next year he joined the New Durham Quarterly Meeting. He was ordained at Canterbury on January 20, 1830. He gathered a church at Lowell. He preached as an evangelist in different towns with much success. At Meredith Village there were many added to the church. After this he was at Farmington and Dover. He in 1852 he started the Belvedere mission in that part of the area called Centreville. He ultimately returned to Meredith Village where he spent his last years

Some people are so afraid to die that they never begin to live
~Henry Van Dyke~

Edwin Byron Stiles
Birth:
January 16, 1860
Albany, Vermont
Death:
1917
New Hampshire
Burial:
Woodstock Cemetery
Woodstock
Grafton County, New Hampshire

He graduated from Bates College in 1885 and from Andover theological Seminary in 1888. He was licensed to preach in 1886 and ordained on February 15, 1888 by the Massachusetts Association. On June 25 he married miss Idaho in. Tucker a college classmate and after it became settled that the foreign mission field was to be his home. They sailed in November as missionaries to India.

Ada Henrietta Tucker Stiles
Birth:
1864
New Hampshire
Death:
1927
New Hampshire
Burial:
Woodstock Cemetery
Woodstock
Grafton County, New Hampshire

The wife of Rev. Edwin Byron Stiles. They married in Lowell, Massachusetts on June 25, 1888. She served as a missionary to India with her husband Edwin.

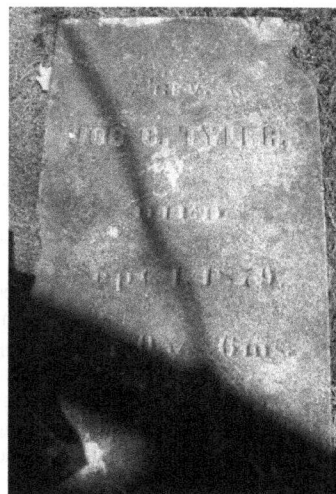

Job C. Tyler
Birth:
unknown
Death:
Sep. 1, 1879
Canaan, New Hampshire
Burial:
Wells Cemetery
Canaan
Grafton County, New Hampshire

He was ordained in 1833 and preached constantly in the towns of Canaan, Orange, Grafton, and Hanover, until by old age. He was a main instrument of revivals in other places especially in East Andover and for years he preached in his own dwelling house. He died at 80yrs. 6mos.

Bartholomew Van Dame
Birth:
Jun. 21, 1807 Netherlands
Death:
Apr. 3, 1872
Nottingham,
Rockingham County,
New Hampshire
Burial:
Epping Central Cemetery,
Epping,, Rockingham County,
New Hampshire

He came over with Capt John C. Long of Portsmouth, New Hampshire in 1819 and came to Epping with Josiah Clark Feb 14, 1822 and served his time with Ensign John Dow from Feb 10, 1824 to June 21, 1828. He suffered many accidents, one that permanently maimed his right arm. In his sixteenth year with John Dow. He began to read, and thirsting for knowledge, he had in Epping acquired a good education. He studied under Dr. Timothy Hilliard, who deeply impressed him and with whom he went on lecture tours. After three terms with Dr. Hilliard he taught three months in Epping, having forty pupils. Again he entered the school of Dr. Hilliard, sometimes acting as his assistant while practicing the most rigid economy. In 1830, he entered New Hampton Institution. He studied mathematics of which he was fond. On Aug. 14, 1830, he was baptized in Epping by Rev. Israel Chesley of Durham. He prepared and published 500 copies of a small hymn-book, partly original. He studied Latin with, Dr. Hilliard, and he taught for three years to gather funds and uniting meanwhile with the Greenfield FWB church under pastor Rev. John Kimball, where his membership remained until his death. He studied Greek under John D. Philbrick, afterward superintendent of the Boston public schools, and read the classics. He entered Strafford Academy in 1835, having Prof. John Fullonton as his classmate in Latin and Greek. He entered the Congregational Theological Seminary at Gilmanton Center soon after his graduation at Strafford. After teaching in various places in Maine and New Hampshire in 1837, he came to Epsom, New Hampshire to supply the vacant pulpit in connection with his teaching, and having a revival he held seventy meetings. Here, April 10, 1838, he was ordained by Arthur Caverno, John Kimball, and Daniel P. Cilley. During forty years, he taught thirty years in all. He was ever a promoter of education. He came and went visiting Washington and the South, looking on statesmen, while thinking and studying about the magnitude of the offense of slavery under his own keen observation. He went to gatherings, sacred, secular, and patriotic, delivering speeches abounding with information, and rendered interesting and fascinating by the quaint individuality of the man.He could hold an audience's attention for hours.

He left a manuscript of 10,000 closely written pages composed since 1834, among them a hymn-book, dictionary, chemistry, arithmetic, geometry, grammar, and lectures on anti-slavery and temperance.

Having willed to several churches and to the benevolent enterprises of his denomination his personal effects, he wrote in his epitaph:"This world I leave without a debt behind,"

Granville C Waterman
Birth:
May 4, 1835
Booth Bay, Maine
Death:
1927
Burial:
Union Cemetery
Laconia
Belknap County,
New Hampshire
Plot: Section 87, Grave 6

He was a son of the Rev. Dexter Waterman. He was converted when 16 years of age and received his education at Litchfield Liberal Institute and Bowdoin College. He received license to preach in 1863 and was ordained on March 23, 1869 by Rev.'s D. Jackson, H. Perry, D. M. Stuart, George H. Ball and A. Aldrich. He held pastorates in New York. New Hampshire and baptized about 60 converts. For some years he was principal at Pike Seminary, New York. He held important positions on the denominational boards. From 1881 to 1886 he was editor of the Sunday school quarterly's and for years has been prominent in Sunday school work. On April 28, 1861 he was married to Miss Julia Mansfield and after her death on December 4, 1873 he married Marietta Stewart. He had several years as a successful professor in Whitestown Seminary and has been active in literary and missionary work.Note: Interred 25 Apr 1927

Abel Wheeler
Birth:
unknown
Death:
Mar. 13, 1870
Burial:
Center Haverhill Cemetery
North Haverhill, Grafton County,
New Hampshire

When about twenty-six years of age he became a Christian. About twelve years afterwards he moved to Haverhill and was one of the original members of the Freewill Baptist church there. He was licensed to preach by the church, and soon after was ordained at Lisbon Quarterly Meeting in 1832. He preached Christ faithfully in several towns until obligated by failing health to retire from the work. He was much respected for his honesty as a man and his consistency as a Christian.He was married to Lipah Wakefield, 23 Oct. 1814, at Newport, NH. In census there is child in 1850 NH census, Lonia M. Wheeler, b. abt 1836.

Frederick L Wiley
Birth:
March 16, 1836
Maryland, New York
Death:
1926
Burial:
Union Cemetery
Laconia
Belknap County, New Hampshire
Plot: Section 505, Grave 1

He received his preparatory education at Whitestown Seminary, New York and graduated from the theological school at New Hampton, New Hampshire in 1868. In 1865 he received license to preach and September 8, 1868 he was ordained by Rev's. J. Mariner, L. B. Tasker, and others. He was married in 1862 Miss Lena L. Smith who died in 1863. In 1868 he was again married to Miss Rebecca Weeks. He held pastorates at Sheffield and Sutton in Vermont; Bath, Maine; Concord, Whitefield and Gilford, New Hampshire. He received 250 people into churches, 127 by baptism. He was a member of the General Conference of 1877. He has for several years been editor of The Messenger. He also wrote *The Life And Influence Of Benjamin Randall;* and *A History Of Free Will Baptists.*
Note: Interred 14 Apr 1926

HE WHO HAS GONE,
SO WE BUT CHERISH
HIS MEMORY, ABIDES
WITH US, MORE
POTENT, NAY,
MORE PRESENT THAN
THE LIVING MAN.

Otis F. Willis
Birth:
1810
Hanover, New Hampshire
Death:
May 8, 1865
Franconia, New Hampshire
Burial:
Willow Cemetery
Franconia
Grafton County, New Hampshire

He was converted in March, 1830 and was baptized by Rev. David Cross. He began to hold meetings, traveling mostly in Vermont and New Hampshire and had several revivals. In 1832, he was licensed by the Strafford Vermont Quarterly Meeting. The same year he moved to Lyndon, Vermont to preach a part of the time at Daniel Quimby's church. In 1834, he was ordained at the request of the church in settled as pastor. In 1835 he entered on a six years pastorate with the church and Sugar Hill, New Hampshire where revivals were enjoyed. In 1841, he moved to Potsdam, New York and in the company of Rev. M. Cole labored in an extensive revival where a church was organized at West Potsdam where he pastored for two years. In 1849, he returned to Sugar Hill. He began

to practice medicine in 1838. The ministry was down neglected for this calling, for the rest of his life. He preached but occasionally and on funeral occasions. He was often heard to regret that he had not followed the work of the ministry.

Winthrop Young
Birth:
1753
Barrington, Strafford County, New Hampshire
Death:
Jan. 6, 1832
Canterbury, Merrimack County, New Hampshire
Burial:
Hackleboro,Canterbury, Merrimack County, New Hampshire

Rev. Young became a school teacher, and after having lived in other locations, moved to Canterbury. Here he was chosen captain of the militia, and his tall, fine figure and courteous manners won him esteem and renown. In August, 1793, Benjamin Randall, visited the town and baptized a number. Finally, becoming deeply interested and zealous, Brother Young was ordained on June 28, 1796, by a council from the Yearly Meeting consisting of Whitney, Buzzell, Randall, Boody and others. He then entered upon a useful pastorate of thirty-five years. In 1798 he baptized thirty in Canterbury. In 1800, a remarkable interest sprang up chiefly through his labors at New Hampton. A church of sixty-four members was organized there by him on Jan. 6th, and for eight months, the glorious work continued, till 114 had been baptized and added to the church, "all or chiefly by our dear and precious brother, Elder Winthrop Young" as Elder Randall, who was present at the last baptism, makes the record. Possessing worldly means, he was benevolent and humble. He was of strong mind and large heart. His deep voice presented petitions in public prayer in such a way that Randall was heard to say, "We have no man among us that can pray like Brother Young." In 1822 at the age of nearly seventy, he was still active, baptizing a number at Northfield. In 1829, Rev. John Harrison was chosen as assistant pastor at Canterbury. Rev. Young died in the 80th year of his age.

Oh, may I join the choir invisible Of those immortal dead who live again.

New Mexico

Lester C. Pinson
Birth:
Mar. 14, 1917
Death:
Jul. 7, 1963
Burial:
Carlsbad Cemetery, Carlsbad,
Eddy County,New Mexico,
Plot: Division F

Waiting and watching within the gate.

New York

Asa G Abbott
Birth:
Sep. 11, 1803
Death:
Feb. 11, 1877
German, N. Y.
Burial:
Westview Cemetery
German Four Corners,
Chenango County, New York

Abbott, Rev. A. G., a native of Pennsylvania. He entered the ministry with the Methodists at an early age, but later moved to Chenango Co., N. Y., and spent the last twenty years of his ministry with the Free Baptists of the McDonoughQ. M. His faith in God survived many afflictions. He was an earnest, thoughtful preacher, and his wise counselshad a wide influence among his brethren by whom he was venerated.

Adon Aldrich
Birth:
Jul. 22, 1795
Uxbridge
Worcester County,
Massachusetts
Death:
Jul. 20, 1853
Ashford
Cattaraugus County,
New York
Burial:
Bond Cemetery
Springville
Cattaraugus County,
New York

He was a minister in the Ontario quarterly meeting in New York State. In 1827 went to Chenango County, where he preached and established the Norwich and New Berlin churches.

John J Allen
Birth:
1822
Death:
May 26, 1899
Burial:
Old Depauville Cemetery
Depauville
Jefferson County, New York

He was educated at Whitestown Seminary and Biblical School. He began to preach in 1849 and was ordained in September 1853. He baptized about 300 converts during his ministry in the area where he had served so long. For 20 years he served as the clerk and treasurer of the Jefferson Quarterly Meeting and had been a delegate to one of the General Conferences.

Albert A. Armstrong
Birth:
1848
Cuba, Allegany County, New York
Death:
1937
Great Valley,
Cattaraugus County,
New York
Burial:
Willoughby Cemetery,
Great Valley,
Cattaraugus County, New York

Albert was educated at the Pike Seminary in Tenbroeck, New York. He received his license to preach in the Free Will Baptist Church in 1869. The year after his conversion, he was ordained by the Cattaraugus Quarterly Meeting June 11, 1878. Except for

a few years in Pennsylvania around 1900, his ministry was continued in Western New York State.

As a well-spent day brings happy sleep, so a life well used brings happy death.

Dr George Harvey Ball
Birth:
Dec. 7, 1819
Sherbrooke, Canada
Death:
Feb. 20, 1907
Burial:
Forest Lawn Cemetery
Buffalo
Erie County, New York
Plot: Section 3

Ball, who was the son of William and Marcy (Harvey) Ball, had his early days in Massachusetts. In 1836 they removed to Ohio, where, while making a home in the wilderness for the family, his used the time to study systematically the evenings until ten o'clock, under the guidance of his mother, and when twenty years of age commenced teaching. During that winter Rev. Ransom Dunn, holding meetings in the schoolhouse, said to him, "Do you think it reasonable and right to serve God?" " Yes," he replied. "And you aim to be a reasonable man do you not?" "Most certainly." "Then you will serve God of course," said the preacher, and passed on. The appeal to reason prevailed, where other appeals had failed. After about two years at Farmington Academy, he spent two years more at Grand River Institute, and preached occasionally in the vicinity, receiving license to preach from the Ashtabula Q.M. in 1843. The next year he went to Ontario, Can., to teach, but was kept constantly at preaching for more than a year, and enjoyed several revivals. He then attended the Biblical School at Whitestown, graduating in 1847. The following year he was married to Maria L. Bensly and entered upon a three years' pastorate at Chester, O. A part of this time he was principal of Geauga Seminary, and numbered James A. Garfield among his pupils. In 1851 he went to Buffalo, N. Y., to plant a church. After four years he settled with the Roger Williams church, Providence, R. I., but soon returned to Buffalo to save the interest there. In 1870 he became New York editor of *The Morning Star*, and the next year editor of the *Baptist Union*. In 1877 he returned to Buffalo,.where he still remains pastor of a flourishing church planted by himself. Bro. Ball has always been a diligent student and an indefatigable worker. He received the degree of Doctor of Divinity from Bates College, Me. He has published several small books of merit, and wrote extensively for the religious and secular press. As a preacher he is argumentative, pungent and direct; as a pastor, sympathetic and helpful. He had a wide influence in the denomination, having served as Trustee of Storer College from its foundation, and of Hillsdale College also, except one term; and being now a member of the Foreign Mission and Conference Boards. In 1886 he visited the General Baptists of England, for the General Conference. His daughter Julia was a graduate of Packer College, Brooklyn, N. Y.,. and Ella J., since completed the Classical Course at Hillsdale College, and for some eight years was lady-principal of Pike Seminary, N. Y.

Velorus Beebe
Birth:
Sep. 10, 1810 Cuba,
Allegany County,
New York
Death:
May 28, 1879
Friendship,
Allegany County,
New York
Burial:
Richburg Cemetery,
Richburg, Allegany County,
New York

He commenced preaching at 18 years of age in Yates County. Travelling as an evangelist he held meetings in many places in Ohio and Michigan. After this he ministered to the church in Bradford, New York, fourteen years; in E. Troy, Pennsylvania, two years; in Veteran, New York, two years, and Wert and Boliver fourteen years. Revivals, some quite extensive in these places. He represented the New York and Pennsylvania Y.M.in the General Conferences of 1847 and 1850.

Yea, saith the Spirit, that they may rest from their labours; and their works do follow them.

Daniel Brown
Birth:
unknown
Death:
Aug. 5, 1882
Dayton, N. Y.
Burial:
Parklawn Cemetery
Wesley, Cattaraugus County,
New York

At the age of twenty-one he professed religion, and united with the Hamburg, N. Y., church. Soon after his marriage to Miss Fanny Perham, in 1841, he moved to Boston, N. Y., and in 1848 to Dayton. He was ordained in 1860. His ministry was confined to the Cattaraugus and Erie Q. M's and was characterized by earnestness, fidelity and self-sacrifice. Aged 69 years 19 days

Nathaniel Brown
Birth:
Apr. 7, 1765,
Warren
Litchfield County,
Connecticut
Death:
Sep. 2, 1844
Bethany Center,
Genesee County,
New York
Burial:
West Bethany Cemetery,
West Bethany,
Genesee County,
New York,
Plot: New Section

He was ordained by the Stratford Association June 27, 1802 and after six years of successful ministry moved in 1808 to Bethany, New York where he purchased a large tract of land and build a sawmill and grist mill. He organized the Bethany Church, the first Free Will Baptist Church west of the Genesee river and remained its pastor until his death for a period of 30 years. Besides this work in New York, he assisted in the organization of the Ohio yearly meeting. He was a prominent member of the first Gen. conference and did much to shape the policy for its future years. Nathaniel was a Revolutionary War veteran. He Enlisted in the Strafford, Orange County, Vermont.

The Dead In Christ Will Rise First.

William C Byer
Birth:
1814
Eaton
Madison County, New York
Death:
Oct. 30, 1868
Fabius
Onondaga County, New York
Burial:
Fabius Evergreen Cemetery
Fabius, Onondaga County,
New York

Rev. Byer, Sr., was a native of Eaton, NY. While attending school in Clinton (NY) he became acquainted with Miss Samantha Ward, who became his wife and helper through life. Her influence was instrumental in leading him to Christ.He was ordained in 1842 to the Freewill Baptist ministry, and labored in Union Yearly Meeting until about 1856, when he became connected with the Burlington Flats Church. He held many protracted meetings and baptized, during his ministry, about five hundred converts. As a preacher he was warm-hearted and earnest. He never feared to rebuke sin, yet was kind and benevolent.The son, William C., Jr., also became a Free Baptist minister. He mar. Inez K. Smith Oct. 18, 1876. He was educated at Whitestown Seminary and received ordination in 1883, taking charge of the North Scriba FB church, where he continued some years. He enjoyed the esteem of his people.

Behold I Come Quickly And Every Eye Shall See Me!

Elder Chester Chaffee
Birth:
Oct. 7, 1791
Death:
Sep. 5, 1876
Arcade, N. Y.
Burial:
Arcade Rural Cemetery
Arcade, Wyoming County,
New York

Chaffee, a native of Grafton, Vt., died at age 85 years. In 1816 he moved to Boston, N. Y., where he served the church as deacon. After fourteen years he moved to Arcade, receiving ordination in 1832, and was connected with the China, Hume and Elton churches. He was a reliable man, faithfulto the trusts committed to him.Parents: David Chaffee (1765–1835) and Anna Johnson (1771–1827)1st Spouse: Abigail _ (1793–1827)2nd Spouse: Mrs. Lydia Jackson (?-1869)

Daniel Chase
Birth:
unknown
Death:
Mar. 2, 1850
Mount Pleasant, NY
Burial:
West Windsor Cemetery
West Windsor
Broome County, New York

Rev. Daniel Chase, born about 1771-72, and died at age 79 years.He began his ministry about 1800, Elder Randall assisting in his ordination. He labored in New Hampshire and Vermont, and in 1816, removed to Jackson, Pennsylvania, being, it is thought, the first minister of the denomination to settle in that state. He rendered faithful service in Susquehanna and Wayne Counties, Pennsylvania, and in Broome County, New York. He represented the Gibson Q.M. Pennsylvania at the organization of the Susquahanna Yearly Meeting.

Ardon Cobb
Birth:
1802
New York, USA
Death:
Aug. 10, 1868
Burial:
Overackers Cemetery
Middlesex, Yates County,
New York

He became a minister after a conversion in 1833, ordained 1840. His labors were with the Danville, Middlesex, North Potter, Sparta, Italy, Scottsburg and Jerusalem churches. He was earnest and active in the work. The Middlesex church especially was blessed under his efforts. His devotion found expression in the frequent inquiry, "How can I render the most efficient service to Christ?".-

Isaiah Bangs Coleman
Birth:
Mar. 7, 1809
Stephentown
Rensselaer County, New York
Death:
Mar. 14, 1883
West Stephentown
Rensselaer County, New York
Burial:
Hillside Cemetery
Stephentown, Rensselaer County,
New York

Coleman died of paralysis at his home age 74 years. He was converted when but a boy, and baptized by Rev. John Allen. His facilities for education were limited, but his studious habits and thirst for knowledge soon prepared him to serve as a teacher for ten years; an advantage to himself, as well as others. May 1, 1834, he married Miss Ann V. Dunham, his companion through life. May 10 of the same year he was licensed to preach, and March 25, 1835, was ordained. He labored with the old Stephentown and Sand Lake churches until Jan. 6, 1844, when he became pastor of the West Stephentown church, then having fifty-eight members. He remained its pastor thirty-nine years, and left it at his death a flourishing church of 180 members, a living testimony to the faithful service rendered. Of those who united with his own church, he baptized 225, besides many who went to other churches. It is said that he married over fourteen hundred couples. Few ministers have attended more funerals than he. His charities were generous and

frequent. He was a strong advocate of temperance and all virtues. His modest, unassuming spirit, together with home duties, confined his helpful influence to narrower limits, though he served as delegate to the General Conference a number of times. On March 3 he told his wife he had had a shock, and could be with her but a short time. In less than an hour his power of speech was gone, and in a few days a vast multitude gathered around his bed, attesting the high esteem in which he was held by the community.He was a teacher, storekeeper, postmaster and minister of the Church he helped found.

Ashel J Cooley
Birth:
July 6, 1826.
Death:
Sep. 25, 1905
Point Peninsula
Jefferson County, N. Y.
Burial:
Woodlawn Cemetery
Elmira
Chemung County, New York

He was married in September, 1846, to Miss Rachel Leonard, and in January,1865, was baptized, uniting with the Three-Mile Bay church, of which his wife was a member. He was ordained June 7, 1874, by the Jefferson Q. M., and was pastor of the Three-Mile Bay church a brief period. He has since served as city missionary at Ithaca, N. Y., in 1880, and as pastor at Dryden, 1881-83; at Stephentown Center, 1883-85, and for a time at Hadley. Died at 82 yrs, 10 mos, 3days Utica, NY

Amos Daniels
Birth:
Aug. 23, 1787
Hartford,
Hartford County,
Connecticut
Death:
Apr. 29, 1873
Burial:
Vestal Park Cemetery,
Vestal,
Broome County, New York

He worked with the Methodists as a licensed preacher, but because of his views on baptism they did not ordain him, and he united with the Free Baptists, receiving ordination at the Owego Q.M. in 1822. He was pastor of the Virgil and Dryden church twenty-five years, reorganized the Dryden church and was its pastor twelve years; organized the Fabius church and was its pastor several years and was also pastor at Jackson, East Troy and other points. He labored extensively in the Susquehanna Yearly Meeting as an evangelist, witnessing many revivals during his ministry. His ministry was over 51 years, and full of usefulness.

Freeman Darte
Birth:
1804

Death:
Jan. 22, 1883
Yorkshire,
Cattaraugus County, New York
Burial:
Delevan Cemetery,
Delevan,
Cattaraugus County, New York

He lived in the Cattaraugus, Yorkshire, area, and farmed to support his family. Freeman was a member, clerk, and then preacher of The First Free Will Baptist Church of East Randolph, NY. He consecrated his life to Christ in 1832, was licensed to preach about 1837 and ordained about 1842, in the Freewill Baptist Church. He was a faithful minister, laboring with good acceptance in many churches of the Erie and Cattaraugus Q.M.'s.

Ira Day
Birth:
Oct. 6, 1818
Burlington, New York
Death:
Jul. 29, 1883
Fabius, New York
Burial:
Willet Cemetery
Willet, Cortland County,
New York

He was converted when thirteen years of age, and joined the Free Baptists soon after moving to Willet, in 1856. He soon began to preach, and ultimately became pastor of the Willet church. Three years before at his death he settled with the Fabius church, which was blessed under his labors. He was a devoted Christian, giving his service and his wealth to the Lord. A gift of $500 to the Norwich church is worthy of special notice. The Central Association, of which he was a trustee, honored him with resolutions of esteem. Spouse: Susannah Whitmore Day (1818 - 1880).
Inscription:
For we know if our earthly house of this tabernacle were dissolved, we have a   building of God an house not made with hands, eternal in the   heavens.
2 Corinthians 5:1

Zebulon Dean
Birth:
1779
New York
Death:
Dec. 4, 1883
Yates County, New York
Burial:
Evergreen Cemetery, Dresden, Yates County, New York

Zebulon settled early in Yates Co., and was ordained a Free Will Baptist minister in 1813, probably in Benton church. It's influence and interest extended over a territory of forty miles in diameter along the western shores of Lake Seneca. He pastored that church and at Barrington in 1829, a church he helped organize in 1819. His ministry was in the surrounding towns and villages In 1819, he with Samuel WIRE, then a licensed preacher, heard that David Marks, a boy preacher of fifteen, was in need of spiritual consolation at Junius, so they went thirty miles and encouraged David and baptized him July 11. Marks was soon afterwards associated in revival meetings with Rev. Dean, who had helped him. In 1829, Rev. Dean attended the third General Conference, at Spafford, N.Y.

Oscar Hanning Denney
Birth:
Jul. 10, 1860
Gallia County, Ohio
Death:
Jan. 7, 1945
Canandaigua
Ontario County, New York
Burial:
Borden-Elk Creek Cemetery
Borden
Steuben County, New York

He was born near Rio Grande, Ohio and was converted in 1869 after which he pursued studies at Rio Grande college and for a season at Hillsdale in Michigan. He received his license to preach in 1879 and was ordained on December 17, 1882. He pastored a number of churches in Ohio before moving to the state of New York where several revivals attended his labors. He also assisted in the organizing of four churches.

Amasa Dodge
Birth:
1768
New London County, Connecticut
Death:
Aug. 13, 1850
Lewis County, New York
Burial:
West Lowville Rural Cemetery
West Lowville
Lewis County, New York

He was ordained that Lowville, New York, April 4, 1818. He was an exhorter rather than a sermonizer; a true man, devoted to the cause of the Master, yet conservative; and when the Free Communion Baptists united with the Free Will Baptist, he, almost alone opposed the union, yet his integrity was never questioned.

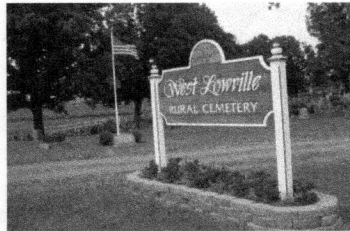

Asa Dodge
Birth:
Apr. 14, 1799
Ludlow, Hampden County, Massachusetts
Death:
Aug. 2, 1877
New York
Burial:
Nanticoke Valley Cemetery
Union Center, Broome County, New York

Rev. Asa Dodge was the son of Asa and Sarah Dodge--one of four sons who were Freewill Baptists ministers [Edward E., Gurley, Calvin and Asa] In 1806, this family settled in New Concord (now Lisbon) N.H. At age 13 yrs, with his brother Edward E, he conducted meetings in which several were converted. He was baptized by Rev. J. Quinby and united with Sugar Hill Church. He attended Morse Academy in Hanover four years, when his family moved to NY. He then entered upon the active life of the ministry. He was licensed by Owego Quarterly Meeting in 1821, and ordained the next year. The first Free Baptist meeting in Troy, NY was held by him in 1822. The Owega QM owes much to him for its prosperity, where most of his ministry was spent. His influence was felt in other QM's as well. He was a successful minister and many souls were converted through his agency.

He occupied a prominent position in the denomination, having represented the Susquehanna, NY Yearly Meeting (YM) in the General Conference of 1829 and several times later. The last ten years of his life was laid aside by infirmities, but he rejoiced in the assurance of a bright home above.

Jacob Hilton Durkee
Birth:
Apr. 30, 1847
Yarmouth
Nova Scotia, Canada
Death:
1925
Monroe County, New York
Burial:
Riverside Cemetery
Rochester
Monroe County, New York
Plot: Sect. M.

Rev. Durkee, was born of Free Baptist parents in Yarmouth Co. Nova Scotia. April 30, 1847. He was converted when about nineteen years of age, and soon entered the New Hampton Institution, N.H., graduating in 1871. Subsequently, he studied about a year in the theological department of Bates College [Maine]. He was ordained a Free Baptist minister at Meredith, N.H., Sept. 28, 1871; a properous pastorate at that place followed. Later he gathered the Free Baptist church of Halifax, N.S., which secured a house of worship under his labors. After supplying the New Market, N.H,, church for a season he went to New York in

1877, where his four years labor at Phoenix and three at Pike resulted in strengthening these churches. He also aided in organizing the Bliss church. In 1884, under direction of the Central Ass'n., he opened a mission at Batavia (NY) which is growing into permanence. Brother Durkee has occupied a prominent position in the Central Association, serving as its corresponding secretary and on its board of trustees.

John Farley
Birth:
1777
New Hampshire
Death:
Dec. 12, 1858
Prospect, Oneida County,
New York
Burial:
Prospect Cemetery,
Prospect, Oneida County,
New York

He was converted at the age of fifteen and at twenty-four commenced preaching with the Open Communion Baptists at Richfield, N.Y. For twelve years he journeyed through the wilderness preaching two or three times a day, and his labors were blessed in the conversion of many souls." He died at the advanced age of 81 years.

James Salmon Gardner
Birth:
Jun. 24, 1822
New York

Death:
Apr. 23, 1881
Whitestown,
Oneida County, New York
Burial:
Grandview Cemetery,
Whitesboro,
Oneida County, New York

Prof. James Salmon Gardner graduated from Whitestown Seminary, N.Y. in 1846, and Hamilton college, Clinton, N.Y, in the class of 1849. In his studies he won the honors for superior scholarship and the degree of Doctor of Philosophy was bestowed by his Alma Mater in 1863. While in school he began teaching and in 1853 he became principal of Whitestown Seminary, a position which he held until his death. While head of the school, he devoted much attention to the successful pursuit of special studies in the sciences, and was interested in every movement for the advancement of education. The year of his graduation, 1849, he married Elizabeth E. PHILLIPS, sister of the Rev. Jeremiah Phillips, the missionary to India.

Levi Geer Gardner
Birth:
1804
Massachusetts
Death:
Apr. 13, 1861
Burial:
Grandview Cemetery
Whitesboro
Oneida County New York

His father served in the Revolution under Gen. Gates. In 1806 the family moved from Worthington, Mass., where Levi was born, to Plymouth, NY. Soon after this they with others united in forming a Free Baptist church under the labors of Elder Campbell. He was baptized by Eld. C. Easterbrooks and soon began to preach, receiving ordination in July 1825. Following the custom of that period, he went forth as an itinerant, preaching much on weekdays, as well as the Sabbath. He had great success in his extended work to the western part of the state and even into Canada. He baptized about 500 converts, nine churches were organized by his assistance, and his counsels were helpful to many, as he encouraged them to higher attainments and to more devoted living.

Squire D. Gardner
Birth:
Feb. 1, 1808
Death:
May 18, 1864
Burial:
Grandview Cemetery,
Whitesboro,
Oneida County, New York

Squire D. was a brother of Rev. Levi Geer Gardner. His father did service in the Revolution under General Gates. He was an ordained Free Will Baptist minister, began preaching in 1841, at the Sherburne church, and was ordained about 1844. He was for seven years pastor of the church in Columbus, where many members were added and a house of worship erected. He was with the Plainfield church four years and saw refreshing seasons, and his labors with the Prospect church were greatly blessed. He was a judicious pastor, an instructive preacher, a candid and prudent councilor, and stood among his brethren in the front rank in the great moral conflict.

Truman Gillett
Birth:
Jul. 23, 1779
Schuyler
Herkimer County, New York
Death:
Feb. 8, 1850
Burial:
Seventh Township Cemetery
Camden
Oneida County, New York

He was converted at 18 years of age. In 1809 he commenced preaching among the Methodists and after six years joined the Free Baptists in Russia, New York receiving his ordination on October 15, 1818. He labored much and had many conversions in Fairfield, Poland, and Oswego County, New York as well as in Canada.Inscription:age 70 yrs 6 mos 16 dys

David Greene
Birth:
Oct. 1, 1807
Hoosick, New York
Death:
Aug. 7, 1882
Fairport, New York
Burial:
Ouleout Cemetery
North Franklin
Delaware County, New York

In his early life he was a resident of Delaware County and with his wife in 1836 joined the Franklin church that had been recently organized. Two years later he was chosen Deacon and in 1842 was ordained as it's pastor, a relationship he continued for 18 years adding to the church by baptisms.

C. E. Hallock
Birth:
July 31, 1847
Constantia, New York
Death:
May 6, 1895
Burial:
Constantia Center Cemetery
Constantia Center
Oswego County, New York

He experienced religion in 1869 and was ordained June 2, 1878 after which he served the Constantia church as pastor. He was actively connected with the temperance work for 18 years.

Ely Hannibal
Birth:
Mar. 18, 1780
Fairfield,
Fairfield County,
Connecticut
Death:
Aug. 28, 1876
Clarkson,
Monroe County,
New York
Burial:
Garland Cemetery, Clarkson,
Monroe County, New York,
Plot: 1 - 8

Freewill Baptist pioneer minister in New York. Rev. Ely was converted Aug. 1806, and two yrs after, he joined a Baptist church; and removing to Yates (later Clarkson), NY, in 1811, he assisted in organizing the church in Sweden. In 1820 he joined a Free Baptist church that was organized in Clarkson; and the church had a council to ordain him on June 12, 1824. A revival immediately began, and fifty were converted. He preached in the surrounding towns and soon became a leader among the people in the rude dwellings of those times, in the big schoolhouses, and in the church, then uncommon, he preached with great earnestness the free gospel of Jesus Christ. There was scarcely a church organized w/o his aid, or a minister ordained without his counsel. He was not a scholar in any modern sense, but was at once popular and successful.

Luther Hanson
Birth:
1820
Death:
1894
Burial:
Glenview Cemetery
Pulteney
Steuben County, New York,

He was licensed in 1845 and attended Whitestown Seminary between the years of 1846-47. His ordination took place June, 1849. His pastorates were in Maine and New York and he had several revivals under his labors. Besides his preaching, he was engaged for several years in teaching. In 1853 he was a delegate to the General Conference.

Isaac Hill
Birth:
1783
Death:
1840
Burial:
West Hill Cemetery
Hornby
Steuben County, New York

He was converted in his youth and ordained on February 22, 1838 and died at the age of 57 years. He was earnest and pointed in preaching, gentleman in manner, and much respected.

Charles H Hoag
Birth:
March 25, 1835
Ridgeway, New York
Death:
Dec. 16, 1904
Burial:
Evergreen Cemetery
Pine Plains
Dutchess County, New York

He turned to God when he was 18 years of age and married Mrs. Minerva Power on December 25, 1858. He received his license to preach in 1876 and was ordained on December 11, 1880. His ministry it was in the Genesee Yearly Meeting most all of his ministry. --Pine Plains Register, 23 Dec 1904.

Death is the crown jewel for the Christian.

Isaac J Hoag
Birth:
Mar. 11, 1819
Chatham, New York
Death:
Mar. 22, 1891
New York
Burial:
Union Cemetery
North Creek
Warren County, New York

Converted at age 15 and became acquainted with the Free Baptists and united with them at West Stephentown. He received license to preach from the Rensselaer Quarterly Meeting in 1846 and supplied two churches for two years in that area. He was ordained on September 10, 1848 where he served pastorates in New York and Massachusetts. He assisted in organizing four churches and baptized nearly 400 converts.

Ephraim Chapelle Hodge
Birth:
Jan. 17, 1876
New York, USA
Death:
Mar. 22, 1941
Jefferson County, New York
Burial:
Adams Rural Cemetery
Adams
Jefferson County, New York

He was ordained at Oneonta Plains in September, 1850 and preached in the churches of the Otsego Quarterly Meeting having ministered the West Onenota church 20 years and for shorter periods other churches in the area. He was held in high esteem by the people of whom he lived around so long. He baptized about 500 converts

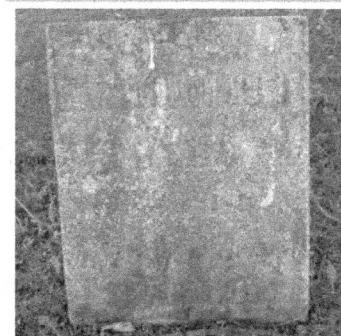

Solomon Howe
Birth:
Nov. 4, 1786
Hillsborough County,
New Hampshire
Death:
May 9, 1859
Smyrna
Chenango County, New York
Burial:
Cincinnatus Cemetery
Cincinnatus
Cortland County, New York

He was converted in 1804, licensed in 1812 and ordained in New Hampshire in 1819. He labored in New Hampshire and Vermont until 1826, when he moved to New York and became one of the honored fathers of the Union Quarterly Meeting. He spent many years in the MacDonough Quarter Meeting and from 1845 to 1850 was in the Nelson Quarterly Meeting.

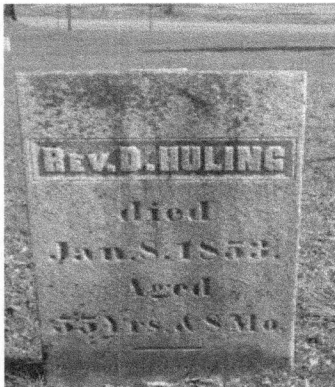

Daniel Huling
Birth:
May 5, 1797
Washington County,
Rhode Island
Death:
Jan. 8, 1853
French Creek,
Chautauqua County,
New York
Burial:
Cutting Cemetery
Cutting
Chautauqua County,
New York

He was converted in 1817 and ordained in 1847.

Robert Hunt
Birth:
Nov. 25, 1792
Schoharie County, New York
Death:
Dec. 7, 1872
Utica
Oneida County, New York
Burial:
Forest Hill Cemetery
Utica
Oneida County, New York
Plot: 30B-1 (Lot 1285)

He was a younger brother of William Hunt and received ordination among the Free Communion Baptists of New York about 1835. He was a man of considerable education, progressive in his tendencies and a good pastor.

A believer believes
A doubter doubts

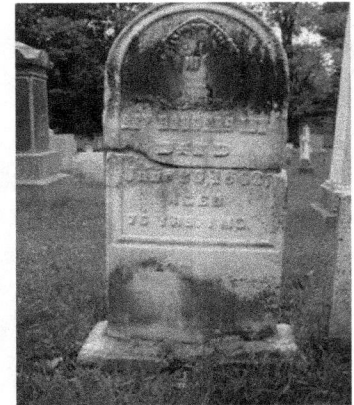

Rogers Ide
Birth:
May, 1788
Vermont,
Death:
Jun. 2, 1863
Spafford
Onondaga County, New York
Burial:
Borodino Cemetery
Borodino, Onondaga County,
New York

Ide fought in the War of 1812, and co-founded the Free Will Baptist Church in Spafford, NY. In 1831 he began preaching, and by 1836 was ordained. Shortly thereafter, he traveled to the southern part of Indiana, where he preached against the sins of slavery, even when slave owners had a reward on his head.

Chester H Jackson
Birth:
Oct. 21, 1834
Death:
Dec. 9, 1912
Burial:
Alger Cemetery
Hume
Allegany County, New York

He was converted in 1849; was a student at Pike Seminary, New York in 1860-61, and received ordination June 7, 1863. He went from Pike, New York to Michigan where he ministered to the Dover Church while pursuing theological studies at Hillsdale College.

Daniel Jackson
Birth:
Apr. 12, 1804
Death:
Dec. 9, 1890
Burial:
Varysburg Cemetery, Varysburg,
Wyoming County, New York

A leading Free Will Baptist minister in New England who was born in Madison, New Hampshire. He received his early religious impressions from Rev. John Colby, and was converted under the labors of Rev. Jonathan Woodman in 1818. He was ordained at East Ossipee, New Hampshire on Sept. 14, 1826. His pastorates were: E. Ossipee (five years), Wheelock, VT (two yrs), Topsham (four yrs), Meredith Village, N.H., Lewiston Falls, ME, Charleston, Mass, Topsham, ME, Saco, South Berwick, Lyndon Centre, VT. and Gardiner City, ME. After 1854, he traveled in the South, and returning, became pastor at Wells, ME. In these pastorates he was successful. At Topsham as a result of one revival ninety-six were baptized. He was active in the general denominational work, having served in the General Conferences of 1827, 1841, and 1880, the centennial meeting.

Nelson A Jackson
Birth:
Dec. 28, 1811
Arcade, N. Y
Death:
Aug. 30, 1871
New Hudson, N. Y
Burial:
Arcade Rural Cemetery
Arcade, Wyoming County,
New York

Jackson was born of Quaker ancestry died at aged 59 years. He was converted under the labors of Elder H. Jenkins when nineteen years of age, and licensed to preach five years later. After spending some time in study, he was ordained in his native town June 6, 1841. His pastorates were with the Varysburgh, Arcade, Elton, Yorkshire, Ashford, and Humphrey and Great Valley churches. But one testimony was borne of him: that he was an earnest, loving, Christian minister. His quiet manner helped to develop thoughtful, abiding piety.

Calvin Jenkins
Birth:
Jan. 18, 1798
Stoddard, Cheshire,
New Hampshire
Death:
Jan. 31, 1882
Burial:
Fullerville Cemetery
Fullerville, St. Lawrence County,
New York

Aged 84 yrs Spouse: Olive Kendall
Jenkins (1798 - 1882)

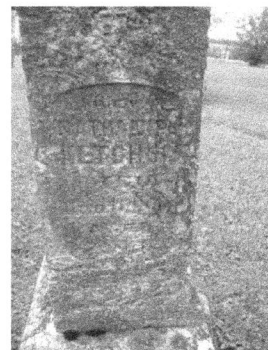

Nathaniel Ketchum
Birth:
unknown
Death:
Jan. 11, 1838
Burial:
Pike Cemetery
Pike
Wyoming County, New York

He was ordained in 1813 and

labored in New York. In 1816 he joined the Bethany Quarterly Meeting and leader in the Erie Quarterly Meeting which was sustained by a very strong revival under his labors.

James Letts
Birth:
unknown
Death:
Dec. 9, 1864
Burial:
Pleasant Lawn Cemetery
Paris, Oswego County, New York

Letts, a native of Ulster, N. Y., was converted in 1850 and united with the Paris church at its organization. He acted as colporteur and agent of the American Tract Society three years, during which time he also held revival services and was connected with the Parish, Lyndon, and Angelica churches. Early in 1858 he held services with the Burns church; many were added and he became its pastor. He was ordained March 3, 1861, and in 1863 returned to the Oswego Q. M., and took charge of the Parish, Redfield, and Constantia churches, holding revivals with them and with the Osceola church the following winter. He was an active, persevering, and successful minister, and died of fever at 40 years of age. The minutes of the national Association of the Randall movement of Free Will Baptists said his death was 1864.

W. A. Lighthall
Birth:
Aug. 22, 1813
Fort Ann, Washington County, New York
Death:
Jul. 8, 1865
Burial:
Pike Cemetery, Pike, Wyoming County, New York

In May 1832, he moved to Weathersfield, and in September became totally blind. But this providence brought to him spiritual light. He was baptized in 1835 and licensed to preach in October, 1837.

Immediately commenced to preach at Middlebury, and in four years the church increased greatly in strength and numbers. At Attica he labored with good success three years. Having thus given proof of his call to the ministry, he was ordained a Freewill Baptist minister at Varysburgh in May, 1845. His later labors were with the churches in Weathersfield, Hamburg, Cowlesville, Ellington, Chautaqua, and Pomfret, besides itinerant preaching. His mind was vigorous and clear; his memory, quickened by loss of sight; was retentive, and his powers were devoted fully to his work

---

Horatio N. Loring
Birth:
1806
Death:
1847
Burial:
Forest Hill Cemetery
UticaOneida County
New York

He was ordained in Rhode Island in 1825. He was one of the four young man, under 30 years of age, who sat in the first General Conference with Rev. Zalmon Tobey. He was delegate to the fourth General Conference in 1830, and Sec. of the sixth General Conference at Meredith, New

Hampshire in 1832. He was pastor of the Broad St. Baptist Church.
Source: Forest Hill burial list carried in the *Utica Morning Herald and Daily Gazette*, May 30 1882.

John H. Loveless
Birth:
1809
Death:
Aug. 22, 1871
Johnsburgh, N. Y.
Burial:
Lynwood Church Cemetery
Hadley, Saratoga County, New York

Loveless died at age 61 years. He was born in Poultney, Vt., and when seventeen years of age united with the Free Communion Baptists in Hadley, N. Y. The following year he began to preach and, being ordained in 1842, continued his labor at Hadley with unremitting ardor. He also labored in Poestenkill, N. Y., and six years in the Monroe Q. M., returning to his former home for the closing years of service. He was an amiable, modest pastor, faithful in precept and example, and his ministry was crowned with success.

Daniel Lyon
Birth:
unknown
Death:
Sep. 23, 1842
Walworth, New York
Burial:
Walworth Center Cemetery
Wayne County, New York

He died at age 47. In 1824 he was ordained and became pastor of the Walworth Church having been a member since its organization in 1816. He was a successful preacher, a wise counselor, a father to his church. More than 300 converts were baptized by him and his death was greatly lamented.

Enoch Mack
Birth:
Jan. 30, 1806
Connecticut
Death:
Feb. 20, 1881
Catskill
Greene County, New York
Burial:
Catskill Village Cemetery
Catskill
Greene County, New York

"Rev. Enoch Mack, M.D., born in Connecticut, in his childhood with his family moved to Susquehanna Co. PA, and here, after graduating in medicine he practiced his profession. After a time, he turned toward the ministry and became interested in temperance and anti-slavery causes. In 1833, he went on horseback to Philadelphia, where, with Garrison, Whittier, and others, he signed the Declaration of Sentiments, put forth by the Anti-Slavery Society. He was attracted to the Free Baptists because of their anti-slavery sentiments, and became an early contributor to the "Morning Star". At the suggestion of Editor William Burr, he was called to Dover. NH, in 1835, and ordained pastor of the first Free Baptist church there. Subsequently, he resigned the pastorate to serve as agent of the Foreign Mission Board, and was also corresponding secretary of the Foreign and Home Mission Societies. During these years and later, he was a frequent correspondent and an editorial contributor of the "Star," and his vigorous pen did much to awaken an interest in missionary work and in the other great moral and Christian enterprises of the day. About 1849, he went to New York City, where he was appointed city missionary for the northern portion of the city. In this capacity he served with earnestness and devotion nineteen years. His last years were spent with his son at Catskill Station in Columbia County.His devoted labors for those causes that would save men from intemperance, give freedom to the bondmen, rescue the heathen millions from idolatry, and lift up the degraded in our great cities, evince the breadth of his sympathies and give him a high place among the benefactors of our race. He was married to Phebe L. Roberts, and they were on 1850 census together, along with Narcissa, a daughter, age 17.On the 1860 census, Enoch stated he was a 'retired minister.'

William Mack
Birth:
1798
Lyme
New London County, Connecticut
Death:
1877
Steuben County, New York
Burial:
Mack Cemetery
Steuben County, New York

He was an active preacher for forty-five years. His labors were mostly in northern Pennsylvania and southern New York, where his ministry was abundantly blessed in the salvation of souls. He assisted in organizing most of the churches of the Tuscarora quarterly meeting. He was the son of Samuel and Mary Mack, Husband of Eliza Kimball. Mack Cemetery is a family cemetery that contains six graves and is located on Mack Road.

Benjamin McKoon
Birth:
Sep. 2, 1799
Death:
Nov. 16, 1880
Columbia, N. Y.,
Burial:
Millers Mills Cemetery
Millers Mills, Herkimer County, New York

Rev. Benjamin, a brother of Rev. D. W. McKoon, died aged 81 years. At the age of seventeen, he obeyed the call to a Christian life and was baptized by Rev. Wm. Hunt. He was ordained at Unadilla Forks in 1823, and for fifty-seven years, he preached the gospel with zeal and earnestness, and often with great power. His early labors were in the Chemung Valley and adjacent country. Afterwards for sixteen years he labored in central New York and in Oswego and Jefferson counties, his efforts being crowned with very marked success. Then, after years of successful ministry in western New York, he moved from Ellington to Hillsdale to educate his children. Returning in 1861, he preached at Columbia, German Flatts, Oxford and Holmesville, and, six years later, took up pastoral work in Chautauqua and Cattaraugus Counties, and continued it until health would no longer permit.

He had baptized about eight hundred converts, and the last three years of life were largely spent in visiting former fields of labor, confirming the saints. Christ and his cross were themes he loved to dwell upon, and the atonement was to him the pivotal point on which rested the great work of the soul's salvation. He was a delegate to the General Conference of 1847 from the Holland Purchase Y. M. His son, Prof. Bela P. McKoon, of Hillsdale College, Whitestown Seminary, and later of Cornell University, in these institutions rendered efficient service as an educator.

Daniel W McKoon
Birth:
Jun. 6, 1811
Herkimer County, New York
Death:
Jan. 4, 1871
Sugartown
Cattaraugus County, New York
Burial:
Sugartown Cemetery
Sugartown
Cattaraugus County, New York

Rev. Daniel William McKoon, a native of Columbia, N.Y., was baptized by Rev. Wm. Hunt when eighteen year of age. He was licensed to preach in 1838 and ordained Feb. 9, 1840 in Free Baptist Church. He commenced immediately a six-years' pastorate with the Newport and Poland church, sixty being added to the church by baptism and lasting good resulted. In 1847 he was prostrated by disease, which so affected the mind that on recovery he found it necessary to

study the alphabet again and regain his former knowledge step by step. After this, twenty years of usefulness remained to him, which were spent in the Cattaraugus and Chautauqua Quarterly Meetings, his last pastorate being with the Ashford church. He died at Orlean aged 59 years. Brother McKoon was a warm-hearted Christian, earnest in every good work and faithful to duty. As a preacher he was systematic and pathetic. In his early ministry he rendered efficient service in securing friends and funds for Whitestown Seminary at a time when both were needed. He represented the Central N.Y. Yearly Meeting in the General Conference of 1844. His son, Newton C. McKoon of Ellicottsville, N.Y., was for many years clerk of the Cattaraugus Q.M., and commissioner of schools for Cattaraugus County.

Newton C McKoon
Birth:
Dec. 17, 1835
Herkimer
Herkimer County, New York
Death:
Aug. 27, 1906
Humphrey
Cattaraugus County,
New York
Burial:
Sugartown Cemetery
Sugartown
Cattaraugus County,
New York

His parents were Rev. Daniel W. McKoon and Jane T. (Young) McKoon.There is an enlistment for him in the Civil War Muster, of 1862, Great Valley, NY. He became a Free Baptist minister and was a leader in the Humphrey Free Bapt Church, where his father ministered. He was also clerk of the Yearly meeting for many years, and was Commissioner of schools.He married Ann Crary (1845-1914), in 1865 per 1900 census.

Asahel Nichols
Birth:
1851
Ames, New York
Death:
unknown
Burial:
Ames Cemetery
Ames
Montgomery County,
New York

He joined the church in his native town, Chesterfield, Massachusetts, in 1840. He later taught two terms at Geauga Seminary, Ohio and graduated from the theological department of Oberlin College, Oberlin, Ohio in 1846. He returned then to preach in Maine and New York.

John Nicholson
Birth:
Mar. 21, 1793
Connecticut
Death:
Apr. 7, 1863
Burial:
Steere Cemetery
East McDonough,
Chenango County, New York

Nicholson was a native of Stonington, Conn., was converted and united with the McDonough, N. Y., church in 1813. He was ordained at the session of the Q. M. held at Plymouth, N. Y., in June, 1833, and continued with the McDonough church, except two years with the Second Otselic and three with the German, 1854-59, until his death, which occurred at the advanced age of 70 years. his wife was the Roby Steere (1798 - 1840).

William Nutting
Birth:
Nov. 6, 1794
Death:
Jan. 25, 1872
Parish, N. Y,
Burial:
Nutting Cemetery
West Monroe, Oswego County,
New York

At the age of twenty-five, after many conflicts, he consecrated himself to the Master's service. His ministry, for nearly forty-five years, was mostly with the churches of the Oswego Q. M. He was an eccentric, zealous man, useful in the work of the Lord. At his death one son was state senator in Virginia and another district attorney of Oswego County, New York.

Death provides the saint to partake of the refreshing of the soul.

Thomas Parker
Birth:
1794
Foster, R.I.
Death:
Aug. 4, 1865
Perrinton (Fairport), N. Y.,
Burial:
Elmwood Cemetery
Perrinton,
Monroe County, New York

He was converted under the labors of Rev. J. Fowler and joined the Walworth church. At the age of twenty-eight he commenced preaching in Penfield, and soon a church was organized there. He was ordained in 1828 and remained pastor of the church twenty-eight years. He also preached in Ontario, Webster, Macedon and Perrinton. For some years before his death he did not have the care of a church, but preached as opportunity presented. During his ministry he baptized over five hundred converts, married 500 couples and attended more than one thousand funerals. His joy was in the Lord, both in life and at its close.

He quicken your mortal bodies by his Spirit.

A. P. Phinney
Birth:
Apr. 8, 1828
Reading, New York
Death:
Nov. 7, 1897
Burial:
Pleasant Lawn Cemetery
Parish
Oswego County, New York

He experienced religion in 1857 in Allegheny County. The same year he was licensed to preach and supplied churches near his home for about three years where his labors were blessed. He moved to Oswego County in 1864 and was ordained on June 10, 1867 under the ministry of the First Parish Church which was greatly strengthened and the Second Parish Church was organized. In 1870 became the pastor of the Hastings church.

Charles Putnam
Birth:
unknown
Death:
Feb. 1, 1878
Byron, N. Y.
Burial:
West Bethany Cemetery
West Bethany, Genesee County,
New York

Putnam was a native of Bethany, died at aged 55 years. After graduating from Union College in 1848, he engaged in teaching at Varysburgh, N. Y. He was converted under the labors of Rev. M. H. Abbey, and after a few months was ordained. After teaching and preaching at Cowlesville, when Pike Seminary was purchased he became its principal, and served the church as pastor. Here his labors were severe and exhaustive, but crowned with generrouis results. Most of his labors were in western New York, his last pastorate being at Byron. He was an excellent minister, in preaching logical, instructive and inspiring, and frequent revivals were enjoyed.

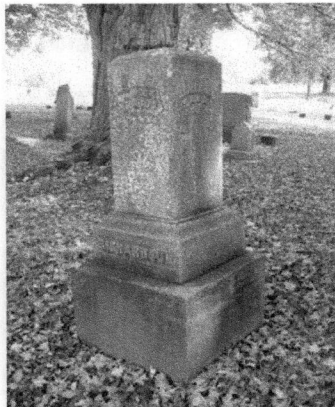

Richard Richardson
Birth:
Jan. 14, 1799
Leek
Staffordshire, England
Death:
Jun. 10, 1872
Varysburg
Wyoming County, New York
Burial:
Cowlesville Cemetery
Cowlesville
Wyoming County, New York

He was a student at the Montpelier and Bates College. He was converted in 1876 and was licensed on June 28, 1885, and ordained July 10, 1887. He also was a student at Cobbett divinity school. He married Elizabeth about 1822 and after her death, he married Sally Munger about 1845

Edson M. Roel
Birth:
December 28, 1858
Dummerston, Vermont
Death:
1939
Burial:
Morningside Cemetery
Hartford
Washington County, New York

On March 1, 1882, he was married to Etta L. Payne. Having given himself to God in the work of the gospel ministry, he was licensed in 1879, and ordained in 1884. He is held pastors in Vermont and New York.

David Valoy Ross
Birth:
1831
Death:
September 6, 1878
Burial:
Forest Lawn Cemetery
Buffalo
Erie County, New York

When five years of age with his parents he moved from Pennsylvania to Clermont, Ohio. In 1861 he entered the Civil War and received an Hon. discharge at the end of three years. He began preaching with the Methodists, but joined the Free Baptists in 1876 and was ordained by the Miami Quarterly Meeting in Ohio the January before his death. His many qualities endeared him to all.

Benjamin Rowland
Birth:
unknown
Death:
Aug. 3, 1872
Sherburne, N.Y.,
Burial:
Christ Church Cemetery
Sherburne, Chenango County,
New York

Rowland, a native of Lyme, Conn., died at age 88 years. Having moved to Burlington, N. Y., he was converted in 1812, three years after his marriage to Miss Seraph Sweetser, and almost immediately began to preach. The next year he was ordained, entering at once upon a seven years' pastorate with the Burlington and Exeter churches. In 1821 he took charge of the Sherburne church, just organized,and remained with it seventeen years, preaching also to other churches. The churches at

Oneonta, Plainfield, Brookfield, Holmesville, Oxford, Lebanon, Smyrna, German Flats, and Columbus were also recipients of his labors, some of them for years. He labored extensively as an evangelist, at one period for seven consecutive years continually in revivals. In 1854 he went to Binghamton, remaining there ten years, and preaching to the Apalachin, Warren, Windham, and Vestal churches. After this he made his home in Sherburne. He was a man of arduous labors. His name was a household word over a large section of country. His baptisms numbered over eight hundred. His preaching was descriptive and hortative. He seemed to embrace the truth with the heart more than the head. He "was an advocate of temperance, a lover of education and missions. His ministry was a ministry of love.

Inscription:
age 88 yr. 6 mo. 22 da.

James Sharp
Birth:
unknown
Death:
May, 18, 1874
Fairport, N. Y.
Burial:
Mount Hope Ceme
tery
Rochester, Monroe County,
New York

A native of Massachusetts, he died at age 76 years. He was converted in youth, his early labors being with the Methodists, much of the time in Canada. The latter part of life he was connected with the Free Baptists in western New York as a pioneer Freewill Baptist minister in Monroe County. Possessing a vigorous intellect, some culture, strong willpower and persistence, with a personal address imposing for a colored person, he had influence with the abolitionist leaders, especially with Gerritt Smith, and took great interest in the progress of their work. The visions of his earlier years were realized in the emancipation of his race (being Black) and in the gift of the elective franchise. He ceased not to thank God for the privilege of labor in this cause and for the results attained.

Cyrus Steere
Birth:
Jun. 3, 1801
Glocester
Providence County, Rhode Island
Death:
Feb. 26, 1878
East McDonough
Chenango County, New York
Burial:
Steere Cemetery
East McDonough
, Chenango County, New York

First pastor of the Free Will Baptist Church, erected in 1831 in East McDonough. Organized churches of the same denomination at German Hollow in 1844 and in Oxford in 1848. Steere, was a native of Burrillville, R. I., began his ministerial labors when twenty-six years of age, and was ordained at East McDonough, N. Y., Aug. 26, 1829. He was a pioneer in the vicinity and assisted in building up and organizing many churches. His labors were chiefly in the McDonough Q. M., and were greatly blessed. He died at aged 76 years

George B Southwick
Birth:
November 22, 1863
Humphrey Ctr., New York
Death:
1923
Burial:
Cherry Creek Central Cemetery
Cherry Creek
Chautauqua County, New York
Plot: 252

He graduated from Pike Seminary, New York in 1885 and student at Bates College and Cobb Divinity School. He received his license to preach in April 1885 pastoring thereafter in New York and Maine.

Ezra P Tallman
Birth:
May 31, 1814
Death:
Aug. 21, 1867
Burial:
Elmwood Cemetery
Perrinton, Monroe County,
New York

Tallman was a native of Galway, N. Y., united with the Penfield church in his twenty-third year, and was ordained when twenty-eight. He became pastor of the Perrinton (Fairport) church, formed at the time of his ordination, and remained with it four years. He then spent nearly three years at the Biblical School at Whitestown, and afterwards was pastor of the Middleville and Norway, Byron, Penfield, and Elba and Alabama churches successively. After caring for his father, Deacon Tallman, in his last sickness, he preached occasionally, and died aged 53 years. He was highly esteemed by his brethren, and his preaching was well adapted to develop spirituality and to establish gospel principles among the people.

William Taylor
Birth:
Mar. 20, 1823
Ontario, Canada
Death:
Apr. 4, 1877
Italy
Yates County, New York
Burial:
Italy-Naples Cemetery
Italy
Yates County, New York

He married Elizabeth Bodine in 1844 and Mary Morse in 1850 and had 10 children. He came to God in 1841 and was ordained in 1858. His labors were in Ontario, Canada, Western New York and Michigan. He aided in building several meeting houses and baptized several hundred converts in represented the St. Joseph's yearly meeting in the General Conference of 1883.

Charles Luther Vail
Birth:
Oct. 21, 1806
Long Island, New York
Death:
Dec. 23, 1887
Windsor, New York
Burial:
West Windsor Cemetery
West Windsor
Broome County, New York

He was 20 at his conversion and joined the church in West Windsor. Here he was ordained on November 3, 1840. His pastorates were West Windsor, New York, South Killingsly Connecticut and Franklin, Oxford, Virgil and Dryden, New York. He continued in active service until 73 years of age.

Freeman VanAmburgh
Birth:
May 1, 1793
Fishkill, Dutchess County, New York
Death:
Aug. 3, 1871
Bath, Steuben County, New York
Burial:
Mount Washington Cemetery
Urbana, Steuben County, New York

Rev. Freeman VanAmburgh, is listed in names of deceased ministers in the "Register of Freewill Baptists", as having "d. Aug. 3, 1871, age 78 yrs, at Bath, N.Y."He was in the War of 1812, proven as his wife, Anna, filed a widow's pension on his service in Capt. Ellis Co., N.Y. Mil., #URS orig 44506.Rev. VanAmburgh settled a few years after his military service at Bath, where he remained for most of life. He was converted in 1824 along with others under the labors of Rev. Z. Dean, and later was organized into a Freewill Baptist church. He was ordained on Sept. 4, 1836, and continued a faithful laborer until strength and life failed.

William Van Tuyl

Birth:
unknown
Death:
Feb. 21, 1829
Burial:
Raplee Family Cemetery
Milo
Yates County, New York
Early Free Will Baptist preacher.

Orrin Wynant Waldron

Birth:
Jul. 13, 1859
North Creek,
Warren County, New York
Death:
1910
Burial:
Ames Cemetery, Ames,
Montgomery County,
New York

He consecrated his life to God in 1878, and was educated at Hillsdale College, Michigan, in the college and theological departments, receiving honors from his literary society for excellence in oratory. While in college he supplied the churches at Scipio, Litchfield and Hadley's Corners, and afterwards became pastor of the church at Marion, Ohio, receiving ordination Oct. 12, 1884 in the Free Will Baptist. After a successful pastorate of three years he entered upon the work with the church at Saco, Me. He has baptized about thirty converts and assisted in revival work. Aug. 5, 1884, he was married to Mary E. Phillips.

Hiram Whitcher

Birth:
Mar. 18, 1809
Danville, Caledonia County,
Vermont
Death:
Jun. 7, 1896
Sweden Center,
Monroe County, New York
Burial:
Lakeview Cemetery,
Brockport,
Monroe County, New York,
Plot: A-111-1

The family moved to Sweden, NY in 1815. Here in 1823, Hiram was converted and uniting with the Union Free Baptist Church of Sweden and Ogden. He received from it a license to preach in 1829. During the summer he was chiefly engaged in study and attended the Middlebury academy. In the spring, he assisted Elder T. Parker in a glorious revival at Penfield and soon joined the church there, after which he was ordained May 30, 1830, by a council of the Bethany Quarterly Meeting. In 1831, he went into Chautauqua County and held revivals in many places and also in Cataraugua County. Many converts were baptized, among them Miss Lavina Crawford and Miss H. Baldwin later to become missionaries, and also Dr. Kingsley, later a bishop of the M.E. church. He held meetings in Ohio, Michigan, and Pennsylvania. In 1834 he settled at Springville and entered the academy, preaching also in the vicinity. In 1840, he with others served as a committee from the General Conference to arrange a union with the Free Communion Baptists. He preached also at Clinton, Poland, Unadilla Forks, and Whitestown, NY. From 1845 to 1854, he labored in Rochester, NY. From there he went to Concord, NH under direction of the Home Mission Society. The following twenty years were spent in Maine, at Booth Bay, Bath, Augusta, Phillips, Falmouth, Saccarappa and elsewhere. After fifty years of active service he accepted a home

provided by his brother, C.J. Whitcher, and moved to Brockport, NY, from which place he has rendered service to several churches. During his ministry, Bro. Whitcher has been engaged in many revivals, and has baptized 680 converts.

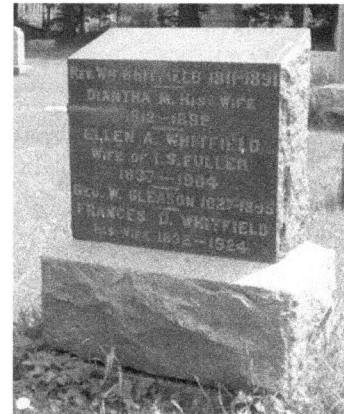

William Whitfield

Birth:
December 27, 1811
London, England
Death:
1891
Burial:
Pierpont Hill Cemetery
Pierpont
St. Lawrence County, New York

He was converted in September 1830 receiving license eight years later and ordination on June 14, 1841. He assisted in organizing the Pierpoint and several other churches. And with the exception of two years in the Jefferson Quarterly Meeting, he has resided at Pierpoint ministering to the people. For 16 years he was clerk of the town and has been for 37 years clerk of the St. Lawrence Yearly Meeting. Among its churches he is had wide influence. He joined in marriage 387 couples. In 1831 he was married to Diantha M. Axtell.

Edwin E. Whittemore
Birth:
Nov. 26, 1850
Oneida County, New York
Death:
1932
Burial:
Prospect Cemetery
Prospect
Oneida County, New York

He married Ellen M. Myers, August 1, 1876. He was educated at Whitestown Seminary, and was principal of the Prospect School six years. He was appointed as village clerk at Prospect. After a religious awakening he turned to God in March 1873, and after serving one year as a licentiate, was ordained by the Whitestown (NY) Quarterly Meeting. He held pastorates at Prospect, Grant and Unadilla Forks and has supplied elsewhere.

Joseph Wilson
Birth:
July 8,.1808
German Flats, N. Y.
Death:
Nov. 12, 1878
Gilbert's Mills, N. Y.

Burial:
Gilbert Mills Cemetery
Pennellville, Oswego County, New York
His spiritual life began in 1835, and he soon received license to preach. In 1840 he was ordained. He was pastor at Granby four years, at German Flats six years, witnessing a gracious outpouring of the spirit, at Gilbert's Mills six years, and also preached in Hastings, Constantia, West Monroe, Parish and other places.He preached a full gospel and was abundant in labors of love. Aug. 29, 1829, he married Ruth Thomas, of German Flats. Benjamin Randall was a great-uncle of Mrs. Wilson.

Amos Wing
Birth:
Nov. 29, 1796
Saratoga County, New York
Death:
Jun. 29, 1879
Oneonta, N.Y
Burial:
Oneonta Plains Cemetery
Oneonta, Otsego County, New York
Plot: Old Section

Son of John and Sylvia Wing. He was Free Baptist clergyman for 45 years in the Freewill Baptist denonimation in various places. History of Second Freewill Baptist, Oneonta, shows that he founded it, and pastored it. He was married on Nov. 12, 1820, to Chloe Lyon, b. 26 June, 1801, and d. 25 April 1823. In 1822 he married a second time to Lucinda R. Newman, b. 26 June 1801, and died 1887. Rev. Amos Wing, died at age 82 years. He was born in Saratoga County, but when young moved to Burlington, where he was baptized by Elder William Hunt. He soon began to preach and spent the remainder of his long life in the ministry, being connected many years with the Oneonta church of the Otsego Quarterly Meeting. He was a good man and God blessed his labors

---

My Hope is in Thee

Joseph Wood
Birth:
1809
Death:
May 3, 1878
Naples, N. Y.
Burial:
Burns Cemetery
Burns, Allegany County, New York

For nearly thirty years he was devoted to the work of the ministry. He preached for some twelve churches in western New York, and in nearly every instance goodresults were manifest. He was a man of excellent judgment and a good minister. The Genesee Y. M. made him a member of the General Conference at Fairport in 1877. His only son fell at Gettysburg.

Inscription:
Age 69 Years
(Civil War Vet)

Ray Woodmansee
Birth:
1794
Death:
Dec. 13, 1875
South New Berlin, N. Y.
Burial:
Riverside Cemetery
South New Berlin,
Chenango County, New York

Woodmansee died at age 8I years. He was son of Joseph Woodmansee, of Richmond, R. I., and received ordination with the Reformed Methodists in 1836. In 1845 he moved to New Berlin, N. Y., and soon joined the Holmesville Free Baptist church and was their pastor several years. With the infirmities of age he retired from the pulpit, but gave the influence of his sweet-spirited life to the cause. He loved every cause that honored God and promoted religion.

Dyer Woodworth
Birth:
Jan. 26, 1798
New York
Death:
Feb. 2, 1859
Burial:
West Hill Cemetery
Hornby
Steuben County, New York

After joining the Calvinistic Baptists when 22 years of age and studying three years in Madison University in preparation for the ministry, he became a Free Baptists in 1840 and was ordained the following year. He was pastor of the Free Baptist Church at Addison, New York for nine years. While living he gave for benevolent purposes about $4000 and he perpetuated his influence by the bequeathing $8000 to the Free Baptist Foreign Mission Societies and the American Bible Society. In his pulpit ministrations he was clear, argumentative and impressive.

William W Young
Birth:
Sep. 22, 1813
Parma
Monroe County, New York
Death:
Oct. 5, 1884
Morganville
Genesee County, New York
Burial:
Morganville Cemetery
Stafford
Genesee County, New York

He was converted in youth and uniting with the Clarkson church, soon began to preach. About 1836, Elders D.(David) Marks, J. N. Hinckley and E. Hannibal, ordained him. His labors were mostly with the churches of the Monroe and Rochester Quarterly Meetings. His sermons were plain and instructive, and many embraced redemption through his instrumentality. His parents were Eli Montgomery Young and Temperance Palmer. He married Hester Ann Knapp, 22 June 1837, in Knapps Corner, NY. at age 23.

For death is no more than a turning of us over from time to eternity.

North Carolina

John William Alford
Birth:
Oct. 3, 1881
Death:
Dec. 5, 1960
Burial:
Kenly Cemetery,
Kenly, Johnston County,
North Carolina

A recognized and respected pastor in eastern North Carolina. Even at age 75 he was driving 100 miles to pastor. He was a brother in law to Mrs. Alice Lupton who was an early leader in the women's movement in North Carolina and on the national level. Records show that he was a member of foreign missions board in the late 50s.

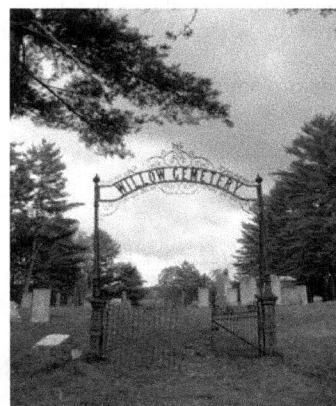

Joseph Garfield Ange
Birth:
Dec. 19, 1922
Martin County, North Carolina
Death:
Jul. 16, 2011
Raleigh, Wake County,
North Carolina
Burial:
Win, Washington County,
North Carolina

Ange pastored Free Will Baptist churches in Tennessee, Michigan, and North Carolina. From 1960 to 1976, he served on the Foreign Mission Board for Free Will Baptists. In 1971, Dr. Ange was awarded an Honorary Doctorate from Bob Jones University. In 1972 he became the director of Religious Activities and the Campus Pastor at Free Will Baptist Bible College in Nashville, TN. Dr. Ange was elected the first full-time President of Southeastern Free Will Baptist College in 1983. He oversaw the construction and occupation of the new campus in 1987. As long as his health permitted, Dr. Ange was a devoted member of Landmark Free Will Baptist Church, where he served as an Adult Sunday School teacher and Senior Saints pastor for 10 years.

He quicken your mortal bodies by his Spirit.

Loy Everett Ballard
Birth:
Mar. 20, 1899
Buncombe County,
North Carolina
Death:
Nov. 19, 1978 Greenville,
Pitt County,
North Carolina
Burial:
Greenwood Cemetery,
Greenville, Pitt County,
North Carolina

He was born in the mountains of Western North Carolina where he spent the majority of his years as a Free Will Baptist ministers within the bounds of the North Carolina State Convention where he served more than 50 years. Not only was his leadership shown as a pastor to the local church, but was very active in organizing the Free Will Baptist League within his area. He also played an active role in establishing and promoting Craigmont Assembly serving 10 years as co-manager with his wife. For 22 years he was Field Sec. of the state Sunday school convention he also served the Free Will Baptist orphanage at Middlesex as director of religious work. He attended Mars Hill College and the Free Will Baptist Seminary in Ayden.

He served pastorates through out North Carolina as well as holding the state and national offices in the denomination as listed. He was known as an avid collector of memorabilia and gave his valuable historical materials about Free Will Baptists to the Free Will Baptist Historical Collection at Mount Olive College. He also wrote for many of Free Will Baptist denominational publications encouraging the gathering of materials about Free Will Baptist history.

He was the father of Dr. Jerry Ballard who held many roles in the national convention and also was director of World Relief of the National Association of Evangelicals.

John Henry Ballard
Birth:
Oct. 23, 1844
Yancey County, North Carolina
Death:
Jul. 8, 1934 Walnut,
Madison County,
North Carolina
Burial:
Ballard Cemetery,
Buncombe County,
North Carolina

Rev. John H. Ballard was an ordained Free Will Baptist minister, being ordained after 1865. He was converted in Oct. 1862, but served in the Union Army for NC, until it ended. Afterward, the Association wanted him to be ordained and he was reluctant because he had limited education. He preached for over fifty years, and had a fruitful ministry. He was a friend of the Temperance movement and all benevolent causes. The French Broad Association, of which he was affiliated, wrote a tribute they published to honor him and his long life of usefulness in the gospel ministry.

Willis W Ballard
Birth:
1868
Death:
1924
Burial:
Ballard Cemetery, Barnardsville,
Buncombe County,
North Carolina

James Moses Barfield
Birth:
Oct. 13, 1838
Greene County, North Carolina
Death:
Sep. 3, 1918
Burial:
Ayden Cemetery, Ayden,
Pitt County, North Carolina

Co-Author of the Barfield and Harrison History of North Carolina Free Will Baptists. He served as a Confederate soldier under the command of Capt. Byrd and in the battalion commanded by Maj. Harding of Greenville. He was licensed to preach the gospel in the year 1867 and was ordained soon after to the full work of the ministry. He was devoted to the Free Will Baptist Denomination and did all in his power to advance their doctrine which he felt was the doctrine of the Bible. It is said that he was not a brilliant speaker, nor great orator and word painter. He was one of the earliest ministers interested in a publication for the denomination which was first published in the town of Fremont, but later moved to Elm City in Wilson County. Later the conferences in North Carolina, with the exception of one, took the matter under their consideration and Elder R. H. Hearn was elected editor and ran the paper in new Bern for several years. Later a Elder Barfield became editor and publisher and soon the office was moved to Ayden by the stockholders in 1897. Elder Barfield was also a pioneer in the work of the Seminary which was started shortly after he moved to Ayden while publishing the *Free Will Baptists,* the state publication.

Jesse Parrott Barrow
Birth:
Oct. 26, 1898
Greene County, North Carolina
Death:
Mar. 11, 1990
Nashville, Davidson County,
Tennessee
Burial:
Hull Road Church Cemetery,
Greene County, North Carolina

Rev. Jesse P. was student at the Free Will Baptist Seminary, Ayden, NC, per his 1917 WW I Draft Registration. In 1920, he was employed in Chicago, perhaps where he met Anna, his future wife. He possibly studied at a College in Nashville, where they were living in 1945-46, per old minutes which stated Nashville as their residence. In the 1949 Nashville City Directory, he and Anna were still in Nashville, with "Free Will Bible College." The 1958 Nashville City Directory showed him employed as Teacher at FWBBC, and Anna as Librarian there. Records show Rev. J. P. Barrow as having served on National FWB Church Boards and committees. He was honored as a leader and minister among the church.

Nigel Bruce Barrow
Birth:
October 23, 1911
Greene County, North Carolina
Death:
March 8, 2004
Greene County, North Carolina
Burial:
Hull Road Church Cemetery,
Greene County, North Carolina

Well-known Free Will Baptist minister in North Carolina and the National Convention in the 50's and 60's, he attended Moody Bible Institute and Northwestern Theological Seminary in Chicago and later attended the graduate school at Texas A&M University. He was ordained to the ministry in 1931 at the Hull Road Original Free Will Baptist Church. He was faithful to his ministry over seven decades and during this period pastored over 30 churches, principally in Eastern North Carolina. He served as the Assistant Superintendent of the Children's Home at Middlesex and was a founding member of the Board of Trustees of Mount Olive College. He managed the denomination's publishing house in Ayden during the 1960s. His family established the Barrow Family Endowment at Mount Olive College endowing professorship in the Department of Religion

Thomas Elijah Beaman
Birth:
Jan. 6, 1899
North Carolina
Death:
Dec. 7, 1961
Goldsboro,
Wayne County, North Carolina
Burial:
Willow Dale Cemetery,
Goldsboro,
Wayne County,
North Carolina

Jesse R Bennett
Birth:
Jul. 1, 1902
Death:
Jan. 17, 1964
Burial:
New Bern Memorial Cemetery,
Trent Woods,
Craven County, North Carolina,
Plot: Section A

Clarence F. Bowen
Birth:
January 5, 1912
Death:
January 22, 1984
Wayne County, North Carolina
Burial:
Stoney Creek, Stoney Creek,
Wayne County, North Carolina
He was a well-known pastor, writer, and denominational leader for the FWB League. He was a past president of the North Carolina state convention and had been honored as Minister Of The Year by the convention. He was a graduate of Campbell and Wake Forest universities. He received his Master's degree at George Peabody College For Teachers in Nashville, Tennessee. He was the pastor of the Pleasant Hill, First Free Will Baptist Church of

Wilson, and Stony Creek Free Will Baptist Churches in N.C. He also had served as pastor of the East Nashville Free Will Baptist Church in Nashville, Tennessee. He was an honorary life member of the North Carolina Free Will Baptist Foreign Mission Board and had for many years been a writer for the Free Will Baptist Church Literature Program.

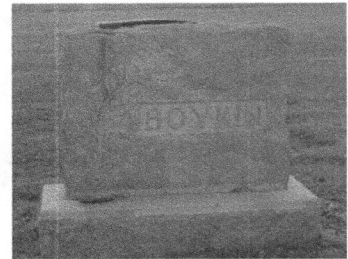

William G. Boykin
Birth:
Oct. 10, 1900
Death:
Mar. 1, 1974
Burial:
Raines Cross Roads Cemetery
Princeton
Johnston County,
North Carolina

An ordained Free Will Baptist minister, whose name appears in early NC records, minutes, etc.

Charles Brown
Birth:
unknown
Death:
Feb. 22, 1998
Goldsboro, Wayne County,

North Carolina
Burial:
Evergreen Memorial Cemetery,
Goldsboro,
Wayne, North Carolina

He had a fruitful ministry of 42 years out of his life of 75. He organized seven churches in three states which included North Carolina, South Carolina and Virginia. His most noted work was the Collingswood Free Will Baptist Church in Portsmouth, Virginia where he pastored 13 years. He also started two other churches in the Tidewater Virginia area. The Great Bridge and Faith Free Will Baptist churches.

Noah D. Brown
Birth:
July 8, 1918
Death:
February 8, 1988
Burial:
Mount Moriah Cemetery, Garner,
Wake County, North Carolina

Seldon D. Bullard
Birth:
unknown
Death:
Sep. 26,
Myrtle Beach,
Horry County, South Carolina
Burial:
Guilford Memorial Park,
Greensboro,
Guilford County, North Carolina

He was a native of Carthage, North Carolina, but moved to Myrtle Beach, South Carolina in 1970 and organized the First Free Will Baptist Church. He had served pastorates in Darlington,

South Carolina; Louisa, Kentucky; Bristol, Tennessee; Glennville, Georgia; Leadington, Missouri; and Morehead city, North Carolina. He received his theological training at Columbia Bible College. He was an active denominational leader serving on the General Board of the National Association of Free Will Baptists, Superintendent of the Kentucky Children's Orphanage in Louisa, Kentucky, and on the National Publications Board.

Tommy Lynn Burch, Jr
Birth:
unknown
Death:
Oct. 26, 2012
Bryson City, Swain County,
North Carolina
Burial:
Cornerstone Wesleyan
Church Cemetery,
Bryson City, Swain County,
North Carolina

A native of Tennessee, Tommy spent over 30 years of his life in Graham and Swain Counties. He was a Minister and Pastored Churches in Elizabethton TN at Moore's Chapel Freewill Baptist Church and in Bryson City at Sawmill Hill Freewill Baptist Church. He graduated from The Freewill Baptist Bible College) with a B.S. degree in Pastoral Administration and also an E.T.T.A. Teaching diploma. He also worked for Swain County West Elementary School for 12 years.

**As the rain from heaven refreshes the parched ground,
so death provides the saint to partake of the refreshing of the soul in the presence of Jesus.**

J. W. Byrd
Birth:
Aug. 30, 1867
Death:
Sep. 7, 1917
Burial:
Saint Mary's Grove Original
Free Will BC Cemetery,
Benson, Johnston County,
North Carolina

J F Casey
Birth:
Sep. 30, 1872
Death:
Dec. 31, 1918
Burial:
Willow Dale Cemetery,
Goldsboro
Wayne County, North Carolina

Floyd B. Cherry
Birth:
April 15, 1916
Dothan, Alabama
Death:
February 24, 2005
North Carolina
Burial:
Selma Memorial Gardens, Selma,
Johnston County, North Carolina

He was an educator, minister, and writer in the Free Will Baptist denomination. Dr. Cherry, was a native of Alabama and was a minister for 65 years beginning at the age of 16. He was ordained a Free Will Baptist minister in Dothan, Alabama on July 16, 1933. He pastored churches in Alabama, Florida, Georgia and North Carolina. He attended Zion Bible school in Georgia; the University of Florida where he received a Bachelor's Degree in Bible Study; and Thomas Edison college, where he received his Masters in Bible Study. He earned his Doctor's Degree from Bob Jones University in Greenville, South Carolina in 1975. He came to pastor the Pine Level Free Will Baptist Church in North Carolina where he was the founder of the Carolina Bible Institute that still continues to this day. He wrote three books and also several pamphlets..

W. Ruffin Coats
Birth:
Dec. 2, 1866
Death:
Sep. 11, 1950
Burial:
Saint Mary's Grove Original
Free Will Baptist church
Cemetery
Benson, Johnston County,
North Carolina

Richard Ray Cordell
Birth:
Aug. 28, 1935
Cincinnati, Ohio,
Death:
Jul. 28, 2011
Goldsboro, North Carolina
Burial:
Evergreen Memorial Cemetery,
Goldsboro,
Wayne County, North Carolina

He served his Lord in ministry for over 54 years and had also served his country in the United States Army. Pastor Cordell was a graduate of the Free Will Baptist College in Nashville, Tennessee, where he received a Bachelor of Science degree in Pastoral Studies. His three pastorates included three states: Indiana, Tennessee, and Alabama. After retiring in Guin, Alabama, Rev. Cordell served for three years as the promotional director for the Alabama Free Will Baptist State Association. He later came to Goldsboro to serve as the Outreach Pastor for Faith Free Will Baptist Church. His greatest joy in life was door-knocking, leading someone to the Lord and asking people to come and visit the church.

Louis N Coscia
Birth:
1926
Death:
May 23, 2010
Burial:
West Memorial Park,
Weaverville,
Buncombe County,
North Carolina

A native of Memphis, Tenn., Rev. Coscia was a Free Will Baptist Missionary serving for 28 years in Brazil. Louis was a running and jogging enthusiast and a gardener. He especially enjoyed growing pansies and is known by many in his area as the "pansy man." He enjoyed reading and writing poetry and had a wonderful sense of humor. A celebration of Rev. Coscia's life was held with Rev. Danny Gasperson officiating.

Clyde W. Cox
Birth:
Mar. 26, 1920
Rowan County, North Carolina
Death:
unknown
Wilson ,Wilson County,
North Carolina
Burial:
Selma Memorial Gardens,
Selma, Johnston County,
North Carolina,

Rev. Cox dedicated his life to the Lord. Throughout his ministry, he was a pastor at 15 churches beginning in 1952 and ending in 2003 at Spring Hill Church in

Goldsboro, N.C. He conducted 274 revivals. He also taught music school in churches throughout North Carolina. He sang, played piano, wrote music and songs and directed music for several revivals. Rev. Cox touched many people's lives over the last 52 years as a dedicated messenger of God. He also served in WWII in the US Navy on the USS Birmingham in the Pacific.

John S. Craft
Birth:
1942
North Carolina
Death:
1980
Burial:
Ayden Cemetery, Ayden,
Pitt County, North Carolina

He was a Free Will Baptist missionary serving in Brazil from 1968-1973.

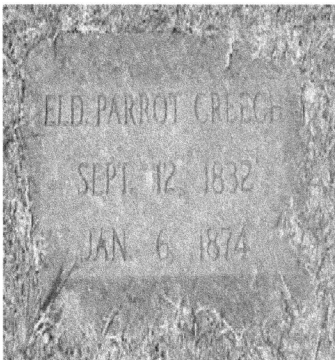

Elder Parrot Creech
Birth:
Sep. 12, 1832
Death:
Jan. 6, 1874
Burial:
Saint Mary's Grove Original
Free Will Baptist Cemetery,
Benson,
Johnston County, North Carolina

Elder Creech was founder of St. Mary's Grove Original Free Will Baptists Church

---

John Linward Crocker, Sr
Birth:
Apr. 1, 1931
Death:
Dec. 12, 2010
Burial:
Branch Chapel Free Will Baptist
Church,
Smithfield,
Johnston County, North Carolina

Funeral services at Branch Chapel Free Will Baptist Church with the Rev. Terry Dennis and Mr. Luby Tyner officiating. Burial was with military honors.

There's nothing certain in a man's life except this: That he must lose it.

Frank Davenport
Birth:
1923
Death:
1997
Goldsboro,
Wayne County, North Carolina
Burial:
Wayne Memorial Park,
Goldsboro,
Wayne County,North Carolina

He was a Church builder organizing 12 churches in North Carolina where he spent most of his ministry. He also helped start four Christian schools. All were in North Carolina. His longest pastorate was a 20 year tenure at the Faith Free Will Baptist church in Goldsboro, one of the 12 churches he organized. His ministry spanned 45 years in North Carolina and Kentucky. He was a native of Pitt County, North Carolina. He was ordained to preach in 1952 at age 29. As a leader he was elected to numerous positions in North Carolina and on the national level. He served six years on the national Home Mission Board and on the national Executive Committee. He Served The North Carolina State Home Missions, and the Bible Bookstore Board. He was also manager of Jubilee, Inc. and as Treasurer of the Free Will Baptist Superannuation Assn.

James Robert Davidson
Birth:
May 28, 1898
Death:
Jan. 9, 1972
Burial:

New Bern Memorial Cemetery, Trent Woods, Craven County, North Carolina, Plot: Section G

Davison is remembered as a long-time crusader for Christian education. Davison made the Board Of Education's report at the 1939 session of the national Association at Bryan, Texas with the proposition of beginning a national Bible college. He at the 1942 meeting in Columbus, Mississippi during his report for that the board was authorized by the convention to open the school in Nashville, Tennessee on September 15, 1942. The first building purchased by the college still bears the name of the man who labored for the college's promotion for so many years. He served on the Board of Trustees of the college in 1943 until 1964. During this 21 year tenure, he served as chairman, vice chairman, and secretary of the board. He also served the as Business Manager during 1942-1944 and again in 1946-1947 He served the National Association as an Assistant Moderator from 1938-1944. At the 1940 for meeting he was elected as Moderator, a post he held until 1946.

Benjamin Bardin Deans
Birth:
Mar. 18, 1866
Death:
Jun. 17, 1934
Burial:
Joseph J. Bissette Cemetery,
Nash County,
North Carolina

Garrett Deweese
Birth:
1772
Botetourt County,
Virginia
Death:
Nov. 28, 1839
Buncombe County,
North Carolina
Burial:
Big Ivy Cemetery,
Barnardsville,
Buncombe County,
North Carolina

He was an early Baptist preacher, but became Free Will and worked in North Carolina and East Tennessee region with Moses Peterson and John Wheeler. At first they were members of the French Broad Association of Baptists. This Assn. became divided over the Calvinistic and the Arminian question. The Arminian group led by Rev. Garrett Deweese, were "Free Will" but practiced close communion. Although the Reverend's Peterson and Wheeler agreed with Deweese on the question of the free moral agency of man and they both invited all Christians to the Communion, they agreed to meet with prayer and settle the questions between them regarding communion. They became known as the "Free Will" Baptist. Not many records exists of Rev. Deweese's detailed ministry, but the records do show he was a faithful man and a leader in his time for his Free Will Baptist church to help serve the spiritual needs of these scattered people. His son, Levi, also became a minister.

Levi Deweese
Birth:
Sep. 2, 1810
North Carolina
Death:
May 25, 1902
North Carolina
Burial:
Gabriels Creek Baptist Church, Cemetery,
Mars Hill, Madison County,

North Carolina

Rev. Levi Deweese was the son of Rev. Garrett and Susannah (Palmer) Deweese..In the Census of 1850, Levi was listed as a head of household in Buncombe Co, NC. .A pioneer Free Will Baptist preacher in North Carolina and East Tennessee..

THE RESURRECTION OF CHRIST, AS IT IS THE JOY OF HIS FRIENDS, SO IT IS THE TERROR AND CONFUSION OF HIS ENEMIES.

Sigbee Bryant Dilda
Birth:
Jan. 8, 1936
Death:
Sep. 11, 2002
Greenville
Pitt County, North Carolina
Burial:
Queen Anne Cemetery
Fountain
Pitt County, North Carolina

Rev Sigbee Dilda, former pastor of Pamplico FWB Church, NAFWB General Board member from South Carolina for many years, and long time soldier of the Cross went to be with the Lord on September 11th. Brother Sigbee had recently resigned from Pamplico FWB Church and moved to Hookerton,NC because of ill health. His wife, Mary, had taught for many years at Maranatha Christian School (First FWB Church, Florence) and is now continuing her labors at Mt. Calvary Christian School; where she lives close to son, Bryant. Daughter, Susanna, is married to Rev Carroll Bazen,Pastor of Grace FWB Church in Lake City, SC.Many things stand out about Brother Sigbee. He was a long time Pastor Glenwood FWB Church (Arkansas) 1965-67; Pamplico FWB Church (SC) 1967-1970; Ruth's Chapel FWB Church (NC) 1970-1980; Great Bridge FWB Church (Virginia) 1980-1983; Tabernacle FWB Church (NC) 1983-89; Lebanon FWB Church (SC) 1989-1990; Pamplico FWB Church (SC) 1990-2002. He believed what he believed and was willing to stand for that belief (A sentiment echoed by all of the speakers at his funeral service). He knew how to have fun but he also knew when to stand firm.And he was a faithful soul winner and soldier for the Lord.

Robert Jefferson Durham
Birth:
Mar. 23, 1927
Wayne County, North Carolina
Death:
Sep. 9, 2012
Rocky Mount, Nash County, North Carolina
Burial:
Rocky Mount Memorial Park, Rocky Mount
Nash County, North Carolina
He was born in Wayne County to the late Jeff and Pearl Harris Durham. He lived with his parents

and helped them run their farm until 1945, when he was drafted into the Army. After being stationed in France and completing his service he returned home and worked as a Deputy Sheriff in Greene County.

He later became Associate Sales Manager with the Western and Southern Life Insurance Company where he worked for eleven years, which moved him to Rocky Mount in 1954; during which time he answered the call to preach. He attended the Evangelical Baptist College and graduated from the William Carter Bible College. In 1960, he founded and organized Grace Free Baptist Church with eleven charter members. Prior to his retirement he saw the church attendance grow to over 500, and in 1976 the church founded Grace Christian School. He had a passion for soul winning and preaching God's word and was honored to see ten of the church members be ordained and begin full-time work for God. Reverend Durham was speaker on the Grace Baptist Hour on WECE radio for 20 years. He served two terms as local moderator and six years as state moderator of the Palmer Association of Free Baptist Churches. After retirement, he held numerous revivals, was interim pastor for several area Baptist churches and continued being a faithful working member of Grace Free Baptist Church. He was survived by his devoted loving wife of 63 years, Gladys Speight Durham.

Nathan Earl Eason
Birth:
Nov. 2, 1932
Greene County, North Carolina
Death:
Apr. 4, 2008
Rocky Mount
Nash County, North Carolina
Burial:
Queen Anne Cemetery
Fountain
Pitt County, North Carolina

Nathan Eason married Mary Agnes Dilda on May 24, 1952 in Greenville, Pitt Co., NC. his parents were James C Eason (1893 - 1975) and Ora Mae Moore Eason (1899 - 1970). He had been the pastor of Grace Free Will Baptist Church in Greenville.

Lonne R. Ennis
Birth:
1895
Death:
1977
Goldsboro,
Wayne County, North Carolina
Burial:
Willow Dale Cemetery, Goldsboro,
Wayne County, North Carolina

Denominational leader, pastor, educator, and conference speaker. He pioneered for a educational program which was greatly needed in our denomination. The Lord equipped to deal with the keen mind and thorough education he acquired abilities that few men among us possessed.. At a time when we needed an educational vision, and someone who could implement that vision, brother Ennis conducted Bible institutes across our denomination. He built an interest in education which finally resulted in Free Will Baptist Bible College being established in Nashville, Tennessee. He stepped into a world of national prominence among Free Will Baptists in 1940 when he preached the opening sermon in the fourth annual session in Paintsville, Kentucky. His sermon *Rivers Of Living Waters* was considered a masterpiece. He was elected as the first executive Sec. of the restless, newly organized denomination in 1940. He served in that position until 1943. He traveled thousands of miles promoting denomination outreach during which time he. pastored three churches at the same time and in addition to his extensive travels. He was summons to Nashville, Tennessee in 1944 where he was appointed president of the Free Will Baptist Bible College serving from 1944 until 1947. His training had been secured from Moody Bible Institute and his diplomatic skills required as an Executive Sec. had been soundly tested for the job. He led the college in purchasing the Sword building in 1945, the same year that the college yearbook, *The Lumen* was dedicated to him. He taught a variety of courses while at the college including English, Sunday School and Church Administration, Bible and others. Ennis remained a guiding voice in his native North Carolina because of his great spiritual strength and wisdom.. He was pastoring two churches at his death at age 81. One of the buildings at Free Will Baptist Bible College is named for him.

James A. Evans
Birth:
November 10, 1905
Death:
October 25, 1999
Lucama, Wilson County,
North Carolina
Burial:
Lucas Cemetery, Lucama,
Wilson County, North Carolina

He was a early Free Will Baptist preacher from Wayne County in eastern North Carolina. He attended Eureka College in Ayden, North Carolina, and was a graduate of the Pastor's Institute of Duke University. In 1994 he received the first honorary Doctor Of Divinity degree given by Mount Olive College. He was an ordained minister for 74 years and served churches in North Carolina, Texas, and Florida. He was selected the outstanding Free Will Baptist Minister of the Year by the North Carolina Association OFWB in 1972. He was the first full-time employee of Mount Olive College where he began in 1954 serving as the Director Of Public Relations. From 1940-1949 he served as the Superintendent of the Children's Home in Middlesex. He was the co-founder of the Free Will Baptist Church Finance Association in 1940 and the first Chairman of Craigmont Assembly of the Original Free Will Baptist Conference Center in 1945.

W. B. Everett
Birth:
1877
Death:
1948
Craven County, North Carolina
Burial:
Cedar Grove Cemetery,
New Bern,
Craven County, North Carolina
Early leader and minister in the eastern area of North Carolina.

James W Everton
Birth:
Nov. 2, 1923
Death:
Mar. 4, 1971
Burial:
East Duplin Memorial Gardens,
Beulaville,
Duplin County, North Carolina

Free Will Baptist preacher and WWII veteran. Inscription:GM3 USNR WWII

William M Ferrell
Birth:
Oct. 25, 1886
Johnston County, North Carolina
Death:
Nov. 6, 1937
Durham,
Durham County, North Carolina
Burial:
Bethel Original
Freewill Baptist Church Cemetery,
Four Oaks,
Johnston County, North Carolina

John Eugene Floyd
Birth:
Jan. 17, 1906
Caldwell County, North Carolina
Death:
Nov. 21, 1996
Charlotte
Mecklenburg County, North
Carolina
Burial:
Hillcrest Gardens
Mount Holly
Gaston County, North Carolina

Rev. John Floyd, 90, of Mt. Holly, a retired Free Will Baptist pastor, evangelist and church planter. He was converted on July 10, 1927 and was ordained in 1946. He overcame tuberculosis at the age of 24, but still refuse to preach. He struggled to accept the call to preach for 15 years because of his fear and an inability to read and his lack of formal education. Six years later at age 30 after over hearing a doctor tell his wife that he would die of pneumonia, he finally accepted the call. He pastored the First Free Will Baptist Church, Marion, North Carolina in 1946 leading the church to grow from 29 members to 412. He pastored several other churches in the 50s and 60s including the Sea Level and Cedar Island Free Will Baptist churches, and the Calvary Free Will Baptist Church in Jacksonville. At the age of 66 he began pastoring the Adawolfe Free Will Baptist Church in Virginia. The church grew from 60 in Sunday school and added 130 members while baptizing 100 members and had four men call to preach and they paid for a new parsonage. He was known as a man of prayer and prayed that 100 men would enter the ministry through his preaching. Some 132 men did answer the call to preach including his son, a son-in-law, two grandsons and a nephew. Also, through his ministry Miss Volena Wilson went to India as a missionary. He preached in 37 states, Canada, Mexico, Puerto Rico and Jerusalem. He organized 15 churches and preached revivals in 100 churches where he witnessed more than 23,000 professions of faith in response to his 7500 sermons which he preached. He also had a continuing the radio ministry for 30 years.

Elder Frederick Asa Fonville
Birth:
Mar. 6, 1770
Alamance County, North Carolina
Death:
Apr. 21, 1835
Alamance County, North Carolina
Burial:
Fonville Family Cemetery
Alamance County, North Carolina

A pioneer Free Will Baptist minister, along with others, who ministered in the remnant left of the Philadelphia Association, in 1832. He was a worthy and faithful man, of good reputation, who stood on his convictions. Beloved son of Stephen Fonville and Lucy Kibble. He was the husband of Rebecca Oliver, whom he married Jan 29, 1790. Their son was William Washington Fonville. After her death in 1793, he married Mary Polly Averett on Dec 12, 1793. Their children were Nathan Fonville; Hannah Fonville; Edna Fonville; John Averett Fonville; Sallie Fonville; and James Roney Fonville. After Mary died in 1816, he married Charity Graham on May 30, 1816 in Orange, North Carolina. Their children were Mary Fonville; Frederick W Fonville; Asa Graham Fonville; Francis Fonville; and Brice Frederick Fonville.
Spouses: Mary Polly Everette Fonville (1775 - 1816). Rebecca Oliver Fonville (1777 -93),
Charity Graham Fonville (1789 - 1858).

William M Fulcher, Jr
Birth:
May 6, 1933
Bridgeton,
Craven County, North Carolina
Death:
Mar. 23, 2004
New Bern,
Craven County, North Carolina
Burial:
Dixon Cemetery, Aurora,
Beaufort County, North Carolina

Bill graduated from the Bridgeton High School in 1952 and thereafter, played baseball for the New Bears. He was drafted into the United States Army in 1953 and served in Korea and Japan. He was trained in radio communication. In 1955 he was honorably discharged from the Army and enrolled in Free Will Baptist Bible College in Nashville Tennessee, to prepare for the Ministry.
He graduated in 1959 with a BA degree. While in school he married Linda Barks in 1957 and during their marriage life they had five children. He pastored the Bethany Free Will Baptist Church in Winterville, North Carolina during 1959-1960. It was at the end of 1960 that he was commissioned as a foreign missionary for the International Mission Board Of Free Will Baptists. He attended the Spanish

language Institute in San Jose, Costa Rica during 1961. From 1961 to 1969 he served in Uruguay, South America and from 1971 through 1979 served in Panama, Central America. He returned to the pastorate in 1979 and served the Bethel Free Will Baptist Church in S. Roxana, Illinois. He served there until 1981 when He was hired by the National Home Mission Board to serve the Spanish-speaking people in Houston, Texas. In 1988 through 1992 he was employed by the Southeastern Free Will Baptist College in Wendell, North Carolina as the Promotional Director. Afterwards he pastored the Faith Free Will Baptist Church in Carrollton, Virginia from 1992 to 2000, and then the Faith Free Will Baptist Church in Maysville, North Carolina from 2000 until 2004 where he was serving when he died.

Houston Owen Ganey
Birth:
Nov. 17, 1931
Death:
Mar. 23, 2003
Nashville, Davidson County, Tennessee
Burial:
Richmond Memorial Park, Rockingham, Richmond County, North Carolina

Brother Ganey was a well respected minister, evangelist and pastor. He was always an encourager to all who knew him. The native North Carolinian was living in Nashville at the time of his death.

Raymond Albert Gaskins
Birth:
Jul. 1, 1921
North Carolina
Death:
Nov. 22, 2010
Ayden, Pitt County
North Carolina
Burial:
Ayden Cemetery,
Ayden, Pitt County,
North Carolina

He graduated as salutatorian of his 1938 Ayden High School class, lettering in football and boxing. In 1943 he completed a three-year Coppersmith apprenticeship from the Norfolk Navy Yard and entered the U.S. Navy, serving as a quartermaster in World War II. He returned to Ayden after the war, attending Banking School at UNC-Chapel Hill, while employed with Planter's Bank and Trust Co. Raymond became a minister in 1957, after completing studies at The Free Will Baptist Bible College in Nashville, Tenn. He served as pastor of Liberty Free Will Baptist Church in Ayden from 1958-2004. He met Beatrice Loftin Gaskins in 1946, marrying her in 1947. She preceded him in death after 57 years of marriage.

Louis H Green
Birth:
Sep. 26, 1940
Death:
Feb. 18, 1986
Burial:
Sweet Hope Freewill Baptist Church Cemetery,
Pitt County, North Carolina

Jesse Christopher Griffin, Sr
Birth:
June 22, 1879
Nash County, North Carolina
Death:
1968
North Carolina
Burial:
Cedar Grove Cemetery,
New Bern,
Craven County, North Carolina

Well-known Free Will Baptist minister, pastor, writer and denominational leader. He was the author of an early Free Will Baptist Minister's Handbook. He was ordained to the ministry on June 10, 1910 just before his thirty-first birthday.

He attended Eureka College and the Free Will Baptist Seminary at Ayden, North Carolina from 1912 until 1914.

During his 57 years of ministry he pastored 28 churches, conducting numerous revivals, funerals, performing marriage rites, and won scores of people to Christ in a ministry that led from the eastern seashore to the mountains of North Carolina as well as extensive work in many other states.

He united with the Free Will Baptist denomination at the White Oak Hill church in Nash County in 1905.

He was manager of the Free Will Baptist Press 1914-16. His column "Notes and Quotes" appeared in the *Free Will Baptist* for 25 years. He was moderator of the Eastern conference of North Carolina Free Will Baptists 1919-1923. He was a member and served as secretary to the Free Will Baptist Orphanage Board between 1923-28.

He was Vice President of the North Carolina State Association 1931-36. President of the North Carolina State Association 1940-42. Field Sec. North Carolina State Association 1942-45. Publicity Director of the General Conference 1929. Statistician of the General Conference-Eastern General 1933-35.

Chairman of the Treatises Committee of the National Association 1935. Member of the Revision Committee of the Treatise 1940.

Chairman of the Board Of Publications and Literature 1942. Re-elected for five years in 1943. He was a member of the General Board of the National Association and a member of the Executive Committee. He did evangelistic meetings in South Carolina, and

Florida, Alabama, Mississippi, Texas, Tennessee and North Carolina. He was the author of many booklets and a book entitled, *The One Foundation*. He was married twice and had a total of 15 children.

John Hall, Jr
Birth:
unknown
Death:
Mar. 11, 1992
Reidsville,
Rockingham County,
North Carolina
Burial:
Evergreen Memory Gardens,
Reidsville,
Rockingham County,
North Carolina

He organized a Free Will Baptist Church in Readsville in 1977 as a home missions project. He served as moderator of the Maryland State Association and editor of the Maryland Newsletter. He had been a schoolteacher, principal and administrator. He attended Free Will Baptist Bible College, Maryland Bible Institute, Covington Theological Seminary and Elkton Bible college.

Charlie Jackson Harris, Sr
Birth:
1870
North Carolina
Death:
1943
Pitt County,
North Carolina
Burial:
Greenwood Cemetery,
Greenville, Pitt County,
North Carolina

He was the first Field Secretary for the N. C. State Convention when it was organized in 1913.

David Wells Hansley
Birth:
Dec. 21, 1909
Folkstone, Onslow Co. N.C.
Death:
Apr. 24, 1989
Burial:
Dalys Chapel Free Will Baptist
Church Cemetery,
Liddell, Lenoir County,
North Carolina

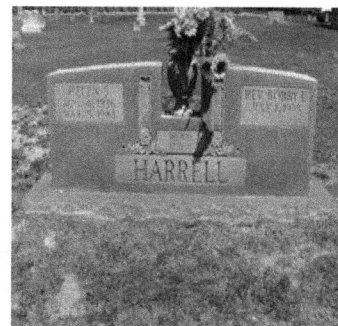

He was an active leader as Chairman of the Board of Directors that led in the creation of the Mount Olive College in North Carolina, a role he held from 1953 to 1963, but continued on the board until 1970. He was a member of the Board of Directors for the Free Will Baptist Press, Ayden, N.C., Chairman of Board of Superannuation and League Board of the National Association. He was a grandson of Jesse Heath an early FWB preacher. He became a minister in 1930 at the age of 21 and served 37 churches in 15 N.C. counties from 1931-1988.

Bobby E. Harrell
Birth:
Jul. 1, 1933
Death:
unknown
Burial:
Dalys Chapel Free Will
Baptist Church Cemetery,
Liddell, Lenoir County,
North Carolina

SHOW THY VACANT TOMB,
AND LET,
AS of old, THE ANGELS SIT,
WHISPERING, by ITS OPEN
door:
"FEAR NOT! HE HATH GONE
bEFORE!"

Thaddeus F. Harrison
Birth:
March 8, 1878
Washington County North
Carolina
Death:
October 24, 1897
Ayden, Pitt County,
North Carolina
Burial:
Ayden Cemetery,
Ayden, Pitt County,
North Carolina

His family gave him all the advantages of an education that they possibly could in his early life.. In 1884 he went to Plymouth High School, then to the Academy at Pantego to study under Prof. A. L. Johnson for 10 months. From there he went to the Carolina Institute to study under Prof.

Rightsell. And from there to Chapel Hill after which he returned home and taught school. Sometime before his last schooling he united with the Disciples church. Not long after he commenced exhorting and speaking in public and soon became dissatisfied and united with the Free Will Baptist at Union Chapel in January of 1894 and was ordained in the same year. He and his twin brother (Theodore) published two books and pamphlets, one containing 10 sermons and the other was on feet washing.. Later he wrote two more pamphlets, one was 100 facts on baptism and another on feet washing. In the spring of 1896 Elder Harrison decided to write a history of the Free Will Baptist of North Carolina. Thus he became a co-author of the *History of North Carolina Free Will Baptist* with J.M. Barfield.

Jeremiah Heath
Birth:
Oct. 4, 1793
North Carolin
Death:
Feb. 22, 1867
Cove City
Craven County, North Carolina
Burial:
Heath Family Cemetery
Craven County, North Carolina

An early Free Will Baptist minister in a remnant of churches in 1832 from the Philadelphia Association. Rev. Jeremiah HEATH's name is found among historical records with early FWB minister's names who contended for, and remained influential in sustaining the Orig. Free Will Baptist church in its early formation and growth, especially the old Bethel Conference, when it could have been merged. He was a leader, with others, during this time who carried forward the FWB cause. Jeremiah was a prominent surveyor in the early formation of the area, to which land records attest; also, he was a Free Will Baptist minister. He organized the Core Creek FWB Church, and also pastored the FWB church at New Bern, NC, and probably others.He raised several children who became worthy citizens. Rev. Jesse Heath's name is known as a prominent leader in the area. (Family papers are held in Joyner Library, East Carolina University, Greenville, N.C. --Index is online). Parents: Rigdon and Elizabeth (Jackson) HEATH. Spouse: Clemmie Holland Jones (NC mar rec'ds)
Inscription:
Organized Core Creek Free Will Baptist Church 1865.

John David Hill
Birth:
Sep. 30, 1924
North Carolina
Death:
Nov. 10, 2008
North Carolina
Burial:
Bethel Original
Freewill Baptist Church Cemetery,
Four Oaks, Johnston County,
North Carolina

Danny H Howell
Birth:
Oct. 19, 1946
Death:
Sep. 4, 1993
Burial:
Fairview Cemetery
La Grange
Lenoir County, North Carolina

While working in the church gymnasium, he climbed a ladder and had a fall which caused his death at age 46. He was called to preach in 1977 and was ordained to the ministry in 1981 pastoring two North Carolina churches; Morehead City and the Goshen church in Mt. Holly. He attended Free Will Baptist Bible College and Lenore Community College, North Carolina and received his Doctor of Ministries from Bethany Theological Seminary, Dothan, Alabama.

Clint Hardrick Holt
Birth:
Mar. 31, 1915
North Carolina
Death:
Dec. 19, 2009
Johnston County, North Carolina
Burial:
Selma Memorial Gardens, Selma,
Johnston County, North Carolina

Holt retired from the NC Dept. of Transportation and was a Free Will Baptist Minister for most of his adult life. He lived in Hendersonville before moving to Smithfield in the early 1980's.

Billy Gray Jackson
Birth:
Jul. 27, 1934
Wilson, Wilson County,
North Carolina
Death:
Mar. 2, 1997
Chapel Hill,
Madison County, North Carolina
Burial:
Onslow Memorial Park,
Jacksonville,
Onslow County, North Carolina

Billy was the pastor of the Cardinal Village Free Will Baptist Church that grew from 30 to a total of 350. He had a high Sunday of 525 on Easter one year. He was truly a man who cared for the people of his church and the entire community. His church loved him so much that they paid for his resting place and for the headstones for he and his wife. His son, Kevin, follows his father in the ministry.

Robert Copps Jackson
Birth:
November 19, 1865
Sampson County,
North Carolina,
Death:
June 21, 1908
North Carolina
Burial:
Roberts Grove
Free Will Baptist Church,
Dunn
Sampson County,
North Carolina

As a young man he joined a Missionary Baptist Church where he was a very faithful member, but in July of 1887 he severed his relationship with this church and united with the Free Will Baptist Church at Shady Grove where he held his membership for several years until he organized a new Free Will Baptist Church near his home. He was licensed to the ministry on August 1, 1891 and the next year in 1892 he was ordained to the ministry. He served for 17 years as a preacher of the gospel of Christ his ministry took him beyond his own state into South Carolina and even as far north as Ohio in his evangelistic work. He was active in the Cape Fear Conference, establishing several Churches of the Free Will Baptist faith.

Roy H Jackson
Birth:
Jun. 20, 1901
Death:
Aug. 31, 1991
Burial:
Pleasant Grove Free Will Baptist
Church Cemetery,
Dunn, Harnett County,
North Carolina

Walter L. Jernigan
Birth:
Mar. 21, 1900
Bladen County, North Carolina
Death:
Nov. 19, 1962 Bladenboro,
Bladen County, North Carolina
Burial:
Lewis Cemetery, Bladenboro,
Bladen County, North Carolina

An ordained Free Will Baptist minister and pastor.

Milton Lee Johnson
Birth:
Aug. 19, 1915
Johnston Co., North Carolina
Death:
February 11 1969
Middlesex
Nash Co., North Carolina
Burial:
Marsh Swamp Church Cemetery,
Wilson, North Carolina

He was a well-known pastor and did a remarkable work throughout the denomination. He was Business Manager of Mount Olive Junior College between 1956-61 He served as the Superintendent of the Free Will Baptist orphanage in Middlesex a total of six years before a heart attack took his life.

Alan Clinton Joyner
Birth:
Oct. 8, 1963
Wilson County, North Carolina
Death:
Oct. 24, 2011
Burial:
Queen Anne Cemetery
Fountain
Pitt County, North Carolina

Son of Llewellyn Brann Joyner and the late Clinton Hubert Joyner, he was a graduate of Wilson Christian Academy. He attended Atlantic Christian College (Barton College) and graduated from Mount Olive College in 2005. He was ordained as an minister in the Original Free Baptist denomination. He served as pastor of the Free Union OFWB Church for eight years where his funeral was held on October 28, 2011, with The Rev. Kelley Smith and The Rev. Dr. David Hines officiating.

Charles Edward Keith
Birth:
Jun. 15, 1922
Dickenson County, Virginia
Death:
Mar. 9, 2008,
Sanford,
Lee County, North Carolina
Burial:
Markham Memorial Gardens,
Durham,
Durham County, North Carolina

A Free Will Baptist minister serving churches in North and South Carolina. Father of N.C. Promotional Director Billy Keith.

Eld. Robert C. Kennedy
Birth:
1881
Death:
1954
Burial:
Whaley Cemetery,
Duplin, County, North Carolina

His son was Rev. Rashie Kennedy (1911 - 2012) who lived to be 100 years of age. He was in the first graduating class of Free Will Baptist Bible College, Nashville, Tennessee in 1942. His ministry among Free Will Baptists is well recorded not only here but in heaven.

Rashie Kennedy, Sr
Birth:
Jul. 15, 1911
Duplin County, North Carolina
Death:
Jun. 19, 2012
Beulaville, Duplin County,
North Carolina
Burial:
East Duplin Memorial Gardens,
Beulaville, Duplin County,
North Carolina

Converted at age 11, Kennedy was licensed to preach in 1940 and ordained in 1941. His 70-year ministry was marked by a passion for prayer and evangelism. Reverend Kennedy sold his North Carolina home in 1942 and relocated to Nashville , Tn. , with his wife and two children to attend FWBBC. He was 31 at the time, three years older than the college president, Dr. L.C. Johnson. While a student at FWBBC, Kennedy organized and pastored Sylvan Park Free Will Baptist Church in West Nashville. He graduated in 1945 and later pastored in North Carolina, Texas, Florida, and Louisiana. His denominational service included eight years on the Free Will Baptist International Missions Board, six years on the Home Missions Board, two years as Texas Executive Secretary, two years on the Oklahoma Bible College (now Hillsdale FWB College) Board and other district and state boards in North Carolina and Texas. He and Myrtle Kennedy were married 63 years. He started a writing career at age 90 by embracing Internet technology and creating a website that featured many of his articles and sermons.

John W Lucas
Birth:
Oct. 23, 1857
Death:
Jun. 14, 1925
Burial:
Pleasant Grove Free Will Baptist
Church Cemetery
Dunn,
Harnett County North Carolina

Reverend J. W. Lucas, a graduate of Wake Forest, was born Averysboro, N. C. in 1850, and was ordained in 1872. For over a quarter of a century, he served as a Free Will Baptist minister and as an educator in East Tennessee. Most of this time he was affiliated with the Union Association. He served as principal of high schools at Parrotsville, Midway, and elsewhere. He succeeded Brother Woolsey as pastor of the Woolsey College Church. His work at the college both as teacher and as pastor was outstanding in quality. He was in attendance at the General Conference at Harper's Ferry, West Virginia, 1901 and again along with Dr. T. H. Woolsey at Hillsdale, Michigan in 1904.
--from One Hundred Years of Paul Woolsey's Free Will Baptist Family, pub. 1949.

Today is not a day of distress, But a day of delight.

Malachi Daniel Lucas
Birth:
Mar. 12, 1884
Wilson County, North Carolina
Death:
Jun. 14, 1909
Wilson County, North Carolina
Burial:
Lucas Cemetery, Lucama,
Wilson County, North Carolina

Patrick Thomas "Elder" Lucas
Birth:
Sep. 8, 1854
North Carolina
Death:
Jul. 2, 1912
Wilson County, North Carolina
Burial:
Lucas Cemetery, Lucama,
Wilson County, North Carolina

Alice Voliva Lupton
Birth:
Oct. 13, 1875
Death:
Jan. 24, 1962
Burial:
Cedar Grove Cemetery,
New Bern, Craven County,
North Carolina

She was one of the earliest organizers for women within the denomination. She organized the first "lady's aid society" in the St. Mary's church in the historic city of New Bern. In May of 1927, a state women's convention was organized in Goldsboro, North Carolina where Mrs. Lupton became the first president of the statewide organization. The 1928 session met at the Eureka College at Ayden, where the work was departmentalized with directors for missions, Christian education, Superannuation, stewardship and youth training. In 1935, a national auxiliary convention was organized at Black Jack church, near Greenville. The North Carolina convention affiliated with it and Mrs. Lupton became it's first president and the North Carolina women joined with others in working toward a Bible college and a foreign missions program. From the earliest days of the women's movement Alice Lupton was always seen at the forefront. She was a author and columnist writing for the *Free Will Baptists* for many years a woman's column. She freely wrote programs for the women's movement and also was the author of one book, *Footprints Of Jesus* which was widely used by women's auxiliaries and ministers and in pre--Easter observations.

Thomas Hillman Matthews
Birth:
Oct. 9, 1830
Nash County, North Carolina
Death:
Sep. 7, 1918
Nash County, North Carolina
Burial:
Thomas H. Matthews Cemetery,
Nash County, North Carolina

Thomas was a Free Will Baptist Minister and served in the Civil War as a Private in the Civil War during 1861-1865, Confederate Regiment State Origin: North Carolina Regiment.

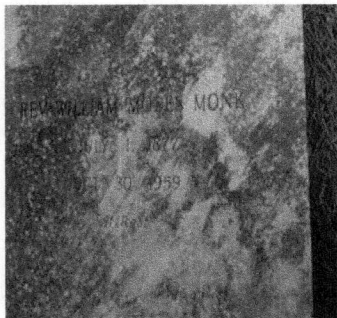

William Moses Monk
Birth:
Jul. 1, 1877
Sampson County, North Carolina
Death:
Oct. 30, 1959
Bell Arthur,
Pitt County, North Carolina
Burial:
Arthur Chapel
FWB Church Cemetery,
Bell Arthur, Pitt County,
North Carolina

Monk was the founding pastor of Arthur Chapel Free Will Baptist Church.

**Today is not a day of defeat
But a day of victory.**

Alfred Moore
Birth:
May 28, 1813
Death:
Aug. 28, 1870
Lenoir County, North Carolina
Burial:
Moore Family Cemetery
Hugo, Lenoir County,
North Carolina

Rev. Alfred Moore was a Free Will Baptist minister for 38 years. He was 59 yrs when he died, leaving his widow and children to mourn his passing. His ministerial work was with the remnant of his church which labored to spread the word after severe hardships. He remained with the part of the dissenting Free Will Baptists who declined to merge with a Disciples coalition in about 1832. His name appears in other records and books. The churches he pastored, are not known, but he remained a faithful minister until death. Several of his children are buried in this cemetery.

Elder J. W. Moore
Birth:
Sep. 22, 1845
North Carolina
Death:
Jan. 27, 1932
North Carolina
Burial:
Bethel Original Freewill Baptist
Church Cemetery,
Four Oaks,
Johnston County,
North Carolina

J. H. Moore
Birth:
Sep. 11, 1874
Death:
Nov. 6, 1950
Burial:
Sweet Hope Freewill Baptist
Church Cemetery,
Pitt County, North Carolina

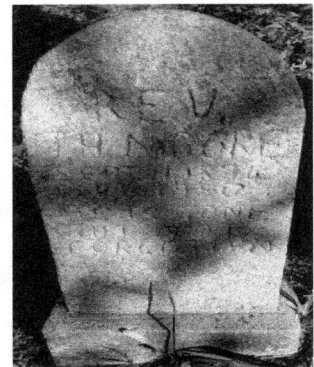

James Moore
Birth:
March 20, 1793
Edgecombe Co. North Carolina
Death:
1882
Greene County, North Carolina
Burial:
Free Union Church Cemetery,
Greene County,North Carolina

He moved from Edgecombe County to Greene County at a very young age and joined the Grimsley Free Will Baptist Church. He accepted the call to preach and was licensed in January 1825 and ordained in February 1827.

He became a very active preacher taking care of many churches in the area. In 1850 he started a church in Greene County that will he named Free Union. It became a flourishing church and he remained a member of the church until his departure in July 1882. Elder Moore served for 53 years as a faithful Minister. Elder J.M. Barfield heard him preach his last sermon which was a funeral service. He was so feeble that two man sat behind him ready to catch him should he began to fall. He had to be ushered in and out of the church building. His funeral was preached by brother Barfield who used the 13th and 14th chapters of the book of Revelation.

John Moore
Birth:
Jun. 1, 1832
Death:
Dec. 13, 1889
Burial:
Hodges Chapel Free Will Baptist Cemetery,
Harnett County, North Carolina

Eld. John Moore was a native of Harnett county, N. C., where he was converted and began to hold prayer-meetings, and was ordained to preach the Gospel, Oct. 13. 1874. He served the remainder of his life in the Master's cause and to Christianize this part of God's moral vineyard.

**Somewhere,
up in the measureless dome,
Beyond the power of the eye to see,
Is the city of Gold-Eternal Home-
Where he is waiting for you and me.**

Edward C Morris
Birth:
Aug. 16, 1891
Death:
Oct. 21, 1976
Burial:
Woodlawn Memorial Park,
Durham,
Durham County, North Carolina,
Plot: Section 5,
lock 12, Lot 15

He moved to Georgia from North Carolina in 1942 to pastor the Glennville and Ebenezer churches in Glennville which at the time were half-time churches. He was the first full-time promotional director in the state of Georgia beginning in 1947 serving through 1961. He worked to unite the state of Georgia. He started printing and sending out a monthly paper which was named *Promotional Bulletin* which is still in use today by the state of Georgia. He was known as a leader, promotional director, editor and publisher, and had an interested in the state youth camp program. During his time the work in Georgia grew and even land given to the state in 1948 for the youth camp. Many new churches were formed, joining the state association which had begun in 1937. By 1953 the state of Georgia had 127 churches. Even though the state Association was relatively young at the time. The Chattahoochee Association, was the oldest Association being organized in 1842 and was the first to have all of its churches participating in the state work.

After his resignation in 1961 Rev. Morris returned to North Carolina.

**Today is not a day of demotion,
But a day of crowning.**

James Clayton Moye
Birth:
Jul. 19, 1890
Greene County, North Carolina
Death:
May 21, 1961
Wilson, North Carolina
Burial:
Snow Hill Cemetery,
Snow Hill,
Greene County,
North Carolina

He attended Ayden Seminary and the Whitsett Institute afterwards, serving Free Will Baptist churches as pastor in. Pitt, Green and Lenoir counties, but had to retire in 1949 because of failing health. He served in the North Carolina

General Assembly as the Representative from Greene County for three terms, 1929, 1931 and 1933. He was Mayor of Snow Hill for six years and served on the Snow Hill School Board. He was also on the Board of Directors of the Free Will Baptist Children's Home in Middlesex. He was a former moderator of the North Carolina Free Will Baptist Convention and was a benefactor of the Free Will Baptist College in Mt. Olive. J. C. Moye Library was named in his honor. He was an extensive farmer and also operated a Chevrolet dealership in the Snow Hill for 27 years.

Addie H Outlaw
Birth:
Aug. 15, 1871
Death:
Nov. 27, 1942
Burial:
Suncrest Cemetery,
Monroe, Union County,
North Carolina

Clarence H Overman, Jr
Birth:
Oct. 31, 1930
Death:
May 23, 2012
Pikeville, Wayne County,
North Carolina
Burial:
Pikeville Cemetery Pikeville,
Wayne County, North Carolina

At the age of fourteen, C.H. joined Union Grove Free Will Baptist Church, where his lifelong career with the Free Will Baptist denomination began. In 1952, he was ordained into the ministry and spent sixty years serving as a Free Will Baptist minister.

He graduated from Atlantic Christian College in 1957 with a degree in Religion and has held numerous pastorates in eastern North Carolina. The Rev. Overman was most recently a member of Rose Hill OFWB Church. C.H. also taught in the public school system for 20 years and was a member of the Ayden Rotary Club for 31 years. Throughout the years he has served as pastor of 12 churches and served on various boards and committees. He served as editor of FWB press for more the 16 years, and general secretary of the OFWB Convention for more than five years.

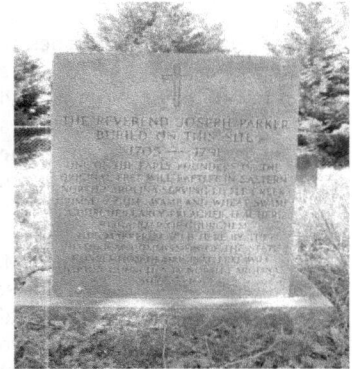

Joseph Parker
Birth:
1705
Death:
1791 Wheat Swamp,
Lenoir County,
North Carolina
Burial:
Private burial ground on
Cajah Barfied place,
Lenoir County,
North Carolina

He was one of the earliest founders and preachers in the Free Will Baptists is North Carolina. The Historical Commission of the North Carolina Original Free Will Baptist erected a highway sign there in 1966.

The marker in at the church started by Joseph Parker at about 1760 and remained a Free Will Baptist Church until 1843 when it was lost to the Disciples of Christ.

Joseph Parker is buried on a private plot near this church.

Christopher Lafayette "C.L."
Patrick
Birth:
Aug. 17, 1911
Death:
Dec. 9, 1996
Burial:
Snow Hill Cemetery,
Snow Hill, Greene County,
North Carolina,

Thomas E. Peden
Birth:
Sep. 13, 1832
Huntington Township,
Gallia County, Ohio
Death:
Feb. 3, 1913
Ayden, Pitt County,
North Carolina
Burial:
Ayden Cemetery,
Ayden, Pitt County,
North Carolina

Ordained Free Will Baptist minister, church planter, college president and a faithful man to his calling. He was ordained May 8, 1859 in Syracuse, Meigs Co. OH, by Elders G. Goler and Ira. Z. Haning. He was still in college at the time but was teaching school and preaching to a congregation in the vicinity of Syracuse. He enlisted in Co. I, Ohio 173rd Infantry,16 Sep 1864 and mustered out 26 Jun 1865, at Nashville, TN (Official Records of the State of Ohio). He was active in the Ohio Yearly meeting, and pastored The Harrisburg Free Will Baptist Church. He served as Associate pastor of Rio Grande Church, Ohio, while connected with the Rio Grande College faculty during the 1870/1880's. He also served on the council when the Gilboa FWB Church Ohio, was organized. He was aware that Free Will Baptists in the north were taking steps toward a union with another denomination, and that there were FWB churches in the South not affiliated with the northern churches, and he envisioned a possible union of these southern branches of FWB into a national organization. He announced through the "Free Will Baptist" that a Gen. Conf. would convene in Nashville, TN. Oct. 7, 1896. Subsequent meetings were held, and Dr. Peden was a leading advocate of this organization hoping to bring a union of North and South, and avert any move toward a merger of the Northern FWB with another denomination.

His dream was not realized, but did succeed in drawing FWB in the South closer together. He was called from Ohio to the Seminary in Ayden, NC, beginning in 1899 (from his diary). He held the principalship until 1910, when he retired because of "age and declining health." Prof. Peden became head of the Theological Dept. when it was started. His tenure as head set the tone of the institution to provide a basic liberal arts education as well as theological training for a number of ministers who would render valuable services. He was well-liked, and esteemed by his peers, and honored for his service in the early beginning of the school. Rev. Robert F. Pittman, a graduate of the Seminary and a member of the faculty, conducted Prof. Peden's funeral.

Moses Washington
Peterson
Birth:
Apr. 14, 1794
North Carolina
Death:
Aug. 1, 1879
Burial:
Peterson Hill Cemetery,
Burnsville,
Yancey County,
North Carolina

A spiritual leader and guide in an early time in our history serving mainly in Western North Carolina.

Edgar T. Phillips
Birth:
Mar. 26, 1857
North Carolina
Death:
Dec. 27, 1945
North Carolina
Burial:
Ayden Cemetery,
Ayden, Pitt County,
North Carolina

Cedric Dixon Pierce, Jr
Birth:
unknown
Wayne County, North Carolina
Death:
Oct. 23, 2012
Greenville
Pitt County, North Carolina
Burial:
Wayne Memorial Park
Goldsboro, Wayne County,
North Carolina

Pauline Pinyan
Birth:
unknown
Death:
Apr. 27, 2010
Kernersville, Forsyth County
North Carolina
Burial:
Eastlawn Gardens of Memory,
Kernersville,
Forsyth County, North Carolina

She was an ordained minister of the North Carolina State Association.

Isaac H. Pipkin
Birth:
Feb. 28, 1835
Death:
Aug. 4, 1917
Burial:
Core Point Free Will Baptist Church Cemetery
Core Point, Beaufort County,
North Carolina

A minister in the early work of Free Will Baptists in North Carolina.Bottom Inscription:"I have fought a good fight, I have finished my course, I have kept the faith." Spouse: Ellen Z Pipkin (1838 - 1915).

Robert F. Pittman
Birth:
Nov. 8, 1883
Jerome, Bladen County,
North Carolina
Death
Jul. 15, 1938
Ayden,
Pitt County,North Carolina
Burial:
Ayden Cemetery,
Ayden,
Pitt County,North Carolina

An ordained Free Will Baptist minister and educator. He taught at Mt. Olive College, NC. He also pastored churches at Sweetgum Grove, Bethany, and Ayden, which erected an imposing stone at his death showing their admiration and esteem for his work among them.

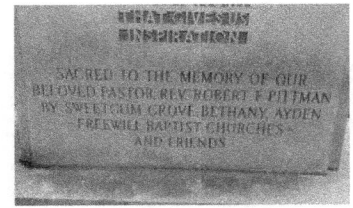

Matthew C. Prescott
Birth:
1873
Death:
1943
Pamlico County, North Carolina
Burial:
Grantsboro Cemetery,
Grantsboro,
Pamlico County, North Carolina

Free Will Baptist minister in eastern North Carolina.

Francis Radford
Birth:
December 1, 1929,
Davidson County,
North Carolina
Death:
Dec. 1, 2009
North Carolina
Burial:
Radford Cemetery
Madison County
North Carolina

Frances was valedictorian of her graduating class at Beech Glen High School when she was 16 years old in 1941. When Frances was a young girl, she went to a secret prayer place beneath a limb of an old fallen chestnut tree and fully surrendered her life to God. This full surrender meant giving up the plans to become a lawyer, and when she was 17 years old she became the first lady licensed to preach the gospel in the Free Will Baptist Churches in her area. Frances had a unique way of preaching the gospel by reaching the heights, depths and sweetness using illustrations in a way that made it a vivid, memorable message. Something you never forgot. It was so plain that the young could understand and so intense that the old were impressed and motivated. During her 60 plus years of active ministry, she served as pastor of several different churches in North Carolina and Tennessee and held revivals in many parts of the United States and Mexico. She was a member of Terry's Fork Free Will Baptist.

William Burkette Raper
Birth:
Sep. 10, 1927
Black Creek
Wilson County, North Carolina
Death:
Aug. 1, 2011
Mount Olive
Wayne County, North Carolina
Burial:
Friendship Free Will Baptist
Church Cemetery
Jones County, North Carolina

After the death of his father in 1936, Burkette entered the Free

Will Baptist orphanage in Middlesex, North Carolina, where he lived until graduation from Middlesex High School in 1944.

He entered the ministry in the Free Will Baptist denomination in 1946 and was ordained by the Western Conference in North Carolina. He served as the pastor of the Oak Grove, Stony Hill, Memorial Chapel of the Free Will Baptist Children's Home in Nash County; Arapahoe in Pamlico County, Friendship in Jones County, Howell Swamp and Hull Road in Greene County. All were in North Carolina. He earned a Bachelor of Arts in Liberal Arts in 1947 from Duke University and a Master of Divinity in 1952 from the Duke Divinity School. He served as the Promotional Director of the Original Free Will Baptist State Convention between 1953 and 1954. On August 2, 1954 he became the president of Mount Olive College, Mount Olive, North Carolina while it was still a two year liberal arts college. At that time he was only age 26, which was the youngest college president in the United States and when he retired as president in January of 1995 he held the distinction of being the current longest tenured president in the nation. During his 40 years as president he guided the development of the college from a two-year junior college to an accredited four-year senior college. In 1960 Atlantic Christian College awarded him an honorary Doctorate of Laws degree. In 1962, he earned a Master of Science in Higher Education from Florida State University. After retirement he served as the college's Director of Planned Giving for 10 years, making his tenure at the college a total of 50 years of service. Prior to his death, he held the distinction of being the longest tenured living ordained minister in the North Carolina Original FWB convention. All together, his ministry to his denomination led him to complete 65 years of service to God and mankind.

Archie W. Ratliff
Birth:
Nov. 29, 1949
Sneedville,
Hancock County, Tennessee
Death:
Dec. 17, 2012
Houston, Harris County, Texas
Burial:
Pinelawn Memorial Park,
Kinston,
Lenoir County, North Carolina

Senior Pastor of Bethel Free Will Baptist Church and Bethel Christian Academy in Kinston, NC, passed away at M.D. Anderson Cancer Center in Houston, Texas. Following graduation from Free Will Baptist Bible College in Nashville, Tn. Ratliff was ordained in 1972 in Glennville, Georgia, where he served five years as pastor of Glennville Free Will Baptist Church. He served as Moderator of the South Georgia Association from 1974 – 1976. and then Peace Free Will Baptist Church, Indianapolis, IN. He served as Moderator of the Indiana State Association for seven of his 14-year tenure there. Archie served as Senior Pastor of Bethel Free Will Baptist Church twenty-two years. Pastor Ratliff battled and defeated esophageal cancer in 2009; however, the radiation and chemotherapy treatments caused him to develop leukemia. Pastor Ratliff was a great respected leader in the Free Will Baptist Denomination. He served 12 years (1996 – 2008) on the Welch College Board of Trustees, including several years as vice chairman. and was very involved with Free Will Baptist International Missions. Pastor Ratliff guided Bethel Church to be globally involved in spreading the Gospel.

Willie E Renfrow
Birth:
Sep. 11, 1914
North Carolina
Death:
Oct. 23, 1970
North Carolina
Burial:
Branch Chapel Free Will Baptist Church
Smithfield
Johnston County, North Carolina

Rev. Willie E. and Sallie Hare Renfrow set up a Renfrow Family Endowment Scholarship for the Christian Ministry.

...he that never doubted of his state, He may, perhaps–he may–too late.

William Walter Reynolds
Birth:
Oct. 25, 1926
Columbia, Tyrrell County, North Carolina
Death:
Dec. 22, 2009
Greenville, Pitt County, North Carolina
Burial:
Hollywood Cemetery, Farmville, Pitt County North Carolina

A veteran of WWII (United States Army), he was ordained to the ministry of the Original Free Will Baptists (Albermarle Conference) on July 30, 1949. He graduated from Free Will Baptist Bible College in Nashville, TN, in 1951. He pastored churches in Tennessee and in North Carolina retiring in 2001.

Gabriel Pinkney Rice
Birth:
Aug. 10, 1854
Marshall, North Carolina
Death:
Jan. 20, 1923
Asheville
Buncombe County, North Carolina
Burial:
West Memorial Park
Weaverville
Buncombe County, North Carolina

He was converted in 1875 and received his ordination on December 14, 1878. His ministry was in the vicinity of Eastern Tennessee, much of it having been spent in evangelistic work; he baptized about 1100 converts.He was the son of Isaac Rachel Elizabeth Arrowood Rice

Roy Lee Rikard, Sr
Birth:
May 27, 1909
Caldwell County, North Carolina
Death:
Mar. 14, 2008
Gastonia, Gaston County, North Carolina
Burial:
Gaston Memorial Park, Gastonia, Gaston County, North Carolina

He was founder of Cramerton Free Will Baptist Church and a Bible Institute.

Fred A. Rivenbark, Sr
Birth:
unknown
Duplin County, North Carolina
Death:
Aug. 23, 2000
Durham, Durham County, North Carolina
Burial:
Woodlawn Memorial Park, Durham, Durham County, North Carolina

He was a resident of Durham for 52 years. Rev. Rivenbark was born in Duplin County, N.C., and was a native of Mount Olive. The Rev. Rivenbark pastored Sherron Acres Free Will Baptist Church, prior to retiring from full-time ministry, and served on staff there as assistant pastor for 25 years. He also pastored Oak Grove Free Will Baptist Church in Durham, St. Paul Free Will Baptist Church, Elizabeth City, N.C., First Free Will Baptist Church, Wilson, N.C., Fairmont Park Free Will Baptist Church, Norfolk, Virginia Beach Free Will Baptist Church, and Stoney Creek Free Will Baptist Church, Goldsboro. In addition to pastoring seven churches, Mr. Rivenbark preached in hundreds of revival meetings.

John Ephriam Sawyer
Birth:
Jan. 26, 1886
Death:
May 15, 1962
Arlington, Virginia
Burial:
Ayden Cemetery, Ayden,
Pitt County, North Carolina

He studied at Ayden Seminary after which he received his ministerial credentials. Later, he was principal at Ayden Seminary and taught at the Seminary for eight years until he was 76 years of age. He believed in a strong academic program coupled with a strong biblical foundation. He was a fluent speaker who took his the ministry seriously.

William Riley Sawyer
Birth:
Jul. 20, 1884
Merritt, Pamlico County,
North Carolina
Death:
Oct. 17, 1922
Pamlico County, North Carolina
Burial:
Trent Free Will Baptist Church
Cemetery
Pamlico County, North Carolina

He was affiliated most of his life with the Trenton Free Will Baptist Church, Merritt, Pamlico County North Carolina. He was associated with the Free Will Baptist Press as early as 1874 as an agent, and was on the Board of Directors from at least 1895 until 1900. He became president of the company in 1901 and continued until 1912. He was the father of John E. Sawyer.

Adam Scott
Birth:
Jan. 23, 1917
Texas County, Missouri
Death:
Mar. 26, 2004
North Carolina
Burial:
Knollwood Cemetery, Clayton,
Johnston County, North Carolina

He was a Free Will Baptist minister and part of a large relationship consisting of ministers with names of Scott, Smith, Vandivort that had ministries across the FWB denomination.

LTC David Leonard Spears
Birth:
Nov. 24, 1960
Vicenza,Veneto, Italy

Death:
Dec. 25, 2011
Sanford, Lee County,
North Carolina
Burial:
Jonesboro Cemetery,
Sanford, Lee County,
North Carolina

A Free Will Baptist minister and Chaplain.

R. B. Spencer
Birth:
Mar. 2, 1886
Pamlico County,
North Carolina
Death:
Jan. 25, 1954
Pitt County, North Carolina
Burial:
Ayden Cemetery, Ayden,
Pitt County, North Carolina

A minister and educator. He was educated in Whitsett Institute and the University of North Carolina. He taught for a number of years. In 1932 he was ordained to the gospel Ministry. He was elected to the position of Editor of "The Free Will Baptist" in 1936, which position he held until September 1953. He was a member of Little Creek Free Will Baptist Church. Funeral services were held at the Free Will Baptist Church by the Rev. R. N. Hinnant, of Micro, assisted by the Rev. Bruce Barrow of Snow Hill, and the Rev. Charles Craddock of Ayden.

Chester V. Stanley
Birth:
1912
North Carolina
Death:
1968
North Carolina
Burial:
Bethel Original Freewill Baptist
Church Cemetery, Four Oaks,
Johnston County, North Carolina

James Dallas Stepps
Birth:
Nov. 2, 1940
Pitt County, North Carolina
Death:
Sep. 2, 2013
Duffield
Scott County, Virginia
Burial:
Pinewood Memorial Park
Greenville
Pitt County, North Carolina,
Rev. James "Dallas" Stepps, 72,a
native of Pitt County, was a
graduate of Hookerton High
School and attended FWB Bible
College in Nashville, TN. He
pastored in TN, SC, NC and in FL
for 30 years, and for 15 years
served as the NC Advancement
Representative for Harvest FWB
Child Care Ministries in Duffield,
VA. He was a member of Unity
FWB Church.

Simon Hill Styron, Jr
Birth:
Mar., 1891
Sealevel
Carteret County, North Carolina
Death:
Dec. 17, 1939
Pine Level,Johnston County, North
Carolina
Burial:
Oliver Cemetery
Johnston County, North Carolina

Early Free Will Baptist minister
serving in North Carolina. He was
married to Ida Oliver.his parents
were Simon Hill Styron (1851 -
1933) Nancy Lupton Styron and
his son was Simon Daniel Styron
(1925 - 1990).

Thomas O. Terry, Jr
Birth:
1921
Death:
2009
Craven County,
North Carolina
Burial:
Greenleaf Memorial Park,
New Bern,
Craven County
North Carolina

He was a Free Will Baptist
minister in eastern North
Carolina.

Jacob Utley
Birth:
Nov. 6, 1803
Raleigh
Wake County, North Carolina
Death:
Mar. 28, 1888
Thomasville
Davidson County, North Carolina
Burial:
Gods Acre
Thomasville
Davidson County, North Carolina

Rev. Jacob Utley, was an early
pioneer Free Will Baptist minister
in NC, whose name appears as one
of the several ministers who
helped sustain the scattered
churches after 1832. On Sept. 1,
1887, he came to the orphanage
as a home for aged ministers. No
others were ever received as the
plan was abandoned.
Spouse: Aplis Wallace Utley
(1810 - 1888).
Inscription:
Native of Wake County, for many
years a missionary pastor in
North Carolina.

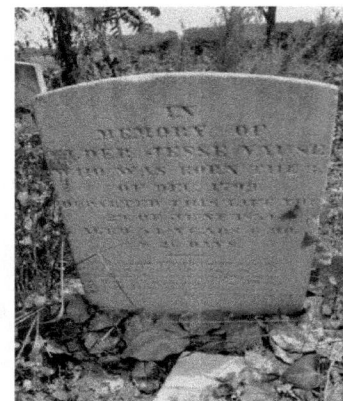

Elder Jesse Vause
Birth:
Dec., 1799
Death:
Jun. 29, 1854
Burial:
Vause Family Cemetery,
Lenoir County,
North Carolina

One of the very early Free Will
Baptist preachers in North
Carolina.

Robert West
Birth:
1947
Death:
2009
Burial:
Hills of Neuse Memorial Gardens,
Smithfield,
Johnston County,
North Carolina

Free Will Baptist pastor and missionary to the Ivory Coast, Africa.

**I bless the Christ of God,
I rest on love divine,
And with unfaltering lip and heart,
I call the Saviour mine.
His cross dispels each doubt;
I bury in his tomb
Each thought of unbelief and fear,
Each lingering shade of gloom.**

Lee Whaley
Birth:
1914
Death:
1988
North Carolina
Burial:
Pinelawn
Memorial Park,
Kinston, Lenoir County,
North Carolina

He was a Free Will Baptist pastor serving in various pastorates and was a home missionary to Alaska.

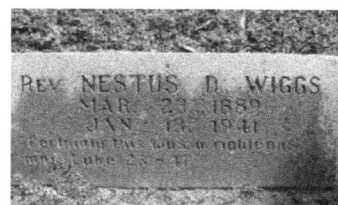

John Wheeler
Birth:
Jan. 1, 1800
North Carolina
Death:
Aug. 15, 1871
Yancey County, North Carolina
Burial:
Silvers Cemetery, Pensacola,
Yancey County, North Carolina

He was a early minister and leader whose legacy spreads across a four state area consisting of N.C., TN., Va. West Va.

Nestus VanDelon Wiggs
Birth:
Mar. 23, 1889
Pine Level, Johnson Co., N.C
Death:
Jan. 13, 1941
Burial:
Cedar Grove Cemetery,
New Bern, Craven County,
North Carolina

He was a member of the Eastern Conference. In 1912 he entered the Free Will Baptists Seminary in Ayden for his Theological study while serving churches in the eastern part of N.C. He was active in revival work and other activities of the Denomination. He served as moderator of the Union Meeting and was a member of the Church Extension Board of the State Convention of N.C. for several years. His funeral was conducted by D.W. Alexander, J.L. Hodges and J.C. Griffin.

Missionary Emma Ruth *Bennett* Willey
Birth:
Dec. 19, 1935
Death:
Dec. 13, 1972
Panama City,
Panama, Panama
Burial:
New Bern Memorial Cemetery,
Trent Woods,
Craven County, North Carolina,
Plot: Section A

Served as a missionary in Panama for Free Will Baptist missions. She served as a missionary in the interior as well as the capital Panama city. She died in the Gorgus hospital in Panama City and was returned to New Bern for her burial. She was the wife of Thomas Willey, Junior

Missionary Zadie Volena Wilson
Birth:
Mar. 11, 1918
Rutherford County,
North Carolina
Death:
Mar. 30, 2001
McDowell County,
North Carolina
Burial:
McDowell Memorial Park,
Marion
McDowell County,
North Carolina

A missionary to India for many years. She later worked for the Presbyterian Journal until her retirement. During her retirement, she continued to be faithful in ministry visiting the hospitals, nursing homes and shut-ins. She also continued to promote the missionary endeavor in India through her many speaking engagements in churches.

Marcellus A. Woodard
Birth:
September 6, 1879
Greene County, North Carolina
Death:
1957
Pitt County, North Carolina
Burial:
Reedy Branch Baptist Church,
Winterville,
Pitt County, North Carolina

An early Free Will Baptist preacher who in 1903 at the age of 24 was licensed to preach the gospel at Howell Swamp Free Will Baptist Church, Greene County, North Carolina. He prepared for the ministry at the Free Will Baptist Seminary, in Ayden and began his early ministry in the Midway Association in South Georgia in 1909. He married the daughter of W.A. McDonald, a pioneer Free Will Baptist minister

in South Georgia. His ministry existed in South Georgia and North Florida until the fall of 1921, when he returned to his native state becoming the pastor of the church in Davis, North Carolina. For 53 years he was a faithful minister the gospel with 32 of those years as a member of the Central conference of North Carolina..

T. E. Woody
Birth:
Apr. 4, 1876
Death:
Dec. 10, 1967
Yancey County,
North Carolina
Burial:
Will Young Cemetery,
Yancey County,
North Carolina

Free Will Baptist preacher in western North Carolina.

Yea, saith the Spirit, that they may rest from their labours; and their works do follow them.

North Dakota

Avery Clark
Birth:
Oct. 17, 1818 Springfield,
Hampden County,
Massachusetts
Death:
Sep. 3, 1863
Dickey County,
North Dakota
Burial:
Whitestone Hill
State Historic Site,
Merricourt,
Dickey County,
North Dakota

Rev. Avery Clark moved to Iowa from his native Mass. in 1846, and began preaching about 1853. He was ordained a Freewill Baptist minister in May 1856 at Delaware Clayton Q.M., Iowa. He was a strong man, positive in his convictions and at Pres. Lincoln's Emancipation Proclamation, he said, "Now I can go." He acted as a "chaplain" in ministering to his regiment, and fell in battle far from home. Enlisted Sept. 22, 1862. Sixth Iowa Cavalry Mustered Sept. 22, 1862. Killed in action Sept. 3, 1863, White Stone Hill, Dakota.

Benjamin Rackliff
Birth:
Jun. 3, 1819
Montville, Maine
Death:
Sep. 10, 1892
Burial:
Prairie Home Cemetery
Gilby
Grand Forks County,
North Dakota

He was ordained in 1858 and was pastor of the church at Wesley, Maine for eight years. He held several local offices and was a representative in the Maine Legislature. He later was a pastor of the Diamond Bluff church, Wisconsin, but much of his ministry was in itinerant work for short periods preaching in a weak churches.

Ohio

Walter Abrams
Birth:
1894
Death:
1979
Burial:
Lagrange Cemetery,
Ironton,
Lawrence County, Ohio

Schuyler Aldrich
Birth:
Apr. 26, 1822
Ontario, Canada
Death:
Sep. 20, 1904
Buffalo, Erie County, New York
Burial:
Evergreen Cemetery, Pierpont,
Ashtabula County, Ohio

He was brought to Christ in 1839, and studied at Oberlin College, Ohio receiving his ordination May 23, 1847. His ministry was with the Mecca, Henrietta. Pittsfield, and Macedonia churches, Ohio, and with the Buffalo, Bethany, Phoenix, Elmira, and Poland churches, N. Y. Several revivals resulted from his labors, and about 200 converts were baptized by him. About 1880, he made his home in Buffalo, N. Y. His devotion to the cause of education is evidenced by a gift of ten thousand dollars to Hillsdale College, to be used in endowing a theological professorship.

Jonas Allen
Birth:
Royalton, Mass.
Death:
Sept. 29, 1864
Madison, Ohio
Burial:
Dock Road Cemetery
Madison, Lake County, Ohio

Allen died aged 86 years. He was baptized by Elder Alva Buzzell, in 1809. At the close of the war of 1812 he began to preach, having his first revival in Charleston, Vt., where a church was organized, and he was ordained in 1824. Soon after churches were organized at East Charleston and at Brighton as a result of his labors. About 1837 he moved to Madison, Ohio, where he continued to preach until more than threescore and ten. He was devoted to every good work, enjoying the work of the ministry and awaiting in confidence for the rest prepared.

James Thornton Arthur
Birth:
Apr. 22, 1853
Pinkerman
Scioto County, Ohio
Death:
Oct. 14, 1925
Scioto County, Ohio
Burial:
Harrison Furnace Cemetery
Minford
Scioto County, Ohio

He was ordained on August 20, 1887 and spent several months in evangelistic work in the Little Scioto Quarterly Meeting in Ohio and then also in the Kentucky Yearly Meeting. At one time he pastored the Harrison church which is at Minford Ohio.

Hobart C. Ashby
Birth:
Nov. 8, 1925
Virginia
Death:
Jan. 16, 1998
Dayton,
Montgomery County, Ohio
Burial:
Miami Valley Memory Gardens,
Centerville,
Montgomery County, Ohio

He was ordained a Free Will Baptist minister in 1956. He began his pastoral duties in 1957 at the Fairborn Free Will Baptist Church where he served three years and in 1961, the Virginia born minister, became the pastor of the First Dayton Free Will Baptist Church, where he served for 33 years. Some 30 men answered the call to the ministry under his ministry. He retired from the church in 1994.

He was a member of the Board of Directors of the Ohio State Association of Free Will Baptists for 22 years. Twice he was moderator of the Ohio State Association. He served six years on the national Home Missions Board. And preached at the national convention in Anaheim, California in 1980. He served in the U.S. Navy during WWII aboard the USS Crux in both the Atlantic and Pacific theaters.

George Washington Baker
Birth:
Oct. 22, 1803
Litchfield Corners,
Kennebec County, Maine
Death:
Oct. 11, 1881
Marion, Marion County, Ohio
Burial:
Marion Cemetery,
Marion, Marion County, Ohio

One of the "Fathers" of the denomination in Ohio. He came from Litchfield, Maine, with his parents in 1822, and settled in Marion, Ohio until his death. He was converted under the labors of Rev. David Dudley and united with the Marion Free Will Baptist Church in 1827.

He received license to preach, though with the firm resolve that he would never be ordained. However, when his labors were crowned with success and he found himself surrounded by many converts who were pressing him to baptize them, he could refuse no longer, and in 1834, was ordained. He was pastor of churches, but he delighted in, and greatly preferred revival work. He was deeply spiritual, affectionate in manner, and a good singer. He was sustained by a large body and a strong constitution. He preached to all classes throughout the region. It is estimated that no less than 3,000 persons became professed Christians under his ministry, and 2,500 of these he baptized. Of these, some twenty-six entered the ministry. He continued to preach until the Fall of 1880. During his long ministry, he took a prominent place in the general state and denominational work. His last sermon was preached August 28, 1881, at a reunion of the pastors and members of the Centreburgh church, one of the first he gathered.

Clifford H. Ball
Birth:
unknown
Death:
Feb. 22, 2007
Kansas City,
Wyandotte County, Kansas
Burial:
Forest Lawn Memorial Gardens,
Columbus, Franklin County, Ohio

Clifford died in Kansas City but was the former pastor at Trinity Free Will Baptist Church and Welch Avenue Free Will Baptist Churches in Columbus, Ohio. He was the current pastor of the Bethel Free Will Baptist Church in Kansas City at his death.

Mance Ball
Birth:
1901,
Death:
1967
Scioto County, Ohio
Burial:
South Webster Cemetery,
South Webster,Scioto County,
Ohio

Early Free Will Baptist minister in southern Ohio

Vernie Bare
Birth:
Oct. 22, 1926
Death:
Dec. 1, 2006
Burial
Ohio Western Reserve National Cemetery,
Rittman,
Medina County, Ohio, Plot: Section 20 Plot 189

Pastor of the Rock of Ages FWB Church.

Peter Barnhart
Birth:
Sep. 22, 1897
Death:
Aug. 8, 1993
Burial:
Lawrence Furnace Cemetery,
Lawrence Furnace,
Lawrence County, Ohio

Free Will Baptist preacher in the early days in southern Ohio.

Selah Barrett
Birth:
1790
Stafford,
Tolland County, Connecticut
Death: there my
Jul. 12, 1860
Rutland, Meigs County, Ohio
Burial:
Miles Cemetery, Rutland,
Meigs County, Ohio
Barrett was baptized by Elder Alva Buzzell at Strafford, Vermont. in 1812. Five years later he moved to Rutland, Ohio, where he was one of the early Free Baptists. He was licensed in 1837 and ordained at Cheshire in 1849. His ministerial labors were with the churches of the Meigs Quarterly Meeting of which he was clerk as early as 1835, and with several in the Athens Q.M.

Selah Hibbard Barrett
Birth:
Feb. 24, 1822
Rutland, Meigs County, Ohio
Sep. 1, 1883
Rutland, Meigs County, Ohio
Burial:
Miles Cemetery,
Rutland, Meigs County, Ohio

Deprived of the advantages of the schools because of ill health, he devoted perseveringly to study at home and gained a knowledge of the branches usually taught in college and afterwards completed courses in law and medicine. He experienced forgiveness of sins in 1838, received license to preach in 1845, and was ordained in 1856 by the Meigs Q. M., his ministry being spent within its bounds. He devoted much time to literary labor, having been a frequent correspondent of the *Morning Star* and other periodicals nearly forty years, and prepared several pamphlets and books, among them "*Memoirs of Eminent Preachers of the Freewill*

Baptist Denomination," and an Autobiography of about 400 pages.

Daniel E. Bates
Birth:
Feb. 2, 1927
Norton, Wise County, Virginia
Death:
Aug. 16, 2010
Ohio
Burial:
Oak Grove Memorial Park,
Lexington,
Richland County, Ohio

Pastor of the Blooming Grove Free Will Baptist Church.

Samuel D. Bates
Birth:
Oct. 13, 1828
Oneida County, New York
Death:
Sep. 17, 1886
Marion,
Marion County, Ohio
Burial:
Marion Cemetery, Marion,
Marion County, Ohio,
Plot: Sharpless Sect. S43 L1

Samuel D. Bates, D.D, in the fall of 1834 moved to Ohio, and settled in Trumbull Co. Samuel was reared on a farm but received his education at Geauga Seminary, which became a part of Hillsdale College, Michigan. He began to teach school when he was 19 years old and in 1848-49 taught the school at which James A. Garfield, afterwards President of the United States, was a pupil. Garfield was three years Mr. Bates' junior, and was persuaded to attend Geauga, from which a friendship existed until President Garfield's tragic death. Of Mr. Bates, Garfield once said, "To him I owe more than to any other living man for what I am today." He continued to teach until he entered the ministry of the Free Will Baptist Church in 1851. The first six years were spent in Trumbull Co. Ohio. In 1857 he came to Marion to accept the charge of the FWB church in that city. He remained pastor of the local church without interruption until 1876, and during his ministry of 19 years built up a strong congregation. When he came to Marion, the Free Will Baptist worshipped in the old church located on Mt. Vernon avenue, but through his energy and executive ability the church on East Center street was built at a cost of $16,000, more than half of which was donated outside of the society. He also was connected with the erection of five other church edifices in the county. He organized the Grand Prairie Free Baptist Church, and was its pastor for nine years. He organized the Claridon Free Will

Baptist Church during the winter of 1870-71, and assisted in building the first church of that denomination in the township. He was pastor of the Claridon Church for 15 years, ministering to the wants of his people until a few months prior to his death. Mr. Bates was zealous in the cause of education as well as religion. He was a trustee of Hillsdale College for 15 years. In 1872 he was elected president of Ridgeville (Indiana) College and so continued up to the time of his death. In June 1884, Ohio Central College, at Iberia, in recognition of his thorough learning and earnest work in behalf of education, conferred upon him the degree of Doctor of Divinity. (Marion County, Ohio, 1907 History, Biography)

"DOTH GOD FAVOUR THEE? FEAR NOT, THOUGH THE WORLD FROWN UPON THEE."

Warner Beebe
Birth:
Feb. 1, 1808
Death:
Oct. 5, 1851
Burial:
Beebe Town Cemetery,
Beebetown,
Medina County, Ohio

He was born Canandaigua, Ontario, NY. By 1825, he was in Liverpool, Ohio, where he united with the Free Will Baptist Church. He was ordained to the gospel ministry in 1835. In 1850, he represented the Ohio Northern Yearly Meeting in the General Conference.

Ben Bird
Birth:
Sep. 1, 1907
Death:
May 11, 1990
Burial:
White Gravel Cemetery,
Minford,
Scioto County, Ohio

Brother Bird's ministry was in the southern part of Ohio.

James Andrew Blair
Birth:
Oct. 10, 1928
Kentucky
Jun. 25, 2004
Crossville,
Cumberland County, Tennessee
Burial:
Miami Memorial Park Cemetery,
Covington, Miami County, Ohio

He was a retired minister, a member of Williams Road

Freewill Baptist Church and attended Crossville First Freewill Baptist. He pastored for more than 30 years in the Ohio area and was the founder of Troy Freewill Baptist Church in Troy, OH. He truly loved taking care of his people in the church. He was also a U.S. Army veteran, having served our country during Korea.

Orvil Blake
Birth:
Apr. 8, 1824
Death:
Aug. 12, 1877
Burial:
Westlawn Cemetery
Mantua, Portage County, Ohio
Plot: Sect A, row 07

Blake, a native of Cornwall, Conn., married in 1850, and two years later moved to Mantua, Ohio, where he lived, labored, and died. His conversion and early labors were with the larger Baptist body, but as they refused him ordination because of his Free Baptist views, he found a home with the latter. He assisted in gathering several churches, and, besides his pastoral work at Mantua, preached also at Brimfield, Troy, Maple Grove, Hiram Rapids and Chester. He was a grand man, loved by all, and his death, at the age of 53 years, was a great loss to the Yearly Meeting. He had lectured on various topics, was correspondent of several journals, and had represented his county in the State Legislature.

John Leonard Blount, Sr
Birth:
Jul. 18, 1930 Ohio
Death:
Apr. 10, 2006 Wilmington,
Clinton County, Ohio
Burial:
Morrow Cemetery Morrow,
Warren County, Ohio

Blount was the pastor of Beech

Grove Church of God that later became the Beech Grove Free Will Baptist Church. He served as pastor from 1988-2006. The last year Rev. Allen Kinard assisted him in his duties.

Marvin Booth
Birth:
unknown
Death:
Feb. 17, 2000
Columbus, Ohio
Burial:
Obetz Cemetery,
Obetz, Franklin County, Ohio,
Plot: Sect 23, lot 91, spc 1

He founded in 1966 the Friendly FWB church in Columbus and pastored it for 25 years. At the time of his death he was pastor of the Reese Community Church. A noted leader and respected minister. He was 65 at his death.,

Charles R. Bowman
Birth:
Jun. 25, 1924
Ramsey,
Nelson County, Virginia
Death:
Apr. 7, 2008
Columbus,
Franklin County, Ohio
Burial:
Alton Cemetery,
Alton, Franklin County, Ohio
He served our country in the United States Army during the Second World War, and had lived in Columbus, Ohio since 1952. He attended Moody Bible Institute and Liberty University. Rev. Bowman was gloriously saved on March 16, 1952 at Old Memorial Hall in Columbus, Ohio, and began preaching in 1953 and would preach everywhere the doors

were opened. Many people accepted Christ as their personal Savior under his ministry. He pastored the Westside FWB Church for 35 years, and faithfully served this church and congregation through 1987. He also pastored in Key West, FL for ten years.

Homer S. Brooks
Birth:
Feb. 9, 1926
Harrogate,
Claiborne County,
Tennessee
Death:
Feb. 11, 2003
Springfield,
Clark County, Ohio
Burial:
Ferncliff Cemetery,
Springfield,
Clark County, Ohio

Rev. Brooks was in the ministry for 54 years. He pastored the South Charleston Church for 35 years. In addition, he pastored the Sunset Church in Springfield for 18 years. For much of his ministry, while he pastored, he would preach 26 weeks of revivals for other churches. He was well known as an evangelist across the region. Brother Homer also was active in denominational roles, holding offices in the Little Miami Conference.

A Righteous Child Has Great Joy.

Morgan Hillman Brown
Birth:
Feb. 16, 1901
Death:
Mar. 8, 1986
Burial:
Vernon Cemetery,
Lyra,
Scioto County, Ohio

Paul Russell Calvert
Birth:
Sep. 26, 1932
Yellow Springs,
Greene County, Ohio,
Death:
Mar. 11, 2010 Springfield,
Clark County, Ohio,
Burial:
Garlough Cemetery,
Pitchin,
Clark County, Ohio,

Rev. Calvert was a member of the Beatty Freewill Baptist Church and was an avid fisherman. He was bi-vocational and was retired form Navistar.

Hamilton James Carr
Birth:
1810
New York
Death:
Apr. 8, 1887
Jackson, Jackson County,
Ohio
Burial:
Fairmount Cemetery,
Jackson, Jackson County,
Ohio

He was the son of Walter Moore Carr. His first wife Rebecca Conaway died in 1845 in Alexander Twp., Ohio. After his wife and father died, he married Ziare and they moved to Jackson, Ohio, where he was a Free Will Baptist preacher until his death. He was pastor of several churches in the Ohio River Y. M. The first two years of his ministry he baptized over 200 persons. He organized many churches and aided in the ordination. of several ministers. He was one of the trustees and an earnest supporter of Rio Grande College. He represented Ohio at the 1880 Centennial Conference in New Hampshire and is pictured in the photo of those over the age of 70 at this meeting. He is in the front row right with Bible in his hand. He was active in his denomination. Mr. Carr was an anti-slavery man and a Republican. During Morgan's raid in Ohio he lost property and subjected to ill-treatment from the rebels.

John Casebolt
Birth:
1872
Death:
1959
Scioto County, Ohio
Burial
Bennett Cemetery,
Minford,
Scioto County, Ohio

Forrest L. Chamberlin
Birth:
Feb. 23, 1922
Scioto County, Ohio
Death:
Jun. 8, 2012
Portsmouth, Scioto County,
Ohio
Burial:
Vernon Cemetery,
Lyra, Scioto County, Ohio

Brother Chamberlin was one of the most respected ministers in southern Ohio. He was a retired barber and Free Will Baptist Minister ordained in 1947. He was the pastor of the Porter, Harrison, Long Run and Germany Hollow Free Will Baptist churches. However, his ministry extended beyond the local level and served on the Board of Directors for the Ohio State Association of Free Will Baptists for a number of years. He was active on various other committees and boards. He was a veteran of the United States Army serving during World War II in Germany and Austria as a radio operator with the 13th armored division.

Clarence O Clark
Birth:
1855
Death:
1943
Burial:
Calvary Baptist Cemetery, Rio Grande, Gallia County, Ohio

He was a very active minister, pastor, leader and professor at Rio Grande College before and after the merger with the Northern Baptist.

Uriah Chabot
Birth:
Feb. 6, 1816
Greene, Ohio
Death
Aug. 18, 1897
Burial:
Powellsville Cemetery
Powellsville
Scioto County, Ohio

He married Luvina Hudson on 29 Sep 1841 in Scioto Co. and they had six children one of which was Dr. G. W. Shabot. He was converted the same year of his marriage and received license to preach in 1854 and was ordained in 1874 after which he became minister to many churches in the little Scioto and Pine Creek Quarterly Meetings.

Rufus B. Clark
Birth:
Nov. 23, 1819
Conneaut,
Ashtabula County, Ohio
Death:
Nov. 25, 1889
Conneaut
Ashtabula County, Ohio
Burial:
City Cemetery, Conneaut,
Ashtabula County, Ohio

Rufus was converted in 1830 and attended Geauga Seminary, and was ordained in 1843. For sixteen years he was pastor of the church in his native town, and he since ministered to the Lenox, Cherry Valley, Burgh Hill, New Lyme, Greenburg and Colebrook, Ohio; Sheffield and Wellsburg, Pennsylvania; Warren, Illinois, and Fon du Lac and Winneconne Wisconsin churches. He was actively identified with the anti-slavery movement. He was a life member of the Home and Foreign Mission Societies. He wrote sketches of the early history of Conneaut and other towns in northern Ohio. He delivered many lectures on various topics and a contributor to the religious and secular press. Rev. Clark wrote a *"Early History of South Ridge"*, about Ashtabula Co, in 1880, and reprinted in 1985, by the Ashtabula County. Genealogical Society.

Sam Crabtree
Birth:
Apr. 17, 1917
Otway, Scioto County, Ohio
Death:
Feb. 4, 1997
McDermott, Scioto County, Ohio
Burial:
Scioto Burial Park,
McDermott, Scioto County, Ohio

Bi-Vocational minister retired from the Empire-Detroit steel Corporation where he was stationary engineer. He was also a Free Will Baptist Minister for 47 years pastoring churches in the area.

But only for a moment.

Phillip E. Crabtree
Birth:
May 5, 1912
Death:
Jan. 14, 1994
Burial:
South Webster Cemetery
South Webster
Scioto County, Ohio

Phillip E. Crabtree, 81, of Oak Hill Branch Road, South Webster, died at a Columbus hospital. The son of the late John A. and Viola Lute Crabtree, he was a miner in a clay mine, a member of the Eifort Free Will Baptist Church, and a Free Will Baptist minister for 54 years. He is survived by his wife Mallie Green Crabtree, who he married Oct. 31, 1932. He has a son who is a home missionary in New Brunswick, Canada.

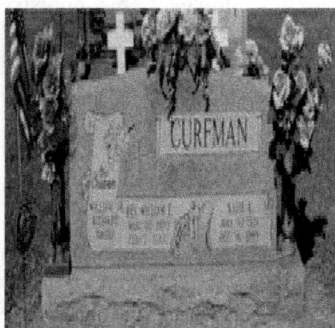

William Ershel Curfman
Birth:
Aug. 8, 1920
Ohio
Death:
Feb. 7, 2000
Gallipolis, Gallia County, Ohio
Burial:
Gravel Hill Cemetery, Cheshire,
Gallia County, Ohio

Ordained October 6, 1951 by the Freewill Baptist Church. He pastored the following Freewill Baptist Churches: Kellys Creek and Spring Hollow, West Virginia, Mt. Olive, Bidwell, Ohio, Coalton, Ohio., Old Kyger, Ohio. and Centerpoint, Ohio., where he was a member. Retired Blacksmith, Kaiser-Aluminum Plant, Ravenswood, W.Va. WW II Marine Veteran, serving when Pearl Harbor, Hawaii, was attacked in 1941. Life member Middleport DAV 53. he was a lifelong member of the Meigs County Free Will Baptist Association and a member of the General Board for the Ohio Association of Free Will Baptists.

Elial Curtis
Birth:
Connecticut
Death:
September 19, 1848
New Haven, Ohio
Burial:
Guinea Corners Cemetery
Huron County, Ohio
He was a native of Connecticut and in his early life moved to New York then

later to Ohio. He was ordained in 1837 and died at New Haven. He was a judicious brother, safe in Counsel, careful in deportment, highly esteemed by a large circle of Christian friends.

Budd L. Darst
Birth:
1900
Gallia County, Ohio
Death:
1993
Gallia County, Ohio
Burial:
Gravel Hill Cemetery,
Cheshire, Gallia County, Ohio

Herbert C. Davis
Birth:
Mar. 21, 1934
Johnson County, Kentucky
Death:
Sep. 3, 2012
Fairborn, Greene County, Ohio
Burial:
Byron Cemetery, Fairborn,
Greene County, Ohio

He was born in Johnson Co., Kentucky, the son of the late James Herbert and Alka (Sadler) Davis. Herb was employed with General Motors as a tool and die maker, retiring in 1982; and was a minister for over 50 years at many churches. One of Herb's hobbies was woodworking and enjoyed playing the violin and singing while Anna played the piano with him.

John Merrill Davis
Birth:
Nov. 16, 1846
Harrisonville,
Meigs County, Ohio
Death:
Nov. 11, 1920
Raccoon Township,
Gallia County, Ohio
Burial:
Calvary Baptist Cemetery,
Rio Grande, Gallia County, Ohio

His childhood education was in the public schools of Scipio Township. He joined the Free Will Baptist denomination in 1860 and in 1863 served the Government as an army teamster during the Civil War. Between March and September of 1865 he served in active duty with the 188th Ohio Volunteer Infantry. He entered Ohio University in 1868 and graduated in 1873. He was ordained in 1872. In 1874, he became President of Ridgeville College in Indiana and pastor of the Free Will Baptist church there. In 1876 He received his M.A. from Ohio University and in 1878 took over Wilkesville Academy in Ohio 15 miles from Rio Grande college where he joined the college staff a year later. In 1887 he became the third president of Rio Grande College at the age of 41.He served Rio Grande College for 40 years and 24 of those as President. He resigned as president in 1911, but remained on the faculty until 1919, also returning to ministerial duties. The University of Wooster conferred upon him the Ph.D. Degree. Ohio University conferred upon him the honorary degree of Doctor of Divinity. He served as President of the Southeastern

Ohio Teacher's Association. President of the Ohio Free Communion Baptist Association. Delegate to several Free Baptist General Conferences between 1883 and 1904. Delegate to the Federal Council of Churches of Christ in Americas. He played an active role in the merger between Free Baptist and the Northern Baptist in 1911.

Alfred Franklin Delawder
Birth:
Jun. 4, 1878
Death:
Jun. 17, 1963,
Jackson County, Ohio
Burial:
Glen Roy Cemetery,
Glen Roy,
Jackson County, Ohio

Early Free Will Baptist pastor in southern Ohio.

Thomas Dimm

Birth:
1810
Pennsylvania
Death:
Jul. 10, 1886
Huron County, Ohio
Burial:
Guinea Corners Cemetery
Huron County, Ohio

A native of Pennsylvania, moved to Ohio in 1834, and united with the Free Baptist Church in Huron, Ohio in 1841. He was ordained in 1844, and for several years labored in the Lake Erie Quarterly Meeting and subsequently with the Seneca, Huron and Lorain Quarterly Meetings. The last years of his life he was afflicted with blindness, but maintain his integrity and his love for Christ and the denomination he had served.

Eusebius M Dodge

Birth:
May 22, 1806
Lyme
New London County,
Connecticut
Death:
Jan. 2, 1852
New Lyme
Ashtabula County, Ohio
Burial:
Dodgeville Cemetery
New Lyme,
Ashtabula County, Ohio

An ordained Freewill Baptist minister from Ohio who was faithful in his service. Rev. Dodge, was the son of Eld. Eusebius and Anna (Merchant) Dodge--family records state that his father was also a Baptist clergyman, as well as Justice of the Peace. Eusebius M. married Hannah H. Hall, Oct. 15, 1826.His parents and extended families moved to Ohio where Rev. Eusebius was ordained as an evangelist, Oct. 15, 1837. He labored with poor churches and in destitute places, and saw many souls converted.He was a man of uncommon power, with great faith and perseverance and love for people. He baptized about a thousand persons.He died at an early age of 45 years.

Cyrus Dudley

Birth:
unknown
Death:
Mar. 3, 1871
Blanchester, Ohio
Burial:
West Woodville Cemetery
Warren County, Ohio

His parents were Peter DUDLEY and Ruby (Soule) DUDLEY.He married Frances Teetor, 1819. They had three children: Hannah, Colmbus J., and Amelia E. There were several "Dudley" families from Maine who migrated to Ohio and began the town, "Maineville," because so many from Maine had come. Rev. Cyrus Dudley, a native of Maine, died at the age of 70 years. When quite young he became a member of the Maineville Freewill Baptist Ohio church. He was married and settled in West Woodville, where he resided until his death. In 1835 he commenced his ministerial duties and until near the close of life was active in the work. He was a man of much power in the pulpit, and successful as an evangelist.

Inscription:
71 yrs 7 mo 23 days

David Dudley

Birth:
Jul. 16, 1791
Mt Vernon, Maine
Death:
May 29, 1867
Waldo, OH
Burial:
Wyatt Cemetery,
Waldo, Marion County, Ohio

He was an early Free Will Baptist Minister, first found in the Ohio records at Rutland, Ohio. He attended the General Conference at Mainsville, Ohio, where he later pastored. However, most of his ministry was to be found in Marion County, Ohio, where many of his churches still exist. He had a powerful influence during his early days in Ohio. source: "Ohio, the cross road of our nation", Vol IV, No. IV. and Alton Loveless.

For those who love history, there were often family members who told the stories that lay behind the photographs, and family.

Moses Dudley
Birth:
1755 Maine
Death:
Nov. 24, 1842
Maineville, Warren County, Ohio
Burial:
Maineville Cemetery,
Maineville, Warren County, Ohio

In 1815, Moses Dudley, with his family, moved from Maine and settled in Maineville. Dudley built the first frame house in the village. The Maineville Free-Will Baptist Church was organized by Elder Moses Dudley, Henry Greely and others as early as 1822 or 1823. It was called Salt Spring Church. For a number of years they worshiped in a schoolhouse east of Maineville, and not far from the Maineville Graveyard. About 1830, they built the present brick building. Elder Moses Dudley was the first pastor of this church.

Thomas Dudley
Birth:
Apr. 18, 1783
Mount Vernon,
Kennebec County, Maine
Death:
Aug. 7, 1860
Pagetown,
Morrow County, Ohio
Burial:
Crossroads Cemetery,
Albany,
Athens County, Ohio

He was the brother of Rev. Moses Dudley, who moved to Ohio and died in Warren, Ohio, and buried in Maineville Cem. At the age of eighteen he joined the church in Mt. Vernon, ME where he was ordained about 1813. In 1836, he moved to Pittsfield ME, where he remained until his removal to Ohio, about 1853, or seven years before his death.

Charles Thomas Dutton
Birth:
Jan. 15, 1927
Dickerson County, Virginia
Death:
Jan. 12, 2004
Marion,
Marion County, Ohio
Burial:
Grand Prairie Cemetery,
Brush Ridge,
Marion County, Ohio

He was a longtime Free Will Baptist Minister serving in the northern Ohio Association.

Donald Enos Ellis
Birth:
Mar. 20, 1931
McDermott, Scioto County, Ohio
Death:
Mar. 4, 2013
Portsmouth, Scioto County, Ohio
Burial:
Rush Townshi
Scioto County, Ohio

He was born a son of the late Charles and Lula Mae Kennard

Ellis. Don was a retired mechanic from Dayton Walther Corp, Pastor of Stoney Run Free Will Baptist Church, and a U.S. Navy Veteran. Funeral services were conducted at the Stoney Run Freewill Baptist Church with Craddock Frye and Roger Clark officiating.

Burial followed where military graveside rites were performed by the William A. Baker and James Irwin Posts of the American Legion.

(Portsmouth Daily Times, March 6, 2013)

John Elswick
Birth:
1891
Death:
1947
Scioto County, Ohio
Burial:
Buckeye Cemetery,
Ohio Furnace,
Scioto County, Ohio

John William Elswick
Birth:
Jul. 27, 1938
Lawrence County, Kentucky
Death:
Jul. 26, 2006
Columbus, Franklin County, Ohio
Burial:
Graham Chapel Cemetery,
Athens County, Ohio

He was the son of the late Fred and Malissia Ellen Boggs Elswick. He was a 1957 graduate of Shade High School. He was retired from Ohio University after 31 years. He was also a minister for the past 38 years. He was recently the pastor of the Carpenter Baptist Church and Poplar Ridge Free Will Baptist Church. He was a member of Grahams Chapel Church. He was involved with the World Christian Outreach Ministry with Rev. Dr. David T. Rahamut.

If you spend all your time worrying about dying, living isn't going to be much fun.

Quentin U. England
Birth:
unknown
Death:
Mar. 30, 2000
Burial:
Obetz Cemetery, Obetz,
Franklin County, Ohio,
Plot: Sect 25, lot 34, spc 1

He was active in the early organization of the Ohio Free Will Baptist Association. He was a member of the Franklin Conference where most of his ministry was.

Floyd J. Estep
Birth:
Jan. 6, 1911
Paintsville,
Johnson County, Kentucky
Death:
Feb. 6, 2009
Portsmouth,
Scioto County, Ohio
Burial:
Evergreen Union Cemetery,
Waverly Pike County, Ohio

He was a member of the Wakefield Free Will Baptist Church, a retired N W Railroad employee, an active Free Will Baptist Clergyman, former pastor of seven Free Will Baptist Churches, Member of Lucasville, Ohio. Life Certificate in Scioto Ministerial Conference of Free Will Baptist and Veteran of WWII.

Calvin Evans
Birth:
Mar. 30, 1930
Death:
Jan. 11, 2006
Tampa,
Hillsborough County,
Florida
Burial:
Highland Memorial Gardens,
South Point,
Lawrence County, Ohio

He was nationally known for founding the Evangelistic Outreach Inc. 48 years ago with a $250 love offering. It grew to spread the word through the Internet, a weekly television show and a daily radio show in numerous markets in the tri-state and throughout the Midwest. He was well-known for his revivals, one of which lasted 13 weeks. Evans started the Spring Jubilee which is held every spring at the Scioto County Fairgrounds. He had worldwide crusades in decade in Jamaica, Uganda and Haiti. He had extended ministries in many countries in the Caribbean. He had thousands to complete correspondence courses in his outreach efforts. Evans, 75, had just entered his fifth decade as an evangelist. He preached his first sermon in 1956 and pastored in churches in Ohio and Kentucky. He was ordained by the Free Will Baptist Denomination and had preached in the national convention in 1974 in Wichita, Kansas to 5000.

Fred C Evans
Birth:
Aug. 7, 1926
Blaine, Kentucky
Death:
Nov. 26, 2001
Burial:
Galena Cemetery, Galena,
Delaware County, Ohio

Rev. Evans was the second pastor of the Welch Avenue Free Will Baptist Church in Columbus, Ohio. He served as Pastor from January 1958 through March 1961 when he left to serve for many years at the Pleasant View Free Will Baptist Church. Afterwards, he began the Greenleaf Road Free Will Baptist Church, which today is called the Southwest Free Will Baptist Church. At the time of his passing, he was 75 years of age and had completed over 52 years in the ministry.

He was pastor of the Faith Harvest Church in Marysville, Ohio at the time of his departure. The funeral services were conducted by Rev. Paul Thompson and the Rev. Glenn Derifield. He was also a veteran of the US Navy serving during WW II.

Vernal Lee Fairchild
Birth:
Jun. 14, 1928
Blaze, Morgan County,
Kentucky
Death:
Sep. 1, 2011
Xenia,
Greene County, Ohio
Burial:
Valley View Memorial Gardens,
Xenia, Greene County,
Ohio

Rev. Fairchild was a graduate of Bethany Bible College where he received his Bachelor of Ministry degree. He also graduated from ITT Technical Institute. He was the Retired Pastor of Fellowship Tabernacle in Xenia; formerly Pastor of Sunset Freewill Baptist Church in Springfield and served as a chaplain with Greene Memorial Hospital. He began his ministry as Director of Xenia Rescue Mission and retired from Wright Patterson Air Force Base.

Today is not a day of defeat.

Isaac Fullerton, Sr
Birth:
Feb. 15, 1809
Greenbrier County,
West Virginia
Death:
Nov. 11, 1886
Scioto County, Ohio
Burial:
Butler & Martin Cemetery,
Minford, Scioto County Ohio

He moved with his parents while still young and settled in Scioto Co., Porter Township, Ohio. He and his sons entered the War in 1861...Rev. Isaac was a Capt. in 59th OH. Rev. Rufus Cheney was the first preacher of the denomination to preach in Scioto Co., in 1816, and he organized the Porter Free Will Baptist Church Sept. 6, 1817, in a schoolhouse on Ward's Run. Rev. Fullerton received license to preach in 1834, and was ordained to the gospel ministry in November 1836. He farmed to provide for his growing family, and most of his long ministry (about 52 yrs) was spent with the FWB churches of Little Scioto Quarterly Meeting, where he had been closely identified with all its work, organizing the FWB church in Wheelersburg, May 17, 1851, and was first pastor of the Sciotoville Church. He attended the General Conference at Marion (1886) as a delegate from the Ohio and Kentucky Y.M. (Info from Ohio records, family genealogy, and Hist. of Ohio, 1884, chap 17, in archives).

William J Fulton
Birth:
1847
Death:
1927
Burial:
Calvary Baptist Cemetery,
Rio Grande, Gallia County, Ohio

Rev. Dr. Wm. Fulton pastored Calvary FWB Church for 40 years, and was teacher in Rio Grande College. He was one of the most popular and respected ministers in Southeast Ohio and especially after the death of Rev. Ira Haning. He died at 80 yrs.

Millard Green
Birth:
1917
Death:
2001
Burial:
Burbank Cemetery
Burbank
Wayne County, Ohio

He was pastor of the Creston church for many years in northern Ohio.

Delbert Glendon Gould
Birth:
Sep. 28, 1908
Tom Corwin,
Jackson County, Ohio
Death:
Jan. 18, 1958
Columbus, Franklin County, Ohio
Burial:
Forest Lawn Memorial Gardens,
Columbus, Franklin County, Ohio

He was converted in the Methodist Church at Glenroy, Ohio. Later he became a member of the Wellston Free Will Baptist Church. He went to Columbus where he united with the Free Will Baptist Church on South Parsons Avenue, which later became the Gibbard Free Will Baptist Church. He was called into the ministry and was licensed in 1949 and ordained in 1950. He served the Rosedale Church and then was chosen as the first pastor of Welch Avenue Free Will Baptist Church in February, 1952 which was started by the Gibbard Ave. church. While pastor of this church he had a massive heart attack on the parking lot of the White Cross hospital where he was going to his doctor. He died at death 49 years. This church continues today as the Heritage Free Will Baptist Church as a large church and multiple staff.

James W. Hall
Birth:
May 28, 1909
Death:
Sep. 25, 1941
Burial:
Butler-Martin Cemetery,
Minford, Scioto County, Ohio.

Ira Z. Haning
Birth:
June 1825
Death:
Sep. 27, 1878
Burial:
Calvary Baptist Cemetery,
Rio Grande, Gallia County, Ohio

Haning was born in Alexander, Ohio.. His parents were first Methodists and later Freewill Baptists, and were faithful in giving religious instruction to their twelve children. Ira was converted in 1843 and joined the church in Lodi, where the family then resided. He studied two years in the University of Ohio at Athens. He also engaged in teaching, and preached at various places acceptably. He received

license in February, 1846, and two years later was ordained at Lodi by Rev's Job Kittle, D. C. Tapping, and S. S. Branch. The churches of the Athens Q. M., then recently formed, needed pastoral care, and he itinerated among them all for several years.. He influenced Deacon Nehemiah Atwood to give $50,000 to start Rio Grande College in southern Ohio which still exist as a popular college.

Joseph Franklyn Harness
Birth:
Mar. 25, 1916
Greene County, Ohio
Death:
Nov. 20, 1995 Portsmouth,
Scioto County, Ohio
Burial:
Lucasville Cemetery,
Lucasville, Scioto County, Ohio

He attended Rio Grande college where he played basketball and received his education. His pastorates were mainly in the Porter Conference in southern Ohio. He was a member of the General Board of The Ohio Association Of Free Will Baptist. He also served as the moderator of the state convention on a number of occasions. His voice was readily heard and respected.

Henry Lee Hawkins
Birth:
May 24, 191
Kentucky
Death:
May 9, 1993
Wheelersburg,

Scioto County, Ohio
Burial:
Memorial Burial Park,
Wheelersburg,
Scioto County, Ohio

Reverend Henry Lee Hawkins was the pastor of several Free Will Baptist churches in southern Ohio, the last of which was Porter Free Will Baptist. He also built many homes and churches in the area and was a skilled craftsman who made many beautiful clocks and pieces of furniture in his later years. He was a strong leader for many years within the Scoio Yearly conference.

Dave A. Hayes
Birth:
Aug. 22, 1889
Lawrence County, Kentucky
Death:
Aug. 28, 1968
Columbus,
Franklin County, Ohio
Burial:
Forest Lawn Memorial Gardens,
Columbus,
Franklin County, Ohio

Retired from Columbus First Freewill Baptist Church in 1964. In the ministry for 50 years. Elected honorary pastor in 1963 Columbus First Freewill Baptist Church.

Herbert J Henson
Birth:
1912
Death:
April 1, 1987
Burial:
Woodlawn Cemetery,
Ada, Hardin County, Ohio

Luther Hecox
Birth:
Dec. 28, 1795
Whitestown, N. Y.
Death:
Sep. 1, 1878
Meigs County, Ohio
Burial:
Brick Cemetery, Meigs County,
Ohio

Hecox was the son of Truman and Sarah Hasford Hecox. His parents settled in Meigs County, Ohio, where he married in 1817 and early became one of the active Free Baptists. After serving as a licentiate several years,he was ordained in 1850, and continued in the work of the Lord in that vicinity until the infirmities of age compelled him to desist. He was a consistent Christian, pathetic and earnest in preaching. Luther was 81 years old when he died. He was the husband of Matilda Dean and the father of Truman.

Kendal F. Higgins
Birth:
March 18, 1813
Cayuga County, New York
Death:
May 8, 1887
Union County, Ohio
Burial:
Oakdale Cemetery
Marysville
Union County, Ohio

He was one of the fathers of the Free Baptist ministry in central Ohio. He experienced religion at the age of 12. He moved to Ohio in early life and felt it an imperative duty to enter the ministry. His ordination took place on April 6, 1845, with Elders G. W. Baker, and Arron Hatch and G. H. Moon serving on the Council.
For over 40 years he was an earnest and successful preacher. He had the care of the churches in central and southern Ohio and Indiana. He had an excellent natural ability and was a strong

reasoner, and his sermons were clear and strong presentations of gospel truth.

Jacob Hisey
Birth:
Jul. 30, 1816
Death:
Dec. 26, 1847
Waynesville, Ohio
Burial:
Miami Cemetery
Corwin
Warren County, Ohio

He was converted in 1836, licensed by the Miami Quarterly Meeting in 1843 and spent some time at the Biblical School at Whitestown, New York.

William Hooper
Birth:
Dec. 2, 1818
Death:
Mar. 21, 1877
Burial:
Miles Cemetery
Rutland, Meigs County, Ohio

Rev. William Hooper, M. D. was a native of New Jersey, was converted at Alexander, Ohio, where he was soon licensed to preach, and ordained a few years later. He labored as an itinerant minister in Athens, Meigs, Gallia, Lawrence and Scioto Counties twelve years, and gathered one or two churches. He then turned his attention to medicine, graduating from the Starling Medical College at Columbus in 1857, and devoted but little time to ministerial duties. He died at age 58 years.

Cyrus Cordon Inman
Birth:
Jan 21, 1839
Spencer, Ohio
Death:
1917
Burial:
Spencer Cemetery,
Spencer
Medina County, Ohio

A worthy and esteemed minister of the Freewill Baptist church in Randall's movement. He attended Hillsdale FWB College in Hillsdale, MI, and organized and pastored churches. He was married to Clemma C. Smith. He was the son of Deacon Stephen Inman, b. 1808 NY, and prob. charter members of that Spencer church. He was for a few years pastor of churches in the Oceana Q. M., Mich. He was ordained in 1869, and not long after returned to Ohio and took charge of the Spencer church, and was pastor of the Beebetown church in the Cleveland Q. M. Cyrus also served in the Civil War from Ohio, Ohio 124th Inf. Regiment, Co. B, as Cpl, then promoted to Sgt. Mustered out 1865.

John Jeffrey
Birth:
unknown
Death:
Ohio
Burial:
Resthaven Memory Gardens
Avon
Lorain County, Ohio

He was an early Free Will Baptist minister in northern Ohio that began the Vincent FWB church. He was a missionary, pastor and known servant.

John Robert Kemper
Birth:
1875
Death:
1957
Scioto County, Ohio
Burial:
Vernon Cemetery,
Lyra, Scioto County, Ohio,

Early pastor in Southern Ohio. Pastor of Union Free Will Baptist church for many years.

Howard Kimble
Birth:
unknown
Death:
unknown
Lawrence County, Ohio
Burial:
Oakland Chapel Cemetery,
Kitts Hill,
Lawrence County, Ohio

A well-known minister in southern Ohio and northeast Kentucky remembered for pastoring Brush Creek in Ky. and the Union Church near Wheelersburg, Ohio. He was a member of the Ohio Board of Directors.

Jobe Kittle
Birth:
Apr. 28, 1805
Death:
Mar. 26, 1877
Scioto County, Ohio
Burial:
Old Wheelersburg Cemetery
Wheelersburg
Scioto County, Ohio

He had been a member of the Porter church 44 years. Receiving ordination to the ministry in 1841, at the hands of Rev. J. M. Shurtliff and others. He labored faithfully for the cause of Christ in the Little Scioto Quarterly Meeting.

Claudis Lewis
Birth:
Jul. 8, 1922
Johnson County, Kentucky
Death:
Sep. 28, 2003
Franklin. Ohio
Burial:
Springboro Cemetery, Springboro,
Warren County, Ohio

Lewis was a World War II veteran of the United States Army and was an escort to Gen. George S. Patton and General Dwight D. Eisenhower. He was a member of the Franklin Free Will Baptist Church. His funeral was held at the Franklin Church with the Rev. Dencil Owsley officiating with full military honors.

Charles Lykins
Birth:
Aug. 7, 1907
Death:
Mar. 5, 1978 Ohio
Burial:
South Webster Cemetery,
South Webster,
Scioto County, Ohio

Minister in southern Ohio.

Bobby J Lyons
Birth:
Mar. 13, 1940
Death:
Oct. 13, 2007
Burial:
Plattsburg Cemetery, Plattsburg,
Clark County, Ohio

He was a member of the Eastside Free Will Baptist church and a Korean veteran.

David Marks
Birth:
Nov. 14, 1805
Shandaken,
Ulster
County, New York
Death:
Dec. 15, 1845
Oberlin, Lorain County, Ohio
Burial::
Westwood Cemetery,
Oberlin, Lorain County, Ohio,
Plot: Sect. F, Lot 5

Rev. Marks, as a child, felt impressed that God was calling him to a great work and began preaching at age 15 years. He traveled all over New England preaching to large crowds wanting to hear "the boy preacher." At 13 yrs of age, he walked over 368 miles from his home in New York to Providence, Rhode Island to attend Brown University where he had free tuition, but no further assistance towards room and board could be rendered; with sad heart, he walked back home. He had a thirst for knowledge and immediately began to study and read while walking or riding horse-back to another preaching appointment in his itinerant ministry. He found he was in sentiment with the teaching of 'Free Will, free grace and free salvation' and united with the Free Will Baptists in July 1819. He became a leader in that church and in the 1831 General Conference, was appointed Agent of the newly established Book Concern, a publishing house, which position he held for four years, leading it to solid footing financially.

DAVID MARKS.

He also was an ardent promoter of Home and Foreign Missions and Education societies. He held pastorates in New Hampshire, Rhode Island, New York, and organized a church in Rochester, New York, and had an iterant ministry all over New England, Upper Canada, and into Ohio. He kept a journal and a "Narrative" of his work and ministry which was printed in 1831, at the insistence of others. After his death, his wife, Marilla, edited *"Memoirs of David Marks"* which was published by the FWB Printing Establishment in 1846; William Burr, Printer. He went to Oberlin College in Ohio, a place of abolitionist creativity and

thought, he having carried the same sentiments in his church and life. He had spoken, written and labored to see slavery abolished. He was without a doubt, one of the most esteemed ministers of his day in his church and in the public's eye. It was while in Oberlin with his wife, that his health failed even more. His great desire to preach even in his weakened condition was so great that he requested that "I be carried to the meeting house to give one more talk for God before I die." This they did, even though it was thought he would die before he finished, but he lived a few weeks longer. Dr. Charles G. Finney, president of Oberlin preached his funeral. Finney said of Mark's "There is none greater among Free Will Baptists."

Herman Marcum
Birth:
Apr. 3, 1933
Wayne County,
West Virginia
Death:
Feb. 7, 2012
Orlando, FL
Burial:
Union Cemetery,
Columbus,
Franklin County, Ohio
He was pastor of the Philadelphia Free Will Baptist Church before his retirement to Florida. For 20 years he raised money locally by coordinating walk-a-thons and rock-a-thons, used for donating fruit baskets to nursing homes in the Columbus area. Rev. Marcum was a member of Faith Freewill Baptist Church in Orlando, FL.

Marvin Dale Markin
Birth:
Aug. 14, 1937
Vinton County, Ohio
Death:
Jun. 3, 2010
Athens, Athens County, Ohio
Burial:
Harkins Chapel Cemetery,
Bolins Mills, Vinton County, Ohio

Free Will Baptist pastor is southeast Ohio and active in his district and state associations. He had been a minister for 53 years with 22 years at Black Oak FWB.

Amos P. Marmon
Birth:
unknown
Death:
Nov. 28, 1879
Burial:
Marmon Valley Cemetery
East Liberty, Logan County, Ohio

Amos Marmon's parents were Edmund Marmon, 1786-1831, and Sarah (Stanton) Marmon, 1788--.He married Cynthia Ann Outland, (1830-1903)Amos P. Marmon, was born in Marmon Valley, Ohio and died near his native place. He was converted under the ministry of Rev. O.E. Baker and united with the East Liberty church in 1853. He proved himself a useful member, and was ordained June 3, 1872. His sermons were thoughtful and carefully prepared, and being deeply emotional, his words touched many hearts.
He was age 53 years, 3 months and 14 days at his death.

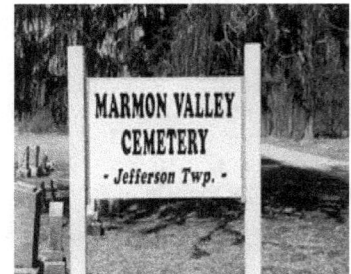

Chester A. Masters
Birth:
Dec. 9, 1928
Lewis Couny, Kentucky
Death:
Jun. 12, 2012
Mansfield, Richland County,
Ohio
Burial:
Franklin Cemetery,
Mansfield,
Richland County, Ohio

He was a bi-vocational Free Will Baptist minister who retired from the Empire Detroit Steel. He was a veteran of the United States Army. At the cemetery he was given full military honors by the Richland County Joint Veterans Burial Detail.

James W Martin
Birth:
Jul. 11, 1829
Guernsey County, Ohio
Death:
Oct. 28, 1899
Athens County, Ohio
Burial:
Crossroads Cemetery
Albany
Athens County, Ohio
Rev. James W. Martin, was the son of James H. and Tracy (Triplett) MARTIN, and was married to Jane Gibson, April 15, 1852. To them were born three children. He was educated at the Albany Academy and the Ohio University; was converted in 1860 and ordained May 23, 1868. He has held the pastorates of several churches in the Ohio River Yearly Meeting to which his ministry has

been spent conducting revivals, baptizing a large number of converts and organizing one church. He has been influential in the local denominational gatherings, and has served as trustee of Rio Grande College and of the Ohio State Association, as president of the board of Atwood Institute, and several times as a delegate to the General Conference.

Eugene Martin
Birth:
1910
Death:
unknown
Scioto County, Ohio
Burial:
Bennett Cemetery,
Minford, Scioto County, Ohio

Moses Walter Martin
Birth:
Apr. 10, 1887
Scioto County, Ohio
Death:
Dec. 18, 1964
Portsmouth,
Scioto County, Ohio
Burial:
Old Wheelersburg Cemetery
Scioto County, Ohio

Moses and his family moved to Portsmouth where he was employed as a street car conductor on the Portsmouth to Sciotoville run. In 1921 the family moved back to Dogwood Ridge in Wheelersburg where he farmed. Later he moved and was employed as a locomotive fireman and engineer at the local Wheeling Steel plant in New Boston. He worked for the steel mill until he retired at the age of 70 (1957). Moses was an ordained Free Will Baptist minister and served several churches in the Scioto County area.

Isaac May
Birth:
Oct. 5, 1796
Strafford
Orange County, Vermont
Death:
Dec. 8, 1874
Clyde
Sandusky County, Ohio
Burial:
Ellsworth Cemetery
Clyde
Sandusky County, Ohio

He was the son of Harvey May Joanne (Wedge); husband of (1) Racheal McMillen, (2) Nancy McMillen. approx 16 children between the two marriages.

He was converted at age 18 and united with the Christian denomination. Later he joined the York church in Ohio and was ordained by the Huron Quarterly Meeting in 1831. For some time he labored as an itinerant: after which he settled at Townsend, and organized a church and remained with it the remainder of his life.

Arthur "Pete" Maynard
Birth:
Jul. 14, 1939
Beauty, Martin County,
Kentucky
Feb. 21, 2002
Washington Court House
Fayette County, Ohio
Burial:
New Holland Cemetery,
New Holland,
Pickaway County, Ohio

He was founder of the Woodlawn Free Will Baptist Church in Washington Court house. He served his country in the United States Navy during the Vietnam era, and as a bi-vocational minister. He was employed as a corrections officer with Ohio Dept. of Corrections in Pickaway County.

Billy O. McCarty
Birth:
Aug. 7, 1926
Salyersville,
Magoffin County, Kentucky
Death:
Jan. 8, 2008
Springfield,
Clark County, Ohio
Burial:

South Vienna Cemetery,
South Vienna,
Clark County, Ohio

He ministered in Free Will Baptist churches in Urbana, West Jefferson, Youngstown, Ohio; California and Georgia during his long ministry. He was actively involved with the Family Life Ministries of Tennessee. He was a man of patient compassion and a wise counselor.

William McCarty
Birth:
Sep. 16, 1938
Death:
Feb. 2, 1984
Lawrence County, Ohio
Burial:
Aid Cemetery,
Aid, Lawrence County, Ohio

He pastored the Fox Hollow and Symes Valley FWB churches in Lawrence Co., Ohio.

Alva McDaniel, Sr
Birth:
1907
Death:
unknown
Scioto County, Ohio
Burial:
White Gravel Cemetery,
Minford,
Scioto County, Ohio

Robert Lee Meade
Birth:
Jul. 11, 1930
Portsmouth,
Scioto County, Ohio
Death:
Mar. 23, 2001
Springfield,
Clark County, Ohio
Burial:
Ferncliff Cemetery,
Springfield,
Clark County, Ohio

He was ordained as minister in 1954 and was State Evangelist for four years. He served as pastor in six different churches from 1956 to 1993: The Shumway Freewill Baptist Church, Houston Hollow Freewill Baptist Church, The Fairborn Church, Turkey Creek Freewill Baptist Church, Belmont Freewill Baptist Church, and twenty-two years at the Forest Valley Freewill Baptist Church, where he was a member.

Redford Meadows
Birth:
Feb. 12, 1925
Wittensville, Ky
Death:
Apr. 6, 2007
Ironton, Ohio
Burial:
Rose Hill Burial Park and Mausoleum, Ashland,
Boyd County, Kentucky, Plot: F

Meadows was a Free Will Baptist Minister for more than 50 years and pastored churches in Michigan, Ohio and Kentucky.

His more recent ministry was at the Union Free Will Baptist Church near Wheelersburg, Ohio

---

Russell Milam
Birth:
1882
Death:
1967
Scioto County, Ohio
Burial:
Bennett Cemetery,
Minford,
Scioto County, Ohio

Early leader in the district, state, and national programs of the Free Will Baptists. His name appears on a regular basis as a representived from Ohio on the national General Board. He was the publicity chairman when the nation convention met in Huntington, WVA..

Bert Miller
Birth:
Feb.21,1913
Death:
Apr. 5, 2001
Burial:
Obetz Cemetery, Obetz,
Franklin County, Ohio

Ordained a Minister in 1935 and instrumental in starting many Freewill Baptist Churches. In 1968 he founded and pastored Lockbourne Freewill Baptist Church in Lockbourne, Ohio. In 1992 Rev. Miller oversaw the building of the new church on Rohr Rd. where he continued to pastor until his death. Past President for 16 years of TWU

Local #208. Retired from COTA after 35 years..

**Today is not a day of despair,
But a day of joy.**

Troy Miller
Birth:
Sep. 11, 1942
Wonder, Floyd County, Kentucky
Death:
Aug. 18, 2012
Jackson, Jackson County, Ohio
Burial:
Franklin Valley Cemetery,
Wellston, Jackson County, Ohio

Troy Miller was born in the hills of eastern Kentucky 30 minutes from the Prestonsburg area. His family moved to West Virginia and Clyde, Ohio before settling in Jackson, Ohio. It was here that he met and married his high school sweetheart, Janice Forshey, in 1958. Together they had 3 sons and 1 daughter: Bob, Julie, Brian, and Jamie.

At the approximate age of 25, Troy accepted Christ as his Savior and soon felt the call to go into the ministry. He would go on to pastor the Coalton Free Will Baptist church on three separate occasions, the Glenroy FWB church (both in Jackson county), and would re-open the Bethesda Chapel FWB church in Pike county

after it had closed its doors several years earlier. During this time he held many revivals, performed hundreds of weddings and funerals and became well known throughout the community. He continued in the ministry until April of 2012 by serving as clergy member for Four Winds Nursing Home in Jackson. In 1995, Troy was diagnosed with kidney cancer and underwent surgery to completely remove one kidney and a portion of the other. He remained cancer free until 2008, when he was diagnosed once again with kidney cancer, this time terminal. Troy Miller passed away in Kingston, Ohio in Ross County at the home of his youngest son.

Troy was formerly employed at Pillsbury in Wellston. He enjoyed visiting and ministering to the residents at Heartland and Four Winds Nursing Homes, as well as ministering to others through his weekly radio broadcasts.

Gerald G. Moore
Birth:
Mar. 9, 1931
Clintwood, Dickenson County,
Virginia
Death:
Jul. 9, 2009
Sandusky County, Ohio,
Burial:
McPherson Cemetery,
Clyde, Sandusky County, Ohio,

Member of the First Freewill Baptist Church in Clyde, Ohio. He served his country in the Air Force during the Korean War. Mr. Moore was a bi-vocational minister had also worked 34 years at the Whirlpool Corp in Clyde.

Tommy Moore
Birth:
Sep. 19, 1928
Adams, Lawrence County,
Kentucky
Death:
Sep. 23, 1967
Burial:
Yatesville Cemetery, Louisa,
Lawrence County, Kentucky

He was the third pastor of the Welch Avenue Free Will Baptist Church in Columbus, Ohio.

*"death smiles
at us all;
all a man can do is
smile back."*

Horace Morse
Birth:
Sep. 19, 1795
Worthington
Hampshire County, Massachusetts
Death:
Nov. 24, 1854

Williamsfield
Ashtabula County, Ohio
Burial:
Richmond Center Cemetery
Richmond Center
Ashtabula County, Ohio

He moved to northern Ohio in 1810 where for several years he was engaged in teaching school. In 1818 he married Lydia, a daughter of Judge S. Stanton. He was converted in the revival which led to the formation of the Williamsfield church, of which he was one of the original members, and he immediately began preaching. He was active in the formation of the Wayne Quarterly Meeting and for some years was a leading minister in the Crawford and Ashtabula Quarterly Meetings.

Inscription:
Rev. HORACE MORSE
WHO DIEDNov. 24, 1854
60 yrs. 2 mos. 6 days(rest of script
not legible from photo)

Kevin Willard Morris
Birth:
Sep. 13, 1978
Mansfield, Richland County,
Ohio
Death:
Nov. 21, 2008
Plymouth,
Richland County, Ohio
Burial:
Greenlawn Cemetery,
Plymouth,
Richland County, Ohio

He preached the Gospel for 12 years, serving as pastor at

Paradise Free Will Baptist Church two years. He graduated from Pioneer Career and Technical Center where he received the Byron Carmean Award- an award granted to non-traditional students and received his Associate's Degree in Early Childhood Education at The Ohio State University. At the age of 11, he underwent a heart transplant, a very special gift allowing him to spend 19 more years with his family and friends.

William Moses
Birth:
unknown
Death:
Oct. 26,1879
Cincinnati, Ohio
Burial:
Spring Grove Cemetery
Cincinnati, Hamilton County, Ohio
Plot: Garden LN, Section 14,
Lot 0, Space 262

Moses was a native of Connecticut and one of the early New York ministers, having been ordained in 1814. In 1832 he was connected with the Betheny Q. M., and after that time, until 1857, with the churches of the Genesee Q. M. Here he preached and labored faithfully. After this he spent about twenty years in Ripon, Wis., and, a year before his death, went to live with his children in Cincinnati. His wife, with whom he had lived sixty-two years

Albanus Avery Moulton
Birth:
Mar. 23, 1848
Massachusetts
Death:
Jun. 22, 1888
Colorado
Burial:
Calvary Baptist Cemetery,
Rio Grande, Gallia County, Ohio

He took the freshman year of his college course at Bates College, the sophomore year at Hillsdale College, and the junior and senior years at Yale College, where he took honors and graduated in 1871. He then completed a course in mathematics and civil engineering in the University of Michigan, and worked for a time at railroad surveying. He was made professor of mathematics at Rio Grande College at its opening in 1876. Three years later he was made president. He discharged the duties of this position for six years with the highest degree of ability, zeal and success. In 1887, it was manifest he could not serve the college longer. His last three years were spent in Colorado, where he worked some at teaching and surveying. His noble Christian spirit made its impression on his schoolmates even, and was felt still more by the young people under his care at Rio Grande. In this influence to shape its opening years, the college was greatly favored.

To Live is Christ
To Die is Gain.

Albanus K Moulton
Birth:
Sep. 26, 1810
Hatley, Quebec, Canada
Death:
Jun. 19, 1873
Linndale,
Cuyahoga County, Ohio
Burial:
Woodland Cemetery,
Cleveland,
Cuyahoga County, Ohio,
Plot: Section 40 Lot 84

Like others of the family he was early converted to Christ, and an accident, partially disqualifying him for manual labor, was the occasion of more schooling than was usually enjoyed by boys in his circumstances. While hesitating to devote himself to the ministry, he providentially found himself in 1837 at Mecca, Ohio, at the August session of the Ashtabula Quarterly Meeting, at which Ransom Dunn was ordained. Brother Moulton's position was understood; and the ordination services, with special prayer for him and special exhortation and persuasion by Rev's Wire, Miller and Dunn, resulted in suspending his journey to the South. A congregation was formed from which other preachers were intentionally detained, and thus he was almost compelled to preach his first sermon. From this time he labored faithfully. In October he received license and the next August was ordained by the Geauga Quarterly Meeting at

Burton.. Many souls were converted and two or three churches organized. under Brother Moulton's labors in the Geauga Quarterly Meeting the next few years. In 1841 he settled with the Washington Street church, Dover, N. H., where an extensive revival was enjoyed, and a house of worship commenced which was completed the year after he left. Early in 1843 he commenced a successful pastorate in Portland, Me., the church being greatly strengthened. The church in Roxbury, Mass., secured his services in 1848, and the outlook became more encouraging than in any previous field but the church in Lowell was in great need and he soon began with them a useful pastorate, during which they erected a house of worship. But in these years of earnest labor his nervous system became debilitated and he retired to the prairies of Iowa, where with returning health he preached some and edited a weekly paper. In 1860 he returned to active work and labored effectually at Great Falls, New Hampshire., Auburn, Maine, Concord, New Hampshire, and Cleveland, Ohio. His death was instantaneous, resulting from a fall from a bridge at Linndale, a suburb of Cleveland.

James R Music, Sr
Birth:
Dec. 22, 1926
Meally,
Johnson County,
Kentucky
Death:
Nov. 10, 2008
Ohio
Burial:
Kingwood Memorial Park,
Lewis Center,
Delaware County, Ohio,

He ministered in several Free Will Baptist churches including Columbus First FWB and Lockbourne FWB.

Homer Nelson
Birth:
1912
Sciotodale, Scioto County Ohio
Death:
Apr. 27, 1985,
Portsmouth, Scioto County, Ohio
Burial:
South Webster Cemetery,
South Webster,
Scioto County, Ohio

He was a active Free Will Baptist pastor and denominational leader. He retired after 50 years service and was a member of the Union Free Will Baptist Church. He was the former pastor of the Germany Hollow, Garden City, Sciotodale, Powellsville, Tick Ridge and the Union churches. He also had been the State Evangelist for the Ohio Free Will Baptist Convention and was the clerk for the Ohio State Association for a number of years. He served as the editor of the *Ambassador Magazine* from 1962 to 1972. His abilities and activities in the denomination are well recorded.

Clarence J. Newman
Birth:
Sep. 30, 1925
Huntington, Cabell County,
West Virginia
Death:
May 18, 2002
Ohio
Burial:
Forest Grove Cemetery.
Plain City. Madison County. Ohio

Rev. Newman was converted at

the age of 12, called to preach in 1957, ordained to the ministry in 1958. His ministry spread over 45 years, with most of it spent in the state of Ohio and with 10 years in Arizona. He was best remembered for his pastorates at the West Jefferson and Marysville Free Will Baptist Churches in Ohio. He served as moderator of the Ohio State Association and as its Promotional Sec. He was a powerful preacher with a distinctive voice conducting revivals in 16 states. He noted his best revival was at the FWB Church in Cleveland in the 1960s, where 75 were saved in one week. During World War II he served in the Merchant Marines. He was a classic car collector and was the 1969 grand national winner with his 1969 Mustang convertible. He was known for taking small churches and building them into a renewable health.

Isaac Tirrell Packard
Birth:
May 3, 1826
Cummington
Hampshire County, Massachusetts
Death:
May 21, 1849
Licking County, Ohio
Burial:
Old Fredonia Cemetery
Licking County, Ohio

Isaac was the son of Theophillus and Esther Packard, born in Mass. When about seven years his father removed to Ohio, where he became an honored resident. His mother died when he was eight yrs of age, missing his best friend and counsellor. He went, after this, to live with a responsible family in Licking Co., where he remained several years. He came under the preaching of Rev. Geo. W. Baker, and at about sixteen years of age he began attending the Granville Academy. Afterward, he entered upon the business of teaching.In 1844, he spent about nine months in KY in this employment, when he was

prevented by an attack of fever, implicating his lungs. After a few weeks recuperating, he returned to Ohio to his family and friends.He united with the Freewill Baptists at Liberty, was baptized by Rev. Goodwin Evans, a FWB minister. He soon felt impressed to enter the work of the Christian ministry. He received license by the First FWB church in Liberty, Licking Co., April 11, 1846. He received public ordination in May 28, 1848.He rode horseback through the western counties of the State, preaching from place to place, then spent the winter teaching and filling in regular preaching appoinments.Again, he entered a course of study in Granville College in early 1848, but constant preaching and studies began to prey upon his feeble bodily powers and his health became much impaired. His disease was such that he knew his time was short. He made disposition of his books to his family, chose President Bailey, of Granville College to preach his funeral. He requested that he be buried beside his mother and sister--- and on May 21, 1849, with his devoted sister and a minister by his bedside, he passed peacefully to the other world.It is written, that "those who knew him best, esteemed him most. He was a young man of uncommon promise. He was mild, modest, and affable in all the intercourse of life, and was greatly endeared to many hearts."

Seth Parker
Birth:
Jul. 7, 1802
New York
Death:
Oct. 19, 1868
New York
Burial:
Steuben Cemetery
Steuben, Huron County, Ohio

Parker was a native of New York and moved to Ohio in 1820. He was converted in 1828, ordained in 1839, and continued with the churches of the Huron Q. M. until his death in Greenfield, Ohio Oct. 19, 1868, aged 66 years. He was twice a delegate to the General Conference, was corporator of the Printing Establishment from 1835 to 1847, and associate judge of the Court of Common Pleas from 1851 to 1858. He read much and was well informed on general topics. He was a faithful minister.

Asa Pierce
Birth:
1809
Berkshire
Berkshire County, Massachusetts
Death:
Jun. 1, 1900
Centerburg
Knox County, Ohio
Burial:
Centerburg Cemetery
Centerburg
Knox County, Ohio

Pierce, Rev. Asa, son of Orange and Ruth (Heath) Pierce. In 1812 his parents went to Ohio and located in Delaware County.In 1843 he was converted,and in 1846 was ordained by Rev's G. W. and O. E. Baker.His first pastorate was the Second Centerburg Free Will Baptist church, since which time he has preached for a number of churches in central Ohio and in Indiana. Many precious revivals have blessed his ministry and resulted in the organization by him of several churches.In 1830 he was married to Margaret Debold. Four children blessed this union. In 1852 he was married to Catherine Myers

James Jasper Perry
Birt h:
Feb. 12, 1884
Martin County, Kentucky
Death:
Aug. 29, 1928
Lyra, Scioto County, Ohio
Burial:
Vernon Cemetery,
Lyra, Scioto County, Ohio

A Free Will Baptist Minister.

The saint of God is escorted to a land where there is no more dying.

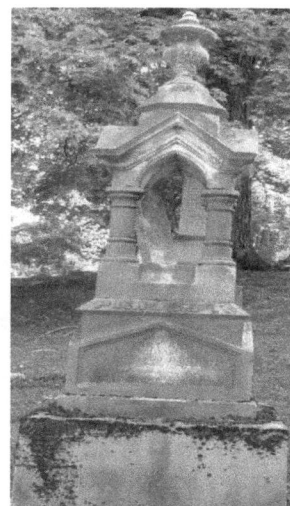

Edwin Pimlott
Birth:
April 10, 1853
Smethwick, England
Death:
May 9, 1890
Burial:
Ferncliff Cemetery
Springfield
Clark County, Ohio
Plot: Section I lot 77

His father, Rev. Frank Pimlott, whose two sons became ministers were associated in England with the Primitive Methodist. Edwin was converted in 1868, educated at Hillsdale College, Michigan, and ordained on December 28, 1879. He became the pastor of the Breech Grove church, Ohio and about 1883 entered upon the pastor of the church in East Kendall, New York. He was engaging revival work baptized 30 converts.

Bill Pitts
Birth:
Sep. 10, 1931
Death:
Feb. 26, 2003
Columbus,
Franklin County, Ohio
Burial:
Harrison Township Cemetery,
South Bloomfield,
Pickaway County, Ohio

Rev. Pitts was the founder and long time pastor of the Greater Columbus Free Will Baptist Church. He was in the ministry for 41 years.

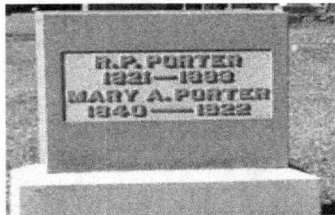

R. P. Porter
Birth:
1821
Death:
1883
Burial:
Mount Tabor Cemetery,
Huntington Township,
Gallia County, Ohio

The Harrisburg Freewill Baptist Church was organized April 4, 1862 with Porter being one of the organizing ministers. He was later a it's pastor.

Raymond Sebastian Powers
Birth:
Mar. 6, 1921
Virginia
Death:
Oct. 23, 1982
Norwalk
Huron County, Ohio
Burial:
Mount Hope Cemetery
Shiloh
Richland County, Ohio

He died from an apparent heart attack at the Crestview-Edison in football game in Milan, Ohio. He moved to Mansfield, Ohio in 1955 and then to Shiloh in 1962. He had been a clerk at the Empire-Detroit Steel company since 1955. He was a Past Master of the Shiloh Masonic Lodge number 542 and Past Patron of the Shiloh Eastern Star number 322. He held the Knights Templar

degree. He was ordained to the ministry in 1949 for the Free Will Baptist denomination. He served with the United States Army Air Force from 1940 to 1945. Services were held at the Wesley Evangelical church in Shiloh by the Rev. Carlos Allen Junior of the Clear Creek Church of Christ, Ashland.

Cecil William Price
Birth:
Mar. 27, 1927
Gallia County, Ohio
Death:
Jan. 6, 1991
Jackson, Ohio
Burial:
Gravel Hill Cemetery,
Cheshire, Gallia County, Ohio
He was a US Navy and Army World War II veteran who retired from the Ohio Valley Electric

Corporation at Kyger Creek. He was a member of the Old Kyger Free Will Baptist Church near Cheshire. He was also a Free Will Baptist preacher.

Pemberton Randall
Birth:
Oct. 6, 1807
Lebanon
New London County, Connecticut
Death:
Jan. 4, 1891
Minneapolis
Hennepin County, Minnesota
Burial:
Spring Grove Cemetery
Medina
Medina County, Ohio
Plot: section 2 lot 97

Medina County Gazette-January 9, 1891: Pemberton Randall - in his book entitled *"The Wonderful Tent"*, Rev. D. A. Randall, D. D., is written, and from which we learn that "Rev. Pemberton Randall was one of seven children born to James Randall and his wife, Joanna Pemberton Randall. The parents were able to bestow upon their children little less than those born with good blood and Christian influences. The Randall's originated in bonnie Scotland, in this stirring annual of which County the family name is not obscure. The Pemberton's sprang from sturdy English stock, possessed of both ability and nobility. Joanna was a direct descendent of Ebenezer Pemberton, D. D., one of the early distinguished pastors of Old South Church, Boston. Both father and mother were native New Englanders. Rev. Pembleton Randall departed this life at the home of his daughter, with whom he and his wife were living. Mrs. Sarah) A. R. (Randall) McGeah, in Minneapolis, Minnesota, at about eight o'clock on Sunday morning, January 4, 1891, being a little past 84 years of age. He was born in Lebanon, Connecticut. In early life, in fact in the autumn of 1826, he and his brother, Rev. Austin Randall, D. D., embraced the Christian religion in a revival meeting held by Rev. David Marks, a Free Will Baptist revivalist who came to a neighboring church and began a series of meetings. In addition to attending the meetings for some three weeks, he and his brothers, alone or in concert, engaged daily in Scripture readings, praying or in meditation. Both made a public profession of religion and on the day before Christmas, by Elder Haskell, pastor of the local church, baptized into Canandaigua Lake. Pemberton adopted the doctrine of the revivalist, and in due time became a cultivated and conscientious minister of the Free Will Church.

Soon after his conversion he removed to Ohio, and after receiving a common school education, he pursued a classical course for two years in Geauga Seminary.

In 1840 he was ordained by Elders Cyrus Coltrim and Warmer Beebe. His labors was with churches in northern Ohio. He has an able preacher, his sermons being clear, logical and strong arguments in favor of the religion of Christ. Young ministers have always considered it a great privilege to listen to his preaching, and although over 80 years of age his mental powers were clear and strong, and the Free Will Baptist Quarterly Meetings were often blessed with his presence and counsel. In

February 1834 he was joined in marriage to Maria T. Beebe, who died in February, 1839, and in 1840 he was married to Sarah C. Foster. He was the father of 10 children; five of whom and his wife survived him.

He was regarded as one of the strongest intellectual scriptural preachers of the denomination, and of which he was a worthy and honored member.

His membership was transferred from Spencer, Ohio, to the Free Will Baptist church of Minneapolis, Minnesota, where his wife is also a member. He was able to converse intelligently to the last, and died trusting in Jesus for the life of one which he has entered in the immortality of the glory world.

His remains in Medina, Ohio on Wednesday morning was, accompanied by his wife and son in law, Mr. J. A. McGeagh, and the funeral services were Thursday afternoon at 2 PM, in Medina in the Baptist church, conducted by Rev. G. H. Damon and assisted by resident and other ministers of other denominations.

Earl E. Rankin

Birth:
Sep. 14, 1897
Olive Hill,
Carter County, Kentucky
Death:
Jan., 1970
Portsmouth,
Scioto County Ohio
Burial:
Salisbury Cemetery
Stockdale, Pike County, Ohio

He was a bi-vocational Minister

and a Free Will Baptist pastor who resided in Scioto County, Ohio for 40 years. As a Free Will Baptist pastor he served the Sciotodale, Bloom, Antioch and Owl Creek churches; Sciotodale Baptist and the Fallen Timber Christian church. He was a retired Detroit Steel Corporation employee and a member of the United Steelworkers union. He was a member of the Scioto Valley Ministerial Association.

David Lyman Rice

Birth:
May 1, 1820
Green, Ohio
Death:
Nov. 19, 1886
Burial:
Westwood Cemetery
Oberlin
Lorain County, Ohio
Plot: H-001-03A

His father resided for a while in Québec but shortly after settled in Ohio before 1820. David was converted in 1834 and baptized the following March by Reverent Ransom Dunn.

His education was obtained at Geauga Seminary. He was licensed by the Green church in 1843 and ordained by the Ashtabula Quarterly Meeting at Lenox on May 17, 1846. After a pastoring a number of churches, he entered another work as an agent for Hillsdale College in 1855. He continued this work until 1876 traveling among the churches conducting revivals and instructing the people as to the needs of the college and its importance to the denomination. In all he gathered more than $50,000 for the endowment of the college and at the same time turning the footsteps of many young men and women toward classic calls and higher life. In 1877 he became pastor of the church at Pierpoint, Ohio and then in 1884 the Burgh church. It was only two years later that he would close his useful life. He is buried in the same Cemetery as the famous Charles Finney and Free Will Baptist leader David Marks.

Melford William Riddlebarger
Birth:
Oct. 10, 1906
Scioto County, Ohio
Death:
Nov. 27, 2003 Portsmouth, Scioto County, Ohio
Burial:
Memorial Burial Park, Wheelersburg, Scioto County, Ohio

He pastored in southern Ohio and was popular among the churches in the area.

Russell Homer Risner
Birth:
Mar. 20, 1934
Death:
Sep. 23, 1987
Burial:
Preston Cemetery, Alger, Hardin County, Ohio

James Richard Roby
Birth:
Jul. 1, 1977
Bellefontaine, Logan County, Ohio
Death:
Aug. 14, 2011
Bellefontaine, Logan County,, Ohio
Burial:
Greenwood Cemetery
De Graff, Logan County, Ohio

Rev. James Richard Roby, 57, of De Graff, was a son of Richard Wilbur Roby of De Graff and the late Shirley Joanne Vaughn Roby. On September 23, 1977, he married Debra Diane Kendall in Bellefontaine.

He was a 1972 graduate of Riverside High School and a graduate of Urbana College. He was the Pastor at the De Graff Freewill Baptist Church.

M. Kenneth Rose
Birth:
Feb. 4, 1932
Emerson, Lewis County, Kentucky
Death:
May 17, 2010
Mansfield, RichlandCounty,Ohio
Burial:
Franklin Cemetery, Mansfield, Richland County, Ohio

Samuel S Schnell
Birth:
Apr. 22, 1854
Liverpool, Ohio
Death:
May 2, 1936
Burial:
Beebe Town Cemetery
Beebetown
Medina County, Ohio

Being converted in 1875, he entered Hillsdale College in 1877 taking the classical course and later at the theological. On September 24, 1883 he was ordained by the Genesee Quarterly Meeting, Michigan, and has since served the churches of Millington and Leslie, Michigan and Lenox, Ohio.

William J. Sheppard
Birth:
1881
Death:
1945
Scioto County, Ohio
Burial:
Vernon Cemetery,
Lyra, Scioto County, Ohio

Early pastor and Ohio leader in the newly formed Free Will Baptists State re-organization.

Jacob Shonkwiler
Birth:
May 1, 1805
Scioto County, Ohio
Death:
Dec. 18, 1882
Lucasville
Scioto County,
Ohio
Burial:
Owl Creek Cemetery,
Beaver, Pike County, Ohio

He was one of the earliest Free Will Baptist ministers in southern Ohio and especially in Scioto County. He was a minister and farmer in this County as well as Pike County, Ohio.

Married twice and had five children by each wife. In August of 1841, he was ordained a Free Will Baptist. He was the pastor of the Hamilton Free Will Baptist Church in 1884, which had been organized in 1881 and a church building was erected that same year. The first pastor of this congregation was Isaac Fullerton. Jacob preached in southern Ohio and in Maysville, Kentucky area. He was a rabid abolitionist and became engaged in the abolition movement. Tradition says that he and his cousin the Rev. Isaac Fullerton, helped slaves escape from Kentucky into Ohio then into Canada.

James A. Shonkwiler
Birth:
Oct. 7, 1877
Pike County Ohio
Death:

October 21, 1955
Hilliard,
Franklin County, Ohio
Burial:
Owl Creek Cemetery
Pike County, Ohio

He was one of the older of the Free Will Baptist ministers in southern Ohio and was a member of the Owl Creek church which still exists.

Carl R. Sizemore
Birth:
July 17, 1917
Death:
2009
Burial:
Puckett Cemetery, Pedro,
Lawrence County, Ohio

Rev. Carl R. Sizemore, 91, of Pedro, Lawrence County, Ohio native was the son of the late Rev, Jesse C. and Hattie Delawder Sizemore. Mr. Sizemore attended Pedro Schools, was a U.S. Army WWII Veteran and a former coal miner for over 40 years with Collins Mining Company. He was a member of Symmes Valley Freewill Baptist Church in Aid, Ohio.

Denver Earl Smith
Birth:
Apr. 8, 1920
Death:
Feb. 14, 1992
Burial:
South Webster Cemetery,
South Webster,
Scioto County, Ohio

Ted B Sowards
Birth:
1905
Death:
1989
Burial:
Friendship Cemetery,
Friendship,
Scioto County, Ohio

Crate D. Sparks
Birth:
Dec. 18, 1934 Culver,
Elliott County,
Kentucky
Death:
Mar. 16, 2012 Mount
Vernon,
Knox County, Ohio
Burial:
Fairview Freewill Baptist Church
Cemetery,
Mount Vernon,
Knox County, Ohio

He began preaching the gospel in 1968. A lifelong servant of God, he founded the Ashley now Victory Freewill Baptist Church. He served the Blooming Grove Freewill Baptist Church, Pleasant Hill Freewill Baptist Church, and founded the Fairview Freewill Baptist Church, where he pastored until 2008. In 1993 he retired from Sunray Stove Company in Delaware, after 33 years of service. A US Navy Veteran, he came to Galena at the age of 18, moved to Mt. Vernon in 1993 and onto Delaware in 2011 to be near his family. Services were held with military honors.

Delmar C Sparks
Birth:
Nov. 7, 1927
Death:
Aug. 17, 2002
Estes Park,
Larimer County, Colorado
Burial:
Blendon Central Cemetery,
Westerville,
Franklin County, Ohio

He was founder of the Westerville Free Will Baptist Church where he served for 31 years. Besides being an outstanding pastor he was a very active denominational leader. He represented the state of Ohio on the General Board of the National Association from 1984-2002. He was also honored to speak at the national convention in 1989 in Tampa, Florida. As a local pastor he served on many district ordaining council's, mission board and moderator. On the state level he served as the moderator of the state Association, served on the State General Board and Executive Board. His early ministry was among the Enterprise Baptist churches before his leaving to organize the Westerville church in 1959. He was a marvelous mentor and fellow servant.

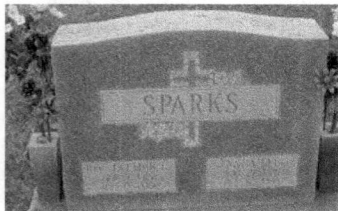

Asa Stearns
Birth:
Feb. 3, 1782
Death:
Sept. 7, 1851
Mercer County, Ohio
Burial:
Elm Grove Cemetery
Saint Marys
Auglaize County, Ohio

Sophia Higley was married to Asa Stearns, a Free Will Baptist preacher, finally settled in Mercer county, Ohio, where they both died. They had four children, Rufus, Amos, Louise, and Joel. Rufus became a doctor and is buried in the same Cemetery with his mother and father. He was connected with the Meigs Quarterly Meeting in South East Ohio in its early years and saw the fruits of his labor they are because many of the churches and influence still exist. An interesting note appears in the history of Athens County Ohio about how the early ministers were supported. "In the Ames Township area secured to the services of Elder Asa Stearns a pioneer Free Will Baptist preacher to preach for them once a month during the year, to be paid with three barrels of whiskey. Rev. Stearns had an arrangement with Ebenezer Currier, at Athens, to take the whiskey and allow him there for $24 be credited him toward the farm he had bought from Judge Currier. The contract was faithfully carried out on all hands, Elder Stearns visiting the congregation every third Saturday and Sunday of each month during the year at the end of which he received a salary of whiskey and made the transfer he did as agreed to Judge Currier."

As a doorman opens the door to a place, so death opens the door for the soul to take its flight.

Eli Stedman
Birth:
Aug. 17, 1777
Tunbridge,
Orange County, Vermont
Death:
Mar. 28, 1845
Rutland, Meigs County, Ohio
Burial:
Miles Cemetery, Rutland,
Meigs County, Ohio

He came to Ohio in 1804, locating in Belpre, Washington county, but removed to Leading Creek in 1805. He was a preacher of the Free Will Baptist denomination. Elihu Stedman was the youngest child of Eli Stedman and wife. He married Adaline Elliott, daughter of Simeon Elliott, Esq., and a sister of Rev. Madison Elliott, at one time principal of the Chester Academy. Elihu Stedman lived in Middleport many years, but moved to Iowa. Eli started the Old Kyger Free Will Baptist Church in 1805 which is the oldest church in Ohio of this denomination which still exists.

Hertis Stone
Birth:
Jul. 30, 1932
Olive Hill,
Carter County, Kentucky
Death:
Sep. 16, 1998
Mansfield, Richland County, Ohio
Burial:
Mansfield Cemetery,
Mansfield,Richland ,Ohio

Although he was a Kentuckian he spent the majority of his adult life in Ohio, where he retired from the General Motors CPC plant.

Brother Stone was pastor of the Wyandotte Free Will Baptist Church of Mansfield for over 20 years. He was also the evangelists for the Northern Ohio Free Will Baptist Conference and was a member of the Cuyahoga-Lorain Free Will Baptists Executive conference board. He also pastored churches in Amherst, Ohio; Huntington, Indiana; Buckeye Lake and Fitchville, Ohio Free Will Baptist churches

J. A. Sutton
Birth:
1847
Symmes township
Hamilton county, Ohio
Death:
1921
LaRue, Ohio
Burial:
LaRue Cemetery
La Rue
Marion County, Ohio

Obit: Rev. Jeremiah Augustus Sutton, LaRue's grand old man, was found dead in bed by his wife. Sunday morning. Death being caused from heart failure. He had

been in his usual health Saturday and was to deliver the sermon at the funeral of Mrs. Milton Anderson, near DeCliff, Sunday afternoon. On the desk in Rev, and Mrs. Sutton's room was the obituary, funeral text and notes on the sermon to be used. The service was conducted by Rev. F. E. Hawes, pastor of Fite Memorial Baptist church, of Marion, who used the text chosen by Rev. Mr. Sutton.Rev. Mr. Sutton was perhaps the most widely known minister in the county and to know him was to win a friend in the truest sense of the word. He had long been called the "marrying and burying parson," having delivered 2,089 funeral sermons and performing 746 marriage services.Rev. Mr. Sutton was ordained to the ministry October 24, 1874. He came to Marion county in 1879 accepting the pastorate in Green Camp Baptist church. This position he held until April 8, 1890 when he was appointed chaplain to the Ohio State penitentiary, which position he filled for about two years. During his pastorate in the institution, Rev. Mr. Sutton organized what was known as the Ohio Penitentiary Sunday-school and through his association had eighty-four conversions. In 1894 Rev. Mr. Sutton moved to LaRue, where he served twelve consecutive years as pastor of the Free Will Baptist church. With the exception of a short time passed as pastor of a charge in West Mansfield, he passed the remainder of his life in LaRue.Rev. Mr. Sutton was twice married, the first wife being Miss Mollie Cox, who died November 28, 1869. March 22, 1883, he was married to Mrs. Helen Kniffin.Rev. Mr. Sutton had held all the offices in the church and a large number of offices in the township and village. He had been a notary public for the past thirty-one years, and at the time of his death was clerk of Montgomery township. He was affiliated with LaRue Lodge, No. 35. F. A. M., and of Green Camp lodge, No. 644,

I.O.O.F. He was also a member of the Eastern Star and Rebekah lodges and of the LaRue Protective association. At one time he was editor of the LaRue News.

Brighton N Tanner
Birth:
1852
Chester, Ohio
Death:
Apr. 1, 1932
Burial:
Lake View Cemetery
Cleveland
Cuyahoga County, Ohio
Plot: Section 42 Lot 782-0

He was educated at Geauga, Ohio. In 1885 he consecrated his life to God and May 20, 1888 was licensed to preach by the Geauga and Portage Quarterly Meeting.

Paul Elden Taylor
Birth:
Aug. 18, 1921
Cheshire,
Gallia County, Ohio
Death:
Dec. 20, 2004
Rutland,
Meigs County, Ohio
Burial:
Gravel Hill Cemetery,
Cheshire,
Gallia County, Ohio

Rev. Taylor served as pastor to the Rutland Freewill Baptist Church for 30 years and he shared his ministry for 12 years in Utah. During World War II he served four years in the U.S. Army in the Philippines as a foot soldier.

Clyde Thompson, Jr
Birth:
Mar. 28, 1939 Grahn,
Carter County, Kentucky
Death:
May 2, 2012 Mansfield,
Richland County, Ohio
Burial:
Mound Cemetery, Piketon,
Pike County, Ohio

He was a veteran of the United States Army and had retired from Wickes Lumber company after driving a truck for over 30 years. He was a Free Will Baptist minister having pastored churches in Ohio and Indiana. He was a member of the Dean Road Free Will Baptist Church in Mansfield, Ohio.

Alvin Trusty
Birth:
1918
Death:
1955
Burial:
Preston Cemetery, Alger,
Hardin County, Ohio
Plot: Section 2
(East), row 18

Benjamin Tufts
Birth:
Feb. 12, 1777
Maine
Death:
Aug. 27, 1849
Maineville
Warren County, Ohio
Burial:
Maineville Cemetery
Maineville
Warren County, Ohio

He was converted in 1802 and became connected with the church in Phillips, Maine where he was ordained in 1822. The same year he moved to Ohio where he United with the main feel, Hamilton County, church and continued to preach as opportunity presented going as far west as Indiana.

Francis Tufts
Birth:
Feb., 1743
Maine
Death:
Oct. 2, 1833
Warren County, Ohio
Burial:
Maineville Cemetery, Maineville,
Warren County, Ohio, Plot: Sec.E

Tufts was a true pioneer. He was born in Medford, Mass., but as Maine and Mass. were one large area, he moved from Medford, MA to Farmington, Maine, and was an early contributor to that area.
He served Maine in the Revolutionary War, enlisting in 1775-1777, in Lincoln Co. Maine. He finally received a pension shortly before his death. Where and when he was ordained was associated with the Farmington Q.M., when it was dealing with Rev. Edward Lock on the subject of open communion before 1800, and the votes came out yeas for Rev. Tufts to have open communion. Rev. Moses Dudley (of Maine) had moved to Ohio from Maine, served in the ministry and meetings in this area. They are both buried in this cemetery. (Maineville history

states that in 1850 this name was adopted because so many citizens had migrated there from Maine). When Samuel Knowlton, a kinsman friend was removing there, Rev. Francis Tufts (at 87 yrs of age) decided to ride horse-back the one-thousand-mile trip with them to get there. They started Sept. 1, 1831, and arrived Oct 13, 1831, went through nine states, stopping only for "the Sabbath" to worship. Rev. Tufts was always invited to preach which he ably did. It was reported he had a retentive memory--well versed in Old and New Testaments that he could quote entire chapters or suitable portions of scripture. Rev. Tufts was in near perfect physical conditions, but two years later, he passed away."*The Story of His Predecessors and Descendants*" by Marion Thomas Whitney, pub. 1995, states that Josiah Tufts (1780-1841), who mar. Jane (Greely) Tufts, was his son. Jane was dau. of Seth Greely (1737-1825) who came to Maineville in 1815.

John F. Tufts
Birth:
Oct. 7, 1829
Barrington
Strafford County, New Hampshire
Death:
May 13, 1873
Warren County, Ohio
Burial:
Maineville Cemetery
Maineville
Warren County, Ohio

His service was among the churches of the Miami Quarterly Meeting. He received license to preach the gospel about 1846 when connected with the Rossbourgh for church and was ordained about three years later. He spent some time at the biblical school in Whitestown, New York. He was a prominent man and much loved in the Miami Quarterly Meeting where he had long service and, noble, and Christian example causing him to be liked by others. He also spent a few years in Iowa. He represented the Ohio Yearly Meeting in the General Conference in 1850.

Clyde Marshall VanHoose
Birth:
Feb. 20, 1933
Johnson County, Kentucky
Death:
Aug. 22, 2011
Burial:
Big Darby Cemetery,
Plain City,
Madison County, Ohio

Employed by Columbus Auto Parts and was the assistant pastor of the North Woodbury Freewill Baptist Church. He was a U.S. Army veteran (1953 to 1955) during the Korean Conflict.

Clovis Vanover
Birth:
Oct. 9, 1933
Laredo, West Virginia
Death:
Columbus,
Franklin County, Ohio
Burial:
Mifflin Cemetery,
Gahanna,
Franklin County, Ohio

He was the founder and Chairman of the C.W. Vanover Evangelistic Association and a member of the Williams Road FWB Church. He as a State-Wide Evangelist for Ohio Free Will Baptists.

Charles H. Webb
Birth:
Mar. 29, 1926
Auxier,
Floyd County, Kentucky

Death:
Mar. 15, 1976
Springdale,
Washington County, Arkansas
Burial:
Woodlawn Cemetery,
Ada, Hardin County, Ohio

Rev. Charles H. Webb, 49 died at of an apparent heart attack in Springdale Hospital, Springdale, Ark. He was an army veteran of World War II, former pastor of the High Street Freewill Baptist, Rt. 2, Ada, a retired factory worker and member of the High Street Freewill Baptist Church.

Eugene Webb
Birth:
Nov. 5, 1931
Bonanza, Kentucky
Death:
Dec. 10, 2010
Dola, Hardin County, Ohio
Burial:
Dola Cemetery, Dola,
Hardin County, Ohio

Free Will Baptist Minister in western Ohio. He and his wife, Carolyn Yoxsimer Webb, worked as house parents at the FWB Home for Children in Greeneville, Tn. for three years and later served as a Field Representative for the home in Ohio for three additional years.
He served his country in the Korean Conflict from 1951-1953 as a member of the U.S. Army 2nd Division.

Harrison Webb
Birth:
May 4, 1927
Lawrence County, Ohio
Death:
Nov. 28, 2007
Ashland, Boyd County, Kentucky
Burial:
Community Missionary Baptist
Church Cemetery,
Lawrence County, Ohio

The Lawrence County, Ohio native, the son of the late Simeon

and Hazel May Fetters Webb. He is survived by his wife, Maxine Faye Littlejohn Webb, whom he married August 18, 1951.Mr. Webb attended Spring Branch Schools. He was a U.S. Army Korean War Veteran serving from 1948-1952 and received a Bronze Star. He was an iron pourer at the Dayton Malleable Iron Company for 27 years, retiring in 1989. He was a member of Symmes Valley Freewill Baptist Church and was a former pastor at several local churches. He lived in this area all his life.

Simeon J Weed
Birth:
1854
Death:
1927
Burial:
Calvary Baptist Cemetery,
Rio Grande, Gallia County, Ohio

Minister, leader, professor at Rio Grande College in Ohio before and after the merger with the Northern Baptists.

John Wheeler
Birth:
Sep. 6, 1787
Rehoboth
Bristol County, Massachusetts
Death:
Aug. 4, 1879
Greenwich
Huron County, Ohio
Burial:
Steuben Cemetery
Steuben
Huron County, Ohio

In 1805 he married Miss Mary Franklin and moved to Richmond, New York. After serving in the Army of the war of 1812 he was converted and in 1818 moved to Greenfield, Ohio where he began to preach, gathered a church and received ordination in September 1825. After the church was put up on a good basis he resigned the pastorate and labored in that region of the country becoming a circuit preacher helping to found several Free Will Baptist Churches. He had two marriages to the following ladies: Huldah Gregory Wheeler Mary Franklin Wheeler

Inscription:
Rev. John Wheeler
DiedAug 4, 1879
Aged 90 years 11 months

Billy Joe White
Birth:
May 8, 1941
Logan, Logan County,
West Virginia
Death:
Aug. 11, 2009
Sullivan, Ashland County, Ohio
Burial:
Southview Cemetery,
Sullivan, Ashland County, Ohio

Billy Joe worked at the Ford Motor Co. in Brook Park for many years, retiring as a general foreman. A man of faith, Billy Joe had served as the pastor of the Free Will Baptist Church in Wellington since 1985. He enjoyed farming.

Philander E. Whittier
Birth:
Aug. 8, 1834
Death:
Oct. 2, 1871
Ohio
Burial:
Cheshire Cemetery
Delaware
Delaware County, Ohio

Rev. Philander Ellis WHITTIER, was the son of John and Loerza Whittier. He was converted in early life, and after various journeyings [lived in Wisconsin], he married in 1863, in Farmington, ME to Mary Parker Tuffs, and soon settled in Ohio. He was licensed to preach by the Richland and Licking Quarterly Meeting in May 1877, and devoted himself to the work of the ministry with goodacceptance, but the end of his labors came soon after.

David Widdig
Birth:
Mar. 17, 1906
Springs, Sciotoville,
Scioto County, Ohio
Death:
Nov. 16, 1993 Huntington,
Cabell County,
West Virginia
Burial:
Memorial Burial Park,
Wheelersburg,
Scioto County, Ohio

He was a retired electrician employed by the Goodyear Atomic Corporation and was a Free Will Baptist Minister for more than 50 years pastoring four churches.

Marion Wilburn
Birth:
1891
Death:
1951
Scioto County, Ohio
Burial:
South Webster Cemetery,
South Webster,
Scioto County, Ohio

Alvin Gardner Wilder
Birth:
Nov. 22, 1828
Chesterfield
Hampshire County, Massachusetts
Death:
Aug. 27, 1875
Berea, Cuyahoga County, Ohio
Burial:
Beebe Town Cemetery
Beebetown,
Medina County, Ohio

Wilder died at aged 46 years. The family moved to Ohio in 1833 and ten years later Brother Wilder was converted, uniting with the Hinckley church. He was ordained Oct. 5, 1856, by a council from the Medina Q. M. His labors were chiefly with the Hinckley, Royalton, Rockport, Liverpool, and Henrietta churches, and in most of them there remained living evidences of the fruit of his labors.

Charlie Wiley
Birth:
Nov. 29, 1929
Stirrat, Logan County,
West Virginia
Death:
Dec. 8, 2010
Columbus,
Franklin County, Ohio
Burial:
Glen Rest Memorial Estate,
Reynoldsburg,
Franklin County, Ohio

Allen Williams, Jr
Birth:
Jan. 9, 1929
Scioto County,Ohio
Death:
Mar. 26, 1996,
Ashland,Boyd County,Kentucky
Burial:
Clapboard Cemetery,Franklin
Furnace,Scioto County,Ohio

He was a son of Allen Williams, Sr and Hazel Ruth Chamberlain. He was a former employee of the Williams Manufacturing Company with 25 years of service. He retired as an employee of Martin Marietta and was a Korean War veteran. He was ordained as a minister in the June, 1957 and served as a pastor of the Pine Creek, Union, Mount Hope and Germany Hollow churches.

Paul Eugene Williams
Birth:
Dec. 8, 1957
Portsmouth,
Scioto County, Ohio
Death:
Jul. 26, 2010
Portsmouth
Scioto County, Ohio
Burial:
Bennett Cemetery,
Minford, Scioto County, Ohio

He was the pastor at Frederick Free Will Baptist Church. Along with Frederick Free Will Baptist Church, he served as pastor at Swauger Valley Free Will, Bloom Free Will, Tick Ridge Free Will and Harvest Chapel Church in Sciotoville. He was a bookkeeper for E.E. Blair Construction Co. in Wheelersburg, and had worked as a bookkeeper for Colonial Florist and Reynolds Bordan and Chapman Accountants in Portsmouth, and the former Nancy Rae Supermarket in Wheelersburg. He was a graduate of Minford High School in the class of 1976, and he was very active in the ministry and work of the Free Will Baptist Denomination.

Joe M. Wireman
Birth:
Sep. 10, 1927
Magoffin County,
Kentucky
Death:
Burial:
Fairmont Cemetery,
Uniopolis,
Auglaize County, Ohio

The Rev. Wireman retired from Boilermakers Local 85 in 1990. He was a member of the Cridersville Church, where he was pastor in previous years and continued to minister throughout his life. He has been a faithful and active member of the church for 58 years.

Leslie Wireman
Birth:
Nov. 14, 1932
Death:
Jan. 22, 2007
Alger, Hardin County, Ohio
Burial:
Preston Cemetery, Alger,
Hardin County, Ohio

Since I accepted Christ, dying is all I've been living for!

Floyd I. Wolfenbarger
Birth:
Feb. 16, 1949
Springfield,
Clark County, Ohio
Death:
May 22, 1985
Little Rock,
Pulaski County, Arkansas
Burial:
Vale Cemetery,
Springfield, Clark County, Ohio

A Free Will Baptist minister, writer and denominational leader. He attended Free Will Baptist Bible College, Oklahoma Bible College, Ohio State University and Cedarville College. Called to preach at age 12 and ordained to the ministry at age 20. He pastored in Oklahoma, Ohio and Arkansas. He was moderator of the Ohio State Association of Free Will Baptists for four years and served eight years as Ohio's General Board Member to the National Association of Free Will Baptists. Six of those years he was a member of the Executive Committee. He wrote articles printed in the *Contact* and *Ambassador Magazines*. A respected leader and minister by his peers.

Andrew Workman
Birth:
Jul. 25
Wayne County, West Virginia,
Death:
Jun. 21
Portsmouth, Scioto County, Ohio
Burial:
Evergreen Union Cemetery
Waverly, Pike County Ohio

Rev. Workman was known throughout the tri-state area of Ohio, Kentucky, and West Virginia as a Free Will Baptist evangelist and preacher. He was short in stature but tall in evangelism.

Gilbert Lafayette Yeley
Birth:
Nov. 2, 1868
Death:
Mar. 1, 1951
Scioto County
Ohio
Burial:
Turner Cemetery
Scioto County
Ohio

He was an early Free Will Baptist preacher in southern Ohio and represents a name that had many other notable Free Will Baptists.

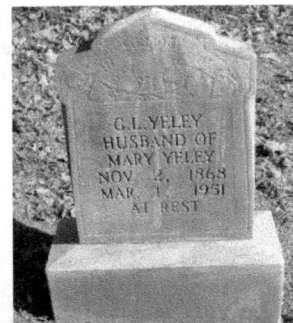

He was farmer and filled pulpits as a Free Will Baptist minister. He was a member of Bloom FWB church. He married Mary Henning in 1890. His sister Miss Bessie Yeley was a missionary.

Bessie N. Yeley
Birth:
Nov. 26, 1895
Death:
Jan. 23, 1969
Wheelersburg,
Scioto County, Ohio
Burial:
Memorial Burial Park,
Wheelersburg,
Scioto County, Ohio

She was ordained by the Porter Conference of Free Will Baptists. In 1936, at the age of 40, Bessie entered Venezuela as a missionary. In subsequent years Bessie served in Cuba under Free Will Baptist Foreign Missions. She also served under the Home

Mission Board in Arizona and Texas along the Mexican border, and later in Miami to Cuban refugees. She was ordained by the Porter Conference.

John Sowers Yeley
Birth:
Feb. 11, 1874
Slocum,
Scioto County, Ohio
Death:
Dec. 26, 1936
Scioto County, Ohio
Burial:
Vernon Cemetery, Lyra,
Scioto County, Ohio

Rev. Yeley began his career as a minister of the gospel at age 31 and continued in the service of Free Will Baptists for 25 years. He was a brother to missionary Bessie Yeley, who at the time of his death was serving as a missionary in Venezula but later in Panama and Cuba. Many notable Free Will Baptists came from the Yeley family in the future years.

Benjamin Franklin Zell
Birth:
August 7, 1833
Warren County, Ohio
Death:
1916
Burial:
Miami Cemetery
Corwin
Warren County, Ohio

He was educated at Mainville Academy and Lebanon normal school. He was ordained in 1862 by Elder Cyrus Dudley, John Hisey and F. Myers. In 1856 he was married to Jane M. Phillips. In 1863 he moved to Salem, Indiana and took charge of the Salem, Ridgeville, and Bear Creek churches. The following year he returned to Ohio and assumed the pastorates of the East Liberty, Union, York and Newton churches. With these churches he labored 14 years. During that time he baptized and received into the churches over 600 persons. Three new meeting houses were built and one church was organized. He served the Ohio and Ohio Central Yearly Meetings as clerk and three times a delegate to the General Conference.

DEATH is THE SUREST CALCULATION THAT CAN bE MADE

Oklahoma

Eldie Clifton Able
Birth:
Aug. 28, 1937
Coweta,
Wagoner County, Oklahoma
Death:
Jan. 5, 2010
Tulsa,
Tulsa County, Oklahoma
Burial:
Vernon Cemetery, Coweta,
Wagoner County, Oklahoma

A retired machinist, Eldie was an active minister who enjoyed mowing, painting cement figurines, horses, reading Westerns and especially his grandchildren.

Maxi Lee Adair
Birth:
Jan. 10, 1940
El Paso, El Paso County, Texas
Death:
Aug. 6, 2012
Muskogee, Muskogee County, Oklahoma
Burial:
Greenhill Cemetery Muskogee, Muskogee County, Oklahoma

Maxi graduated from Tahlequah High School in 1959. In 1960, he joined the United States Army and received an honorable discharged in 1963. He worked for Acme Engineering beginning in 1965 until his retirement in 2002. Maxi gave his life to God on March 14, 1969 and surrendered to preach New Year's Eve 1974. He pastored the Grovania Free Will Baptist Church, Fort Gibson Free Will Baptist Church, Hitchita Free Will Baptist Church, and the First Free Will Baptist Church in Muskogee.

Elder William Charles Austin
Birth:
Jun., 1864
Savannah,
Hardin County, Tennessee
Death:1933
Shawnee, Pottawatomie County,
Oklahoma
Burial:
Fairview Cemetery,
Shawnee, Pottawatomie County,
Oklahoma

He was an ordained Free Will Baptist preacher, but research is needed to obtain the date he was ordained. His name is in old church records as having preached several years before statehood in 1907. He was a prominent preacher and able debater in the central part of Oklahoma, and western Arkansas. He was an acceptable orator, and a great preacher. Many were converted under his ministry, and it is unknown just how many churches he organized, but he did a good work. He was editor of a church paper, *The Pruning Hook,* for a few years and was always putting forth the gospel.

Starks Washington Baldwin
Birth:
Jun. 23, 1865
Tawamba County, Mississippi
Death:
Jan. 27, 1920
Wister,Le Flore County,
Oklahoma
Burial:
Ellis Chapel Cemetery,
Wister,Le Flore County,
Oklahoma

Jerry Cleo Banks
Birth:
Aug. 3, 1948
Tulsa,
Tulsa County, Oklahoma
Death:
Jan. 6, 2005
Oklahoma
Burial:
Moore Cemetery, Moore,
Cleveland County
Oklahoma

Jerry served as a missionary in Japan for 19 years and a pastor in Colquitt, Georgia, and Cushing, Oklahoma. He was also an instructor at Hillsdale FWB College as is his wife Dr. Janice Banks. He also was serving as pastor of Kingsview FWB Church, So. OKC, when he was tragically killed in an auto accident

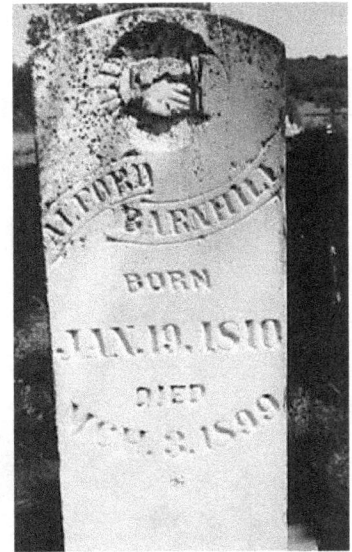

Alford Barnhill
Birth:
Jan. 19, 1810
Tennessee
Death:
Mar. 3, 1899
Arpelar, Pittsburg County,
Oklahoma
Burial:
White Chimney Cemetery,
Stuart,
Pittsburg County Oklahoma

He was ordained as Free Will Baptist preacher, but unknown when and where. He came into Indian Territory, in what is now Oklahoma, where these pioneer ministers preached and organized churches for the settlers. When several churches were organized, they met at Nubbin Ridge school house, near Spiro, Choctaw Nation, Sept. 1, 1894, and formed the Territorial Association of Free Will Baptists. Eld. A. Barnhill, was elected the first moderator, Eld. O.J. Taylor, Ass't Moderator, and Eld. I.W. Graham, clerk. Eld. A. Barnhill's name appears in old Territorial marriage records of those he performed.

You Are Home At Last!

John E. Bean
Birth:
1876
Texas
Death:
May, 1961
Edmond,
Oklahoma County, Oklahoma
Burial:
Sunny Lane Cemetery, Del City,
Oklahoma County, Oklahoma

He was an ordained Free Will Baptist minister. His brother, Will L. Bean, was also a preacher. In Oklahoma during the 1920's through 1950's. Rev. Bean was very active, and known as an outstanding evangelist. He was chosen to preach in the 1932 and 1934 Oklahoma FWB State Associations. He authored the book, *"What Would the World Be Without the Bible,"* a book that defends the Biblical record in various aspects of its historical statements. He is also author of a number of poems based on Bible subjects, and being a natural elocutionist, he often recited from memory upon request.

Ransom "Rance" Bess
Birth:
Apr. 22, 1844
Grenada,
Grenada County, Mississippi
Death:
Aug. 5, 1932
Pontotoc County, Oklahoma
Burial:
Egypt Cemetery, Ada,
Pontotoc County, Oklahoma

Early pioneer minister of the Chickasaw Nation (Pontotoc Co. OK). He was well-liked and esteemed and ministered to many. Civil War Veteran Pvt. Co. F, 18th TX Ochiltree's Inf. CSA

Paskel Dale Bevan
Birth:
Apr. 15, 1946
Death:
Sep. 3, 2010
Burial:
Friends Church Cemetery,
Cromwell,
Seminole County Oklahoma

Paskel was the owner and operator of Seminole Sheet Metal for many years. He was also a longtime minister of the Friends Free Will Baptist Church of Seminole County. Paskel also enjoyed reading his Bible and helping build missionary churches.

W. M. Bingham
Birth:
Feb. 26, 1871
Death:
Mar. 11, 1947
Burial:
Sub-Station Cemetery,
Freedom Hill,
Creek County, Oklahoma

Kenneth Brandon
Birth:
Sep. 6, 1921,
Death:
Jan. 29, 2008
Talihina, Le Flore County,
Oklahoma
Burial:
Macedonia Cemetery,
Pocola,
Le Flore County, Oklahoma

Rev. Brandon was a veteran of World War II, where he served in the Marine Corps, receiving a Purple Heart for wounds received during the Bougainville Island campaign. He started and pastored many Freewill Baptist Churches in his lifetime. He never had much in the way of material wealth; he gave everything he had to the less fortunate.

William "Bill" Bratcher
Birth:
Oct. 16, 1916
Garvin County, Oklahoma
Death:
Mar. 31, 2012
Oklahoma
Burial:
McGee Cemetery, Stratford,
Garvin County, Oklahoma

The Ada Newspaper: April 3, 2012 Stratford —Mr. Bratcher was ordained in the Free Will Baptist church in the late 1940's, in Pontotoc Co. OK. He preached and ministered to churches throughout the area.

Ernest E. Bristow
Birth:
Aug. 31, 1894
Tecumseh,

Pottawatomie County, Oklahoma
Death:
Nov. 26, 1941
Asher, Pottawatomie County,
Oklahoma
Burial:
Wanette Cemetery, Wanette,
Pottawatomie County, Oklahoma

After he finished college, he taught school in many small oil towns in south central Okla. He was also an ordained minister, and music instructor, and often led the singing in many churches. He taught "singing schools" in communities all over that area. Related to teaching school, his name is found in the old 1920's Ada Weekly newspaper with items such as, "E.E. Bristow, Stratford, teacher, for 8 terms; then "Prof. Bristow with his able corps of teachers attended teachers meeting Thursday, Friday and Saturday." He had left Oklahoma to find work in California due to hardships following dustbowl. He worked one day there, had a heart attack and returned to Oklahoma where he died a few months later. In the book, *"History of Oklahoma Free Will Baptist State Association, 100 Years, 1908-2008"*, pub. 2008, it records that in 1926, "Eld. E. E. Bristow, was Rep. from Center to the State Ass'n of FWB, and in the 1932 annual state Association, he was elected clerk of that organization.

Edna Hunt Buckelew
Birth:
1909
Death:
1985
Burial:
McGee Cemetery,
Stratford,
Garvin County, Oklahoma

She was a Free Will Baptist minister in the early part of Center Association, OK.

Robert William Carter
Birth:
Apr. 30, 1916
Ola, Yell County, Arkansas
Death:
Sep. 5, 2001
Broken Arrow,
Tulsa County, Oklahoma
Burial:
Park Grove Cemetery,
Broken Arrow,
Tulsa County, Oklahoma

A Free Will Baptist minister, Rev. Carter was licensed in 1957 and ordained in 1958. He pastored churches in California, Arkansas, Missouri and Oklahoma.

James Nathaniel Caton
Birth:
Oct. 14, 1862
Cooper County, Missouri
Death:
May 18, 1953
Ada, Pontotoc County, Oklahoma
Burial:
Oakman Cemetery,
Oakman,
Pontotoc County, Oklahoma

Old Brother" Caton, as he is known to his innumerable friends, was born in Missouri where he grew to young manhood, and remembered back as he tells of the time when the "Bluecoats," part of Custer's army, passed through his town on their way to the badlands of South Dakota. He left his home state of Missouri in

1886 for Texas. He was a farmer, made a few crops in Texas, moved to Oakland, Indian Territory, and made a crop, then back to Texas and in 1895, he moved to a place near Allen and lived in Pontotoc County. Definitely an Ada pioneer. Rev. Caton, a Free Will Baptist preacher since 1902, has probably married and buried as many people in the county as any other preacher. Even at 85, he still performed these ministerial duties. He has pastored at nearly every small community in the northern part of the county. His first pastorate was at Sikes school, where Atwood now stands. Other places where he pastored are Black Rock, Happyland, Cedar Grove, Yeager, Center, Culley west of Sasakwa, Pecan Grove, Stedman, McCalls Chapel, and Big Springs south of Wewoka. He was pastor of the Oakman church, his home community, for 19 years. At age 84, he was recalled as pastor with an assistant to take his place if he was unable to appear. Preaching in the "good old way," Caton would have four or five churches at the same time preaching in them only about once a month. He would arrive on Saturday in the community where he was pastor and hold one service that day, another on Sunday morning, another Sunday evening. During the summer session, he would hold revival meetings from two to five weeks long in each community he pastored.

Marion L. Caton
Birth:
Aug. 12, 1898
Pontotoc County, Oklahoma
Death:
Sep., 1965
Oklahoma City,
Oklahoma County, Oklahoma
Burial:

Arlington Memory Gardens, Oklahoma City, Oklahoma County, Oklahoma

He grew up around Oakman, Pontotoc Co. Oklahoma attending schools there. He was an ordained Free Will Baptist minister and pastor.

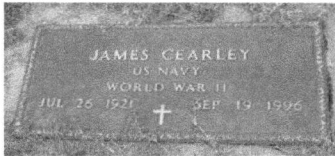

James Cearley
Birth:
Jul. 26, 1921
Death:
Sep. 19, 1996
Burial:
Tecumseh Cemetery, Tecumseh, Pottawatomie County Oklahoma

He was a Free Will Baptist minister and a member of the US Navy during WW II.

James B. Chism
Birth:
May 12, 1925
Tupelo, Mississippi
Death:
Sep. 9, 2007
Tulsa, Oklahoma
Burial:
Floral Haven Memorial Gardens, Broken Arrow, Tulsa County, Oklahoma, Plot: Sermon on the Mount Garden

He grew up in East Tupelo where he played football and the clarinet in the band. After graduation he became a medic in the United States Army during World War II. After his discharge he married Imogene Martin on October 15, 1946. They both graduated from Bob Jones University in Greenville, S. C. where he earned a Masters Degree in Church History in 1952. He became the Minister of the Horse Branch Free Will Baptist Church in Turbeville, South Carolina. Later the First Free Will Baptist Church in Newport News, Virginia. In 1967 he moved his family to Tulsa to become the pastor of the New Home Free Will Baptist Church where he was pastor until 1988 where he retired.

He founded the greater Tulsa the seniors organization OASIS and was very active on the Oklahoma State Mission Board starting churches across the state. They served over six decades in the ministry.

Claude C. Chisum
Birth:
Mar. 25, 1894
Texas
Death:
Jun. 6, 1962
Hughes County, Oklahoma
Burial:
Non Cemetery, Non, Hughes County, Oklahoma

He served in the Infantry WW I, where he was exposed to mustard gas which caused him health problems thereafter. He lived in the Non community where he served the FWB church as a deacon for many years. He then was ordained as a minister of the gospel and pastored churches in the area, among them; Crossroads, Calvin, and others, and preached wherever he was needed. He attended the Quarterly and State Association meetings.

William M. Coggins
Birth:
unknown
Texas
Death:
1946
Oklahoma
Burial:
McGee Cemetery, Stratford, Garvin County, Oklahoma

W. M. Coggins came to Indian Territory, probably after 1900, from Wise Co. Texas, upon request by a letter from Eld. Tom J. Townsend, an early arriver to the Indian Territory, asking him to come and help form some four churches into an association and preach for them. By 1904, he was preaching in the area churches from which the Center Association was formed in 1893 of Chickasha Nation. He was elected to be moderator of this Center Association in 1906, following Rev. Mark Harris's move to Arkansas. He continued in this position for years, in most every session until his late retirement. He was pastor of several churches throughout the years, that included Blanchard in McClain Co., and his name appears in many old church records as having preached or pastored there. He was the elected delegate by this group to represent them in the Southwestern Association of Free Will Baptists, which met Nov. 1906 at Decatur, Texas. He was always in the forefront of leadership in the support of the Tecumseh FWB College which had been started in 1917. At the August 1946 session, it was reported that "our old beloved moderator has passed away;" then it was voted "for the Association to place a monument at his grave."

The day is coming when all will hear His voice.

Albert Lee Collier
Birth:
Jul. 25, 1918
Death:
Mar. 19, 2008
Burial:
Highland Cemetery,
Okemah,
Okfuskee County,
Oklahoma

He spent the majority of his life in and around the Okemah area. At the time of his death Albert was a member of the Okemah Free Will Baptist Church. He was ordained as a deacon in the Schoolton Free Will Baptist Church west of Okemah, April 10, 1949, and was ordained as a Free Will Baptist minister on May 20, 1951. He received a certificate of award from the Oklahoma Bible College on May 15, 1961. He helped organize Schoolton Free Will Baptist Church. He preached his second sermon after the organization of the church that Saturday on Schoolton corner. He preached his third sermon at Pleasant Oak School. His first pastorate was at the Schoolton Free Will Baptist Church. He also pastored Free Will Baptist Churches at Hannah, Sunnylane in Del City, Wewoka, Prague, Henryetta, Calvin, and Faith Free Will Baptist Church in Holdenville. He built or remodeled every place he pastored. He built an educational wing a new sanctuary at Sunnylane, a completely new facility at Wewoka, remodeled the

facility at Prague and totally remodeled the Henryetta church. Brother Collier was instrumental in founding of the Okemah Free Will Baptist Church and labored in the construction of the facility under the pastorate of Brother Frank Young. The north wing of the church was dedicated in his honor. He served on the Oklahoma State Church Training Board, Oklahoma State Mission Board, and moderator of many associations while serving on several district boards. He celebrated 50 years of ministry on December 30, 2001. Records show that during his ministry he preached 170 funerals, 24 weddings, 56 revivals.

Leonard Crowder
Birth:
Apr. 12, 1917
Death:
Nov. 19, 2009
Barling,
Sebastian County,
Arkansas,
Burial:
Stigler Cemetery,
Stigler, Haskell County,
Oklahoma,

He was a Free Will Baptist Minister and a member of the Bethlehem Free Will Baptist Church of Van Buren, Arkansas.. He served in many churches in the area over the years but served as Pastor of the Walnut Street Free Will Baptist Church for over 30 years. He served in the Civil Conservation Corp and was an active member of the Ministerial Alliance of Fort Smith for many years.

Marvin P Dalton
Birth:
Mar. 9, 1906
Arkansas
Death:
Nov. 28, 1987
Tulsa County, Oklahoma
Burial:
Floral Haven Memorial Gardens,
Broken Arrow,
Tulsa County, Oklahoma

Well-known gospel song writer who was the son of William Henry Dalton and Effie (Thomas) Dalton. who were both Free Will Baptist preachers in Arkansas and Oklahoma. Marvin, a noted and published song writer, with *"Looking for a City", "When Jesus Passed By"*, and *"O' What a Saviour"* being the most popular of his songs. He attend Free Will Baptist Bible College in the late 40's. He directed music at the First Free Will Baptist Church in Tulsa under John West, but at the time of his passing was a member of the Assembly of God which had been the denomination of his wife.

Stephen Andrew Dame
Birth:
Feb. 9, 1847
Jasper, Marion County,
Tennessee
Death
Apr. 3, 1927
Burial:
Center Cemetery, Center,
Pontotoc County, Oklahoma,
Plot: Dame Family
(near entrance)

As a young boy, Stephen brought food and supplies to his older brother who was fighting in the Civil War. They moved from Jasper to Randolph County, Arkansas, in about 1878 or 1880. They lived in a tiny community known both as Water Valley and DeMun. Here, they built a log cabin. and farmed in Randolph County. Stephen was called to preach the Gospel at a young age. He could not read or write, but his wife could. She would read him passages from the Bible and he learned to read it. The Bible was the only thing he ever learned to read. He was a Freewill Baptist preacher. A man of great stature, Stephen stood 6'4" and was very slim. The obituary in the Ada Evening News (Ada, OK), read:"Rev. S. A. Dame, aged 82, died Sunday at 1 o'clock at his home at Center. Funeral services were set for this afternoon. Internment in Center cemetery. "Mr. Dame was a pioneer Freewill Baptist minister who had spent many years of his life in this country, doing his part in reclaiming it and making it a better place for later comers. He was highly respected by all who knew him."

William David "Voss" Dame
Birth:
Dec. 31, 1881
Death:
Jul. 23, 1957
Burial:
Center Cemetery, Center,
Pontotoc County, Oklahoma

William Edward Dearmore
Birth:
May 25, 1881
Arkansas
Death:
Dec. 12, 1945
Wanette,
Pottawatomie County, Oklahoma
Burial:
Wanette Cemetery, Wanette,
Pottawatomie County, Oklahoma

Dearmore, was an ordained Free Will Baptist minister, coming into Oklahoma from his native state of Arkansas. His name appears in 1924 Free Will Baptist State Minutes as being elected Ass't Moderator of the State meeting, and Moderator of the 1935 thru 1939 meetings. He was one of a committee selected in the 1935 conference to represent Oklahoma in Nashville, Tennessee, about forming a National Association. He was active in his local, state and national meetings.

Othel Thomas Dixon
Birth:
Jun. 20, 1919
Hector,Pope County, Arkansas
Death:
Oct. 27, 2007
Claremore,
Rogers County, Oklahoma

Burial:
Greenlawn Cemetery, Checotah,
McIntosh County, Oklahoma

He was the first Dixon to achieve outstanding All Star Basketball Player status. He graduated from Checotah High School in 1940. He moved to Oklahoma City working as a clerk at the Veterans Administration.

O.T. moved to Enid where he went to work at Vance Air Force Base as Personnel Director for the Army Air Corp. He was discharged from the Army Air Corp. in San Antonio, Texas.

They moved to Arkansas where he attended John Brown University and then College of the Ozarks where he obtained a degree in Education in 1952.

He pastored several Free Will Baptist Churches and built new buildings for the churches. He was ordained in May 1948 having served as pastor and evangelist for 59 years. Throughout his preaching career, he held many revivals throughout the United States. In the 1950's he published a book of sermons called, *Meetin' Time In The Ozarks*. He began a radio ministry while pastoring churches in Arkansas and Missouri. New buildings of worship were built during his pastorate at Charleston and Russellville, Arkansas, Mountain Grove and Springfield Missouri, and Norman, Oklahoma.

In the late 1960's he obtained a Masters Degree in Counseling from Oklahoma City University. In 1976 he became the chaplain of the Oklahoma City Dept. of Corrections where he developed the Chaplaincy Program. He was a son of Rev. Thomas H. Dixon.

OTHEL T DIXON
SGT US ARMY AIR FORCES
WORLD WAR II
JUN 22 1919   OCT 27 2007

Thomas H Dixon
Birth:
Jun. 21, 1887
Hector,
Pope County,Arkansas
Death:
Feb. 14, 1973
Muskogee,
Muskogee County,
Oklahoma
Burial:
Greenlawn Cemetery,
Checotah,
McIntosh County, Oklahoma

A prominent Free Will Baptist preacher and church organizer, During his long tenure as pastor, Rev Dixon established several Free Will Baptist churches. He organized the Hitchita Free Will Baptist church in 1932 and served as pastor until 1937. In 1939 he organized the First Free Will Baptist Church in Checotah and served as pastor 11 years. He organized the Harmony Free Will Baptist Church at Hilltop and was its pastor at the time of his death. He pastored churches in both Arkansas and Oklahoma and served as state moderator for both Arkansas and Oklahoma.

Jerry D. Dudley
Birth:
Oct. 2, 1927
Oklahoma
Death:
Jan. 2, 1988
Garvin County, Oklahoma
Burial:
McGee Cemetery,
Stratford,
Garvin County,
Oklahoma

Jerry was a WW II Navy veteran. He was raised by pious parents and early in life he became a Christian, and then entered the ministry. He entered ministerial studies at Nashville, Tennessee at Free Will Baptist Bible College in the late 1940's/1950's. His parents moved to California and Jerry and Bea began a pastorate at First FWB Church in Bakersfield, California. He pastored Tulare, CA where he saw the church grow and add members. He started a church in Oregon, and later was elected as Exec. Secretary of California FWB, where he helped edit *"The Voice"* the state paper. He accepted a pastorate in Oklahoma City, at Southern Oaks, where he built an additional facility. After several years, he entered the pastorate in Stratford FWB Church and at Choctaw. He was always active in his denomination's work, holding positions in the district, as well as state and national. sadly, one daughter, Kaye, and her husband, John, who were on their itinerary for a mission assignment to Brazil, were killed in a tragic auto accident.

D. B. Duniphin
Birth:
Feb. 22, 1858
Arkansas
Death:
Aug. 8, 1927
McClain County, Oklahoma
Burial:
Fairview Cemetery
Tuttle, Grady County, Oklahoma
Plot: Blk D, Lot 117

His parents were Burrel S. Duniphin and Nancy Jane "Annie" Gilmore. He married 1st: Mary Elizabeth STOVER, and they had several children. She died in 1900, and he married, 2) Mrs. Nannie J. Welsh Aug. 29, 1900, in Garvin Co. OK (from Kinard Files, on Indian Terr. marriages, Garvin Co, OK).When he entered the ministry is not known; but there is a record of The Southwestern Convention meeting at Tecumseh College, Dec. 26-30, 1917, recorded in G.W. Million's book, "History of Free Will Baptist," pub. 1958, that "at 7 o'clock, Rev. I.W. Yandell and Rev. D.B. Duniphin, preached uplifting discourses..."

Claud Freeman, Jr
Birth:
Oct. 10, 1926
Stratford, Garvin County,
Oklahoma
Death:
Aug. 2, 198 6
Ada, Pontotoc County, Oklahoma
Burial:
McGee Cemetery,
Stratford, Garvin County
Oklahoma

As a bi-vocational minister, he pastored many area churches. He retired from the Stratford Fire Department.

Cecil R. Fassio
Birth:
Jan. 18, 1927
Wilburton,
Latimer County, Oklahoma
Death:
Dec. 6, 2008
Hartshorne,
Pittsburg County, Oklahoma

Burial:
Springhill Cemetery,
Le Flore County, Oklahoma

He began his ministry in the 1950's and later became a Free Will Baptist ordained minister in 1966. He pastored various churches in Oklahoma and at Bell Gardens, California and in 1972 returned to Oklahoma to the Wilburton Free Will Baptist Church. He later made home in Stonewall, where he pastored the FWB church from 1979 to 1983. He moved to Hartshorne and be began pastoring the Hartshorne FWB Church until 1994, and later the Pittsburg FWB until 2001.They owned and operated the Little Rascals Day Care for more than 23 years.

Ward W Fellabaum
Birth:
Jun. 21, 1916
Death:
Feb. 21, 2001
Burial:
Tamaha Cemetery
Tamaha, Haskell County,
Oklahoma

James Anderson Fergueson
Birth:
May 15, 1916
Olney, Texas
Death:
Mar. 28, 2011
Ardmore,
Carter County, Oklahoma
Burial:
Hall Cemetery, Antlers,
Pushmataha County, Oklahoma

Fergueson, known as J. A., died at the age of 94. J.A. married Velma Ella Ford on December 28, 1940, in Stephenville, Texas. He lived in this area since 1962, was a rancher, and raised dairy and beef cattle. J. A. also enjoyed hunting coyotes and wolves. He served his country as an artillery soldier in World War II, where he shot the big guns. He was a Free Will Baptist preacher and pastored the Mt. Zion, Pleasant View, Hall and the Free Will Baptist Church of Antlers.

William G Fields
Birth:
May 2, 1870
Cedar County, Missouri
Death:
Nov. 25, 1943
Seminole,
Seminole County, Oklahoma
Burial:
Tecumseh Cemetery, Tecumseh,
Pottawatomie County,
Oklahoma,
Plot: A2B8-R12-20

Rev. Fields was listed as an ordained Free Will Baptist minister in the Roll of Ministers in the old Center Association (Pontotoc Co) Minutes, as early as 1915, pastoring a church at Woodland. His name appears frequently in their records after 1917, preaching, pastoring and serving on boards and committees. In the 1919 Minutes, this is recorded, "Rev. W.G. Fields was elected delegate to the Co-Operative General Association which meets at Nashville, Tennessee." In his ministerial report of 1924, "travelled 1,430 miles; preached 106 sermons; conversions witnessed: 100; baptized 9; married two couples; conducted two funerals; receipts, $170.00." He was living at Wanette, Pottawatomie, Oklahoma in the 1930 census and gave his occupation as teaching. He also pastored a church at Trousdale.

Sadie E Fincher
Birth:
Jul. 10, 1894
Indian Territory, Oklahoma.
Death:
Apr. 18, 1987
Burial:
Fairlawn Cemetery
Cushing
Payne County
Oklahoma,
Plot: Blk 10

Rev. Sadie Fincher, a former pastor of the Olive Free Will Baptist Church and Silver City Free Will Baptist Church, She was 92 and born in Indian Territory, Oklahoma.

Jesse Augustus Fox
Birth:
May, 1861
Pike County, Arkansas
Death:
Aug. 8, 1932
Asher, PottawatomieCounty,
Oklahoma
Burial:
Vista Cemetery,
Asher, Pottawatomie County,
Oklahoma

Between 1910-1920, he came to Antlers, Pushmataha Co., Oklahoma where he and his wife, Savanna, were enumerated in 1920. In the southeastern Oklahoma marriage records, at Darwin, his name was listed as a "Free Will Baptist minister" who performed marriages there. Nothing is known where he was ordained, or of his ministerial labors.

Let other's seek a home below,
Which flames devour,
or waves o'er flow
Be mine a happier lot to own
A mansion in glory,
my own new home.

James Albert Franklin
Birth:
Sep. 29, 1910
Crawford County,
Arkansas
Death:
Aug. 23, 2003
Ada, Pontotoc County,
Oklahoma
Burial:
Fairlawn Cemetery,
Cushing,
Payne County, Oklahoma,
Plot: Blk 9

Rev. Franklin was an ordained minister of the Free Will Baptist Church for well over 60 years, pastoring churches in Arkansas, Oklahoma, and California. He was still active up until his death, supplying pulpits for pastors as needed.

Howard Joe Gage
Birth:
Aug. 24, 1914
Death:
Aug. 24, 2005
Oklahoma
Burial:
Graham MemorialCemetery,
Pryor,
Mayes County, Oklahoma
An ordained Free Will Baptist minister, pastor, missionary, and evangelist. Country Missionary Work and taking the Good News here and to different Countries.

As a missionary he served some time as a builder in the Ivory Coast, West Africa. He was also a member of the arm services achieving the rank of T Sgt U S Army World War Ii.

Jake W. Gage
Birth:
Feb. 5, 1891
Madison County, Arkansas
Death:
Mar., 1984
Pryor,
Mayes County, Oklahoma
Burial:
Fairview Cemetery, Pryor,
Mayes County, Oklahoma

In 1932, Jake was visiting an old-time preacher, Rev. George Washington Benton, on his farm, and was led to become a Christian. He began at once to witness to his friends, not intending to become a minister, but when a dear friend, Bob McClendon, died whom he had led to Christ, he was asked to preach his funeral. Jake's first revival was at the Paris School House by Spavinaw Creek. He said he really didn't know anything about the Bible, but the people didn't either, and his love and compassion must have shown through to them as there were 33 conversions. In 1936, Jake left his son, Howard, to help care for the farm and his wife, Callie and children, and walked to Arkansas for a series of revivals. At Kingston there were 105 conversions, and baptized 65 of them. A pool hall, whiskey store, and a beer joint closed. Five

hundred persons attended the baptizing that followed the meeting. He also held revivals in the court houses of Berryville, and Eureka Springs. After eight weeks of revival, he had walked 300 miles and was carrying his offerings of $18.00, tied in a hankerchief. He built and pastored the Cole Free Will Baptist Church for eight years. Other pastorates were Lowery, for eight years, where he built a church; First FWB Church in Pryor for six years, resigning to go into full time evangelistic work. He preached revivals in 125 different churches in Oklahoma, Arkansas, Missouri, California, New Mexico, and Idaho.

To be absent in body is to be present with the Lord.

Richard Henry Gallant
Birth:
May 22, 1945
Death:
Jan. 30, 1994
Arizona
Burial:
Oakland Cemetery,
Poteau,
Le Flore County,
Oklahoma,
Plot: Section L

He was born in Boston, Massachusetts, but came to the state of Oklahoma. He pastored for a time the Poteau Free Will Baptist Church then became a staff member for the Hillsdale Free Will Baptist college in Moore, Oklahoma. He ran for the Senate in the state of Oklahoma but did

not achieve his goal. He moved to the state of Arizona and developed Valley fever while there and died.

Shelby Van Greeson
Birth:
Dec. 30, 1933
Oklahoma,
Death:
Jun. 8, 2008
Oklahoma City,
Oklahoma County, Oklahoma
Burial:
Sunny Lane Cemetery,
Del City,
Oklahoma County, Oklahoma

He attended Oklahoma City schools, and Hillsdale College, and completed his Master's in Theology. He was also retired from the US Post Office. His last pastorate was First FWB Church in Oklahoma City.

Johnie Eli Hale
Birth:
Nov. 4, 1924
Theodosia, Ozark County, Missouri
Death:
Jun. 23, 2008
Burial:
Wann Cemetery, Oologah, Rogers County, Oklahoma

He pastored three churches in Oklahoma, five in Arkansas and two in California. He organized the church in Mountain Home, Arkansas and also served under the State Mission Boards in Arkansas and California starting the churches in Ash Flat, Arkansas., and Anderson, California. He preached revivals in Oklahoma, Missouri, Arkansas, Michigan, and to supplement his income while he worked as a tile setter and had his own business in Mountain Home, Ark.

John R. "J.R." Hall
Birth:
Dec. 8, 1927
Pottawatomie County,
Oklahoma,
Death:
Oct. 18, 2004
Blanchard,
McClain County, Oklahoma
Burial:
Lexington Cemetery,
Lexington, Cleveland County,
Oklahoma,
Plot: SW

He was an ordained minister of the Free Will Baptist Church. He had preached over fifty years, and always was successful. He served in the U.S. Navy with honor. They lived in California and Oklahoma where he pastored churches and he died while pastor at First Free Will Baptist Church, Blanchard, Oklahoma, where he had completed twenty years.

Lonnie Hall
Birth:
Oct. 18, 1912
Hercules,
Taney County, Missouri
Death:
Dec. 2, 2003 Sapulpa,
Creek County,
Oklahoma,
Burial:
Green Hill Memorial
Gardens Cemetery, Sapulpa,
Creek County, Oklahoma

He preached at churches in Oklahoma and Texas.

Ralph Clayton Hampton, Sr
Birth:
Mar. 3, 1915
Oklahoma
Death:
Dec. 29, 1986
Pottawatomie County, Oklahoma
Burial:
Resthaven
Memorial Park, Shawnee,
Pottawatomie County, Oklahoma

He was an Minister for Free Will Baptist all his life. Three of his sons all became ministers and professors. Ralph Clayton Jr, Charles Edgar, James A, Larry Don. FWB Ministers. Ralph, Jr, and Charles Edgar, became college professors. Larry was editor at Thomas Nelson, Randall House Publications, and ACE publications.

George Washington Hanks, Jr
Birth:
Nov. 23, 1872
Texas
Death:
Mar. 16, 1958
Keller, Carter Co., Oklahoma
Burial:
Keller Cemetery,
Carter County, Oklahoma

Inscription:Married Aug. 2, 1911

Ernest Harrison
Birth:
May 4, 1920
Henrietta, Oklahoma
Death:
Sep. 10, 1985
Henrietta, Oklahoma
Burial:
Henryetta Cemetery, Henryetta,
Okmulgee County, Oklahoma

He pastored churches in Oklahoma at Weleeka, Henrietta, McAlester, Allen, and other places. He held positions in his local District Associations wherever he lived, and was elected to the Clerk position of the State Sunday School Board. He was elected as Ass't moderator of the State Association in 1970. He was always actively engaged in the work of the ministry and church. While at Weleeka, he was burned badly in an accidental fire on his job, and it was doubtful for awhile he would survive. He recovered and went right back to his ministry, serving faithfully until his death. He had a brother, Harold, who became a noted minister, and he also left a son, Ernest, Jr., who is a successful pastor and administrator.

In death we feel the presence of the Holy Spirit brush across our souls with a deep settled peace.

Elder William H. Hearron
Birth:
1882
Death:
1957
Burial:
Dibble Cemetery,
Dibble County,Oklahoma

An early FWB minister. Great leader.

J. Arthur Hearron
Birth:
1905
Death:
1968
Burial:
Dibble Cemetery,
Dibble,
McClain County,
Oklahoma

A good preacher and singer. He was the son of Eld and Mrs. W.H. Hearron.

Robert Dean Hidde
Birth:
Oct. 23, 1950
Fort Smith
Sebastian County, Arkansas
Death:
Mar. 15, 2013
Tulsa
Tulsa County, Oklahoma
Burial:
Memorial Park Cemetery
Tulsa
Tulsa County, Oklahoma

Bob Hidde was born to Robert and Nadine Hidde in Ft. Smith, Arkansas. He graduated from Tulsa Central High School in 1968 and went on to obtain his Doctorate in Sacred Theology at Princeton University in Princeton, New Jersey. On July 3, 1969, he married Vicki Reynolds. They welcomed a daughter Leah, on August 6, 1971.Bob answered God's call to ministry and began preaching at the age of 15. He served as a Free Will Baptist pastor for over 40 years. Churches he served included First Free Will Baptist in Tulsa, West Tulsa Free Will Baptist in Tulsa, Madison Avenue Free Will Baptist in Tulsa, Rose Hill Free Will Baptist in Monticello, Ark, Ballews Chapel Free Will Baptist in Grubbs, Ark, and most currently, Northside Free Will Baptist in Broken Arrow. He believed in being prepared for ministry at a moment's notice. Pastor Hidde was in ministry as the on-call chaplain for Ninde Funeral Home for 25 years, ministering to thousands of Tulsa families and beyond. Since 1999, he was the Managing Trustee for Memorial Park Cemetery. He served as the Moderator for the Tulsa Free Will Baptist Association and sat on the Credential Boards. He was the past President for the Oklahoma Personnel Consultants. He was also a member of the Tulsa Men's Club, the Tulsa Summit Club and the University of Arkansas Alumni Association. Along with his wife, Vicki, he owned and worked in their career development business, Resume Source, Inc., helping thousands of people and companies around the United States.

Herbert Curtis Hogue
Birth:
Apr. 16, 1931
Roff
Pontotoc County, Oklahoma
Death:
Mar. 17, 2013
Oakman
Pontotoc County, Oklahoma
Burial:
Francis Cedar Grove Cemetery
Francis
Pontotoc County, Oklahoma
Curtis Hogue, 81, of Ada, at his home.He attended Steedman and Byng grade school and graduated from Byng High School. He attended Hillsdale Bible College in Moore.Mr. Hogue pastored Free Will Baptist Churches for many years. He operated a Christian Bookstore for 10 years and formerly owned and operated Yard Ornaments, Etc. Mr. Hogue was a longtime active member of the First Free Will Baptist Church in Ada where he taught Sunday School Class for over 50 years.

Henry S Huckeby
Birth:
May 8, 1858
Arkansas
Death:
Jan. 26, 1913
Garvin County, Oklahoma
Burial:
McGee Cemetery, Stratford,
Garvin County, Oklahoma,
Plot: Sect 3, Row 13

He was the son of George and Lucinda Huckeby, and was in Chickasaw Nation in the 1900 census with wife, Annice who he married 27 Apr. 1879 in Madison Co. AR. In the 1900-1901 Center Ass'n Minutes it is recorded "Rev. H.S. Huckeby as pastor at Summers Chapel" Maxwell, (Pontotoc Co) OK.

He was in a list of preacher's names the association accepted as ordained ministers after examination, and issued them a Certificate of Ordination showing they had recently come into the area.

In the 1902 session, he was elected to preach and then was elected to be Moderator. In 1908, he is credited with organizing the Non, FWB church, Hughes Co. OK, that produced so many FWB preachers just after statehood.

James D. Huling
Birth:
May 17, 1827
South New Berlin
Chenango County, New York
Death:
Nov. 6, 1900
Kingfisher County, Oklahoma
Burial:
Oak Grove Cemetery
Dove, Kingfisher County,
Oklahoma

Rev. J. D. Huling, whose parents were Daniel and Lydia (Burlingame) Huling, was born in Willett, Broome Co., N.Y., May 17, 1827. In September 1852, he was married to Mary W. Moore.

In 1870 he was ordained, and labored from 1870 to 1875 in connection with Rev. J. B. Fast in evangelistic work in the Cherokee Co. Quarterly Meeting.. In 1877 he organized the Caney church and with Brother Fast they organized the Montgomery Q.M., and also the church in Nevada, Kansas. Increasing infirmities prevented his holding a pastorate, but he still preached as opportunity offered and strength permitted.

Inscription:
"J. D. HULING,
CO.I., 15 ILL. INF."

George M. Isham
Birth:
Sep. 9, 1848
Tennessee
Death:
Nov. 10, 1938
Henryetta,
Okmulgee County, Oklahoma
Burial:
Oakman Cemetery, Oakman,
Pontotoc County, Oklahoma

He became a minister and joined the Free Will Baptist where he was found in Chickasaw Nation (Pontotoc Co. OK) by 1900. During the next several years he was active in the old Center Association, and his name appears in the Minutes of its meetings. He was elected its moderator in the 1900 session at Oakman Church. In this 1900 account, he was listed as pastor of Egypt Church, and Union Arbor at Midland, west of Ada. In 1902, he was pastor of four churches...one each Sunday. (This was frequently done then to supply the churches part of the time with a minister).These four churches were: Egypt, Summers Chapel, Union, and Union Arbor. His address was Ada, Indian Territory. In 1903, he was pastor of Oakman church. He was frequently called upon to preach at these meetings. He moved to Stephens Co, and 1920 census, he was a widower at age 67; by 1930.

Clarence Albert Jarrett
Birth:
Sep. 13, 1925
Missouri
Death:
Sep. 14, 2008
McAlester,
Pittsburg County, Oklahoma
Burial:
Tannehill Cemetery, McAlester,
Pittsburg County, Oklahoma

He joined the U.S. Navy and served during WWII in the Aleutian Island Campaign. Albert worked as an auto mechanic and painting contractor. He built and pastored Crowder Free Will Baptist Church, North McAlester Free Will Baptist Church and Fellowship Free Will Baptist Church in McAlester. He assisted with building other churches and was an active member of the Gaines Creek Free Will Baptist Association. He was a member of the American Legion and served as chaplain for the Harrison Powers Post #79 of McAlester for many years. He was a member of Canadian Shores Free Will Baptist Church.

Earl Jenson
Birth:
Jun. 18, 1911
Pittsburg County,
Oklahoma
Death:
Feb. 21, 1985
McAlester,
Pittsburg County,
Oklahoma
Burial:
Indianola Cemetery,
Indianola,

Pittsburg County, Oklahoma

He was serving as pastor of the Lone Oak Free Will Baptist Church at the time of his death. He was ordained as a Free Will Baptist Minister Aug. 14, 1943 and pastored churches in Oklahoma, California and Missouri.

Wade T. Jernigan
Birth:
Sep. 25, 1927 Bladenboro,
Bladen County, North Carolina
Death:
May 15, 2006
Tulsa, Tulsa County, Oklahoma,
Burial:
Willow View Cemetery,
Cleveland County, Oklahoma

The ministry of the well-known Free Will Baptist preacher and educator spanned more than 60 years. His education included an English Bible diploma, a bachelor of science of arts, a master's degree and doctorate in Theology. Five colleges and universities have conferred honorary degrees upon him. He was 17 when he announced his call to preach on March 25, 1945, at his home

church, Oak Grove Church in Bladenboro, N. C. He was licensed to preach the following Sunday and preached his first sermon April 8, 1945, at Oak Grove Church. He has conducted more than 800 revivals, pastored 14 churches including the First Free Will Baptist Church in Miami, and served four churches as interim pastor. He was involved in church pioneering and was instrumental in starting 25 churches. He was referred to across the United States as "Mr. Free Will Baptist." He helped start Oklahoma Bible College (now Hillsdale Free Will Baptist College), and was a member of the Christian Education Board. Most recently, he served as a Professor of Homiletics and in Public Relations with the office of Institutional Advancement at Hillsdale Free Will Baptist College. Jernigan's bold style and gift for doctrinal preaching made him a popular conference and revival speaker. He was a leader wherever he served: Moderator of the Oklahoma State Association, Executive Secretary of the California State Association, Chairman of the national Home Missions Board, member of the Commission on Theological Liberalism, Home Missionary to Idaho, member of both the national General Board and Executive Committee. Wade was a member of the five-man committee that recommended starting in 1958 what is now Hillsdale FWB College. However, his signature work in education came during a nine-year span (1969-1978) when he served as president of California Christian College in Fresno. A prolific writer, Jernigan produced four books, including his best-known work published in 1975, The Unsealed Book, an Amillennial commentary on the Book of Revelation. He also wrote 60 songs, poetry, and numerous articles.

Scott Jones
Birth:
Aug. 8, 1910
Death:
Jan. 15, 1976
Burial:
Francis Cedar Grove Cemetery,
Francis,
Pontotoc County, Oklahoma

William Chapman "Bud" Jones
Birth:
Feb. 3, 1856
Death:
Sep. 5, 1944
Burial:
Rosedale Cemetery,
Ada, Pontotoc County, Oklahoma,
Plot: West-26-5-5

A minister and son-in-law of Rev. Ransom Bess.

George Earl Judd
Birth:
Mar. 9, 1915
Death:
Feb. 21, 1989
Burial:
Sub-Station Cemetery,
Freedom, HillCreek County,
Oklahoma
He served as a PVT.in the U.S. Army during World War Two.

Richard P. Kennedy
Birth:
Oct. 10, 1949
Richmond,
Contra Costa County,
California
Death:
Aug. 10, 2012
Owasso,
Tulsa County, Oklahoma
Burial:
Graceland Memorial
Park Cemetery, Owasso,
Tulsa County, Oklahoma

Dr. Kennedy served in the ministry of Jesus Christ for 30 years. His formal education began at California Christian College in Fresno, California, where he received his Bachelor of Science Degree. He continued his education at Golden Gate Baptist Seminary in Mill Valley, California, where he began his Master of Divinity Studies.

He then attended Liberty University in Lynchburg, Virginia, and completed his Masters and his Doctor of Ministry at Fuller Theological Seminary in Pasadena, California. Always venturesome, Dr. Kennedy began two churches; Temple Church, Greenville, North Carolina, and Northside Church, Stockton, California. Both grew at record rates and continue to impact people's lives around the world. He was Co-Pastor at Big Valley Grace Community Church in Modesto, California, for seven years and ended his career as head pastor of Los Gatos Christian Church, Los Gatos, California. Dr. Kennedy also served as an adjunct professor for Oklahoma Wesleyan University and Hillsdale Free Will Baptist College.

Bob L. Ketchum
Birth:
Jul. 30, 1936
Liberty,
Tulsa County, Oklahoma
Death:
Feb. 28, 2010
Tulsa,
Tulsa County, Oklahoma
Burial:
Bixby Cemetery, Bixby,
Tulsa County, Oklahoma

Bob received and accepted the call to the ministry during his teenage years, preaching his first sermon in May 1953 at Shahan. Shortly after ordination in 1955, he was asked to preach two Sundays each month at Duck Creek Church and twice monthly at Hitchita Free Will Baptist Church. His pastorates included Okmulgee, Cushing, Shady Grove in Tennessee, Central in Tulsa, Owasso and Grace North of Indian Springs, Broken Arrow. He served the Lord as founder, then pastor of Grace for 25 years. During his years of pastoring, he served the Free Will Baptist denomination in various positions. For several years he was a member of the Board of Trustees of Free Will Baptist College in Nashville, TN, his alma mater. He was selected to preach at the Free Will Baptist National Convention at Macon, Georgia in 1973. He also was privileged to serve the Oklahoma Free Will Baptists on several boards and committees during these years and two as the state moderator.

William O. "Bill" Ketchum
Birth:
unknown
Death:
Jul. 15, 2004
Oklahoma
Burial:
Prairie Gardens Cemetery,
Liberty,
Tulsa County, Oklahoma

The Rev. Bill Ketchum, 86, of Bixby, an ordained Free Will Baptist minister for many years. He pastored churches and was used extensively as an evangelist. (Sapulpa Herald)

John Dudley Kimbrough
Birth:
Nov. 17, 1880
Alabama
Death:
Jan. 3, 1958
Oklahoma
Burial:
Allen Cemetery,
Allen, Pontotoc County,
Oklahoma

John D. Kimbrough was an ordained Free Will Baptist minister, where and when he was ordained is unknown, but probably as a very young man. He was one of those who preached and ministered in Indian Territorial days (before 1907) and afterward. No record is available that tells the number that he baptized, churches organized, weddings or funerals that he was the officiant, but he is acknowledged by descendants of those who knew him that he was well-loved, engaged in his work and did a great service for his Master. His name and picture in the book, *"History of the First Hundred Years 1908-2008,"* show his name is still honored today for his labors. In the *"Annuals of Red Oak*, pg 153, his name is listed with a few other ministers that preached at the Norris FWB church, even back to 1890's.

Richard G. Lane
Birth:
Feb. 28, 1896
Texas
Death:
Jun. 16, 1959
Arkansas
Burial:
Little Cemetery, Little,
Seminole County, Oklahoma

He was a Free Will Baptist minister and pastor from Sulphur, Oklahoma. Much of his ministry was in central Arkansas at the Pleasant Grove Free Will Baptist Church in Greenbrier and later he organized the First Free Will Baptist Church in Conway. His daughter, Jean, was the wife of J. Reford Wilson who became the National Director for Foreign Missions in Nashville Tennessee for the National Association of Free Will Baptists.
(He was the authors pastor when he was a boy. Mom Lane impacted me dearly. J.Reford Wilson conducted our marriage).

Harry L. Lee
Birth:
Feb. 11, 1914
Death:
Nov. 19, 1996
Burial:
Arpelar Cemetery
Arpelar, Pittsburg County,
Oklahoma

Ordained Free Will Baptist minister/pastor. He pastored churches in his locality, while also being bi-vocational, and helping others. He was a quiet, mild-mannered man, who was esteemed by all who knew him.

John Alvin Lee
Birth:
Sep., 1862
Illinois
Death:
Jun. 4, 1951
Pontotoc County, Oklahoma
Burial:
Francis Cedar Grove Cemetery,
Francis,
Pontotoc County, Oklahoma

John moved to Oklahoma in 1887. Elder Lee was ordained a Free Will Baptist minister in 1894. His name appears often in old church records, having served as pastor of several churches, and moderator of the Center Association in 1900. He preached, performed weddings, conducted funerals, and was active in revival work.

William E Lindsey
Birth:
1873
Death:
Jul. 24, 1945
Burial:
Oak Park Cemetery, Chandler,
Lincoln County, Oklahoma,
Plot: Section 9, Lot 69

He was a FWB pastor in the early years.

John W. Lunsford
Birth:
Apr. 21, 1850
Tennessee
Death:
May 17, 1928
Oklahoma
Burial:
West Hill Cemetery,
Roff, Pontotoc County, Oklahoma

John was a Free Will Baptist minister in the old Center Ass'n, (Pontotoc Co)of churches where he is shown to have pastored various churches. In 1912, he was pastor at Shady Grove, Dolberg, Pontotoc Co. He had a brother, W.G. Lunsford, also a minister listed in the names of a committee in a 1902 meeting, of this same Center Association.

Marvin Kenneth Mann
Birth:
Sep. 19, 1928
Briartown
Muskogee County, Oklahoma
Death:
Jul. 14, 2013
Tulsa
Tulsa County, Oklahoma
Burial:
Greenlawn Cemetery
Checotah
McIntosh County, Oklahoma

His life was service to his Lord and Savior Jesus Christ, to love on his family and serve with his church family. He enjoyed golf and raising cattle. He was preceded in death by his parents, Rev. LW and Lula Belle Mann. He honorably served our nation in the United States Army and was proud to be a veteran. Along with his brother Bill, he started Ace Fence Company in November 1953 in which he operated until his retirement in 1990. He and a brother planted churches and denominational associations and in the early days preached revivals together. They labored together. He was ordained as a preacher of the gospel on September 11, 1960 in Broken Arrow, OK. The fruit from the churches planted and many souls led to Christ will only be fully known in Heaven. After years of pastorates, he cherished being the moderator of the Arkansas Valley Association of Free Will Baptist as well as serving in the General Board of the Oklahoma Association of Free Will Baptist. He preached his last sermon one week before his home-going. He was thrilled to see his grandsons continue his passion of church-planting in Texas and Illinois.

David T. Mansker
Birth:
Jun. 4, 1847
Johnson County, Arkansas
Death:
Mar. 6, 1929
Paden, Okfuskee County, Oklahoma
Burial:
Lambdin ,Prague, Lincoln County, Oklahoma

His great-grandfather was George Mansker, born about 1747 in Germany; his grandfather was William Mansker, born about 1774 in Pennsylvania; and his father was John R. Mansker, born in Tennessee. During the 1830s, the Manskers moved from Tennessee to Arkansas. By 1834, Thomas Mansker's father and mother were married in Lawrence County, Arkansas, one of the first counties to be settled in the state. By at least 1836, they had moved into Johnson County, Arkansas, where Tom was born on the 4th of June 1847. When he was 17, and at the point of enlistment, all the males of his family were already active in military service except for his youngest brother. Tom Mansker enlisted into the 7th Missouri Cavalry of the Confederate States of America. Tom was assigned to Captain Nathan Horn's Company, Lieutenant Colonel C. H. Nichol's Regiment of Colonel Sidney D. Jackman's Brigade under General Sterling Price. The Manskers came into Indian Territory probably after September 1891 to an area opened up to White settlement. Sometime between 1900 and 1910, David Thomas Mansker received his call and appointment to the ministry, a calling he pursued to the end of his life. Sometime between 1910 and 1920, Tom Mansker and his wife Martha Jane moved to Ontario, Malheur County, Oregon. However, before another two years had passed, they were back in Oklahoma, but this time in Paden, Okfuskee County, Oklahoma. In the obituary of Martha it read, "They lived and bore the trials and hardships of the early life of Oklahoma. She was converted about the age of 27 and ever afterwards lived a beautiful devoted Christian life, her companion being a minister of the gospel of the Free Will Baptist Church. "Reverend McElvaney officiated. Published in The Prague Record, Thursday, November 17, 1921. Seven and a half years after her death, the Rev. Mansker died in Paden, and was buried beside Martha Jane. After the funeral, Elder Epperson wrote these words about his friend and colleague: David Thomas Mansker "came nearer being loved by everybody than any man I ever knew. He had been preaching some forty years, after having come to Oklahoma in an early day. He was as faithful to his church as he was to his family. You can't say too much for him as a man or as a minister—he was the best pastor I think I ever saw. To make it plain, it will take all eternity to tell about Brother Mansker. We know where to find him. Oh, I could say so much, but he will tell us all about it over there." ("Obituary for Elder David Thomas Mansker", published in The Free Will Baptist Gem, April 1929, p. 12)On his next birthday, he would have been 82 years old. The funeral was held in the Free Will Baptist Church in Paden. Several preachers were in attendance and had a part in the funeral. The services were conducted by Elder A. B. Epperson. Reverend McElvany, of Prague, a life-long friend of Tom's, talked at the gravesite.
Inscription:
Co. C. Mo. Cav. CSA

Lester James Maynard
Birth:
Mar. 3, 1915
Death:
Jun. 27, 2002
Burial:
Blanchard Cemetery,
Blanchard,
McClain County,
Oklahoma

He was a minister over 50 years.

Alvis Lee McAffrey
Birth:
Sep. 23, 1914
McGee, Garvin County,
Oklahoma
Death:
Nov. 9, 1994
Madill, Marshall County,
Oklahoma
Burial:
Woodberry Forest Cemetery,
Madill, Marshall County,
Oklahoma

He was ordained a Free Will Baptist minister when a young man, and then pastored churches throughout the area, among them were Stratford, Gaar Corner, and a long pastorate at First Free Will Baptist Church in Sulphur; Non FWB, and Memorial at Sulphur. He was a minister for over 50 years. He served on boards for his association and was active in the Oklahoma State Association of FWB.

Furman Archie McCage
Birth:
Nov. 22, 1907
Stigler, Haskell County,
Oklahoma
Death:
Dec. 29, 1972

Oklahoma City, Oklahoma County, Oklahoma
Burial:
Stigler Cemetery, Stigler, Haskell County, Oklahoma

Ordained Free Will Baptist minister/pastor in Oklahoma and California where he held various positions in the denomination.

Joshua E. "J.E." McGee
Birth:
Sep. 20, 1857
Fayette County, Alabama
Death:
Jan. 21, 1923
Oklahoma,
Burial:
Garwin Cemetery, Antlers,
Pushmataha County, Oklahoma

Eld. J.E. McGee was a pioneer Free Will Baptist minister in the Indian Territory and after statehood until his death. He was a great evangelist who did a great work in the Choctaw Nation. In 1885, he began a work at CullaChaha, near Cameron, and was one of the founders of the Old Territorial Association organized at Nubbin Ridge, near Spiro, Oklahoma, in 1894. The boundaries were from 18 miles west of Tahlequah, to the Arkansas line at Fort Smith and south to Antlers. Later, the growth produced two associations, and one carried the name, Roberts-McGee, after two of the founding fathers.

Dottis McGehee
Birth:
Jan. 29, 1881
Thackerville, Love County, Oklahoma
Death:
Sep. 26, 1939
Pontotoc County, Oklahoma
Burial:
Oakman Cemetery, Oakman, Pontotoc County, Oklahoma

Rev. McGehee was ordained a Free Will Baptist minister in 1927 (per old minutes) of the Center Association where he chiefly labored.

Cecil E. McKenzie
Birth:
Aug. 14, 1902
Death:
Apr. 19, 1976
Burial:
Holdenville Cemetery,
Holdenville, Hughes County, Oklahoma

Martin M McKee
Birth:
Oct. 1, 1889
Nelson, Choctaw County Oklahoma
Death:
Nov. 14, 1947
Paris, Lamar County, Texas
Burial:
Soper Cemetery, Soper, Choctaw County, Oklahoma

He was an ordained Free Will Baptist minister, who preached, pastored, baptized and performed weddings all over southeastern Okla. in the 1920-1940's. He was active in Associational meetings, often writing an article about it for a church publication. His name appears in old records of the church. In 1929, he was elected Moderator of the Oklahoma State Ass'n of FWB. We know he was a beloved and faithful minister. He died in a Paris, TX hospital.

Edward E Morris
Birth:
Jun. 8, 1897
Arkansas
Death:
Feb., 1987
Oklahoma City
Oklahoma County, Oklahoma
Burial:
Memorial Park Cemetery,
Ada, Pontotoc County, Oklahoma

E. E. Morris, was born in Arkansas, but soon was living in Oklahoma. He served in the U.S. Army in WWI. He was an ordained Free Will Baptist minister and pastored churches in Oklahoma and California for many years pastoring the Ada First FWB for several years in the 1930-40's, then the Capitol Hill FWB Church, in Oklahoma City, where it grew and he carried on a weekly radio program. He was used as an evangelist frequently. He served on State Boards and also in local

Districts. He served a term as the moderator of the National Association in its early days. He was a promoter of the denominational enterprises. He pastored in California where his wife, died in 1957. He later served as California State Promotional Director. He pastored other churches at Tulare and Arvin, California. He was known for his strong positions on issues he believed in and was a leader in those things. He was a "hands on" pastor, frequently using a carpenter's tools to get a job finished.

J C Morgan
Birth:
May 6, 1931
Death:
Aug. 23, 2013
Burial:
Bixby Cemetery
Bixby
Tulsa County, Oklahoma

Shortly after High school, J. C. married the love of his life, Lila Fay James in Bixby Oklahoma. In those early years J.C. worked as a welder for Yuba Heat Transfer and McNamara Tank in Tulsa.
J.C. was led to Christ by Reverend Ray Gwartney at the Bixby Free Will Baptist Church. He became an ordained minister in December of 1961. Shortly thereafter he accepted his first pastorate at Pensacola Free Will Baptist church near Grand Lake. Under his guidance and Lila Faye's support, the church grew and thrived. In the early 1960's the family moved to Oklahoma City where he and Lila Faye managed the Free Will Baptist Bible book store. J.C. attended the Hillsdale Free Will Baptist Bible College at night during this time, and honed his preaching style at numerous small churches throughout Oklahoma. The Lord led J.C. to Pastor Churches in Chickasha and Lawnwood Free Will Baptist church in Tulsa, where he retired. After his retirement in the mid 1990's, J.C. and Lila Faye returned

to their hometown of Bixby where they continued to serve in local churches. All in all he preached over 4,000 sermons, and hundreds of baptisms, funerals and weddings. He always challenged young people to trust God and live the Christian life. In retirement, he served as an interim pastor at Lewis Avenue Free Will Baptist church. In the past few years he has served in various roles, including the senior's ministry at the Bixby Free Will Baptist church.

B C Munkus
Birth:
Nov. 20, 1876
Ellis County, Texas
Death:
Sep. 15, 1952
Norman, Cleveland County, Oklahoma
Burial:
Moore Cemetery, Moore, Cleveland County, Oklahoma

He left home at an early age, and moved to the Oklahoma Indian Territory before 1900. He was a Free Will Baptist minister & evangelist and was active in the early years of the Oklahoma FWB State Association.

John Columbus Newby
Birth:
Oct. 30, 1884
Arkansas
Death:
Aug. 12, 1957
Le Flore County, Oklahoma
Burial:
Ellis Chapel Cemetery, Wister, Le Flore County, Oklahoma

Newby, known affectionately as "Clum" Newby, was an ordained Free Will Baptist minister. When he came from Arkansas to Indian Territory he soon found and worked with others of like faith, such as Eld. J.M. Roberts, who in 1894, gathered some of them together to form a Territorial Association. An old Latimer Co. record, *"Annals of Red Oak"*, page 153, we find his name among the earliest ministers, alone with Wilson Yandell, Rouche Allen, Mr. West, Clum (Columbus) Newby, Jack Shipman and Elzie Yandell, who preached at Norris Church (outside Red Oak) as early as 1890. We find his name in old minutes, where he preached and organized churches all over eastern Oklahoma. He was in the group of ministers who helped form the State Association of FWB, in 1908, at Holdenville, (Hughes Co) Oklahoma.

Father, into thy hands I commend my spirit."

Luke 23:46

Dennis H O'Donnell
Birth:
Oct. 17, 1907
Death:
Sep. 3, 1991
Burial:
Little Cemetery, Little,
Seminole County, Oklahoma

A Free Will Baptist minister and pastor.
(Bro. to Rev. E.A. O'Donnell).

Emris Allen O'Donnell
Birth:
Feb. 9, 1900
St. Clair County, Alabama
Death:
Mar., 1979
Holdenville,
Hughes County, Oklahoma
Burial:
Fairlawn Cemetery, Chickasha,
Grady County, Oklahoma,
Plot: Blk 5 Lt 14 Sp 8 SE/4

He was an ordained minister of the Free Will Baptists. He pastored FWB churches in Oklahoma where he was involved in their ministries, serving in various positions, and was editor of a state church paper, *"The Gospel Truth"* at one time. He had a great singing and speaking voice, and a pleasant personality. He was a WW I veteran.

James Montgomery Pannell
Birth:
Jun. 3, 1856
Tishomingo County, Mississippi
Death:
Jul. 16, 1909
Pontotoc County, Oklahoma
Burial:
Maxwell Cemetery, Oil Center,
Pontotoc County, Oklahoma

Parents were Bartlet Pannell Cecilla. Married to Nancy Melvina Burgess 6 April 1877. An ordained minister in the Free Will Baptist Center Association, Pontotoc/Garvin counties. His death is recorded in its old Minutes.: Nancy Ann Melvina Burgess Pannell (1857 - 1941).

Isaac Newton Pate
Birth:
Dec. 22, 1870
Pike County, Arkansas
Death:
Jun. 22, 1951
Antlers, Pushmataha County,
Oklahoma
Burial:
Antlers City Cemetery,
Antlers, Pushmataha County,
Oklahoma
Pate was a pioneer Free Will Baptist preacher in Oklahoma.

David Leroy Poynor
Birth:
Jul. 3, 1820
Death:
Nov. 12, 1903
Burial:
Shahan Cemetery
Broken Arrow
Wagoner County, Oklahoma

A leader in the early beginnings in NW AR/MO for his church and association of churches. Raised a large family.

Johnny H. Priest
Birth:
Dec. 30, 1920 Non, Hughes County,
Oklahoma
Death:
Dec. 16, 1988
Boise City,
Cimarron County, Oklahoma
Burial:
McGee Cemetery,
Stratford,
Garvin County, Oklahoma

He entered WWII military service and served his country. He announced his call to preach in the Free Will Baptist Church of Non and began to preach in area churches. He began a Free Will Baptist Church in the panhandle of Oklahoma at Boise City.

Ulis C. Purdom
Birth:
Jan. 8, 1906
Piette, Arkansas
Death:
Aug. 16, 1989
Quinton, Pittsburg County,
Oklahoma
Burial:
McLain Cemetery
Muskogee, Muskogee County,
Oklahoma

He was an ordained FWB minister, and his name appears in old minutes, and in 1966, he was the District evangelist for Gaines Creek Association. His parents were M. D. Purdom (1859 - 1941) and Louisa Purdom (1865 - 1952) and his wife was Cora Brumley Purdom (1913 - 1978).

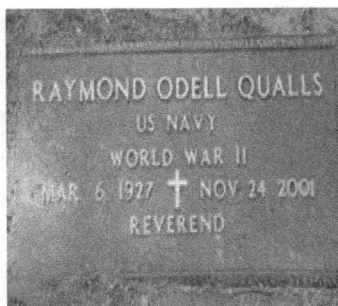

Raymond Odell Qualls
Birth:
Mar. 6, 1927
Mulberry, Crawford County,
Arkansas
Death:
Nov. 24, 2001
Fort Smith, Sebastian County,
Arkansas
Burial:
Maple Cemetery
Maple, Sequoyah County,
Oklahoma

Funeral services for Rev. Raymond QUALLS, 74, of Muldrow, were held Wednesday, at 10 a.m. at the Eastside Freewill Baptist Church, with Revs. Wade Jernigan, Gilbert Pixley and Jerry Copeland officiating. His wife was Lona Mae Viles Qualls (1929 - 2011).

James W "Jim" Ragland
Birth:
Oct. 10, 1864
Tennessee
Death:
Oct. 23, 1950
Oklahoma
Burial:
Oakman Cemetery,
Oakman, Pontotoc County
Oklahoma

A Free Will Baptist pioneer minister, ordained in 1919, serving in the Center Association of churches (Pontotoc Co. OK) as its moderator in 1899. He held various offices of leadership through 1934.

William Clay Richey
Birth:
Jan. 29, 1904
Aspermont,
Stonewall County, Texas
Death:
Sep. 3, 1961
Blanchard,
McClain County, Oklahoma
Burial:
Dibble Cemetery, Dibble,
McClain County, Oklahoma

He moved with his family from Texas to Oklahoma, attended schools and grew to manhood in around Grady and McClain counties, Oklahoma. He yielded his life to God's call to the gospel ministry in 1933 at once began "to preach Christ" in the local churches. He was ordained in the Free Will Baptist Church in 1933. He studied the scriptures assiduously, while gaining knowledge of parliamentary law, greatly aiding his denomination in its conference deliberations, he being selected to be the 'parliamentarian' for several sessions. He ably served the Oklahoma. State Association of FWB as moderator for several years, and his name appears in their minutes in other positions where he served. He was a good speaker and preacher. He reasoned the scriptures and had a forceful delivery. He was esteemed among his peers. In 1959, he preached the funeral of his old mentor, Dr. I.W. Yandell, in Oklahoma City. He pastored churches at Dibble, Bryant, Springhill (at Lexington), and Pleasant Hill churches, and organized the First Church at Blanchard, before he died suddenly.

W. G. Ridge
Birth:
May 25, 1856
Death:
Apr. 3, 1937
Burial:
Laverty Cemetery, Chickasha,
Grady County, Oklahoma

Tombstone has his name as Rev. W.G. Ridge

Albert S. Roberts
Birth:
May 7, 1877
Death:
Mar. 22, 1937
Burial:
Palestine Cemetery
Russellville, Pittsburg County,
Oklahoma

He was the grandson of Olive Branch Roberts from North Carolina. Olive Branch had 16 children and one was named Pleasant, John Pleasant who was a N.C. state legislator for over 20 years. John Pleasant moved to Arkansas and had five children. His baby's name was Albert Slayton, born in 1879. He had six children and the youngest was Rev. William Thomas Roberts.

James M. Roberts
Birth:
Jul. 20, 1852
Death:
Dec. 26, 1940

Burial:
Garland Cemetery, Stigler,
Haskell County, Oklahoma

Elder Roberts was an early Oklahoma pioneer Free Will Baptist preacher from Arkansas. His own words from old letters and diaries best describe his life and labors. "In the year of 1884 I moved from Sebastian County, Arkansas to the Cherokee Nation near Weber Falls on the Arkansas River, rented a farm, and soon began preaching on Saturdays and Sundays in the little school houses here and there and underbrush arbors and shade trees. I had a wife and seven children at that time, for which I made a living on the farm, so it took a lot of my time. I had an appointment ten miles north of Weber's Falls near McClain at the old Buckhorn schoolhouse and other places too numerous to mention. In 1892 Brother O .J. Tailor (Taylor), a Free Will Baptist preacher from Texas, located near McClain and I soon formed his acquaintance, and we began preaching together. In the latter part of 1892, he and I organized the Concord Church at the old Buckhorn school house which was the first Free Will Baptist church organized in the Cherokee nation. Bro. Tailor and I worked together for six years and organized churches in many places." He wrote, "These were trying times. There was no money, no roads, and no bridges." Elder Roberts made many of these long trips on foot while carrying his Bible and a change of clothing in a small satchel. Many times he waded the streams, even in winter. Sometimes he slept with his Bible for a pillow and his bed a pile of leaves or grass with the pale moon and the twinkling stars as a covering."The second church to be organized was the old 'Fields Chapel' Church Northeast of Porum, Oklahoma. It was then Star Villa, I.T. In 1885, another church was organized at old Cullachaha near Cameron in the Choctaw Nation, and Elder J. E.

McGee began a work in that part of the country." A group of churches gathered near the old Scullvill Stant, in 1894 in the Choctaw part at a little school house known as Nubbin Ridge. There they were organized as the Territorial Association. But it was not perfected until Sept. 1894. Roberts was in the very formation of the Oklahoma FWB.

William Thomas Roberts
Birth:
Dec. 17, 1910
Mena,
Polk County, Arkansas
Death:
Mar. 29, 2000
Tulsa County, Oklahoma
Burial:
Floral Haven Memorial Gardens,
Broken Arrow,
Tulsa County, Oklahoma

Rev. Tommy Roberts was born to Rev. Albert Slayton Roberts and Nora Roberts. His father took his family from Arkansas to Oklahoma after their baby son, William Thomas was born.
Tommy resisted the call of God on his life, but at the age of 19 he accepted the Lord as Savior and the calling to preach God's Word. He married Lucy Marie Laughlin when he was 19 and she was 15. They had six children. When he passed away on March 29, 2000 he was probably the oldest FWB minister in Oklahoma at that time with 70 years of ministry and marriage.
He and his wife, Marie, pastored churches in Oklahoma, Kansas and California.

He "pastored" four churches at a time in the Stigler area. Some of them met in school houses with pot-bellied stoves. He didn't need a microphone or loud speaker because his voice carried strongly and he sang an impressive low bass.

Bro. Tommy was called to the New Home Free Will Baptist Church in Berryhill, Oklahoma in the 50's. He moved his family of six children and continued in the area of Tulsa, Oklahoma for many years. He also pastored Airport FWB Church, Cincinatti FWB Church, two FWB churches in Claremore. He began the church in Owasso FWB and was it's second pastor.

From Oklahoma he went to the Shawnee Mission FWB Church in Kansas City, Kansas. From there he went to California to pastor the Modesto FWB Church.

He was called to help struggling churches and with his wife, Marie, by his side with her great alto voice and gift for hospitality and evangelism, they left churches with increased attendance and sometimes with a remodeled church and church parsonage. A contractor by trade, he built churches, parsonages, dormitories, altars, benches and whole neighborhoods. Being his own boss, he took time off for all district and state and national meetings. He served on boards in whatever state they were in and he loved his denomination.

The couple supported FWB Christian education, whether it was in Nashville, Oklahoma or California. He enjoyed helping in camp ministries and improving camp ground properties.He was a great supporter of his local communities. Missions was a part of his message. "Either you go or you send," he preached. Missionaries, foreign and home, were always in their home and were supported by them.

He wore many hats throughout his life and ministry and has left his legacy. From his talent as a skilled workman, eight of his offspring have gone into the profession of construction or engineering. As a community spirit, eleven teachers from his family have participated in the public school and colleges. Others serve in the field of medicine, government, law enforcement, banking,chemistry, photography, transportation, business, and many other trades. As a man of God, thirty-three of his offspring have served in the ministry as preachers, deacons, youth ministers, gospel singers, and missionaries.

J W Strawn
Birth:
Jul. 24, 1823
Hawkins County, Tennessee
Death:
Oct. 1, 1904
Beckham County, Oklahoma
Burial:
Ural Cemetery
Beckham County, Oklahoma

He was the son of John Strawn, of Tenn. He was married to Mary A. Jennings in 1847, and experienced religion two years later. He received license in 1881, ordination in 1883, from a council of Free Will Baptists from the Row Valley Q.M. Kansas, and had pastoral charge of the Bethsaida church.

Carl David Shivers
Birth:
Sep. 14, 1925
Death:
Mar. 23, 2009
Burial:
Little Cemetery, Little,
Seminole County, Oklahoma

Carl served in the infantry of the U. S. Army during World War II from 1943-1946, achieving the rank of one of the youngest first sergeants. While in Germany he received many medals and commendations, including two bronze service stars. God called him into the ministry in August 1948 to preach the word of God for the Free Will Baptist denomination. Since that time he has pastored twelve churches which included: Paden, Vanzant, Prague, Sante Fe, Calvin, Stratford, Springhill, Gaar Corner, Mustang, campground, Cedar Grove, and Memorial of Sulphur. He helped organize and start three churches, Prague, Okemah, and Stroud. He has enjoyed preaching for Free Will Baptists and was a staunch believer in the Bible. Along with pastoring and preaching he was a farmer, rancher, oil field pumper, auctioneer, and real estate salesman. The ministry was always first in his life.

Camey Alexander Sledge
Birth:
May 16, 1870
Toccopola,
Pontotoc County, Mississippi
Death:
Feb. 5, 1951
Valliant
McCurtain County, Oklahoma

Burial:
Felker Free Will Baptist Church
Cemetery, Felker,
McCurtain County, Oklahoma

Rev. C.A. Sledge's parents were Lemuel M. and Nancy Jane Terry Sledge, of Pontotoc Co. MS. On Sept. 14, 1892, in Pontotoc Co. MS, he married Miss Mary Susan DAVIS. It is unknown at this time when and where he was ordained a Free Will Baptist minister. They have an infant, born and died July 18, 1893, bur. MS, so it is easily assumed they came after this date but before 1904. They were found living in eastern Oklahoma, then Indian Territory. His name is in old church records showing that in 1904, he helped Rev. McGee form the Territorial Association of Free Will Baptists, to which Rev. Sledge belonged. This Association of early churches grew rapidly in the early 1900's, so that it was divided to further the progress; one was East Territorial and West Territorial, finally becoming Grand River. Rev. and Mrs. Sledge were early pioneers in all this work.

A Majesty Truly Regal Reigns

Ira W Smithey
Birth:
Oct. 22, 1896
Death:
Aug. 2, 1971
Burial:
Green Hill Cemetery,
Davis, Murray County,
Oklahoma,
Plot: Griffin Section,
Block North 5

Rev. Ira Smithey was the son of a pioneer Oklahoma preacher, Rev. J. W. Smithey. Ira worked bi-vocational, and while doing so, organized a church in Oklahoma City.

We must not demean life by standing in awe of death.

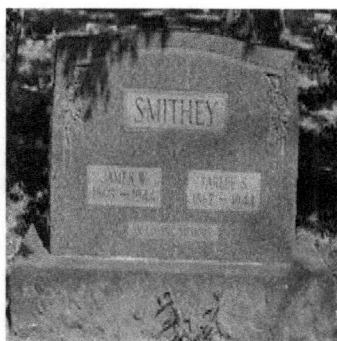

James William Smithey
Birth:
Jan. 9, 1865
Death:
May 15, 1944
Sulphur,
Murray County, Oklahoma
Burial:
Green Hill Cemetery, Davis,
Murray County, Oklahoma,
Plot: Old South, S5, row 14

Elder Smithey was ordained at Boyd schoolhouse near Bonham, TX. He came to Chickasaw Nation Territory in the early part of his ministry and began immediately to do evangelistic work throughout the old Chickasaw Nation and portions of the old Oklahoma Territory. In the 1915 Center Ass'n minutes, his name appears as having been elected to bring a message. We have no record of the number of conversions in his ministry nor the number of churches that he organized. We know that he was constantly engaged in evangelization of the old Chickasaw Nation and that a number of churches were organized as the direct result of his labors. Eld. Smithey possessed great power as an evangelist and his method of reasoning on the FWB doctrine was that he convinced ministers of other denominations to take membership in the church. He was a good organizer and did the more prominent work in the organization of the Oklahoma Association. His son, Ira J. Smithey, was also a minister.

Elder Aaron W Solomon
Birth:
Nov. 23, 1844
Death:
Jan. 6, 1920
Burial:
Lightning Ridge Cemetery,
Roff, Pontotoc County, Oklahoma

Aaron W. Solomon, was an ordained active minister of the Free Will Baptist church before statehood and after until his death.

Harry E Staires
Birth:
Jun. 19, 1904
Thayer,
Oregon County, Missouri
Death:
Sep. 30, 1985
Drumright,
Creek County, Oklahoma
Burial:
Drumright North Cemetery,
Drumright,
Creek County, Oklahoma

The Rev. Staires served as pastor of the Drumright Church a total of 21 years, serving for the first time in the 1930s during which time the church had a membership of over 400. He organized 12 new churches in Oklahoma including the Oilton Church, where he served as pastor, resigning in 1952. He assisted in organizing 25 other churches. Active in the Free Will Baptist administration, he served on the National Home Mission Board for 25 years, serving six of those years as chairman of the board. He was a moderator of the Oklahoma Association eight years and served six years on the Oklahoma Executive Board. In addition to Drumright and Oilton, he pastored churches in Tulsa, Duncan, Oklahoma City, Blackwell and Okmulgee.

I knew a man who once said, "death smiles at us all; all a man can do is smile back."

Elmer F Steelman
Birth:
1918
Death:
1985
Burial:
Laflin Creek Cemetery, Alex,
Grady County, Oklahoma

Jessey D. Stepp
Birth:
Jun. 10, 1915
Death:
Sep. 30, 1994
Burial:
Bixby Cemetery, Bixby,
Tulsa County, Oklahoma

An ordained Free Will Baptist minister who pastored Bixby and other area churches for several years.

Roma Stewart
Birth:
Oct. 16, 1927
Death:
Apr. 6, 1983

Burial:
Non Cemetery,
Non, Hughes County, Oklahoma

An ordained Free Will Baptist minister who first pastored in California and then in several churches in Oklahoma.

J. B. Stone
Birth:
Feb. 6, 1878
Heber Springs, Cleburne County,
Arkansas
Death:
Mar. 13, 1934
Ada, Pontotoc County, Oklahoma
Burial:
Egypt Cemetery,
Ada, Pontotoc County, Oklahoma

Moved to Oklahoma and settled in Pontotoc County where he farmed and preached. He and his wife were long-time members of the Free Will Baptist Church.

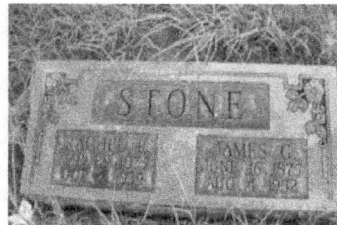

James Gilbert Stone
Birth:
Jun. 16, 1875
Death:
Aug. 4, 1952
Burial:
Lightning Ridge Cemetery,
Ruff, Pontotoc County,
Oklahoma

Edward S. Sunday
Birth:
Jan. 1, 1912 Oklahoma
Death:
Mar. 7, 1966 Guymon,
Texas County,
Oklahoma
Burial:
Stigler Cemetery,
Stigler, Haskell County, Oklahoma
His family was from the Cherokee Nation area of the Indian Territory. He was educated at Tahlequah and University of Tulsa, where he received a B.A. Degree. He was ordained a Free Will Baptist minister, and pastored churches in eastern Oklahoma at Checotah, Stigler, and others.

During early 1950's, he pastored at Healdton and Guymon, Oklahoma, where he died, from cancer. Rev. Sunday was a Cherokee Indian, and made his family proud. He was a soft-spoken person, and a very articulate and informed speaker. He was elected moderator of almost every association of churches where he pastored because he was a good parliamentarian and could move business along smoothly.

W. Bailey Thompson
Birth:
Nov. 7, 1931
Lexington, Oklahoma
Death:
Aug. 23, 2008
Burial:
Oakland Cemetery
Poteau, Le Flore County,
Oklahoma

He was born to the late Wooson and Trula (Johnson) Thompson. Rev. Thompson was called to preach at the age of 16 years and happily answered God's call on March 2, 1950. Rev. Thompson married Barbara Jean (Hickson) Thomspon. they welcomed to their lives, Jerry, Bob and Von Thompson. Rev. Thompson began pastoring the Freewill Baptist Church in Poteau, Oklahoma. He conducted over 350 revivals and served as Dean of Men at the Hillsdale Free Will Baptist College and as a moderator of the states of Oklahoma, Texas, and Arizona. His service was held at the Community Free Will Baptist Church in Pocola, Oklahoma. Rev. Bob Thompson, Rev. Cory Thompson and Rev. Keith Burden officiated the service.

Thomas Jefferson Townsend
Birth:
Jul. 4, 1856
Texas
Death:
Jan. 26, 1931
Wetumka,
Hughes County, Oklahoma
Burial:
Wetumka Cemetery,
Wetumka, Hughes County,
Oklahoma, Plot: Block 26

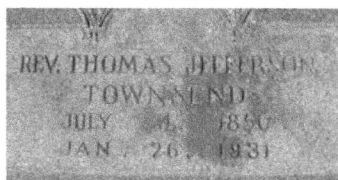

Rev. Townsend was a pioneer in spreading the gospel in the Indian

Territory and later after it was called Oklahoma. His name is an honored name in the foundation of the Free Will Baptist work.

James L Van Winkle
Birth:
Jun. 22, 1928
Death:
Mar. 10, 2000 Stillwater,
Payne County,
Oklahoma
Burial:
Highland Cemeter, Pawnee,
Pawnee County, Oklahoma,
Plot: Gate 6 East Section

He was bi-vocational minister pastoring seven churches in Oklahoma. He was a SGT in the US ARMY serving in Korea. He was also commissioned to serve with the special services missile unit in Washington, D.C. and later served in Germany. He taught auto body repair at the Tulsa Vo-Tech for 17 years until retiring.

William Luther Waddle
Birth:
Jun. 5, 1875
Coryell County,Texas
Death:
Nov. 6, 1956
Cleveland County, Oklahoma
Burial:
Lexington Cemetery
Lexington, Cleveland County,
Oklahoma

Lonnie E. Ward
Birth:
May 14, 1883
Texas
Death:
Apr. 7, 1958
Oklahoma
Burial:
Dibble Cemetery, Dibble,
McClain County, Oklahoma,
Plot: Sec 1, Row 7

An early FWB preacher. When he was ordained is unknown, but on his WWI Draft Registration on Sept. 1918, he stated his occupation as "minister." His ministry was long, and mostly confined to his home area in McClain and Garvin counties, where he preached and pastored churches with good success. His name appears in old church records as "delegate from Dibble to State Ass'n,1935".

*Thou art not dead! Thou art the whole
Of life that quickens in the sod.*

John H. West
Birth:
Nov. 24, 1901
Missouri
Death:
Apr., 1981
Tulsa,
Tulsa County, Oklahoma
Burial:
Rose Hill Memorial Park,
Tulsa, Tulsa County, Oklahoma

At first he worked in the oil industry as a pumper. Sometime during this period he entered the ministry, and was ordained a Free Will Baptist minister, date is unknown, but before 1935, for his name appears in the records that year as one of the speakers at the State FWB Ass'n. He entered upon a long pastorate at the First FWB Church, Tulsa, where his ministry was blessed with success. He became known among his brethren as "Mr. Sunday School." His influence extended to young ministers whom he offered training and help to them. He was always active and working towards better education, and was involved in the establishment of the Hillsdale FWB College. The administration building now bears his name. He retired before his death and filled in for pastors and preached at meetings when called upon. He was a member of the national association Sunday school board and very instrumental in its progress.

William R West
Birth:
Apr. 14, 1857
Death:
Oct. 2, 1926
Oklahoma
Burial:
Vista Cemetery, Asher,,
Pottawatomie County,
Oklahoma

A Free Will Baptist minister who preached in the early territory churches.

James O Williams
Birth:
Jul. 17, 1929
McCurtain, Haskell County,
Oklahoma
Death:
Aug. 6, 2012
Muskogee, Muskogee County,
Oklahoma
Burial:
Keota Cemetery, Keota,
Haskell County, Oklahoma

Bro James, as he was lovingly called, graduated from Keota Oklahoma in 1947 and enlisted in the US Navy in September 1947 and was discharged in 1951 as a Korean War Veteran Radioman reaching the grade of E-5 Petty Officer 2nd class. He spent all 4 years in San Diego, California where he sang with the Melodyaires Quartet for 2 years. He returned to Oklahoma in 1952 and entered Eastern A&M College in Wilburton graduating with an Associate Science degree. While there he organized and sang with a gospel quartet. The Lord called him into the ministry in 1960 and he was ordained as a Free Will Baptist minister in September 1961. Over the next 52 years he preached in churches all over Haskell County, Quinton and the Muskogee First Free Will Baptist Church for 10 years and 13 years at the Porum Free Will Baptist Church. He saw many people converted during his ministry. Next to his preaching, James loved gospel singing, playing the piano for over 60 years. He wrote several gospel songs and was published by Albert Brumley Music Company and Texas Legendary Music Company.

Muril Wilson
Birth:
Jun. 5, 1917
Death:
Oct. 18, 2002
Coalgate, Coal County,
Oklahoma
Burial:
Francis Cedar Grove Cemetery,
Francis,
Pontotoc County, Oklahoma

Ordained Free Will Baptist minister at Happyland Church, who also pastored other Oklahoma churches.

J Reford Wilson
Birth:
Apr. 3, 1924
Death:
Jan. 5, 1995
Burial:
Lexington Cemetery
Lexington Cleveland County
Oklahoma, Plot: E-R6-10

He was a visionary who pushed Free Will Baptist Foreign Missions in his leadership of 13 years. (1962-1975). The Oklahoma native's ministry spanned 50 years becoming active immediately after his conversion at age 16 in the Spring Hill Free Will Baptist Church in Lexington, Oklahoma. He was the agency's third director and during his tenure the number of adult foreign missionaries increased from 38 to 93. He was an conference speaker, journalist and administrator. He traveled extensively to the mission field to serve a missionary needs, consult the missionaries, attend strategy meetings with field counsels and speak at retreats around the world. In 1965 alone, he toured 13 countries in three months visiting major Free Will Baptist mission fields and doing initial work to open new fields. In 1979, in an article he wrote on world missions, he stated, " No church is properly functioning with real life unless the fire of missions is burning on its altar." He resigned in 1975 and returned to Oklahoma to teach four years

Bible and Missions at Hillsdale Free Will Baptist College. In 1979, his final pastorate was at the Butterfield Free Will Baptist Church in Aurora, Illinois where he invested 11 years of his life with that congregation. In 1991, after retiring, he began serving again as Missions professor at Hillsdale College. He pastored six churches in four states: Oklahoma, Tennessee, Arkansas and Michigan. Three times, he was elected to three terms on the Foreign Missions Board. Four times, the Arkansas State Ass'n elected him as their moderator. He also served six years on the Board of Directors with the Evangelical Foreign Missions Association. He also served as president of the Oklahoma FWB League Convention, conducted weekly radio broadcast as pastor in Pocahontas, Arkansas, and wrote curriculum for the Sunday School Department. He studied in several educational institutions: Oklahoma State University, Free Will Baptist Bible College, California Christian College, University of Tennessee and Southern Baptist Seminary.

Harry W Withers
Birth:
unknown
Death:
Jul. 29, 2013
Burial:
Vernon Cemetery
Coweta
Wagoner County, Oklahoma

An Oklahoma Free Will Baptist minister/pastor in the Tulsa area.

He fulfilled righteousness

Frances M Wood
Birth:
Sep. 9, 1909
Arkansas
Death:
Feb. 12, 1996
Oklahoma County, Oklahoma
Burial:
Memorial Park Cemetery,
Ada, Pontotoc County, Oklahoma

He moved with his family to Oklahoma a few years after 1907 statehood. They lived and farmed around Stratford. F.M. was one of the younger of their children, Vard and Walter, also sons. Rev. F.M. was converted in a revival near Stratford, along with his brothers. He entered the ministry in the Free Will Baptist, and pastored churches in the Center Association and surrounding. He also was used as an evangelist. Preachers during these depressed, economic times were more than likely to farm or have other income to care for their family. Rev. F.M. worked some with the Rail Road. He and his wife had one daughter, the late Marie Wood, who married Rev. James Murray, who is a leader in the church. He was widowed at the time of his death and was living near his daughter, in OKC where he died. He was well-thought of, and was a good preacher.

Weldon V. Wood
Birth:
Nov. 9, 1926
Oklahoma
Death:
Jun., 1967
Burial:
Memorial Park Cemetery, Ada,
Pontotoc County, Oklahoma

He was the son of Rev. Vard Wood. He grew up in Pontotoc Co. and was active in church activities from his youth. He married and raised three children, Jan Cason, (dec); Bruce Wood, and Tim Wood, a pastor in CA. He worked hard in the District and State Youth programs, which was called the "League" at that time. He was converted early in life. He was elected as State Clerk of the State Association of FWB, at age 25 yrs, and served for several years until his move to CA. He pastored Ada FWB church, and Capitol Hill in OKC, and probably others before these. He had a big smile, and very likeable personality. He was said to be "a rising star" when he was tragically killed in an auto accident on way from CA to OK, about 41 years of age.

William Vard Wood
Birth:
Mar. 5, 1890
Arkansas
Death:
Apr. 9, 1979
Pontotoc County, Oklahoma
Burial:
Memorial Park Cemetery,
Ada, Pontotoc County, Oklahoma

W. Vard Wood, was known in his adult years by the name "Vard". He was the son of James Perry Wood, and Melinda Elizabeth (McBee) Wood, of Arkansas, who moved to OK, early on and died near, or at Stratford. When he was ordained is unknown at this time, but he was converted in a large revival held in the late 1920's or early 1930's and entered the ministry soon afterward, and he served faithfully until his death. He was not college educated, but applied himself in study of the Bible, and other, learning where he found opportunity during those early times. He became one

of the leaders in his Oklahoma Free Will Baptist church. He was used often in evangelistic meetings with great success. He was known to lead an exemplary life and his preaching was with power. He had a habit of quoting, verbatim, a verse of scripture, while gesturing as if he was reading it from his hand. His pleasant voice and kind-sounding speech made him immediately affable to meet, and converse with. No known statistics of the number of revivals, converts and baptisms, he had, or the churches he pastored. But he had great success. He was loved and esteemed by all who knew him.

Dr Isaac Wilson Yandell
Birth:
Jul. 16, 1876
Scott County, Arkansas,
Death:
Dec. 19, 1959
Oklahoma City,
Oklahoma County, Oklahoma,
Burial:
Lexington Cemetery, Lexington,
Cleveland County, Oklahoma,
Plot: SW-R4-41

He entered the gospel ministry at age 16, ordained in 1894, in Scott Co. Arkansas. He moved from Arkansas with his family before 1900, to Indian Territory (Okla.). He studied medicine at the Vance School in Northwest Arkansas and passed the Federal Medical

Examination at McAlester and began helping the settlers with their medical needs. He also farmed as most old-time preachers did as they received hardly any support from churches. He farther studied medicine, and again passed the Federal Examination in McAlester, I.T. He attended the Academy at Kully Chaha, an Indian School the government had set up, and took extended courses at various schools, working at any menial task to support his studies. Kully Chaha debating team would hold debates with the Presbyterian school team at Cameron, where he participated, and acquired a love of polemics. He studied law and parliamentary procedure. His family moved into LeFlore Co., I.T. where his father died at age 49, and is buried in Royal Oak cemetery of that county.

He preached for the Free Will Baptist Church for 67 years, in Arkansas, Texas, California, and in Oklahoma. He was a leader in the organization of the Oklahoma. State Association of churches and served as its moderator. He served in many positions and offices of the FWB.

He served as president of the Old Southwestern Convention, before 1935, and offered advice and counsel towards forming the National body.

He was active and instrumental in organizing over fifty FWB churches. Many young ministers were under his tutelage.

During his time and era, the ministry demanded many sacrifices from which he did not draw back.

He was a great orator, preacher and debater, and as a speaker was always in demand wherever he went. He never ceased to study, even though he lost his eyesight several years before his death. He could recite many, many scriptures verbatim, and one time after he was blind, he counted 120 hymns of which he knew every stanza. He possessed an unusually keen and retentive mind and wisdom that had to 'be from above.' His wit and humor were enjoyed by all his friends and family alike wherever he went. He lived a life with many hardships, but he always saw a positive side and an uplifting attitude which served him well.

DeArthur Yandell
Birth:
Mar. 22, 1934
Alex,Grady County, Oklahoma
Death:
Sep. 1, 2009
Chickasha,
Grady County, Oklahoma
Burial:
Non Cemetery,
Non, Hughes County, Oklahoma

He was born to Dr. Isaac Wilson and Dovie Lee. DeArthur dedicated his life as a young man to serving the Lord and others with all his heart. He ministered for 58 years. DeArthur pastored churches in Oklahoma and California for many years, and the Chickasha Freewill Baptist from 1999 until he preached his last

sermon on Easter Sunday 2009. DeArthur annually attended the Oklahoma State and National Associations of Freewill Baptist Churches, and the State Ministers Conference of Free Will Baptists, where he made many friends.

L D Yandell
Birth:
Jan. 5, 1923
Denison, Grayson County, Texas
Death:
Oct. 23, 2009
Oklahoma City, Oklahoma County, Oklahoma
Burial:
Lexington Cemetery, Lexington, Cleveland County, Oklahoma

He was preceded in death by his parents, Dr. Isaac Wilson and Dovie Lee Yandell. He was ordained in the Oklahoma District Association, and pastored Glendale FWB Church for over nine years. He was bi-vocational and preached and "filled in" when asked, after his pastorate. He also

labored with his brother, Rev. DeArthur Yandell, in Trinity FWB Church in Oklahoma City. Only a robbery by two gunmen, with guns on him and his wife while made to lie on the floor, caused him to decide to retire from that occupation.

Homer Lee Young
Birth:
Feb. 2, 1929
Death:
Oct. 10, 2007
Burial:
Little Cemetery,
Little, Seminole County, Oklahoma

He was a graduate of Connors State College, Oklahoma Bible College (Hillsdale) Tulsa Univ., where he studied theology. Ordained as a Free Will Baptist minister in 1952. He established and worked as pastor in several churches. First in Henryetta, then to Cushing, Stillwater, Tulsa, OKla. C,ity Moore, McAlester, El Reno, Wilburton, Wewoka, Chickasha. He also served as the Okla. Free Will Baptist State Exec. Sec. He was not only a minister, but a member of the State Minister's Quartet for forty years, which went everywhere singing in conventions, revivals and homecomings.

Everett Eugene Zoellers
Birth:
Nov. 1, 1927
Kansas City,
Jackson County, Missouri
Death:
Jan. 2, 2010
Dallas, Dallas County, Texas
Burial:
Hillcrest Memorial Park,
Ardmore, Carter County,
Oklahoma

Gene and Barbara (Thompson) were wed on November 12, 1945, in Ardmore, Okla. For most of his adulthood Gene was a minister. He pastored at Westside Free Will Baptist Church, Midland, Texas for several years. They then lived and ministered in Dallas.

"As the image on the seal is stamped upon the wax, so the thoughts of the heart are printed upon the actions."

Pennsylvania

R. E. Anderson
Birth:
1809
Norwich, Massachusetts
Death:
Feb. 27, 1888
Burial:
Bethel Cemetery
Franklin
Venango County,
Pennsylvania

The common school of his area formed the basis of his education. In 1848 he was ordained in the Wesleyan Methodists and afterwards joined the Free Baptists movement. He pastored in Pennsylvania as well as Conneaut and Chester, in Ohio. In his 50 years of service he baptized over 2000 people. When he was a Wesleyan Methodists he had served as the Pres. of the conference and afterwards as a Free Will Baptist was a delegate to the General Conference. He was also a delegate to the National Free-Soil Convention in 1852. In the contest against intemperance and slavery he has been a persistent worker.

Hiram Bacon
Birth:
Jul. 18, 1808
Death:
Nov. 12, 1886,
Burial:
Austinburg Pioneer Cemetery,
Austinburg,
Tioga County, Pennsylvania

Erastus Sterling Bumpus
Birth:
May 3, 1815
Death:
Jan. 23, 1880
Pennsylvania
Burial:
Plum Church Cemetery
Cooperstown, Venango County,
Pennsylvania

Bumpus was converted at the age of 14. In July 1837, he married Annette Shirley, and soon moved to Waterford, Pennsylvania, and then to Ohio, where he joined the Pierpoint church, and was ordained to the gospel ministry in the Free Will Baptist church, in the Ashtabula Quarterly Meeting. In 1853, he returned to Pennsylvania and ministered to the Big Bend, Croton, Plumb, Canal and other churches, remaining with the Cancul church nine years. He was a good man, generous and charitable. His preaching was plain, practical and earnest.

Seldon Butler
Birth:
Jul. 15, 1806
Rochester,
Windsor County, Vermont
Death:
Oct. 19, 1888
Tioga County, Pennsylvania

Burial:
Butler Hill Cemetery,
Tioga County, Pennsylvania

Rev. Butler was licensed to preach in 1841, and ordained in February, 1843, in the Freewill Baptist Church. Rev. Wm. Mack and others served on his council. His ministry from the first was in one vicinity, commencing in the Bradford and Tioga Quarterly Meeting. He held revivals, baptized three hundred and fifty converts and organized six churches. He was active in his community and raised a large family while doing the work of a minister.

James Calder
Birth:
February 16, 1826
Harrisburg, Pennsylvania
Death:
1893
Burial:
Harrisburg Cemetery
Harrisburg
Dauphin County,
Pennsylvania
He was married on December

25, 1850, to Ellen C. Winebrenner, eldest daughter of Rev. John Winebrenner, the founder of Church of God.
She died in 1858 and he later married Elizabeth DD Murphy of Harrisburg.
His son Rev. William Calder was a missionary to Rangoon, Burma. His only daughter was the wife of Prof. J. W. Preston of Pennsylvania State college. He pursued his preparatory studies in Harrisburg and Bristol, Pennsylvania and Norwich, Vermont.
He graduated from the Wesleyan University, Middletown, Connecticut on August 1, 1849.
He was converted on February 11, 1837 and United with the Methodist Episcopal Church receiving license in 1847 and entering the Philadelphia conference. In October, 1850 he was appointed a missionary to China; and after receiving his ordination in December he sailed for China on March 1851.
In November 1853, because of a change of belief as to baptism and church policy, he was baptized at Hong Kong, withdrew from the Methodist Episcopal Church and returned to America in 1854 and united with the Church of God.
He served as pastor of the church in Harrisburg until 1859 when he and a majority of the members organized the first Free Baptist Church of which he continued to pastor until 1869 when he became the Pres. of Hillsdale College, in Michigan and was the pastor of the church at that place.
In 1871 he accepted the presidency of Pennsylvania State college where he remained until 1880. He then became pastor of the church at Harrisburg again. He was the editor of the *Church Advocate* from 1856-1858, and was principal of the

Shippensburg Collegiate Institute, then professor of Belles-Letters in Pennsylvania Female College and was a Trustee of Storer college from its organization.

Bela Cogswell
Birth:
Jan. 10, 1817
Death:
Dec. 2, 1900
Burial:
Cogswell Cemetery, Silvara
Bradford County, Pennsylvania

He started out his career in the ministry as a Methodist, but changed his viewpoint towards religion about 1850 when he became a Freewill Baptist, a group who stood up against Slavery. He was a founder of the Silvara Freewill Baptist church in 1856. He improved those which he had to the best advantage studying and reading as far as he could, until the people thought he was qualified to teach, when he taught several terms. Previous to 1837, before he was twenty years old, he was licensed to preach the gospel, and for more than forty years he has been engaged in the work of the ministry and preached to the same people.

He was one of the original members of the Free Will Baptist church on the Tuscarora, and was mainly instrumental in its organization, and in erecting the

Pleasant Church edifice, which is used by the congregation. This church as a marble pulpit of unique construction, and on the marble tablets surrounding it are the names of the members, pastors, contributors, etc., a constant reminder of the worshipers of those who are affiliated with them in the ties of the spiritual brotherhood. Mr. Cogswell has been their first and last pastor. In addition to his duties as pastor, he has frequently had to perform the official duties of a citizen, having, besides other township offices, been justice of the peace fifteen years.

Asa Dodge
Birth:
1829
Death:
August 3, 1883
Burial:
Wellsboro Cemetery
Wellsboro
Tioga County, Pennsylvania

He commenced preaching in 1851, having been approved by the Ridgeway church, and received a Quarter Meeting license and in 1854 and was ordained by the Tioga County Quarterly Meeting in 1867. He did good work as an evangelist rather than as a pastor and at his death resolutions appreciative of his character and youthfulness were passed by the Potter County and Tioga County Quarterly Meetings within the bounds of which his labors were chiefly spent. Had three bros. who were also FB ministers.

Calvin Dodge
Birth:
Oct. 12, 1814
Lisbon
Grafton County, New Hampshire
Death:
May 15, 1882
Cadis
Bradford County, Pennsylvania
Burial:
Cadis Cemetery
Cadis, Bradford County,
Pennsylvania

Rev. Calvin Dodge was one of four brothers who were Free Baptist ministers: Gurley, Edward, and Asa Dodge, whose parents were Asa and Sarah DODGE.He married Charlotte Allen in 1844.He was licensed for the ministry at 25 yrs, and three years later was ordained by the Owego Quarterly Meeting at Dryden, N.Y., while engaged in a Revival with the Troy church. He held revivals after license at Cuba, Wirt, and Bolivar.He was a useful man. Died age 67 years.

Edward E Dodge
Birth:
1794
New Hampshire, USA
Death:
May 4, 1837
Cadis, Bradford County,
Pennsylvania
Burial:
Cadis Cemetery
Cadis, Bradford County,
Pennsylvania

Rev. Edward E. Dodge, brother of Rev. Asa Dodge, was converted in 1812, he was baptized by Rev. Joshua Quinby, and united with the Free Baptist church at Lisbon, N.H. He soon after began to conduct meetings. About 1819 he removed to Dryden N.Y., near the head of Lake Cayuga, and united heartily with Rev. John Gould, the only Free Baptist preacher in the great state, in breaking to the people the bread of life.In 1821, after two years of successful labor, he attended the Vermont Yearly Meeting held at Turnbridge, and was there ordained.He returned to labor with Gould and to organize churches at Berkshire, Candor, and Owego, and Choconut in Pennsylvania. On May 27, 1820, they met in conference and organized the Owego Quarterly Meeting, consisting then of an isolated band of one hundred and sixty brethren. He was untiring in his labors in the revival of 1825 in that region.

Daniel Mcbride Graham
Birth:
Nov. 17, 1817
Huron County, Ohio
Death:
Dec. 21, 1888
Philadelphia
Philadelphia County,
Pennsylvania
Burial:
Mount Moriah Cemetery
Philadelphia
Philadelphia County,
Pennsylvania

His parents, reverent Lemuel L. And Hannah were of Scottish descent and gave their son religious instructions. He was baptized in the LaGrange County, Indiana in 1839 and entered the sophomore class of Oberlin college in the spring of 1841. He lived part of his time with Prof. Charles G. Finney, and the degree of Master of Arts was conferred in 1847. The degree of Dr. of Divinity was conferred by Bowdoin college in 1863. Graham received license from the Calhoun Quarterly Meeting in 1844, and was ordained by the same body three years later. He was president of Michigan Central college at Spring Arbor, Michigan, 1844-48. He then ministered to the church in Saco, Maine two years and that the New York City church for 11 years. Then at Portland, Maine and Chicago Illinois in the years that followed. In 1871 he became Pres. of Hillsdale College filling that position with credit for three years. For several years he was editor of the *Free Will Baptist Quarterly* also of the *Christian Freeman.* He was a frequent contributor to the columns of *The Morning Star*, *The Free Baptists,* and the *Religious Intelligencer* of New Brunswick. He held various positions on many of the denominational boards and aided in securing the cooperation of brothers in New Brunswick and Nova Scotia in foreign missionary work. And in 1860 served the denomination as delegate to the General Baptists of England. His later ministry was with the church at East Somerville, Massachusetts and churches in Philadelphia, Pennsylvania where his last pastorate was. His ministry was attended with divine blessings. His records show that he had more than 1000 converts and baptisms during his years of service

Behold the Lamb of God

Oliver Clinton Hills
Birth:
June 8, 1824
Death:
1913
Roulette
Potter county, Pennsylvania
Burial:
Wellsboro Cemetery
Wellsboro
Tioga County, Pennsylvania

He experienced the new birth in February, 1843 and was licensed to preach on December 23, 1854. He was ordained by a Council of the Spafford Quarterly Meeting on September 9, 1855. His early ministry was in the Spafford and Troy Quarterly Meetings. He ministered to churches in the New York and Pennsylvania Quarterly Meetings and had revivals each year of his ministry. He organized six churches and baptized 221 converts. He assisted in raising funds for building several meeting houses during, 1868-70, he engaged in church extension work under the direction of the Pennsylvania Missionary Society receiving cash and subscriptions for church buildings amounting to more than $9000. Twice to served as a delegate to the General Conference. He was in the ministry for many years, having been pastor of several churches in Tioga county and was for some time chaplain at the Tioga County Home. The funeral services were at the Free Baptist church on East avenue, Rev. A.C. Shaw, D.D. officiated.He was one of those plain unassuming preachers whose chief aim in life was that of doing good in a quiet, but effective manner, which gained for him many friends among those with whom he came in contact.

Daniel W. Hunt
Birth:
April 21, 1821
Otsego County, New York
Death:
Oct. 31
Knoxville, Pennsylvania
Burial:
Woodlawn Cemetery
Austinburg
Tioga County, Pennsylvania

He studied in the Deerfield, Pennsylvania school where he was brought to God in 1855. In the same year received license to preach. He was ordained on September 26, 1858 being connected with the Brookfield church of the Tuscarora Quarterly Meeting. Hunt, aged 81, died in Knoxville at the home of his son, Mr. John B. Hunt. When a youth he removed with his parents and their many children to Brookfield township, where he remained nearly 30 years and where his marriage to Miss Ann Wakley took place. After living in Troupsburg, N.Y., for a time they moved to Knoxville for the

remainder of his life. When still a young man Mr. Hunt became a member of the Free Will Baptist Church, and for many years had been a licensed preacher in the denomination. His funeral service was largely attended and was held on Sunday afternoon, at the Free Will Baptist church in Austinburg, Brookfield township, where Mr. Hunt had been a member for nearly half a century.

John Welsley Ingerick
Birth:
Apr. 24, 1831
Rutland
Tioga County, Pennsylvania
Death:
Sep. 13, 1915
Wellsboro
Tioga County, Pennsylvania
Burial:
Wellsboro Cemetery
Wellsboro
Tioga County, Pennsylvania

He was licensed in the Tioga Quarterly Meeting, February, 1884 and did a good work in serving the outlying districts in the word of life. He served for 10 years as the quarterly meeting clerk.

Info: Wellsboro Gazette, September 14, 1950, page 3

Chester Prince
Birth:
Jun., 1792
Dudley, Worcester County, Massachusetts
Death:
May, 1867
Rome, Bradford County, Pennsylvania
Burial:
Rome Cemetery
Rome, Bradford County, Pennsylvania

He was converted at the age of sixteen, moved in 1815 to Bradford County, Pa., where he died. He joined the Rome church at an early day, being a pioneer, Died age 74y 11m

Caleb S Rogers
Birth:
Mar. 14, 1791
Bennington County, Vermont
Death:
Aug. 15, 1879
Greenfield, Pennsylvania
Burial:
Lowville Cemetery
Wattsburg, Erie County, Pennsylvania
Plot: Sect or Lot 7

His parents were Nehemiah and Lydia (Smith) Rogers, who moved to Luzerne Co. Pennsylvania, at an early day. He was converted in western New York when twenty-seven years of age under the labors of Rev. J. Parmenter, and licensed at the Bethany Quarterly Meeting on Jan 24, 1825. A year later he was ordained. He labored in Genesee and Livingston Counties until 1836, and at Freedom, N.Y., until 1841. Then he moved to Sparta, PA. in the Washington and French Creek Q.M's until his death. Here, though so aged, he had preached only the Sabbath before. He traveled extensively, and was well known and highly esteemed throughout this region. (This was found in the History of Genesee Co. online:"The Freewill Baptist church, organized in 1809, was the first in town." (Bethany). Area where Rev. C.S. Smith was active in early times). He married Chloe Warriner, 13 April 1815, Bennington, NY. They had several children, When a very young man, he served in the Navy in the War of 1812.

Cary Rogers
Birth:
Aug. 22, 1815
Grafton, Rensselaer County, New York
Death:
Aug. 30, 1894
Cranesville, Erie County, Pennsylvania
Burial:
Hope Cemetery
Cranesville, Erie County, Pennsylvania

Rogers, was an ordained Freewill Baptist minister.. His parents were Nathan and Sarah (Steward) Rogers, who were of English and Scotch descent. His wife was Mary Rogers, who he married on 1/17/1848. He was licensed in 1876 and ordained in 1878. He assumed the pastoral care of the Pageville, Pennsylvania, church in 1877 and continued his labors

with them until 1887, when failing health caused him to resign his position as pastor.

Samuel Buck Seaman
Birth:
Aug. 4, 1810
Tioga County, Pennsylvania
Death:
Mar. 3, 1854
Wilmore
Cambria County, Pennsylvania
Burial:
Wilmore United Brethren Church Cemetery
Wilmore
Cambria County, Pennsylvania

He was engaged in ministerial labor several years have been be connected with the Jefferson church of the Cook's town quarterly meeting, Pennsylvania since his ordination about 1844.His wife was Anne Ashbaugh Seaman (1819 - 1899)*

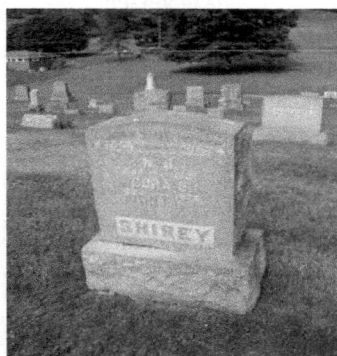

Nicholas J. Shirey
Birth:
Jul. 24, 1846
Death:
1931
Burial:
Barren Run Methodist Cemetery
Smithton
Westmoreland County, Pennsylvania

Rev. N.J. Shirey, was educated at Mt. Pleasant and at Edinboro' Normal School, PA, and received ordination Nov. 16, 1879, into the

Freewill Baptist church. He has ministered to the Jenner and Dunnings Creek churches two years, to the Deanville and Oakland churches one year and is now [1889] with the Brookfield and Cameron, N,Y., churches. He has labored as an evangelist, and baptized ninety-one converts.In August 1884, he was married to Cora E. Bailey.

Joshua G Shoemaker
Birth:
Oct. 7, 1830
Death:
Dec. 11, 1900
Burial:
Deanville Cemetery
Deanville
Armstrong County, Pennsylvania

His father with the Rev. George Shoemaker, who was a founder of the Church of the Brethren in Christ. Brother Shoemaker became a Free Baptist in 1880 and was minister of the Deanville church. His early ministry was devoted to itinerant work with the Church Of Brethren In Christ. His son, M. N. Shoemaker was a student in the theological Department of Hillsdale College Michigan.On August 4, 1861, Joshua married Elizabeth Ann Myers 1839-1892 and to them seven children were born. Later he married Nancy J Miller but there were no children to this union.

John Corydon Steele
Birth:
Mar. 4, 1834
Boston
Erie County, New York
Death:
Jun. 3, 1910
Burial:Non-Cemetery Burial
Pennsylvania

He began the Lord's service in 1852 and received his license to preach in 1854. He was ordained by the Erie Quarterly Meeting in New York in 1862. The same year he was married to Caroline Griffith and they had two daughters. His ministry has been with the church at Attica, Warsaw, Chagrin Falls and Parma, Ohio. Most of his work was done in the state of New York organizing churches and laboring to build up the cause under the direction of the Home Mission Society. Besides revival meetings in all these places some of them were largely successful. He was very active not only in revivals and organizing churches but had great influence in the Western part of New York State. He was very prominent in the work of the Central Association and also served as a delegate to the General Conference.

Benjamin Towner
Birth:
July 8,1803
Rome, Pa.
Death:
Apr. 2, 1866
Lawrence, Pa.
Burial:
Evergreen Cemetery
Tioga, Tioga County, Pennsylvania

His early religious experiences were with the Methodists, but he did not agree with them and was told that he was a Free Baptist, the first he had ever heard of the denomination. He immediately sought them, and spent some years in the ministry. He was especially giftedin singing and aided much in revival services.

Henry H Van Amringe
Birth:
Jan. 13, 1796
Philadelphia, Pa.
Death:
May 24, 1862
Philadelphia, Philadelphia County, Pennsylvania
Burial:
Laurel Hill Cemetery
Philadelphia, Philadelphia County, Pennsylvania

He was graduated honorably by Columbia college, New York city, in 1815. Immediately after graduating he studied law, and in 1818 was admitted to practice in the Supreme Court of the State of New York. He subsequently settled at Westchester, Chester Co., Pa., and by his ability and integrity soon gained a distinguished position at the bar. During the administration of Gov. Shulze he was appointed by Attorney General Ellmacher his deputy for Chester County. This office he resigned in 1835. He became Recorder of Pittsburgh, Pa., in 1840, by appointment of the Governor. He resigned the Recordership in 1844, and, though he had a brilliant legal and political career open before him, he quit forever the practice of the bar to devote himself to the Chrisatian ministry. From this time forward he labored assiduously to disseminate the gospel. He itinerated through various parts of Pennsylvania, New York, Ohio, Illinois and Wisconsin, as an evangelist and a lecturer on such practical reforms as he deemed best calculated to secure to all free homes, personal liberty, education, and the perpetuity of our republican institutions. His influence had much to do with the passage of a homestead exemption law by Wisconsin, which still remains in force. He wrote much for the papers, many pamphlets on subjects of religion and reform, and several religious works.In 1854 he united with the F. W. Baptists, and became pastor of their church near Burlington, Wis.. His arduous labors shattered his constitution, and he was compelled at last to yield through physical exhaustion. He resigned the pastorship of the Freewill Baptist church at Prairie Centre, Illinois, in the latter part of 1859, and by invitation west to live in Philadelphia with his sister and her family, by whom he was attended with the most devoted and untiring affection till his death. Though he was afflicted with paralysis, which extended gradually over his body and affected at last even his speech, and, at times, with acute neuralgic and rheumatic pains, no impatient or complaining word ever escaped his lips. He seemed not to think of himself, but was the charm of the family from the uniform cheerfulness and sweetness of his temper, the inexhaustible fund of information which he was ever ready and pleased to impart, the tender interest he manifested in the welfare of all about him, and the noble Christian example his daily life afforded. His death was as calm as his hope was steadfast. As he approached his end, the paralysis in a great measure left him, and he slept himself away as gently as an infant. His friends scarecely knew that he had gone till his silent pulse informed them that his spirit rested in the bosom of his Father. After his death there were found among his private papers two of what he had terms "Books of Remembrance." In one of them was the following remarkable entry. "Faithfully did he keep the vows here made and most signally were his prayers answered." In the early part of the evening on which this entry was made he had recorded that he was reading Upham on Christian Perfection and in conformity with direction consecrated himself solemnly to God.

David Winton

Birth:
Jan. 25, 1825
Centerville, Crawford County,
Pennsylvania
Death:
Dec. 29, 1870
Pierpont, Ashtabula County,
Ohio
Burial:
Hope Cemetery, Lundys Lane,
Erie County, Pennsylvania

At the age of fifteen, he was converted and the next year commenced the work of an evangelist. He traveled in Crawford, Venango and Erie Counties. In April 1846, he became pastor of the Free Baptist Church of Wellsburg, and for six years labored incessantly, preaching in Lockport, Girard, Franklin and Pikeville. He spent three months in western New York. In August, 1854, he became pastor of the church in Jackson, Mich., and for several years he labored with the Jackson and Spring Arbor churches. He served three years as a chaplain and two years as general agent of the Michigan State Prison. In 1869, he returned to Pennsylvania, and the following February took up the work at Pierport, Ohio, where after a brief illness he died, Dec. 29th. Rev. Winton's gift was that

of a revivalist. He was an able preacher. Temperance, education and freedom had in him a strong advocate.

The Dead In Christ Will Rise First.

Rhode Island

Thomas L. Angell

Birth:
Nov. 10, 1837
Greenville
Providence County
Rhode Island
Death:
1923
Burial:
Smith Lot
Smithfield
Providence County
Rhode Island

When 3 years old he began to attend the common school of Greenville, and continued in this school several years with the loss of only one term. December 1855, he went to Thetford, Vt., and remained two terms. The next two years he was at the Wesleyan Academy, Wilbraham, Mass., fitting for college. He entered Brown University in 1858, and graduated in 1862. The following winter he taught the school in Greenville. In November, 1863, He entered the Theological School at E. Windsor, Conn. The next spring he taught school in Greenville again, and in the fall of 1864, became an assistant of Rev. B. F.

Hayes in Lapham Institute. He was for three years Principal of that school, until the Summer of 1868 In January 1869, he entered upon the Professorship of Modern Languages in Bates College. After the close of the college year, he spent a year in Europe in study. In early years he had marked religious impressions through parental instruction and the powerful influence of the devout teacher of the Greenville school.He was baptized by Rev. James McKenzie. He preaches more or less along with his work in the college. His first sermon was preached in the F. B. Church of Harrison, Me., Jan. 5, 1873. On July 31, 1862, he married Miss Emily Brown of Providence, R. I. His only daughter, Miss F. Angell, entered Bates College in 1886.

A Day of Victory

Reuben Allen
Birth:
Sep. 4, 1793
Gilmanton
Belknap County New Hampshire,
Death:
May 30, 1872
North Scituate, Providence
County
Rhode Island, USA
Burial:
Smithville Cemetery
North Scituate
Providence County Rhode Island

In October, 1811, while apprenticed to a blacksmith, he experienced a radical change of heart and at age 19, after a struggle back from death's door, he yielded his life to the Lord and began holding a revival meeting at Northfield, where 35 were converted. In 1818, he went to Vermont, where he preached alternately at Wheelock and Cabot. His labors were blessed, he was ordained to the ministry; fifty persons were baptized and two churches organized. Early in 1820 he traveled and preached in Burlington, St. Albans and other towns in VT. In 1821, he visited Rhode Island, reaching Burrillville on horseback, Oct. 13, for the organization of the RI Quarterly Meeting. The next day he preached the sermon at the ordination of Daniel Green, the first Freewill Baptist ordination which took place in the state. His labors were prolific in Vermont and Rhode Island.

Alfred Williams Anthony
Birth:
Jan. 13, 1860
Death:
Jan. 20, 1939
Burial:
Swan Point Cemetery,
Providence,
Providence County, Rhode Island

Anthony was born in Providence, Rhode Island on January 13, 1860 to Lewis Williams Anthony and Britannia Franklin (Waterman) Anthony. He was a descendant of Rhode Island founder, Roger Williams. Anthony graduated from Brown University in 1883 and Cobb Divinity School in 1885, which was then affiliated with Bates College. Anthony also received an A.M. degree from Brown in 1886.

In 1887, he was appointed to a professorship at Cobb Divinity School and went on to publish various books and articles. When the Divinity School merged with the College religion department, he became a religion professor at Bates College serving from 1908 to 1911. Anthony was active in various Freewill Baptist institutions and served as President of the Board of Trustees of Storer College in West Virginia. He travelled to Africa and Asia as

Secretary for the Free Will Baptist Home Missions Council. Anthony also as a Trustee for Bates College, Hillsdale College, and Brown University.

A Prof. at Bates College and the author of various notable books including *An Introduction to the Life of Jesus* (1896) and *The Method of Jesus* (1899) and *Bates College and Its Background* (1936). He received an honorary D. D. from Bates in 1902, Brown in 1908, and an L.L.D. from Colby in 1914. He had a strong influence on the merger with the Northern Baptists.

Allen Brown
Birth:
Mar. 31, 1788 Providence,
Providence County, Rhode Island
Death:
Nov. 6, 1860
Providence,
Providence County, Rhode Island
Burial:
North Burial Ground,
Providence,
Providence County, Rhode Island

He enjoyed the privileges of the best schools his city afforded. He united early with the First Congregational church under the care of Rev. Mr. Wilson. After serving an apprenticeship in the hardware store of Governor Jones, he went for a year in 1810, to Savannah, GA, and engaged in business for himself. He then established the business under the name of Dyer and Brown in Providence. Feeling a call to the ministry, he entered on a course of study in Philadelphia, and on graduating returned to Providence and took the pastoral charge of the Third Baptist church, then just organized. During the six years that followed he witnessed many conversions. His views were decidedly Arminian and he was ordained not without hesitation by the council. He was a member of the "Union Conference," with Zalmon Tobey, Henry Tatem, and Ray

Potter, which ordained Martin Cheney, April, 24, 1825.

In 1827, at the expiration of his pastorate with the Third Baptist church, feeling he had no sympathy from the Baptist brethren, he joined the Olneyville, R.I., Freewill Baptist church under Rev. Martin Cheney, and also the Q.M.

During the next thirty years of his life he held no pastorate. He was bookkeeper in Merchants' Bank of Providence for twenty years. He then entered the counting-room of Dr. Samuel B. Tobey as confidential clerk.

On the opening of the Dexter Asylum, he became chaplain, preaching regularly to the unfortunate for more than twenty years till his last sickness laid him aside for over a year.

To the Freewill Baptist Foreign Mission Society he bequeathed the sum of five hundred dollars. For many years he was well known to the readers of *The Morning Star* by his contributions in poetry and prose over the signature "A.B." He is also profiled in the book, *"Memoirs of Eminent Preachers In The Freewill Baptist Denomination (1874)"*, by Selah Hibbard Barrett of Rutland, Ohio.

Gideon A. Burgess
Birth:
May 29, 1854
Death:
Mar. 4, 1945
Burial:
North Burial Ground,
Providence,
Providence County,
Rhode Island

Burgess, Rev. Gideon A., son of Albert Williams and Mary B. (Williams) Burgess, was born in Providence, R. 1., May 29, 1854. He descended through both parents from Roger Williams, and by paternal descent from Rev. Samuel Winsor, father and son, who held the pastorate of the First Baptist church, Providence, 1732-71. He graduated from the Providence High School in 1874, Brown University in 1878, and Bates Theological Seminary in 1881. Converted Oct. 6, 1872, he was baptized by Rev. J. Mariner in January, 1873, uniting with the Greenwich Street church. Having been licensed by the Rhode Association in 1878, he was ordained at Greenville, R. I., as pastor of the First Smithfield church, Nov. 22, 1882, the Rev. J. Mariner preaching the sermon. He has baptized 40, solemnized 37 marriages, and attended 111 funerals. He was Secretary of the Rhode Island Sunday-School Union from 1883, resigning the office to assume the pastorate of the First church in Minneapolis, Minn. , Jan. 1, 1889. He has been Corresponding Secretary of the Free Baptist Education Society since 1886. He was chosen state agent for the Church Extension fund, and a member of the Minnesota State Mission Board in 1889. He is one of the editors of the Free Baptist Cyclopcedia published in 1889. He married Jan. 1, 1884, Miss Emma A., daughter of Simon S. Steere, of Greenville, R. I.

Maxcy Whipple Burlingame
Birth:
May 5, 1805
Gloucester,R. I.
Death:
Mar. 4, 1879
Georgiaville, R. I.
Burial:
Winsor-Hunt Lot
Glocester, Providence County,
Rhode Island

He was the youngest of ten children of Stephen and Abigail Burlingame. His father was a farmer of respectable standing, and both his parents were Christians. He could not remember the time when he was not accustomed to pray. During his childhood he often wished he might participate in a revival of religion. At the age of nineteen he made a public profession, was baptized by Rev. Joseph White in September, 1825, and united with the church in Gloucester. He now became sensible that he must have experienced religion when but a child. The impressions in regard to preaching were renewed with increased power, and though his diffident and sensitive spirit sought to stifle them, at length an abiding and increasing sense of duty lead him to consecrate himself to the work of the ministry. He attended a grammar school for some time in Killingly, Conn., and afterward the Wilbraham Academy. At the latter place he had the society of a number who were preparing for the ministry. In May, 1828, he received license to preach from the Rhode Island Q. M. His family then moved to Deerfield, Pa., where he taught and preached. Conversions resulted, and a church was organized. He returned to Rhode Island in the spring of 1829 and preached through the summer to several churches. He was ordained at Chepachet. January 28, 1830, he was married to Miss Harriet Winsor, of Gloucester. Soon after, he began to preach at Chepacher and Blackstone, Mass:, regularly, and fifth Sundays at Burrillville for a time. He soon dropped the latter appointment. Revivals occurred at the othe places and considerable additions to the churches. In the summer and autumn of 1834 he preached a part of the time at Pautucket with success. In the following winter he took charge of a school in Georgiaville, which had been broken up. He succeeded in the school. A revival resulted from his labors which induced him to move there in the spring of 1835. A church was soon organized and during the two years that he was pastor about fifty persons were baptized, among them his wife. Two of the earlier members became ministers. He had continued to preach at Blackstone, Mass., a part of the time, and now, in 1837, moved there and devoted all his time to that interest.He labored there in all over sixteen years. About 550 persons were received into the church. After four years a new house of worship was built. He also preached occasionally at Saundersville, in Grafton, Mass., and was instrumental in the organization of a church there afterward the Farnumsville church. He left there in 1846. The next three years he preached at Greenville and then at Chepachet. After a short time at Gilford Village, N. H., he settled at New Market, N. H. Other pastorates were in Danville, N. H., and Topsham, Me. He preached also in North Berwick, New Gloucester and Cornish, Me., at West Scituate, R. I., and East Killingly, Conn. About nine years before his death he returned to Georgiaville. He served as pastor there four years, and preached also at Tiverton and Carolina Mills, R. I., and Westford, Conn. He was more than fifty years in the ministry. At his death no Free Baptist minister in Rhode Island had performed more service than he. He promoted missions, education and reform. From 1844 to 1859 he was a corporator of the Printing Establishment. He was efficient in originating the Smithville Seminary. He was a member of several General Conferences. His usefulness was not from superior intellect or talent in preaching, though he was above the average, but from loyalty to Christ and sympathy for men. He was very sensitive, but as tender toward others as he would have others be to him. His overflowing sympathies were governed by discretion. Ten ministers participated in his memorial service at Georgiaville, and five others were present.

Martin Cheney
Birth:
Aug. 29, 1792
Death:
Jan. 4, 1852
Burial:
Pocasset Cemetery, Cranston,
Providence County, Rhode Island

He was born in Dover, Massachusetts. Ordained to Preach April 28, 1825. Was installed Pastor over the First Free Will Baptist Church in Olneyville (Providence, Rhode Island) on Nov. 7, 1828 and continued until his death Jan. 4, 1852. His last words were "I have a hope that endureth to the end.

William Crookes
Birth:
1824
England
Death:
Jan. 18, 1893
Rhode Island
Burial:
North Burial Ground
Providence
Providence County, Rhode Island

He was converted at age of 14 and was licensed to preach on January 29, 1863 and ordained on September 19, 1840 by Rev. J. A. Mckenzie, and George Wheeler and others. His pastorates were basically in the Rhode Island area where he witnessed extensive revivals under his labors from which he baptized about 100 converts. At Maple Root church he had 175 come forward during six weeks; and at West Greenwich he had about 40 and at Ash Mills 60. He had a circuit of four churches, one for each Sunday during the month during his profitable ministry.

David Culver
Birth:
Apr. 30, 1795
Death:
Jun. 10, 1866
Pontiac, R. I.
Burial:
Greenwood Cemetery
Coventry, Kent County, Rhode Island

Fifty years of his life were spent in the ministry, mostly among the Methodists. After his union with the Free Baptists, he evinced strong sympathy with reforms, discretionin counsel, energy in work and faithfulness in pastoral duties.

George T. Day
Birth:
Dec. 8, 1822
Day Center,
Saratoga County, New York
Death:
May 21, 1875 Providence,
Providence County,
Rhode Island
Burial:
Pocasset Cemetery, Cranston,
Providence County,
Rhode Island

He was baptized by Martin Cheney in May 1840 uniting with the church at Olneyville. Attended Smithfield Seminary in 1845 he entered the biblical school at Whitestown, New York. In 1850 he moved to Chester, Ohio to become principal at Geauga Seminary. In 1852 he became the successor of Martin Cheney as the Pastor of Olneyville Free Baptist Church 1852-1857. Pastor, Roger Williams Free Baptist Church 1857-1867. Editor, *The Morning Star* 1867-1875. Possessing great natural ability, broad culture, deep piety, commanding eloquence and thorough devotion to principle. He was a prominent denominational leader, a successful Christian worker and a valued personal friend. In 1876 the Biography of Dr. Day, was written by Rev. Wm. H. Bowen,

D.D., printed by the Free Will Baptist Printing Establishment, Dover, New Hampshire. He was a convert of Rev. Martin Cheney, at Olneyville, and a life-long friend.

Wilbur Eugene Dennett
Birth:
Jun. 22, 1852
Buxton
York County, Maine
Death:
1938
Biddeford
York County, Maine
Burial:
Locust Grove Cemetery
Providence
Providence County,
Rhode Island

He was converted in boyhood and graduated from the scientific Department of the University of Wisconsin in 1879 and from the theological Department of Hillsdale College in 1883. License to preach was granted him in 1880 and on April 8, 1883 he was ordained to the ministry. His ministry has been with the churches at Cambridge Rome, Michigan and later in the state of New York where his labors were blessed immensely.

Edmund G. Eastman
Birth:
Feb. 16, 1846
Madison, New Hampshire
Death:
Jan. 21, 1908
Burial:
Pocasset Cemetery
Cranston
Providence County, Rhode Island

He was converted in 1858, and licensed by the Exeter, Maine Quarterly Meeting in March, 1875, and ordained in March 1776. He pastored numerous churches in Maine and New Hampshire before becoming the pastor of the Warwick Central church in Rhode Island in 1884, where 49 united with the church. He served in the Civil War over two years and was overseer of the poor and first selectmen in Parkman, Maine.

Herbert Ruthwen Farnum
Birth:
Aug. 19, 1853
Death:
Dec. 13, 1901

Burial:
Swan Point Cemetery,
Providence,
Providence County, Rhode Island

He was superintendent of the Bernon Mills for many years, and has given his influence heartily for the church in all its lines of usefulness, and for the general good of the community. To his effort and care the continued exclusion of the liquor traffic from the village is largely due.

Caleb Greene
Birth:
August 31, 1803
West Greenwich, Rhode Island
Death:
Dec. 27, 1894
Rhode Island
Burial:
Greene-Waite Lot
West Greenwich
Kent County, Rhode Island
He was converted in March, 1823, license in 1838, and ordained June 18, 1840 as the pastor of the Warwick and East Greenrich church. In 1843 he organized a church at West Greenwich and was its pastor for seven years.

George Ellison Hopkins
Birth:
Dec. 18, 1811
Foster, Rhode Island
Death:
May 21, 1890
Burial:
Acotes Hill Cemetery
Glocester

Providence County, Rhode Island

He studied at Scituate Academy and Westfield (Conn) Academy. He was ordained in about 1837, and was pastor of Foster Free Will Baptist Church ten years, where membership tripled. He served as pastor at Chepachet, Westford, and East Putman churches. He was two years representative in the Legislature and had been superintendent of schools in Foster, Glouscester and Scituate. He also taught for many years. His seven children were all teachers, two sons having graduated from Brown University.

Ezekiel R. Littlefield
Birth:
1815
Rock Island, Rhode Island
Death:
1891
Burial:
John R. Dodge Cemetery
New Shoreham
Washington County, Rhode Island

The Rev. Ezekiel Littlefield's gravestone is surprisingly small for a member of such a highly esteemed profession. Located in the NE quarter of the cemetery, its inscription simply reads "aged 76 years" His mother was the daughter of Rev. Enoch Rose, who was a devoted and acceptable Free Baptist minister who had been ordained in 1817. Ezekiel was converted in 1830 and was licensed in 1843 and later ordained in 1845 by Rev. J. A. Mackenzie, Silas Hall, a Calvinistic Baptists; and John Tillinghast, a six principle Baptist. Soon after his ordination, he lost nearly all of his left hand by the explosion of a blasting powder. Because of this he was only able to baptize two people, yet he held extensive revivals. He ministered the Second New Shoreham church and supplied some 20 years. In 1835 he married Lucretia, the, daughter of Capt. Robert C. Hodge.

Salome *Lincoln* Mowry
Birth:
Sep. 13, 1807
Raynham, Bristol County,
Massachusetts
Death:,
Jul. 21, 1841
Warwick,
Kent County, Rhode Island
Burial:
Pleasant View Cemetery,
Tiverton, Newport County,
Rhode Island

An early female preacher. About 1823, she was baptized with nine others, by Rev. Ruben Allen, a Free Will Baptist minister, who was pastor of the church at Taunton, where she united at that time. Her mind was upon religious thoughts and she read her Bible faithfully. She somehow, felt a deeper duty to do more for God but wrestled with the question because she was a woman. This was very rare in that time for a woman to speak publicly. She however, thought if she didn't, she would not be obedient to God. She preached her first sermon, Oct. 17, 1827. However, she was never ordained by any church. But she became a voice for good. She behaved in a most appropriate manner and deportment throughout her life. She dressed suitably and had few gestures when speaking, but her deep toned and heavy voice commanded attention, and large audiences could hear her. Her sermons were of substance and many times there was no standing room when she preached. She was welcomed in most places by other clergy to a pulpit; the Reformed Methodist pastor, in the town where she lived, wrote a letter of commendation for her testifying to her character. On Dec. 2, 1835, she was married to Rev. Junia S. MOWRY, a Free Will Baptist minister. Her burial took place at mid-night, due to having to go by boat across the bay and the tide was not favorable. The delay because of winds caused them to not arrive until midnight at the place of burial. (From *"The Female Preacher, or Memoir of Salome Lincoln..."* by Almond H. Davis, 1843 Providence, R.I.)

William N. Patt
Birth:
November 17, 1808
Scituate, Rhode Island
Death:
Apr. 29, 1891
Burial:
Smithville Cemetery
North Scituate
Providence County, Rhode Island

His father was a sea captain for over 20 years. William was the next to the youngest of nine children and received early Christian training from an earnest Christian mother. He went away to school in at the age of 16 and was qualified to teach. He also served an apprenticeship as a carpenter and a builder in Providence. He became a Christian on January 16, 1827 and thereafter his motto was, "Holiness Of Heart And Life." After years of thought and struggle, he began his ministry in 1842 was licensed to by the Rhode Island Quarterly Meeting. He preached in a number of churches in Rhode Island and in Maine. And after serving one of their churches in Rhode Island, he was ordained in 1847 by Reverend's M. W. Burlinggame, M. J. Steere and D. Williams and continued his pastorate for two years longer. He also preached in Connecticut. He labored with his hands for his daily support and has given of his earnings $1500 to the aid of the cause of Christ, besides traveling 100,000 miles mostly on foot to attend religious meetings, and preaching some 1200 times, attending 3000 conferences and prayer meetings. He was very earnest in temperance and anti-slavery support.

**Oh self-denying love, which felt alone
For needs of others, never for its own!"**

Benjamin D Peck
Birth:
Apr. 11, 1813
Bristol
Bristol County, Rhode Island
Death:
Jun. 11, 1896
Burial:
Oak Hill Cemetery
Woonsocket
Providence County, Rhode
Island
Plot: D 0035

Rev. B.D. Peck, was brought up by pious parents, especially his mother, who influenced his upbringing. He was baptized in a revival as a young man, and united with the Freewill Baptist church where he lived. He felt that he needed to do more and began to study for his life-work, at Belton Academy, for two years. He preached his first sermon Nov. 1838, and the next spring, began as successor of Rev. Martin J. Steere. In 1840, he received a call to the church in Grafton, MA, where he was ordained on June 4th of that year. Here he remained for six years as pastor, as the church grew. His next pastorate was Waterford, successor to Rev. Burlingame. He was nominated by the Free Soil Party as candidate for the Massachusetts Legislature and, receiving a large vote, was elected while still pastor of the church. At the close of the Legislative session in 1848, he removed to Portland. Rev. Peck was prominent in the Temperance Movement in that state. He was an active member in the Temperance Watchman organization from Maine, and became editor of *"The Watchman"*, a FWB temperance paper, pub. at Portland. He did this while carrying on his pastoral labors. He served his denomination as member of several benevolent boards and societies, and was esteemed as a worthy man.

---info on his ministry taken from *"The Rhode Island Pulpit,"* pub. 1852, by Rev. A. D. Williams.

Benjamin Phelon
Birth:
Jun. 1, 1806,
Halifax, England.
Death:
Jul. 18, 1882
Providence
Providence County, Rhode Island
Burial:
Major General George Sears
Greene Lot
Warwick, Kent County, Rhode
Island
Plot: 00050

His parents were Christians, and he had faithful Sabbath-school instruction.He was converted at sixteen and united with the General Baptist church at Haley Hill in his native town. He preached his first sermon in a private house in Halifax, Jan. 30, 1825. He preached two years with good acceptance and then entered the General Baptist Academy at Heptonstall Slock, under the charge of Rev. Richard Ingham. He supplied churches during the three years of this course and for three years afterwards. In the summer of 1834 he spent several months at Derbyshire studying under the direction of Rev. J. G. Pike and supplying pulpits of neighboring churches. In December of that year he came to America. A note from Mr. Sutton, who was then in this country, induced him to visit New England. By his advice, also, he went to Apponaug, R. I., where soon after a church was organized, with which he remained two years and a half.He preached in Boston, Mass, one year, Centredale, R. I., one year, again ·in Boston two years, in Nashua, N. H., one year, and then spent six years in Fall River, Mass., building up a new interest. By vigorous and ceaseless toil he succeeded. A church was formed, and eventually a meeting-house erected. In 1849 he returned to Apponaug and remained there more than twenty years,until failing health compelled him to resign. He spent the remainder of his days in Providence. A part of the time he was able to serve churches. Especially valuable was his work at Tiverton during the long sickness of their pastor, Rev. J. A. McKenzie. His classical tastes he retained and in a measure gratified. He was an early and persistent abolitionist and teetotaler. He was a good man, an able and faithful minister, and universally respected.

James A. McKenzie
Birth:
Dec. 3, 1812
Newport, R. I.
Death:
Apr. 10, 1873
Tiverton, R. I.
Burial:
Pleasant View Cemetery
Tiverton, Newport County,
Rhode Island

He was decidedly unique in his religious experience and in other characteristics. His father was a Scotchman, and a ship captain. His mother was a native of Newport. At the age of twelve. he was returning from berrying, and coming through a swamp to a dry knoll, he knelt and prayed, "And," he said, "I beheld the glory of God; I felt changed; I was at one "with God." Knowing of no company of disciples nor of any social meetings, he began to gather the boys from their plays, "and then tell them what I knew of the Word and work of grace on the soul, and whereunto I saw it would lead. After awhile they became so taken with it that we found a place for our meetings. The first we had was a 10ft in the barn, and after that the best rooms in marry and good houses. But somehow or other, the best meetings we had were those in the barn chamber. These boys eventually formed themselves into a sort of society, consisting of upwards of forty, and saved somewhat from their spending money every week for the benefit of the poor. The most of these boys became good and honorable men in the churches of Christ. Several became ministers of the gospel" He finally united with the First Baptist church in Newport and was encouraged to take part in the meetings,which he did very acceptably. After a lengthy examination of the Scriptures, he was not satisfied with the sprinkling he had received in infancy, and was immersed, March, 1828, at the age of fifteen,and united with the church. He was encouraged to preach by the church and became assistant to the aged pastor, the Rev. Mr. Eddy. A portion of the church began a new interest, which was afterwards known as the Fourth Baptist church. Mr. McKenzie was ordained August 12, 1830, in his eighteenth year, and became pastor of this church. Two years after, he joined the Rhode Island Q. M. of Free Baptists,and in 1838 the church also united with that Q. M. After this he was settled for a time in Portsmouth, N. H. He was seven years pastor of the Roger Williams church, Providence, R. I., during which time the church prospered greatly and many were added to its membership. He left there in 1847 to go to Tiverton, where he would receive half the salary, because he thought he could do more good there. In this and many other cases he was actuated to a considerable extent by what he termed" divine suggestions. He remained at Tiverton till 1853, when he became pastor at Greenville (First Smithfield). After three years here and three years in Providence with the Third church, he returned to Tiverton. He was original in his preaching and possessed some oddities both as a preacher and as a man. Once when he had preached in a Close Baptist church, a communion service was held from which he, of course, was left out. He rose in the pulpit, and looking down upon them, said with the simplicity of a child: "I'll tell my Father of you." He was remarkably gifted in prayer. He was a guileless man and greatly beloved.

Mowry Phillips
Birth:
Aug. 20, 1820
Lancaster, N. Y.
Death:
Jul. 4, 1881
Gloucester, R. I.
Burial:
Oak Hill Cemetery
Woonsocket, Providence County,
Rhode Island

His grandmother and mother lived at Pascoag, where they were baptized by John Colby. When fifteen years of age, his mother died at Marcellus, N. Y., where the family then resided. She was the only Christian in the family. Years after, he thus speaks concerning himself at that time: "At this time I was a wicked, prayer less boy, yet when the truth flashed upon me that my mother was no more, I rushed to a solitary place, threw myself upon my knees, and prayed as sincerely and earnestly as I ever did, that God would bless the stricken flock; and shelter those little ones left without a mother's care. However, this was the only vocal prayer which I offered for months, or even years. Soon after his father gave him his time. He worked in Manchester, N. Y. two years, in Marcellus one year, a few months in Michigan, and then attended school at

Alexander Academy, New York. While there he was cheered with the news that his father was converted. Returning home in the spring of 1841, he himself yielded to Christ, was baptized, and joined the M. E. church in Marcellus. He then studied at the Onondaga Academy. Moving to Rhode Island, he united with the Free Baptist church at Waterford. The following year he was licensed to preach. He was acting pastor of the Reformed Methodist church at Millville, Mass., two years. March 1, 1845, he was ordained at Pascoag by the Western Rhode Island Q. M. In April, 1846, he became pastor of the Georgiaville church. During this pastorate of eighteen years many were converted and the church edifice was built. He was next pastor of the Pascoag church ten years, during which time many were gathered into the church, and the church edifice was refitted and enlarged. On account of sickness, he moved to a farm in Gloucester. After years of rest he became pastor of the West Scituate church, six miles away, but did not change his residence. He preached his last sermon in the fall of 1880, when he was so feeble through consumption that he was obliged to sit during the discourse. He was a man of fervent piety and greatly beloved. A Freewill Baptist clergyman. He preached the funeral sermon of Rev. Reuben Allen, in 1872.

Stephen Phillips
Birth:
Oct. 6, 1833
Marcellus
Onondaga County, New York
Death:
May 13, 1904
Wisconsin
Burial:
Slatersville Cemetery
North Smithfield
Providence County, Rhode Island

Phillips, Rev. Stephen, brother of Rev. Mowry Phillips, was born in Marcellus, Onondaga County, N. Y., Oct. 6, 1833. He studied three years at Smithville Seminary under Hosea Quinby. Converted in 1847, he was licensed in 1859 by the Rhode Island Q. M., and was ordained in 1863, by the Western Rhode Island Ministers' Conference. He was pastor of the West Seituate church from 1862-70. In 1865-66 he baptized twenty as the result of revivals. From 1870-80 he was confined at home by sickness. In 1883 he entered pastorate at North Foster. He married, Oct. 24, 1855, Mary E. S. Brown, and May 27, 1858, Abby L. Paine. He had five children, four of whom were teachers.

Amarancey Paine Sarle
Birth:
1812
Death:
1882
Burial:
Pocasset Cemetery
Cranston
Providence County, Rhode Island

Dau. of Squire and Amy (Hills)

Paine. Married Orris Sarle, who only lived six yrs more. She was a lover of books, and charitable service. A member of the Freewill Baptist church, Olneyville, RI.

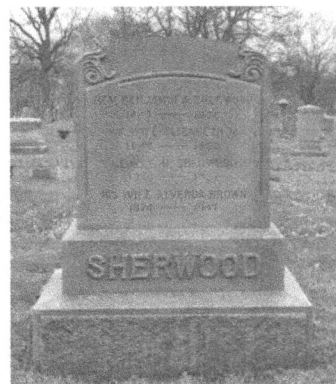

Benjamin A. Sherwood
Birth:
1843
Death:
1930
Burial:
Pocasset Cemetery
Cranston
Providence County,
Rhode Island

Graduated Bates Theological School, in 1875. An ordained Free Communion Baptist, and pastored Free Baptist churches in several states with good success.

Charles Shippee
Birth:
Mar. 6, 1809
East Greenwich, Rhode Island
Death:
Mar. 18, 1896
Burial:
Joseph Carpenter Lot
East Greenwich
Kent County, Rhode Island

He was converted in 1835 and ordained in 1852 by T. Tillinghast, J. Place, B. B. Cottrell, and P. Harrington. During his ministry he baptized over 150 converts in 1832 he was married to Jane Tarbox.

Daniel Angell Sweet
Birth:
1805
Death:
Jun. 28, 1861
Johnston, Rhode Island
Burial:
Reverend Daniel A Jenckes Lot
Johnston
Providence County, Rhode Island

He began to preach about 1842 and was ordained by the Six Principle Baptist about 1845 but holding views on open communion differing with them, he with his church in 1856 united with the Free Baptist Quarterly Meeting. In 1858 he added 23 to his church by baptism. His funeral was preached by Rev. Rueben Allen.

Nathaniel Sweet
Birth:
1806
Death:
Nov. 13, 1873
Johnston, Rhode Island
Burial:
Sweet Lot
Johnston
Providence County, Rhode Island

He was a brother to the Rev. Daniel Sweet and served in the ministry nearly 50 years.

When we die, we will not die alone because we will be with Jesus forever.

Martin J Steere
Birth:
Oct. 15, 1814
Providence
Providence County,
Rhode Island
Death:
Jan. 18, 1877
Athol
Worcester County, Massachusetts
Burial:
North Burial Ground
Providence
Providence County,
Rhode Island

Rev. Martin Jenckes Steere, son of Stephen, a grandson of Elisha, was born in Smithfield. In 1834 he joined the Second Smithfield Free Baptist Church, at Georgiaville. He wished to prepare himself for the ministry, and with this end in view fitted for college at Fruit Hill Seminary, near Manton, R.I., but ill health oblidged him to relinquish for a time his further course of study. However, in May 1837, he was ordained by the Rhode Island Conference, and the same year succeeded the Rev. M.W. Burlingame as pastor of the Georgiaville church, remaining until 1839. He then was appointed assistant editor of the "Morning Star," the organ of the denomination and editor of the Sunday-school paper. He then pastored the Apponaug church for three years, then went to North Scituate, where he labored for three years.He also spent one year at Waterford, Mass. He wrote and published at the request of the General Conf., a book entitled "The Friend of Chasity."After twenty years of active service in the ministry of the Free Baptist denomination, a change in his theological views led him, in April, 1859, into the Universalist Church. He pastored several church in Lawrence, W. Haverhill, MA, Lewiston, ME and Maridon, Conn, and Mechanics Falls, ME. His health suffered from the severities of his labors and the harshness of the climate and he was compelled to desist. He removed in June 1876, to Hardwich, MA, where he purchased a small estate, hoping still to preach and write for the press.He died from pneumonia at the house of his daughter, Mrs. Horace C. Smith, (Sarah Frances) Athol, MA while on a visit Jan. 18, 1877.

Elder Abel Thornton
Birth:
Aug. 16, 1799
Death:
Oct. 14, 1827
Burial:
Robert Thornton Cemetery,
Johnston,
Providence County, Rhode Island
In 1820 he was captivated by the earnest preaching of Ms. Clarissa H. Danforth and the Elder Joseph White of the Smithfield "Free Will" Baptist Church. Abel became increasingly active in this Christian society. He died of consumption October 14, 1827, while wandering around New England as an itinerant preacher, spreading the word of God to all who would listen. His "diary," *The Life of Elder Abel Thornton,* was printed in Providence by the Free Will Baptists in 1828.

Charles Wade

Birth:
Jun. 27, 1790
Glocester,
Providence County,
Rhode Island
Death:
Apr. 13, 1883
Norwich,
New London County, Connecticut
Burial:
Swan Point Cemetery,
Providence
Providence County,
Rhode Island

He was converted through the faithfulness of an old friend, and was baptized and joined the Foster Free Will Baptist church in Nov. 1828, four months after its organization, Rev. Daniel Williams being pastor. He was ordained as deacon of this church Nov. 7, 1825, with Rev's Reuben Allen and Joseph White's assistance, he preached his first sermon, Feb. 12, 1826. In 1837 he returned to his farm and lived there for thirty-seven years. In 1841, he was ordained a Free Will Baptist minister, and before 1843, working with the church sixty-one converts had been baptized to the church. The Morning Star church was organized in 1846, and he was called as its first pastor. He continued with this church until his seventieth year, when he baptized some thirty-four converts and retired from active ministry. He took the church paper, "Morning Star" from the first, and was attached to his denomination and was a close student of God's word. He died in his 93rd year, April 13, 1883. His son, Almon Wade, has for many years been a prominent member of the Roger Williams church, Providence, R.I.

David Richards Whittemore

Birth:
Jul. 31, 1819
Salisbury, Merrimack County,
New Hampshire
Death:
Mar. 23, 1888 Providence,
Providence County,
Rhode Island
Burial:
Pocasset Cemetery, Cranston,
Providence County,
Rhode Island

As a student in Dracut Academy, and the publishing agent of "Zion's Banner," a weekly religious newspaper, he was especially active in religious work. Early in 1842 he removed to Rhode Island, and in October of that year was ordained as Free Will Baptist pastor of the church in North Providence. Rev. Martin Cheney and Rev. James A. McKenzie were members of the council. In 1846, he became pastor of the South church in Newport. Since 1849 he has resided in the western part of Providence. He has been deeply interested in organizing and perfecting the work of the association, and has aided many of its churches in securing supplies and settling pastors. He long cherished the plan of securing the best possible historical and literary facilities for the denomination. Through his zeal the *"Free Baptist Cyclopeaedia"* was undertaken. For many years he was an active agent in the association for the *"Register"* and *"Morning Star."* He was an outspoken Abolitionist when it cost much to be outspoken; he was always an advocate of total abstinence and prohibition; for many years he has held office in the Rhode Island Peace Society. He has successfully prosecuted at the same time the insurance and other business. Incisiveness of intellect, correctness of judgment, and positiveness of opinion have been traits which have made him to many a wise counselor and bold leader.

Clarence O. Williams

Birth:
Nov. 10, 1859
Foster,
Providence County,
Rhode Island
Death:
Sep. 10, 1889
Burial:
Williams Lot, Foster,
Providence County,
Rhode Island

He prepared for college in the Grammar and High School, Providence, and graduated at Brown University in 1883. From 1883 to 1886. He was professor of Latin and metaphysics at New Hampton Institution in New Hampshire. In 1886-87 he attended Bates Theological School and taught mathematics in Nichols Latin School. At the same time he preached for the South Lewiston church. He was then elected to the chair of Latin in Hillsdale College, Michigan.

Henry Williams

Birth:
Feb. 10, 1823
Death:
Mar. 5, 1900
Burial:
Williams Lot, Scituate,
Providence County, Rhode Island

His father was a descendant of Roger Williams, and his mother a descendant of King Phillip. His parents and grandparents all died in triumphs of faith in Christ. He was converted March 1849, and joined a Christian Union church at Rice City, Coventry, Rhode Island. After preaching from place to place, he took a letter and joined the Six Principle Baptist church of Crompton. After six months trial he was ordained March 17, 1874. He afterwards joined the Free Baptist church in West Greenwich. Many have been converted under his labors.

Irving Winsor
Birth:
Nov. 20, 1859
Smithfield
Providence County, Rhode Island
Death:
Jul. 29, 1933
Rhode Island
Burial:
Colonel Abraham Winsor Lot
Smithfield
Providence County, Rhode Island

He studied at New Hampton College, NH, and graduated from Cobb Divinity School in 1889. He entered the ministry of the Freewill Baptist and was licensed in 1888. He preached at West Bethel and Winningham.

Joseph Winsor
Birth:
Oct. 4, 1714
Death:
Sep. 4, 1802
Burial:
Winsor Lot
Glocester, Providence County, Rhode Island
His parents were Samuel Winsor (1677 - 1758) and Marcy Harding Winsor (1683 - 1771) and his wife was Deborah Mathewson Winsor (1716 - 1785).

Samuel Winsor, II
Birth:
Nov. 18, 1677
Death:
Nov. 17, 1758
Burial:
North Burial Ground
Providence, Providence County, Rhode Island

Pastored the Roger Williams Bapt. Church in Providence. His parents were Samuel Winsor (1644 - 1705) and Mercy Williams (1640 - 1705) he was married to Mercy Harding on 7 Jan 1703

South Carolina

Wilburn Beasley
Birth:
unknown
Marion County, Alabama
Death:
Mar. 19, 2002
Turbeville, Clarendon County, South Carolina
Burial:
Horse Branch
Free Will Baptist Cemetery, Turbeville, Clarendon County, South Carolina

He was a Free Will Baptist Minister having graduated from the Free Will Baptist Bible College in Nashville, Tennessee in 1954. Afterwards, he pastored the Beech Springs Free Will Baptist Church in Mississippi, the Glennville Free Will Baptist Church in Georgia, the Horse Branch Free Will Baptist Church, Turbeville, and High Hill Free Will Baptist Church in Lake City, both in South Carolina. He was very active in the denomination on all levels and was a member of the Board of Retirement and Insurance for 12 years in Nashville, Tennessee.

Jimmie William Brown
Birth:
May 29, 1924
Chesterfield County
South Carolina
Death:
Mar. 1, 2002
Nashville, Tennessee
Burial:
Elmore Cemetery, Coward,
Florence County, South Carolina

He was a veteran of World War II and the Korean War serving both in the United States Navy and the United States Marine Corps. He was also active in the United States Army reserves and National Guard spending a combined total of more than 20 years. He attended the Free Will Baptist Bible college from 1956 to 1960 and worked in campus maintenance during this time. Afterwards, he pastored churches in Brilliant Alabama; Townley, Alabama; and Hartselle, Alabama for about 10 years. Then, he served as house parents at Free Will Baptist Home for Children in Greenville, Tennessee and Virginia Baptist Children's Home in Salem, Virginia for a total of eight years. Upon his retirement in 1985 he returned to the Free Will Baptist Bible College to do part-time maintenance for several additional years.

Joseph Lee Cagle
Birth:
Jul. 12, 1938
Johnsonville,
Florence County, South Carolina
Death:
Feb. 13, 2011
Florence,
Florence County, South Carolina
Burial:
New Prospect Free Will Baptist
Church,

Pamplico,
Florence County, South Carolina

Rev. Cagle was currently serving as Pastor at Little Bethel FWB Church. His other pastorates included New Prospect FWB Church, Mill Branch FWB Church, St. John FWB Church, and Hillside FWB Church. Under God's guidance and direction, he helped start the New Prospect Christian School. Rev. Cagle was a National Association of FWB General Board member.

Percy Rufus Coffey
Birth:
Nov. 15, 1926
Death:
Feb. 12, 2001
Massachusetts
Burial:
Bowman Memorial Cemetery,
Bowman,
Orangeburg County,
South Carolina

A pastor and denominational leader. His early pastorates were among the Southern Methodists before uniting with the Free Will Baptists in 1954 for whom he also pastored in South Carolina, Tennessee and Virginia. In 1962

he served five years as the Director of Missions Education for the Foreign Missions Department and thereafter was elected the Executive Secretary of the National Association of Free Will Baptists where he served until 1979 when he returned to the pastorate. He was a graduate of Bob Jones University and later studied at Vanderbilt University. His ministry spanned 54 years.

Robert Edwards
Birth:
1937
Death:
2000
Burial:
Clarendon Memorial Gardens
Manning
Clarendon County, South Carolina

He was a well-known state and national minister and leader.

Webster Pressley Gause
Birth:
Jun. 5, 1863
Death:
Nov. 24, 1918
Burial:
High Hill Cemetery
Scranton
Florence County, South Carolina

He was the son of William Nelson Gause (1834 - 1899) and Jane D. Gause (1831 - 1885) He was married Ellen Cornelia Evans Gause (1867 - 1942).

Norwood A. Gibson, Sr
Birth:
Mar. 5, 1928
Florence,
Florence County, South Carolina
Death:
Apr. 22, 1999
Florence County,SouthCarolina
Burial:
Florence Memorial Gardens,
Florence,
Florence County, South Carolina

He was a Free Will Baptist pastor and Promotional Sec. for the South Carolina Association of Free Will Baptists. He led this Association to be one of the best giving Associations to missions and the national departments. He also served on the Foreign Mission Board of the national Association. He was also proud that he had served in the U.S. Army for his country.

Moab Hewitt
Birth:
1795
Death:
1863
Florence County, South Carolina
Burial:
Lynch's Memorial
Gardens Cemetery,
Florence County, South Carolina

A early South Carolina Free Will Baptist Minister.

Elijah Myers Hicks
Birth:
Jan. 15, 1853
Death:
Sep. 29, 1921
Burial:
Bethel Baptist Cemetery
Olanta
Florence County,South Carolina
Plot: c117

He was the son of Elijah Hicks (1812 - 1881) and Francis R. Myers Hicks (1814 - 1878). He married Elizabeth Welsh Hicks (1854 - 1932).

**Today is not a day of distress
But a day of delight.**

Herman A. Hyman
Birth:
Aug. 5, 1938
Pamplico, Florence County
South Carolina
Death:
Jan. 3, 2007
Florence, Florence County,
South Carolina
Burial:
Mount Elon Freewill Baptist
Church Cemetery, Pamplico,
Florence County, South Carolina

Free Will Baptist pastor and patriot. He was educated in the Florence school system, Florence Darlington Technical College and after his call to the ministry, he was a student at Bethel Bible Institute. He founded the Immanuel Free Will Baptist church in Santee in 1986 and served as Orangeburg County Sheriff's Department as a chaplain from 1995-2006. He was pastor of the Immanuel Free Will Baptist Church for 19 1/2 years before going to Auburndale, Florida to pastor. Due to bad health he returned back to his home in Santee. He served in the United States Navy from 1958 through 1960.

Arthur F Lawter
Birth:
Jun. 24, 1904
Death:
Jan. 31, 1965
Lockhart,
Union County, South Carolina
Burial:
Whitney Cemetery, Spartanburg,
Spartanburg County,
South Carolina

Reverend Lawter was the pastor of Lockhart Free Will Baptist Church

---

Miller H Mellette
Birth:
Jul. 6, 1888
Death:
May 19, 1960
Burial:
Horse Branch Free Will Baptist
Cemetery,
Turbeville, Clarendon County,
South Carolina

Redding Floyd Moore
Birth:
Feb. 18, 1903
Death:
Aug. 7, 1981
Burial:
Carolina Memorial Park,
North Charleston,
Charleston County,
South Carolina

Samuel M. Moore, Jr
Birth:
Mar. 25, 1912
Death:
Mar. 16, 1997
Burial:
Evergreen Cemetery,
Chester,
Chester County, South Carolina

A Day Of Crowning.

Mancy C Noles
Birth:
Sep. 9, 1933
Death:
Sep. 6, 2002
Burial:
Evergreen Memorial Park
Sumter
Sumter County, South Carolina

Walker's Chapel FWB Church, Sumter was organized on April 21, 1974 by Rev. Mancy Noles with 12 charter members. Services were held for 2 years in a single wide mobile home put in front of a 4 room house (Whose rooms were used for Sunday School). In 1976 the building the Church now occupies was constructed on 2 lots of land donated by Rev. Noles. Later an addition was built onto the back of the church for Sunday School Rooms and rest rooms. Then, as the Church grew, a fellowship building was built behind the Church and eventually a drive thru covered walk way was added. The Fellowship Building also contained more rest rooms and the baptismal pool. And all the buildings and land are completely paid for. Brother Mancy was the Pastor of this church until his death on September 6th. He suffered a stroke in 1999 which affected his

speech. More strokes eventually confined him to a wheel chair but he continued to faithfully do all he could in the Church.

James Benjamin Rice, Jr
Birth:
Feb. 27, 1928
Death:
Sep. 10, 1993
South Carolina
Burial:
Hillcrest Memorial Gardens,
Greer, Spartanburg County,
South Carolina

He was a Free Will Baptist pastor and denominational leader, serving in South Carolina and Georgia. He established the First Free Will Baptist Church in Greer, S.C., as a joint project with the Beavercreek Home Mission Board and the National Home Mission Board of the National Association of Free Will Baptists. Afterwards, he became the Superintendent of the Free Will Baptist Children's Home, where he served for 11 years prior to his death. He was a graduate of University of Georgia and a United States Navy veteran serving during World War II. Inscription: HA1 US Navy World War II

Evander S Robinson
Birth:
Oct. 26, 1860
Death:
Jan. 27, 1944
Burial:
Horse Branch Free Will Baptist
Cemetery,
Turbeville, Clarendon County,
South Carolina

His funeral was conducted by two other early preachers: George C. Vause and M. H. Mellette.

Stephen Elias Smith
Birth:
Sep. 27, 1849
Death:
Sep. 1, 1921
Burial:
Oak Ridge Memorial Cemetery
Williamsburg County,South
Carolina

Early Minister.

Sam Richard Truett
Birth:
Sep. 24, 1945
Death:
Aug. 7, 2001
South Carolina
Burial:
Grove Hill Cemetery,
Darlington,
Darlington County,
South Carolina

He was a Free Will Baptist pastor for 33 years pastoring four churches in South Carolina and one in North Carolina. He was ordained to preach at age 23 in September of 1968. He was an active denominational leader both in North and South Carolina and on a national level. He spoke twice at the national convention of Free Will Baptists. First in Louisville, Kentucky in 1981 and 1989 in Tampa, Florida. He was a skilled journalist and wrote Sunday school literature for Randall House Publications. He also served 15 years on the Board of Trustees at Free Will Baptist Bible College. He earned both a Bachelors and Masters Degree from Bob Jones University in Greenville, South Carolina. He had one son, Rev. Chris Truett who is a very versatile and talented Minister.

Jason B Turner
Birth:
Jul. 23, 1971
Death:
Apr. 5, 1998
Burial:
Oak Grove Methodist Cemetery,
Manning,Clarendon County,
South Carolina

Cornelius Acue Vause
Birth:
Sep. 1, 1893
Death:
May 16, 1967
Burial:
Bethany Cemetery,
Florence County,
South Carolina

He was a very early South Carolina leader and preacher. He was a Veteran, WW I.

Julius B Vause
Birth:
May 10, 1904
Death:
Feb. 3, 2001
Burial:
Bethany Cemetery,
Florence County, South Carolina

Early South Carolina leader and organizer. He was honored by the South Carolina Conference Home Mission Board for 20 years of service. He was a pastor for more than 30 years, which included five years as Superintendent at the Free Will Baptist Children's Home.

Wright Wilson
Birth:
Mar. 17, 1811
Death:
Jan. 28, 1887
Clio, Marlboro County, South
Carolina
Burial:
McLucas Cemetery,
Clio,
Marlboro County,
South Carolina

He served Free Will Baptist long before the present national convention.

South Dakota

Laban Clark Cobb
Birth:
Feb. 6, 1810
Buckland, Massachusetts
Death:
Jan. 30, 1885
Colman, South Dakota
Burial:
Union Cemetery
Flandreau
Moody County
South Dakota
Plot: 14-2-1

Rev. Cobb was born in Massachusetts, but early removed to Monroe County, New York where he was converted under the labors of Rev. Eli Hannibal. He was married on December 30, 1834 to the daughter of Rev. William Greenleaf, who was born in Columbus, New York on September 2, 1817. After their marriage they were active members of the church, together moved to Wisconsin in 1849 where they entered into a wider field of usefulness. They preached in new and destitute localities, and the spirit of God worked through them with great power. Both he and his wife, Minerva, were both licensed to preach at the Marquette Quarterly Meeting in Wisconsin about 1858 and In 1864 they went to Winona County, Minnesota where they labored in the Root River Quarterly Meeting and was ordained in 1868 in connection with the Root River Quarterly Meeting in Minnesota. They continued many years to work with marked success. Later their health impaired and they moved in 1879 to Colman South Dakota. He was known to be a man of great power in prayer.

Minerva U. Cobb
Birth:
Sep. 2, 1818
Columbus, New York
Death:
Mar. 5, 1890
Colman, South Dakota
Burial:
Union Cemetery
Flandreau
Moody County, South Dakota
Plot: 14-2-2

She was the daughter of Rev. William Greenleaf, who was born in Columbus, New York on September 2, 1818. After her marriage to Laban Clark Cobb, they were active members of the church. Together they moved to Wisconsin in 1849 where they entered into a wider field of usefulness. They preached in new and destitute localities, and the spirit of God worked through them with great power. Both she and her husband, were both licensed to preach at the Marquette Quarterly Meeting in Wisconsin about 1858 and In 1864 they went to Winona County, Minnesota where they labored in the Root River Quarterly Meeting and was ordained in 1868 in connection with the Root River Quarterly Meeting in Minnesota. They continued many years to work with marked success. Later their health impaired and they moved in 1879 to Colman South Dakota.

John Gilbert Hull
Birth:
Nov. 5, 1822
Vermont
Death:
Feb. 29, 1884
Souix Falls,
South Dakota
Burial:
Mount Pleasant Cemetery
Sioux Falls, Minnehaha County,
South Dakota

He was converted at nineteen years and began to preach immediately. After a few months, he went to Biblical School at

Whitestown, NY, where he remained a year. Then he pastored successively Phoenix, Amboy, Hastings, Parish and Union churches, NY. In 1855 he moved to Wisconsin and was active with churches in Rock and Dane Quarterly Meetings, living in Jefferson Co. Wisconsin. He was zealous for souls even to the end. His labors were made more efficient by the assistance rendered by his devoted wife, formerly Miss Lois A. Higbee, whom he married in 1846. Their son, John J., b. 1847, also became a Free Baptist minister, later located in Wisconsin, and was very effective. He also went to Dakota when his father died where he gathered a church in Souix Falls.

"I think that if you compare the fruitfulness of one with another, while something may be due to superior activity, and something to ordinary worldly causations, yet there be multitudes of men whose usefulness cannot be accounted for on any other principle than that they have received this gift of the Holy Ghost, and that this gift makes more of them than is made of men who are ten times their superiors in natural endowments."

-Henry Ward Beecher

Tennessee

James Richard Adams
Birth:
unknown
Death:
Mar. 2, 2012
Antioch,
Davidson County, Tennessee
Burial:
Evergreen Cemetery,
Erwin, Unicoi County, Tennessee

Dr. Adams was born in Erwin, TN, and lived there until he moved to Nashville to attend Free Will Baptist Bible College. After graduating in 1966, Richard and his beloved wife Carolyn, moved to Kannapolis, NC, where he became the pastor of Ben Avenue Free Will Baptist and stayed until 1970. At that time, the couple, along with their two children moved to Elizabethton, Tennessee when "Preacher Adams" served as the much-loved pastor of East Side Free Will Baptist Church for twenty years. In January of 1990, the Adams' family moved to Nashville, TN, where Richard became the Director of Development with Free Will Baptist Home Missions North America. Over the next eighteen years, Richard directed the Church Extension Loan Fund which enabled church planters to buy land and build facilities all across North America. Richard worked the Build My Church Campaign raising millions of dollars for Home Missions. He and Carolyn traveled around the world to Canada, Mexico, the Virgin Islands, Puerto Rico, and the United States, representing the cause of Christ and Home Missions. In honor of Richard's tireless work for missions, the Free Will Baptist Home Missions Board named the million-dollar endowment of funds he raised in his name-the Richard and Carolyn Adams Endowment. Dr. Adams made a tremendous impact of the cause of Christ and for Free Will Baptists around the world. He will be sorely missed not only by family, but also by literally hundreds of friends across our nation.

Randall Adkins
Birth:
Apr. 15, 1805
Tennessee
Death:
Aug. 16, 1888
Tennessee
Burial:
Adkins Cemetery, Oak Grove, Campbell County, Tennessee
Broken Headstone Looks like the death date on stone could read August 6, 1888 but others have August 16, 1888.

W. S. Adkins
Birth:
unknown
Death:
Mar. 25, 1904
Burial:
Adkins Cemetery, Oak Grove, Campbell County, Tennessee

Member of Church for 15 years) age 51 years.

J A Albright
Birth:
Jun. 21, 1840
Death:
Nov. 30, 1921
Burial:
Albright Cemetery
Dickson County, Tennessee

He was one of the early Free Will Baptist ministers and central Tennessee and was affiliated with the Ashland Quarterly Meeting.

Hildon Clarence Beasley
Birth:
May 15, 1916
Stewart County, Tennessee
Dec. 21, 2003 Erin,
Houston County, Tennessee
Burial:
McIntosh Cemetery,
Houston County, Tennessee

He was a Free Will Baptist Minister.

Charlie Bennett
Birth:
unknown
Death:
May 22, 2011
Johnson City
Washington County Tennessee
Burial:
Roselawn Memorial Park,
Johnson City,
Washington County, Tennessee

He was 93 at the time of his passing. He was a member and pastor of the True Gospel Free Will Baptist Church for nearly 50 years.

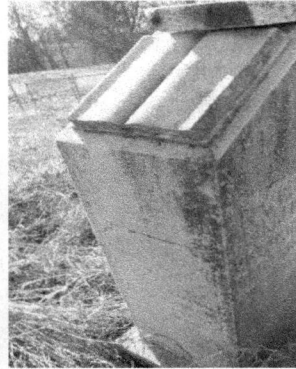

G. W. Binkley
Birth:
Oct. 17, 1850
Tennessee, USA
Death:
Mar. 21, 1903
Davidson County, Tennessee
Burial:
Turrentine-Binkley Cemetery
Ashland City
Cheatham County, Tennessee

George Washington Binkley was the son of Turner and Martha (Mayo) Binkley. On Nov. 17, 1870, Binkley married Florence Waggoner. In 1888 he was a member of the Ashland Quarterly Meeting in which he served as a Free Will Baptist minister.

The idea is to die young as late as possible.

James B Bloss
Birth:
1884
Death:
1959
Burial:
Polk MemorialGardens, Columbia,
Maury County, Tennessee

An ordained Free Will Baptist minister who pastored in Tennessee and Alabama. (WWI) Soldiers Grave Pearl Rivers. He was also a member of the Foreign Missions Board of the National Association.

Terry Lockert Boyd
Birth:
unknown
Death:
Jan. 26, 2005
Pleasant View, Cheatham County,
Tennessee
Burial:
Pleasant View
Methodist Church Cemetery,
Pleasant View, Cheatham County,
Tennessee

A Free Will Baptist minister and owner of the Boyd Funeral Home in Ashland, Tennessee. He was a member of the Good Springs Free Will Baptist Church in Pleasant View, Tennessee.

Fred L Bradshaw
Birth:
May 8, 1909
Death:
Mar. 5, 1963
Burial:
Highland Cemetery,
Sparta,
White County, Tennessee,

Fred Arvel Brewer
Birth:
Jul. 18, 1942
Johnson County,Tennessee
Death:
Apr. 20, 2002
Sullivan County, Tennessee
Burial:
Rainbow Cemetery
Mountain City
Johnson County, Tennessee

He was a Freewill Baptist Minister for 31 years. He had pastored several churches in Johnson City, Washington County and Sullivan County. He sang with his family in churches all over North Carolina, Virginia and Tennessee.He was preceded in death by two brothers, Ernest Brewer and Rev. Bill Brewer.

William Lafayette Bright
Birth:
Jul. 4, 1883
Death:
Apr. 9, 1951
Burial:
Corinth Cemetery, Loudon,
Loudon County, Tennessee

Corp A H Burgess
Birth:
Apr. 17, 1844
Death:
May 14, 1922
Burial:
Liberty Freewill Baptist Church
Cemetery,
Old Washington County,
Tennessee

He served in the 2nd NC Mounted Infantry Co E.

Behold He Lives!

Herman Christian
Birth:
Apr. 6, 1928
Death:
Jun. 9, 2008
Burial:
Centerhill Cemetery,
Warren County, Tennessee

Thomas Charles Cofer
Birth:
Aug. 19, 1836
Death:
Aug. 10, 1885
Tennessee
Burial:
Carney Cemetery # 1
Whites Creek,
Davidson County, Tennessee

Thomas C. Cofer organized the a Free Will Baptists church in 1880 at William T. Trotter's home. Trotter lived in a Civil War barracks on a dirt road, Buena Vista Pike. Pastor Cofer led in erecting a building at the corner of Buena Vista and Scott Street. He served as pastor of the church until his death in 1885.
The first Free Will Baptist church in Nashville, called the North Nashville Free Will Baptist

Church, changed its name to honor the founder. That first building burned about ten years later and the city bought the lot for Buena Vista School on the street called Ninth Avenue North.
The church rebuilt on Arthur Avenue near what is now Garfield. In 1930 the congregation bought the brick building at 1600 Tenth Avenue North. The church built a parsonage there in 1952 for $8,000.
It was at this church that in 1935 the National Association of Free Will Baptists was formed through the efforts and leadership of the pastor of more than 40 years, John L Welch. Free Will Baptist Bible College in 2012 changed the name to Welch College in honor of him and his wife who had been a librarian and at the college for many years. He was also very influential in the early days of the college and very instrumental in it being in Nashville, Tennessee.
Cofer was married on May 14, 1857 to Florissa Moses who was born in 1836. Thomas was a Free Will Baptist preacher. They had the following children: William T.1858; James M. 1862; Sarah F. 1865; Johanna 1866; Charles M. 1869; David 1871; and Flora 1879.

Inscription:
Rev. T. C. Cofer
born aug. 19, 1836
died aug. 10, 1885
Blessed are the pure in heart for they shall see God

Robert Barrett Crawford
Birth:
Jun. 21, 1913
Death:
Aug. 9, 2001
Burial:
Gibbs Cemetery, Ashland City,
Cheatham County, Tennessee

A minister, denominational leader and the first full-time Executive-Secretary of the National Association of Free Will Baptists. He was converted to Christ at age 12, ordained to preach age 21, and pastored churches in Alabama, Tennessee, North Carolina and Florida. He was the founding pastor of the Trinity Free Will Baptist Church in Greenville, North Carolina. He graduated from the University of Alabama and attended the Vanderbilt Divinity school. For 20 years he served in the Public Relations Department of Free Will Baptist Bible College in Nashville, Tennessee. He was active in ministry for 65 years and was one of the founders and shapers of the Free Will Baptist denomination.

Ronald Creech
Birth:
unknown
Death:
Aug. 16, 2005
Burial:
Woodlawn Memorial Park,
Nashville,
Davidson County, Tennessee

A Free Will Baptist pastor, state Executive Secretary for the state of North Carolina Free Will Baptists. He retired from Free Will Baptist Bible College in Nashville Tennessee where he served as the Director Of Development.

No one can confidently say that he will still be living here tomorrow.

Missionary Daniel Wickert Cronk
Birth:
February 28, 1923
Detroit Michigan
Death:
November 20, 1997
Nashville,
Davidson County, Tennessee
Burial:
Cremated

He graduated from Hazel Park High School, Detroit, Michigan; Free Will Baptist Bible College, Nashville, Tenn.; Columbia University, Columbia, South Carolina and Middle Tennessee State University, Tennessee. He was ordained to the gospel ministry in 1943 and served his denomination as a missionary to India for 25 years, a professor at Free Will Baptist Bible College for nine years and a member of the Board Of Foreign Missions for 15 years.

Missionary Trula *Gunter* Cronk
Birth:
Jun. 7, 1924
Greene County, Tennessee
Death:
Dec. 22, 2009,
Thailand
Burial:
Shelton Mission Cemetery,
Greystone,
Greene County, Tennessee

Mrs. Cronk grew up in the school

years at Zion Mission, a circuit of schools and churches, which was started by the United Presbyterian missionaries from Pennsylvania.

She lived her teen years at Free Will Baptist Children's Home, located near Camp Creek School. Rev. I.L. and Mary Frances Stanley were very instrumental in her life. Later, the Rev. Paul and Nelle Woolsey would come to oversee the home and take Trula in as their own. She was the valedictorian of her graduating class at Camp Creek High School. With the love and support of "mom and dad" Woolsey, she was able to attend college and fulfill her calling to be a missionary to India. At the Free Will Baptist Bible College, in Nashville, where she would meet her future husband, Daniel Cronk, who was from Michigan. Together they went on to graduate from Columbia College in South Carolina. Trula also attended Peabody College."They served the Lord as Free Will Baptist Pioneer Missionaries in India. The couple relocated to Nashville in 1972, where the Rev. Cronk was professor of the missions program at the Free Will Baptist Bible College and Mrs. Cronk taught school in 1994. The home in which she lived at the Free Will Baptist Children's Home was given the name 'The Trula Gunter Cronk Home for Children' in honor of her being the first resident there. *"Over Mountain or Plain or Sea"* was published in

2003 and is a two-part autobiography detailing parts of Mrs. Cronk's childhood and her many years as a missionary."In 2004, Mrs. Cronk moved back to Greeneville. Although she had lived in the Himalayas, traveled the Nile at midnight, seen the Taj Mahal, Buckingham Palace, the Louvre in Paris, Pharook's Palace in Alexandria, walked the Sahara Desert, climbed the Leaning Tower of Pisa and Cheops Pyramid, vacationed on beautiful Dal Lake in Sri Nafar, sipped tea with movie stars, world statesmen, and Scottish tea planters, shared seats with Mother Teresa, hunted crocodiles, tigers and rode camels, visited Japan, China, Germany, Russia and traveled the world over, no place was ever as dear to her as Greene County. In November of 2006, she left the mountains of East Tennessee to live with her son, Randall, a resident of Thailand.

Robert M Cutshall
Birth:
Aug. 23, 1912
Death:
Dec. 10, 1990
Burial:
Burnetts Chapel Cemetery,
Greene County, Tennessee

James Thomas Davis
Birth:
unknown
Death:
Aug. 11, 2001
Burial:
Williamson Memorial Gardens,
Franklin,
Williamson County
Tennessee

Dr. Davis was a minister, church planter, pastor, professor and research scientist. He was a founder of a number of churches in central Tennessee and at his retirement was pastor emeritus of the Franklin Community Church. He had been a professor at Free Will Baptist Bible College and was a Bio-Chemist with the Vanderbilt University Medical School

F. A. Dewitt
Birth:
Mar. 9, 1883
Death:
May 21, 1970
Burial:
McMinn Memory Gardens,
Athens,
McMinn County, Tennessee

Robert H Doan
Birth:
Mar. 25, 1907
Virginia
Death:
Nov. 9, 2001
Medina County, Ohio
Burial:
Morning View Cemetery
Bluff City
Sullivan County, Tennessee

Early Free Will Baptist pastor who served in West Virginia pastoring the Ansted Free Will Baptist Church in 1955-56. He also spent time in Ohio.

George D. Dunbar
Birth:
Aug. 13, 1889
Tennessee
Death:
Jun. 20, 1968 Washington County, Tennessee
Burial:
Liberty Freewill Baptist Church Cemetery,
Old Washington County
Tennessee

George Dobson Dunbar In June 1917, registered for WW I Draft. He was described as tall and of medium build, blue eyes and brown hair. He was a minister in the Free Will Baptist Church where he was ordained, and became a leader in the eastern Tennessee Free Will Baptist churches. He was Pastor, Evangelist and Exec. Sec'y of the Union FWB Ass'n, in Washington Co. in the 1940's. He was responsible for the preparation, arrangement and publication of *"God, A Hundred Years and A Free*

Will Baptist Family" by Rev. Paul Woolsey, a FWB Missionary to India, a book which preserved many historical facts and accounts that could have been lost had it not been published.

Zadock D. Duncan
Birth:
Feb. 1, 1830
Death:
Feb. 1, 1921
Burial:
Hoodoo Cemetery
Hoodoo
Coffee County, Tennessee

He was a Free Will Baptist minister affiliated with the New Union Association which belong to the state of Tennessee. He served in the Military - Lt, Co., I, 34th TN Infantry, C.S.A

Kenneth Paul Eagleton
Birth:
Jul. 1, 1928
Death:
Aug. 26, 1999
Burial:
Middle Tennessee State
Veterans Cemetery,
Nashville,

Davidson County,
Tennessee, Plot: PP 02 15

Minister, missionary to Brazil for International Missions of the Free Will Baptist denomination. He was a graduate of Free Will Baptist Bible College in Nashville, Tennessee. He was a veteran of the United States Air Force and achieved the rank of staff Sgt. and served in Korea.

Missionary Marvis Eagleton
Birth:
Apr. 27, 1926
Death:
Feb. 21, 2003
Burial:
Middle Tennessee State
Veterans Cemetery,
Nashville,Davidson County,
Tennessee, Plot: PP 02 15

She was a missionary to Brazil for the International Board of Foreign Missions for the Free Fill Baptist denomination. She was a graduate of Free Fill Baptist Bible College in Nashville, Tennessee.

Herman Hughes Ellis
Birth:
Jul. 2, 1934
Gause, Tennessee
Death:
Jul. 19, 2006
Cedar Hill, Tennessee
Burial:
Heads Free Will Baptist Church
Cemetery,
Cedar Hill,
Robertson County, Tennessee

He was saved in July of 1960, and later attended the Free Will Baptist Bible College and ordained as a Minister of the gospel at Head's Free Will Baptist Church in 1961. He was a pastor in Michigan, Alabama and Tennessee and used as an evangelist across the entire nation.

George W. Farless
Birth:
Apr. 15, 1885
Death:
Apr. 24, 1968
Burial:
Gnat Hill Cemetery
Manchester
Coffee County, Tennessee

He was a minister in the New Union Association of Free Will Baptists.

Harrison William Farrell
Birth:
Jan. 15, 1848
Coffee County, Tennessee
Death:
Aug. 6, 1924
Warren County, Tennessee
Burial:
Hillsboro Cumberland
Presbyterian Cemetery
Hillsboro
Coffee County, Tennessee

He was a minister that was affiliated with the new Union Association, which had been affiliated with the United Baptists, and the state of Tennessee

Winford R Floyd
Birth:
1932
Death:
1995
Burial:
Happy Valley Memorial Park,
Elizabethton,
Carter County, Tennessee,
Plot: Mausoleum of Peace

He was a well-known Minister in eastern Tennessee and active in denominational leadership.

Joe T Fort
Birth:
Dec. 27, 1866
Death:
May 22, 1924
Burial:
Fort Family Cemetery,
Clarksville,
Montgomery County, Tennessee

Estel M French
Birth:
Sep. 12, 1902
Death:
Apr. 21, 1978
Burial:
Mosheim Central Cemetery,
Mosheim, Greene County,
Tennessee

"As the image on the seal is stamped upon the wax, so the thoughts of the heart are printed upon the actions."

Malcolm Craig Fry
Birth:
Jun. 6, 1928
Detroit,
Wayne County, Michigan
Death:
Aug. 24, 2007
Locust Grove,
Mayes County, Oklahoma
Burial:
Hermitage Memorial Gardens,
Old Hickory,
Davidson County, Tennessee

He was a Free Will Baptist minister and a denominational leader. He was the National Church Training Service Director and Adult Curriculum Director at Randall House in Nashville Tennessee. He was an outstanding pianist and singer and made many recordings. He also served with the U.S. Army and was also a U.S. Air Force Veteran;

Willie M. "Bill" Gardner, Jr
Birth:
Unknown
Norfolk,
Norfolk City, Virginia
Death:
Jun. 15, 2001
Nashville,
Davidson County, Tennessee
Burial:
Woodlawn Memorial Park,
Nashville,
Davidson County, Tennessee

A well-known pastor, recording artist and denominational leader whose singing ability brought many pulpit opportunities. During his ministry, he pastored churches in four states; Tennessee, Indiana, Mississippi and Georgia. He attended Free Will Baptist Bible College, with later studies at North Carolina State University, and earned a Masters degree in music at Mississippi State University. He was known for his clear, high tenor voice singing frequently at many national conventions, state associations and Bible conferences. He was a member of the Music Commission and Media Commission. His last recording effort occurred during the production of *"He Keeps Me Singing"* video which featured 50 Free Will Baptist singers and musicians. He was a role model for many musicians and singers.

Benjamin F Garland
Birth:
1846
Death:
September 15, 1887
Burial:
Garland Cemetery
Carter County, Tennessee

He was a Free Will Baptist minister and died at age 35. The Headstones Provided for Union Soldiers.
Inscription:
Co L, 13th Tenn Cav.

H. Wilks Gower
Birth:
Aug. 3, 1842
Death:
Feb. 5, 1924
Burial:
Heads Free Will Baptist Church
Cemetery, Cedar Hill
Robertson County, Tennessee

James W Gower
Birth:
Aug. 30, 1821
Robertson County, Tennessee
Death:
Jul. 29, 1886
Robertson County, Tennessee
Burial:
Heads Free Will Baptist Church
Cemetery
,Cedar Hill,
Robertson County, Tennessee

Was a minister in the Free Will Baptist Church for 29 yr. (written on tombstone)

And every eye shall see him

Paul Frederick Hall
Birth:
Feb. 20, 1938
Durham, Durham County,
North Carolina
Death:
Nov. 5, 2008
Nashville,
Davidson County, Tennessee
Burial:
Spring Hill Cemetery, Nashville,
Davidson County, Tennessee

He graduated from Durham High School in 1956, That fall he entered FWBBC. After attending two years he married Ruthann Edwards from Illinois in August 1958. Fred was called as assistant pastor at Swannanoa FWB church. During that time their first child was born. The family returned to Nashville to continue his education. After another year of college, Fred was called to be minister of music and assistant pastor at Central FWB church in Royal Oak, Michigan.. After two years the desire to finish his education led Fred to resign and return to Nashville. Finally in 1964 he received his BA degree. Fred served churches in North Carolina, South Carolina, Tennessee, Illinois, Kentucky and Michigan during his years of ministry. Fred wrote Sunday School literature for Randall House Publications several years and served in several roles in the denomination. Many people knew him for his beautiful singing voice and while he loved to sing, his first love was preaching and teaching. In 1984 Fred earned a Master of Arts Degree in Pastoral Studies from FWBBC. In 2000 he earned a second Master's degree from this Pensacola Christian Seminary in Bible Exposition. He had started work on a doctor's degree from Pensacola Christian Seminary, but by this time his health was failing and was not able to attain that goal. He loved to study and maintained a 4.0

grade average in both of his masters programs. During his lifetime Fred had built up quite a library. When he passed away, his family gave it to Trinity FWB Church in Bowling Green, KY. The "Rev. Fred Hall Memorial Library" was established in his honor. They had celebrated their 50th wedding anniversary on August 17 of that year while he was in the hospital.

Charles Edgar Hampton
Birth:
Mar. 25, 1938
Blanchard,
McClain County, Oklahoma
Death:
Mar. 5, 2007
Nashville,
Davidson County, Tennessee
Burial:
Harpeth Hills Memory Gardens,
Nashville,
Davidson County, Tennessee

Dr Hampton is an alumnus of Free Will Baptist Bible College, Oklahoma Baptist University,

Oklahoma University, and the University of Texas. He also retired from the Free Will Baptist Bible College after 26 years. Funeral services was at the Free Will Baptist Bible College with Dr Paul Harrison officiating.

Ralph C. Hampton
Birth:
Dec. 13, 1934
Dibble, McClain County,
Oklahoma
Death:
Sep. 7, 2012
Nashville. Davidson County.
Tennessee
Burial:
Harpeth Hills Memory Gardens,
Nashville,
Davidson County, Tennessee

The Oklahoma native was converted at age 12 during a youth camp and ordained to preach in 1960. Hampton's ministry to the broader denomination included six pastorates in Tennessee and Missouri, articles for *Contact* and *ONE Magazine,* and curriculum writing for Randall House Publications. His signature leadership role came during a 15-year span when the National Association of Free Will Baptists elected him moderator nine times (1987-1996) and assistant moderator six times (1981-1987). He moderated during several controversial and pivotal sessions, including the emotionally charged 1995 national convention. Ralph began his 50-year tenure at Welch College in 1958 at age 23. Like most young educators, he wore several hats, which meant that he taught 15 hours per semester, served as Christian Service Director, and was the dormitory supervisor. The son of a Free Will Baptist preacher and oldest of four brothers, he spent half a century changing the landscape of denominational education, preparing students for ministry in a world-wide community, and raising a family of three children with his wife Margaret—all three children graduated from Welch College. He pushed himself hard as an educator, earning five degrees —A.A. degree from East Contra Costa Junior College (1955), B.A. degree from Welch College (1958), M.A. degree from Winona Lake School of Theology (1961), M.Div. from Covenant Theological Seminary (1970), and the D.Min. (ABD) from Trinity Evangelical Divinity School. He was the former chairman of the Biblical and Ministry Studies Department at Welch College and a member of the college faculty for 50 years, died after a two-year battle with cancer.

R S Harris
Birth:
1870
Death:
1940
Burial:
Troy Cemetery
Troy
Obion County, Tennessee

He was a member of the Clinch River Association which was situated west of the John Wheeler Association in Virginia and Tennessee. And was one of the early ministers the Association.

Steven Robert Hasty
Birth:
Jun. 15, 1949
Death:
Apr. 21, 1998
Tennessee
Burial:
Greenbrier Cemetery,
Greenbrier
Robertson County, Tennessee

A Free Will Baptist pastor for 25 years serving five churches in Michigan, Tennessee, Florida and Georgia. He was a prolific writer and noted historian serving 10 years on the National Historical Commission. He launched *"The Time Machine"* for the Georgia FWB Historical Society and *"Resources for Free Will Baptist History"* for the national commission. He researched and wrote a 35 chapter historical novel about the denomination which was in its final stages when he died.

William H. Head
Birth:
Mar. 31, 1839
Death:
Jul. 10, 1923
Burial:
Heads Free Will Baptist Church
Cemetery,
Cedar Hill,
Robertson County, Tennessee

Herman Lawrence Hersey
Birth:
Jan. 1, 1926
Chicago,
Cook County, Illinois
Death:
Jan. 26, 2008
Jackson,
Madison County, Tennessee
Burial:
Highland Memorial Gardens
Jackson
Jackson County, Tennessee

A Free Will Baptist minister, pastor and denominational executive. A minister of the gospel for 58 years serving churches in North Carolina and was the

Director of the Board Of Retirement And Insurance for the National Association Of Free Will Baptists. He was a graduate of Bob Jones University, Chicago Musical College and attended the St. Louis Institute of Music at George Washington University. He is remembered as an outstanding pianist.

William J. Hill
Birth:
Jan. 10, 1928
Death:
Aug. 17, 2001
Burial:
Green Acres Memorial Gardens,
Crossville,
Cumberland County, Tennessee

Hill was a Minister that span 50 years and was the college chaplain at Taylor University in Indiana. He spoke in many universities in the United States as well as abroad. He began his ministry in 1948 as Minister of the first Free Will Baptist Church in Myrtle, Missouri. Later he pastored churches in Tennessee and Michigan and later the Evangelical Mennonite church in Indiana and Ohio. He was a graduate of the Free Will Baptist Bible college in Nashville and did graduate work at the University of Detroit in Michigan and Anderson College in Indiana. And was author Of "Organizing The Free Will Baptist Sunday School" printed by Randall house publications.Two other brothers were also noted ministers, namely; Bob Hill and Dr. Don Hill.

Critt Holman
Birth:
Sep. 6, 1908
Death:
Sep. 27, 2002
Burial:
Stewart Cemetery,
Cookeville,
Putnam County, Tennessee

Nathan Honeycutt
Birth:
Jul. 20, 1824
Buncombe County,
North Carolina
Death:
1907
Burial:
Nathan Honeycutt Cemetery,
Tiger Valley,
Carter County, Tennessee
Nathan was an early Free Will Baptist minister and was noted in Paul H. Woolsey's *"My Woolsey Free Will Baptist Family"*, pub. 1949:"Reverends Nathan Honeycutt and "Bobby" Moore's labors were especially blessed in Carter County, Tennessee. Today (1949) there are more Free Will Baptist Churches in this than any other county in the state - some twenty, belonging to the Union and Toe River Associations. Brother Honeycutt was the first

minister to enter the young association after its birth in 1850. Of all the other early leaders, Brother Honeycutt proved to be the most earnest and efficient helper, outside the Union Association, in the planning and building of a denominational school. Soon after commencement of Free Will Baptist work in this vicinity Father Woolsey began correspondence with the General Conference of the North. It was Brother Honeycutt who stood with him for the unification of the work with the entire denomination. In those formative years many questions of policy, doctrine and rules had to be adopted."His ability and leadership was instrumental to the church's growth in that part of Tennessee.

Jesse E Hudgens
Birth:
Dec. 5, 1862
Cheatham County, Tennessee
Death:
Aug. 17, 1952
Ashland City
Cheatham County, Tennessee
Burial:
Hudgens Cemetery
Cheatham County, Tennessee

He gave fifty years of ministry and service to the Free Will Baptist denomination.

Richard M Johnson
Birth:
1851
Death:
1913
Burial:
Alder-Livesay Cemetery,
Kyles Ford,
Hancock County, Tennessee

Paul Jackson Ketteman
Birth:
Jul. 24, 1924
Illinois
Death:
May 21, 1987
Nashville,
Davidson County, Tennessee
Burial:
Harpeth Hills Memory Gardens,
Nashville,
Davidson County, Tennessee

Paul J. Ketteman, was on the college's first graduating class in 1942. In May 1945, Paul graduated from the new school's two year program after working hard to pay for his education. He immediately enrolled in Columbia Bible College, Columbia, S. C. To finish his degree in 1947. Paul pastored first at Mt. Elon FWB Church, then at Edgemont FWB Church in Durham, North Carolina, then back to Mt. Elon (this time full-time), and later at First FWB Church, Columbus, Mississippi. He served four years as clerk of the National Association of Free Will Baptists and nine years on the Bible college Board Of Trustees. He worked for the college 25 years in fundraising and public relations. His wife, Mrs. Helen Ketteman, taught business 20 years at the college.

Paul was a native of Illinois and was raised in a minister's home. His life was totally dedicated to his Lord and the college that he represented. He began the annual Christmas fund drive that was given his name after his death. He understood better than most how costly it is to provide Christian education. The idea of challenging churches and individuals to operate the college for a day originated with the Paul J. Ketteman, long time public relations director at FWBBC.

Dewey R Kirk
Birth:
Jan. 18, 1937
Death:
Jun. 25, 1982
Burial:
Island Ford Cemetery,
Lake City,
Anderson County,
Tennessee

Jesse Laws
Birth:
1889
Death:
1931
Burial:
Laws-Green Cemetery,
Cocke County, Tennessee

William Wallace Lee
Birth:
Nov. 26, 1857
Hawkins County, Tennessee
Death:
Aug. 28, 1944
Sullivan County, Tennessee
Burial:
Collins - Gravelly Rd
Sullivan County, Tennessee

His name is in early FWB records. Pastored at the Morning Star Freewill Baptist Church Hawkins County, TN

James Willard McCarroll
Birth:
Aug. 12, 1935
Death:
Jan. 5, 2009
Joelton,
Davidson County,
Tennessee
Burial:
Joelton Hills Memory Gardens,
Joelton,
Davidson County,
Tennessee

He was a Minister of the Gospel for over 45 years and pastored four churches; Harper Road Free Will Baptist Church, Mount Zion Free Will Baptist Church, First Free Will Baptist Church of McEwen and was currently serving the Olivet Free Will Baptist Church in Clarksville, all in Tennessee.

Death is beautiful when seen to be a law, and not an accident - It is as common as life.

Henry Melvin
Birth:
Jul. 8, 1905
Death:
Jun., 1971
Nashville, Davidson County,
Tennessee
Burial:
Spring Hill Cemetery,
Nashville,
Davidson County, Tennessee

Brother Melvin was saved in a Methodist revival in Kynesville, Florida at the age of 17 and later surrendered to God's call to the ministry. He was ordained on October 3, 1925 in that city. In his early ministry. He pastored in Florida and Georgia. Prior to the formation of the National Association in 1935 brother Melvin attended the General Conference for the first time in 1927. This conference dates back to 1920. Melvin preached the opening sermon the very next year in 1928. He was a frequent program personality thereafter, including messages in 1928 and 1932. He was a leader in Christian Education illustrated by his service on the annual education committee in 1929 and in 1931. In 1929 he was elected General Secretary Of Young People Word for the General Conference. Many acknowledge that the most significant contribution to his denomination was his ministry to the youth--first with the League Board and later the Church Training Service Board. Altogether, he served 39 years with The League and CTS board.

He was known for his energetic and visionary leadership which kept the youth board moving ahead for Christ. He showed his interest in missions early serving on the annual missions committee of the convention in 1927 and again in 1932. The 1932 minutes show that his sermon was on "The Church" and he strongly emphasized the church's mission in bringing the world to Christ. In 1935, he was very instrumental in producing an atmosphere of optimism in the merger of the Western and Eastern conferences. Following the report of the committee, brother Melvin suggested that all stand and sing, *Blessed Be The Tie That Binds,* as a token of the reality of the coming tie. In the mid-30's brother Melvin pastored the Edgemont Free Will Baptist Church in Durham, North Carolina. It was here that a close relationship between he and Thomas and Mabel Willey came into existence and he introduced them to the Free Will Baptist Missions program where they later served under their auspices. At the Seventh Annual Session of the national association in Nashville, Tennessee in 1943, the Board Of Foreign Missions commended him for his involvement in the missions program by sponsoring a trip for him to Cuba in February, 1943, during which time he assisted Rev. and Mrs. Willey in the organization of the Cuban national convention.. In 1946 he was elected to the Free Will Baptists Bible College Board of Trustees. He was the college business manager the following year. Because of his strong musical talents he was selected to the 1964 music committee for the new Free Will Baptist hymn book. He was a well-respected pastor with at least 26 sons in the ministry during those pastorates. His son, Dr. Billy Melvin, became the Executive-Secretary of the National Association of Free Will Baptists and later the Director of the National Association Of Evangelicals.

LaVerne Dale Miley
Birth:
Sep. 9, 1928
Kirksville,
Adair County, Missouri
Death:
Mar. 15, 2005
Nashville,
Davidson County, Tennessee
Burial:
Woodlawn Memorial Park,
Nashville,
Davidson County, Tennessee

A Free Will Baptist minister, medical doctor, missionary, and college professor. He opened the medical work in the Ivory Coast, Africa, where he served as a medical missionary for 19 years. For many years he was a professor at the Free Will Baptist Bible College in Nashville, Tennessee and served as a medical consultant for Free Will Baptist International Missions. He also worked with the Navajo Indians in the western United States and served in the Men of Valor Prison Ministry and was a longtime member of Cofer's Chapel Free Will Baptist Church in Nashville, Tennessee.

William H Morelock
Birth:
1875
Death:
1956
Burial:
Beech Creek Missionary Baptist Church Cemetery, Rogersville, Hawkins County, Tennessee

Howard T. Munsey
Birth:
Jun. 27, 1926
Death:
Aug. 14, 2009
Burial:
Jefferson Memorial Gardens
Cemetery, Jefferson City,
Jefferson County, Tennessee
He was the founding pastor of Peace Free Will Baptist Church in Morristown, delivered his first sermon in 1953 at Greenville First Free Will Baptist Church. He joined the U.S. Navy in 1942 and served during World War II and the Korean War, achieving the rank of petty officer first class. Rev. Munsey worked for Magnavox, built homes, and later part-owner of Hearthstone Log Homes in Dandridge during the 1970s and 1980s. During his lifetime, he organized two and pastored seven other Free Will Baptist churches. He had an effective revival and pulpit-supply ministry. Rev. Munsey served as the president, until his death, of Berea Ministries Inc., a mission organization he created in the 1950s to support the ministry of national pastors in Mexico. It was first chartered as the mission arm of a radio ministry called "Cross Beams Missions."

Death is the opening of the gate to eternal joy.

James Alan Munsey
Birth:
Aug. 10, 1950
Death:
Feb. 3, 2001
Texas
Burial:
Union Cemetery, Newport,
Cocke County, Tennessee

Munsey built the Free Will Baptist Church in Weslaco, Texas, while he worked with Free Will Baptist churches in Mexico. He was very instrumental in building many churches in Mexico and organizing numerous ones. He also was instrumental in building a Free Will Baptist Institute for the training of Mexican pastors. He was the son of Howard Munsey.

William Henry Oliver
Birth:
Nov. 4, 1903
Indian Mound
Stewart County, Tennessee
Death:
May 15, 1991

Nashville
Davidson County, Tennessee
Burial:
Forest Lawn Memorial Gardens
Goodlettsville
Davidson County, Tennessee

Rev. Dr. William Henry Oliver, a Free Will Baptist minister for 68 years, in Nashville. Hundreds attended his funeral May 18 at East High School where he served 18 years as principal (1939-1957).Rev. Oliver once said in an interview that he had three goals in mind when he started college---to become a preacher, a teacher and a writer. He eventually accomplished all three."I felt the Lord wanted me to be a preacher. I had to be a teacher, and I wanted to be a writer," he said. Mr. Oliver began teaching in Nashville city schools in 1930 at Hume Fogg HS. He taught algebra and English and coached the school's boxing and baseball teams, leading the baseball players to a city championship.He received his bachelor's degree from Vanderbilt University in 1926, and later received master's degrees in arts and education at George Peabody College.In 1957, the Nashville Board of education elected Mr. Oliver as city school superintendent. He retired in 1963 after the city and county government merged.He taught at Belmont College for the next seven years and then took a similar position at Free Will Baptist Bible College (1970-1977).He was ordained a minister in 1924 and later founded and became the first pastor of the East Nashville Free Will Baptist Church. He wrote literature and poetry including one well received poem titled At Twilight. In 1987 he was awarded an honorary Doctor of Literature Letters from Cumberland University. He was a member of the Kappa Alpha fraternity, Civitan, the Red Cross board, past president of the East Nashville YMCA and a past member of the Nashville Chamber of Commerce.

Hardy C Pace
Birth:
May 30, 1846
Death:
Oct. 16, 1928
Burial:
Taylor Cemetery
Stewart County, Tennessee

He served as a Free Will Baptist minister in the Ashland Quarterly Meeting in the late 1800s. He was married to   D Attie Wallace Pace (1847 - 1929)

Jerry Franklin Presley
Birth:
Jan. 16, 1932
Death:
Sep. 28, 1993
Tennessee
Burial:
Sweetwater Valley Memorial Park, Sweetwater, Monroe County, Tennessee
He was a Free Will Baptist minister and pastor for 26 years in Tennessee and Illinois until poor health forced him to resign from full-time pastoral service. He held numerous denominational positions, including Promotional-Secretary for the Tennessee Union Association, Youth camp Director, and 10 years as clerk of the Union Ministerial Association. He taught school in four Tennessee counties. He served in Korea with the U.S. Army.

Cleo Pursell
Birth:
Feb. 16, 1918
Fort Worth,
Tarrant County, Texas
Death:
Dec. 17, 2009
Nashville,
Davidson County, Tennessee
Burial:
Woodlawn Memorial Park and Mausoleum, Nashville, Davidson County, Tennessee

She became the first full-time Executive Sec. of the Women's National Auxiliary Convention and led the organization for 22 years (1963-1985). The headquarters of this woman's organization is located in Nashville, Tennessee and is part of the National Association of Free Will Baptists. The ministry flourished under her capable leadership and eventually she led the membership to an all-time high. She was a prolific writer of books and pamphlets as well as writing a regular feature for *Contact* Magazine called "Words for Women". She will be remembered for her far-reaching vision and constant leadership. She was 91 at her passing. She was an ordained minister and outlived her minister husband, Rev. Paul Purcell, who is buried in Oklahoma.

Roger C Reeds
Birth:
Sep. 16, 1928
Saint Louis,
St. Louis City, Missouri
Death:
May 2, 2007
Joelton,
Davidson County, Tennessee
Burial:
Joelton Hills Memory Gardens, Joelton, Davidson County, Tennessee

A Free Will Baptist pastor, author, and denominational leader. Converted in November 9, 1947 and called to preach the next year. He pastored churches in Missouri, North Carolina, and Tennessee. He was the founding Director of Randall House Publications, in Nashville, Tennessee, where he served 31 years, and was on the committee of founders of Donelson Christian Academy. He held degrees from Free Will Baptist Bible College, Middle Tennessee State University and Luther Rice Seminary.

Norman Howard, Richards
Birth:
Sep. 30, 1938
White County, Arkansas
Death:
Aug. 22, 2013
Nashville
Davidson County, Tennessee
Burial:
Mount Olivet Cemetery
Nashville
Davidson County, Tennessee

Norman age 74, of Nashville, passed away at the Vanderbilt Medical Center. He faithfully loved and served the Lord as a Missionary in Africa and as a Minister, presently with The Donelson Fellowship Church. He was preceded in death by his parents; 2 brothers and 1 sister. Rev. Richards is survived by his loving wife of 50 years, Bessie Richards; sons, Gene Richards (Patti), and Randal Richards (Patty); 4 grandchildren, Wesley, Julia, Olivia, and David; 2 brothers, Wayne Richards (Patsy) and Claude Presnell (Juanita); and 3 sisters, Mildred Sowell, Juanita Dickson (Ray), and Madie Walker (Don). Funeral services were conducted at the church with the Rev. Robert Morgan officiating. A private family graveside service was conducted in the Mount Olivet Cemetery.

Charles Raymond Riggs
Birth:
Oct. 15, 1915
Randolph County, Arkansas
Death:
Apr. 13, 2009
Burial:
Crest Lawn Cemetery,
Cookeville,
Putnam County, Tennessee

In November of 1934, he was married to Velma Staten and she passed away two months later. He then was united in marriage to Winona Mae Gates on October 25, 1936. She preceded him in death in March 1999.
Then he married Burnice Davis on July 22, 1999, in Cookeville, Tennessee. Brother Riggs was in his early ministry a school teacher, and as a minister known for his singing. He became an outstanding pastor and minister in the Detroit area. Under his leadership as the first Director Of Foreign Missions for the National Association of Free Will Baptist the organization grew. He is remembered as an early statesman for the denomination and has left a legacy of having many sons and grandchildren as ministers within the denomination.

Death has no strength; Jesus has subdued its power

Carol A. Waring Robirds
Birth:
Mar. 8, 1938
California
Death:
Mar. 30, 2010
Brentwood,
Davidson County, Tennessee
Burial:
Woodlawn Memorial Park and Mausoleum, Nashville,
Davidson County, Tennessee

Carol and her husband, Don, served as FWB missionaries in Brazil from 1964 to 1971, when Don was asked to join the office staff in Nashville as Dir. of Communications. Carol served as his assistant for several years.

Willie B Rodgers
Birth:
Jun. 14, 1918
Putnam County, Tennessee
Death:
Feb. 7, 2005
Cookeville
Putnam County, Tennessee
Burial:
Rodgers Cemetery
Baxter
Putnam County, Tennessee

Rev. Willie B. Rodgers passed away at his home. He was 86 years of age, and a native of Putnam Co. TN. Bro. Rodgers had a very fruitful ministry in South and North Carolina, and Tennessee. Most of his ministery was in Tenn. Churches he pastored: Antioch; Lily's Chapel; Duncan's Chapel; Manchester First; Trinity (Nashville); Taylor's Providence; Post Oak Shade; Algood First; United Hensley's Chapel; Taylor's Seminary; Cedar Hill; and Community Church.Rev. Jack Taylor conducted his service. He commented that he had many times sought good counsel from Bro. Rodgers. He was a devoted Bible student. He lived what he preached and was a great influence to many people. He married Velma Ramsey Rodgers.

Inscription:
Married April 28, 1950;
PFC US Army WWII

Melvin R Sanford
Birth:
Jan. 31, 1920
Death:
Oct. 17, 1993
Burial:
Fairview Free Will Baptist Church Cemetery
Anderson County, Tennessee

He ministered for over 54 years and started several churches in West Virginia pastoring numerous churches there. He also pastored churches in Ohio and Florida. He was known for his revivals some of which went as much as six weeks or more.He saw a great number of converts during his ministry. He was married to Helen L Sanford (1925 - 1998)

Inscription:
Married June 23, 1943

Ernest Sawyer
Birth:
unknown
Death:
Aug. 2, 2012
Del Rio, Cocke County, Tennessee
Burial:
Fugate Free Will Baptist Church Cemetery,
Del Rio, Cocke County, Tennessee
He pastored the Fugate Free Will Baptist church near Del Rio for 29 years.

Donald Ray Sexton
Birth:
July 9, 1930
Kentucky
Death:
1997
Tennessee
Burial:
Happy Valley Memorial Park Elizabethton
Carter County, Tennessee
Plot: Mausoleum of Peace

Sexton was licensed of preach in 1950 and ordained in 1951. He was a native of Jenkins, Kentucky. He graduated from Free Will Baptist Bible college in 1960 and attended language school in Switzerland and France. He served as Tennessee's first state missionary in 1963 and moderated the Tennessee State Association between 1967-71. He pastored six churches, four in Tennessee and two in Kentucky. He and his wife Billie were missionaries to France beginning in 1971 and served until 1979 when Don was diagnosed with Parkinson's disease. During his ministry in France, Sexton started the First Free Will Baptist Church in in Nantes. He was elected the Field Director in 1976. After he returned to the states, Sexton was asked by the Foreign Mission Board to promote foreign missions in the United States. For the next 13 years he traveled, informed and motivated Free Will Baptist about foreign missions. He resigned in 1990 due to his health problems. From his efforts the Don and Billi Sexton walk-a-thon became one of the most successful efforts in the denomination raising nearly 1,000,000 for missionary support.

As the rain from heaven refreshes the parched ground, so death provides the saint to partake of the refreshing of the soul in the presence of Jesus.

Robert Logan Shockey
Birth:
Sep. 16, 1927
Clay City,
Powell County, Kentucky
Death:
Mar. 7, 2008
Chapmansboro,
Cheatham County, Tennessee
Burial:
Bet
Ashland City,
Cheatham County, Tennessee

He was called to preach in 1955 and ordained to preach in 1956.His education consisted of Bible Diploma/Free Will Baptist Bible College in Nashville, Tennessee, in 1958. His pastorates included Raccoon Free Will Baptist Church in Greenup, Kentucky. from 1954-55; Bethlehem Free Will Baptist Church in Ashland City, Tennessee. from 1955-1957; Donelson Free Will Baptist Church in Nashville, Tennessee. from 1957-1959; Second Free Will Baptist Church in Ashland, Kentucky, from 1959-68 and 1973-74; Dothan Free Will Baptist Church in Dothan, Alabama from 1971 to 1973; Heritage Temple Free Will Baptist Church in Ashland, Kentucky from 1978-1984; Portland Free Will Baptist Church in Portland, Tennessee. in 2004. Denominational positions included: Moderator: Kentucky State Association of Free Will Baptists from 1959-1966; Moderator: Blue Grass Conference/Kentucky; Pastor of the Year Kentucky 1964;

President: Bethel Bible Institute Paintsville, Kentucky from 1982-1984. Home Missions Department from 1961-1978; Member: Home Missions Board (1961-1966); Promotional Secretary (1967-1971); General Director (1972-1978) (includes Director of Evangelism and Director of Military Chaplains); Free Will Baptist Bible College 1984-1995; Campus Pastor, Christian Service Director, Ministerial Fellowship Director, Director of Student Support. National Radio Speaker Radio & TV Commission, Victorious Faith Program. Evangelist 1954-2008; United States/Canada/Mexico/ Virgin Islands. His publications included Let's Go Fishing (pamphlet); How to Call a Pastor (pamphlet); Five Smooth Stones (pamphlet); The Teacher (pamphlet); Bus Ministry (pamphlet); How to Go Soulwinning (pamphlet). Tracts include Gods Simple Plan of Salvation; Tip; Now That You Are Saved; Keys to a New Life. Other accomplishments include: United States Navy, Psychiatric Nurse, Served two enlistments.

Rolla Darrell Smith
Birth:
Dec. 29, 1920
Norwood, Wright County, Missouri
Death:
Mar. 15, 2013
Nashville, Davidson County, Tennessee

Burial:
Hermitage Memorial Gardens
Old Hickory, Davidson County, Tennessee

He pastored at Hazel Creek Free Will Baptist (FWB) Church (MO), Fellowship FWB Church (Flat River, MO), Donelson FWB Church (Nashville), First FWB Church (Savannah, GA) and Grant Avenue FWB Church (Springfield, MO). He was a man of ordinary means yet rich in what matters most...love for God, love for family and love for friends. He was the General Director at FWB International Missions Department from 1960-1962 and 1975-1986 and Missions Instructor at Welch College from 1987-1989. Honorary Pallbearers were missionaries and staff members from the FWB International Missions Department and members of the Harvesters Sunday School Class at Cross Timbers FWB Church.A life celebration service was held at Harpeth Hills Funeral Home with Dr. Paul Harrison officiating.

Sam Peyton Stewart
Birth:
Jan. 18, 1857
Death:
Jun. 3, 1910
Burial:
Stewart Cemetery, Cookeville, Putnam County, Tennessee

Rev. S. P. Stewart died at his home in the Seventh district. The news writer extends his sympathy to the bereaved family and friends. He was a Free-will Baptist minister. [Date 6/16/1910, Vol. VIII, No. 24, Page 8]

William Horace Teague
Birth:
Aug. 2, 1918
Death:
Nov. 1, 2000
Burial:
Union Cemetery, Newport
Cocke County, Tennessee

He was called to preach in 1943 and was ordained in 1947 by Tennessee's union Association. He began passing immediately at Johnson's Chapel Free Will Baptist Church.He was a Free Will Baptist minister for 53 years and pastored a church is in his home state of Tennessee and for five years a church in Michigan. He then returned to Newport, Tennessee where he continued his ministry. He served as the moderator of the Tennessee state Association. He was a dedicated man who slap was fully yielded to Christ and he sacrificed for the ministry and suffered in order to preach the gospel. He had two sons that likewise became ministers Rev. Harold Teague of Beckville, Texas and Jim Teague of Chuckey, Tennessee

Elbert Worth Tippett
Birth:
Dec. 19, 1940

Portsmouth,
Portsmouth City, Virginia
Jan. 5, 2011
Nashville,
Davidson County, Tennessee
Burial:
Harpeth Hills Memory Gardens,
Nashville,
Davidson County, Tennessee

Bert Tippett was the long-time voice of Free Will Baptist Bible College as he headed the media office for numerous years. He was a great preacher, gentleman and a person of sterling character.

R. Eugene Waddell
Birth:
1935
Death:
Oct. 21, 2007
Burial:
Harpeth Hills
Memory Gardens, Nashville,,
Davidson County, Tennessee

He served with distinction churches in South Carolina, Virginia, and North Carolina before becoming pastor of Cofer's Chapel FWB Church in Nashville, Tennessee, a position he held from 1964 - 1981. He joined FWB International Missions where he was the Associate Director and then Director, until he retired in 1998. As the Director of International Missions, Mr. Waddell traveled to more than 40 countries, ministering to both the unchurched and the churched, and to the missionaries who called him their pastor. During his tenure the Mission began ministering in Russia, Mongolia, China, and Central Asia. Under his leadership contact with Cuba was reinstated, 64 missionaries were appointed, overseas church attendance almost doubled, and the TEAM summer missions program for high school students was initiated. In addition to his time as general Director, Waddell served as Associate Director for five years (1981-1986) and completed over 20 years (1959-1981) as an active member of the Board of Free Will Baptist Foreign Missions. Following his December 31, 1998, retirement, he served as Minister of Care and, more recently, Pastor Emeritus at Cofer's Chapel FWB Church in Nashville, Tennessee. Waddell leaves behind an impressive legacy of faith, love, resilience, passion for reaching unreached peoples, integrity, compassion, mediation, vision and servanthood. Mr. Waddell earned a B.A. from FWBBC in Nashville and a M.A. from Columbia (SC) International University.

John L. Welch
Birth:
unknown
Death:
Jul. 24, 1988
Nashville,
Davidson County, Tennessee
Burial:
Spring Hill Cemetery,
Nashville,
Davidson County, Tennessee

He had early influence in both conferences of the East and West, and had much to do in bringing them together as a denomination in 1935. The meeting was held at the Cofer's Chapel Free Will Baptist Church where he pastored. Reverend Welch was the first moderator of the National Association of Free Will Baptists in 1935. He also had influence in the beginning the Free Will Baptist Bible College to Nashville, Tennessee., and served 12 years as a member of the college's Board of Trustees, and pastored Cofer's Chapel Free Will Baptist Church in Nashville 53 years.

Mrs. Mary Welch served faithfully as a secretary at the college, spent nearly 60 years as a pastor's wife, and was a leader in the women's movement. For the past five decades, there has been a building on campus named in honor of John and Mary Welch — the historic Welch Library. He was 94-years-old at the time of his death. Free Will Baptist Bible College in 2012 renamed the school Welch College in their honor.

All say, "How hard it is that we have to die" - a strange complaint to come from the mouths of people who have had to live.

WELCH, Rev. John L— Sunday morning July 24, 1983 at a local infirmary. Age 94 years. Survived by daughter, Mrs. William M. (Jean) Henderson, Joplin, Mo.; daughter-in-law, Mrs. Bessie Welch Smalley; four grandchildren; eleven great grandchildren. His remains are at the Eastland Chapel, 904 Gallatin Road. The remains will lie in state at the Cofer's Chapel Free Will Baptist Church, 4300 Clarksville Highway Tuesday afternoon from 1 until time of services at 2 p.m. with the Pastor Billy Gene Outland, Dr. Robert E. Picirrille, Rev. R. Eugene Waddell, Rev. Henry Oliver, and Dr. D. Michael Henderson officiating. Interment Spring Hill Cemetery. Honorary Pallbearers: Ministers of Cumberland Association, Free Will Baptist Headquarters, and Free Will Baptist Bible College. Active: Bill Smith, Jimmie Carter, Scybert Basford, Jack Trotter, Jack Nicholson, John Boyte, Willie Owen, Jarman Goodman, and Webb Cofer. IN LIEU OF FLOWERS, MAKE CONTRIBUTIONS TO COFER'S CHAPEL FREE WILL BAPTIST CHURCH OR TO THE FREE WILL BAPTIST BIBLE COLLEGE. ROESCH PATTON DORRIS & CHARLTON, Eastland Chapel, 904 Gallatin Road, 244-6480

Juna J Wilkerson
Birth:
Jun. 2, 1910
Death:
Dec. 19, 1994
Burial:
Carters Chapel Cemetery,
Greene County,
Tennessee

Homer Emerson Willis
Birth:
May 8, 1924
Clintwood,
Dickenson County, Virginia
Death:
Feb. 17, 2005
Nashville,
Davidson County, Tennessee
Burial:
Woodlawn Memorial Park,
Nashville,
Davidson County, Tennessee

A Free Will Baptist pastor, evangelist and denominational leader. He was converted to Christ at age 15 and ordained to the ministry at age 18. He graduated from Free Will Baptist Bible College in Nashville, Tennessee in 1946 and also Trinity College. He pastored churches in Michigan, Tennessee, Kentucky and North Carolina. He was General Director of the National Home Mission Board of Free Will Baptists from 1956 until 1973. During his tenure the department planted churches in 33 states and he opened the work in Canada, the Virgin Islands, Puerto Rico, and extended the work in several states of Mexico. He was founder and editor of *Mission Grams*, the Director Of Evangelism, founder of the Church Loan Fund Program and the Director of the Chaplain's Ministry. He preached in all 50 states and Canada, Mexico, Puerto Rico, the Virgin Islands, Germany, Israel and Egypt. His ministry took him to every continent except Australia. He was an honorary life member of the Gideon's, a past Lieutenant Governor of Kiwanis International, an organization that he had served for 50 years. He was a member of the Who's Who in Tennessee.

Paul H. Woolsey
Birth:
Nov. 23, 1908
Death:
Jun. 19, 1989
Burial:
Burial:
Harris Memorial Cemetery
Greene County
Tennessee

Rev. and Mrs. Paul Woolsey were tremendously interested in the educational system of the county in East Tennessee. Woolsey served on the Greene County Board of Education for six years, two of which he was chairman of the board and one year due to the sickness of the superintendent, most of the work of that office fell to him. When he accepted the call to the mission field, he and Mrs. Woolsey were teaching in the elementary school of Cedar Creek, formerly the Cedar Creek Presbyterian Academy.
Rev. and Mrs. Woolsey worked in the local church and continued their visits in the interests of the entire work of the denomination during the year and a half that they were in the community. They not only supported the school in every possible way, but contributed liberally to their equipment fund for India.

They left America from New York City April 10, 1947, and arrived in Bombay Monday on May 5. They proceeded to Kotagiri, Nilgiris, South India and joined Miss Barnard in her labors there during the hot season. In the month of July they entered the Language School at Landour, Mussoorie, in the United Provinces of North India, preparatory to the opening of a new work in North India. Turbulent India, about to gain her complete independence, is a long way from the peaceful home where the family had dwelt since the days of the independence of the United States. Much of the history of the Woolsey family can be found in the book he wrote entitledl, *"God, A Hundred Years And A Free Will Baptist Family."*

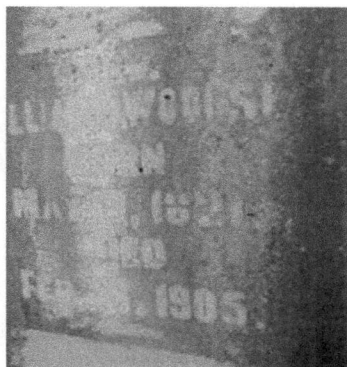

William B. Woolsey
Birth:
May 19, 1821
Greene County, North Carolina
Death:
Feb. 10, 1905
North Carolina
Burial:
Harrison Cemetery, Greystone, Greene County, Tennessee

He was converted at the age of 21 yrs and joined the Nebo Baptist Church. He soon felt his calling to further endeavors and began to preach, being licensed in 1843. However, his strong views on Arminism vs Calvinism, saw a break and along with two other

older talented ministers, Moses Peterson and John Wheeler, they withdrew and formed the Toe River Association of Free Will Baptists with six churches, scattered between the mountains. William Bonaparte was elected clerk and remained so for eighteen years. By 1854, they had twelve ministers and more churches. He, though not afforded a formal education, began at once to study, buy Bible helps, and classics, as he could, and soon rose to a place of leadership among the people. He knew the value of education, sought it himself, and promoted it for others. He was self-educated and had a wise head about him. He, and others, established the Woolsey College, going far and near to try to secure funds or support, to build it, which they did, so that the youth could attend school and have some training after the devastation suffered by the Civil War. He organized Horse Creek Church in 1849; assisted in organizing Dry Fork FWB; and Nebo. He lived an active life in the ministry, and raised a large family who followed his footsteps. (*"My Free Will Baptist Woolsey Family"*, by Rev. Paul H. Woolsey, pub 1949" a great-grandson.)

Established 1812

Texas

H, Zirl Cox
Birth:
unknown
Texas
Death:
1993
Duncanville,
Dallas County, Texas
Burial:
Vashti Cemetery,Vashti,
Clay County, Texas

The Antelope, Texas, native served as pastor of the First Freewill Baptist Church from 1947 until his retirement in 1986. He entered the ministry in 1939 and served in the Army from 1943 to 1945 as a medic and chaplain's assistant. He was also a partner in Cox Real Estate firm in Dallas from 1968 until his death. Mr. Cox received his Bachelor's Degree in Bible education from Dallas Bible College in 1951. He earned his Master's Degree In Theology from Bible Baptist Seminary in Fort Worth in 1953.

A. F. Ferguson
Birth:
Nov. 8, 1909
Memphis,
Shelby County, Tennessee
Death:
Apr. 18, 2008 Georgetown,
Williamson County, Texas
Burial:
Tyler Memorial Park and
Cemetery, Tyler,
Smith County, Texas

A. F. Ferguson, 98, pastored 16 churches and started two over a period of 60 years in Texas, Oklahoma, Mississippi and California. He was a member of Lake Hills Freewill Baptist Church of Cedar Park, and a junior founder of Justin Boot Co. in Fort Worth. Published in the Tyler Morning Telegraph on 4/21/2008.

W D Haston
Birth:
May 10, 1860
Death:
Jun. 4, 1929
Burial:
Buck Creek Cemetery,
Paducah,Cottle County, Texas

At about 30 years of age, he entered the ministry and affiliated with the Free Will Baptists. He married Sallie McLemore, 16 Sept. 1880, Yell Co. AR. He and Sallie later moved to Texas and continued in work and raising a large family.

A short notice/bio of his death appeared in the Free Will Baptist paper, *"The Gem"* July 1929 issue, in Missouri, where Eld. J. A. Edmondson, wrote that he was called to conduct his fellow minister's funeral in Paducah, TX. He stated Eld. W.D. Haston "had for over 40 years, preached all over and organized churches."

Everett D. Hellard
Birth:
Sep. 29, 1923
Death:
Feb. 11, 2007
Texas
Burial:
Garden Park Cemetery,
Conroe,
Montgomery County, Texas

He pastored churches in many

areas for the Free Will Baptist and was a leader at all levels. His beautiful tenor voice caused him to have many invitations to sing at many of the conventions. *Ship Ahoy* was always asked as the song for him to sing.

J. W. Johnson
Birth:
Aug. 4, 1845
Death:
Jul. 24, 1899
Burial:
King Cemetery
Henderson County, Texas

In1888 he was one of the ministers in the Denton Creek Association of Free Will Baptist which is located northwest of Dallas. Inscription:Co K3 Texas Cav C.S.A.

Billy Marion Jones
Birth:
Feb. 3, 1937
Houston Harris County Texas
Dec. 19, 2011
Fort Smith
Sebastian County, Arkansas
Burial:
Steep Hollow Cemetery,
Bryan,Brazos County, Texas

Bill was a minister, pastor, missionary to Ivory Coast for 10 years, editor of *"Heartbeat"* a missions magazine in Nashville, TN, President of Hillsdale Free Will Baptist College in Moore, OK for 8 years, Director of Oklahoma Missions for 2 years, served on the Foreign Mission Board for 26 years, professor of Theology at the college, Senior Adult pastor Poteau FWB Church.

J W Loftis
Birth:
Nov. 8, 1869
Death:
Jan. 8, 1906
Burial:
Jacksonville City Cemetery
Jacksonville
Cherokee County, Texas

He was one that the earlier pastors in the Brazos Quarterly Meeting which was started in 1887.

Isaac Martin
Birth:
Dec. 31, 1812
Death:
Nov. 2, 1888
Burial:
Alto City Cemetery
Alto
Cherokee County
Texas

He was one of the early ministers in Chattahoochee Association and is recorded in the 1842 minutes.He married Mary Polly Truitt on June 6, 1834 in Jasper County, Georgia; she died in 1890 in Cherokee County, TX; Reverend and Mrs. Martin had eleven children. His parents were James Martin (1788 - 1869) and Hester Bogan Martin (1789 - 1867) who is buried in Georgia and was the parents of four preachers one of which started the Martin Association in the state of Georgia.

Elder Samuel Crawford Martin
Birth:
Jan. 20, 1825
Alabama
Death:
Dec. 23, 1903
Steep Hollow
Brazos County, Texas
Burial:
Steep Hollow Cemetery
Bryan
Brazos County,Texas
Plot: Section 2, Space 278

Transcription of Obiturary from The Bryan Eagle, Thursday, 24 Dec. 1903. REV. S. C. MARTIN DEAD. Venerable Pioneer Baptist Preacher Gone to his Reward. Brazos county mourns the loss of one of her oldest, noblest and best citizens, and the holidays have been darkened in homes throughout the length and breadth of the county, where his name was a household word, by the death of Rev. S. C. Martin at his home in the Steep Hollow community on Wednesday morning, December 23, 1903, at 8:30 o'clock.Rev. Martin, infirm with the weight and labors of 79 years, has been in failing health for some time and ill for several weeks, so that his death was not unexpected. Nevertheless, it was a sad blow to the family and host of friends when the news came from the darkened chamber that his noble spirit had taken its flight. Rev. Martin was a native of Alabama and came to Texas before the civil war, locating in Tyler county. He moved to Brazos county more than thirty years ago and has since resided in the Steep Hollow community. For more than half a century he preached the gospel and his labors were graciously blessed in the salvation of soul. Not only did he serve as pastor of nearly every Baptist church in Brazos county, but though out his life he did much successful revival work.He was sincere, earnest, uncompromising, unselfish and consecrated. He labored as faithfully without reward as when his labors were abundantly rewarded. In deed his best service was given to the Master with numerically weak and struggling churches, and it may be truly said that he gave his life to the gospel, the church and humanity. His brother was the founder of the Martin Association in the state of Georgia and had at least two other brothers who were Free Will Baptist preachers as well. His ancestry has roots in South Carolina with one of them buried in the Horse Branch Free Will Baptist Cemetery. I am strongly assuming that he was also a Free Will Baptist preacher even though I have not been able to find verification of that in the state of Texas.

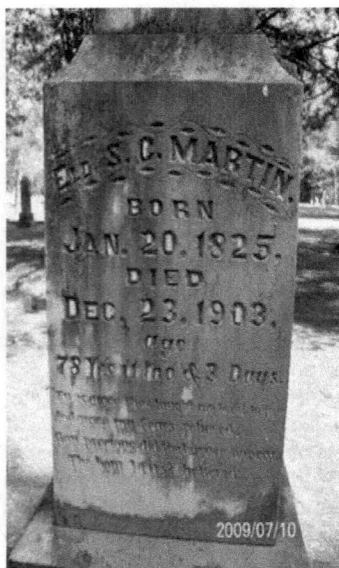

Elizabeth R McAdams
Birth:
Oct. 1, 1884
Luverne, Alabama
Death:
Sep. 1, 1964
Burial:
Falba Cemetery,Huntsville,
Walker County, Texas

At 13 she recalls she wanted to be a missionary. At 25 she felt that God was calling her to preach. She was licensed to preach in October, 1910. In 1911 she married Rev. Hiram McAdams and they established themselves as an evangelistic team in North Carolina, Missouri, Texas, Oklahoma, Arkansas etc. Elizabeth became known as Lizzie, or Sister Lizzie, realized her teenage dream of being a missionary when she, her husband, and 6 year old Naomi Rebecca went to Barbados, British West Indies, in 1918 as missionaries. They spent a short time on the island and then returned to the States as evangelists. Back in the States Mrs. McAdams worked hard at trying to bring Free Will Baptist in

the West and East together. At the meeting in Cofer's Chapel in 1935, she stood and made the motion that East and West unite as the National Association of Free Will Baptists, and without a reading of the committee's report on the Treatise, the motion passed and the National Association became a reality. At her death at the age of 80, she had spent 54 years in the ministry. In her book, *Rolling Stones,* she summed up her ministry: "We have preached in 17 states, have held about 300 revivals with about 10,000 professions of faith in the Lord Jesus, organized 11 churches and numerous Auxiliaries and Leagues in different states. During this period of time, spent four years as home missionaries. She also wrote *My Experiences, Six Gospel Sermons, Rolling Stones, Go Tell that Fox, Getting a Shave in the Devil's Barbershop, My Trip to the West India Islands,* and *Woman's Bible Right to Preach the Gospel.* She was also a member of the national home mission board in the early years of the denomination. She was active in travielng among our churches. She was an evangelist, a promotional Secretary for various departments, and was pastor of a number of churches.

Hiram Mullens McAdams
Birth:
Jun. 18, 1879,
Walker County, Texas,
May 24, 1964
Huntsville,
Walker County, Texas,
Burial:
Falba Cemetery, Huntsville,
Walker County, Texas

McAdams married Elizabeth Rachel Lawlis, in 1911.They had a daughter, Naomi R., in 1913, born in Texas. Rev. Hiram and his wife, Rev. "Lizzie" as she was affectionately called, were ordained as ministers in the 1920's in the Free Will Baptist Church. They were co-pastors, and an evangelistic team holding large revivals in North Carolina, Texas, Alabama, Oklahoma, Missouri, and Nebraska. They organized churches and promoted Tecumseh College in Oklahoma, and was active in church missions throughout. In 1918, they acquired passports and went to Barbados, West Indies, as missionaries for a short time, before they returned to become very involved in mission work in the states. His wife wrote several books, some of which described their work. They were respected and held in esteem by those who knew them, and in memory by those who read and know of their labors. It is noteworthy that Rev. "Lizzy" outlived her husband only three months and 8 days.

Oliver Roy Norie, Jr
Birth:
Jul. 24, 1923
Death:
Jul. 19, 1998
Burial:
Crestview Memorial Park,
Wichita Falls,
Wichita County, Texas
Most of his life and ministry was invested in Texas Free Will Baptist churches. In his early years he traveled the state promoting home and foreign missions and gave every month to missions work in Texas. At the time of his death he was the pastor of the new Salem Free Will Baptist Church.

Judson B Palmer
Birth:
April 25, 1851
Orangeville, Ohio
Death:
1937
Burial:
Galveston Memorial Park
Hitchcock
Galveston County, Texas
Plot: Section B
He attended Hillsdale College in Michigan where he assisted in teaching and graduated from the theological department. He was ordained in May, 1873 with Reverent's A. A. Smith, A. H. Chase and other serving on the Council. He served as a teacher in the Cairo mission for two years and as a state missionary. His pastorates consisted in churches in Michigan, Wisconsin, and Iowa. He was engaged in many revivals where

the presence of the spirit was manifest and he baptized over 150 converts. He became the general secretary of the YMCA a Galveston, Texas where he died.

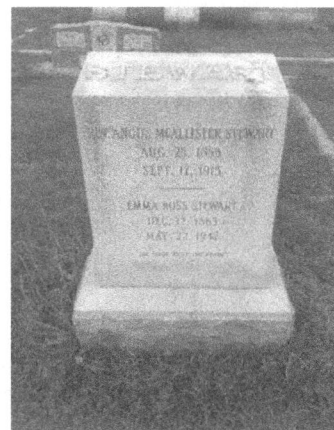

Angus McAllister Stewart
Birth:
Aug. 25, 1853
Death:
Sep. 17, 1913
Burial:
Odd Fellows Cemetery
Carthage
Panola CountyTexas

In 1878 a number of churches in Panola County entered into an organization which became known as the Texas Association. He was very instrumental in to organize associations as well as local churches.

Milton L Sutton
Birth:
Jan. 25, 1899
Louisiana
Death:
Nov. 1, 1980
Wichita Falls,
Wichita County, Texas
Burial:
Buffalo Springs Cemetery,
Buffalo Springs,
Clay County, Texas

He was an ordained pastor and leader in the Texas church. He pastored at Ft. Worth for years.

Obediah J. Taylor
Birth:
Feb. 14, 1851
Anderson County,
South Carolina
Death:
Feb. 14, 1939
Smith County, Texas,
Burial:
Hopewell Cemetery,
Swan, Smith County, Texas

His father died in 1864, in Franklin, Tennessee, Civil War, which left his mother a widow. She died about 1880 when they were in Mountain Home, Logan Co. Arkansas. After this is when he probably migrated to Indian Territory in eastern Oklahoma, for they were in the Chickasaw Nation census of 1900, Township 6, with six children. *"First Hundred Years of Oklahoma Free Will Baptist,"* pub. 2009, states that in Rev. J.M. Robert's diary,

"O.J. Tailor (sic), was in Indian Territory in 1894, and preached with Rev. J. M. Roberts. In meeting minutes of Sept. 1, 1894, organization of churches in Indian Territory, 'Rev. O. J. Taylor, was elected ass't moderator' of their group. Where he was ordained and where his ministry took him is not known. It's possible he was ordained in Arkansas after they moved there. His occupation was always listed as "farmer" as most of the old pioneer ministers were, as they received precious little money for their ministerial labor.

Harold R Teague
Birth:
Nov. 30, 1937
Newport
Cocke County, Tennessee
Death:
Jan. 2, 2012
Burial:
Rusk County Memorial Gardens
Henderson
Rusk County, Texas

He attended Free Will Baptist Bible College in Nashville, Tennessee. He was a pastor and began his career preaching in Springfield, Tennessee in 1959. He then pastored Harris Memorial Freewill Baptist Church in Greeneville, Tennessee, First Freewill Baptist Church in Henderson, Texas, Longview Freewill Baptist Mission in Longview, Texas, Union Arbor Freewill Baptist in Beckville, Texas and returned again to First Free Will Baptist Church in Henderson where he retired in July 2007. Throughout his career, he held many positions of leadership in the Free Will Baptist Denomination at the district, state, and national level. He was honored as Who's Who in American Religion and touched many lives throughout his ministry career. He also worked for many years on the campuses of the schools for Pine Tree ISD. He was a member of the Lion's Club of Henderson, Texas. He was

an incredible husband, father, grandfather, friend and pastor, but most of all he was a devoted follower of Jesus Christ.

Charles B. Thompson
Birth:
Mar. 17, 1890
Death:
Sep. 2, 1977
Burial:
Bryan City Cemetery
Bryan
Brazos County, Texas
Plot: Block 21

PVT US Army World War II.Spouse: Annie Lawless Thompson (1897 - 1988)*

It is not a day of disappointment, But a day of excitement.

W. T. Wood
Birth:
Apr. 18, 1845
Death:
Feb. 6, 1910
Burial:
Bright Light Cemetery
Bryan
Brazos County, Texas

He was a minister in the Brazos County Association which was organized by the Rev. T.H. Adams with the assistance of Rev. A.M. Stewart in the late 1800s
Inscription:
"A truer nobler heart never beat within a human heart"

Utah

Eugene Zephaniah Whitman
Birth:
Dec. 6, 1850
Woodstock
Oxford County, Maine
Death:
Dec. 4, 1930
Bountiful
Davis County, Utah
Burial:
Bountiful Memorial Park
Bountiful
Davis County, Utah

He was the son of Zephaniah Benson Whitman and Eliza Chase. On October 20, 1873 he was converted. He was a student at Kent's Hill Academy and was licensed as a Methodist April 7, 1875 and held three pastorates enjoying one revival in which 25 were baptized. On December 29, 1883, he was licensed by the Free Baptists and was ordained at the Waterville and Sydney churches, March 27, 1884. He entered of 1889 in the Cobb Divinity School at the same time serving the church at West Bowdoin. In 1888, he took the pastoral care of the Sabattus where a revival of 38 were added to the church.

I'm Looking for a City

Vermont

Mason Hezekiah Abbey
Birth:
Aug. 9, 1821 Westminster,
Windham County, Vermont
Death:
Jan. 8, 1895
Newport,
Orleans County, Vermont
Burial:
Sutton Village Cemetery,
Sutton,
Caledonia County, Vermont

He was educated at Clinton Seminary and entered the Free Baptist, holding pastorates at Harrisburg, Attica, Varysburgh, Warsaw, Philadelphia and Lowville, N. Y. In 1864 he served three months as missionary among the freedmen around Norfolk, Va. He was for fifteen years in evangelistic work. In 1884, he became pastor at Allegheny, Pa., where he remained for ten years, going from there to West Charleston, Vt.

Shubel Boston
Birth:
1790
Death:
Dec. 23, 1841
Burial:
South Wheelock Cemetery
Wheelock
Caledonia County, Vermont

In 1826 he was ordained and became an itinerant preacher of the Parsonsfield Quarterly

Meeting, Maine. In 1833 he moved to Wheelock Quarterly Meeting, in Vermont where he had a long and useful ministry until his death. He was pastor at St. Johnsbury from 1835 to 1839 and afterwards resided at Sheffied.

Joseph Bruce
Birth:
December 31, 1821
Springfield, Vermont
Death:
Dec. 16, 1860
Vermont
Burial:
Lower Branch Cemetery
Braintree
Orange County, Vermont

He was the grandson of a Calvinistic Baptist preacher. He moved with his father in 1822 to Schoon, Essex County, New York. He felt God was calling him as early as eight years of age but yielded finally in 1838 uniting with the Methodists. He was licensed in that body the year of his conversion, and he saw 15 converted in Chester and 30 in Horicon. His license was renewed in 1840 and, till 1858, he continued to preach in different circuits in Vermont but became dissatisfied with this form of church and government, and their policy on the question of slavery. He joined the Free Baptists in 1857 and in June 1858 was ordained. During 1858 he preached over 300 sermons going from place to place on foot. About this time he moved to Boldon. In the

spring of 1859 he served the church at South Bolton and organized a church at Trout Lake. In the fall of that year his labors at Ford Ann were blessed with a revival. He continued to preach with a failing health till October 14 in 1860 when he preached his last sermon in Middlesex, Vermont. He died in his 40th year after having a ministry of Twenty-two years.

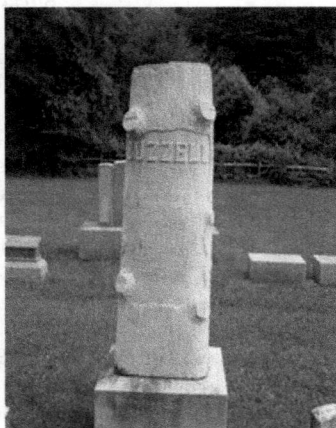

John F. Buzzell
Birth:
1836
Northfield, Vermont
Death:
1900
Burial:
Waitsfield Village Cemetery
Waitsfield
Washington County, Vermont

His father was Eli Buzzell and his mother was the daughter of Elder Aaron Buzzell. He became a Christian in 1859 and on January 1 of that year he was married to Martha meal. They had 10 children altogether. He was ordained by the Huntington Quarterly Meeting the limits of which he labored during his ministry. He was the superintendent of schools for 12 years.

Benjamin Chatterton
Birth:
1781
Acworth,
Sullivan County, New Hampshire
Death:
Jun. 11, 1855,
Middlesex,
Washington County, Vermont
Burial:
Chatterton Cemetery,
Middlesex,
Washington County, Vermont

Elder Benjamin Chatterton was a founder of the Freewill Baptist Church in Middlesex, Vt, now the Shady Rill Baptist Church. The cemetery is a small private cemetery up on McCullough Road, known as East Hill Road in the 19th century. Ben was active on the local school board and town committee's during his life in Middlesex. A biography on him can be found in *Hemenway's Gazetteer* of Washington County.

Joshua Coffrin
Birth:
Feb. 20, 1816
Waterbury, Vermont
Death:
Oct. 28, 1891
Burial:
Hope Cemetery
Waterbury
Washington County, Vermont

He was converted on January 1837 and was licensed to preach on November 18, 1843. He was ordained in Morristown by the Huntington Quarterly Meeting. He became pastor of the Franklin church where he was for 25 years and preached at other notable churches in the area for years. He was known for his many revivals and had baptized over 200 during a series of time he organized two churches.

David Cross
Birth:
1786
Wilmot, N.H,
Death:
Jun. 22, 1870
Newark,Vt.
Burial:
Sutton Village Cemetery
Sutton, Caledonia County,
Vermont

Cross died age 84 years and 6 months. He was occupied with farming until he settled in life for himself. After his marriage and when about thirty years of age he was converted and soon began the work of the ministry. Many were converted under his preaching, several who became earnest ministers. After preaching about ten years in several places in New Hampshire with good success, he settled at Sutton, Vt., where he lived and preached more or less for forty years. He always owned a farm from which he largely obtained his support.

Amos Davis
Birth:
Sep. 26, 179
Bakersfield
Franklin County, Vermont
Death:
1841
Bakersfield, Vermont
Burial:
Maple Grove Cemetery
Bakersfield
Franklin County, Vermont

He experienced religion early in life among the Methodists and united with the Free Will Baptist Church in Fairfield in the earliest history of the Enosburg QM. He was ordained at South Fairfield and rendered effectual service in building up the quarterly meeting.

Frank E Davison
Birth:
1853
Death:
1932
Burial:
South Hero Cemetery
South Hero
Grand Isle County, Vermont

Minister/pastor in several states for the Free Baptist; then later with the Congregational Church.

Lewis Dexter
Birth:
1824
West Topsham
Orange County, Vermont
Death:
1921
Burial:
West Topsham Cemetery
West Topsham
Orange County, Vermont,

Rev. Lewis Dexter was the son of Parker and Betsey (King) Dexter, of Topsham, VT. His parents were members of the West Topsham church. He became a Christian at ten. July, 1864, he enlisted in Co. H., Ninth Regiment, Vermont Volunteers, and served in the army till the war closed. He graduated at New Hampton Institution (NH) in 1869, and from Bates Theological School (Lewiston, ME) in 1872. In July he was ordained by Prof. J. Fullonton and others, and settled at Sabattusville, where he had already preached a year. He was licensed by the Corinth, Vermont quarterly meeting, in 1870. Soon after his ordination, Oct 17, he married Miss Clara Evans. During his three years at Sabattusville he baptized thirty and received forty-five into the church. From Oct. 1, 1874-June 1, 1878, he was pastor at Georgiaville, R.I., and added fifty-seven to the church. He was then called to the Greenwich Street church, Providence, where he lifted an oppressive church debt of over $8,000. He baptized eleven and received twenty-one into the church during two years. From Sept. 1, 1880, to March 1, 1887, he was pastor of the church at Blackstone, Massachusetts where he baptized twenty-nine and added fifty to the church. The vestry of the church was remodeled. March 1, 1887, he accepted a call to the Doughty Falls church, North Berwick, Maine. He has succeeded in developing a deep interest in Sunday-school, missionary and temperance work. The Sunday-school normal instruction he introduced at Ocean Park (ME). He was clerk of the Ministers' Conference of the Rhode Island Association ten years. At the General Conference in 1880 he was delegate from Rhode Island."

Orange Dyke
Birth:
Jul. 8, 1799
Huntington, Chittenden
County, Vermont
Death:
Aug. 19, 1875
Westford
Chittenden County, Vermont
Burial:
Maplewood Cemetery
Huntington
Chittenden County, Vermont

Rev. Orange Dike, was born on 8 Jul 1799, and Huntington, Chittendon, Vt. to Jonathan Dike (II) (1751-1826) and Abigail Brown Dike (1757-1840), he married first on 19 Mar 1818 to Lois Mix and second he married on 23 Jun 1841 to Lois Randall Pine. Excerpts from *History of Chittenden County, Vermont With Illustrations and Biographical Sketches of Some of Its Prominent Men and Pioneers.*"The first house built expressly for purposes of worship was erected at the north village in 1836 by the Methodists and Freewill Baptists. Another smaller house was built at the south village in 1841, and was owned chiefly by Calvinistic Baptists. Nearly all the denominations have at one time or another sustained services in Huntington, though the only regular organization now acting in town is the Freewill Baptist. The first preacher of this persuasion in town was Elder Charles Bowles, colored, who

came here in the summer of 1817, and at various times has been succeeded by the following preachers: Benajah Maynard, Josiah Wetherbee, Orange Dike. The first post-office opened in town was established near the commencement of the century, at the house of Jabez FARGO, who was postmaster. As it did not quite pay expenses it was soon discontinued, and no other took its place until 1828, when Amos DIKE received the appointment and opened an office at the south village. In 1829, on application to the general department, it was transferred to the north village and Alexander Ferguson was appointed. Since then the postmasters at the north village (Huntington), have been as follows: 1829 to 1841 inclusive, Alexander Ferguson; 1842, Cyrus Johns; [April 2 1842-] 1843 To 1845, Orange Dike; 1846-47, ..."_The Freewill Baptist Quarterly. Volume VI._ Dover: Freewill Baptisti Printing Establishment. Wm. Burr, Pinter, MDCCCLVIII, Page 83.

Edward Fay
Birth:
May 6, 1783
Buckland, Franklin County,
Massachusetts
Death:
Feb. 7, 1860
Jericho,
Chittenden County, Vermont
Burial:
Jericho Center Cemetery,
Jericho,
Chittenden County, Vermont

He began preaching about forty years of age (abt 1823) and was ordain in 1826, by the Free Will Baptist church. He was pastor of the church in Underhill, VT for thirteen years; then he returned to his former charge and retained it until his death. He preached much to the destitute churches of the Enosburg Quarterly Meeting.

John Forrest
Birth:
Apr. 18, 1831
Sutton, Vermont
Death:
Jan. 20, 1912
Burial:
South Barton-Willoughby
Cemetery
Barton
Orleans County, Vermont

He was converted to the age of 12, in 1843, and licensed by the Methodists as a local preacher in 1880. He united with the Free Baptists in 1884, and was ordained by them May 13 following at South Barton. The church was built up under his faithful labors.

John Garfield
Birth:
April 15, 1801
Barre, Vt.
Death:
Jan. 8, 1878
West Wheelock, Vt.
Burial:
West Wheelock Cemetery
Wheelock, Caledonia County,
Vermont

When quite young, his parents moved to Glover. When about seventeen he was converted under the labors of Elder Fisk and joined the M. E. church. His unwillingness to preach caused him to backslide. He was awakened about six years afterward, and preached with the Methodists about twenty years. In Stannard, in 1841, his labors resulted in a great revival. September 11, a Free Baptist church was organized and he was ordained as pastor. He held the office fourteen years. The last seven years his health was poor. When unable to speak aloud, he would whisper words of comfort to the little band that gathered in his home for prayer and conference.

Peleg Hicks, Sr
Birth:
1738
Rehoboth
Bristol County,
Massachusetts
Death:
1826
Burke Hollow
Caledonia County,Vermont
Burial:
Burke Green Cemetery
Burke
Caledonia County, Vermont

He was a Baptist minister with two churches that united with the Wheellock, Vermont, Quarterly Meeting on August 29, 1802. He was ordained about 179-.

Mark Hill
Birth:
May 22, 1796
Buxton, Me.
Death:
Nov. 3, 1866
Sutton, Vt.
Burial:
Sutton Village Cemetery
Sutton, Caledonia County,
Vermont

Son of Nathaniel and Martha Crockett Hill was the youngest of thirteen children,

all of whom he survived. Converted in the fall of 1817 he was baptized by Rev. Clement Phinney, and feeling called to the ministry he spent two years in preparatory studies at an academy. In 1820 and 1821 he was principally engaged in teaching. The next year he went to Rhode Island to confer concerning his call to the ministry with Rev. J. White, and soon found his place on the walls of Zion. He preached in Maine, and emigrated to Vermont.In 1825 he bought a farm in Lyndon of Rev. Joseph Quinby, on which he worked, teaching winters and preaching with Quinby and others. In 1827 he married Arvilla Ruggles, of Lyndon, and the same year united with the church there, being chosen its clerk. At the time of his marriage, of the three hundred dollars he possessed two hundred dollars had been loaned to the Free Baptist. Printing Establishment in Limerick. In 1833 he moved to a farm in Sutton. In 1834 he was ordained in Lyndon. He preached chiefly in Sutton, Sheffield, Wheelock, Lyndon, and South Bartol, and saw many conversions. For twenty-five years he was clerk of the Wheelock O. M. He acquired a competence, and gave liberally for education and missions, generously remembering them in his will. His last public utterances were at an anti-slavery meeting.

Paul Holbrook
Birth:
unknown
Death:
Dec. 3, 1821
Burial:
Tinkham Cemetery
East Montpelier
Washington County, Vermont

He was ordained in 1805 and died after a ministry of only about 20 years in Vermont.

Isaac Hyatt
Birth:
February 22, 1837
Quebec, Canada
Death:
1910
Vermont
Burial:
Riverside Cemetery
Swanton
Franklin County, Vermont

His father died when he was five years of age leaving the mother with two children. He went to live with Jacob Hyatt, his grandfather, and had an early had a thirst for knowledge. He graduated from the Biblical School at New Hampton in 1862. He was pastor in Tunbridge, Vermont and Rochester, New Hampshire where a church was organized and a house of worship built. After which he pastored in Pawtucket, Rhode Island where 37 additions were made. Then he returned back to Vermont subsequently pastoring in the Rhode Island, Maine, and New York.

Daniel W. Jackson
Birth:
Mar. 25, 1839 Starksboro,
Addison County, Vermont
Death:
Jan. 27, 1860
Burial:
Starksboro Village Cemetery,
Starksboro,
Addison County, Vermont

In 1855 he was converted, and a few months later was baptized. In 1856, feeling a call to preach, he consulted with Rev. Mark Atwood, and passed the winter in southern Starksborough, preaching and teaching school. In Sept. 1857, he was licensed by the Huntington Q.M. He spent the year in over a dozen places in Vermont and Canada, and had revivals in Huntington Gore, VT, and in Farnham, P.Q. In March, 1858, he went to the Biblical School in New Hampton, N.H., preaching in the vicinity. In the fall he visited Putnam, NY and returning to Vermont in January, he began traveling as an evangelist in the Huntington Q.M. He was ordained Feb. 13, 1859, by the Q.M. at West Berlin. In May, his health improving, he returned to the New Hampton Biblical School.

Joseph W Jackson
Birth:
1839
Richland
Kalamazoo County, Michigan
Death:
Sep. 13, 1865
Hinesburg
Chittenden County, Vermont
Burial:
Rhode Island Corners Cemetery
Hinesburg, Chittenden
County, Vermont

He was born in Richland, Kalamazoo County, Mich., and moved with his father to Starksborough, Vt., at the age of ten. Brought up in a Christian home, he found Christ at seventeen and soon joined the church. He began, after hesitation, his ministry in 1861. At the September session of the Huntington Q. M. he was licensed, and in the spring of 1862 he settled with the Middlesex church. The coming summer he preached half of the time in Lincoln, where a church was organized and a house of worship built. The following December he was ordained as pastor of this church. In April, 1863, he gave half of his time to the Starksborough church, and continued pastor of both churches till his death.

Alanson Kilburn
Birth:
1786
Litchfield, Connecticut
Death:
Oct. 28, 1855
Vermont
Burial:
Enosburgh Center Cemetery
Enosburg Center
Franklin County, Vermont

When he was two years of age, his father in family moved to Castleton, Vermont. At 18 he went to New Haven, Vermont where he remained about three years. During this period he was converted and joined the Methodist Church where he became a class leader. After which, he moved to Dunham, Quebec, where he united with the Wesley Methodist and continued as class leader and received a license to exhort. He labored there are under the direction of English missionaries until 1825, when he joined the Free Baptist Church in farnham, Quebec. On April 9, 1826, he was ordained by a Council of the Enosburg Quarterly Meeting. Here he labored for five more years until his death came from Palsy which greatly impaired his speech.

George King
Birth:
Dec. 16, 1815
Orange County, Vermont
Death:
Nov. 1, 1872
Sutton
Caledonia County, Vermont
Burial:
Sutton Village Cemetery
Sutton, Caledonia County,
Vermont

When about twelve years of age, he was converted and united with the church in Topsham, Vt. He was licensed in 1850, and ordained at Goshen Gore, Oct. I, 1856, at the age of forty. He preached as an evangelist in Eden, Craftsbury, Albany and many other towns. In some places he witnessed many conversions. His last pastorate was at South Wheelock. He purchased a farm in Sutton, on which he lived the remainder of his life. He still preached occasionally in destitute places. He saw all of his large family of children converted before his death, and gave liberally for the support of the benevolent causes of the denomination.he He was the son of George and Mehitable Noyes King. He married 1st Diana Darling on Oct.13,1811 in Corinth,Vt.and 2nd Rebekah Burbank on Sep.29,1845 in Washington,Vt.

Live every day so as not to be afraid of tomorrow

Nathaniel King
Birth:
Apr. 4, 1767
Hampstead,
Rockingham County,
New Hampshire
Death:
Oct. 18, 1852
Northfield,
Washington County, Vermont
Burial:
Mount Hope Cemetery,
Northfield,
Washington County, Vermont

As a early Father of the Denomination, history states he moved with his father at the age of eight to Sutton, NH, where he resided till he was twenty-one. He then visited Turnbridge, VT and purchased a tract of land which he soon began to improve. In 1794, he married Miss Lydia Noyes, and for fifty-eight years. Early in 1799, Daniel Batchelder and Nathaniel Brown held meetings in Turnbridge, and in the revival which followed Nathaniel King was converted March 31, 1799. A church was soon after organized. At Bro. King's house the persecuted Free Baptist preachers found a refuge and home. He himself soon began to conduct meetings. July 1, 1804, he was ordained in the Turnbridge church by Rev's. John and Aaron Buzzell, and Pelatiah Tingley. He was active in meetings and revivals and saw many people added. His labors were not

confined to his own parish. For forty-two years he served the Turnbridge church, for seven, the Randolph church and for fourteen the Northfield. He held offices of trust and confidence. For thirteen years he represented Turnbridge in the Legislature of the state. In 1811 he visited, in company with Rev. John Buzzell, churches in central Vermont. The same year he added thirty-two to his church. That year his Y.M., appointed him to collect funds for the poor. In 1819, he with two others crossed the Green Mountains, and organized the Huntington Q.M. In 1821, he was elected president of the Vermont Charitable Society at its organization. Benevolence was a leading trait of his character. He gave $100 for endowment of Biblical School at Whitestown, NY; $150 for the Bible cause; $350 for Missions and other benevolent purposes. He was interested in the anti-slavery movement. He was moderator of the second General Conference. Near the end of his life he repeatedly assured his friends that the doctrine he had preached for more than half a century sustained him in the time of trial.

Samuel Lord
Birth:
1780
Barnstead, New Hampshire
Death:
Dec. 27, 1849
Waterbury, Vermont
Burial:
Waterbury Center Cemetery
OldWaterbury Center
Washington County, Vermont

He accepts religion when but 10 years of age and entered the ministry in his 19th year. He was ordained in Maine in 1801 and the same year moved to Vermont and was among the earliest founders of the denomination in that state. He was active in organizing many churches and in the saving of souls.

John Moxley
Birth:
unknown
Death:
Sep. 7, 1884, USA
Burial:
Hutchinson Cemetery
East Orange
Orange County, Vermont

As a young man he felt call to the ministry but did not accept that call. He served his town as Selectman, Justice Of The Peace, and a representative to the legislature. At the age of 55 years great sorrowed over the death of his two children led him to consecrate himself to the ministry. He was ordained at the session of the Strafford Quarterly Meeting on June 24, 1871. He later served many churches in that region. He also worked successfully with the Y.M.C.A. He was also clerk of the Stafford Quarterly Meeting for 15 years and was a delegate from Vermont yearly meeting to the Gen. conference in Fairport, New York.

Jonathan Nelson
Birth:
1777
Barnstead, New Hampshire
Death:
Nov. 26, 1843
Burial:
Old Wheelock Village Cemetery
Wheelock
Caledonia County, Vermont

At the age of twenty-five married there Miss Betsey Collins. He did much hard work on a farm and reared a family of nine children, yet he found time to do public service for the Lord's people. Converted at the age of twenty-eight, he was baptized and joined the Methodists, by whom he was licensed to preach. He settled in Wheelock, Vermont, and was ordained by the Freewill Baptist Wheelock Quarterly Meeting in 1819. He served for years the churches of that section. In the great revival of 1823 he baptized sixty or seventy. In 1841, he went into Lower Canada, where he was stricken with fever, and lived long enough to send for his wife and two sons.He died in his 67th year, and was carried to Wheelock for funeral services and burial. He possessed sound judgment, was well versed in the Scriptures, and was hospitable and benevolent.

J. M. Nelson
Birth:
Feb. 20, 1822
Hardwick, Vermont
Death:
Jul. 29, 1895

He was a student at Peachham Academy. Converted in 1854, he received his license by the Wheelock quarterly Meeting two years later and in 1861 was ordained by the Enosburgh Quarterly Meeting. His ministry was basically within Vermont.

David Norris
Birth:
unknown
North Danville, Vermont
Death:
Nov. 21, 1839
Burial:
Stanton Cemetery
North Danville
Caledonia County, Vermont

He was aged 71 at his death and for 47 years had been a Christian and Free Will Baptist Minister.
Inscription:
age 71 yrs
He was the son of Samuel Norris 1734-1816 and Huldah Bartlett 1734-1780

John Calvin Osgood
Birth:
Feb. 14, 1841
East Randolph
Orange County, Vermont
Death:
Jul. 14, 1907
Burial:
East Randolph Cemetery
East Randolph
Orange County, Vermont

He was the son of Dea. William and Almira (Dibbell) Osgood.He served in the military from Vermont in the Civil War.He married Miss Mary G. Flanders, July 15, 1868, and had one son living, Ernest Erle Osgood, who became a clergyman, and is buried in Virginia.He was an ordained Freewill Baptist clergyman. He became a Christian when about nineteen years of age.

He received his preparatory education at New Hampton Institution, and graduated from the Theological School in 1868. He was licensed by the Strafford Quarterly Meeting, while a student, and was ordained at Gilmanton Iron Works, N.H., in the fall of 1868, by Rev's E.P. Ladd, A.D. Smith, J.M. Durgin, and others. He was pastor at Gilmanton Iron Works, Natick, Mass, Contoocook and Pittsfield, N.H., South Strafford, VT, Springvale, ME, and in 1887 pastor of the church at South Berwick, ME. He has had success and conversions in his pastorates, and has baptized about sixty converts.

Benjamin Page
Birth:
Jun. 9, 1780
Death:
Nov. 9, 1869
Burial:
Pleasant View Cemetery
Ludlow
Windsor County, Vermont

He was ordained in 1803 in Vermont. For some years he worked with the Hardwick Quarterly Meeting and his ministry prospered. Becoming alienated from his brethren, he confessed that for three years did not feel right, nor added a single member to his church. From general loving treatment he felt better. He joined the Christian order later, but at the January quarterly meeting in 1823 he returned making a confession for an satisfactory. Then preached to a deeply interested people a sermon that was full of power.

Charles Sumner Perkins
Birth:
October 25, 1836
Walden
Caledonia County, Vermont
Death:
Aug. 3, 1909
Walden
Caledonia County, Vermont
Burial:
South Walden Cemetery
South Walden
Caledonia County, Vermont

He prepared for college at the Lewiston Falls Academy, in Auburn; graduating from Bowdoin college in 1860 and from Bangor Theological Seminary in 1864. He became a Christian in 1857 was licensed by the Bowdoin Quarterly Meeting in 1863 and ordained by a Council of the same body on October 6, 1864. After his graduation from the theological Seminary he supplied the Free Baptist Church in New York City for one year, then in 1865-66 he supplied the Roger Williams church, Providence, Rhode Island in the absence of Dr. George Day. During the year his labors were rewarded with nearly 100 conversion. Afterwards, he became pastor of the Park Street church, Providence for six years the church and led it to reorganize, its location change from N. Main St. and the present location on Park Street. After pastoring in Rhode Island, he spent time in Portland Maine and then Boston, Massachusetts. He then became pastor of eight church in Lyndon Ctr., Vermont where he baptized

over 200 people. He held numerous denominational positions. He was the record and corresponding secretary of the Foreign Mission Society, member of the foreign mission and home mission boards, on the executive committee of these and the education society, overseer of Bates College and member of four Gen. conferences. He married on November 30, 1864 to Mary Murray of Brunswick, Maine. Children:

Daniel Quimby
Birth:
Dec. 26, 1773
Weare,Hillsborough County
New Hampshire
Death:
Nov. 29, 1850
Lyndon, Caledonia County
Vermont
Burial:
Lyndon Center Cemetery
Lyndon, Caledonia County
Vermont

A document (deed) of land sold to Daniel Quimby on February 1, 1815 for $440 which was the middle third (110 acres) of the original tract of land bought by Jeremiah Olney, Lot #62, in Lyndon, in the County of Caledonia in the State of Vermont. The location of this piece of property was not in town but north of the village near Burke. According to a researcher from Lyndonville, VT, "an old book in

Sutton, VT mentions the ordination of Brother Daniel Quimby as an Evangelist. Joshua Quimby gave the charge on September 16, 1819. Several books mention his name as a pastor, minister, leader in the FWB Randall movement. He was an esteemed man and loved.

Rev. Daniel died in Lyndon 29 November 1850 (says the Free Baptist Cyclopedia, p. 550); "Rev. Jonathan Woodman preached his funeral sermon."

Fernando Randall
Birth:
1831
Death:
Mar. 22, 1880
Bulwer, Québec, Canada
Burial:
Lyndon Center Cemetery
Lyndon
Caledonia County, Vermont

He was converted and baptized while in the Army and for over year he was a chaplain. After being in business for a time. He answered the call to the ministry, and was ordained by a Council at the Wheelock Quarterly Meeting on February 17, 1870 at Newark. He was a member of the Lyndon Vermont church and labored with good success. In June, 1878, he went to Bulwer and built up a strong and thriving church and brought in valuable members. He was greatly beloved.Note: *He was a captain in Co. G 7th Vt. Vol.

Ophir Shipman
Birth:
Jan. 25, 1801
Washington
Orange County, Vermont
Death:
Oct. 10, 1874
West Topsham
Orange County, Vermont
Burial:
West Topsham Cemetery
West Topsham
Orange County, Vermont

Rev. Ophir Shipman, died at age 73 years. He was converted in 1829, was baptized by Rev. Timothy Mores, and united with the church in Northfield. After three years the church called a council which ordained him June 10, 1832. He continued pastor of this church seven years. He has since had pastorates at West Topsham, West Fairlee, Williamstown, and Middlesex. He also labored as an evangelist in different parts of the state. A few years before his death he moved to West Topsham in failing health, and purchased a home.

S. W. Stiles
Birth:
Sept. 26,1827
Danville, Vt
Death:
Aug. 26, 1877
Newport Centre, Vt.
Burial:
Pine Grove Cemetery
Newport, Orleans County,
Vermont

S. W. was a brother of Rev. Horace Stiles, At the age of sixteen he became a Christian and felt called to preach when twenty-one. Ten years later he began his ministry, giving a part of his property for the Master's use, as a thank offering. His first efforts at Hyde Park in December, 1845, resulted in many conversions. The next month he was licensed by the wheelock Q. M. He was ordained the following June. He served the churches in Newark, South Barton, Glover Centre and Sheffield. At Newton Centre he toiled hard, and a house of

worship was built. He was taken with hemorrhage of the lungs, but kept at work and concealed his suffering still two weeks before his death. He was a sympathetic and faithful pastor.

Joshua Tucker
Birth:
Jun. 20, 1800
Leicester, Worcester County,
Massachusetts
Death:
Aug. 7, 1877
Lincoln, Addison County,Vermont
Burial:
Green Mount Cemetery
Starksboro, Addison
County,Vermont

Tucker died at aged 77 years.He was converted in 1829, baptized by Rev. Stephen Leavitt, and united with the church in Washington, Vt. He soon began to preach, and was ordained in Williamstown in 1835 as pastor of the church there. He held this pastorate most of the time for ten years, during which more than fifty were added to the church. After 1845 he lived and preached most of the time within the limits of the Huntington Q. M. He was pastor at Starksboro' and other places. He was successful as an evangelist and was highly esteemed by all who knew him.

Jonathan Woodman
Birth:
Mar. 27, 1798
Wheelock,
Caledonia County, Vermont
Death:
Jan. 18, 1888
North Tewksbury,
Middlesex County,
Massachusetts
Burial:
Sutton Village Cemetery,
Sutton,
Caledonia County, Vermont

A Noted Free Will Baptist Minister. At age 17, he was in "trials of his mind regarding his duty to preach" when he met Daniel Quimby, who gave him relief, and Jonathan began a lifetime of useful labors. He was soon after licensed by the Sutton Free Will Baptist Church. In summer of 1816, he crossed NH on foot to attend the meeting of the NH Yearly Meeting at Parsonfield, ME. He offered to care for the horses at the meeting, and was admitted for entertainment to the house of Eld. John Buzzell. Multitudes assembled which the meeting house could not hold. Finally Sunday came, Eld. John Buzzell arose, but after a few words he confessed, "brethren, I have not got the word; if anyone has it, let him stand forth." Immediately the Vermont boy, trembling by the pulpit stairs, and the burden of God upon his soul, arose to his feet and began to deliver his message. Then Eld. Buzzell said, "Hold on lad!" rising in his pulpit. "Brethren, shove some planks out of the window and give the boy a chance." They removed one of the side windows, made him a platform where he could stand and preach to the throng outside as well as the multitude within the house. His text, "the spirit of the Lord is upon me, because He hath anointed me to preach good tidings unto the meek." He poured forth his message; strong men wept, sinners trembled, and confessed, and there was not a day like that in the history of that church. And when in after time, candidates for baptism were examined, more than a hundred dated their conviction for sin and beginning of a life of consecration from the sermon of that day. Jonathan Woodman was ordained in 1818 at age twenty, as pastor of the Effingham, N.H. church. In 1825, he was one of the nine who perfected plans and bore the financial responsibility for the publication of *"The Morning Star."* He suggested the name for the paper and rode forty miles through the mud to purchase the paper for the first issue. For two years he was one of the proprietors of the Printing Establishment, for seven years a trustee, and for 31 years a corporator. He became the first president of the Anti-Slavery Society in 1843. For two terms he sat in the Vermont Legislature. In 1828 he was chaplain to that body. In 1848, he was chosen by the FWB Gen. Conference to be a delegate along with another minister, to England's General Baptist Conference, and while away kept a diary of his travels, which diary is now in Bates College Edmund Muskie Archives and Special Collections, Lewiston, ME., He was a powerful and acceptable preacher, especially gifted in prayer, mighty in the Scriptures, a man of blameless life, a Christian eminently spiritual and cheerful. The whole denomination looked up to him with reverence.

Virginia

Hobert Monroe Addington
Birth:
Apr. 11, 1919
Wise,
Wise County, Virginia
Death:
Oct. 6, 2008
Wise,
Wise County, Virginia
Burial:
Wise Cemetery, Wise,
Wise County, Virginia

Rev. Hobert Monroe Addington lived to the age of 89. He was a member of the Esserville Freewill Baptist Church, a pastor for several Freewill Baptist churches in the area, a member of the UMWA and was an employee of Old Ben Coal Co. for over 33 years.

Howard T Bostic
Birth:
May 31, 1905
Swords Creek,
Russell County, Virginia
Death:
Jul. 4, 1987
Swords Creek,
Russell County,Virginia
Burial:
Bostic Call Cemetery,
Swords Creek
,Russell County, Virginia

Missionary Zalene Lloyd Breeden
Birth:
Jun. 22, 1916 Durham, Durham County,
North Carolina
Death:
Dec. 14, 2004
Buena Vista, Rockbridge County, Virginia
Burial: Green Hill Cemetery, Buena Vista,
Rockbridge County, Virginia

At the age of 32, and single, she boarded with Dan and Trula Cronk on August 8, 1948 for India assigned by the Free Will Baptists missionary board to work with Laura Belle Barnard who had been in India several years. Midway through her term she resigned as a Free Will Baptist missionary and to work for Dr. Graham's homes in Kalimpong, West Bengal, situated in the Himalayan foothills in Northeast India. On her return back to the United States another classmate Marie Hanna and her husband were beginning their service in India.

On November 27, 1954, she married Robert F. Breeden, to whom she would become a devoted wife, mother, homemaker and pastor's wife. Afterwards, serving as a home missionary and pastor's wife in North Carolina, New Jersey, Alaska, New Hampshire, Maine, Wisconsin, Tennessee and Virginia. They celebrated their 50th wedding anniversary on November 27, 2004.

She was a graduate of Free Will Baptist Bible college in Nashville, Tennessee and Nyack college, Nyack, New York.

Gird Ashby Cave
Birth:
Mar. 16, 1884
Madison County
Virginia
Death:
Jul. 10, 1972
Burial:
Victory Baptist Church Cemetery
Comertown
Page County, Virginia

Rev. Gird Ashby Cave, 88, of Comertown died at home after a lingering illness. He had been a frequent patient in Harrisonburg and Luray hospitals. Mr. Cave was a preacher at Comertown's Independent Church and a country store merchant 35 years in Comertown. He was well-known throughout the county as a preacher, frequently heard on local radio stations and conducting street corner services in Luray. He was a son of the late John Isaac and Mary Katherine Offenbacker Cave. His wife the former Dorothy Ann Thomas. The couple celebrated their 67th wedding anniversay Dec 26.

John A Cave
Birth:
1812
Death:
Nov., 1899
Burial:
Calvin H Cave Cemetery
Mauck
Page County, Virginia

He was an early minister in

Virginia. His Wife was Mary Ann Phillips Cave who he married on August 31, 1835 in Virginia.

Waymond Larson Cave, Sr
Birth:
Aug. 4, 1933
Death:
Jan. 24, 1994
Burial:
Victory Baptist Church Cemetery
Comertown
Page County, Virginia

Rev. Cave died at age 60. He was pastor of the Comertown FWB Church in Shenandoah. He was ordained in Nov. 1, 1969. He was the co-founder of the Comertown church where he pastored for 25 years until his health failed. He played the guitar and sang gospel songs with his father and much of his encouragement came from his grandfather, Rev. G.A. Cave who gave the property for the church and who preached for 67 years before his death. His parents were Ralph William Cave and Elsie Lillian Breeden Cave.

John Colby
Birth:
Dec. 10, 1787
Death:
Nov. 30, 1817
Burial:
Saint Paul's Episcopal Churchyard, Norfolk, Norfolk City, Virginia

At age 30 Years he died while on a long preaching trip to Ohio and was on his way back home to Vermont. He died in Norfork, Va. is in buried in a quaint gravesite near the Episcopal Church. His ministry, while short, touched many lives and many came to Christ a list of ministers accepted the call to preach became of him. A memorial to him is in the Sutton Village cemetery at Sutton, Vermont. He was a very talented rising star and mourned by his denomination when he died. A autobiography of his life was written and published by Free Will Baptists.

Albert Dingus
Birth:
Mar. 3, 1945
Death:
Feb. 25, 2008
Burial:
Laurel Grove Cemetery,
Norton,
Wise County, Virginia

He bgan preaching in October 1927 with Ben and Wade Powers at the FWB church on Mudtown Hill in Jenkins, Kentucky. He was ordained on April 21, 1928. He and 8 other believers organized the Burdine Free Will Baptist Church in Jenkins. For over 56 years he was the faithful and loving pastor of that church. His ledger contained more than a 1000 names of those he baptized, married and held funeral. In 1936 he was instrumental in organizing the Letcher County Conference of FWB which united with the John Thomas Association. More that 50 men surrendered to preach under his ministry. At a Bible Conference held at FWBBC in Nashville, Tenn. in 1982, he was asked to stand and was acknowledged as one of the outstanding pastors among Free Will Baptists.

Robert Aston Dingus
Birth:
Jul. 13, 1883
Virginia
Death:

Feb. 21, 1951
Virginia
Burial:
Sabras Chapel Cemetery,
Dungannon,
Scott County, Virginia
World War I Draft

Harley Graham Dye, Sr
Birth:
Sep. 30, 1903
Swords Creek
Russell County, Virginia
Death:
Oct. 25, 1993
Oak Ridge
Anderson County, Tennessee
Burial:
Greenhills Memory Gardens
Claypool Hill
Tazewell County, Virginia

He was a FWB preacher for 45 years conducting revivals and pastor numerous churches in the John-Thomas Association. He served on the New Durm Ordaining Council was a member and Honorary Pastor of the East Lebanon FWB church.

James Edward Dye
Birth:
Jun. 16, 1921
Drill
Russell County, Virginia
Death:
Nov. 5, 2011

Oakwood
Buchanan County, Virginia
Burial:
Haywood Wilson Cemetery
Swords Creek
Russell County, Virginia

Rev. James Edward Dye, age , 90, spent his early life in Drill, moving to Buchanan County in 1940. A United States Army veteran, serving serving in Europe during World War II. A retired coal miner, And a member of UMWA Local 2372 in Jewell Valley. He was a member of Guiding Light Free Will Baptist

Church and had been a minister for over 60 years In the John-Thomas Association. Military honors were conducted by VFW Post 9864 of Lebanon, Virginia.

Finas "Bud" Arlin Hill
Birth:
Nov. 22, 1936
Death:
Aug. 10, 2002
Burial:
Hill Family Cemetery
Haysi
Dickenson County,Virginia

He was a minister in the Dickenson County Conference Of the John-Thomas Association, for 22 years. He was a member of Splashdam Freewill Baptist Church in Haysi and Pastor of Phillips Chapel freewill Baptist Church in West Dante.He worked for Chevrolet's Warren, Mich., plant for 14 years, a member of UAW Local No. 909. He worked for Island Creek Coal Comoany's No. 1 mine for 19 years and was a member of UMWA Local No. 1509.

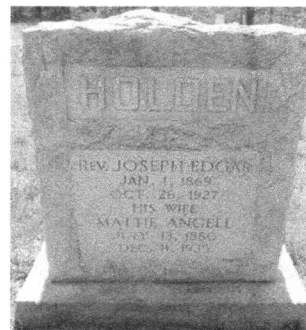

Joseph Edgar Holden
Birth:
Jan. 1, 1869
Death:
Oct. 26, 1927
Burial:
Mayo Baptist Church Cemetery
Spencer
Henry County, Virginia
He was a member of the John Wheeler Association which helped its seventh anniversary on

September 1, 1887 this Association had churches or were located in the extreme northwest part of North Carolina and the northeast part of Tennessee, with his territory extending northward even into Virginia. Rev. Holden was a member of this large body of Free Will Baptists.

Monroe Hubbard
Birth:
Dec. 4, 1883
Death:
Apr. 10, 1977
Burial:
Dewey Memorial Cemetery,
Wise County, Virginia

Ezra Johnson
Birth:
Feb. 19, 1916
Dickenson County, Virginia
Death:
Dec. 19, 1986
Burial:
Dewey Memorial Cemetery
Wise County, Virginia

He was a Free Will Baptist Preacher For Almost 50 Years And He Loved To sing and taught sing and to anyone who wanted to learn. He taught all of his children to sing and he baptized and married six of them.

Emmett J Kilgore, Jr
Birth:
Aug. 8, 1914
Death:
Nov. 12, 2001
Burial:
Greenwood Memorial Gardens,
Coeburn, Wise County, Virginia

Kyle Wilson Hubbard
Birth:
1902
Death:
March 4, 1990
Bristol, Virginia
Burial:
Russell Memorial Cemetery
Lebanon
Russell County, Virginia

He was a faithful member of the Tunnel Hlll Free Will Baptist Church where he was ordained into the ministry in The John-Thomas Association, November, 1940 at this church and at the time of his death was the pastor emeritus.

Harold Kilgore
Birth:
Feb. 13, 1931
Death:
Dec. 4, 1999
Wise,
Wise County, Virginia
Burial:
Wise Cemetery, Wise
Wise County, Virginia

He was a bi-vocational Free Will Baptist minister and was a book keeper for a large mining concern. His two sons also became FWB ministers as well.

James Patton Lambert
Birth:
Oct. 25, 1904
Death:
Mar. 11, 1983
Abingdon
Washington County, Virginia
Burial:
Sullivan Cemetery
Bee
Dickenson County, Virginia

He was a FWB and a member of the John-Thomas Association

William Henry Large
Birth:
Dec. 30, 1861
Hawkins County, Tennessee
Death:
Sep. 10, 1951
Blountville,
Sullivan County, Tennessee
Burial:
Johnson Cemetery,
Washington County, Virginia

S. M. McFall, Sr
Birth:
Jan. 30, 1887
Death:
Jan. 8, 1977
Burial:
Kilgore Cemetery,
Banner, Wise County, Virginia
Ordained a Freewill Baptist
Minister, in Nov 1910 by Elders
W. R. Stallard, Cain Counts, and
John Pennel.

Vester McKinney
Birth:
Nov. 15, 1901
Death:
Mar. 21, 1989
Tazewell County, Virginia
Burial:
Ramsey Cemetery
Clinchco
Dickenson County, Virginia

He was a former employee of the
WM Ritter lumber company, a
retired coal miner, a minister of
the Free Will Baptist
denomination for 45 years In the
John-Thomas Association, and a
United States Army veteran.

Ersel McPeek
Birth:
Oct. 17, 1908
Death:
Sep. 18, 1994
Burial:
Dewey Memorial Cemetery
Wise County,Virginia

He was a member of the
John-Thomas Assn. and a FWB
preacher.

STORE UP YOUR TREASURES IN HEAVEN

Daniel James Merkh, Sr
Birth:
1928
Death:
Apr. 12, 2002
Burial:
Holly Lawn Cemetery,
Suffolk, Suffolk City, Virginia

He was a student at the Free Will
Baptist Bible college in Nashville,
Tennessee and after his
graduation he and his wife,
Margaret, were commissioned in
1957 as missionaries. Rev. Merkh
and family spent one year in
Lausanne, Switzerland to learn
the French language, four years in
the Ivory Coast of West Africa and
nine and a half years in France as
missionaries. After these times of
service they retired from foreign
mission service in 1975. He was
both a teacher and church planter
on the mission field Rev. Merkh, a
native of Camden, N.J., also served
as a pastor in Tennessee, South
Carolina and Virginia for 20 years
and lastly serving the First Free
Will Baptist Church in, Richmond,
Virginia where he retired. He was
a member of Ryanwood Free Will
Baptist Church, Vero Beach,
Florida., and a veteran of the U.S.
Marines during World War II.

Missionary Margaret Lucille
Johnson **Merkh**
Birth:
Jan. 29, 1930
Death:
Feb. 21, 2012
Burial:
Holly Lawn Cemetery
Suffolk Suffolk City, Virginia,

She was predeceased by her
husband of 54 years, Rev. Daniel
James Merkh, Sr. Rev. Merkh,
Margaret, and family spent one
year in Lausanne, Switzerland to
learn the French language, four
years in the Ivory Coast of West
Africa, and nine and half years in
France as missionaries. After
returning to the United States,
Margaret later went on to work
and retired as an executive
secretary for Dominion Power.
She was a member of the Free
Will Baptist Church in Carrollton,
Virginia.

Ben Powers
Birth:
unknown
Death:
1983
Virginia
Burial:
Temple Hill Memorial Park
Castlewood
Russell County, Virginia

His lineage was from a circuit
riding Methodist preacher
background. He helped organize
23 Free Will Baptist Churches in
the 1940's in Wise County, Va. and
portions of Kentucky. He and his
brother Wade Powers were used
in numerous revivals in

surrounding counties. They would stay with people in the community for two to three weeks at a time, from house to house, and then preach revivals during the evening hours. They would receive poundings of food items as honorariums.

David D. Powers, Sr
Birth:
Jul. 17, 1920
Death:
Sep. 3, 1993
Burial:
Laurel Grove Cemetery,
Norton, Wise County, Virginia

Inscription: PFC US Army World War II

A man's dying is more the survivors' affair than his own.

R Harlis Powers
Birth:
Jun. 26, 1855
Scott County, Virginia
Death:
Jan. 14, 1922
Wise County, Virginia
Burial:
Round Top Cemetery,
Wise, Wise County, Virginia

Wade H Powers, Sr
Birth:
1894
Death:
1970
Burial:
Perry Cemetery,
Wise, Wise County, Virginia

He and his brother Ben Powers were used in numerous revivals in surrounding counties. He preached as far as Louisa, Kentucky. They would stay with people in the community for two to three weeks at a time, from house to house and then preach revivals during the evening hours.

Eli E. Reedy
Birth:
1879
Death:
1950
Burial:
Clinch Valley Memorial Cemetery
and Mausoleum,
Richlands,
Tazewell County, Virginia

Howard Reynolds
Birth:
Mar. 29, 1925
Russell County, Virginia
Death:
Dec. 19, 2007
Lebanon
Russell County, Virginia
Burial:

Reynolds Family Cemetery
Honaker
Russell County, Virginia

Reynolds, 82,of Honaker, was a lifelong resident of Russell County, and a member and pastor of Tunnell Hill Freewill Baptist Church for 14 years in the John-Thomas Association.

George Wythe Salyers
Birth:
Aug. 1, 1918
Death:
Jan. 4, 1986
Burial:
Rugsby Church Cemetery
Dickenson County, Virginia

He was a member of the Rachel Chapel Free Will Baptist Church and a minister for 25 years. He served on the ordaining Council for 15 years and served as pastor of the Yates Chapel church for 24 years. He was a veteran of World War II having served in the United States Army.

Glen W Stevens
Birth:
May 7, 1917
Virginia
Death:

May 21, 1988
Virginia
Burial:
Bowen Cemetery
Russell County, Virginia

He was a retired coal miner and a member of the Mt. View Freewill Baptist church on Combs Ridge. He was a Free Will Baptist minister With the John-Thomas Association.

Roy C. Vanover
Birth:
Dec. 5, 1918
Death:
Mar. 25, 2003
Burial:
Powell Valley Memorial Gardens
Big Stone Gap
Wise County, Virginia

He was called to preach in September 24, 1968 and was ordained on October 25, 1969. He served as pastor of the Pyles Memorial, Ferbie Chapel, and Lone Pine Chapel Of the John-Thomas Association. He was very active in many of the churches throughout the area in his preaching, singing and praying. He was a member of the Lone Pine Chapel. In his early years he sang with the Friendly Four Quartet. He was a member of that Dickenson County conference and was a member of this ordaining Council. He served on the Board of Directors also for

Camp Jacob. He worked in the coal mines for 39 years and was a member of the UWMA union. He retired from Bethlehem Steel at the age of 55.

Ralph Edward Vicars
Birth:
unknown
Death:
Mar. 29, 2009
Norton, Wise County, Virginia
Burial:
Wise Cemetery
Wise, Wise County, Virginia

He was the pastor of the Burdine Free Will Baptist church.

Ralph Lee Weaver
Birth:
Nov. 10, 1915
Kannapolis
Cabarrus County, North Carolina
Death:
Oct. 21, 1992
Durham
Durham County, North Carolina
Burial:
Roselawn Burial Park
Martinsville
Martinsville, Virginia
Plot: 16-245

Rev. Ralph Lee Weaver, 76-year-old pastor of Woodland Heights Free Will Baptist Church, Martinsville, VA, since 1948, died from complications of bypass heart surgery in Duke University Hospital, Durham, NC. He preached his last sermon Sunday morning, Sept. 27th, after suffering chest pains all night.

Weaver was the son of Ira Samuel and Margaret Ada (Bullard) Weaver, one of several children.Rev. Weaver served as moderator of the Maryland Association, and was a life member o f the Martinsville/Henry Co. Rescue Squad where he served as as chaplain.His long ministry at Woodland Heights began in 1948, with 12 members where he built the membership until the congregation outgrew their facility and purchased land in 1956 and began a building program in 1959, on the present location.Rev. Weaver was graduated from Martinsville Bible College and attended Patrick Henry Community College.

Harry Paul Whitaker
Birth:
Jul. 27, 1922
Bostic
Rutherford County, North Carolina
Death:
Mar. 29, 1994
Russell County, Virginia
Burial:
Temple Hill Memorial Park
Castlewood
Russell County, Virginia

He entered the ministry in 1955 and was ordained as a Free Will Baptist minister In the John Thomas Association on November 30, 1957. He dedicated 40 years serving the Straight Hollow Free Will Baptist where he pastored for 22 years.

Washington

Charles Henry Alborn
Birth:
Jul. 14, 1870
Blue Earth, MN
Death:
Feb. 27, 1936
Burial:
Sumner Cemetery
Sumner, Pierce County,
Washington

He accepted the Lord Jesus Christ in a little Methodist church in 1887. Taught his first school 1890-1891 in the Stormy Creek School, Eagle Bend, Minnesota. He also preached his first sermon at that school. He taught at Spruce Hill school 1891-1892 also near Eagle Bend, Minnesota. Charles Married Clara Kyes at Eagle Bend, Minnesota November 26, 1892. Charles, with a man named Joe Carter built a United Brethren Church in Eagle Bend, Minnesota and he was licensed to preach after the church was organized. Charles and Clara lived in a little log house he built in Eagle Bend. They lived in that house until they moved to Wood Lake, Minnesota in the summer of 1893. Then they moved back to Eagle Bend in the same fall for school again. Here is where their first child was born (Everett Robert) on September 2, 1893. For the next school year he taught the Kohlhouse School near Bertha, Minnesota in Todd County 1893-1894. He taught summer school in the Carter district 1894 then taught in the same school 1895-1896. Lizzie Rebecca was born November 7, 1895 in Eagle Bend. He taught in the Coon school house 1896-97. Their 3rd child Jay Dewey was born on March 12, 1898. Their fourth child, Gladys Ellen was orn October 7, 1899 and she died October 14, 1900. They moved to Gray Eagle, Minnesota where he also taught school there in 1901 and 1902. Evan William was born here July 7, 1901. From here they moved to Hewitt, Minnesota and he taught school there and also pastored a United Brethren church in Wrightstown a few miles out of Hewitt 1902-03. Philip William was born in Hewitt, MN on June 13, 1903. Floyd Wayne was also born in Hewitt March 26, 1905. In June 1905, they moved to Glenville, MN and he pastored a United Bretheren Church June 1905 and this is where on September 4, 1906 Lila Ruth was born. In October 1906 they moved to Myrtle, MN to pastor a United Brethren Church until the autumn of 1908 when they moved to London, MN where he built and pastored the United Brethren Church until the autumn of 1909. They then moved back to Glenville, MN where Nettie May was born September 29, 1909. They moved in June of 1910 to Winneconnie, WI and until the spring of 1911 he pastored the Free Will Baptist Church there. They moved to Wyocena, WI where Edith Adell was born June 4, 1911. He pastored the Baptist Church of Wyocena until 1913 when he started to pastor the Hillsdale, WI church. Around this time he served a church out in West Dallas, driving a team out from Wyocena for a little time. Having moved to Barron, WI, From the fall of 1921 until the fall of 1922 Charles pastored the Colville, WA Baptist church. June 1932. he moved to Sumner, WA to pastor the Sumner Baptist church until his death.

Inscription:
In Memory Of
Romans 8:28

Lewis Woodbury Gowen
Birth:
Apr. 15, 1850
Sanford,
York County, Maine
Death:
Jun. 9, 1935
Waitsburg,
Walla, Walla County,
Washington
Burial:
IOOF Cemetery,
Waitsburg,
Walla Walla County,
Washington,
Plot: Block 32B; Lot 3; Space 5

On 1 June 1873 he entered the ministry and 3 June 1876 was ordained a minister of the Free Baptist denomination at Ossipee in Carroll County, New Hampshire. In 1881 he graduated from the theological department of Bates College at Lewiston, Androscoggin County, Maine. He preached at Effingham in New Hampshire; Parsonsfield, Milo, and LaGrange in Maine; Cape Sable Island in Nova Scotia; and Evansville in Wisconsin. Sometime after 1883 Lewis brought his family west in a wagon train, driving a 'hack' [a short bed wagon with a rounded canvas dome top]. On a good day they traveled 20 miles, driving from sun-up to sun-down. About 1885 he accepted a call to the Baptist Church at Alexandria in Nebraska. While serving as Pastor of at Boise, Idaho he helped raise funds to build a church. The name 'Reverend L. W. Gowen' is printed in one of the stained glass windows. After holding a number of pastorates in the east and middle west, he accepted a call to the First Baptist Church at Boise, Idaho in 1888; afterwards serving in Pullman, Caldwell, Emmett, and, Weiser. Because of failing eyesight he gave up the active ministry in 1898 when he and Mrs. Gowen began work as colporters for the American Baptist Publication Society serving in Southern Idaho and Western Oregon. For over 13 years they covered this territory distributing Bibles and religious literature, organizing churches and Sunday Schools in neglected districts. In 1911 they retired because of Mr. Gowen's eyesight and moved to Waitsburg. He was totally blind for the last ten years of his life but learned to read with two sets of raised print systems and spent the last years of his life with his Bible.

Inscription:
'Rev.' LEWIS W. GOWEN
April 15, 1850 - June 9, 1935
'Minister of the gospel'

He said no one comes to the Father except through Him;

Benjamin F Paul
Birth:
Jul. 27, 1867
North Norwich, New York
Death:
Jan. 23, 1924
Burial:
Parkland Evangelical Lutheran
Cemetery
Tacoma
Pierce County, Washington

He studied that the Cortland Normal School, New York and was converted in April, 1885, and was licensed to preach by the McDonough Quarterly Meeting

the following June. He attended Hillsdale College in Michigan for two terms, and assisted in a revival at Globleville, Michigan and was employed as the evangelist by the Wisconsin Yearly Meeting. In May 1886, he entered the pastorate of the church at Warren, Illinois and received his ordination at Wayne, Wisconsin the following month.

YOU'RE NOT GOOD ENOUGH TO MAKE IT TO HEAVEN

–AND YOU NEVER WILL BE.

PUT ON THE RIGHTEOUSNESS OF CHRIST AND TRUST HIM AS THE ONLY WAY TO ETERNAL LIFE.

West Virginia

Andrew J Adkins
Birth:
May 25, 1887
Death:
Mar. 2, 1964
Burial:
White Chapel Memorial Gardens
Barboursville
Cabell County, West Virginia
Plot: T   V Lot 111D SP 3

He was one of the early for pastors of the Union Free Will Baptist Church, Griffinsville, West Virginia which was founded in 1897 making it one of the oldest Free Will Baptist Church in West Virginia.

Dallas Carlton Adkins
Birth:
Jun. 6, 1924
Key rock, West Virginia
Death:
Aug. 20, 1992
Beckley, West Virginia
Burial:
Blue Ridge Memorial Gardens,
Prosperity,
Raleigh County, West Virginia

Rev. Adkins was a 40-year resident of Pierpoint, a member of the Beckley Conference of

Freewill Baptist Church, where he pastored for 24 years. He pastored Camp Creek Freewill Baptist Church, Ghent Freewill Baptist Church, Ury Freewill Baptist Church and Midway Freewill Baptist Church, Christiansburg, VA.

Rev. Adkins was a World War II Army veteran, chaplain and member of the Varney Cline American Legion Post No. 133 of Pineville and was second lieutenant in the Civil Air Patrol, serving as cadet leader teaching moral education. He was a member of the West Virginia Assn. Of Retired School Employees. Military graveside rites were conducted by the Varney Cline American Legion Post No. 133 of Pineville.

Roy W. Adkins
Birth:
unknown
West Virginia
Death:
Jan. 25, 2013
Logan County, West Virginia
Burial:
Highland Memory Gardens
Cemetery
Pecks Mill, Logan County,
West Virginia

Roy was born in Putnam, West Virginia and at his death at 80 lived in Whitman. He was a U.S.Army veteran, a member of the Monahill Free Will Baptist Church, and a retired salesman and ministe.

Ernold J. Barker
Birth:
Nov. 12, 1909
Death:
1974
Burial:
Barker Cemetery
Ashford
Boone County, West Virginia

Rev. Ernold Barker and Paul Barker were early ministers of the Emmons Free Will Baptist Church in West Virginia.

Paul Barker
Birth:
Jul. 7, 1895
Death:
Apr. 7, 1979
Burial:
Barker Cemetery
Ashford
Boone County,West Virginia

Rev. Ernold Barker and Paul Barker were early ministers of the Emmons Free Will Baptist Church in West Virginia.

Nathan Cook Brackett
Birth:
Jul. 28, 1826
Phillips Corner
Somerset County, Maine
Death:
Jul. 20, 1910
Burial:
Harpers Cemetery
Harpers Ferry, Jefferson County,
West Virginia

Founder of Storer College, Nathan Cook Brackett (July 28, 1836-July 20, 1910) was born in Phillips, Maine. He was a minister of the Free Will Baptist Church. Graduating from Dartmouth College in 1864, he joined the U.S. Christian Commission and was stationed in the Shenandoah Valley to assist both Union and Confederate soldiers and freed slaves. After the war, Brackett served his church's mission to educate freed slaves by supervising 25 young female teachers from the North, scattered in Free Will Baptist schools throughout the valley from Harpers Ferry and Martinsburg to Lynchburg, Virginia. He proposed that his church's best service would be to equip blacks to teach other blacks, rather than relying only on missionary teachers from New England. The church leaders embraced the idea and raised the necessary funding to establish Storer College at Harpers Ferry. The college opened in October 1867, with Brackett as its first president. Brackett retired from Storer's presidency in 1897, although he continued as treasurer until his death. Brackett was respected by blacks and whites alike. He served on the Harpers Ferry Town Council and was for two years the superintendent of free schools there. He was a regent of the Bluefield Colored Institute (now Bluefield State College) for eight years, four as president of the board. He received the degree of Doctor of Philosophy from Bates College, Lewiston, Maine, at its Commencement in June, 1883. he purchased a Summer residence in Phillips, Maine, his native town, and bought the local paper, The Phillips Phonograph. His religious preferences are Free-Will Baptist; in politics, he is a Republican. He was married October 16, 1865, to Miss Louise Wood, of Lewiston, Maine. Source: "Memorialia of the Class of '64 in Dartmouth College" complied by John C. Webster, Shepard Johnston, Printers, 1884, Chicago.

Thomas Preston Bell
Birth:
Mar. 22, 1889
Logan County, Kentucky
Death:
Oct. 19, 1928 Williamson,
Mingo County,
West Virginia
Burial:
Milton Cemetery, Milton
,Cabell County, West Virginia

Arthur C. Berry
Birth:
1887
Death:
1963
Burial:
Richwood Cemetery,
Richwood, Nicholas County,
West Virginia

Orvil Clinton Berry
Birth:
May 23, 1902
West Virginia
Death:
Dec. 5, 1980
Kanawha County, West Virginia

He was on the Brotherhood Conference council that met to organize the Springdale Free Will Baptist Church, Hurricane, West Virginia on July 24, 1955. His parents were David Franklin Berry (1864 - 1943) and Sarah Ann Woodard Berry (1870 - 1967) His wife was Sena May Berry (1904 - 1984).

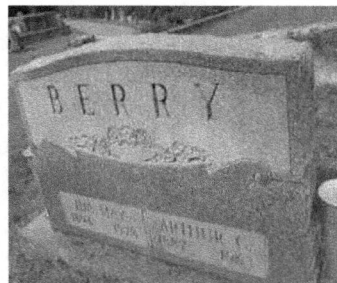

Ernest F Bias
Birth:
1906
Death:
1986
Burial:
Enon Cemetery, Salt Rock
,Cabell County, West Virginia

Reverend Ernest Franklin Bias was the son of Evermont V. Ellender Rose (Hoskinson) BIAS.

Harry Herbert Booth
Birth:
Mar. 6, 1929
Stagle, West Virginia
Death:
Mar. 25, 2012
Charleston, West Virginia
Burial:
Highland Memory Gardens
Cemetery
Pecks Mill
Logan County, West Virginia

He was a son of the late John and Rebecca Clay Booth. Harry enjoyed fishing, hunting, telling jokes, family functions, attending church, visiting the nursing home, cooking, canning, gardening, woodworking and reading the Bible, but more than anything he enjoyed witnessing for the Lord. Harry served as the Chaplain for the VFW, was a veteran of the US Army serving in the Korean War and retired from the coal mines. He was also in the nursing home ministry at Boone Nursing Home and a member of the Monclo Freewill Baptist Church.

Floyd Brown
Birth:
Oct. 24, 1834
Boone County, West Virginia
Death:
Dec. 6, 1923
Burial:
Coon Cemetery
Boone County, West Virginia

He and his wife had 13 children. His conversion took place in 1867 and he was licensed to preach in 18 seven day. He pastored several churches in West Virginia

Noah Estil Buckner
Birth:
Mar. 24, 1921
Morehead
Rowan County, Kentucky
Death:
Jul., 1979
Princeton
Mercer County, West Virginia
Burial:
Roselawn Memorial Gardens
Princeton
Mercer County, West Virginia

He was the first pastor of the Lashmeet Free Will Baptist Church. Records show that he was on the ordaining Council that ordained Rev. Jeff Dishner who later became the pastor of the Lashmeet Free Will Baptist Church, Princeton, West Virginia.

Freedom prospers when religion is vibrant and the rule of law under God is acknowledged.

George Joseph Burns
Birth:
Jan. 30, 1933
Pleasants County, W.Va.
Death:
Sept. 9, 2008
St. Marys, W.Va..
Maple Lane Masonic Cemetery
Hebron, W.Va

He was a son of the late Charles Francis and Agnes Cecelia Nichols Burns. George was a 1951 graduate of St.Marys High School, a U. S. Navy veteran and had retired from the Pleasants County School System. He was a full-time minister at Beech Run Freewill Baptist Church. Services were Maple Lane Freewill Baptist Church, Hebron, W.Va., with the Rev. Bud Corbin officiating. He was a member of the Beech Run FWB Church, the Upper Ohio Valley Conference of FWB, and the WV State Association of FWB.

Wilson C Cadle
Birth:
1866
Death:
1945
Burial:
Jordan Harper Cemetery,
Walton,
Roane County, West Virginia

Fermon C Calhoun
Birth:
Jun. 6, 1912
Newland, very County,
North Carolina

Death
Oct. 17, 1973
Raleigh County, West Virginia
Burial:
Blue Ridge Memorial Gardens,
Prosperity,
Raleigh County, West Virginia

He was a retired miner, a member of the UMWA and had pastored the Bethel Freewill Baptist Church for 10 years, prior to his retirement..

William Fleetwood Chapman
Birth:
Dec. 19, 1918
West Virginia
Death:
Aug. 19, 2002
Elkview
Kanawha County, West Virginia
Burial:
Elk Hills Memorial Park
Big Chimney
Kanawha County, West Virginia

He was the son of George W and Verna Chapman He was elected pastor in 1954 and served until January 1963 the Loudendale Free Will Baptist Church near Charleston, West Virgini. Several successful revivals were held while Rev. Chapman was pastor and many of the present members of the church United with the church at that time.
Inscription:
PVT US ARMY WORLD WAR II

Carter Clark
Birth:
1872
Death:
Oct. 6, 1941
Burial:
Comer Cemetery
Loudendale
Kanawha County,
West Virginia

He was one of the leaders in getting the Little Harts Creek Free Will Baptist Church started along with Rev. John George and Rev. Willis

Comer. An interesting note:' I'm the daughter of Nellie Clark Workman and she always told me stories about poppy Clark taking her with him to church. She said he would hold her hand and sit her up front so he could keep an eye on her while he preached. My mom loved her poppy.'

Arthur J. Collins
Birth:
Aug. 9, 1925
Death:
May 7, 1982
Burial:
Grandview Cemetery,
Grandview,
Raleigh County, West Virginia

William Cecil Combs
Birth:
Feb. 19, 1912
Honaker, Russell County,
Virginia
Death:
Nov. 14, 2003
Sophia,
Raleigh County, West Virginia
Burial:
Blue Ridge Memorial Gardens,
Prosperity,
Raleigh County, West Virginia

Cecil Combs was a native of southwest Virginia. His father was a farmer, and his mother a homemaker who was active in founding Sunday Schools in the rural area in which they lived. Cecil loved nature and was an avid hunter. He spent countless hours in the woods and farm country learning much about animals, plants, and trees. He was preceded in death by his parents Cecil married Norma Elizabeth Ball in 1932 in Lebanon, Virginia. They moved to West Virginia in 1934, where their fifteen children were born and where they raised fourteen children to adulthood. The Combs lived in West Virginia until 1964 when they moved to central Florida with the intention of establishing a Free Will Baptist Church. During his ministry Bro. Combs pastored churches in Georgia, Florida, and West Virginia. Although an humble man, he emerged as a leader early in his ministry. Bro. Combs helped to lead Free Will Baptists in West Virginia to organize the State Association of Free Will Baptists. A CPA, he was elected Clerk, and served both the W Va. State Association and the Beckley Conference as moderator numerous times. Cecil Combs was a minister during the days when few Free Will Baptist Churches had full-time pastors. A builder by trade, he left a physical legacy as well as a spiritual one. He built hundreds of homes in Raleigh County, WV. In every church he pastored, he used his building skills to construct, remodel, or build additions to the churches, educational units, parsonages and youth camps. Bro. Combs and his son Billy helped construct the large Vehicle Assembly Building which houses rockets at the Kennedy Space Center on Merritt Island. This close proximity to Cocoa Beach brought a burden upon his heart for the town, leading him to establish the Cocoa Free Will Baptist Church, where he pastored for five years. He led in the building of the church facility at the Cocoa Church; youth

camps both in West Virginia and Bonifay, Florida; gymnasium and classroom building in Sophia, WVa.; and additions to the parsonages at Piney Grove Church in Chipley, Florida, and in Sophia, W Va. He led the construction project for the West Virginia Cottage at the Free Will Baptist Children's Home in Greenville, Tennessee during his ministry in the 1950s. During his years in central Florida, Bro. Combs assisted in organizing Free Will Baptist churches in nearby Vero Beach and Titusville, organized the Indian River Association, which he served as moderator. He also served as the moderator of the Florida State Association and published the Free Will Baptist State Paper both in Florida and West Virginia. Bro. Combs was preceded in death by his wife Norma of 58 years. Several of their descendants are in ministry. Among them are sons Bob Combs, WVa. pastor and a former Georgia pastor; Jim Combs, missionary to Brazil; sons-in-law Ed Cook, Kentucky pastor; Jim Puckett, Oklahoma pastor; grandsons Randy Puckett, Home Missionary in Texas; and John Hornsby, chaplain for the H. B. Zachry Company in San Antonio, Texas. The Lord blessed Bro. Combs with a sharp mind and the ability to recite a great body of scripture by heart. He was well-known for his Biblical knowledge, and especially of eschatology. Although retired after fifty years in the ministry, Bro. Combs continued to serve, conducting a weekly service at Heartland Nursing Home, and filling the pulpit at Sophia in the absence of his pastor.

Willis C Comer
Birth:
1867
Death:
1942
Burial:
Comer Cemetery
Loudendale
Kanawha County, West Virginia

He was the first they had pastored the Little Harts Free Will Baptist Church and did so a number of times preceding his death. His wife was Lucinda Clark Comer (1869 - 1958).

Carl Joseph Cooper
Birth:
Death:
Feb. 9, 2011
Milton, WV.
Burial:
Forest Memorial Park,
Milton, WV.

Pastor Carl Joseph Cooper, age 78, of Milton, WV, beloved husband of Nelma Young Cooper, and faithful servant of the Lord Jesus Christ.

After beginning his preaching ministry in December of 1964, Pastor Cooper served faithfully through evangelistic work, Pastor of several churches, active involvement in local, State, and the National Association of Free Will Baptists. Pastor Cooper served as a Home missionary to Wheeling, WV. He authored a book entitled Two Covenants and taught numerous Bible studies, many of them on the subject of The Wilderness Tabernacle using a scale model that he constructed. In addition to his life in ministry, Pastor Cooper was a builder by trade and former owner of White Oak Lumber Company. Pastor Cooper was preceded in death by his parents, Pastor J.W. Cooper and Ada Leslie Nugen Cooper, and his brother Pastor Lloyd Cooper. He is survived by his faithful and loving wife of 59 years, Nelma Young Cooper, brother, Ezra Cooper, sister, Lorene Rooper, sons, Wesley Edward Cooper (Debbie), Pastor Daniel Joseph Cooper (Sandie), Paul Keith Cooper (Sandra), and daughter, Julie Cooper McCoy (Pastor Dale), seven wonderful grandchildren, and two very special great-grandchildren. Pastor Cooper was extremely proud that all his children and their families are faithfully serving the Christ he so loved and proclaimed.

James Wesley "J.W." Cooper
Birth:
Jan. 19, 1908
Death:
Jan. 7, 2002
Burial:
Forest Memorial Park
Milton
Cabell County, West Virginia

The Rev. James Wesley "J.W." Cooper, 93, of Milton widower of Ada Nugen Cooper, died Monday, January 7, 2002 in Teays Valley Nursing and Rehabilitation Center. He was a coal miner, carpenter, building contractor and pastor. Survivors include two sons, the Rev. Carl J. Cooper of Milton and W. Ezra Cooper of Hurricane; and one daughter, Lorene Rooper of Barboursville.

Roy Lee Cox
Birth:
April 8, 1933
Gillespie,
Ritchie County, W.Va.
Death:
June 20, 2009
Marietta, Ohio
Burial:
Maple Lane Masonic Cemetery
Hebron, Pleasants County, W.Va.

A son of the late Jacob and Nina Coss Cox. Roy was a graduate of St. Marys High School with the class of 1951 and was retired from the Pleasants County School System as a maintenance supervisor. He was known to his many friends as the "fix-it-man." He loved gospel music and singing in church, as well as being a member of the singing group "The Relative Quartet." He was the founder, member, and the retired pastor of the Beech Run Freewill Baptist Church at Arvilla, W.Va. He was a member of the Beech Run FWB Church, the Upper Ohio Valley Conference of FWB, and the WV State Association of FWB A Celebration of Roy's life and ministry was held at the Beech Run Freewill Baptist Church at Arvilla, WV with Pastor Robert Cornell and the Rev. Rex Cox officiating.

Moss A Craddock

Birth:
May 5, 1907
Hewett
Boone County, West Virginia
Death:
Aug. 23, 1993
Burial:
Forest Lawn Cemetery
Pecks Mill
Logan County, West Virginia

Well-known Free Will Baptist preacher and pastor. He helped to organize the Chapman Memorial Free Will Baptist Church, Harts, West Virginia, along with Oliver Privett, Wayne Damron, J. A. Rakes.

Wayne Damron

Birth:
unknown
West Virginia
Death:
Apr. 21, 1978
Logan County, West Virginia
Burial:
Forest Lawn Cemetery,
Pecks Mill,
Logan County, West Virginia

Well respected minister for Free Will Baptists in West Virginia. His last pastorate was at the Trinity FWB church in Henlawson.

Owen R Estep

Birth:
January 10, 1854
Boone County, West Virginia
Death:
Dec. 4, 1909
West Virginia
Burial:
Estep Cemetery
Ameagle
Raleigh County, West Virginia

He was ordained in March, 1884, by the Kanawha Quarter Meeting and since that time is been engaged continually in revival in organizing work. He organized over 15 churches and now is pastor of the Liberty, New Salem, Jarrett's Valley and

Fifteen mile churches. His labors were largely among a poor people but few will it the R could do the work so efficiently with so little pay for his labors and travels.

Arthur G. Frye

Birth:
Feb. 2, 1923
Lincoln County, West Virginia
Death:
Aug. 10, 1991
West Virginia
Burial:
Franklin Cemetery
Branchland, Lincoln County,
West Virginia

He was a member of Chapman Memorial Church, previous West Virginia Promotional Director. He was retired from Columia Gas. He served as a Free Will Baptist minister for 43 years.

John E Garrido

Birth:
Jan. 27, 1934
Death:
unknown
Burial:
Docks Creek Cemetery
Kenova
Wayne County, West Virginia

He was the first pastor of the Good Shepherd Free Will Baptist Church in Huntington, West Virginia which was organized on March 19, 1966.Note: A date of death is NOT listed on this marker

Ottis Hensley

Birth:
unknown
Death:
Oct. 4, 1993
Charleston
Kanawha County, West Virginia
Burial:
Blue Ridge Memorial Gardens
Prosperity
Raleigh County, West Virginia

Hensley was returning home from a preaching appointment when he stopped and fell down a steep embankment breaking his neck in the fall. He was the West Virginia Promotional Director, editor of the Messenger, and manager of the state book store. He was also in his fourth year as pastor of the Kilsyth FWB church. He was previously chairman of the State Home Mission board and served on the Steering Committee in 1991 when the West Virginia association hosted the National Association in Charleston. He was a graduate OF Bethany Bible College in Bethany, Alabama. He was 51 at the time of his death and has been a minister 23 years.

John M. Henson

Birth:
Feb. 22, 1898
Mercers Bottom,
Mason County, West Virginia
Death:
May 17, 1984
West Virginia,
Burial:
Valley View Memorial Park,
Hurricane,
Putnam County, West Virginia

He was definitely one of the pioneer Free Will Baptist preachers in the tri-state area of West Virginia, Kentucky, and Ohio. He was a friend to all pastors and ministers keeping the Free Will Baptist doctrine known where ever he preached. He knew ministers far and wide and did his portion of revivals where ever he could. And in his day he had to travel anyway possible. Before he passed into eternity wrote his life's story in his book *"My Journey with Jesus"* filled with hundreds of names of people he baptized and preachers with whom he fraternalized. Rev. Hansen was a veteran of World War I serving in Company B 52nd infantry. He served in England, France, and Germany. He joined the Free Will Baptist denomination on December 28, 1928.

John Hockenberry
Birth:
1921
Death:
1985
Burial:
Forest Memorial Park
Milton Cabell County
West Virginia,

Hockenberry was a very respected Minister in West Virginia. He died in the pulpit while preaching at the Prince of Peace Free Will Baptist Church in Huntington, West Va. where he was pastor for many years. He served in the United States Navy during World War II.

C.C. Lett
Birth:
1888
Death:
1971
Burial:
Woodmere, Memorial Park,
Huntington,
Cabell County, West Virginia

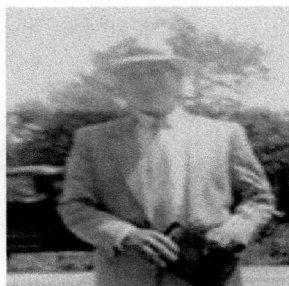

Leslie Allen Lilly, Sr
Birth:
Aug. 30, 1898
Camp Creek community
Mercer County, West Virginia
Death:
Sep., 1976
Camp Creek community
Mercer County, West Virginia
Burial:
Roselawn Memorial Gardens
Princeton
Mercer County, West Virginia

Father: John Wallace Lilly and his Mother was: Mary Ellen Epling He joins the ranks of many whose last name is Lilly who were Free Will Baptist preachers. He spent the majority of his life in the Camp Creek area of West Virginia and ministered basically in that area.

Andrew Jackson Linville
Birth:
Dec. 20, 1843
Kanawha County, West Virginia
Death:
Apr. 21, 1920
Charleston
Kanawha County, West Virginia
Burial:
Spring Hill Cemetery
Charleston
Kanawha County, West Virginia

He served as a federal soldier during the rebellion, and married Nancy Stowers in 4 Oct 1865. They had eight children. He was ordained among the free salvation Baptists in 17 scratch that 1875 and became a free Baptist minister in 1885. Most of his ministry was in the first Kanawha quarterly meeting where he engaged in revival work in which he had been very successful.

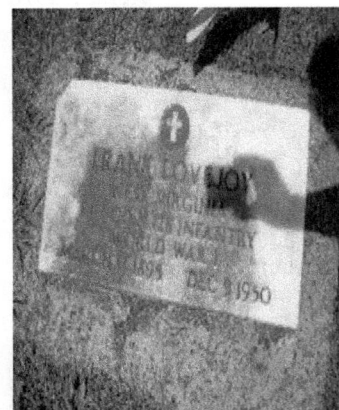

Frank Lovejoy
Birth:
Mar. 17, 1895
Death:
Dec. 9, 1950
Burial:
Lovejoy Cemetery, Palermo,
Lincoln County, West Virginia

The Rev. Lovejoy was a veteran attached to the 128th division in World War I during which he was wounded. He was a member of the Freewill Baptist Church.

Albert Meade
Birth:
Apr. 14, 1888
Wayne County, West Virginia
Death:
Apr. 15, 1943
Logan County, West Virginia
Burial:
Pack Cemetery
Atenville
Lincoln County, West Virginia

He was the founder of the Little Harts Freewill Baptist Church, Little Harts Creek Road, Harts (Atenville), Lincoln County, WV, and was from Wayne County, WV

Tillman Clayton Morgan
Birth:
Aug. 13, 1909
Lewis County, West Virginia
Death:
1988
West Virginia
Burial:
Woodmere Memorial Park
Huntington
Cabell County, West Virginia

He was the son John Dallas Morgan and Bertha May (Walker). He began his ministry with Free Will Baptist in the fall of 1945 and continued preaching until his death in 1988. He served the brotherhood conference as clerk for several years. He was also clerk and Treas. of the West Virginia state Association. During these years he pastored several churches in West Virginia. He served for two terms as mayor of the town of Nettie and he traveled thousands of miles among his churches while living in Huntington.

Alexander Hatch Morrell
Birth:
Oct. 10, 1818
Berwick
York County, Maine
Death:
Dec. 25, 1885
Irvington
Essex County, New Jersey
Burial:
Harpers Cemetery
Harpers Ferry
Jefferson County, West Virginia

Alexander Hatch "Alex" Morrell was the son of Josiah Morrell, Jr and Sarah Quint his wife, who for many years were members of the Society of Friends. At 18 years of age he united with the Free Will Baptist Church in Litchfield, Maine. He served as a book salesman in Kentucky. He was ordained at Phillips, Maine in 1850. His work there and surrounding towns continued until 1861. His pastorates in Maine were very successful until in 1867 the Home Mission Board asked him to work in the Shenandoah Mission and there after became the soliciting agent for Storer College. He is known for being an ideal pastor and had a clear and forcible voice and a good sermonizer. On 8 Jun 1845 in Hall County, Maine, Alex married Eliza "Lizzie" Seavey of Georgetown, Sagadahoc County, Maine. He was an ordained Freewill Baptist minister, who felt a mission to help educate freed slaves, and began a very useful work at Storer College, in Harper's Ferry, Jefferson County,

West Virginia. He retired and died in New Jersey, but his body was taken to Harper's Ferry where he is buried.

James Edwards Mounts
Birth:
Nov. 12, 1934
Ranger, Lincoln County, West Virginia
Death:
Apr. 20, 2011
Ranger, Lincoln County, West Virginia
Burial:
Frye-Nelson Cemetery, Ranger, Lincoln County, West Virginia

Rev. Mounts was a tipple mechanic for Pittston Coal Group at Loredo, and he was the pastor of the East Fork Freewill Baptist Church of Ranger for 40 years.

Sam Mullins
Birth:
Jul. 3, 1877
Virginia
Death:
May 30, 1956
West Hamlin
Lincoln County, West Virginia

Burial:
Lucas
Harts
Lincoln County, West Virginia

Helped to organize the new Zion Free Will Baptist Church between 1910 and 1915 along with H. H. Daniels which is near Logan, West Virginia.

Eldon M. Pauley
Birth:
Jan. 22, 1877
Death:
May 23, 1943
Burial:
Indian Mills Cemetery,
Indian Mills,
Summers County, West Virginia

George Pauley
Birth:
unknown
Death:
May 23, 1974
West Virginia
Burial:
Blue Ridge Memorial Gardens,
Prosperity,
Raleigh County, West Virginia

The service for Rev. Pauly was in the Bradley Free Will Baptist Church. This information came from the Beckley Post Herald on May 26, 1974.

James Albert Rakes
Birth:
Jun. 11, 1897
Lincoln County, West Virginia
Death:
Jan. 22, 1960
ManLogan County, West Virginia
Burial:
Forest Lawn Cemetery
Pecks Mill
Logan County, West Virginia

He was the son of Amos Rakes who was born on Oct 1873 in Lincoln County, WV. and his mother was Nancy M. Vance born Apr 1879 in Lincoln County, WV. and who died on 18 Jul 1930 in

Lincoln County, WV. He helped to organize the Chapman Memorial Free Will Baptist Church in harts, West Virginia, along with Oliver Privett, Moss Craddock, and Wayne Damron.

Paul J. Scarbro
Birth:
Feb. 22, 1921
Rock Creek, West Virginia
Death:
Nov. 7, 2008
Beckley, Raleigh County,
West Virginia
Burial:
Blue Ridge Memorial Gardens,
Prosperity, Raleigh County,
West Virginia

He was of the Free Will Baptist faith and was a minister and pastor for over 50 years. Among the churches he pastored were Packsville Baptist, Shumate Branch, Coal City Free Will Baptist, Price Hill Free Will Baptist, and North Sand Branch Baptist.

Henry W. Scott
Birth:
1888
Death:
Apr. 11, 1975
Charleston,
Kanawha County, West Virginia
Burial:
Sunset Memorial Park,
South Charleston,
Kanawha County, West Virginia

The Rev. Henry W. Scott was a retired Freewill Baptist minister after 45 years of service.

James Harold Shafer
Birth:
unknown
Death:
Jun. 14, 2011
Elkview,
Kanawha County,
West Virginia
Burial:
Elk Hills Memorial Park,
Big Chimney,
Kanawha County, West Virginia

He retired from Union Carbide with 34 years of service and was a minister throughout his life. He was a member of Meadowbrook FWB church and the Kanawha Free Will Baptist Conference. He pastored several FWB churches in West Virginia

Abram Clark Shaver
Birth:
Jul. 21, 1842
Scalia County, Ohio
Death:
Oct. 13, 1923
Kanawha County, West Virginia
Burial:
IOOF Cemetery
East Bank
Kanawha County, West Virginia

He was converted in 1860 and baptized by Rev. Thomas E. Peden. After serving in the army, he settled in West Virginia and married in 1869 Miss M. Baker. For some years he was manager of a large mercantile establishment. His faithfulness and influence aided materially in establishing the cause of Free Will Baptists in the Kanawha Valley. Where he served the Lord with great interest in his church and vicinity.

Sherman Sizemore
Birth:
Jul. 4, 1918
Death:
Oct. 13, 1985
Burial:

Grandview Memorial Park
Dunbar
Kanawha County, West Virginia

One of the pastors and the early members of the Herndon Free Will Baptist Church, Herndon, West Virginia. His wife was Olivia Mae Selbe Sizemore (1920 - 2006)

Roy Lee Stanley
Birth:
Nov. 16, 1943
Death:
Jan. 15, 2011
Burial:
Independence Cemetery, Sandyville,
Jackson County, West Virginia
He was an ordained minister serving many congregations throughout the region prior to his retirement. He was also a proud veteran of the United States Air Force.

Gaylord M. Shrewsbury
Birth:
Jul. 19, 1940
Death:
Aug. 3, 2000
Burial:
Shrewsbury Cemetery at Beeson
Beeson
Mercer County, West Virginia

He was pastor for 18 years the Old State Road Free Will Baptist Church in Beeson, West Virginia.

Inscription:
He Fought A Good Fight.
He Kept The Faith.
Military Marker:EN 2 U. S. Navy
July 19, 1940 - Aug. 3, 2000

John H. Surratt
Birth:
Jan. 20, 1847
Fayette County, Virginia
Death:
May 9, 1933
Burial:
Alexander Cantley Cemetery
Rock Creek
Raleigh County, West Virginia

He married Jannette Cantley in 1868 and with his wife joined the Free Baptists in 1884. The same year he received license to preach and own June 13, 1886 he was ordained. His labors were as an evangelist in the Raleigh Quarterly Meeting of which he was the clerk.

William Travis
Birth:
May 30, 1923
Ceredo, WV
Death:
November 9, 1994
Burial:
Docks Creek Cemetery,
Kenova, Wayne County,
West Virginia

He served in the U.S. Navy during WWII. Transferred to the U.S. Army after the war, hoping to make a career of the military. He was saved in 1952, kneeling at a tree stump in the woods in Texas where he was working for the Texas State Prison system as a building superintendent. He loved working their annual rodeos. He discharged from the Army after becoming a Christian and answered the call to preach soon thereafter. He was ordained in 1953 and began preaching as a "fill-in" preacher in various towns in Texas. He once held a 6-week revival in China Grove, Texas, under a thatch roofed structure and was paid with vegetables from the people's gardens. For several months, he drove 100 miles each way to fill in at a part-time church which only met every other week. In 1955, he felt the call to the mission field and went to the Bible College for a year studying missions. Then, in 1956, he took his family to Pinar del Rio, Cuba to work at Los Cedros del Libano (Cedar of Lebanon) Bible Institute with Mom and Pop Willey and fill-in for missionaries who were on leave of absence. They filed for permanent residence papers so they could stay and work as full-time missionaries, but were refused after Batista lost the war to Castro. There were many times, the Institute's bus was stopped, torn apart and searched by Communist soldiers. Daddy joined the other men from the Seminary to help the people in neighborhood villages that were burned at night by Castro's army. It was there we saw first-hand the work of Satan as his demons possessed people who would run wildly on the Seminary grounds, then saw the miraculous work of our Savior as he healed those people following times of severe stress and mighty prayers. He was forced to leave the island after being there only 6 months. He moved to Ft. Lauderdale to fill in at the FWB church, and later was called to his first full-time pastorate. Later a small group began meeting in a childcare facility in nearby Deerfield Beach, and the church grew from there. Deerfield Free Will Baptist church was built and today supports a school with grades K4-12. He was bi-vocational while pastoring there. After 7 years in Florida moved Jasper, Alabama in 1963 where he pastored the First FWB Church in Jasper for about 7 years. Then he answered to call to Thomaston, Georgia. The church in Thomaston was built from two used Army barracks that were bought and brought to the church property. He was in Thomaston till around 1980-1981, then moved to Hazelhurst, Georgia and pastored there about 3 years; and his final pastorate was in Millen, Georgia, where he passed away in 1995.

Roy Alex Tyree
Birth:
Mar. 19, 1917
Beckley
Raleigh County West Virginia
Death:
Apr. 16, 2007
Beckley, Raleigh County
West Virginia,
Burial:
Blue Ridge Memorial Gardens,
Prosperity,
Raleigh County, West Virginia

Mr. Tyree was a retired miner and a member of UMWA District 17, and a retired Free Will Baptist minister with more than 50 years of service, having officiated a host of weddings and funerals. During his ministry, he pastored: Terry Community Church, Weirwood Community Church, Willis Branch Community Church, Naomi Free

Will Baptist Church, Fairdale Free Will Baptist Church, Maple Fork Community Church (three times), Rock Lick Community Church, Oak Grove Baptist Church at Backus Mountain, Layland Community Church, Zickafoose Memorial Church at Landisburg, Charmco Free Will Baptist Church, North Baptist Church at Sand Branch and the Spruce Tabernacle. Rev. Tyree was also on WOAY Radio for 23 years and was on WOAY-TV for 2 1/2 years.

Dell Upton
Birth:
Aug. 2, 1854
Leon, Mason County,
West Virginia
Death:
Jul. 15, 1942
Mason County, West Virginia
Burial:
Wolfe Valley Cemetery,
Leon, Mason County,
West Virginia

Rev. Upton was a leader in the Free Will Baptist church of which he ministered until his death. His name is found in many records, one, in which he was pastor of Cofer's Chapel FWB Church, Nashville, TN in the early decade of 1900's: "Coming as pastor in 1907 was Dr. Dell Upton from Leon, West Virginia. Perhaps only in heaven will he know that he gave Cofer's Chapel a start in directions which continue to this day. December 17, 1907, he gathered a group of women in his home and organized what they called 'The Ladies' Aid Society.' In the organization were such women as Fanny Polston, Mrs. Ed Parker, and a teenager, then known as Annie Weaver (later Mrs. Mary Ann Welch, affectionately known as Miss Mary.)"(Taken from Dr. Mary Ruth Wisehart's *History of Cofer's Chapel*, 2008 Homecoming History of church.). Dr. Upton envisioned a FWB college in Nashville in 1907, and obtained a charter, but for whatever reason,

it did not materialize at that time. He was awarded the Doctor of Divinity degree for his work and leadership abilities. He was one of the ministers who opposed the merger of FWB with the Northern Baptists in 1911.

Carl Wesley Vallance
Birth:
Mar. 18, 1918
Holden,
Logan County, West Virginia
May 27, 2006 Huntington,
Cabell County, West Virginia
Burial:
White Chapel
Memorial Gardens,
Barboursville,
Cabell County, West Virginia

He was graduated from Kitt's Hill High School, Ohio, in 1936, with highest-grade honors in his class. For many years Carl was bi-vocational, working full time as a master carpenter in the Huntington area, building, selling and remodeling homes. His greatest joy in woodworking was cabinet construction. He also served as a church pastor for over 68 years of active ministry. Carl considered the most important happening in his young life occurred May 10, 1938, when he asked Jesus Christ to forgive his sins, and was saved. He immediately began to preach, was licensed and ordained in the West Virginia Yearly Meeting of Free Will Baptists, which later became a part of the National Association of Free Will Baptists and was faithful in his service to God for all his life. More than 20 men accepted the call to preach through his ministry. His work included numberless revivals from Canada to Florida. His spiritual impact on West Virginia, the United States and worldwide, will continue through the many lives he touched with the message of the Gospel. He always promoted Bible education, missions and the denominational ministries of Free Will Baptists. His first pastorates included these churches in Logan County, WV: Holden No. 7 and No. 8 Community Church, Holden No. 22 Community Church, Pine Creek Church at Omar, and Monaville Community Church, which through his leadership became Monaville Free Will Baptist Church. While there, he once preached to over 3,000 in an open-air service without aid of voice amplification. He was noted for the loudness of his voice, his knowledge of the scripture, his authority in the pulpit and his abiding concern for the spiritual needs of the people as he preached. In October 1950 the family moved to Huntington, in Cabell County, W.Va., when he accepted the pastorate of Thomas Memorial FWB Church. He served there for 26 years, until 1976. In those years the church enjoyed growth to over 500 in attendance, and underwent several expansions of the property. Pastor Vallance and his wife hosted 15 trips to Israel, beginning in Christmas of 1969. They introduced hundreds to the awesome experience of walking in the footsteps of Jesus in the Holy Land. He became founding pastor of Central FWB in Huntington in 1976, where he ministered until retirement in 1994. During his pastorate the church purchased property at 6th Ave and 5th Street. He was overseer of construction of the new worship center in 1980, using plans drawn by his son, Robert, a civil engineer. With Carl's leadership the church purchased four plots of property to provide growth

opportunity for the church. In the service of his denomination, Carl began his ministry in the Yearly Meeting of Free Will Baptists in West Virginia. He was in attendance at the organizational meeting of the WVa. Free Will Baptist State Association, and was a pioneer in this ministry. He served in such positions as Moderator, Parliamentarian, and Foreign Missions Board member. He was elected as the General Board member, making him the representative of the WVa. state ministry to the National Association. He began attending the National Association of FWB in 1947, and only missed three meetings. He served as Executive Committee member on the national level, helping to oversee the ministry operations of the National Executive Office, and plan programs for annual National Conventions.

Preston Vance
Birth:
Apr. 4, 1919
Beauty, Fayette County,
West Virginia
Death:
May 6, 2012
Logan, Logan County,
West Virginia
Burial:
Forest Lawn Cemetery,
Pecks Mill,
Logan County, West Virginia

A well-known area minister, Vance, 93, of Chauncey, died at

Logan Regional Medical Center. He was a son of the late Everest and Audrey Sullies Vance. Rev. Vance was a retired coal miner, a member of the UMWA, a former employee of the WVa. Coal and Coke Company and a veteran of the U.S. Army where he served as Staff Sergeant of the 94th Infantry Division during World War II. Rev. Vance was the founder of the Beth Haven Christian School at Omar. He was a minister for 53 years. During this time, he was pastor of the Mt. Calvary Freewill Baptist Church at Atenville for 12 years and pastor of the Walnut Grove Freewill Baptist Church at Chauncey for 23 years. He was also a member of the New Life Freewill Baptist Church at Rossmore and a member of the Huff Creek Freewill Baptist Conference.

Robert Lee Vance
Birth:
Jan. 19, 1910
West Virginia
Death:
Dec. 28, 1985 Ferrellsburg,
Lincoln County,
West Virginia
Burial:
Robert Velva Vance Farm (Little Harts Creek) Harts,Lincoln County
West Virginia

He was pastor of the Little Harts Freewill Baptist Church, Little Harts Creek Road, Harts, WV, and was retired from the West Virginia Dept. of Highways.

Ward Vance
Birth:
Apr. 1, 1943
Harts, Lincoln County
West Virginia
Death:
Sep. 2, 2009
Logan, Logan County,
West Virginia
Burial:
Forest Lawn Cemetery,
Pecks Mill,
Logan County, West Virginia

Pastor of the Little Harts Freewill Baptist Church, Harts, WV. He pastored "officially" for 24 years and was a member for about 45 years. He was an Assistant Pastor to his father for many years prior his pastoring. He served as a deacon for nine years helping his father with pastoral duties. He loved the Church greatly. He worked at Sunset Furniture in Huntington, WV, in the mid-1960s, Vance's Amco at Atenville, WVa., as a mechanic, and served as a State Inspector for the State of West Virginia. He later started his own business, Ward's Workshop, as a building contractor until he got hurt in 1986. He was a member of the United States Chamber of Commerce.

Chester C. Wainwright
Birth:
1847
Jefferson County, West Virginia
Death:
Aug. 13, 1902
Charles Town
Jefferson County, West Virginia
Burial:
Fairview Cemetery
Gibsontown
Jefferson County, West Virginia
He married Lizzie Dunlap on December 27, 1877. He was ordained about 1875, pastoring of the churches at Charlestown and Shepherdstown. He was a student at Storer college, Harpers Ferry, West Virginia, about 1876-78, and ministered the Charlestown church to which more than 100 have been added by baptism.

Earl Austin Whitmore
Birth:
Dec. 25, 1917
Death:
Jun. 16, 1996
Cabell County, West Virginia
Burial:
Greenbottom Cemetery
Green Bottom
Cabell County, West Virginia

One of the former pastors of the Good Shepherd Free Will Baptist Church, Huntington, West Virginia.

Samuel Franklin Wills
Birth:
Mar. 3, 1855
Raleigh County, West Virginia
Death:
Mar. 26, 1936
Burial:
Barker Cemetery
Ashford
Boone County, West Virginia
In 1875, he married Paulina Webb and was ordained at December 6, 1886. His pastorates was with the

New Hope and Rock Creek churches in West Virginia

Omer L. Williams
Birth:
Aug. 18, 1913
Death:
Jun. 18, 1976
Burial:
Sunset Memorial Park
Beckley
Raleigh County, West Virginia
Plot: Locustvale Section

He founded the Shelton Free Will Baptist Church in Shelton, West Virginia and served as its pastor from 1958 until 1963.

If the Spirit of him that raised up Jesus from the dead dwell in you, he that raised up Christ from the dead shall also quicken your mortal bodies by his Spirit that dwelleth in you.
Romans 8:11

Wisconsin

George C Alborn
Birth:
1877
Death:
1956
Burial:
Wauwatosa Cemetery
Wauwatosa, Milwaukee County,
Wisconsin

Rev. Alborn, a graduate of Hillside College, a Free Baptist institution and the first college in Michigan to organize under the general college law in 1853, was a prolific and scholarly writer, publishing a novel (Ish Kerioth, 1904), a history (History of the First Baptist Church if Bricelin, Minnesota, 1933) and a collection of poetry (Rhythms of Life), 1941, He served as pastor of the Burnett church (Dodge County) from 1899 to 1901, the Fairwater (Fond du Lac County) and Grand Prairie (Green Lake County) churches from 1902 to 1905, the Greenbush church (Sheboygan County) from 1906 to 1907, the Allenville church (Winnebago County) from 1908 to 1909, and the Oak Center and Oakfield churches (Fond du Lac County) in 1911. Following the dissolution of the Wisconsin Freewill Baptist church, he also served other congregations including the Underwood Memorial church in Wauwatosa.

Rev. Alborn also served as secretary of the Home Mission Board of the Wisconsin Freewill church and was instrumental in promoting the merger of the Freewill church with the general Baptist church, as reported in the May, 2007, newsletter of the historical society:

The topic of reunion remained relatively quiet until 1904, when it was raised again during Yearly Meetings in Wisconsin, Minnesota and Maine in the belief that the Baptist church had grown closer to the theological positions of the Freewill church. Among other initiatives, Rev. George C. Alborn, pastor of the Fairwater congregation, advanced a resolution at the Wisconsin Yearly Meeting calling for a merger of the two denominations. In response, the national General Conference created a committee to study the issue.

In accordance with an act passed by the 1913 legislature authorizing the change, the trustees of the Wisconsin Yearly Meeting of Freewill Baptists, in session at Fairwater, Wis., September 23, voted to dissolve the corporation. The resolution filed with the secretary of state provides that all property coming to the corporation shall inure to the benefit of the Wisconsin Baptist state convention, and that the affairs of the corporation shall be wound up. Rev. P. Kisner is president and Rev. George C. Alborn secretary of the convention. (September 30, 1913, Janesville Daily Gazette)

Jesse Burnham
Birth:
May 16, 1778 Lee,
Strafford County,
New Hampshire
Death:
Dec. 5, 1869
Janesville,
Rock County, Wisconsin
Burial:
Mount Pleasant Cemetery,
Rock County, Wisconsin

He moved to Sebec, Maine, in 1806, and began to preach there with success. Jointly with Rev. Mr. Sealels and Rev. Mr. Libby organized a church there. Baptized many hundreds in the region where now are the towns of Atkinson, Charlestown, Garland, Corinth, Dexter, Exeter, Bradford, Dover, Foxcroft, Sebec, Brownsville, Milo, Medford and other places and gathered them into the Sebec Quarter Meeting. He was ordained in 1808 in New Hampshire, and He moved to Maxfield, ME, 1815, and Howland, ME, 1818. Organized a church there. Afterward, organized churches at Passadumkeng, ME, another at Lincoln, and Lowell, ME. In 1840 he moved to Janesville, Wisconsin, being the second Free Will Baptist minister in WI, after Rev. Mr. Cheney, together, organized the First QM in Wisconsin. He organized Prairie du Sac church in 1841. He assisted in organizing the Honey Creek Q.M. and was also in the Yearly Meeting. He did good service as a pioneer preacher on the prairies of Wisconsin and northern Illinois. He labored many years and died in his 86th year, preaching till within four weeks of his death.

Richard M Cary
Birth:
Dec. 10, 1794
Williamsburg,
Hampshire County,
Massachusetts
Death:
Oct. 16, 1868
Rock County ,Wisconsin
Burial:
North Johnstown Cemetery,
Milton,
Rock County, Wisconsin

In 1806, when still a young boy his family moved to western New York, which was rugged and wild with no neighbor south or west, for 40 miles. He had limited opportunity for education or religious training, but by untiring effort he began to study and received a common English education. No minister was near when needed for a funeral, so his father often said the words of comfort; this the father did for Richard's brother, Calvin, who was killed at Buffalo, NY in War of 1812. His brother's death affected Richard deeply. In 1814, a Freewill Baptist missionary, the Rev. Jeremiah Folsom, visited this newly settled country, and he embraced the earliest opportunity of hearing the stranger. In Sept. 1816, he was baptized with seven others and organized with them into a Freewill Baptist Church. He

felt impressed with a duty to preach. On Oct. 3, 1816, Erie Co. NY, he delivered his first sermon. He was ordained in June 1820 to the ministry. He began to hold meetings and baptize a number of converts. In Nov. he organized a church, and pastored the church for a portion of the time for the next twenty years. In Aug. 1821 he assisted in the organization of the Holland Purchase Yearly Meeting, which included all twenty-seven churches. At this time, he became acquainted with David Marks, a lad of 15 years, who was out on his first preaching tour. They together, at Eden, had a large number they organized into a church. He continued in ministry until 1842 when he moved out West, to Johnstown, Wis. where he soon organized a church. He took a leading part in planting other churches and in organizing the Wisconsin Y.M. He also pastored two years in Cherry Valley, IL in the 1850's. Elder Cary was a man of unbiased judgment and earnest convictions, with more dignity than is usual, tall, slender, and of a very fine and graceful figure. He was prematurely gray from ill health. His preaching was Biblical and impressive. He and his wife were companions for more than half a century. Their son, Roswell, educated at Hillsdale College, was a pre-eminent member of the Tennessee bar, but died suddenly in Feb. 1868. Of their seven children who survived at his death, Benjamin, who died earlier, had served as a member of the Wisconsin Legislature, and for six years as Treasurer of Rock County. His own words, "...about five hundred have received baptism at my hands." He planted twelve churches and assisted in several others. He assisted in ordaining about twenty ministers and preached about six hundred funeral sermons. The denomination lost one of its early pillars, and the church one of its wisest counselors.

Rufus Ellis Cheney
Birth:
May 4, 1780 Hillsborough
County,
New Hampshire
Death:
Aug. 30, 1869
New Berlin,
Waukesha County, Wisconsin
Burial:
Sunnyside Cemetery,
New Berlin,
Waukesha County, Wisconsin

Cheney was born in Antrim, New Hampshire. He began to preach about twenty-three years of age, and was ordained in 1810. After residing for a time in Vermont, near St. Johnsbury, he moved to Attica, New York, where, with the assistance of Rev. N. Brown, he was instrumental in gathering a church. During his three years at that place it increased to 120 members. In 1817 he settled in Porter, Ohio, and organized a small church, which soon numbered more than 100. (This church still exists and the pastor is the moderator of the Ohio State Association and active in the national convention.) In his labors the Little Scioto Quarterly Meeting had its origin. Returning to New York, he ministered to the Attica church several years, and built there a house of worship. In 1837 he settled in Wisconsin, where he organized the New Berlin church in 1840, and the Honey Creek church in 1841,-the first churches gathered in the state. He was the father of the Honey Creek Quarterly Meeting, and, with Cary and others, took an important part in building up the Wisconsin Yearly Meeting. He enjoyed the confidence of all who knew him.

DON'T WORRY ABOUT TOMORROW BECAUSE GOD HAS ALREADY TAKEN CARE OF IT.

Joseph Clough
Birth:
Oct. 9, 1813
Gilmanton, Belknap County, New Hampshire
Death:
Dec. 12, 1894
Burnett, Dodge County, Wisconsin
Burial:
Hyland Prairie Cemetery
Oak Grove, Dodge County, Wisconsin

He was an ordained Freewill Baptist minister, and settled in 1848 on a farm in Burnett, (Dodge Co) Wis., where he died.He united with the Rolling Prairie church at its organization; received license to preach in August, 1854, and was ordained by the Waupun Quarterly Meeting, in February, 1858. He was at different times pastor of some of the churches in the vicinity, and was respected by all.

Abner Coombs
Birth:
Dec. 1, 1794
Brunswick, Cumberland County, Maine
Death:
Mar. 15, 1880
Honey Creek, Walworth County, Wisconsin
Burial:
Honey Creek Cemetery
Honey Creek, Walworth County, Wisconsin
Plot: Block 3 Lot 2

He was converted when twenty-two years of age and married to Annstrus Melcher two years later. His ordination by the Sebec, Quarterly Meeting took place Sept. 22, 1830. Residing at Foxcroft, he organized a church there and at Sangerfield, and assisted in gathering several others.Removing to Wisconsin in 1842, he soon united with the Honey Creek church, and remained in it until his death. He was pastor of that church seven years, also for a time at Pike Grove and Wheatland, Sharon and other places also enjoyed his labors. He baptized 178 converts, was thoroughly evangelical and never swerved from the plain precepts of the Bible.

Isaac G Davis
Birth:
Mar. 18, 1819
Canada
Death:
Dec. 23, 1862
Fayette, Lafayette County, Wisconsin
Burial:
Fayette Cemetery
Fayette, Lafayette County, Wisconsin,

His parents were Silas L. Davis and Phoebe (Bennett) DAVIS. His family had moved to Vermont and his brother, Rev. Jairus E. Davis was in a protracted meeting when Isaac G. declared that from 'from that moment on he was for the Lord.' He began to feel it his duty to preach, and in 1838, he began holding meetings and studying with reference to the great work. His efforts were favorably looked on and the Huntington Quarterly Meeting of Freewill Baptist, gave him license in June 1839 to preach. He was ordained the next year on the 26th of Sept. 1840. He was accepted by the Missions Board as a foreign missionary, but it was finally concluded that his health would not endure the climate of India. However, his heart was always enlisted in the cause of Missions, and he gave of his scanty means, as well as his life going and preaching, to help. While attending Biblical School at Lowell, he labored with the church in Roxbury, MA, which was greatly increased in strength and numbers.In Aug. 8, 1843, he was married to Almira Bullock, in Lowell, Mass. They spent one year in Portsmouth, NH, then two years of faithful service to Deerfield, NH. A trip to Nova Scotia and New Brunswick was made where his labors were successful.After a three-month supply of the desk at Lawrence, he removed West.For several years, with the exception of a year or two spent in Elgin, Ill., most of his time was given to missionary labors in Boon and McHenry Quarterly Meetings and in other parts of Illinois and Wisconsin.In 1855, he took the pastoral care of the FWB Church in Fayette, WI, where (with exception of one year in Warren, Ill) he continued faithfully until his death. He enjoyed the confidence of his congregation. In Dec. 1862, he served as moderator in Quarterly Meeting, apparently in good health; was immediately taken ill, and died in eleven days. Prof. Ransom Dunn, whom he had selected, addressed a large and deeply-affected audience upon the occasion, from II Corinthians 4:17-18.His life and example were unusually blameless. His friends were many; his enemies, none. He left the inestimable treasure of a good example to the world.He left four brothers,--Mr. Silas A. Davis, the Yearly Meeting Clerk; Deacon W. Bennet Davis, and Revs. Jairus E. and Kinsman R. Davis. Also, three or four sisters, and an aged father, who, for more than fifty years, has been a faithful member of the Freewill Baptist Denomination. His own family consisted of a daughter and three sons, the oldest of whom went in the army, and the youngest--a child two years old--to heaven, having departed two days in advance of his father. He was aged 43 years.Source: Info is from an old book, "Memoirs of Eminent Preachers In The Freewill Baptist Denomination (1874)," by Selah Hibbard Barrett. (copyright is public domain). Also, a short bio confirms relationships to his minister brothers, etc, in *"Cyclopedia of Free Baptist,"* pub. 1889, by Burgess and Ward as well as a short bio of Isaac G.Family

Samuel Drown
Birth:
Mar. 10, 1796
Sheffield,
Caledonia County, Vermont
Death:
Sep. 9, 1884
Beaver Dam,
Dodge County, Wisconsin
Burial:
Oakwood Cemetery,
Beaver Dam,
Dodge County, Wisconsin,
Plot: Sec 1b

He was ordained a Free Will Baptist minister in 1831 in New Hampshire, and labored for a time in the Wheelock Quarterly Meeting, and also, in New Hampshire, where he was a member of the Legislature three years. In 1845. He moved to Dodge Co., Wisconsin, and obtained land, and continued to reside at Beaver Dam until his death. He was treasurer of Dodge Co. in 1847, and connected with the Jefferson QM of FW Baptists, being widely known and respected.

Benjamin Garret Fowler
Birth:
1774
Death:
Dec. 12, 1848
Burial:
Union Cemetery
Brothertown, Calumet County,
Wisconsin

Fowler, a native of Mohegan, Conn., and one of the Brothertown Indians, was ordained in New York in 1819, and died in Manchester, Wis., Dec. 12, 1848, aged 73 years. "This may certify that Benjamin Fowler is acknowledged as a public administrator in the Free-Will Baptist connection.- Done by order of the Union Yearly Meeting Council at Sherbum, June 14, 1845. Samuel Nichols, Yearly Meeting Clerk."

He was much loved as a good citizen and philanthropist and was respected as a faithful minister. In his advanced years he supplied the Manchester church, preaching his last sermon December 2. He was marshal of the town for several years, and a peacemaker from 1808 to 1811. In religious affairs he was a leader, and ministered as an elder of the Freewill Baptist order. He removed to wisconsin with his family, and aged 74. His gravestone bears the tribute: 'He spoke the language of his Master, 'little children, love one another',

Josiah Fowler
Birth:
Jul. 29, 1794
Thetford,
Orange County, Vermont
Death:
Dec. 29, 1864
Wyocena,
Columbia County, Wisconsin
Burial:
Wyocena Cemetery,
Wyocena,
Columbia County, Wisconsin

His father was a native of England, a cooper by trade and lived in humble circumstances, which compelled the children early to form habits of industry. Rev. Fowler at 13 years of age, gave himself to God; he became connected with the Free Baptists when twenty-one, and while teaching in Camillon, New York, preached his first sermon in his schoolhouse. He received license in Apr 1816, and ordination Aug. 20, 1819, Rev's N. Brown, N. Ketchum and N. Hinckley serving on the council. He had great success as an evangelist and in surrounding towns he baptized multiplied converts which enabled him to organize churches. Out of the many converts, nine became ministers. In 1836, Rev. Fowler became a member of the Ohio and Pennsylvania Y.M., and was active in the work, serving as pastor at Mecca, Ohio., Wellsburgh and Big Bend, Pennsylvania, health permitted. A few months before his death he sought relief in a change of climate, but without avail, and died in Wyocena, Wisconsin. Rev. Fowler was esteemed as one of the church's ablest ministers. He had strong religious sensibilities, and was greatly blessed of God in his chosen line of work. Two of his sons served as officers in the Civil War; one became an attorney and one professor of mathematics in Hillsdale College.

Waiting

Emeline *Wade* Griffin
Birth:
Mar. 29, 1817
Ontario, Canada
Death:
Sep. 1, 1906
Hortonville,
Outagamie County, Wisconsin
Burial:
Allenville Cemetery, Allenville,
Winnebago County, Wisconsin

Married Jacob Griffin 06 Oct. 1836, in Canada. Her husband was a minister, who went from Canada to United States and back, finally to Wisconsin, where they for 35 years together, had been successful in their preaching and church endeavors. She, successfully preached alongside her husband, as per written records. Their work resulted in much good. she died at age 89.

Jacob Griffin
Birth:
Nov. 5, 1815
Lincoln County, Ontario, Canada
Death:
Jan. 26, 1901
Hortonville,
Outagamie County, Wisconsin
Burial:
Allenville Cemetery, Allenville,
Winnebago County, Wisconsin

His parents held loyalist sentiments and went to Canada to escape. It was mostly an untamed area, and Jacob did not have many educational opportunities, but at age 16 years, he heard Rev's David Marks and Obadiah Jenkins preach. After the meeting he joined the Free Will Baptist Church there. He began to preach in 1843, and ordained in Canada in 1844. At once he began in evangelizing and organizing churches. On 06 Oct. 1836, he married Emeline WADE, and shortly thereafter, they migrated to Illinois. He was useful there in that state, but moved back to Canada in 1852, remaining until 1867, when he accepted a call to Winnebago and Vineland churches in Wisconsin. He was abundant in his labors, pastoring and evangelizing in the region. Over 700 were baptized by him. He was a sympathetic friend, a true minister, who sought neither wealth nor the praise of men. His wife Emeline survived him; two sons, Rev. Z.F. Griffin of Keuka College, New York, who for ten years was a missionary in India;

Norvell W. Griffin, a farmer in Oklahoma. A short funeral service was held at his home, then his body was carried by train to the Free Baptist Church, in Allenville, where the Rev. J. M. Kayser, long-time friend, and fellow churchman, officiated at his service.(more information can be found on the Wisconsin Free Will Baptist Historical Society web site, History of Nebraska, Vol 3, by Julius S. Morton).

Nathaniel Harvey
Birth:
Jan. 9, 1788
New Hampshire
Death:
Jun. 4, 1870
Fulton, Rock County, Wisconsin
Burial:
Mount Pleasant Cemetery
Janesville, Rock County, Wisconsin

Harvey was born in Nottingham, N. H., and was converted in early life under the labors of Elder Benjamin Randall. He began to preach when eighteen years of age, and was ordained in 1812, when he settled at Atkinson, Maine., where he remained pastor about thirty years. In 1844 he moved to Fulton,Wisconsin, where he remained until about four years before his death, at Evansville. While in Wisconsin, Brother Harvey was connected with the Calvinistic Baptists.

The Day Is Near

Herman Jenkins
Birth:
1785
Massachusetts
Death:
Jul. 23, 1855
Heart Prairie
Walworth County
Wisconsin
Burial:
Millard Cemetery
Millard
Walworth County
Wisconsin
Plot: Sec. A, Row 4

He was converted in a revival immediately following the organization of the Bethany, NY, church in 1809, about twenty-four years of age. The second session of the Bethany Free Will Baptist Quarterly Meeting (Q.M.) was held at his house in Batavia in May 1813, and he was ordained Aug. 20, 1814. He remained connected with the Bethany church until 1840, when he went to Ashtabula Co. Ohio, and in 1843, he settled in Wisconsin. His death occurred at his house on Heart Prairie, Wis., July 23, 1855.His education was limited, but his acquaintance with human nature and experimental religion, and his great familiarity with the Bible enabled him to labor with great success. The venerable Nathaniel Brown being also with the Bethany church, Bro. Jenkins was permitted to

labor much abroad. His firm health permitted him to indulge his ardent zeal. He was at Boston, NY, in 1817; at Middlebury, NY in 1824, and saw here and elsewhere the abundant blessing of God. He made an exploring tour into Canada in 1822, assisting Elder Banghart at Dunwich, and another tour in 1828, gathering the church in Southwold. He was especially successful at Trumbull and Hart's Grove, OH. Having preached at Penfield, NY in 1830, a revival began, which was continued by others and over fifty persons dated their conviction to his sermons. Few men on the Western frontier have done more efficient service.

He is the beginning and the end

J. M. Kayser
Birth:
Mar. 19, 1831 Columbiana
County, Ohio
Death:
Dec. 21, 1913
Seattle,
King County, Washington
Burial:
Allenville Cemetery, Allenville,
Winnebago County, Wisconsin

He was ordained a Free Will Baptist minister, in Athens, Ohio Quarterly Meeting in 1862. He had been licensed by same, on Nov. 23, 1861. During his first two years of ministry, he traveled as evangelist with the Rev's I. Z Haning and B. V. Tewksbury. He prepared in the Atwood, Ohio Institute for one year, then finishing with the University of Ohio for three years. His pastorates included: Albany, Ohio; Liberty, Illinois; Gobleville and Waverly, Michigan; and Winneconie, Wisconsin, where his labors were blessed. He has filled the Chair of Mathematics at Atwood Institute for three years; was a delegate to the General Conference, was president of the Wisconsin Home Mission Board. He also served in Nebraska Free Will Baptist churches doing mission work and helping there, before going to Wisconsin, where he spent 36 years of his ministry. He was used in many funerals and weddings as he ministered in Wisconsin.

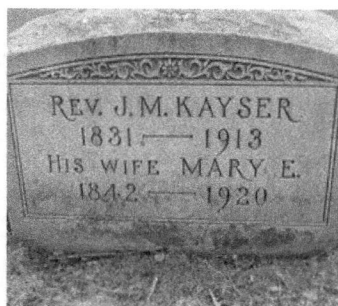

William Mitchell
Birth:
Mar. 5, 1821
Death:
Jan. 8, 1904
Burial:
Union Cemetery
Hortonville, Outagamie
County, Wisconsin

Rev. William Mitchell was born at New Portland, Maine and married to R.C. Staples in 1847. Twenty-seven years later [1874] he was married again to B.L. Raymond. He was converted in 1840, and ordained in 1844.
His ministry of more than forty years has been spent mostly in Wisconsin with the Fairwater, Harrisville, Rosendale, Eldorado, Greenbush, South Prairie, Winnebago, Vinland, Hortonville and Dale churches. The church at Hortonville, where he served as pastor at intervals, in all amounting to more than twenty years.

Augustus Phillips
Birth:
Mar. 27, 1825
Marcellus, New York
Death:
Apr. 30, 1907
Eau Claire, Wisconsin
Burial:
South Lawrence Cemetery
De Pere,
Brown County, Wisconsin

The first two decades of Wrightstown's Freewill Baptist congregation are inexorably tied to the career of Augustus Phillips, one of northeastern Wisconsin's most remarkable religious figures in the second half of the nineteenth century. Three of Phillips' five brothers became Freewill Baptist ministers serving congregations in New England. Phillips apparently received no formal education. He left home at the age of eleven and went to Ohio, then back to New York, and then to Rhode Island, working as a farm laborer and woolen goods manufacturer. In 1846 he married Minerva Greene, and in 1851 the couple moved to Wisconsin, where he purchased 160 acres of land in an unincorporated settlement known as Sniderville, approximately 2 miles northwest of the village of Wrightstown. This farm, later expanded with the purchase of additional acreage, was the family's home for the next 54 years. In September 1864 Phillips enlisted in Company E of Wisconsin's 42nd

Infantry Regiment; he was mustered out in June 1865, after distinguished service, with the rank of corporal. Phillips' religious activities began soon after he arrived in Wisconsin.

He served as a lay preacher beginning in the mid-1850s at the "earnest request" of his neighbors, preaching to Methodist congregations, a practice he may have continued for ten years. He was ordained a Freewill Baptist minister in 1866.

On January 6, 1866, Phillips and fourteen men and women met and organized Wrightstown's Freewill Baptist congregation. Two years later they acquired land and began constructing their church in the village. Within a few years, some of the original members organized separate Freewill Baptist congregations at Sniderville and at Greenleaf, another unincorporated settlement approximately four miles east of Wrightstown. Phillips is credited with establishing all three of these congregations, and he served all three as pastor until 1885. In that year he withdrew from the pastorates of Wrightstown and Greenleaf but continued as pastor at Sniderville, finally retiring from that pulpit in 1905.

Phillips was known for leading successful revivals through out his pastorate. In September 1876 a revival began in Wrightstown "which bids fair to be equal to the one recently held over at Greenleaf, where between 40 and 50 conversions.

In addition to preaching in the three churches at Wrightstown, Greenleaf, and Sniderville, Phillips also exchanged pulpits with other Freewill Baptist ministers throughout the region, including Kaukauna, Oshkosh, Shiocton, and Hortonville, preaching to the

latter congregation every other week "for quite a long time. Phillips and lay members of the Wrightstown church also attended Quarterly Meetings of the Waupun District at various communities throughout northeastern Wisconsin. In October 1905 Phillips preached his farewell sermon to the Sniderville Baptist congregation; Baptists from Wrightstown, Kaukauna, Appleton "and other places" attended. Phillips died in Eau Claire. His body was returned to northeastern Wisconsin by train, his funeral "very largely attended, people from Menasha, Greenleaf, Kaukauna, Wrightstown and De Pere being present." Phillips was buried in the Sniderville Baptist cemetery. Phillips' wife Minerva died on January 6, 1913, and is buried next to him in the Sniderville cemetery (now the South Lawrence Cemetery).

Mowry Phillips
Birth:
Mar. 16, 1857
Death:
Jan. 27, 1942
Burial:

South Lawrence Cemetery
De Pere, Brown County,
Wisconsin

Parents: Augustus Phillips (1825 - 1907) Minerva A. Greene Phillips (1825 - 1913)

James Raymar Pope
Birth:
May 13, 1819
Windsor
Hartford County, Connecticut
Death:
Jun. 8, 1897
Clinton
Rock County, Wisconsin
Burial:
Clinton Cemetery
Clinton
Rock County, Wisconsin

Rev. James Raymar Pope 9th child of Dr. Samuel Pope and Freelove Waterman Pope of Union, Broome Co., NY., and Freelove Pope of Janesville, Rock Co., WI.At the age of 5 years his father Samuel Pope, was a prominent physician, moved to Broome Co., NY. At the age of fifteen James' father died, leaving a family of nine children, of which he was the seventh son. In 1839 Mr. Pope came to Wisconsin probably with mother and brother Cyrus Waterman Pope, settling in Rock County, near Janesville where other brother Virgil Pope resided Section 14, Janesville. At the age of twenty-two he began the study of law, but was converted a year later and joined the Free Will Baptist Church. He abandon the bar and took the pulpit, and began preparation for the same at once. In June 1848 Bro. Pope was ordained to the gospel ministry and in 12 June 1851 in Harmony, Rock Co., WI., was united in marriage to Justina V. Miller a daughter of Cornelius Miller and wife Selinda Smith Miller.In 1889 he was pastor of Longbranch Free Will Baptist Church, located 6 miles southeast of Tecumseh, Johnson Co., Nebraska.

W. A. Potter
Birth:
Jan. 23, 1820
Bennington, Vermont
Death:
Jul. 23, 1880
Monticello, Wisconsin
Burial:
Zwingli Cemetery
Monticello
Green County, Wisconsin

A. B. Taylor
Birth:
unknown
Southwold,
Ontario, Canada
Death:
Jan. 28, 1876
Burial:
Rienzi Cemetery,
Fond du Lac,
Fond du Lac County,
Wisconsin

Rev. Taylor, when nineteen years of age, became a follower of the Saviour, and soon after began preaching. During his labors in Canada he was permitted to see the results of his efforts, and conversions among those with whom he toiled were of frequent occurrence. But as a sense of the paramount importance of the work in which he was engaged came to be fully recognized by him, he felt the need of greater educational advantages than he had yet enjoyed accordingly and soon after entered the Theological department of Hillsdale College. During the time he spent here he was continually at work for the Master, usually preaching three times upon the Sabbath. Revivals seemed to be a natural outgrowth of his labors, and he was permitted to be largely instrumental in the organizing of two or more churches in southern Michigan. So zealously did he labor that it was said of him by one of the teachers, "He has done a lifework before his graduation."Completing his studies in June, 1873, he received a call to the pastorate of the Free Baptist church in Fond du Lac, and soon after entered upon his work. There he continued to labor until a few weeks before his death.

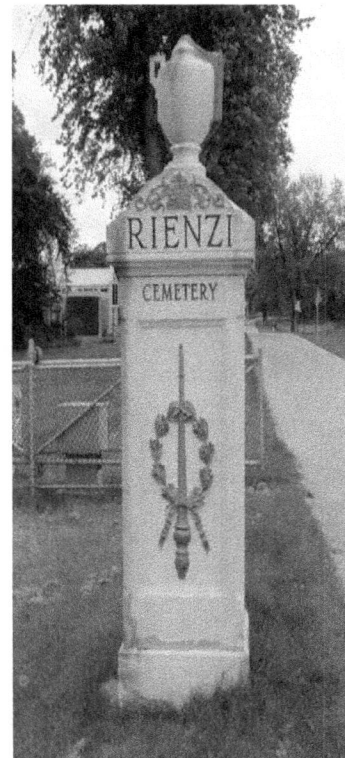

George A. Taylor
Birth:
Nov. 13, 1842
Huntington
Huntington County, Indiana
Death:
Jun. 29, 1913
Los Angeles
Los Angeles County, California
Burial:
Greenwood Cemetery
Dallas
Barron County, Wisconsin

He died at the Pacific Branch, National Home for Disabled Veteran Soldiers, Los Angeles County, California, aged 70 years, 7 months and 16 days, where he had been admitted November 7, 1912. His remains were shipped to Dallas, Barron County, Wisconsin, and buried there beside the remains of his wife Nancy in Greenwood Cemetery.On November 24, 1859, George was united in marriage to Nancy Alvise Rogers, by Reverend G. Dissmore, at Lindina, Juneau County, Wisconsin. Nancy was born August 17, 1838, in Indiana. She died December 29, 1905, aged 67 years, 4 months and 12 days, and was buried in the Taylor family plot in Greenwood Cemetery. They were the parents of nine children.George was a Civil War veteran who enlisted March 10, 1865, at St. Paul, Minnesota, to serve one year as a Private in the 1st Minnesota Infantry, and was mustered into Federal service with Company C the next day at the same location. At that time he received 1/3 of his $100.00 enlistment bounty and was listed as a 22 year and 3 month old, 5'8" tall farmer, with brown hair, brown eyes and a fair complexion, born in Huntington, Indiana, and from Mapleton, Cottonwood Township, Brown County, Minnesota. On March 5, 1865, his name was on a roll of men at the Draft Rendezvouz at Ft. Snelling, St. Paul, Minnesota.On July 14, 1865, George was discharged with Company C, at Jeffersonville, Indiana. His original discharge is in his pension file at the National Archives. On their muster out roll it was noted that he was due 1/3 of his enlistment bounty less $6.00 for arms retained.After his discharge, George returned to Minnesota. He was ordained by the Blue Earth Valley Quarter Meeting in Minnesota, June 13, 1869. He assisted in the organization of the Medo, Minnesota and Dallas, Wisconsin churches and was formerly clerk of the Blue Earth Valley Quarterly Meeting. He was also the first clerk of the Minnesota Southern Yearly Meeting, was a clerk of the St. Croix Quarter Meeting, and was a member of the Minnesota yearly Meeting Home Mission Board. As a citizen he held the office of accessor, town clerk, chairman of the Board Of Supervisors, Justice of the Peace, member of the school board.

He resided there until 1870, when he moved to Mauston, Juneau County, Wisconsin. In 1871, he moved to Colby, Clark County, Wisconsin, and in 1875, to Huntington, Huntington County, Indiana, returning the same year to Mauston. In 1876, he moved to Dallas, Barron County, Wisconsin. He farmed near Dallas and Hillsdale, in that county, and nearby Ridgeland, Dunn County, Wisconsin, until 1908, when he moved to Cauldwell, Idaho. In 1912 he moved to Los Angeles County, California.

Orin Haines True
Birth:
May 30, 1831
Moultonborough, Carroll County, New Hampshire
Death:
Nov. 27, 1913
Burial:
Maple Hill Cemetery
Evansville, Rock County, Wisconsin
Plot: Original Block 1, Lot 135

His parents, Asa W. and Rebecca (Haines) TRUE, gave him early instruction in religion and he was converted when about five years of age. He graduated from the literary department of the New Hampton Institution in 1858, and subsequently from the theological.

He married Miss Sarah L. Bean, of Candia, NH, on Aug. 22,1860 and after her death, fourteen years later, he married Mrs. E. H. Hudson, of Johnstown, Wis. His ordination took place June 20, 1861, his subsequent ministry being with the churches at Lisbon and W. Lebanon, ME, N. Scituate, R.I., Nekimi, Rosendale, Fond du Lac, Evansville, Oakland, York Prairie, Monticello, Scott, Marcellon and Winneconne, Wisconsin. Much of the time his pastoral care has been bestowed upon two of these churches simultaneously. Revivals have attended his ministry, and the churches have been strengthened.

A Light that still Shines

Amos Tyler
Birth:
Apr. 11, 1802
Piermont, N. H.
Death:
Aug. 13, 1876
Big Spring, Wis.
Burial:
Big Spring Cemetery
Big Spring, Adams County,
Wisconsin

Tyler died at age 74 years. His early ministry as a licentiate was with the Methodists. In 1834 he moved to Hatley, Québec, Canada, where he united with the Free Baptists, and was ordained Oct. 2I, 1836. Here he preached in various townships until 1855, when his health became impaired and he moved to Newport,Wis. With returning health he again engaged in ministerial work, gathered the Big Spring and Kilbourn City church, and engaged in many revivals in the Sauk County Q. M. He was eminently social, very helpful in prayer and exhortation, and benevolent in his gifts, especially to the needy interestnear his home. His daughter is Mrs.Rev. W. E. Dennett.

J. J. Wakefield
Birth:
Sep. 15, 1821
Death:
Jul. 28, 1865
Burial:
Beaver Dam City Cemetery
Beaver Dam, Dodge County,
Wisconsin
Plot: L-29

Wakefield was a native of Cornish, Me., died at age 33 years. Such was the type of his piety that the church urged upon him a license to preach, and he was ordained May 30, 1853, at Neenah, Wisconsin. He preached to destitute churches for a time and in 1854 became pastor of the Berlin and Fairwater churches. After four years he settled with the Johnstown church; but in 1860 he moved his family to La Crosse and traveled for his health, yet continued to work for the Master. His gifts were admirably adapted to winning souls, and his early death was widely lamented. recorded in the morning star on September 6, 1865.

Comfort Babcock Waller
Birth:
Jul. 24, 1813
Washington County,
New York
Death:
Feb. 23, 1891
Fond du Lac County,
Wisconsin
Burial:
Oak Center Cemetery,
Fond du Lac County,
Wisconsin

He became a minister just prior to his marriage. and was among the first to pioneer Freewill Baptist work in Wisconsin. He married Nancy Batchelder in 1832 in New York. They moved to Ohio where he was involved in the ministry until 1842 when he removed to Trenton, Washington County, Wisconsin. A little later he moved back and forth serving both the Trenton Freewill Church and one in Scott, Scheboygen County, Wisconsin. Grieved by the loss of his son, David (Co. D 12th Wisconsin Infantry) a prisoner in Andersonville, he decided that a change was in order, so he moved to Fond du Lac County. He did continue to preach and gave his last sermon in the Boltonville Freewill Baptist Church in the fall of 1890.

Peter Warren
Birth:
Jan., 1818
Maine
Death:
Mar. 10, 1856
Burial:
Woodland Cemetery
Kohler
Sheboygan County, Wisconsin

Rev. Peter Warren, was converted at the age of sixteen and soon began preparation for the ministry. He graduated at Redfield, Maine, and was in the Biblical School 1843-45. He sought improved health in the West, where he taught schoolHe was ordained by the Fond du Lac Quarterly Meeting, Wisconsin, June 6, 1852. The next August he became pastor of the Boston, New York, church and later of the Attica church. But health failing, he returned to Greenbush, Wis., where he died in the 39th year of his age.He possessed a mind of high order and was an able minister. Inscription:Aged 38 years

William Warner
Birth:
October 25, 1796
England
Death:
Dec. 3, 1885
Wisconsin
Burial:
Oaks Cemetery
Valton
Sauk County, Wisconsin

He fought in the British ranks at the battle of Waterloo. After coming to America he enlisted in the Army of Jesus Christ in 1820 and soon received license to preach. His early labors were in Quebec, Canada and his ordination being received at Hadley, Quebec, Canada on January 17, 1837. Continuing in the Canadian Province most of the time until about 1848 when he moved to Enfield, New Hampshire and labored there and in the vicinity of a number of years. He then moved to New Hampton and while there gave a very able lecture on the Battle of Waterloo. About 1864 he moved to Clementsville21, Wisconsin uniting with the Vineland church. He was an able minister serving his generation faithfully.

Hiram Watrus
Birth:
Jan. 26, 1815
Williamson
Wayne County, New York
Death:
Jan. 25, 1874
Boscobel
Grant County, Wisconsin
Burial:
Boscobel Cemetery
Boscobel
Grant CountyWisconsin

He was converted in 1833, while living in Geneva, Ohio, and ordained in 1861. While at Scott, Wis. He engaged actively in the work of the ministry in Crawford and Grant Counties, residing ten years at Marion and in 1873 went to Boscobel, where he hired a house of worship and soon organized a church.'He was rich in all the Christian graces,'and his death was felt to be a great loss."

Historial Photos
in Authors Files:

Elizabeth Marks, sister of David Marks and first female gradute of Oberlin College. Residence: Iowa.

Manning Bible Institute, Cairo, Ill.

FWB Seminary-Waterbury, Vt.

Parsonfield Seminary,Parsonfield, Me.

W. Va. College,Flemington, WVA

List of Ministers

Abbey	Mason Hezekiah	407
Abbott	George	119
Abbott	William	120
Abbott	Asa	240
Able	Eldie Clifton	325
Abrams	Walter	289
Adair	Maxi Lee	325
Adams	Amos Banks	47
Adams	John Quincy	120
Adams	James Richard	381
Addington	Hobert Monroe	417
Addison	William Amos	47
Adkins	W. S.	381
Adkins	Roy	426
Adkins	Dallas Carlton	425
Alborn	Charles Henry	424
Alborn	George C.	439
Albright	J. A.	382
Aldrich	Adon	241
Aldrich	Schuyler	289
Alford	J. W.	261
Allen	Matthew R.	193
Allen	John	241
Allen	Jonas	290
Allen	Reuben	364
Allred	O. T.	196
Altis	Earl Edward	196
Altman	Benny Allen	47
Amburgey	John R.	47
Amerson	W. L.	47
Ames	Moses	120
Ammons	H. A.	48
Anderson	R. E.	356
Andrews	Otis	121
Ange	Joseph Garfield	262
Angell	Thomas	363
Anthony	Leonard Short	48
Anthony	Alfred Williams	364
Ard	Allen Bruce	48
Armstrong	Albert A.	241
Arnold	John Calvin	48
Arthur	James	290
Asberry	A. L.	85
Ashby	D. W.	85
Ashby	Hobart C.	290
Ashley	James	170
Atkins	Randall	381
Atkins	Andrew	425
Atwood	Brian	9
Atwood	Hezekiah	121
Austin	William Charles	326
Avery	Austin	212
Ayer	Aaron	121
Babb	J. Franklin	212
Babcock	William S.	213
Bacheler	Henry M.	213
Bacon	Hiram	356
Bagwill	J.H.	86
Bailey	John	121
Baker	Oscar E.	101
Baker	George Washington	290
Baker, Jr	Matthew	86
Ball	John C.	167
Ball	George	241
Ball	Clifford H.	291
Ball	Mance	291
Ballard	Loy Everett	262
Ballard	Willis W.	263
Ballard	John Henry	262
Ballwin	Starks Washington	326
Banks	John J.	122
Banks	Jerry Cleo	326
Bare	Vernie	291
Barfield	J. M.	263
Barker	Lewis P.	197
Barker	Ernold	426
Barker	Paul	426
Barnard	Laura Belle	48
Barnes	John Nelson	49
Barnhart	Peter	291
Barnhill	Alford	326
Barrett	Selah	291

Barrett	Selah Hibbard	292		Bird	Ben	293
Barrow	Nigel Bruce	263		Bixby	Loren	86
Barrow	Jesse Parrott	263		Bixby	Newell	101
Bartlett	Favel	123		Bixby	Ruby Knapp	102
Batchelder	Otis Robinson	213		Blackwelder	Isaac Joshua	43
Batchelor	John Lewis	49		Blair	Roger Lee	115
Batchelor	Johnny Ralph	49		Blair	James Andrew	293
Batchelter	John	123		Blake	Edwin	123
Bates	Daniel E.	292		Blake	Israel	214
Bates	Samuel D.	292		Blake	Orvil	293
Bathrick	Stephen	86		Blanks	J. W.	15
Batson	John D.	187		Blanton	Isaac J.	50
Baxley	Gerald	49		Blanton	David W.	50
Baxter	George	170		Bloss	James B.	382
Bayless	Joseph	110		Blount, Sr.	John Leonard	293
Beach	L. R.	49		Boatright	David Louis	50
Beaman	Thomas Elijah	264		Bond	Walter	9
Bean	Benaiah	213		Bone	Zachariah Taylor	50
Bean	John E.	327		Boody, Jr.	Joseph	214
Beasley	Wilburn	375		Booth	Marvin	294
Beasley	Hilton Clarence	382		Booth	Harry	427
Beatty	Harry Howard	197		Bostic	Howard T.	417
Bedell	Isaiah M.	167		Boston	Shubel	407
Beebe	Velorus	242		Bowden	Stephen	123
Beebe	Warner	293		Bowen	Thomas J.	51
Beers	Ed C.	49		Bowen	Seaborn	51
Bell	Ralph J.	50		Bowen	Clarence F.	264
Bell	Thomas Preston	427		Bowman	Charles R.	294
Bennet	Archibald	170		Boyd	Terry	382
Bennett	Jesse R.	264		Boykin	William	264
Bennett	Charlie	382		Brackett	Levi	124
Bequette	Lue	197		Brackett	Nancy Cram	124
Berry	Arthur C.	427		Brackett	Nathan Cook	426
Berry	Orvil Clinton	427		Braddy	Joe Burney	15
Bess	Ransom	327		Bradley	Barney B.	51
Betchelder	Tappan	101		Bradley	Richard A.	86
Bevan	Paskel Dale	327		Bradley	William	87
Bias	Ernest F.	427		Bradshaw	Fred L.	382
Bickford.	Lewis P.	214		Branch	Samuel S.	87
Bingham	Manuel Eugene	197		Brandon	Kenneth	327
Bingham	W. M.	327		Branham	Steve	115
Binkley	G. W.	382		Brasher	Miles Evans	197

Braswell	David Rowan	51	Bumpus	Erastus	356
Bratcher	Benjamin F.	51	Burch	Tommy Lynn	10
Bratcher	William	327	Burch, Jr	Tommy Lynn	265
Breeden	Zalene Lloyd	417	Burgess	Gideon A.	365
Brewer	Fred	382	Burgess	A. H.	383
Bridges	Henry Elmer	51	Burkholder	Julia Phillips	171
Bridges	Oscar C.	52	Burlingame	Maxcy Whipple	366
Bright	William Lafayette	383	Burnett	Robert L.	52
Bristol	Ernest E.	327	Burnham	Jesse	439
Brodnax	James Edward	52	Burns	William	170
Brooks	Nahum	215	Burns	George	428
Brooks	Homer S.	294	Burr	William	215
Brown	J. A.	9	Burris, Jr	George Washington	16
Brown	Henry P.	15	Burton	William	88
Brown	James F.	15	Butler	John J.	171
Brown	Bobby Lee	30	Butler	Oliver	122
Brown	Gerald E.	52	Butler	Seldon	356
Brown	Henry	87	Buzzell	Hezekiah D.	216
Brown	Ebenezer	124	Buzzell	John F.	408
Brown	Jonathan	124	Buzzell	John	122
Brown	David D.	170	Buzzell	Aaron	216
Brown	Benjamin F.	197	Buzzell	Alvah	216
Brown	Daniel	242	Byer	William	243
Brown	Noah D.	264	Byrd	J. W.	265
Brown	Floyd	428	Cadle	Wilson C.	428
Brown	Amos	215	Cagle	Joseph Lee	376
Brown	Nathaniel	243	Calder	James	357
Brown	Charles	264	Calhoun	Furman C.	428
Brown	Morgan Hillman	294	Calley	David	217
Brown	Allen	365	Calvert	Paul Russell	294
Brown	Jimmy William	376	Campbell	Clarence Elijah	16
Bruce	Joseph	408	Campbell	Cyrus	125
Bryan	Claude R.	198	Campbell	Glynn	16
Bryant	James Earl	52	Campbell	Cecil	198
Bryant	Obed W.	88	Carr	T. P.	53
Bryant	George	124	Carr	Hamilton James	295
Buckelew	Edna Hunt	328	Carroll	William N.	53
Buckner	Noah Estil	428	Carter	J. C. Hubert	53
Bullard	Seldon D.	265	Carter	T. M.	53
Bullock	Almira Wescott	125	Carter	Robert William	328
Bullock	Jermiah	125	Carveno	Arthur	217
Bullock	Wescott	125	Cary	Richard M.	439

Casebolt	John	295		Clay	Jonathan	128
Casey	J. F.	265		Clearly	James	329
Cason	Martin Franlin	53		Cleaver	Mike	198
Castle	Scott	115		Cleveland	Edward	128
Caton	Marion L.	328		Clough	Joseph	440
Caton	James Nathaniel	328		Coats	Romanzo	84
Catrett	Henry L.	53		Coats	David	102
Cave	Gird Ashby	418		Coats	Ruffin	266
Cave	John A.	418		Cobb	Jackson Malone	10
Cave	William Larson	418		Cobb	William	129
Cavin	C . Z.	115		Cobb	Ardon	244
Chabot	Uriah	295		Cobb	Laban	380
Chadbourne	Joseph	126		Cobb	Minerva	380
Chadwick	Edward	126		Coburn	Greenleaf H.	129
Chaffie	Chester	243		Cofer	Thomas Charles	383
Chamberlin	Forrest L.	295		Coffey	Percy Rufus	376
Chambless	L. J.	54		Coffman	Arthur Edward	16
Champlin	David E.	102		Coffman	Joseph Dempsey	17
Chandler	Hubbard	127		Coffman	Lawnie	17
Chapman	William Fleetwood	428		Coffrin	Joshua	408
Chase	Albert H.	40		Coggins	William M.	329
Chase	Daniel	243		Cogswell	Bela	357
Chase	Lyman	88		Colby	George	129
Chase	George Colby	127		Colby	Joshua	130
Chatterton	Benjamin	408		Colby	John	418
Cheney	Oren Burbank	126		Cole	Samuel	218
Cheney	Martin	366		Cole	Solomon	219
Cheney	Rufus Ellis	439		Coleman	W. C.	54
Cherry	Floyd B.	265		Coleman	Isaiah	244
Cheshire	Edward S.	54		Collett	Caleb	95
Childers	Claude B.	88		Collier	Albert Lee	330
Chism	James B.	329		Collins	George W.	54
Chisum	Claude C.	329		Collins	Arthur J.	429
Christian	Herman	383		Colliver	Lawrence	115
Clark	Aaron	128		Combs	William Cecil	429
Clark	John	128		Comer	Fred E.	198
Clark	Dudley E.	172		Comer	Willis C.	430
Clark	Peter	218		Condit	William E.B.	30
Clark	Avery	289		Conley	Harvey Burns	115
Clark	Clarence O.	295		Conley	John Elliott	115
Clark	Rufus B.	296		Cook	John	130
Clark	Carter	428		Cook	Elijah	172

Cooley	Ashel	244		Crowell	William D.	38
Coombs	Lavina Carr	130		Crumb	Luther R.	31
Coombs	Abner	440		Culver	David	367
Cooper	Freeman	131		Curfman	William Ershel	296
Cooper	Carl Joseph	430		Curtis	Elial	296
Cooper	James Wesley	430		Curtis	Silas	220
Cordell	Richard Ray	266		Cutshall	Robert M.	385
Corey	A. P.	187		Dalton	Marvin P.	331
Corrales	Osmondo	31		Dame	Charles Dwight	85
Corson	Charles	219		Dame	Stephen Andrew	331
Cosia	Lewis N.	266		Dame	William David	331
Couillard	Jacob	130		Damron	Wayne	431
Coursey	C. C.	54		Daniel	Joshua Edward	55
Cox	John	95		Daniels	Scott	116
Cox	Authur Elmes	219		Daniels	Amos	245
Cox	Clyde W.	266		Darling	James Harvey	173
Cox	H. Ziri	402		Darling II	Thomas J.	96
Cox	Roy Lee	430		Darst	Budd L.	297
Crabtree	Philip	296		Darte	Freeman	245
Crabtree	Samuel D.	296		Davenport	Frank	267
Craddock	Charles B.	10		Davidson	James Robert	267
Craddock	Moss	431		Davis	Winford C.	199
Craft	John S.	267		Davis	Herbert C.	297
Crase	Henry Clay	198		Davis	Amos	409
Crawford	Robert Barrett	384		Davis	Isaac	440
Crawley	William Robert	51		Davis	Kinsman	208
Creech	Tunis Michael	10		Davis	John Merrill	297
Creech	R. Paul	55		Davis	James Thomas	385
Creech	Parrot	267		Davison	Frank	409
Creech	Ronald	384		Dawson	Willie	55
Crews	William Elvin	199		Day	Tommy Sewell	17
Crocker, Sr.	John L.	267		Day	Willard C.	18
Crockett	Charles	131		Day	Ira	245
Cronk	Trula Gunter	384		Day	George T.	367
Cronk	Daniel Richard	384		Dean	Zebulon	245
Crook	Madison Lamarr	55		Deans	Benjamin	268
Crookes	William	367		Dearmore	William Edward	331
Cross	Gene Autry	55		Dees	Christian Benjamin	199
Cross	Jesse	219		Delawter	Alfred Franklin	297
Cross	David	409		Dell	G. Thomas	55
Crouch	John M.	17		Dell	G. Thomas	55
Crowder	Leonard	330		Dennett	Wilbur	367

Denny	Oscar	246		Dudley	Edward	103
DePuy	Wellington	173		Dudley	Cyrus	298
Deweese	Garrett	268		Dudley	Jerry D.	332
Deweese	Levi	268		Dudley	David	298
DeWitt	William	209		Dudley	Moses	299
Dewitt	F. A.	385		Dudley	Thomas	299
Dexter	Lewis	409		Dunaway	Israel Bunyan	32
Dick	William	41		Dunbar	George D.	386
Dickey	Alice M.	199		Duncan	Zadock D.	386
Dickey	Robert	220		Duniphin	D. B.	332
Dilda	Sigbee Bryant	268		Dunlap	Harold Keith	57
Dills	John B.	116		Dunn	James M.	57
Dimm	Thomas	298		Dunn	Ransom	172
Dingus	Albert	419		Dunn	Francis Wayland	173
Dingus	Robert Aston	419		Dupree	J. H.	57
Dipboye	Glenn G.	18		Durfee	Gilbert	173
Dixon	Othel Thomas	331		Durgin	Frank Llewellyn	187
Dixon	Thomas H.	332		Durgin	Lucy Marilla	188
Doan	Robert H.	376		Durham	Robert Jefferson	269
Doan	Robert	386		Durkee	Jacob	246
Dodd	Damon C.	55		Dutton	Charles Thomas	299
Dodd	Sylvia	56		Duvall	Adrian	18
Dodge	Milo William	110		Dye	James Edward	419
Dodge	Amasa	246		Dye, Sr.	Harley Graham	419
Dodge	Asa	246		Dyer	Joseph	131
Dodge	Eusebius	298		Dyke	Orange	410
Dodge	Asa	358		Eagleton	Marvis	386
Dodge	Calvin	358		Eagleton	Kenneth Paul	386
Dodge	Edward	358		Eason	Nason Earl	269
Doggett	Oris	18		Eastman	Andrew J.	220
Dore	TRUE	131		Eastman	Edmund	368
Doss	Orbin Hurst	32		Eaton	Ebenezer G.	132
Dotson	Claude A.	199		Eaton	Ebenezer	132
Doyle	Jefferson Davis	18		Edgar	William Henry	209
Drake	W. A.	56		Edwards	James Thomas	57
Drake	E. Allen	56		Edwards	Robert	376
Drew	Isaac W.	102		Edwards	Eunice	200
Driggers	William S.	56		Elkins	Daniel	221
Driver	William	199		Elliot	George Columbus	10
Drown	Samuel	442		Ellis	Donald	299
Duckworth	Earl B.	57		Ellis	Herman Hughes	387
Duckworth	Dyer	261		Elswick	John William	300

Elswick	John	300		Findley	Hoyd Duard	59
Emanuel	Adolphus	58		Finley	Hoyt Duard	59
Emanuel	John M.	58		Flanders	Thomas	133
Embry	George Troup	58		Florence	Virgil	39
Emerson	William H.	58		Floyd	Drew	59
England	Quentin	300		Floyd	John Eugene	271
Ennis	Lonne R.,	269		Floyd	Winford R.	387
Estep	Floyd E.	300		Fondren	William	193
Estep	Owen	431		Fonville	Frederick Asa	271
Etheridge	Charles B.	58		Forrest	John	410
Etheridge	Grady C.	58		Fort	Joseph O.	59
Evans	James A.	270		Fort	Joe T.	387
Evans	Fred C.	301		Foss	Joseph	133
Evans	Calvin	300		Foster	Charles	133
Everett	W. B.	270		Fowler	Herschel Greeley	59
Everson	Alton	59		Fowler	Benjamin	442
Everton	James W.	270		Fowler	Josiah	443
Ewer	Daniel	174		Fox	Jesse Augustus	334
Ewer	Nathaniel	174		Foy	William	133
Fairchild	Vernal Lee	301		Franklin	Warren	200
Fairfield	Micaiah	174		Franklin	James Albert	334
Farless	George W.	387		Frederick	Joe Sephus	11
Farley	John	247		Freeman, Jr	Claud	333
Farnum	Herbert Ruthwen	368		French	Estel M.	387
Farrell	Harrison William	387		Fry	Malcolm Craig	388
Farwell	Josiah	132		Frye	Arthur G.	431
Fasion	Kenneth	59		Fulcher, Jr.	William M.	271
Fassio	Cecil R.	333		Fuller	Jarius	134
Fast	John	111		Fullerton,Sr	Isaac	301
Fay	Edward	410		Fulton	William J.	301
Fellabaum	Ward	333		Gage	Jake W.	335
Felt	L. D.	103		Gage	Howard Joe	334
Felt	Marcus	103		Gallant	Richard Henry	335
Fenner	Louisa	41		Gallison	William F.	134
Fergueson	James Anderson	333		Ganey	Houston Owen	272
Ferguson	Tom C.	200		Gann	Milton	11
Ferguson	A. F.	402		Gardner	James Salmon	247
Ferrall	William M.	270		Gardner	Levi	247
Fields	O. L.	11		Gardner	Squire	247
Fields	William G.	334		Gardner, Jr	Willie M.	388
Fifield	William Penson	174		Garfield	John	410
Fincher	Sadie E.	334		Garland	David	221

Garland	Benjamin	388		Green	Louis H.	272
Garrido	John E.	431		Green	Millard	301
Garrision	Cecil Oliver	18		Greene	Ted	116
Gaskins	Raymond Albert	272		Greene	David	248
Gates	Newton Preston	174		Greene	Caleb	368
Gause	Webster Pressley	376		Greenway	Virgil R.	200
George	W. E.	44		Greenwood	Herman A.	19
Getchell	Mark	134		Greeson	Shelby Van	335
Getchell	William	134		Griffin	Emmaline	443
Gibson	Luther D.	193		Griffin	Benjamin J.	61
Gibson, Sr	Norwood A.	377		Griffin	Jacob	443
Giddens	Harvey W.	59		Griffin Sr	Jesse Christopher	272
Giddens	Murray Elvin	60		Grimsby	William Thomas	62
Giddens	Teedom M.	60		Grimsley	E. C.	61
Gidney	Harry	135		Grinnell	Thomas	175
Gifford	Henry	103		Gross	Stephen	137
Gilbert	Chester A.	60		Guinn	William M.	19
Gilkey	Phillip	135		Guthrie	Don	19
Gill	Walter D.	60		Guyton	Whitaker	11
Gill	Benjamin Terrell	60		Guyton	Whitaker	15
Gillett	Truman	248		Hackett	Moulton	221
Gilliland	James Charles	89		Hadden	Claude H.	62
Given	Lincoln	135		Haggett	S. M.	137
Gleason	Abel	103		Hale	Johnie Eli	335
Goodrich	Bernard	136		Hall	James M.	302
Goodwin	Joseph	136		Hall	John R.	336
Goolsby	Richard M.	16		Hall	Lonnie	336
Goolsby	Richard Harrell	60		Hall	Paul Frederick	388
Gordon	George Alexander	89		Hall Jr	John	273
Goss	Kyle	19		Hallock	C. E.	248
Gould	Delbert Glendon	302		Halsted	David	104
Gowen	Lewis Woodbury	424		Ham	Ezra	221
Gower	H. Wilkes	388		Hames	Claudie	32
Gower	James W.	388		Hampton	Ralph C.	389
Graham	Daniel M.	359		Hampton	Charles Edgar	389
Grant	John	136		Hampton, Sr	Ralph Clayton	336
Graves	Josiah	41		Haning	Ira Z.	302
Gray	William H.	60		Hanks, Jr	George Washington	336
Gray	Andrew	137		Hanna	Marie	95
Green	Benjamin Franklin	61		Hannibal	Ely	248
Green	Doctor Evan	51		Hanscom	Pelatiah	222
Green	Ross H.	200		Hansley	David Wells	273

Hanson	Moses	222
Hanson	Luther	248
Harding	Ephraim	137
Harding	Elisha	175
Harley	Floyd	89
Harman	Lot	138
Harness	Joseph Franklyn	303
Harper	Joseph	222
Harrell	Kelly C.	62
Harrell	C. W.	62
Harrell	Bobby E.	273
Harriman	David	223
Harrington	John	223
Harris	Mark Metcher	20
Harris	James G.	62
Harris	R. S.	390
Harris	James G.	62
Harris, Jr	Charlie Jackson	273
Harrison	Thaddeus F.	273
Harrison	Ernest	336
Hartley	John R.	20
Harvery	Erastus	104
Harvery	Nathaniel	444
Harvey	C. J.	62
Haskell	George	138
Haston	W. D.	402
Hasty	Stephen Robert	390
Hathaway	Asa	139
Hathaway	Leonard	139
Hathorn	Samuel	138
Hawkins	Henry Lee	303
Hayden	Wentworth	188
Hayes	R. Staten	62
Hayes	David A.	303
Hayes.	James A.	116
Head	William H.	390
Heard	Chester	38
Hearron	William H.	337
Hearron	J. Author	337
Heath	Josiah Lorenzo	188
Heath	Jeremiah	274
Hecox	Luther	303

Hellard	Everett D.	402
Henderson	Benjamin F.	200
Hensley	Ottis	431
Henson	John M.	431
Henson	Herbert	303
Hersey	Herman Lawrence	390
Hershey	Evelyn	89
Hewitt	Moab	377
Hicks	James Walter	89
Hicks	Elijah Myers	377
Hicks	Peleg	411
Hidde	Robert Dean	337
Higgins	Joseph	139
Higgins	Kendal	303
High	Carl Leo	20
Hill	Joel	62
Hill	Albert	140
Hill	William C.	201
Hill	Samuel	223
Hill	Isaac	249
Hill	William J.	391
Hill	John David	274
Hill	Mark	411
Hill	Finas Arlin	419
Hillis	Bessie Widener	62
Hillis	Bessie Widener	62
Hills	Clinton	359
Hills	Marilla Turner	223
Hiltibidal	John	89
Hiltibidal	Opal	89
Hilton	Charles	188
Hisey	Jacob	304
Hix	Orrin	104
Hoag	Charles	249
Hoag	Isaac	249
Hobson	Andrew	140
Hockenberry	John	432
Hodge	Ephriam	249
Hodges	Elmer	201
Hogue	Herbert Curtis	337
Holbrook	Paul	411
Holden	Joseph Holden	419

Holland	Terrell	20		Hull	John Gilbert	380
Hollis	Daniel G. W.	12		Hulsey	Thomas Russell	12
Hollis	Martin Luther	194		Hunt	Daniel	360
Holloman	James Monroe	20		Hunt	Robert	250
Holman	Critt	391		Huntoon	Henry	224
Holmes	Robert W.	63		Hutchins	Samuel	141
Holmes	W. H.	63		Hutchins	Leonard	141
Holmes	Hiram	224		Hutchins	Elias	224
Holroyd	Charles	104		Hutchinson	Asa	142
Holt	Clint H.	275		Hyatt	Isaac	411
Holton	George Sharrod	63		Hyman	Herman A.	377
Honeycutt	Nathan	391		Ide	Rogers	250
Hooper	William	304		Ingerick	John W.	360
Hoover	Arlie	111		Inman	Cyrus	304
Hopkins	George	89		Irvin	Dennis Oliver	63
Hopkins	George	368		Irvin	Von Deron	64
Hopson	Pelathiah M.	140		Irvin	Paul H.	63
Hopson	Andrew	167		Isbell	William Sherman	21
Horne	Benjamin Franklin	53		Isham	George M.	338
Hoskinson	Andrew	90		Jackson	Chester	250
Houghton	Alphonso	141		Jackson	Nelson	251
Houston	Carlton Robert	63		Jackson	Roy H.	275
Howard	Eugene	12		Jackson	Daniel W.	411
Howard	Francis	141		Jackson	Joseph	412
Howard	George	175		Jackson	Daniel	251
Howell	Danny H.	274		Jackson	Billy Gray	275
Howes	Edward	175		Jackson	Robert Copps	275
Howes	Solomon	249		James	John Pierce	64
Hubbard	George	90		Jaques	Benjamin	142
Hubbard	Kyle Wilson	420		Jarrett	Clarence Albert	338
Hubbard	Monroe	420		Jeffers	Lorenzo	225
Huckaba	Gaylord	20		Jeffrey	John	304
Huckeby	Henry Sanford	337		Jeffreys	Lloyd	201
Huckins	Thomas	176		Jeffreys L.	Opal	201
Huddleston	Truman	32		Jenkins	John H.	64
Hudgens	Jesse	391		Jenkins	Enoch	105
Hudguns	King David	201		Jenkins	Herman	444
Hugguns	Orville	90		Jenkins	Calvin	251
Hughes	William Bonnie	12		Jenne	Alonzo	176
Huling	Daniel	250		Jenness	Rubin V.	225
Huling	James	338		Jenson	Earl	338
Hull	John Jay	33		Jernigan	Walter L.	275

Jernigan	Wade T.	339		Kennedy, Sr	Rashie	276
Jobe	William Rufus	21		Kenny	Moses R.	177
Johns	Edward	33		Kern	Arthur W.	90
Johnson	Keith	21		Ketcham	Samuel	177
Johnson	Jennie	38		Ketcham	Nathaniel	251
Johnson	Linton C.	65		Ketchum	Bob L.	340
Johnson	David	111		Ketchum	William O.	340
Johnson	M. L.	275		Ketteman	Columbus Jackson	91
Johnson	Richard M.	391		Ketteman	Paul J.	392
Johnson	J. W.	402		Keyes	Samuel	112
Johnson	Ezra	420		Kicenki	Arthur A.	201
Jones	G. W.	65		Kilburn	Alanson	412
Jones	Spurgeon	64		Kilgore	Harold	420
Jones	M. H.	96		Kilgore, Jr	Emmett J.	420
Jones	Ichabod	96		Killingsworth	John A.	195
Jones	Abner	226		Kimble	Howard	305
Jones	Daniel Wyatt	195		Kimbrough	John Dudley	340
Jones	Scott	339		King	George	412
Jones	William Chapman	339		King	Nathaniel	413
Jones	Billy Marion	403		Kingsbury	Elijah	177
Jordan	John	142		Kingsbury	Leonard	177
Joslin	David A.	21		Kinney	William	142
Joslin	Joel Arthur	22		Kirk	Dewey R.	392
Joyner	Alan Clinton	276		Kirkland	Zane T.	23
Judd	George Earl	339		Kittle	Jobe	305
Kalar	Anson	176		Knight	Arnold	177
Kayser	J. M.	445		Knighton	Hiram Leroy	65
Keith	Ruth	188		Knowles	Samuel	227
Keith	Charles Edward	276		Knowlton	Ebenezer	143
Kellam	Charles Rice	22		Knowlton	Zina	144
Kelly	Hughie J.	65		Lamb	John	144
Kelton	Darwin Eugene	22		Lamb	George	144
Kemper	John Robert	305		Lambert	James Patton	420
Kenerson	Francis	226		Lane	William B.	65
Kenison	Spencer	226		Lane	Richard G.	341
Keniston	Thomas	227		Laney	Greenville	66
Kennan	Ralph	44		Lang	Larkin	167
Kennan	Ida M.	176		Lansing	Peter Alexander	209
Kennedy	Paul	33		Large	William Henry	420
Kennedy	Richard P.	340		Lash	John	178
Kennedy	Ernest McKinley	23		Latham	W. R.	13
Kennedy	Robert	276		Latimer	George	112

Lawhorn	William Randolph	66		Lord	Samuel	413
Lawhorn	Simeon Roy	66		Loring	Horatio	52
Lawless	Winston Benton	33		Lothrop	Nathan	227
Lawrence	Richard	43		Lovejoy	Frank	432
Laws	Jesse	392		Loveless	John	252
Lawter	Arthur F.	378		Lovering	James B.	68
Leach	Zachariah	144		Lovett	L.O.	68
Leatherbury	Glennda	9		Loyless	J. W.	68
Leavenworth	J. B.	178		Lucas	John W.	277
Ledbetter	Willis Jackson (Jack)	112		Lucas	Malachi Daniel	277
Lee	George Cullen	195		Lucas	Patrick Thomas	277
Lee	Harry	341		Lumpkin	Henry Lewis	58
Lee	William Wallace	392		Lumpkin	Johnnie B.	68
Lee	John Alvin	341		Lumpkin	William Robert	68
Lee, Jr.	Robert	23		Lunsford	John T.	69
Lesher	John	105		Lunsford	John W.	341
Lett	C.C.	432		Lupton	Alice Voliva	277
Letts	James	252		Luther	Israel	96
Lewis	Herman A.	23		Lybarger	Curtis Lee	23
Lewis	Samuel	145		Lyford	Francis	227
Lewis	Lincoln	227		Lykins	Charles	305
Lewis	Claudis	305		Lyon	Daniel	252
Libby	Almon	145		Lyons	Bobby J.	305
Libby	David	145		Mack	Enoch	253
Libby	James	145		Mack	William	253
Lick	Absalon S.	202		Maddox	Walter B.	23
Lighthall	W. A.	252		Magoon	Josiah	228
Lightsey	Tom Joseph	67		Malone	Wallace	91
Lightsey	Ralph	66		Malvern	Lewis	168
Lilley, Sr.	Leslie Allen	432		Mankster	David T.	342
Limbocker	Henry S.	112		Mann	Charles Earl	202
Lindsey	William E.	341		Mann	Thomas J.	202
Linville	Andrew Jackson	432		Mann	Marvin Kenneth	341
Lisle	Bruce V.	66		Manning	Levi B.	69
Little	James D.	67		Marcum	Samuel H.	202
Little	Joel H.	67		Marcum	Herman	306
Little	S. N.	67		Marie	Hyatt	201
Littlefield	Ezekiel	368		Mariner	John	146
Lofts	J. W.	403		Markin	Marvin Dale	306
Long	Theron W.	67		Marks	Ives	97
Loomis	Amaziah	105		Marks	William	209
Lord	David	178		Marks	David	305

Marmon	Amos	306		McDaniel	John D.	70
Marshall	Albert Josiah	189		McDaniel	Walter Ballenger	70
Marston	James	105		McDaniel	Alva	308
Martin	C.C.	69		McDonald	Warren Arthur	70
Martin	Robert	119		McFadden	Richard B.	71
Martin	James W.	307		McFall, Sr.	S. M.	421
Martin	Isaac	403		McGee	W. H.	13
Martin	Samuel Crawford	403		McGee	Wilton R.	97
Martin	Eugene	307		McGee	Joshua E.	343
Martin	Moses Walter	307		McGehee	Dottis	343
Massey	Newton Elmore	69		McGray	Asa	39
Massey	Roger M.	69		McKee	William Franklin	24
Masters	Chester V.	307		McKee	Martin	343
Matthews	Woodrow	13		McKenzie	Cecil E.	343
Matthews	Thomas Hillman	277		McKenzie	James	371
Mauck	Joseph William	178		McKindsley	Elbridge L.	146
Mawhorter	Thomas J.	97		McKinney	Vester	421
May	Isaac	307		McKoon	Benjamin	253
Mayhall	Trellis L.	13		McKoon	Daniel W.	254
Mayhew	Archie	33		McKoon	Newton	254
Maynard	John H.	179		McKown	John D.	202
Maynard	Authur	308		McLendon	Seab A.	71
Maynard	Lester James	343		McMillan	Clarence	71
Mayo	Elihue Roy	13		McMillan	John W.	91
McAdams	Elizabeth R.	404		McMillan	George	91
McAdams	Hiram Mullens	405		McMinn	Thomas	92
McAffrey	Alvis Lee	343		McPeek	Ersel	421
McAlister	Doice Lee	34		Meade	Jesse	116
McBride	Leon	91		Meade	Robert Lee	308
McCage	Furman Archie	343		Meade	Albert	433
McCarroll	James Willard	392		Meadows	Reford	308
McCarty	Billy O.	308		Mellette	Thomas B.	71
McCarty	William	308		Mellette	Milton H.	378
McCellan	James Samuel	24		Melvin	Henry	393
McCellan	Elbert	24		Merkh	Daniel James	421
McClain	George W.	34		Merkh	Margaret Lucille	421
McClain	Peter	71		Merrill	Asa	228
McClary	John	228		Merrill	Nathan	229
McCorvey	Solomon Oscar	70		Meservey	Atwood B.	229
McCullers	Jordan	70		Milam	Russell	309
McCutcheon	James	228		Miley	Laverne Dale	393
McDanal	Frank Seeley	70		Millard	William F.	202

Miller	John	146
Miller	George	202
Miller	Bert	309
Miller	Troy	309
Miller.	James F.	202
Million	George W.	24
Mills	Henry	71
Mills	Michael	98
Mills	Charles Blunt	179
Milton	Nathan H.	229
Miner	Jared H.	98
Minton	George W.	92
Mishler	William J.	92
Mitchell	William	445
Mock	Cecil C.	71
Modlin	Samuel E.	92
Monk	William Moses	278
Montgomery	H. S.	71
Moody	David	146
Moody	Samuel A. J.	179
Mooneyham	Walter Stanley	34
Moore	Roy M.	25
Moore	Donald	72
Moore	Tommy	117
Moore	Alfred	278
Moore	J. W.	278
Moore	J. H.	278
Moore	James	279
Moore	John	279
Moore	Gerald G.	309
Moore	Tommy	310
Moore	Redding Floyd	378
Moore, Jr.	Samuel M.	378
Morelock	William H.	393
Morgan	J.C.	344
Morgan	Tillman C.	433
Morrell	Alexander Hatch	433
Morrill	Benjamin L.	107
Morrill	Samuel Plummer	147
Morris	Edward C.	279
Morris	E. E.	344
Morris	Kevin Willard	310
Morrow	John	209
Morse	Horace Washington	113
Morse	Timothy	230
Morse	Horace	310
Moses	William	310
Moulton	Thomas	106
Moulton	Levi	147
Moulton	Franklin	189
Moulton	Albanus Avery	311
Moulton	Albanus K.	311
Mounts	James E.	433
Mowry	John Russell	106
Mowry	Junia Smith	106
Mowry	Salome Lincoln	369
Moxley	John	413
Moye	James C.	279
Mugg	Marcus	179
Mullins	Earlist	117
Mullins	Sam	433
Munkus	B. C.	344
Munsey	Howard T.	394
Munsey	James Alan	394
Musgrove	George N.	35
Musgrove	Isaac Frank	72
Music, Sr	James R.	311
Myers	Seaborn Franklin	72
Nance	Luther	13
Nealy	William	230
Nelson	Jonathan	413
Nelson	J. M.	414
Nelson	Homer	312
Newbold	Joshua G.	107
Newby	John Columbus	344
Newell	Francis	113
Newman	Clarence	312
Nichols	Asahel	254
Nicholson	John	254
Nickerson	Joseph	147
Nickerson	Samuel	230
Noble	Joseph N.	147
Noble	John N.	203
Noles	Mancy C.	378

Norie, Jr	Oliver Roy	405	Patrick	Christopher	281
Norris	John	231	Patt	William . D	369
Norris	David	414	Paul	Benjamin	425
Northrup	William A.	113	Pauley	Eldon M.	434
Norton	Lemuel	148	Pauley	George	434
Norton	Erastus	180	Payne	L. D.	25
Norton	William R.	180	Payne	Kelvin	93
Norwood	James H.	195	Pease	Albert	148
Noyes	Eli	98	Peaslee	A. C.	231
Nutting	William	255	Peaslee	Isaac	231
Odell	Nathaniel	107	Peck	Benjamin	370
O'Donnell	Herman	14	Peden	Thomas E.	281
O'Donnell	Dennis H.	345	Pelt	Daniel F.	44
O'Donnell	Emris Allen	345	Pelt	Chester H.	44
Oliver	William Henry	394	Pembrook	Roy E.	35
Osgood	John Calvin	414	Pennington	Charlie	117
Otis	Micajah	231	Perkins	Seth	149
Outlaw	Addie H.	80	Perkins	Charles Sumner	415
Overman	C. H.	280	Perry	Oliver Hazard John	73
Overstocker	Jacob	92	Perry	Peter Wells	93
Pace	Hardy C.	395	Perry	James Jasper	313
Packard	Isaac t.	312	Peters	August Jonathan	73
Page	Ezekiel Gilman	148	Peterson	Moses Washington	281
Page	John	148	Phelon	Benjamin	370
Page	Benjamin	414	Phillip	Edgar T.	282
Paine	William	149	Phillips	Mary R.	182
Palmer	Asahel	107	Phillips	Mowry	371
Palmer	Judson B.	405	Phillips	Augustus	445
Pannell	James Montgomery	345	Phillips	Mowry	446
Park	William T.	72	Phillips	Bruce Erwin	25
Parker	Benjamin P.	149	Phillips	Jeremiah	181
Parker	Thomas	255	Phillips	Nellie Maria	181
Parker	Joseph	280	Phillips	Ida Orissa	182
Parker	Seth	313	Phillips	Stephen	372
Parkman	William H.	72	Phinney	Clement	150
Parmelee	Linus S.	180	Phinney	Joseph	150
Parrish	Neal H.	72	Phinney	A. P.	255
Parsons	William C.	99	Pierce	Cedric	282
Patch	Orrin D.	93	Pierce	Asa	313
Pate	Isaac Newton	345	Pike	John	150
Patrick	James Monroe	25	Pimlott	Edwin	313
Patrick	Raymond	25	Pinkham	John	150

Scott	Linza D.	78	Small	James	156
Scott	Henry W.	134	Small	Humphrey	156
Scott	George Washington	204	Small	James	156
Scott	Adam	285	Smart	Wiley L.	94
Seaman	Samuel Buck	361	Smith	Sheldon	36
Sellards	James W.	205	Smith	Charles	113
Sellers	Farest W.	78	Smith	Tilton E.	184
Sellers	Willie A.	78	Smith	Andrew	191
Senters	Carl Lee	117	Smith	Samuel	210
Sewell	Caleb	94	Smith	Stephen Elias	379
Sexton	Donald Ray	397	Smith	Denver Earl	317
Shafer	James Harold	434	Smith	Rolla Darrell	398
Sharp	Levi N.	190	Smithey	Ira W.	349
Sharp	James	257	Smithey	James William	349
Shattuck	Charles	83	Smutz	David	108
Shaver	Abram Clark	434	Snow	Fred Albertis	156
Shaw	Sargent	155	Solomon	Aaron W.	349
Shelton	Melvin	27	Southwick	George B.	257
Shelton	Robert S.	27	Sowards	Ted B.	317
Sheppard	William J.	316	Sparks	Paul M.	184
Sherwood	Benjamin A.	372	Sparks	Crate D.	317
Shipley	H. D.	27	Sparks	Delmar C.	318
Shipman	Ophir	415	Spears	David Leonard	285
Shippee	Charles Henry	372	Spencer	R. B.	285
Shiry	Nicolas	361	Springfield	Thomas Woods	14
Shivers	Carl David	348	Springfield	William James	14
Shockey	Robert Logan	398	St. Claire	Eugene Louis	74
Shoemaker	Joshua G.	361	Staab	J. J.	14
Shonkwiler	Jacob	316	Stafford	Warren Chase	168
Shonkwiler	James A.	317	Stahl	Berne Ora	28
Shrewsbury	Gaylord M.	435	Staires	Harry E.	349
Shutes	Kenneth	77	Standley	Richard Milo	205
Silvernail	John	183	Stanford	Federal A.	184
Simpson	Elzie Elisha	205	Stanley	Iris Lyndon	196
Sinclair	John L.	236	Stanley	Chester V.	286
Sisson	George W.	210	Stanley	Roy Lee	435
Sizemore.	Carl R.	317	Starbird	Freelon	156
Sizemore.	Sherman	434	Starr	Norman	184
Sledge	Camey Alexander	348	Staten	Charles R.	28
Sleeper	Levi	236	Staten	Ralph Lee	28
Slone	Joe	118	Stearns	Asa	318
Small	William	108	Stedman	Eli	318

Steele	Cyrus	257	Sweetland	Virgil	158
Steele	John Corydon	362	Swett	Jesse	158
Steelman	Elmer F.	350	Swett	David	158
Steere	Martin	373	Sylvester	Bradbury	159
Stepp	Jessey D.	350	Tallman	Ezra	258
Stepps	James Dallas	286	Tally	John H.	205
Stevens	Moses	156	Tanner	Brighton N.	319
Stevens	Hiram	237	Tappan	Edmund M.	168
Stevens	Glen W.	422	Tasker	Friend D.	159
Stevenson	William S.	156	Taylor	John	78
Steward	Justice H.	108	Taylor	William	258
Stewart	Angus McAllister	405	Taylor	Obediah J.	406
Stewart	Roma	350	Taylor	A. B.	447
Stewart	Sam Peyton	398	Taylor	Paul	319
Stiles	Ada Henrietta Tucker	237	Taylor	George A.	448
Stiles	Edwin Byron	237	Teague	Harold R.	406
Stiles	S. W.	416	Teague	William Horace	399
Stilson	Cyrus	157	Tedder	J. L.	79
Stinson	Joseph	157	Tedford	Charles	169
Stinson	William C.	157	Terry	Grover V.	205
Stogsdill	William Preston	205	Terry, Jr.	Thomas O.	286
Stone	Hertis	318	Thigpen	Jonathan Noel	94
Stone	J. B.	350	Thomas	Rue	85
Stone	James Gilbert	350	Thomas	Sophia	159
Stoup	James R.	78	Thomas	John	184
Stout	Alvah	157	Thomas	Nelson	185
Stout, Jr.	James	157	Thomas	Roena C.	206
Stovenour	Frederick	99	Thomas.	Roy L.	40
Straight	Freeborn W.	191	Thompson	Paul Timothy	15
Strawn	J. W.	348	Thompson	Roy Lathan	28
Strickland	Thomas J.	78	Thompson	James Alford	79
Styron, Jr.	Simon H.	286	Thompson	George W.	114
Sullivan	Glover Cleveland	78	Thompson	Thomas	159
Summerlin	Spencer	108	Thompson	Lawrence D.	206
Sunday	Edward S.	350	Thompson	Bailey	351
Surratt	John	435	Thompson	Charles	406
Sutton	J. A.	319	Thompson, Jr	Clyde	319
Sutton	Milton L.	406	Thornton	Abel	373
Swaffer	John C.	205	Thorton	Allen L.	79
Sweatt	John	109	Tingley	Pelatiah	161
Sweet	Daniel Angell	373	Tippett	Elbert Worth	399
Sweet	Nathaniel	373	Tobey	Zalmon	42

Tomlinson	A. J.	79		Vance	Robert Lee	437
Toothacker	Edward	159		Vance	Ward	438
Touchton	Moutrie H.	79		Vanhoose	Eliphas Preston	118
Touchton	Thomas T.	79		Vanhoose	Frew Stewart	118
Towner	Benjamin	362		Vanhoose	Millard	118
Townsend	Thomas Jefferson	351		Vanhoose	Clyde M.	321
Tracy	Christopher	159		Vanhoose	Richard Scott	118
Tracy	Etta G.	160		Vanover	Roy C.	423
Tracy	Jonathan	160		Vanover	Clovis	321
Tracy	Olin Hobbs	160		Vaughn	Henry W.	100
Travis	William	435		Vause	Jesse	286
True	Orin Haines	448		Vause	Cornelius Acue	379
Truett	Sam R.	379		Vause	Julius B.	379
Trustry	Alvin	320		Venable	Ruben B.	29
Tucker	Wayne	28		Vicars	Ralph	423
Tucker	William	100		Vickers	Julian	80
Tucker	David A.	100		Von Dame	Bartholomew	238
Tucker	Joshua	416		Waddell	R. Eugene	399
Tufts	Francis	320		Waddle	William	351
Tufts	John	320		Wade	Edgar Jackson	80
Tufts	Benjamin	320		Wade	Frank W.	80
Turner	Willie Gus	79		Wade	Charles	374
Turner	Jason B.	379		Wages	George W.	196
Turner	Abel	160		Wainwright	Chester C.	438
Turner	Kenneth	206		Wakefield	J. J.	449
Tyler	Job C.	237		Wakely	Sidney	162
Tyler	Amos	449		Waldron	Orrin	259
Tyree	Roy Alex	436		Walker	Charles P.	169
Uhles	Emma Serena	94		Wallace	John	162
Ulmer	Matthias	162		Waller	Comfort Babcock	449
Upton	Dell	436		Walrath	Joseph Harvey	185
Urury	James	79		Waltman	John Alexander	36
Utley	Jacob	286		Ward	John T.	185
Vail	Charles Luther	258		Ward	George Douglas	95
Valentine	Robert T.	109		Ward	Lonnie E	351
Vallance	Carl Wesley	436		Warner	Robert J.	206
Van Tuyl	William	259		Warner	William	450
Van Winkle	James L.	351		Warren	Peter	449
VanAmburgh	Freeman	258		Waterman	Ira	206
VanAmringe	Henry H.	362		Waterman	Granville C.	238
Vance	Leon	14		Waterman	Dexter	162
Vance	Preston	437		Watkins	Samuel	80

Watrus	Hiram	450		Whitney	John	165
Watson	Benjamin Blanton	80		Whitney	William E.	186
Weaver	Ralph Lee	423		Whittemore	Joseph	109
Webb	Reece G.	29		Whittemore	Edwin E.	260
Webb	Charles	321		Whittemore	David Richards	374
Webb	Eugene	321		Whittler	Philander E.	322
Webb	Harrison	321		Widdig	David	322
Weed	Simeon J.	321		Wiggs	Nestus D.	287
Weeks	John R.	81		Wilburn	Marion	322
Welch	John W.	399		Wilder	Alvin	322
Wellbaum	Mary Elizabeth	207		Wiley	Green Thomas	82
West	John H.	352		Wiley	William T.	82
West	William R.	352		Wiley	Frederick L.	239
West	Robert	287		Wiley	Charlie	323
Weston	Willie K.	207		Wilkerson	Junis J.	400
Weymouth	Nathaniel F.	163		Wilkinson	Samuel Longstreet	82
Whaley	Lee	287		Willey	Mabel Alice	45
Wheeler	John B.	81		Willey	Emma Ruth	288
Wheeler	Samuel	163		Willey, Sr.	Thomas	45
Wheeler	Austin	192		William	Omer	438
Wheeler	Wilmetta Marks	211		Williams	E. C.	82
Wheeler	Abel	238		Williams	Jules Legender	114
Wheeler	John	322		Williams	Alvin Dighton	211
Wheeler	John	287		Williams	Allen	323
Whitaker	Alexander H.	186		Williams	James O.	352
Whitaker	Harry Paul	423		Williams	Clarence O.	374
Whitcher	Hiram	259		Williams	Daniel	42
Whitcom	Samuel	186		Williams	Paul	207
Whitcomb	Simeon Coffin	163		Williams	Paul Eugene	323
White	James E.	29		Williams	Henry	374
White	Stanton B.	29		Williamson	Charles Cecil	46
White	William Pleasant	30		Williamson	Stephen	164
White	Will S.	30		Willis	Kinnebrew	82
White	Connie C.	81		Willis	Otis	239
White	Joseph	164		Willis	Homer Emerson	400
White	Billy Joe	322		Willis, Sr.	Kennebrew	82
White, II	Thomas	164		Wills	Samuel Franklin	438
Whitfield	Wilson	259		Wilson	Harvey J.	83
Whitley	James L.	81		Wilson	Joseph	260
Whitley	L. B.	81		Wilson	Zadie Volena	288
Whitman	Eugene Zephaniah	407		Wilson	J. Reford	353
Whitmore	Earl Austin	438		Wilson	Muril	352

www.ingramcontent.com/pod-product-compliance
Lightning Source LLC
Chambersburg PA
CBHW081142270326
41930CB00014B/3012